Contemporary Advancements in Information Technology Development in Dynamic Environments

Mehdi Khosrow-Pour
Information Resources Management Association, USA

A volume in the Advances in Systems Analysis, Software Engineering, and High Performance Computing (ASASEHPC) Book Series

An Imprint of IGI Global

Managing Director: Lindsay Johnston
Production Editor: Jennifer Yoder
Development Editor: Allison McGinniss
Acquisitions Editor: Kayla Wolfe
Typesetter: Kaitlyn Kulp
Cover Design: Jason Mull

Published in the United States of America by
Information Science Reference (an imprint of IGI Global)
701 E. Chocolate Avenue
Hershey PA, USA 17033
Tel: 717-533-8845
Fax: 717-533-8661
E-mail: cust@igi-global.com
Web site: http://www.igi-global.com

        Library of Congress Cataloging-in-Publication Data

Contemporary advancements in information technology development in dynamic environments / Mehdi Khosrow-Pour, editor.
      pages cm
  Includes bibliographical references and index.
    ISBN 978-1-4666-6252-0 (hardcover) -- ISBN 978-1-4666-6253-7 (ebook) -- ISBN 978-1-4666-6255-1 (print & perpetual access) 1. Information technology. I. Khosrow-Pour, Mehdi, 1951- editor.
  T58.5.C6675 2014
  004--dc23
                    2014012884

This book is published in the IGI Global book series Advances in Systems Analysis, Software Engineering, and High Performance Computing (ASASEHPC) (ISSN: 2327-3453; eISSN: 2327-3461)

British Cataloguing in Publication Data
A Cataloguing in Publication record for this book is available from the British Library.

All work contributed to this book is new, previously-unpublished material. The views expressed in this book are those of the authors, but not necessarily of the publisher.

For electronic access to this publication, please contact: eresources@igi-global.com.

Advances in Systems Analysis, Software Engineering, and High Performance Computing (ASASEHPC) Book Series

Vijayan Sugumaran
Oakland University, USA

ISSN: 2327-3453
EISSN: 2327-3461

MISSION

The theory and practice of computing applications and distributed systems has emerged as one of the key areas of research driving innovations in business, engineering, and science. The fields of software engineering, systems analysis, and high performance computing offer a wide range of applications and solutions in solving computational problems for any modern organization.

The **Advances in Systems Analysis, Software Engineering, and High Performance Computing (ASASEHPC) Book Series** brings together research in the areas of distributed computing, systems and software engineering, high performance computing, and service science. This collection of publications is useful for academics, researchers, and practitioners seeking the latest practices and knowledge in this field.

COVERAGE

- Computer Networking
- Storage Systems
- Computer System Analysis
- Performance Modelling
- Computer Graphics
- Human-Computer Interaction
- Distributed Cloud Computing
- Virtual Data Systems
- Network Management
- Enterprise Information Systems

IGI Global is currently accepting manuscripts for publication within this series. To submit a proposal for a volume in this series, please contact our Acquisition Editors at Acquisitions@igi-global.com or visit: http://www.igi-global.com/publish/.

Titles in this Series

For a list of additional titles in this series, please visit: www.igi-global.com

Contemporary Advancements in Information Technology Development in Dynamic Environments
Mehdi Khosrow-Pour (Information Resources Management Association, USA)
Information Science Reference • copyright 2014 • 320pp • H/C (ISBN: 9781466662520) • US $205.00 (our price)

Systems and Software Development, Modeling, and Analysis New Perspectives and Methodologies
Mehdi Khosrow-Pour (Information Resources Management Association, USA)
Information Science Reference • copyright 2014 • 365pp • H/C (ISBN: 9781466660984) • US $215.00 (our price)

Handbook of Research on Emerging Advancements and Technologies in Software Engineering
Imran Ghani (Universiti Teknologi Malaysia, Malaysia) Wan Mohd Nasir Wan Kadir (Universiti Teknologi Malaysia, Malaysia) and Mohammad Nazir Ahmad (Universiti Teknologi Malaysia, Malaysia)
Engineering Science Reference • copyright 2014 • 686pp • H/C (ISBN: 9781466660267) • US $395.00 (our price)

Advancing Embedded Systems and Real-Time Communications with Emerging Technologies
Seppo Virtanen (University of Turku, Finland)
Information Science Reference • copyright 2014 • 502pp • H/C (ISBN: 9781466660342) • US $235.00 (our price)

Handbook of Research on High Performance and Cloud Computing in Scientific Research and Education
Marijana Despotović-Zrakić (University of Belgrade, Serbia) Veljko Milutinović (University of Belgrade, Serbia) and Aleksandar Belić (University of Belgrade, Serbia)
Information Science Reference • copyright 2014 • 476pp • H/C (ISBN: 9781466657847) • US $325.00 (our price)

Agile Estimation Techniques and Innovative Approaches to Software Process Improvement
Ricardo Colomo-Palacios (Østfold University College, Norway) Jose Antonio Calvo-Manzano Villalón (Universidad Politécnica De Madrid, Spain) Antonio de Amescua Seco (Universidad Carlos III de Madrid, Spain) and Tomás San Feliu Gilabert (Universidad Politécnica De Madrid, Spain)
Information Science Reference • copyright 2014 • 399pp • H/C (ISBN: 9781466651821) • US $215.00 (our price)

Enabling the New Era of Cloud Computing Data Security, Transfer, and Management
Yushi Shen (Microsoft, USA) Yale Li (Microsoft, USA) Ling Wu (EMC, USA) Shaofeng Liu (Microsoft, USA) and Qian Wen (Endronic Corp, USA)
Information Science Reference • copyright 2014 • 336pp • H/C (ISBN: 9781466648012) • US $195.00 (our price)

Theory and Application of Multi-Formalism Modeling
Marco Gribaudo (Politecnico di Milano, Italy) and Mauro Iacono (Seconda Università degli Studi di Napoli, Italy)
Information Science Reference • copyright 2014 • 314pp • H/C (ISBN: 9781466646599) • US $195.00 (our price)

www.igi-global.com

701 E. Chocolate Ave., Hershey, PA 17033
Order online at www.igi-global.com or call 717-533-8845 x100
To place a standing order for titles released in this series, contact: cust@igi-global.com
Mon-Fri 8:00 am - 5:00 pm (est) or fax 24 hours a day 717-533-8661

Table of Contents

Detailed Table of Contents

e-Government services have to operate in dynamic environments, and there is a limited time for adaptation in terms of legislation, society, and economy. Maintaining reliable services is even more difficult with continuous changes, like mergers and acquisitions, supply chain activity, staff turnover, and regulatory variation. The nature of the changes has become discontinuous; however, the existing approaches and IT solutions are inadequate for highly dynamic and volatile processes. The management of these challenges requires harmonized change management and knowledge management strategy. In this chapter, the selected change management strategy and the corresponding knowledge management strategy and their IT support are analyzed from the public administration point of view. SAKE (FP6 IST-2005-027128) and SMART projects (LLP 201-1-ES1-LEO05-49395) approaches and IT solutions are discussed to demonstrate the strategic view and to solve the knowledge management and change management related problems and challenges in public administration. Pilots of the projects are focusing on the challenge of dynamically matching educational system offer and job market demand. SAKE provides holistic framework and tool for an agile knowledge-based e-government, while SMART offers an innovative learning environment that will match labour market needs with the training offer.

This chapter examines the effects of perceived information quality, perceived system quality, and perceived flow on mobile Social Networking Sites (SNS) users' trust. Pearson correlations via SPSS 21.0 computer program was used for data analysis as it has the ability to ensure the consistency of the model with the data, to provide information necessary to scrutinize the study hypotheses, and to estimate associations among constructs. Each correlation coefficient was assessed as significant at the 0.01 level, and the overall model was determined to fit the data well as multicollinearity was absent. In terms of the associations with perceived user trust, perceived flow had highest significant positive correlation coefficients, followed by perceived information quality and perceived system quality. Next, further investigation of the study encountered that perceived flow is significantly associated by both perceived system quality and perceived information quality of mobile SNS, respectively. The chapter concludes with directions for future research.

The rapid development of complex virtual worlds (most notably, in 3D computer and video games) introduces new challenges for the creation of virtual agents, controlled by Artificial Intelligence (AI) systems. Two important sub-problems in this topic area that need to be addressed are (a) believability and (b) effectiveness of agents' behavior (i.e. human-likeness of the characters and high ability to achieving their own goals). In this chapter, the authors study current approaches to believability and effectiveness of AI behavior in virtual worlds. They examine the concepts of believability and effectiveness and analyze several successful attempts to address these challenges. In conclusion, the authors provide a case study that suggests that believable and effective behavior can be achieved through learning behavioral patterns from observation with subsequent automatic selection of effective acting strategies.

In recent years, a large number of impressive face and object recognition algorithms have surfaced, both computational and biologically inspired. Only a few of these can detect face and object views. Empirical studies concerning face and object recognition suggest that faces and objects may be stored in our memory by a few canonical representations. In cortical area V1 exist double-opponent colour blobs, also simple, complex, and end-stopped cells that provide input for a multiscale line and edge representation, keypoints for dynamic feature routing, and saliency maps for Focus-of-Attention. All these combined allow us to segregate faces. Events of different facial views are stored in memory and combined in order to identify the view and recognise a face, including its expression. The authors show that with five 2D views and their cortical representations it is possible to determine the left-right and frontal-lateral-profile views, achieving view-invariant recognition. They also show that the same principle with eight views can be applied to 3D object recognition when they are mainly rotated about the vertical axis. Although object recognition is here explored as a special case of face recognition, it should be stressed that faces and general objects are processed in different ways in the cortex.

The increasing capabilities of Internet have caused a qualitative change in the management of spatial information while recent advances in Web 2.0 technologies have enabled the integration of data and knowledge in intuitive thematic maps. This has wide-ranging indirect effects in supporting the ways stakeholders make a decision based on information coming from various distributed resources, but the real question is, What applications and technologies are in place to deal with these decisional environments? Aiming at giving an answer to this question, this chapter explores the feasibility of a computational environment that supports the Web-based exploration and the spatial analysis in real estate decisional processes. It relies on the concept of dataspace as a new scenario for accessing, integrating, and analyzing geo-spatial information regardless of its format and location. Built on top of a cloud environment, it is made up of specialized modules, each of which provides a well-defined service. Mash-ups integrate data from different resources on the Internet and provide the user with a flexible and easy-to-use way for geo-referencing data in the maps provided by Google Maps and Google Earth. Through an interactive process, the user arrives at some interesting maps, glimpses the most important facets of the decisional problem, and combines them to fashion a solution. Applicative experiments demonstrate the effectiveness of the computational environment proposed.

This chapter describes the performance of a compute cluster applied to solve Three Dimensional (3D) molecular modelling problems. The primary goal of this work is to identify new potential drugs. The chapter focuses upon the following issues: computational chemistry, computational efficiency, task scheduling, and the analysis of system performance. The philosophy of design for an Application Framework for Computational Chemistry (AFCC) is described. Eighteen months after the release of the original chapter, the authors have examined a series of changes adopted which have led to improved system performance. Various experiments have been carried out to optimise the performance of a cluster computer, the results analysed, and the statistics produced are discussed in the chapter.

The purpose of this chapter is to present current research on the modern Bulgarian language. It is one of the oldest European languages. An information system for the management of the electronic archive with texts in Bulgarian language is described. It provides the possibility for processing the collected text information. The detailed and comprehensive researches on the letter and the word frequency in the modern Bulgarian language from varied sources (fiction, scientific and popular science literature, press, legal texts, government bulletins, etc.) are performed, and the obtained results are represented. The index of coincidence of the Bulgarian language as a whole and for the individual sources is computed. The results can be utilized by different specialists – computer scientists, linguists, cryptanalysts, and others. Furthermore, with mathematical modeling, the authors found the letter and word frequency distributions and their models and they estimated their standard deviations by documents.

Various attempts are made by researchers on the study of vagueness of data through Intuitionistic Fuzzy sets and Vague sets, and also it is shown that Vague sets are Intuitionistic Fuzzy sets. However, there are algebraic and graphical differences between Vague sets and Intuitionistic Fuzzy sets. In this chapter, an attempt is made to define the correlation coefficient of Interval Vague sets lying in the interval [0,1], and a new method for computing the correlation coefficient of interval Vague sets lying in the interval [-1,1] using α-cuts over the vague degrees through statistical confidence intervals is also presented by an example. The new method proposed in this work produces a correlation coefficient in the form of an interval. The proposed method produces a correlation coefficient in the form of an interval from a trapezoidal shaped fuzzy number derived from the vague degrees. This chapter also aims to develop a new method based on the Technique for Order Preference by Similarity to Ideal Solution (TOPSIS) to solve MADM problems for Interval Vague Sets (IVSs). A TOPSIS algorithm is constructed on the basis of the concepts of the relative-closeness coefficient computed from the correlation coefficient of IVSs. This novel method also identifies the positive and negative ideal solutions using the correlation coefficient of IVSs. A numerical illustration explains the proposed algorithms and comparisons are made with some existing methods.

Chapter 9

In this chapter, the authors establish decomposition theorems of Generalized Interval-Valued Intuitionistic Fuzzy Sets (GIVIFS) by use of cut sets of generalized interval-valued intuitionistic fuzzy sets. First, new definitions of eight kinds of cut sets generalized interval-valued intuitionistic fuzzy sets are introduced. Second, based on these new cut sets, the decomposition generalized interval-valued intuitionistic fuzzy sets are established. The authors show that each kind of cut sets corresponds to two kinds of decomposition theorems. These results provide a fundamental theory for the research of generalized interval-valued intuitionistic fuzzy sets.

This chapter examines the graph coloring problem. A graph strict strong coloring algorithm has been proposed for trees in Haddad and Kheddouci (2009). In this chapter, the authors recall the heuristic-based algorithm for general graphs named GGSSCA (for Generalized Graph Strict Strong Coloring Algorithm) proposed in Bouzenada, Bensouyad, Guidoum, Reghioua, and Saidouni (2012). The complexity of this algorithm is polynomial with considering the number of vertices. Later, in Guidoum, Bensouyad, and Saidouni (2013), GGSSCA was applied to solve the graph distribution problem.

Chapter 11

In the era of medicine, the heart and cardiovascular system has become one of the standard observation targets. Palpation and auscultation in the precordial area is performed as part of the regular physical examination to detect possible cardiovascular and pulmonary problems. However, due to the large number of people suffering from cardiovascular problems, labor-intensive methods such as auscultation might be inefficient in preventive cardiovascular condition screening. Seismocardiography (SCG) could have the potential to be a part of the solution to this problem. SCG is one of many modalities of cardiac-induced vibration measurements, and it has been shown to be of use in detecting coronary artery disease and assessing myocardial contractility. Lately, due to advances in sensor technologies, the SCG measurement is being developed by introducing three-dimensional measurements. Three-dimensional approach is considered to yield more information about the cardiovascular system than any single uniaxial approach. In conclusion, SCG seems to have the potential to offer a complementary view to cardiovascular function and a cost-effective method for screening of cardiovascular diseases. SCG is explored in this chapter.

Francisco Torrens, Universitat de València, Spain
Gloria Castellano, Universidad Católica de Valencia, Spain

The existence of Single-Wall C-Nanocones (SWNCs), especially nanohorns (SWNHs), and BC$_2$N/ Boron Nitride (BN) analogues in cluster form is discussed in solution in this chapter. Theories are developed based on models bundlet and droplet describing size-distribution function. The phenomena present unified explanation in bundlet in which free energy of (BC$_2$N/BN-)SWNCs involved in cluster is combined from two parts: volume one proportional to the number of molecules n in cluster and surface one, to n$^{1/2}$. Bundlet enables describing distribution function of (BC$_2$N/BN-)SWNC clusters by size. From geometrical differences bundlet [(BC$_2$N/BN-)SWNCs] and droplet (C$_{60}$/B$_{15}$C$_{30}$N$_{15}$/B$_{30}$N$_{30}$) predict dissimilar behaviours. Various disclination (BC2N/BN-)SWNCs are studied via energetic and structural analyses. Several (BC$_2$N/BN-)SWNC's ends are studied that are different because of closing structure and arrangement type. Packing efficiencies and interaction-energy parameters of (BC$_2$N/BN-)SWNCs/ SWNHs are intermediate between C$_{60}$/B$_{15}$C$_{30}$N$_{15}$/B$_{30}$N$_{30}$ and (BC$_2$N/BN-)Single-Wall C-Nanotube (SWNT) clusters: in-between behaviour is expected; however, properties of (BC2N/BN-)SWNCs, especially (BC$_2$N/ BN-)SWNHs, are calculated closer to (BC$_2$N/BN-)SWNTs. Structural asymmetry in different (BC2N/ BN-)SWNCs characterized by cone angle distinguishes properties of types: P2. BC$_2$N/BN, especially species isoelectronic with C-analogues may be stable.

Amro Shafik, University of Toronto, Canada
Salah Haridy, Northeastern University, USA

Computer Numerical Control (CNC) is a technology that converts coded instructions and numerical data into sequential actions that describe the motion of machine axes or the behavior of an end effector. Nowadays, CNC technology has been introduced to different stages of production, such as rapid prototyping, machining and finishing processes, testing, packaging, and warehousing. The main objective of this chapter is to introduce a methodology for design and implementation of a simple and low-cost educational CNC prototype. The machine consists of three independent axes driven by stepper motors through an open-loop control system. Output pulses from the parallel port of Personal Computer (PC) are used to drive the stepper motors after processing by an interface card. A flexible, responsive, and real-time Visual C# program is developed to control the motion of the machine axes. The integrated design proposed in this chapter can provide engineers and students in academic institutions with a simple foundation to efficiently build a CNC machine based on the available resources. Moreover, the proposed prototype can be used for educational purposes, demonstrations, and future research.

Folasayo Enoch Olalere, Universiti Malaysia Kelantan (UMK), Malaysia
Ab Aziz Bin Shuaib, Universiti Malaysia Kelantan (UMK), Malaysia

This chapter investigates the knowledge regarding how user-centered design can be achieved during ceramic product development with the aid of computer-aided ceramic design. The chapter gives the general overview of ceramics, computer-aided design, and its application in ceramic product development. It also illuminates on product emotion, its influence on consumers' behaviour, and how it can be integrated into new products. With reference to desire emotion, the chapter elaborates on the determining factors and the resulting appraisal that will elicit the desire emotion. Furthermore, it analyses the systematic approach in building user-centred design in new products. Based on this understanding, a study is described where a newly developed mug design and a multi-functional ceramic pot were tested to know emotive responses of people towards the products. The results from the study show some interesting findings by demonstrating the theories in practice and also reveal the viability of computer-aided design as a tool for building user-centered design.

The move towards a low-carbon world, driven partly by climate science and partly by the business opportunities it offers, will need the promotion of environmentally friendly alternatives, if an acceptable stabilisation level of atmospheric carbon dioxide is to be achieved. This requires the harnessing and use of natural resources that produce no air pollution or greenhouse gases and provide comfortable coexistence of humans, livestock, and plants. This chapter presents a comprehensive review of energy sources, and the development of sustainable technologies to explore these energy sources. It also includes potential renewable energy technologies, efficient energy systems, energy savings techniques, and other mitigation measures necessary to reduce climate changes. The chapter concludes with the technical status of the Ground Source Heat Pumps (GSHP) technology. The purpose of this chapter, however, is to examine the means of reduction of energy consumption in buildings, identify GSHPs as an environmentally friendly technology able to provide efficient utilisation of energy in the buildings sector, promote using GSHPs applications as an optimum means of heating and cooling, and to present typical applications and recent advances of the DX GSHPs.

Evolutionary Algorithms (EAs) are well-known optimization techniques to deal with nonlinear and complex optimization problems. However, most of these population-based algorithms are computationally expensive due to the slow nature of the evolutionary process. To overcome this drawback and to improve the convergence rate, this chapter employs Quasi-Opposition-Based Learning (QOBL) in conventional Biogeography-Based Optimization (BBO) technique. The proposed Quasi-Oppositional BBO (QOBBO) is comprehensively developed and successfully applied for solving the Optimal Reactive Power Dispatch (ORPD) problem by minimizing the transmission loss when both equality and inequality constraints are satisfied. The proposed QOBBO algorithm's performance is studied with comparisons of Canonical Genetic Algorithm (CGA), five versions of Particle Swarm Optimization (PSO), Local Search-Based Self-Adaptive Differential Evolution (L-SADE), Seeker Optimization Algorithm (SOA), and BBO on the IEEE 30-bus, IEEE 57-bus, and IEEE 118-bus power systems. The simulation results show that the proposed QOBBO approach performed better than the other listed algorithms and can be efficiently used to solve small-, medium-, and large-scale ORPD problems.

Chapter 17

T. Ganesan, Universiti Teknologi Petronas, Malaysia
I. Elamvazuthi, Universiti Teknologi Petronas, Malaysia
K. Z. K. Shaari, Universiti Teknologi Petronas, Malaysia
P. Vasant, Universiti Teknologi Petronas, Malaysia

Many industrial problems in process optimization are Multi-Objective (MO), where each of the objectives represents different facets of the issue. Thus, having in hand multiple solutions prior to selecting the best solution is a seminal advantage. In this chapter, the weighted sum scalarization approach is used in conjunction with three meta-heuristic algorithms: Differential Evolution (DE), Hopfield-Enhanced Differential Evolution (HEDE), and Gravitational Search Algorithm (GSA). These methods are then employed to trace the approximate Pareto frontier to the bioethanol production problem. The Hypervolume Indicator (HVI) is applied to gauge the capabilities of each algorithm in approximating the Pareto frontier. Some comparative studies are then carried out with the algorithms developed in this chapter. Analysis on the performance as well as the quality of the solutions obtained by these algorithms is shown here.

Preface

Throughout time, information technology has continuously improved on how we process, retrieve, and distribute data. New types of technology are continuously being developed and implemented to aid all different enterprises, such as some discussed in this book, being information and knowledge quality, facial recognition, cloud computing, sustainable development, artificial intelligence, and many more. It is important to understand the successful uses of information technology and also mismanagement of information technology in order to improve future implementations in all types of settings. *Contemporary Advancements in Information Technology Development in Dynamic Environments* discusses progressive research in interdisciplinary areas of information technology relating to the ever-changing world.

The book is organized into 17 chapters. A brief description of each of the chapters can be found below:

e-Government services have to operate in dynamic environments, and there is a limited time for adaptation in terms of legislation, society, and economy. Maintaining reliable services is even more difficult with continuous changes, like mergers and acquisitions, supply chain activity, staff turnover, and regulatory variation. The nature of the changes has become discontinuous; however, the existing approaches and IT solutions are inadequate for highly dynamic and volatile processes. The management of these challenges requires harmonized change management and knowledge management strategy. In "Knowledge-Based E-Government Solutions in Dynamic Environment," Chapter 1, by Andrea Kő, Barna Kovács, and András Gábor, the selected change management strategy and the corresponding knowledge management strategy and their IT support are analyzed from the public administration point of view. SAKE (FP6 IST-2005-027128) and SMART projects (LLP 201-1-ES1-LEO05-49395) approaches and IT solutions are discussed to demonstrate the strategic view and to solve the knowledge management and change management related problems and challenges in public administration. Pilots of the projects are focusing on the challenge of dynamically matching educational system offer and job market demand. SAKE provides holistic framework and tool for an agile knowledge-based e-government, while SMART offers an innovative learning environment that will match labour market needs with the training offer.

Chapter 2, "Effects of Perceived Information Quality, Perceived System Quality, and Perceived Flow on Mobile Social Networking Sites (SNS) Users' Trust," by Norazah Mohd Suki and Norbayah Mohd Suki examines the effects of perceived information quality, perceived system quality, and perceived flow on mobile Social Networking Sites (SNS) users' trust. Pearson correlations via SPSS 21.0 computer program was used for data analysis as it has the ability to ensure the consistency of the model with the data, to provide information necessary to scrutinize the study hypotheses, and to estimate associations among constructs. Each correlation coefficient was assessed as significant at the 0.01 level, and the overall model was determined to fit the data well as multicollinearity was absent. In terms of the associations with perceived user trust, perceived flow had highest significant positive correlation coefficients, followed by perceived information quality and perceived system quality. Next, further investigation of the study encountered that perceived flow is significantly associated by both perceived system quality and perceived information quality of mobile SNS, respectively. The chapter concludes with directions for future research.

In Chapter 3, "Creating Believable and Effective AI Agents for Games and Simulations: Reviews and Case Study," Iskander Umarov and Maxim Mozgovoy study current approaches to believability and effectiveness of AI behavior in virtual worlds. They examine the concepts of believability and effectiveness, and analyze several successful attempts to address these challenges. In conclusion, they provide a case study that suggests that believable and effective behavior can be achieved through learning behavioral patterns from observation with subsequent automatic selection of effective acting strategies.

Chapter 4, "Face and Object Recognition Using Biological Features and few Views" by J.M.F. Rodrigues, R. Lam, K. Terzić, and J.M.H. du Buf, discusses facial recognition advancements. In recent years, a large number of impressive face and object recognition algorithms have surfaced, both computational and biologically inspired. Only a few of these can detect face and object views. Empirical studies concerning face and object recognition suggest that faces and objects may be stored in our memory by a few canonical representations. In cortical area V1 exist double-opponent colour blobs, also simple, complex, and end-stopped cells that provide input for a multiscale line and edge representation, keypoints for dynamic feature routing, and saliency maps for Focus-of-Attention. All these combined allow us to segregate faces. Events of different facial views are stored in memory and combined in order to identify the view and recognise a face, including its expression. The authors show that with five 2D views and their cortical representations it is possible to determine the left-right and frontal-lateral-profile views, achieving view-invariant recognition. They also show that the same principle with eight views can be applied to 3D object recognition when they are mainly rotated about the vertical axis. Although object recognition is here explored as a special case of face recognition, it should be stressed that faces and general objects are processed in different ways in the cortex.

The increasing capabilities of Internet have caused a qualitative change in the management of spatial information while recent advances in Web 2.0 technologies have enabled the integration of data and knowledge in intuitive thematic maps. This has wide-ranging indirect effects in supporting the ways stakeholders make a decision based on information coming from various distributed resources, but the real question is, What applications and technologies are in place to deal with these decisional environments? Aiming at giving an answer to this question, Michele Argiolas, Maurizio Atzori, Nicoletta Dessì, and Barbara Pes explore in Chapter 5, "Improving Spatial Decision Making in Cloud Computing," the feasibility of a computational environment that supports the Web-based exploration and the spatial analysis in real estate decisional processes. It relies on the concept of dataspace as a new scenario for accessing, integrating, and analyzing geo-spatial information regardless of its format and location. Built on top of a cloud environment, it is made up of specialized modules, each of which provides a well-defined service. Mash-ups integrate data from different resources on the Internet and provide the user with a flexible and easy-to-use way for geo-referencing data in the maps provided by Google Maps and Google Earth. Through an interactive process, the user arrives at some interesting maps, glimpses the most important facets of the decisional problem, and combines them to fashion a solution. Applicative experiments demonstrate the effectiveness of the computational environment proposed.

Chapter 6 by J. Tindle, M. Gray, R.L. Warrender, K. Ginty, and P.K.D. Dawson, "Further Development of an Application Framework for Computational Chemistry (AFCC) Applied to New Drug Discovery," describes the performance of a compute cluster applied to solve Three Dimensional (3D) molecular modelling problems. The primary goal of this work is to identify new potential drugs. The chapter focuses upon the following issues: computational chemistry, computational efficiency, task scheduling, and the analysis of system performance. The philosophy of design for an Application Framework for Computational Chemistry (AFCC) is described. Eighteen months after the release of the original chapter, the authors have examined a series of changes adopted which have led to improved system performance. Various experiments have been carried out to optimise the performance of a cluster computer, the results analysed, and the statistics produced are discussed in the chapter.

The purpose of Chapter 7, "Research on Letter and Word Frequency and Mathematical Modeling of Frequency Distributions in the Modern Bulgarian Language," by Tihomir Trifonov and Tsvetanka Georgieva-Trifonova is to present current research on the modern Bulgarian language. It is one of the oldest European languages. An information system for the management of the electronic archive with texts in Bulgarian language is described. It provides the possibility for processing the collected text information. The detailed and comprehensive researches on the letter and the word frequency in the modern Bulgarian language from varied sources (fiction, scientific and popular science literature, press, legal texts, government bulletins, etc.) are performed, and the obtained results are represented. The index of coincidence of the Bulgarian language as a whole and for the individual sources is computed. The results can be utilized by different specialists – computer scientists, linguists, cryptanalysts, and others. Furthermore, with mathematical modeling, the authors found the letter and word frequency distributions and their models and they estimated their standard deviations by documents.

Various attempts are made by researchers on the study of vagueness of data through Intuitionistic Fuzzy sets and Vague sets, and also it is shown that Vague sets are Intuitionistic Fuzzy sets. However, there are algebraic and graphical differences between Vague sets and Intuitionistic Fuzzy sets. In Chapter 8 by John Robinson P. and Henry Amirtharaj E.C., "Vague Correlation Coefficient of Interval Vague Sets and its Applications to Topsis in MADMProblems," an attempt is made to define the correlation coefficient of Interval Vague sets lying in the interval [0,1], and a new method for computing the correlation coefficient of interval Vague sets lying in the interval [-1,1] using α-cuts over the vague degrees through statistical confidence intervals is also presented by an example. The new method proposed in this work produces a correlation coefficient in the form of an interval. The proposed method produces a correlation coefficient in the form of an interval from a trapezoidal shaped fuzzy number derived from the vague degrees. This chapter also aims to develop a new method based on the Technique for Order Preference by Similarity to Ideal Solution (TOPSIS) to solve MADM problems for Interval Vague Sets (IVSs). A TOPSIS algorithm is constructed on the basis of the concepts of the relative-closeness coefficient computed from the correlation coefficient of IVSs. This novel method also identifies the positive and negative ideal solutions using the correlation coefficient of IVSs. A numerical illustration explains the proposed algorithms and comparisons are made with some existing methods.

In "Decomposition Theorem of Generalized Interval-Valued Intutiionistic Fuzzy Sets," Chapter 9, Amal Kumar Adak, Monoranjan Bhowmik, and Madhumangal Pal establish decomposition theorems of Generalized Interval-Valued Intuitionistic Fuzzy Sets (GIVIFS) by use of cut sets of generalized interval-valued intuitionistic fuzzy sets. First, new definitions of eight kinds of cut sets generalized interval-valued intuitionistic fuzzy sets are introduced. Second, based on these new cut sets, the decomposition generalized interval-valued intuitionistic fuzzy sets are established. The authors show that each kind of cut sets corresponds to two kinds of decomposition theorems. These results provide a fundamental theory for the research of generalized interval-valued intuitionistic fuzzy sets.

Chapter 10, "A Generalized Graph Strict Strong Coloring Algorithm: Application on Graph Distribution," by Meriem Bensouyad, Mourad Bouzenada, Nousseiba Guidoum, and Djamel-Eddine Saïdouni, *examines the graph coloring problem. A graph strict strong coloring algorithm has been proposed for trees in Haddad and Kheddouci. In this chapter, the authors recall the heuristic-based algorithm for general graphs named GGSSCA (for Generalized Graph Strict Strong Coloring Algorithm) proposed in Bouzenada, Bensouyad, Guidoum, Reghioua, and Saidouni. The complexity of this algorithm is polynomial with considering the number of vertices. Later, in Guidoum, Bensouyad, and Saidouni, GGSSCA was applied to solve the graph distribution problem.*

Chapter 11, "Precordial Vibrations: Seismocardiography – Techniques and Applications," by Mikko Paukkunen and Matti Linnavuo, discusses SCG measurement. In the era of medicine, the heart and cardiovascular system has become one of the standard observation targets. Palpation and auscultation in the precordial area is performed as part of the regular physical examination to detect possible cardiovascular and pulmonary problems. However, due to the large number of people suffering from cardiovascular problems, labor-intensive methods such as auscultation might be inefficient in preventive cardiovascular condition screening. Seismocardiography (SCG) could have the potential to be a part of the solution to this problem. SCG is one of many modalities of cardiac-induced vibration measurements, and it has been shown to be of use in detecting coronary artery disease and assessing myocardial contractility. Lately, due to advances in sensor technologies, the SCG measurement is being developed by introducing three-dimensional measurements. Three-dimensional approach is considered to yield more information about the cardiovascular system than any single uniaxial approach. In conclusion, SCG seems to have the potential to offer a complementary view to cardiovascular function and a cost-effective method for screening of cardiovascular diseases.

The existence of Single-Wall C-Nanocones (SWNCs), especially nanohorns (SWNHs), and BC_2N/Boron Nitride (BN) analogues in cluster form is discussed in solution in Francisco Torrens and Gloria Castellano's Chapter 12, "Nanostructures Cluster Models in Solution: Extension to C, BC_2N, and BN Fullerenes, Tubes, and Cones." Theories are developed based on models bundlet and droplet describing size-distribution function. The phenomena present unified explanation in bundlet in which free energy of (BC_2N/BN-)SWNCs involved in cluster is combined from two parts: volume one proportional to the number of molecules n in cluster and surface one, to $n^{1/2}$. Bundlet enables describing distribution function of (BC_2N/BN-)SWNC clusters by size. From geometrical differences bundlet [(BC_2N/BN-)SWNCs] and droplet (C_{60}/$B_{15}C_{30}N_{15}$/$B_{30}N_{30}$) predict dissimilar behaviours. Various disclination (BC_2N/BN-)SWNCs are studied via energetic and structural analyses. Several (BC_2N/BN-)SWNC's ends are studied that are different because of closing structure and arrangement type. Packing efficiencies and interaction-energy parameters of (BC_2N/BN-)SWNCs/SWNHs are intermediate between C_{60}/$B_{15}C_{30}N_{15}$/$B_{30}N_{30}$ and (BC_2N/BN-)Single-Wall C-Nanotube (SWNT) clusters: in-between behaviour is expected; however, properties of (BC_2N/BN-)SWNCs, especially (BC_2N/BN-)SWNHs, are calculated closer to (BC_2N/BN-)SWNTs. Structural asymmetry in different (BC_2N/BN-)SWNCs characterized by cone angle distinguishes properties of types: P2. BC_2N/BN, especially species isoelectronic with C-analogues may be stable.

Computer Numerical Control (CNC) is a technology that converts coded instructions and numerical data into sequential actions that describe the motion of machine axes or the behavior of an end effector. Nowadays, CNC technology has been introduced to different stages of production, such as rapid prototyping, machining and finishing processes, testing, packaging, and warehousing. The main objective of Chapter 13 "An Integrated Design for a CNC Machine" by Amro Shafik and Slah Haridy, is to introduce a methodology for design and implementation of a simple and low-cost educational CNC prototype.

The machine consists of three independent axes driven by stepper motors through an open-loop control system. Output pulses from the parallel port of Personal Computer (PC) are used to drive the stepper motors after processing by an interface card. A flexible, responsive, and real-time Visual C# program is developed to control the motion of the machine axes. The integrated design proposed in this chapter can provide engineers and students in academic institutions with a simple foundation to efficiently build a CNC machine based on the available resources. Moreover, the proposed prototype can be used for educational purposes, demonstrations, and future research.

Chapter 14, "Computer-Aided Ceramic Design: Its Viability for Building User-Centered Design" by Olalere Folasayo Enoch and Ab Aziz Bin Shuaib, investigates the knowledge regarding how user-centered design can be achieved during ceramic product development with the aid of computer-aided ceramic design. The chapter gives the general overview of ceramics, computer-aided design, and its application in ceramic product development. It also illuminates on product emotion, its influence on consumers' behaviour, and how it can be integrated into new products. With reference to desire emotion, the chapter elaborates on the determining factors and the resulting appraisal that will elicit the desire emotion. Furthermore, it analyses the systematic approach in building user-centred design in new products. Based on this understanding, a study is described where a newly developed mug design and a multi-functional ceramic pot were tested to know emotive responses of people towards the products. The results from the study show some interesting findings by demonstrating the theories in practice and also reveal the viability of computer-aided design as a tool for building user-centered design.

The move towards a low-carbon world, driven partly by climate science and partly by the business opportunities it offers, will need the promotion of environmentally friendly alternatives, if an acceptable stabilisation level of atmospheric carbon dioxide is to be achieved. This requires the harnessing and use of natural resources that produce no air pollution or greenhouse gases and provide comfortable coexistence of humans, livestock, and plants. This chapter presents a comprehensive review of energy sources, and the development of sustainable technologies to explore these energy sources. It also includes potential renewable energy technologies, efficient energy systems, energy savings techniques, and other mitigation measures necessary to reduce climate changes. The chapter concludes with the technical status of the Ground Source Heat Pumps (GSHP) technology. The purpose of Abdeen Mustafa Omer's Chapter 15, "Clean and Green Energy Technologies, Sustainable Development, and Environment," however, is to examine the means of reduction of energy consumption in buildings, identify GSHPs as an environmentally friendly technology able to provide efficient utilisation of energy in the buildings sector, promote using GSHPs applications as an optimum means of heating and cooling, and to present typical applications and recent advances of the DX GSHPs.

Evolutionary Algorithms (EAs) are well-known optimization techniques to deal with nonlinear and complex optimization problems. However, most of these population-based algorithms are computationally expensive due to the slow nature of the evolutionary process. To overcome this drawback and to improve the convergence rate, Chapter 16, "New Efficient Evolutionary Algorithm Applied to Optimal Reactive Power Dispatch" by Provas Kumar Roy, employs Quasi-Opposition-Based Learning (QOBL) in conventional Biogeography-Based Optimization (BBO) technique. The proposed Quasi-Oppositional BBO (QOBBO) is comprehensively developed and successfully applied for solving the Optimal Reactive Power Dispatch (ORPD) problem by minimizing the transmission loss when both equality and inequality constraints are satisfied. The proposed QOBBO algorithm's performance is studied with comparisons of Canonical Genetic Algorithm (CGA), five versions of Particle Swarm Optimization (PSO), Local Search-Based Self-Adaptive Differential Evolution (L-SADE), Seeker Optimization Algorithm (SOA), and BBO on the IEEE 30-bus, IEEE 57-bus, and IEEE 118-bus power systems. The simulation results show that the proposed QOBBO approach performed better than the other listed algorithms and can be efficiently used to solve small-, medium-, and large-scale ORPD problems.

Many industrial problems in process optimization are Multi-Objective (MO), where each of the objectives represents different facets of the issue. Thus, having in hand multiple solutions prior to selecting the best solution is a seminal advantage. In Chapter 17, "Multiobjective Optimization of Bioethanol Production via Hydrolysis using Hopfield-Enhanced Differential Evolution," T. Ganesan, I. Elamvazuthi, K.Z.K. Shaari, and P. Vasant use the weighted sum scalarization approach in conjunction with three meta-heuristic algorithms: Differential Evolution (DE), Hopfield-Enhanced Differential Evolution (HEDE), and Gravitational Search Algorithm (GSA). These methods are then employed to trace the approximate Pareto frontier to the bioethanol production problem. The Hypervolume Indicator (HVI) is applied to gauge the capabilities of each algorithm in approximating the Pareto frontier. Some comparative studies are then carried out with the algorithms developed in this chapter. Analysis on the performance as well as the quality of the solutions obtained by these algorithms is shown in the chapter.

Mehdi Khosrow-Pour
Information Resources Management Association, USA

Chapter 1
Knowledge–Based E–Government Solutions in Dynamic Environment

Andrea Kő
Corvinus University of Budapest, Hungary

Barna Kovács
Corvinus University of Budapest, Hungary

András Gábor
Corvinus University of Budapest, Hungary

ABSTRACT

e-Government services have to operate in dynamic environments, and there is a limited time for adaptation in terms of legislation, society, and economy. Maintaining reliable services is even more difficult with continuous changes, like mergers and acquisitions, supply chain activity, staff turnover, and regulatory variation. The nature of the changes has become discontinuous; however, the existing approaches and IT solutions are inadequate for highly dynamic and volatile processes. The management of these challenges requires harmonized change management and knowledge management strategy. In this chapter, the selected change management strategy and the corresponding knowledge management strategy and their IT support are analyzed from the public administration point of view. SAKE (FP6 IST-2005-027128) and SMART projects (LLP 201-1-ES1-LEO05-49395) approaches and IT solutions are discussed to demonstrate the strategic view and to solve the knowledge management and change management related problems and challenges in public administration. Pilots of the projects are focusing on the challenge of dynamically matching educational system offer and job market demand. SAKE provides holistic framework and tool for an agile knowledge-based e-government, while SMART offers an innovative learning environment that will match labour market needs with the training offer.

DOI: 10.4018/978-1-4666-6252-0.ch001

BACKGROUND

There are constant changes in the political, economic and legal environment of public administration, especially since the economic crisis started around 2008. Eastern and Middle European countries are highly affected by these changes since their economic environment was generally vulnerable at that time when every one of those countries expected the continuation of the economic prosperity. All of the issues of the economic crisis increased the burden on public administration, requiring more agile responses in decision-making, as well as more flexible processes and systems that are able to align with the changes within this highly dynamic environment. These challenges are quite new to European countries, as well as to Eastern and Middle European ones, like Latvia, Hungary of Poland.

The increasing dynamism of the environment imposes new challenges to public administration. As an example, increasing information overload of public servants can be mentioned as factor jeopardizing the organizations' capability of adaptation to its environment's dynamism. Increasing information complexity, as well as the rising amount and types of information systems available for a certain problem area make information management more difficult (Bray, 2008; Himma, 2007). New decisions and regulations have to be constructed quickly; "time-to-market" of regulations has to be reduced, which necessitates the support of public administration in order to produce agile responses. Management of changes requires a systematic approach as explained by Abrahamson (2000) and Kotter (2011), since changes in one part of the information assets can imply difficulties in other parts of the e-government system.

Knowledge has been and still is government's most important resource (Heeks, 2006), its management is therefore a crucial task. Unpredictability and dynamism of the environment require adaptive, fast and knowledge-based decisions (Riege, 2006). There are multiple examples avail-

able where knowledge-intensive work of public administration can be observed. As a suitable example, UK Government's Knowledge Network can be mentioned, which is a government-wide electronic communication tool helping government department to share knowledge and collaborate online with colleagues across government; or the knowledge management initiatives in the Federal Government in US (Barquin, 2010).

In order to comply with the permanent renewal need of knowledge, special knowledge management techniques and systems are needed (Jashapara, 2011; Kő & Klimkó 2009). These systems have to cope with the fast changing, context-sensitive character of knowledge; meanwhile they have to support the externalization of knowledge (Holsapple, 2003).

The researches detailed in this chapter aimed to a) analyze the challenges regarding change management and knowledge management in the area of public administration; b) investigate the relationship of change management and knowledge management strategies within the viewpoint of public administration and c) provide holistic frameworks and tools for an agile knowledge-based e-government that is reflecting the challenges collected in a) and expected to be sufficiently flexible to adapt to dynamic environments and applicable for the needs of public administration.

First, knowledge management and change management-related problems and challenges in public administration are detailed. Next, relationships between change management and knowledge management strategies are detailed and analyzed from the public administration perspective, followed by their appropriate IT support. SAKE project approach and IT environment is presented as an example of compliance with needs arising from change management and knowledge management strategies. SMART solution is detailed as another approach to manage the needs coming up from the dynamic nature of job market. Finally an overview about the SAKE and SMART cases are discussed.

SETTING THE STAGE

Change management, knowledge management and information technology are overlapping disciplines, also interwoven in practice. Change management strategy applied by the organization influences the types of knowledge that it will draw upon, which will take effect on the knowledge management strategy, which, in turn, determines information technology used in the organization.

In this section, the nature of changes and change management issues are discussed while main knowledge management strategies, and relationships between change and knowledge management strategies are detailed, also highlighting their IT support.

Knowledge is a strategic resource of companies, also being a decisive factor of public administrations' success. All knowledge management initiatives, such as implementing new technical solutions, reorganization or promoting knowledge-sharing culture provide substantial challenges. Continuous challenges force companies to take the approach of change management into consideration. Different approaches and success factors of changes are hot topics in the literature (Jashapara, 2011; Dalkir 2013). The nature of change became discontinuous from the 1970s (Jashapara, 2011), when the consequences of the rising oil price shocked companies and forced organizations to manage such unpredictable surprises. Public bodies are subject of change as well, especially nowadays considering economic restrictions and their effects. Employees often resist change, because they have to work in a different environment, give up their work and modify their behavior. Personal response to change can be various, from shocking to adaptation, according to the transition phases in the cycle of change (Hayes, 2002). Commitment of employees has crucial role in the success of change management. According to Strebel, three dimensions are important to reach their commitment (Strebel, 1996): "formal dimension (job description, tasks and processes, relationships,

compensation), psychological dimension (equity of work and compensation) and social dimension (unwritten rules, values)."

Kotter stated that organizations successfully change in a slow-moving world in a very calculated, controlled way that is mostly a management process (Kotter, 1997). He analysed the failure factors of change processes (Kotter, 1995) and identified 8 steps of the change management process: feeling of urgency for change (which is a starting condition), forming a good team (supportive coalition), create a vision of change, communicate the vision, remove obstacles, change fast (create short term wins), consolidate results and keep on changing while embedding changes into culture. These steps require a knowledge management strategy that emphasizes the importance of tacit knowledge and long-term management.

Today, due to the fast-changing environment people are forced to take larger leap, like perform organization-wide reengineering projects. Lewin suggested three phases of change management for helping individuals, groups and organizations (Lewin, 1951):

- *Unfreezing and Loosening* current sets of behaviors, mental models and ways of looking problem.
- *Moving* by making changes in the way people do things, new structures, new strategies and different types of behaviors and attitudes.
- *Refreezing* by stabilizing and establishing new patterns and organizational routines.

Lewin's approach is cited frequently in the literature, as being general model of change management, which can be applied together with the decisive knowledge management strategies.

Several other change management theories and assumptions were published, like Lippitt's Phases of Change Theory (Lippitt, 1958), Prochaska and DiClemente's Change Theory (Prochaska & DiClemente, 1986), Social Cognitive Theory, and the Theory of Reasoned Action and Planned Behavior.

Organizations facing the need of change management utilize a variety of resources supporting them in reaching their goal. Based on the Resource-Based View (RBV) of the firm, change management strategy has to focus on the acquisition and use of resources, like new competencies (Barney, 1991; Wernerfelt, 1984). According to this approach, organizations can select between the following alternatives (Bloodgood & Salisbury, 2001):

- Reconfigure existing resources;
- Acquire new resources with reconfiguration;
- Acquire new resources without reconfiguration, or they may;
- Preserve the status quo and engage in a business as usual strategy.

This Resource-Based View is applied in the analyses of relationships between change management strategy, knowledge management strategy and their IT support. The key question is what kind of information technology should be applied in the organization in order to support these strategies.

Knowledge Management Strategies

Based on the KM strategy literature and consultancy, common form of knowledge management strategies are codification and personalization strategies (Hansen et al. 1999). Codification strategy relies mainly on information technology and often uses databases to codify and store knowledge. This approach emphasizes the importance of explicit knowledge and externalization (Nonaka & Takeuchi, 1995). It is a risk-avoiding approach, because there is a little room for innovation and creativity, they use the tried and tested methods. Personalization strategy is more about people; the focus is on tacit knowledge and on its sharing. It is a creative, networking-based approach, which can result high profit through unique and innovative

solutions. This strategy requires high level of rewards for knowledge sharing and dialogues. Form of strategy proposed is characterized as dialectic between the forces of innovation (personalization strategy oriented) and efficiency (codification strategy oriented) (Mintzberg, 1991).

Finding a proper ratio between personalization and codification is difficult for public administration since the obligatory tradition of codification, conforming to regulations and the nature of the work; but personalization is required by the rapid changes in their environment, like economic downturns and political changes.

Several other knowledge management strategies have been proposed in the literature emphasizing different aspects of knowledge management. Some KM strategies focus on the type of knowledge, others on the business processes/areas, and others on the end results. Karl Wiig (1997) and the APQC (American Productivity and Quality Center) identified six emerging KM strategies, reflecting the different natures and strengths of the organizations involved (Wiig, 1997; Manasco, 1996). Day and Wendler of McKinsey & Company distinguished five knowledge strategies employed by large corporations, (Day & Wendler, 1998). Knox Haggie and John Kingston provided guidance for KM strategy selection (Haggie & Kingston, 2003). Table 1 based on Bloodgood and Salisbury (2001) approach highlights relationships between change strategies, knowledge management strategies and their IT support.

Reconfiguring existing resources strategy aims to achieve a better fit to the current external environment by changing the way existing resources are used by the organization. This approach mainly requires personalization, because knowledge assets of the organization have already been codified but the way of usage is different. Tacit knowledge and socialization have key role in this process. IT support is targeting network creation; forums, groupware are typical IT solutions used in this approach.

Table 1. Relationships between change strategies, knowledge management strategies and their IT support

Change Strategies	Knowledge Type Emphasized		Knowledge Management Strategy		Typical IT Support
	Explicit	*Tacit*	*Codification*	*Personalization*	
Reconfigure existing resources	Low	High	Low	High	Create networks
Acquire new resources with reconfiguration	Moderate	Moderate	Moderate	Moderate	Create networks and codifying knowledge
Acquire new resources without reconfiguration	High	Low	High	Low	Codifying knowledge

Acquiring new resources with reconfiguration strategy combines codification and personalization strategy; both explicit and tacit knowledge are emphasized. Socialization and externalization are appropriate approaches, making knowledge repositories and groupware suitable forms of IT support.

Acquiring new resources without reconfiguration strategy concentrates on explicit knowledge and emphasizes codification strategy. Competitive advantage is gained through fast knowledge transfer. This strategy focuses on IT usage, relying typically on knowledge repositories and ontologies.

Nowadays, the economic downturn forced public administration to apply reconfiguring existing resources strategy in most of the cases, increasing the importance of personalization strategy. IT support has to concentrate on network creation, emphasizing solutions assisting socialization.

SAKE IT solution provides an example of compliance with the needs arising from change management and knowledge management strategies. Before discussing its features an overview about the underlying knowledge management system development methodology is presented.

Knowledge Management System Development Methodologies

Different approaches to knowledge management can be distinguished on the basis of the investigated research questions, as the learning focused approach; the process focused approach; the technology focused approach; the environment focused (ecological) approach and the purpose focused approach (Klimkó, 2001). Researchers following the technology focused approach consider knowledge as a transferable object.

The first step of a technology based approach is often to set up a knowledge repository (Davenport, 1998), in which proper search capabilities has to be offered. A similar approach with different starting point is the one dealing with the so-called organizational memory, which is considered to be a real object that can be constructed with the tools of information technology. Abecker and his co-authors want to facilitate context-sensitive searching in the organizational memory by using different levels of ontologies (company, business area, information level) (Abecker et al., 1998).

In order to set up a knowledge repository (or sometimes referred as to build a knowledge-base or simply knowledge system) a proper methodology is required. One of the most wide-spread approaches among suitable methodologies is the CommonKADS method (Schreiber et al., 2000). The authors of CommonKADS wanted to provide a structured, verifiable and repeatable way for building a (software) system. Knowledge acquisition is done by engineering-like methods, with the help of knowledge engineering. The underlying assumption of CommonKADS is that knowledge engineering means description of the knowledge from different viewpoints, being a modelling activity where an aspect model is a proper abstraction of reality itself. CommonKADS assumes that knowledge has a stable internal structure that can be analyzed by describing different roles and knowledge types. This assumption is analogous with the stability of data models in structured methodologies that help building up traditional data processing systems.. The base of the methodology is a set of models consisting of six model types (Schreiber et al., 2000):

- **Organizational model:** Describing the organizational environment.
- **Task model:** Collecting tasks, which are considered relevant subsets of business processes. The task model globally analyses entire tasks: inputs, outputs, resources, conditions and the requirements of execution.
- **Agent model:** Representing agents performing processes described in the Task model.
- **Communication model:** Describing communication, information exchange, and interaction between agents.
- **Knowledge model:** Consisting of an explicit, detailed description of the type and the structure of knowledge used in the course of execution.
- **Design model:** Defining a technical system specification based on the requirements specification determined by the models detailed above.

Recently performed researches applying agile methods form the software engineering community (like eXtreme Programming) in the knowledge management (Hans, 2004) seem to be very promising for the management of changes. Indeed, the characteristic of agile methodologies is their attempt to shift the company's organizational and project memory from external to tacit knowledge, i.e. written documentation is replaced by communication among team members. In the SAKE project, this idea is extended by introducing

semantic technologies that enable a formal and explicit representation of all factors that implement changes and their relations to knowledge and knowledge workers in order to resolve the problem of the consistent change propagation accounted in the previously mentioned system. Auer and Herre (Auer & Herre, 2007) proposed RapidOWL methodology for collaborative knowledge engineering. The major aim of RapidOWL is to make the elicitation, structuring and processing of knowledge and thus the cooperation of domain experts and knowledge engineers more efficient. The RapidOWL methodology is based on the idea of iterative refinement, annotation and structuring of a knowledge base. In SMART solution this iterative refinement and structuring of a knowledge base is performed.

CASE DESCRIPTION

The SAKE methodology constitutes a hybrid composition of approaches and methodologies. Specifically, the proposed methodology takes in account a) the Know-Net method, that has been designed as a supporting tool to help the design, development, and deployment of a holistic Knowledge Management Infrastructure, b) the CommonKADS methodology (Schreiber, et al., 2000), that supports structured knowledge engineering, and c) the DECOR Business Knowledge Method (Abecker, et al., 2003) that constitutes a business process oriented knowledge management method consisting of a structured archive around the notion of the company's business processes which are equipped with active, context-sensitive knowledge delivery, to promote a better exploitation of knowledge sources. The *Know-Net method* elaborated by KNOW-NET (Esprit EP28928) project provides a holistic corporate knowledge management method and tool integrating content management and collaboration with advanced search and retrieval. The method is based on a knowledge asset centric framework combining the process-centred view of knowledge management (treating knowledge management as an interpersonal communication process) and the product-centred approach (which focuses on the artefacts for knowledge). The method claims that knowledge assets and knowledge objects are the common unifiers of a holistic organization-wide knowledge management environment that integrates process and content. This solution was further enhanced and tested in the LEVER project (IST-1999-20216) that helped four user companies set up knowledge repositories, facilitate knowledge exchange in communities of practice and implement procedures for capturing and diffusing best practices. CommonKADS methodology is detailed in the previous section. A structured archive has been provided by DECOR, enriching business processes with active, context-sensitive knowledge delivery to promote a better exploitation of knowledge sources. The core of the DECOR Business Knowledge Method is an extended Business Process Modelling method, including automatable knowledge retrieval activities, additional knowledge management tasks,

sub-processes, and additional process variables. It provides methodological guidance for running a Business-Process Oriented Knowledge Management (BPOKM), which includes a) business process identification and analysis b) task analyses c) business process design d) ontology creation and refinement.

The objectives of the SAKE methodology are to:

- Facilitate the planning of necessary organizational changes (processes, actors, systems);
- Facilitate the (re-)structuring of PAs' knowledge resources (processes, actors, systems etc.);
- Support the adaptation of changes in policy, strategy and law from the public sector (e.g. continuous harmonization with EU regulations).

Figure 1 provides a diagrammatic overview of the SAKE methodology.

Figure 1. Overall SAKE methodology (Papadakis, 2006)

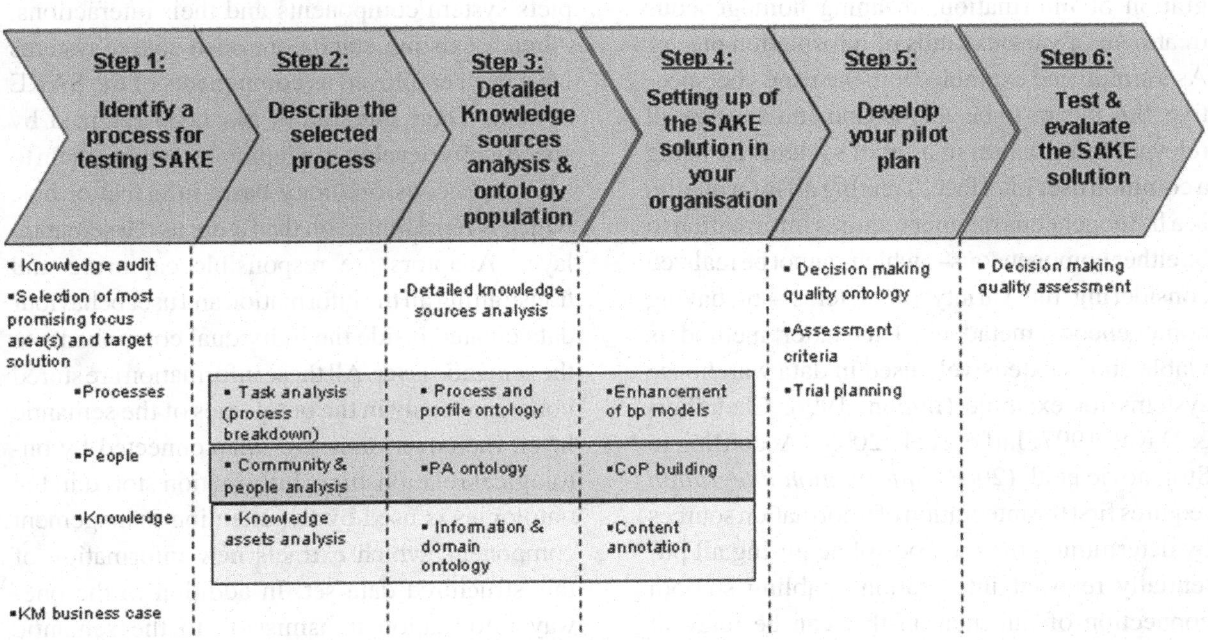

The SAKE methodology consists of the following steps:

- Knowledge "as is" analysis aiming to identify the current state of the Knowledge Infrastructure from the perspectives of currently existing and missing elements.
- Knowledge sources analysis involving the identification and specification of knowledge sources existing in the organization (PA).
- Ontology creation and population that involves the design and development of pilot-specific extensions and instances of the pre-developed ontologies that realize the conceptual framework of SAKE approach.
- Deployment of basic functionality and process modelling aiming the deployment of the basic functionality of Groupware and Content Management Systems in order to get a hands-on understanding of the basic SAKE functionality and provide user feedback on functionality issues.
- Testing, evaluating pilot solution.

Focus of the SAKE system itself is the integration of information, meaning homogeneous treatment of various kinds of information pieces. As a simplified example from the user's perspective, this means to be able to find and manage all relevant information in a set of systems by using a common user interface. Treating all information in a homogeneous manner requires information to be either homogeneous—which cannot be realized considering the variety of systems—or having homogeneous metadata. This latter method is viable and is extensively used in data warehouse systems for example (Inmon, 1996; Chaudhuri & Dayal, 1997; Jarke, et al., 2003). According to Stojanovic et al. (2008), *information integration* requires first the integration of information sources by determining the methods of acquiring all potentially relevant information enabling smooth connection of information that can be relevant

for a decision making process of an organization. Second requirement is the integrated processing of all information, ensuring a common view in order to get the most useful outcome for the decision making process. Finally, the integration of information flow with the current process and user context is necessary for defining the importance of information to the user. Information integration provides a framework for knowledge repositories needed to serve knowledge codification, acquisition and leveraging. SAKE system itself aims the realization of these requirements through offering an IT environment providing appropriate answers to the challenges of the public administration. The system consists of various components reflecting to these requirements, offering solutions to the above-mentioned problems of the public administration by being enhanced via means of information integration.

Overview of SAKE System Components

This section provides an overview about SAKE system main components, presenting them from the viewpoint of the functionalities. Figure 2 depicts system components and their interactions. Already existing, standalone open-source systems have been employed as components of the SAKE system. Their integration has been realized by specifically developed adaptors, attaching them to a homogeneous, ontology-based information bus, which is represented on the figure as the semantic layer. Adaptors are responsible capturing and transmitting all the information and user behaviour data created inside the individual components to the semantic layer. All these information are stored homogeneously in the ontologies of the semantic layer, moreover, they are interconnected by ontological relationships. Information stored in the ontologies is used by the attention management component, which extracts new information of this structured data set. In addition to the one-way information transmission to the semantic

Figure 2. SAKE system components (Stojanovic, et al., 2008)

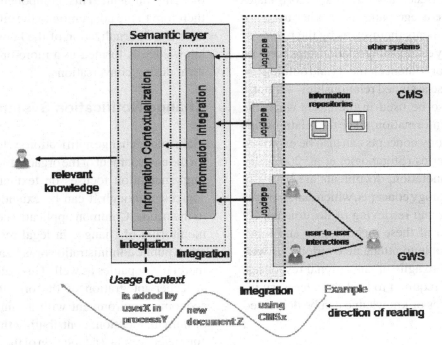

layer, functionalities of the components are also extended by ontology-based functions that are detailed later. These functions realize integration between the components themselves. On the top, a homogeneous, web-based common user interface applying portal technologies has been developed.

In the followings, details of the components are presented, also emphasizing the compliance for the requirements detailed before.

Content Management System

Most frequent sources of knowledge in an organization are various textual content, or in other words, documents. This form is used widely, is usually understood by every partners in a communication process, it is easy to update, index and provide searching facilities based on its content, and can be processed by humans and software as well. Content management systems can also manage other types of content like audio or video, querying facilities however are inadequate to cope with them effectively. Currently, full-text search is one of the most used means to retrieve information stored in textual form; however, it has several shortcomings, like homonyms, synonyms and other linguistic problems, also including the problem of different languages. By the introduction of ontologies as part of a semantic layer behind the components, it is possible to homogenize information stored in various types of content in the content management system, as well as to enrich the stored content with contextual information, including the current business process, activity, and task; as well as user information. The availability of this additional information enables several features that can support the work of public administrators. The typical overload situation of the administrators can be alleviated by filtering information according to the contextual information available in the semantic layer. This way, in the case of content management system, documents and knowledge that are relevant to the current processes or activities can be offered automatically. Necessary information originates either from the usage patterns of other users, or from the documents themselves by the means of indexing and by establishing relationships between the document or content elements and ontological concepts. These assigned relationships—annotations—can also be used in the cases when the users look for information, since the relationships between ontology concepts can also be exploited during the queries (Stojanovic, et al, 2007). By having this annotation, documents are basically mapped to ontology concepts, which can also ease the processing and retrieving of documents. By the application of these technologies and functions it is possible to attenuate overload, as well as enabling more agile organizational responses, since the time required to find the necessary information pieces or knowledge can be decreased significantly.

Groupware System

The information that is hidden in communication processes can also provide a great added value to the organization, when they can be exploited to some extent. Groupware system supports communication and collaboration activities by offering common facilities like discussion forums, shared calendars and notification services. This component also employs the functions of the semantic layer, meaning that all information created in the component's facilities is also stored in the ontologies, together with contextual information that was detailed in the case of content management system. As an additional feature, annotation is also present in this component via the means of ranking, indicating the usefulness of a conversation item for solving the targeted problem. Besides, usage patterns are also recorded in the ontologies, which contribute to the preciseness of information retrieval. Facilities of the groupware system contribute to the preservation of knowledge as communication in the organization usually contains the fastest reflections to the changes of

the environment. This component contributes therefore to the adaptation to the changes as well as to the externalization of the knowledge, since knowledge is formed in a more-or-less tangible form during conversations.

Change Notification System

Main role of change notification system is to monitor the environment of the organization. Its current implementation focuses on textual information sources, although it can be extended according to the needs. Common application of CNS is the monitoring of changes in legal regulations that affect public administration organizations or commercial companies as well. This facility provides a deeper integration of the organization in its economic environment with a minimal amount of human attention, contributing this way to the competence of fast adaptation of the organization. The changes noticed in the monitored environment are delivered to the ontologies and are processed by the public administrators, since it is still not a realistic requirement to have the external sources automatically processed and incorporated into the common knowledge of the organization.

Workflow Management System

Business processes are key points in SAKE system operation as providing contextual information to other components, as well as guiding the users during problem solving processes. In a public administration environment processes are determined strictly by legal regulations. These processes can be described in a process model and a workflow can be built upon that. In the case of SAKE system, processes are modelled using an ontological description in order to be able to integrate them with other information in the system through the ontologies. This model is converted into an executable format and fed to a workflow engine, which offers a performance gain as compared to an ontological execution.

During the process execution, all information provided by the users and all events happened in the context of the process are stored in instances of the process in the ontology. Ontology always provides this way an adequate picture of the current state of the process, constituting also the business context, which is used by every other component as described before. It has to be considered, however, that knowledge-intensive processes cannot be described fully in a formal way. In the case of the Hungarian pilot detailed below, a ministerial proposal has to be developed by a consulting body, which involves mainly experts' discussion. In this case, support of the workflow system is limited to the frames of the process, while the components of the system are used upon need, providing all additional semantic information as described above. According to the discussion above, having well-defined processes and workflows contribute to the transparency of the operation of public administration institutions. This approach also represents a way to preserve organizational knowledge crystallized in best practices by means of formalizing them into processes.

Attention Management System

The Attention Management System (AMS) component of the SAKE system provides information according to the semantic information stored in the ontologies of the semantic layer. AMS employs a reasoner (KAON2 has been selected in the project for performance reasons) and executes various predefined and ad-hoc queries, delivering information to the user that are thought to be relevant according the rules. AMS is used for providing the semantics-related functions described above, like the delivery of context-related documents and discussions in a given environment, as well as finding content-related information to a specific domain.

SAKE components support acquiring new resources with reconfiguration change strategy; they facilitate network creation (e.g. groupware

component) and knowledge codification (e.g. content management component) as well. Next section details SAKE solution validation through the Hungarian pilot.

The Hungarian Pilot: Higher Education Portfolio Alignment with World of Labour Needs

SAKE solution was validated on three cases of PA organizations located in three different countries: Hungary, Poland, and Slovakia. Pilots were set up and organized according to SAKE methodology described above.

Higher education in Hungary had to face several challenges recently, like decreasing student population, stronger competition between higher education institutes, capacity overflow and compliance to the reforms of European Higher Education initiated by Bologna declaration. Hungarian Government decided a large-scale reform aiming to modify the Hungarian higher educational system, both the educational structure and the operating model. By connecting to the European Higher Education Area, Hungary needs to modernize operating processes, improve quality radically, and introduce strategic human resource management. The labour market demands three times more persons from vocational training, compared to the graduated number of students. Structure of the higher education shifted towards the humanities, arts, legal studies and business administration in Hungary and in most countries of Europe, compared to engineering and education in applied sciences. Structural problems require restructuring the educational portfolio and a sharp modification in teachers' education. Restructuring is also a strategic human resource management task with several risks. Hungarian case in SAKE project aimed higher education portfolio alignment with world of labour needs, which means the support of validation. Purpose of validation is to match the individual's competences with the needs of the labour market (Thomsen, 2008). The alignment process is a "strategic" problem at the field of education, which consists of knowledge intensive tasks. Different domains and cultural backgrounds of the players in the pilot process require unified and consistent interpretation, which is provided by underlying ontologies. Additional challenge is the reconciliation of the central planning and higher educational institutes' autonomy.

Main steps in Hungarian pilot process were the following:

- Description of the educational output by the Higher Education Manager (supported by SAKE semantic layer and CMS).
- Updating the database containing the actual figures of education (like number of students, who can start their studies in a certain year).
- Data collection about job opportunities, labour requirements (supported by SAKE CMS and CNS).
- Job profiling (supported by SAKE semantic layer and CMS).
- Comparison of existing job profiles and educational output (supported by SAKE semantic layer).
- Labour market forecast preparation for 3-5 years (supported by SAKE groupware and CMS).
- Job profiling – determination of world of labour needs (supported by SAKE groupware and SAKE semantic layer).
- Comparison of forecasted job profiles and educational output (supported by SAKE semantic layer).
- Planning further actions (supported by SAKE Groupware and CMS).

All steps were supported by workflow component. Higher education portfolio means the offer for the students in order to achieve their smooth integration to the labour market after their graduation. Higher education portfolio is normally prepared by public servants five or three years before the exact needs and situation of the labour market demands are known. Educational output (educational offer) is determined by higher educational portfolio, it contains the details of degree programs. Job profiling provides a job profile document for SAKE system. Job profiles are stored by CMS and their annotations are maintained in the semantic layer. Forecasting of labour market needs is a must, meanwhile codification of demands are also needed. Two primary roles are decisive in the pilot process, the Higher Education Manager and Educational Planner. Higher Education Manager is responsible for the educational output, while Educational Planner prepares the job profiles, detailing educational demand of labour market. SAKE system is an excellent candidate to support PA employees in the above mentioned pilot process, because of the following reasons:

- Higher Education Manager and Educational Planner are facing with information overload; educational output, job profiles, regulation, economic environment have to be processed during the planning process.
- More accurate planning is needed, due to the fast changing demographic and economic tendencies.
- Pilot process requires collaboration and cooperation among the partners involved in the process.
- Knowledge used in the pilot needed codification.
- "Matching" had no IT support earlier.
- Pilot process requires a conceptual framework.
- Pilot process needs documentation and strong control.

Higher educational portfolio determines the higher education offer, which consists of graduated students. From the labour market perspective the most important characters of the offers are the graduated students' competencies, namely their skills, abilities and knowledge, which make them a proper candidate to comply with a certain job. These competencies are defined by higher education degree programs. World of labour needs is the educational demand of labour market, which is described by job profiles collected from the publicly available resources, like recruitment databases and decisive Hungarian job portals. Educational output (degree programs), the offer and the job profiles the demand are compared in terms of competencies. Competencies are used as specific statements of areas of personal capability that enable to perform successfully in their jobs by completing tasks effectively (Mentzas et al, 2006).

Development of domain ontology for the Hungarian pilot was the most important task of system implementation and customization. This ontology contained descriptions of the above-mentioned competencies and educational outputs. In this phase of implementation, domain experts have been invited to cooperate on the development

of ontology to ensure a common model. In addition, documents of accredited qualifications and courses have been processed in order to determine detailed competencies offered and get adequate data on higher educational output.

During the operation of the system, job profiles have been processed as annotated documents, during which relationships have been established between the job profiles and competencies. Ontological reasoning have been employed to realize the matching between educational outputs and annotated job profiles in order to provide input for the rest of decision making preparation process (see Figure 3).

The following user scenario presents SAKE system's support for Higher Education Manager during the educational planning process.

Higher Education Manager is preparing the educational output, which he already did many times before. However, the corresponding law

Figure 3. Screenshot from SAKE system

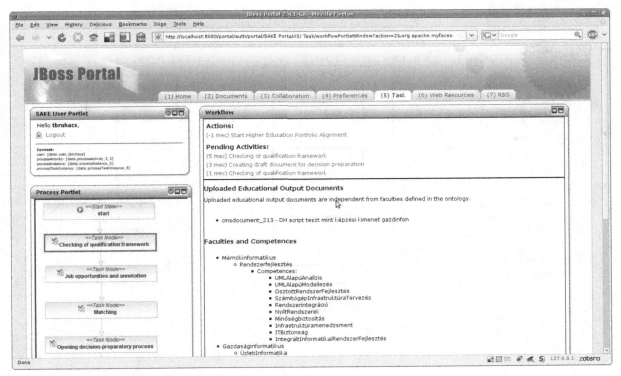

(Act on Higher Education, 2004) has been changed recently, so that CMS system warns him that he should be more careful in the resolution. Indeed, the context of the case is recognized and the module Attention Management searches for the semantically relevant recent changes in documents that are related to the given case, in order to inform the user. Moreover, the changed parts of relevant documents can be highlighted (Figure 4).

Users' Experiences and Feedback

The Hungarian trial team comprised of labour market experts, higher education experts and ministry staff responsible for higher education development. Overall, users were satisfied with the system capabilities. Several improvements were identified as a result of SAKE's intervention, as the possibility of involving more stakeholders in the process in timely manner; or making complex decision making easier (Samiotis, 2009).

User feedback was positive on system components: content management was found useful – especially the annotation and classification features –, groupware system supported the collaboration effectively; workflow has contributed to the transparency of the process. Users highlighted that the ability to have the educational output and the labour market demand represented in competencies (the annotation feature) is valuable by itself, moreover the reasoning capability on the top of this was also found very interesting and promising by the users. Similar impression has been expressed for the semantic search. Overall, having a central document management solution and improved cooperation in the specific working environment was found a very useful approach.

Collaboration functions of the system were found to be a new way of communication among colleagues, which presupposes the adoption of a new mentality and a new way of working and dealing with workflow processes. Content-wise, the operation of the system depends greatly on

Figure 4. Higher education manager is coping with changes in law

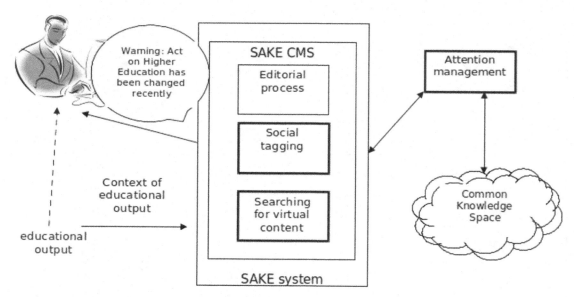

the information created, uploaded and exchanged by its users. If these prerequisites are fulfilled then SAKE could act and react to users' requests responsively and timely. Users have found pushing of information as a strong feature of SAKE, although it should be refined more in the future. As a conclusion, it is agreed that effectiveness of this feature depends largely on the users' contribution.

On the negative side, users have mentioned difficulties of navigation inside the system as well as the immature graphical user interface, which are caused by the fact that during the prototype development, more attention was paid to the functionalities than to the user experience.

The knowledge management-based approach of this pilot process was beneficial for PA's from several aspects:

- It helped to refine knowledge and change management strategy of the PA
- Pilot process became more transparent, faster, documented and controlled easier than before
- Knowledge used by the pilot process was codified and available as explicit knowledge for another processes
- Matching of educational output and labour market demands got IT support
- Common conceptual framework was provided.

Higher education portfolio planning got useful feedback from the system, e.g. by highlighting those competencies, which are required by the labour market, but not available in the higher education. Important experience of the pilot was that the introduction of an innovative solution, like SAKE requires special knowledge management related techniques, like the customization of organizational culture in order to make public servants more committed and motivated. Hungar-

ian pilot highlighted that SAKE system can support lowering the unemployment rate through the more precisely planning of higher education portfolio.

SAKE Solution Summary and Conclusion

SAKE main components provided several tangible, beneficial features for PA organization and its employees as well; amongst other it supported to refine their change management and knowledge management strategy. Satisfying the need for adaptive, fast and knowledge-based decisions was facilitated by semantically-enhanced components. Change management component has provided quick discovery of changes in the environment of the organization. Semantic-enhanced content management system has offered more effective information retrieval via mapping content elements to ontology concepts. Groupware system has facilitated decision preparatory discussions by annotation functions. Workflow system has orchestrated the decision preparation process by offering the framework of activities. Finally, attention management system has filtered semantic information captured in all other components during the operation of the system by applying pre-defined and ad-hoc rules. SAKE system provided several added values for public administrators' work, like the improved communication and collaboration quality. Threads, "comment on comment" support has made communication more structured. SAKE system provided a framework for knowledge externalization; educational demand and job profiles are structured, organized and annotated. Semantic layer offered common terminology and taxonomy, which are important where several stakeholders with different background are working in the same process. Another useful feature is the notification of potentially interesting changes. Main results of SAKE project were the following:

- SAKE methodology;
- SAKE ontologies;
- SAKE components (code and documentation);
  - Semantic Layer;
  - Attention Management System;
  - Change Management System;
  - Workflow Management System;
  - Content Management System;
  - Groupware System.

IMPROVED SAKE CASE: SMART APPROACH

SAKE solution was improved and applied in other projects and pilots. OntoHR project (LLP-1-2009-1-HU-LEONARDO-LMP) utilized SAKE IT solution and Hungarian pilot case experiences. The project aimed to facilitate competency based selection and recruitment with ontology supported information system (Kismihók, 2010). In UbiPOL project (FP7-ICT-2009-4, ICT-2009.7.3: ICT for Governance and Policy Modelling), the SAKE workflow solution lessons learnt was investigated and utilized in workflow modelling (Tsohou, 2012). SMART research extended and further developed SAKE solution, meanwhile utilized SAKE pilot experiences. SMART (Skill MAtching for Regional developmenT) aims similar target domain as SAKE Hungarian pilot. It seeks answer the need of matching between educational system supply and the job market's professional requirements by the design of an innovative system able to map profiles required by the job market and the job seekers' competences and to improve the collaboration among Vocational Education and Training (VET), institutional and business sectors. SMART solution is supported through the implementation of a dynamic ontology-based adaptive tool inspired by the competence's approach, which is able to identify and anticipate the new emerging jobs and market's needs and to

support the adaptation of the learning outcomes of the educational regional system. The project focuses on education and job balance in Andalusia region featured by high rates of unemployment and overqualification.

The project adapted and enriched results of the partners' previous EU projects in order to define common operative frames and anticipate the market needs: MISLEM proved efficient methodologies and procedures to match skills and competences developed by educational and VET institutions and labour market requirements. STUDIO developed an ontology-driven approach and tools that map and anticipate needs of companies and educational competences (see Figure 5).

The logic of the SMART solution is summarized in Figure 5. Labour market needs are captured from job requirements available in job offers online in the Internet. Job offers are identified and collected with web mining techniques. These job offers further analyzed with text mining pre-processing component to provide input for the ontology learning tool, which is supporting the labour market ontology construction. Labour market ontology has similar meta structure as SAKE Hungarian domain ontology. Educational system supply is managed by the STUDIO ontology driven adaptive knowledge evaluation and testing environment. Tourism educational ontology of STUDIO environment provides a structure for educational output. Ontology matching part is comparing tourism educational ontology and labour market ontology revealing the gap between educational output and labour market needs.

CURRENT CHALLENGES

Nevertheless, SAKE's propositions for work were not assimilated by the end users to the desired level. This finding has a huge value for this project and also for other similar initiatives. It proved again that technological interventions cannot be capi-

Figure 5. SMART solution overview

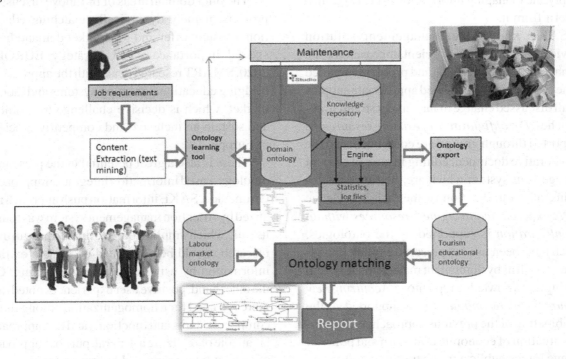

talized unless the organizational environment is prepared to do so. One way to tackle this problem is to offer methodological support in all phases of the technology intervention, from introduction, familiarization, adaptation, rethinking, up to operalization, then to re-invention and back to adaptation again. This issue was attempted to be addressed by the SAKE methodology, but further work should be done for the confrontation of organizational barriers and the prescription of countermeasures.

SAKE, OntoHR and SMART solutions have proven that despite any difficulties it is worthwhile to invest in knowledge management. SAKE as an ICT tool realizes in its functionalities i.e. content management, groupware, workflow, all basic KM manifestations for the creation, sharing and application of knowledge. It also introduces a novel approach in KM through the notion and implementation of attention management, which is shifting KM's support from pull-based to push-based approach.

It has been concluded that ontology engineering is a difficult task and can be a bottleneck in knowledge acquisition, but the chosen methodology has a decisive role regarding the quality of the end product and facilitates development. Building ontology is a cooperative task of many experts requiring a collaborative environment during the development. By the inclusion of the environmental changes, SAKE system supports the creation of a common organizational knowledge repository, which helps avoiding knowledge inconsistencies and ambiguities in the organization. SAKE system had some disadvantages as well, like ignorance of recipients against continuous notifications. Lack of computer skills or missing trust can cause difficulties in the systems' operation. The system may appear too complicated, which can hinder its usage. Lessons learnt, experiences gained in SAKE project were utilized in several other fields and projects; especially in the investigation of job market needs, educational system supply and managing information overload gained benefit from it.

SAKE knowledge management solution provided effective and efficient approach for the management of challenges and problems detailed in the first section. It provided appropriate support for all discussed change management strategic approaches. *Reconfiguration of existing resources* is supported through groupware component and the collaborative document editing feature of content management system which are the functions focusing on the utilization of the tacit knowledge of PA experts. *Acquiring new resources without reconfiguration* is supported by the ontologies, which have been used to preserve explicit knowledge; as well as by the content management system serving as a knowledge repository. *Acquiring new resources with reconfiguration* is supported via the combination of the previous approaches. The current situation of economic downturn and political change forces public administration to follow the reconfigure existing resources strategy, which is appropriate on the short run, however the authors are convinced that the combined application of personalization and codification strategy results in long-term success. Ratio between personalization and codification strategy is influenced by environmental effects and change management strategies.

According to the experiences gained during the system development, ontology development is one of the most complex and time consuming tasks that requires professional experience involving a lot of expert discussions and efforts. On its technological side, currently available ontology reasoners applied in the system require many resources in terms of computing time and operative storage capacities. Development of more efficient reasoning engines or enabling parallel processing of ontologies can encourage the development of information integration solutions, like the one depicted in this article.

The pilot domain areas of the above discussed projects, namely dynamically matching educational system offer and job market demand have special importance in EU strategy EUROPE 2020. SMART research deals with the approaches bridging educational/training systems and labour market, which is decisive challenge to promote and sustain an inclusive and competitive society in Europe.

There is also a great potential in the presented ontology-based information integration approach. On one side, SAKE information push approach realized by Attention management system was found useful, which implies on one hand that further research should be conducted on how to extract information by using ontological reasoning. On the other hand, positive user experiences noted that there is a need for a homogenization among these complex systems and functions, and this approach is capable of realizing a general-purpose approach of system integration and homogenization.

ACKNOWLEDGMENT

Project SAKE (IST-2005-027128) is funded by the European Commission's 6th Framework Programme. This publication reflects only the author's views. The European Community, represented by the Commission of the European Communities is not liable for any use that may be made of the information contained herein. Further information regarding SAKE can be found at http://www.sake-project.org/.

SMART (Supporting dynamic MAtching for Regional developmenT) Leonardo da Vinci Transfer of Innovation Project; Reference: 201-1-ES1-LEO05-49395

TÁMOP-4.2.1/B-09/1/KMR-2010-0005 is a research and innovation program of the Corvinus University of Budapest aiming ICT-based analyses of knowledge transfer, sharing and knowledge codification fields.

REFERENCES

Abecker, A., Bernardi, A., Hinkelmann, K., Kühn, O., & Sintek, M. (1998). Toward a Technology for Organisational Memories. *IEEE Intelligent Systems*, *13*(3), 40–48. doi:10.1109/5254.683209

Abecker, A., Mentzas, G., Ntioudis, S., & Papavassiliou, G. (2003). Business Process Modelling and Enactment for Task-Specific Information Support. *Wirtschaftsinformatik*, *2003*(1), 977–996.

Abrahamson, E. (2000). Change Without Pain. *Harvard Business Review*, (July-August): 75–79.

Auer, S., & Herre, H. (2007). RapidOWL - An Agile Knowledge Engineering Methodology. In *Perspectives of Systems Informatics* (pp. 424–430). Springer Berlin Heidelberg. doi:10.1007/978-3-540-70881-0_36

Barney, J. B. (1991). Firm resources and sustained competitive advantage. *Journal of Management*, *17*(1), 99–120. doi:10.1177/014920639101700108

Barquin, R. (2010).: Knowledge Management in the Federal Government: A 2010 Update; http://www.b-eye-network.com/view/14527

Bloodgood, J. M., & Salisbury, W. D. (2001). Understanding the influence of organizational change strategies on information technology and knowledge management strategies. *Decision Support System Journal*, *31*, 55–69. doi:10.1016/S0167-9236(00)00119-6

Bray, D. A. (2008). *Information pollution, knowledge overload, limited attention spans, and our responsibilities as IS professionals*. Paper presented in Global Information Technology Management Association (GITMA) World Conference. Atlanta, GA.

Chaudhuri, S., & Dayal, U. (1997). An overview of data warehousing and OLAP technology. *SIGMOD Record*, *26*(1), 65–74. doi:10.1145/248603.248616

Dalkir, K. (2013). *Knowledge management in theory and practice*. Routledge.

Davenport, T. H., Long, D. W., & Beers, M. C. (1998). Successful Knowledge Management Projects. *Sloan Management Review*, *39*, 43–57.

Day, J. D., & Wendler, J. C. (1998). Best Practice and Beyond: Knowledge Strategies. *The McKinsey Quarterly*, *1*, 19–25.

Gruber, T. R. (1993). A translation approach to portable ontology specifications. *Knowledge Acquisition*, *5*(2), 199–220. doi:10.1006/knac.1993.1008

Haggie, K. & Kingston, J. (2003, June). Choosing Your Knowledge Management Strategy. *Journal of Knowledge Management Practice*, 1–24.

Hans, D. D. (2004). Agile Knowledge Management in Practice. In G. Melnik, & H. Holz (Eds.), *Advances in Learning Software Organizations* (Vol. 137–143). Lecture Notes in Computer Science Heidelberg: Springer-Verlag.

Hansen, M. T., Nohria, N., & Tierney, T. (1999). What's Your Strategy for Managing Knowledge? *Harvard Business Review*, (March-April): 106–116. PMID:10387767

Hayes, J. (2002). *The theory and practice of change management*. Palgrave, Basingstone.

Heeks, R. (2006). *Implementing and Managing eGovernment*. London: Sage Publications.

Himma, K. (2007). The concept of information overload: A preliminary step in understanding the nature of a harmful information-related condition. *Ethics and Information Technology*, *9*(4), 259–272. doi:10.1007/s10676-007-9140-8

Holsapple, C. W. (2003). Knowledge and its attributes. In C. W. Holsapple (Ed.), *Handbook on Knowledge Management 1: Knowledge Matters*. Heidelberg: Springer-Verlag. doi:10.1007/978-3-540-24748-7

Inmon, W. (1996). The data warehouse and data mining. *Communications of the ACM*, *39*(11), 49–50. doi:10.1145/240455.240470

Jarke, M., Lenzerini, M., Vassiliou, Y., & Vassiliadis, P. (2003). *Fundamentals of data warehouses*. Springer Verlag. doi:10.1007/978-3-662-05153-5

Jashapara, A. (2011). Knowledge Management: An Integrated Approach (second edition). Prentice Hall, Pearson Education Limited, United Kingdom.

Kismihók, G., Mol, S., Sancin, C., Van der Voort, N., Costello, V., Sorrentino, G., & Zoino, F. (2010). Ontology based competency matching between the vocational education and the workplace: The OntoHR project. *Proceedings of AICA, l'Aquila, Italy*.

Klimkó, G. (2001). *Mapping Organisational Knowledge*. (Unpublished doctoral dissertation). Corvinus University of Budapest, Budapest, Hungary

Kő, A., & Klimkó, G. (2009). Towards a Framework of Information Technology Tools for Supporting Knowledge Management. In E. Noszkay (Ed.), *The Capital of Intelligence - the Intelligence of Capital* (pp. 65–85). Budapest: Foundation for Information Society.

Kotter, J. (2011). Change management vs. change leadership: What's the difference? *Forbes*. Retrieved April 15, 2013

Kotter, J. P. (1995). Leading change: Why transformation efforts fail. *Harvard Business Review*, (March-April): 59–67.

Kotter, J. P. (1997). On leading change: A conversation with John P. Kotter. *Strategy and Leadership*, *25*(1), 18–23. doi:10.1108/eb054576

Lippitt, R., Watson, J., & Westley, B. (1958). *The Dynamics of Planned Change*. New York: Harcourt, Brace.

Manasco, B. (1996). Leading Firms Develop Knowledge Strategies. *Knowledge Inc.*, *1*(6), 26–35.

Mentzas, G., Draganidis, F., & Chamopoulou, P. (2006). An Ontology Based Tool for Competency Management and Learning Path. Presented on I-KNOW 06 conference, Graz, Austria

Mintzberg, H. (1991). The effective organization: forces and forms. *Sloan Management Review*, *32*(2), 57–67.

Nonaka, I., & Takeuchi, H. (1995). *The Knowledge-Creating Company: How Japanese Companies Create the Dynamics of Innovation*. Oxford University Press.

Papadakis, A. (2006). *D5 - As Is Analysis*. SAKE Project Documentation.

Prochaska, J. O., & DiClemente, C. C. (1986). Toward a comprehensive model of change. In W. R. Miller, & N. Heather (Eds.), *Treating addictive behaviors: processes of change* (pp. 3–27). New York: Plenum Press. doi:10.1007/978-1-4613-2191-0_1

Riege, A., & Lindsay, N. (2006). Knowledge management in the public sector: stakeholder partnerships in the public policy development. *Journal of Knowledge Management*, *10*(3), 24–39. doi:10.1108/13673270610670830

Samiotis, K. (Ed.). (2009) *D28 Evaluation Report*. SAKE Project Documentation.

Schreiber, G. (2000). *Knowledge Engineering and Management, The CommonKADS Methodology*. The MIT Press.

Stojanovic, N., Apostolou, D., Dioudis, S., Gábor, A., Kovács, B., Kő A., … Kasprzycki, J. (2008). *D24 – Integration plan.* SAKE Project Documentation.

Stojanovic, N., Kovács, B, Kő, A., Papadakis, A., Apostolou, D., Dioudis, D., Gabor, A., … Kasprzycki, J. (2007). *D16B – 1st Iteration Prototype of Semantic-based Content Management System.* SAKE Project Documentation.

Strebel, P. (1996). Why Do Employees Resist Change? *Harvard Business Review*, (May-June), 86–92.

Thomsen, R. (2008). *Elements in the validation process.* Retrieved 05.03.2008, from http://www.nordvux.net/page/481/cases.htm

Tsohou, A., Lee, H., Al-Yafi, K., Weerakkody, V., El-Haddadeh, R., & Irani, Z. et al. (2012). Supporting Public Policy Making Processes with Workflow Technology: Lessons Learned From Cases in Four European Countries. *International Journal of Electronic Government Research*, *8*(3), 63–77. doi:10.4018/jegr.2012070104

Wernerfelt, B. (1984). A resource-based view of the firm. *Strategic Management Journal*, *5*, 171–180. doi:10.1002/smj.4250050207

Wiig, K. M. (1997). Knowledge Management: Where Did It Come From and Where Will It Go? *Expert Systems with Applications*, *13*(1), 1–14. doi:10.1016/S0957-4174(97)00018-3

KEY TERMS AND DEFINITIONS

Attention Management: Refers to models and tools for supporting the management of attention at the individual or at the collective level, and at the short-term (quasi real time) or at a longer term (over periods of weeks or months).

Change Management: Is an approach to transitioning individuals, teams, and organizations to a desired future state (Kotter, 2011).

Change Management Strategy: Refers strategy for managing change.

E-Government: Refers to the utilization of ICTs to improve and/or enhance the efficiency and effectiveness of service delivery in the public sector.

Knowledge: Is actionable information (Jashapara, 2011).

Knowledge Management: Is the effective learning process associated with exploration, exploitation and sharing of human knowledge (Jashapara, 2011).

Knowledge Management System (KM System): Refers to a (generally IT based) system for managing knowledge in organizations for supporting creation, capture, storage and dissemination of information.

Knowledge Management Strategy: Refers strategy for managing knowledge.

Ontology: Formally represents knowledge as a set of concepts within a domain, using a shared vocabulary to denote the types, properties and interrelationships of those concepts (Gruber, 2003).

Chapter 2
Effects of Perceived Information Quality, Perceived System Quality, and Perceived Flow on Mobile Social Networking Sites (SNS) Users' Trust

Norazah Mohd Suki
Universiti Malaysia – Sabah, Malaysia

Norbayah Mohd Suki
Universiti Malaysia – Sabah, Malaysia

ABSTRACT

This chapter examines the effects of perceived information quality, perceived system quality, and perceived flow on mobile Social Networking Sites (SNS) users' trust. Pearson correlations via SPSS 21.0 computer program was used for data analysis as it has the ability to ensure the consistency of the model with the data, to provide information necessary to scrutinize the study hypotheses, and to estimate associations among constructs. Each correlation coefficient was assessed as significant at the 0.01 level, and the overall model was determined to fit the data well as multicollinearity was absent. In terms of the associations with perceived user trust, perceived flow had highest significant positive correlation coefficients, followed by perceived information quality and perceived system quality. Next, further investigation of the study encountered that perceived flow is significantly associated by both perceived system quality and perceived information quality of mobile SNS, respectively. The chapter concludes with directions for future research.

INTRODUCTION

Social networking sites, such as Facebook, MySpace, Twitter and LinkedIn, which accessed via mobile phones is known as mobile social networking sites (SNS) incorporates the social connections of users by social networking services, and communication channel. Users could enjoy the portability of the mobile device for SNS in terms of create a profile and connect their profile

DOI: 10.4018/978-1-4666-6252-0.ch002

to others, sharing text, images, and photos (Boyd & Ellison, 2008). The advent of SNS is rapidly altering human interaction (Counts & Fisher, 2010; Zhong, Hardin & Sun, 2011). For instance, Facebook has 167,431,700 active users in United States and 13,577,760 active users in Malaysia in 2013 (Socialbakers, 2013). This number continues increasing globally due to millions of people worldwide are living much of their lives on SNS and is quickly becoming one of the most popular tools for social communication and entertainment.

What at people do with SNS? People shared 30 billion pieces of content (i.e. web links, news stories, blog posts, notes, photo albums, pokes, status, photos, news feed, tag, market place, instant messaging and video etc.) via SNS each month and more than 900 million objects that they interact with (i.e. pages, groups, events and community pages). This study is helpful to mobile SNS providers as it discusses the effect of perceived information quality, perceived system quality, and perceived flow on mobile social networking sites (SNS) users' trust. If the mobile SNS provider wishes to retain and increase their customers, special attention will need to be paid towards the information and system quality provided. Apart from that, the variety of SNS management team such as Facebook and Twitter will benefit from this study as well because they are capable of altering and providing the perceived enjoyment to their users. Hence, this study intent to examine the effects of perceived information quality, perceived system quality, and perceived flow on mobile Social Networking Sites (SNS) users' trust.

This chapter is structured as follows. The next section review literature on perceived information quality, perceived system quality, perceived flow, and perceived user trust with deriving testable hypotheses. The ensuing section describes the research methodology used in conducting the research. Section 4 reports the results of the study while section 5 discusses the research findings. The chapter rounds off with conclusions and direction for future research.

PERCEIVED INFORMATION QUALITY

Perceived information quality is related to the amount of information, variety of information, content richness and navigation (Ilsever, Cyr, & Parent, 2007). It is a prevalent social concept and a key antecedent of overall user satisfaction (Aggelidis & Chatzoglou, 2012; Chang, Li, Wu, & Yen, 2012; Zhou, 2013), which impacted the perceived value of the e-commerce system, and information systems success (DeLone & McLean, 1992). It is essential in the creation of a trust building relationship (Fung & Lee, 1999; Keen, Balance, Chan & Schrump, 2000; Kim & Park, 2013; Wong & Hsu, 2008) via the reliable, relevant and personalisation of information exchanges (Yvette & Karine, 2001). Moreover, information quality presented on the Internet has a significant impact on the user flow experience (Chau, Au & Tam, 2000) in terms of the pleasure in using mobile SNS when conduct multiple tasks while surfing the Internet to acquire information or entertaining themselves. For instance, users will most likely form negative perceptions about the information quality of mobile SNS platform if the mobile service provider cannot provide accurate, comprehensive and timely information to its users. Thus, it is posited that:

H1: Perceived information quality of mobile SNS is positively correlated with perceived user trust.
H2: Perceived information quality of mobile SNS is positively correlated with perceived flow.

PERCEIVED SYSTEM QUALITY

Perceived system quality is related to the existence of a fast, reliable links for navigation in processing a request which influences the user's intention to re-enter a website (Chiou, 2005; Garrett, 2003; Hsu & Lu, 2004; Nelson & Todd, 2005). System quality impacts user trust in mobile commerce technologies (Gefen, Pavlou, Benbasat, McKnight, Steward, & Straub, 2006; Vance, Christophe, & Straub, 2008), user satisfaction (Aggelidis & Chatzoglou, 2012; Zhou, 2013), and perceived ease of use (Chen & Hsiao, 2012). Website quality tends to be a stronger predictor of trusting beliefs (McKnight, Choudhury, & Kacmar, 2002). Positive perceived flow engendered during searches at a website helps to produce a remarkable experience among users (Deighton & Grayson 1995). Indeed, inefficient system quality weakens flow experiences (Aladwani & Palvia, 2002). Accordingly, the following hypothesis is developed:

H3: Perceived system quality of mobile SNS is positively correlated with perceived user trust.

H4: Perceived system quality of mobile SNS is positively correlated with perceived flow.

PERCEIVED USER TRUST AND PERCEIVED FLOW

Perceived user trust is related to users' believes that using mobile service will be free of security and privacy threats (Doney & Cannon 1997; Wang, Wang, Lin, & Tang, 2003), which will reduce perceived uncertainty and risks, thus reduce the effort spend on monitoring the mobile service provider, subsequently enhancing users' perceived control (Pavlou, Liang, & Xue, 2007) and improving their experience. Kim & Park (2013) found that transaction safety had significant effects on trust. If users trust mobile service providers, they expect positive flow of future experiences (Kim, Shin, & Lee, 2009). Preceding research found that trust affects the online travel community users' flow experience (Wu & Chang, 2005). Hence, it is proposed that:

H5: Perceived flow is positively correlated with perceived user trust.

Figure 1 illustrates the proposed theoretical framework based on the aforementioned literature.

METHODOLOGY

Out of 250 questionnaires administered to university students studying at the Universiti Malaysia Sabah Labuan International Campus from 26th January 2011 to 27th February 27 2011, 200 questionnaires were gathered and suitable for data analysis, leading to a response rate of 80% by utilizing purposive sampling technique. This sample size is practical as Roscoe (1975) noted that the sample size between 30-500 samples is considered satisfactory. They were randomly intercepted in the university campus who have at least a social networking site account such as Facebook, MySpace, Twitter or LinkedIn and have experience browse it via mobile phone, including smartphone. Indeed, their participation is purely voluntary. The balance 50 questionnaires were eradicated for analysis of data due to the error of a large amount of responses.

The structured close-ended questionnaire comprised three sections. The first section consisted of demographic characteristics of respondents. The ensuing section aimed at collecting information concerning their mobile SNS experiences using frequency distribution statistics. The final section measured their perception on perceived flow, perceived system quality, perceived information quality and perceived user trust. Twenty-two

Figure 1. Theoretical framework

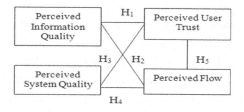

questionnaire items were used to measure the variables on a five-point Likert scale ranging from 1 strongly disagree to 5 strongly agree and derived from the following sources: perceived information quality (DeLone & McLean, 1992), perceived system quality (Armstrong & Hagel, 1996; Chiou, 2005; Nelson & Todd, 2005), perceived enjoyment (Davis, Bagozzi, & Warshaw, 1992; Koufaris, 2002), perceived control (Macan, Shahani, Dipboye, & Phillips, 1990), attention focus (Intriligator & Cavanagh, 2001; Pylyshyn & Storm, 1988), and perceived user trust (Berry & Parasuraman, 1991).

Pearson correlations via Statistical Package for Social Science (SPSS) 21.0 computer program was used for data analysis as it has the ability to ensure the consistency of the model with the data and to estimate associations among constructs.

DATA ANALYSIS

Table 1 presents the distribution of respondents' demographic characteristics with out of 200 respondents, 49% males, and 51% females. Respondents were mainly aged 21 to 25 years earn a monthly allowance of lesser than RM300. In terms mobile SNS experiences, Facebook is the most frequently visited mobile SNS i.e. 74% respondents as compared to Twitter and MySpace. Descriptive results show that 18% of the sample group uses mobile SNS for more than 15 times in a week. There is more than one-quarter (i.e. 27.5%) of the respondents' have the experience using mobile SNS for a period of more than 6 months.

FACTOR ANALYSIS

Principal component analysis with varimax rotation was used in this factor analysis. The Bartlett test of sphericity was significant ($\chi^2 = 1815.224$, $p<0.01$) and the Kaiser-Meyer-Olkin measures of the sampling adequacy was far larger than 0.50 which was 0.896, indicating sufficient in-

tercorrelations (see Table 2). Igbaria, Livari, and Maragahh (1995) claimed that only measurement items with the loading superior than 0.50 and cross loading lesser than 0.35 were determined to have a unique relationship with the construct. Inspection of the anti-image of the correlation matrix was well exceeding the satisfactory level of 0.50. In reference to the eigenvalues, there was only one factor with the value greater than one has been extracted, and used for further analysis with 57% of the variance has been explained.

Specifically, the pattern matrix has condensed the initial three independent variables with eleven items i.e. perceived enjoyment (4 items), perceived control (3 items), and attention focus (4 items), to one main factor with ten items. These dimensions are interchangeable and significantly correlated among each other (Huang, 2006; Koufaris, 2002). Results have suppressed small coefficients of absolute value below 0.50 for item 'when using this mobile SNS, I felt confused' and deleted it for reason does not fulfilling this requirement. After rereading the grouping of the factors, the new label for this factor is perceived flow, which is closely reflected the indispensable contents confined in the constructs (Siekpe, 2005; Wang, Baker, Wagner, & Wakefield, 2007). Rotation was not needed, as only a single factor was extracted. Table 2 exemplified factors loading in perceived flow. Results discovered that item loadings ranging from 0.685 to 0.848 with item 'I felt that using this mobile SNS is interesting' has a relatively highest loading on perceived flow, followed by item 'I felt that using this mobile SNS is enjoyable', and item 'I felt that using this mobile SNS is exciting'. The data were used for the calculation of reliabilities by means of the reliability coefficient of Cronbach's alpha.

RELIABILITY ANALYSIS

The Cronbach's alpha value was used to test the reliability of the items measuring each variable to reflect how well items in a set are positively

Table 1. Socio-demographic profile of respondents

	Frequency	Percentage
Gender		
Male	98	49.0
Female	102	51.0
Age (years old)		
< 20	26	13.0
21 – 25	168	84.0
26 – 30	4	2.0
> 31	2	1.0
Monthly Allowance		
< RM 300	160	80.0
RM 301 - RM 400	13	6.5
RM 401 - RM 500	7	3.5
> RM 501	20	10.0
Amount of time mobile SNS used in a week		
1 to 5 times	125	62.5
6 to 10 times	32	16.0
11 to 15 times	7	3.5
> 15 times	36	18.0
Experience of mobile SNS usage		
0 to 2 months	97	48.5
2 to 4 months	34	17.0
4 to 6 months	14	7.0
> 6 months	55	27.5
Most frequently visited mobile SNS		
Facebook	147	73.5
MySpace	2	1.0
Twitter	5	2.5
MSN	9	4.5
Yahoo Messenger	10	5.0
Others	27	13.5

correlated to one another. Hair, Black, Babin, Anderson, and Tatham (2010) stated that all constructs had no problems in reliabilities when the Cronbach's alpha values exceeded the criterion of 0.70. Results presented in Table 3 enumerate that the Cronbach's alpha value of all variables were above 0.70, ranging from 0.824 to 0.962. Thus, all variables were reliable to measure all constructs consistently, free from random error, and had high internal consistency.

CORRELATION ANALYSIS

A Pearson correlation is performed to investigate the interrelationships between the four constructs. The average score of the multi-items for a construct

Table 2. Factor analysis of perceived flow

Items	Loading
I felt that using this mobile SNS is interesting	0.848
I felt that using this mobile SNS is enjoyable	0.841
I felt that using this mobile SNS is exciting	0.822
When using this mobile SNS, I was intensely absorbed in the activity	0.815
I felt that using this mobile SNS is fun	0.810
When using this mobile SNS, I concentrated fully on the activity	0.782
When using this mobile SNS, my intention was focused in the activity	0.781
When using this mobile SNS, I felt calm	0.721
When using this mobile SNS, I was deeply engrossed in the activity	0.719
When using this mobile SNS, I felt in control	0.685
Total variance explained	6.275
Percentage of variance explained	57.043
Kaiser-Meyer-Olkin measure of sampling adequacy	0.896

was computed and the score was used in correlation analysis. Lind, Marchal, and Wathen (2010) noted that the correlations is strong when the value is $r=0.50$ to 1.0 or $r=-0.50$ to -1.0. Moreover, Simon ((2008) stated that correlation values at $+0.01$ and above are significant but show slight association while values beyond $+0.7$ to $+1.0$ infer strong positive association.

Table 4 exposes that correlations between the variables are positively significant at 0.01 level

Table 3. Summary of reliability analysis

Variables	Number of items	Cronbach's alpha
Perceived Information Quality	4	0.962
Perceived System Quality	4	0.824
Perceived Flow	10	0.912
Perceived User Trust	3	0.865

and finds that all of them are correlated. This is hardly surprising, as all are perceptions from the same minds. There is considerable psychology evidence that when people make a choice, they adapt their cognitive structures to support it. Hence it is not surprising that every perception correlates significantly at 0.01 with every other one. One suspect that any perceptions measured would do the same. With regards to means distribution, the perceived flow had the highest mean value on a five-point Likert scale of 1 = strongly disagree to 5 = strongly agree i.e. 4.608, trailed by perceived system quality (means=4.580), and perceived information quality (means=4.465). Next, perceived user trust had lowest mean value i.e. 4.287.

The skewness of all the items ranges from -0.219 to -0.591 below ± 2.0. Similarly, the values for kurtosis ranges from 0.023 to 0.846 well below the threshold of ± 10. Both the skewness and kurtosis are low for the most part, specifying that the scores approximate a "normal distribution" or "bell-shaped curve".

CORRELATIONS WITH PERCEIVED USER TRUST

The correlation coefficients for the hypotheses testing is obtainable in Table 4 which enumerated that all hypothesized paths were significantly associated with perceived user trust at $p<0.01$. Explicitly, results via Pearson correlations exposed that perceived flow had highest significant positive correlation coefficients with perceived users trust ($r=0.643$, $p<0.01$). Thus, HI is maintained. The next vital pair of correlations appeared between perceived information quality and perceived user trust i.e. $r=0.625$, $p<0.01$, signifying H3 is retained. Likewise, the final analysis which investigate the association between perceived system quality and perceived user trust produce comparable significant results, that is H5 is supported ($r=0.608$, $p<0.01$).

Table 4. Inter-construct correlations

	Mean	Std. dev.	Skewness	Kurtosis	Correlations with	
					Perceived user trust	Perceived flow
(1) Perceived information quality	4.465	1.250	-0.483	0.357	0.625(**)	0.564(**)
(2) Perceived system quality	4.580	1.175	-0.591	0.761	0.608(**)	0.750(**)
(3) Perceived flow	4.608	1.382	-0.339	0.023	0.643(**)	-
(4) Perceived user trust	4.287	1.147	-0.219	0.846	-	-

** Correlation is significant at the 0.01 level (2-tailed).

CORRELATIONS WITH PERCEIVED FLOW

Pearson correlation analysis is conducted on the three variables to determine the strength and direction of the linear association between independent variables (i.e. perceived information quality and perceived system quality) and the dependent variable (i.e. perceived flow). The results of the inter-correlation of the variables displayed that Pearson correlations ranging from 0.564 to 0.750 (see Table 4). The first value refers to the correlation coefficient for perceived information quality factor with perceived flow, implying that the posited hypothesis, i.e. H2 is preserved. The latter value belongs to perceived system quality factor which had highest significant positive correlation coefficients with perceived flow. Consequently, the proposed hypothesis, i.e. H4 is conserved.

DISCUSSION

This study examined the effects of perceived information quality, perceived system quality, and perceived flow on mobile Social Networking Sites (SNS) users' trust. Empirical results via Pearson correlations provide information necessary to scrutinize the study hypotheses. Each correlation coefficient was assessed as significant at the 0.01 level, and the overall model was determined to fit the data well as multicollinearity was absent.

In terms of the associations with perceived user trust, perceived flow had highest significant positive correlation coefficients, followed by perceived information quality and perceived system quality, satisfying H1, H3 and H5. The mobile SNS provider and have a better perceived flow compared to those in doubt. Users reported that being confident was important and stressed the value of being able to explore new things in online environments (Hassanein & Head, 2007). This result is analogous to earlier research discoveries (i.e. Fung & Lee, 1999; Keen, Balance, Chan & Schrump, 2000; Kim & Park, 2013; Wong & Hsu, 2008) which noted that the quality of the information posted on the company website or mobile portal has a direct impact on potential customers' perception and trust of its products and services. Davis (1989) and Sledgianowski and Kulviwat (2009) found that user's thinking as to the usefulness of a system has great influence and is positively related to adoption of information technology thereafter will develop higher trust in the mobile SNS platform.

Further investigation of the study encountered that perceived flow is significantly associated by both perceived system quality and perceived information quality of mobile SNS, respectively, thus H2 and H4 were sustained. Prior discoveries by Pilke (2004) found that informative and pleasant visualization was quite frequently mentioned in by participants as an element that facilitates flow. If the information provided via the mobile SNS are accurate and of high quality, users will have a better perceived flow. Zhou, Li and Liu (2010) noted that mobile SNS platforms that are unreliable and have slow responses or where services are abruptly interrupted will seriously affect users' experience including enjoyment, attention focus and control which are the three reflective dimensions of flow. This result is consistent with the findings of previous studies (i.e. Gefen et al., 2006; Kim & Park, 2013; Kim et al., 2009; Vance et al., 2008; Wu & Chang, 2005).

CONCLUSION AND RECOMMENDATIONS

Empirical results via Pearson correlations revealed that both perceived information quality and perceived system quality affected the perceived flow and perceived users' trust. Furthermore, perceived flow is regarded as the strongest factor that significantly affected users' trust on mobile SNS. Mobile SNS providers need to consider user perceived flow to enhance users' trust. Thus, mobile SNS providers should implement steps to increase the perceived information quality and perceived system quality in order to build and enhance users' trust level and further provide users with a compelling experience.

This research offers important theoretical contributions as most existing studies only addressed the concern of user acceptance of online social networking sites utilizing theory of technology acceptance model. This study adopts a comprehensive approach to explain the effects of perceived information quality, perceived system quality, and perceived flow on mobile Social Networking Sites (SNS) users' trust. In addition, the research model providing support to an integration of cross-disciplinary studies in virtual community research.

On the practical side, the results provide some tangible recommendations for helping enhance their SNS users' trust thereafter could bring continued profitability and business success. It is also important to make efforts by policy makers to outline strategies through its white papers to encourage usage of social networking sites as avenue to strengthen business activities more competitively by emphasizing on aspects of perceived information quality, perceived system quality, and perceived flow on mobile Social Networking Sites (SNS) users' trust.

Further research is deemed essential to expand the sample size and investigate at different geographical location by considering several social groups beyond Malaysia, such as other Asian countries, Europe, and USA, to improve the generalizability of findings as most of the current samples are university students in the very same university and leaning more towards students and not the general public or adults, as different working professionals demographic would use mobile SNS differently which introduces a big bias. It also recommended to empirically test and estimate the proposed hypothesised relationships via Structural Equation Modeling (SEM) technique as it has the ability to ensure the consistency of the model with the data and to estimate effects among constructs instantaneously.

REFERENCES

Aggelidis, V. P., & Chatzoglou, P. D. (2012). Hospital information systems: Measuring end user computing satisfaction (EUCS). *Journal of Biomedical Informatics*, *45*, 566–579. doi:10.1016/j.jbi.2012.02.009 PMID:22426283

Aladwani, A. M., & Palvia, P. C. (2002). Developing and validating an instrument for measuring user-perceived web quality. *Information & Management*, *39*(6), 467–476. doi:10.1016/S0378-7206(01)00113-6

Armstrong, A. G., & Hagel, J. (1996). The real value of online communities. *Harvard Business Review*, *73*(3), 134–141.

Berry, L. L., & Parasuraman, A. (1991). *Marketing services: Competing through quality*. New York, NY: The Free Press.

Boyd, D. M., & Ellison, N. B. (2008). Social network sites: Definition, history and scholarship. *Journal of Computer-Mediated Communication*, *13*(1), 210–230. doi:10.1111/j.1083-6101.2007.00393.x

Chang, I. C., Li, Y. C., Wu, T. Y., & Yen, D. C. (2012). Electronic medical record quality and its impact on user satisfaction - Healthcare providers' point of view. *Government Information Quarterly*, *29*, 235–242. doi:10.1016/j.giq.2011.07.006

Chau, P. K., Au, G., & Tam, K. Y. (2000). Impact of information presentation modes on online shopping: An empirical evaluation of a broadband interactive shopping service. *Journal of Organizational Computing and Electronic Commerce*, *10*(1), 1–22.

Chen, R. F., & Hsiao, J. L. (2012). An investigation on physicians' acceptance of hospital information systems: A case study. *International Journal of Medical Informatics*, *81*, 810–820. doi:10.1016/j.ijmedinf.2012.05.003 PMID:22652011

Chiou, J. S. (2005). The antecedents of consumers' loyalty toward Internet service providers. *Information & Management*, *41*(6), 685–695. doi:10.1016/j.im.2003.08.006

Counts, S., & Fisher, K. E. (2010). Mobile social networking as information ground: A case study. *Library & Information Science Research*, *32*(2), 98–115. doi:10.1016/j.lisr.2009.10.003

Cyr, D., Head, M., & Ivanoc, A. (2006). Design aesthetics leading to m-loyalty in mobile commerce. *Information & Management*, *43*(8), 950–963. doi:10.1016/j.im.2006.08.009

Davis, F. D. (1989). Perceived usefulness, perceived ease of use, and user acceptance of information technology. *Management Information Systems Quarterly*, *13*(3), 319–340. doi:10.2307/249008

Davis, F. D., Bagozzi, R. P., & Warshaw, P. R. (1992). Extrinsic and intrinsic motivation to use computers in the workplace. *Journal of Applied Social Psychology*, *22*(14), 1111–1132. doi:10.1111/j.1559-1816.1992.tb00945.x

Deighton, J., & Grayson, K. (1995). Marketing and seduction: Building exchange relationships by managing social consensus. *The Journal of Consumer Research*, *21*(4), 660–676. doi:10.1086/209426

DeLone, W. H., & McLean, E. R. (1992). Information systems success: The quest for the dependent variable. *Information Systems Research*, *3*(1), 154–171. doi:10.1287/isre.3.1.60

Doney, P. M., & Cannon, J. P. (1997). An examination of the nature of trust in buyer-seller relationships. *Journal of Marketing*, *61*(2), 35–51. doi:10.2307/1251829

Fung, R. K. K., & Lee, M. K. O. (1999). EC-Trust (trust in electronic commerce): Exploring the antecedent factors. In *Proceedings of the 5th American Conference on Information Systems*, (pp. 517-519). Academic Press.

Garrett, J. J. (2003). *The elements of user experience: User-centered design for the web*. Indianapolis, IN: New Riders.

Gefen, D., Pavlou, P. A., Benbasat, I., McKnight, D. H., Stewart, K., & Straub, D. W. (2006). Should institutional trust matter in information systems research? *Communications of the AIS*, *19*(7), 205–222.

Hair, J. F., Black, B., Babin, B., Anderson, R. E., & Tatham, R. L. (2010). *Multivariate data analysis: A global perspective*. New Jersey: Pearson Education Inc.

Hassanein, K., & Head, M. (2007). Manipulating social presence through the web interface and its impact on consumer attitude towards online shopping. *International Journal of Human-Computer Studies*, *65*(8), 689–708. doi:10.1016/j.ijhcs.2006.11.018

Hsu, C. L., & Lu, H. P. (2004). Why do people play games? An extended TAM with social influences and flow experience. *Information & Management*, *41*(7), 853–868. doi:10.1016/j.im.2003.08.014

Huang, M. H. (2006). Flow, enduring, and situational involvement in the web environment: A tripartite second-order examination. *Psychology and Marketing*, *23*(5), 383–411. doi:10.1002/mar.20118

Igbaria, M., Livari, J., & Maragahh, H. (1995). Why do individual use computer technology: A finish case study. *Information & Management*, *29*(5), 227–238. doi:10.1016/0378-7206(95)00031-0

Ilsever, J., Cyr, D., & Parent, M. (2007). Extending models of flow and e-loyalty. *Journal of Information Science and Technology*, *4*(2), 10–13.

Intriligator, J., & Cavanagh, P. (2001). The spatial resolution of visual attention. *Cognitive Psychology*, *43*(3), 171–216. doi:10.1006/cogp.2001.0755 PMID:11689021

Keen, P., Ballance, C., Chan, S., & Schrump, S. (2000). *Electronic commerce relationships: Trust by design*. Upper Saddle River, NJ: Prentice Hall.

Kim, G., Shin, B., & Lee, H. G. (2009). Understanding dynamics between initial trust and usage intentions of mobile banking. *Information Systems Journal*, *19*(3), 283–311. doi:10.1111/j.1365-2575.2007.00269.x

Kim, S., & Park, H. (2013). Effects of various characteristics of social commerce (s-commerce) on consumers' trust and trust performance. *International Journal of Information Management*, *33*, 318–332. doi:10.1016/j.ijinfomgt.2012.11.006

Koufaris, M. (2002). Applying the technology acceptance model and flow theory to online consumer behavior. *Information Systems Research*, *13*(2), 205–223. doi:10.1287/isre.13.2.205.83

Lind, D. A., Marchal, W. G., & Wathen, S. A. (2010), Basic statistics for business and economics. 7thed. United States: McGraw-Hills.

Macan, T. H., Shahani, C., Dipboye, R. L., & Phillips, A. P. (1990). College students' time management: Correlations with academic performance and stress. *Journal of Educational Psychology*, *82*(4), 760–768. doi:10.1037/0022-0663.82.4.760

McKnight, D. H., Choudhury, V., & Kacmar, C. (2002). The impact of initial consumer trust on intentions to transact with a web site: A trust building model. *The Journal of Strategic Information Systems*, *11*(3-4), 297–323. doi:10.1016/S0963-8687(02)00020-3

Nelson, R. R., & Todd, P. A. (2005). Antecedents of information and system quality: An empirical examination within the context of data warehousing. *Journal of Management Information Systems*, *21*(4), 199–235.

Pavlou, P. A., Liang, H., & Xue, Y. (2007). Understanding and mitigating uncertainty in online exchange relationships: A principal-agent perspective. *Management Information Systems Quarterly*, *31*(1), 105–136.

Pilke, E. M. (2004). Flow experience in information technology use. *International Journal of Human-Computer Studies*, *61*(3), 347–357. doi:10.1016/j.ijhcs.2004.01.004

Pylyshyn, Z. W., & Storm, R. W. (1988). Tracking multiple independent targets: Evidence for a parallel tracking mechanism. *Spatial Vision*, *3*(3), 179–197. doi:10.1163/156856888X00122 PMID:3153671

Roscoe, J. T. (1975). *Fundamental research statistics for the behavioural sciences* (2nd ed.). New York: Holt, Rinehart and Winston.

Siekpe, J. S. (2005). An examination of the multidimensionality of the flow construct in a computer-mediated environment. *Journal of Electronic Commerce Research, 6*(1), 31–43.

Simon, S. (2008). *Definitions of correlation. Children's Mercy.* Retrieved February 9, 2014, from http://www.childrens-mercy.org/stats/definitions/correlation.htm.

Sledgianowski, D., & Kulviwat, S. (2009). Using social network sites: The effects of playfulness, critical mass and trust in a hedonic context. *Journal of Computer Information Systems, 49*(4), 74–83.

Socialbakers. (2013). *Malaysia Facebook statistics.* Retrieved January 2, 2014 from http://www.socialbakers.com/facebook-statistics/malaysia.

Vance, A., Christophe, E. D. C., & Straub, D. W. (2008). Examining trust in information technology artefacts: The effects of system quality and culture. *Journal of Management Information Systems, 24*(4), 73–100. doi:10.2753/MIS0742-1222240403

Wang, L. C., Baker, J., Wagner, J. A., & Wakefield, K. (2007). Can a retail web site be social? *Journal of Marketing, 71*(3), 143–157. doi:10.1509/jmkg.71.3.143

Wang, Y. S., Wang, Y. M., Lin, H. H., & Tang, T. I. (2003). Determinants of user acceptance of Internet banking: An empirical study. *International Journal of Service Industry Management, 14*(5), 501–519. doi:10.1108/09564230310500192

Wong, Y. K., & Hsu, C. J. (2008). A confidence-based framework for business to consumer (B2C) mobile commerce adoption. *Personal and Ubiquitous Computing, 12*(1), 77–84. doi:10.1007/s00779-006-0120-5

Wu, J. J., & Chang, Y. S. (2005). Towards understanding members' interactivity, trust, and flow in online travel community. *Industrial Management & Data Systems, 105*(7), 937–954. doi:10.1108/02635570510616120

Yvette, S., & Karine, F. (2001). Information quality: Meeting the needs of the consumer. *International Journal of Information System, 21*(1), 21–37.

Zhong, B., Hardin, M., & Sun, T. (2011). Less effortful thinking leads to more social networking? The associations between the use of social network sites and personality traits. *Computers in Human Behavior, 27*(3), 1265–1271. doi:10.1016/j.chb.2011.01.008

Zhou, T. (2013). An empirical examination of continuance intention of mobile payment services. *Decision Support Systems, 54*, 1085–1091. doi:10.1016/j.dss.2012.10.034

Zhou, T., Li, H., & Liu, Y. (2010). The effect of flow experience on mobile SNS users' loyalty. *Industrial Management & Data Systems, 110*(6), 930–946. doi:10.1108/02635571011055126

Chapter 3
Creating Believable and Effective AI Agents for Games and Simulations:
Reviews and Case Study

Iskander Umarov
TruSoft International Inc., USA

Maxim Mozgovoy
University of Aizu, Japan

ABSTRACT

The rapid development of complex virtual worlds (most notably, in 3D computer and video games) introduces new challenges for the creation of virtual agents, controlled by Artificial Intelligence (AI) systems. Two important sub-problems in this topic area that need to be addressed are (a) believability and (b) effectiveness of agents' behavior (i.e. human-likeness of the characters and high ability to achieving their own goals). In this chapter, the authors study current approaches to believability and effectiveness of AI behavior in virtual worlds. They examine the concepts of believability and effectiveness and analyze several successful attempts to address these challenges. In conclusion, the authors provide a case study that suggests that believable and effective behavior can be achieved through learning behavioral patterns from observation with subsequent automatic selection of effective acting strategies.

INTRODUCTION

What is a Virtual World?

Virtual worlds provide a basis for many popular video and computer games (e.g. Half-Life, The Sims), "life simulators" (e.g. Second Life, Entropia Universe), and virtual military training grounds (e.g. Virtual Battle Space). The use of such worlds becomes more and more widespread, as typical hardware is now able to perform realistic 3D real-time rendering, and the coverage of broadband Internet connection constantly increases. Furthermore, virtual worlds get new applications, most notably in the area of education and "serious

DOI: 10.4018/978-1-4666-6252-0.ch003

games." One can note, for instance, the existence of "virtual classrooms" in Second Life.

It is interesting to note that while the term "virtual world" is commonly used, only few authors provide its precise definition. Bell (2008) tried to combine previous definitions, found in the literature, into the following formula: "a synchronous, persistent network of people, represented as avatars, facilitated by networked computers." This definition, though, ignores an important observation: modern virtual worlds can be inhabited not only with human-controlled characters, but also with AI-based virtual agents, serving as non-participating world's "native population," hostile opponents or friendly teammates. Furthermore, it is still unclear what kinds of computer-generated environments qualify for the name of "virtual worlds." The work by Mitchell (1995) "From MUDs To Virtual Worlds" suggests a clear distinction between MUDs (Multi-User Dungeons, text-based multiplayer games) and virtual worlds. Mitchell notes the lack of immersion, caused by limited visual capabilities of MUDs, and suggests that virtual worlds should combine MUD-styled gameplay with vivid 3D graphics. Though the discussion of features that turn a virtual simulation into a virtual world are beyond the scope of this chapter, it is natural to presume that "a world" should possess certain high degree of complexity and audiovisual interaction, not found in simpler computer-simulated environments.

Virtual World's AI-Controlled Inhabitants

As noted by Bell, the primary population of a virtual world is constituted by real people, represented as human-controlled agents or *avatars*. A world can be also inhabited by computer-controlled agents, also known as *NPCs* (non-player characters). Their role depends on the nature of the given world: serving as elements of the world's setting (Milward, 2009), being used for research purposes (Friedman, Steed, & Slater, 2007) or even being

completely prohibited as violating the intended world's configuration (Blizzard, 2010).

The case of our interest is AI systems that can substitute human players or even *pretend* to be humans. This scenario is very common in the domain of computer games: if you play a computer chess match, fighting game, or a soccer tournament, you naturally assume that it is possible to choose either human- or computer-controlled opponent. Complex computer games and virtual worlds demand high-quality AI systems, able to control characters satisfactorily. The success of such AI is determined by the (human) users of a virtual world or a computer game. The factors that contribute to the overall user satisfaction are not obvious: successful AI systems are not necessarily the strongest game characters.

Consider the simplest example: in the classic Pac-Man game a human player has to eat all the "pills" located on the level, avoiding computer-controlled ghosts. It is not hard to program "optimal ghosts" that easily capture the protagonist; however, a player will be doomed to defeat in such a game, making the whole game project unejoyable and thus unsuccessful. The same problem arises in chess, since the best AI systems are able to play at grandmaster level, while not all human participants are eager to compete with grandmasters all the time.

With games being the way in which many people around the world are learning how to use computers, and one of the primary reasons people spend time with computers, questions regarding how to improve the quality of the virtual worlds (and the AI agents in them) is an interesting challenge and opportunity for the field of computer science. This chapter is focused specifically on the analysis of the current state of affairs and possible further directions in AI agents' development for virtual worlds.

This chapter is organized as follows. We begin with an overview of the research regarding what makes games fun and engaging, or "fun factors," then looking specifically at how AI Agents in

Virtual worlds can contribute to or distract from these factors, and the overall success of that game. We then examine what it is that makes AI agents "believable" and "effective," and address what are the practical challenges that exist in AI development of these characteristics? We outline some of the potentially promising experimental approaches to AI development (including which testbeds can be used, how to test believability, which research projects have contributed to creating believable behavior, and which research projects have contributed to creating effectiveness). Using the background of the existing research, we then look at a specific case study: a 3D boxing video game environment. We experiment with and research the practical application of creating AI agents that: (a) increase "believable" behavior through learning by observation and case-based reasoning; (b) optimize "effective" behavior by means of reinforcement learning; and thus (c) outperform built-in handcrafted AI agents in evaluation with Turing tests and automated scoring schemes (Mozgovoy & Umarov, 2010a, 2010b). We conclude with discussion, conclusions, and some suggestions for future research.

FUN FACTORS AND REALISM

The Pac-Man and chess examples show that the quality of AI agent's decision making, in terms of achieving own goals in the game, is not the only criterion to measure the quality of a computer-controlled opponent. A game should be *enjoyable*, and virtual training environment has to be *realistic*, and AI features should be consistent with these goals. As Paul Tozour (AI Programmer for Deus Ex 2 game) notes, "The whole point is to entertain the audience, so no matter what you do, you need to make sure the AI makes the game more fun. If a game's AI doesn't make the game a better experience, any notions of 'intelligence' are irrelevant" (Eyewitness: Complete AI Interviews. 2002).

General Game Fun Factors

While the concept of *realism* leaves little ambiguity[1], the factors that contribute to the overall game enjoyability are not easy to reveal. These factors (often called "fun factors") serve as a subject of research activities for decades. Perhaps, the earliest attempts to analyze them are found in Malone (1981). Malone lists the following factors as the most important: (a) the existence of clear goals; (b) the presence of hi-score table; (c) good audiovisual effects; (d) the presence of randomness in the gameplay.

More recent studies have shown the differences in perceived importance of particular fun factors between game developers and players, and across game genres (Choi, Kim, & Kim, 1999). Furthermore, the conclusions often depend on the used research basis and methods. Many researchers, for example, rely on the Flow Theory (Csikszentmihalyi, 1991). As shown by Csikszentmihalyi, most Flow (i.e. deep enjoyment of a certain activity) experiences are caused by goal-directed, rule-bounded activities that require appropriate skills and mental energy. These observations were applied to the domain of game worlds by Sweetser and Wyeth (2005), who list the following factors, affecting user enjoyment:

1. **Concentration:** Games should require concentration, and the player should be able to concentrate on the game.
2. **Challenge:** Games should be sufficiently challenging and match the player's skill level.
3. **Player Skills:** Games must support player skill development and mastery.
4. **Control:** Players should feel a sense of control over their actions in the game.
5. **Clear Goals:** Games should provide the player with clear goals at appropriate times.
6. **Feedback:** Players must receive appropriate feedback at appropriate times.

7. **Immersion:** Players should experience deep but effortless involvement in the game.
8. **Social Interaction:** Games should support and create opportunities for social interaction.

However, systematic study of game reviews performed by Wang, Shen, and Ritterfeld (2009) shows that professional reviewers mention other game attributes as key fun factors:

1. Technological capacity (various technological aspects of the game).
2. Game design.
3. Aesthetic presentation (audiovisual experience and game style).
4. Entertainment gameplay experience.
5. Narrativity / storyline features.

Certain fun factors can be identified even for very simple games. For instance, Yannakakis and Hallam (2004) express the following suggestions for the Pac-Man game: (a) the game should be neither too hard nor too easy; (b) there should be a diversity in ghosts' behavior over a series of games; (c) the ghosts' behavior should be aggressive rather that static.

AI as Fun Factor

So how does this relate to AI agents in virtual worlds? The above lists of fun factors may not provide direct guidance on the role of computer-controlled characters in overall success of a computer game or virtual world, but can help frame the discussion. Additionally, it is clear that the importance of high-quality AI varies from genre to genre: in computer chess, AI is the most valuable game subsystem; in an online arcade tank battle game Tanki Online[2] AI-controlled characters are absent, so game enjoyability is completely defined by other factors.

If we presume that a certain virtual world is inhabited with AI-controlled characters, it is important to examine the impact of AI quality on the overall user experience. Technically we can connect AI with the factors 1 to 6 in Sweetser and Wyeth's list, and with the factors 1, 2, & 4 in the list composed by Wang et al. Indeed, Sweetser and Wyeth mention AI as an important source of game challenge. Explicit views on this issue are expressed in the works by Yannakakis and Hallam (2004, 2005). The authors show how AI quality affects player's enjoyment in the games that involve interaction with computer-controlled opponents. They conclude that more enjoyment comes with non-trivial adaptive opponents, which means they exhibit a variety of different behavioral styles and are able to respond to changing human strategies.

What other features, besides adaptivity, help make AI an enjoyable opponent? Numerous researchers (e.g., Choi, Konik, Nejati, Park, & Langley, 2007; Glende, 2004; Taatgen, van Oploo, Braaksma, & Niemantsverdriet, 2003) mention *human-likeness* of computer-controlled opponents as one of the primary attributes of a successful AI system. To quote Taatgen et al., "a computer opponent becomes more interesting and enjoyable to play against as it behaves more like a person"[3]. In case of virtual worlds, inhabited with human-like creatures, human-likeness of their behavior (fulfilled by an AI system) is essential, since it contributes to the overall realism of the world. Players may expect human-like behavior from human-like characters even in simpler game environments, not necessarily qualifying for a status of a full-fledged virtual world.

Since *game challenge* is a widely recognized fun factor, we can identify the following two attributes of a successful AI system: realism / human-likeness, and high skill level. In the subsequent sections, we will have a more detailed look at these attributes and examine, what is it that makes AI agents "believable" and "effective."

BELIEVABLE AND EFFECTIVE AI AGENTS

Realism and human-likeness of AI-controlled agents are related to the general principle of *believability*. Following the concept of "believable character" in the Arts, the term "believable agent" is used in computer science literature to denote realistic interactive characters, inhabiting virtual worlds. Defined in (Bates, 1994) as the "one that provides the illusion of life, and thus permits the audience's suspension of disbelief," a believable agent is usually characterized with human-like peculiarities, such as capabilities to learn, to "think" between the decisions, to make mistakes, to adjust own strategy in response to opponent's actions. Furthermore, a believable agent should not be given "god abilities," such as seeing hidden objects, having extra-fast reaction or controlling several army squads simultaneously.

Identifying individual AI features, leading to believability, is a worthwhile research topic. Jones et al. (1999) propose the following basic principles for building a believable agent: (a) it should have roughly the same basic data processing structure as human players; (b) it should have the same basic sensory and motor systems as human players; (c) it should have the same knowledge as human players.

The acceptance of these general principles still leaves enough room for their interpretation and implementation in actual virtual worlds. For example, the work by Choi et al. (2007) adds three more features for a human-like agent: (a) hierarchical organization of knowledge; (b) goal-directed but reactive behavior; (c) incremental learning schemes.

The developers of computer games are well-aware of the positive impact which believability of AI agents makes on the user's gaming experience. For example, the authors of built-in Counter-Strike bots specifically mention human-likeness of their AI features, such as "behave in a believably human manner," "communicate with teammates," respect "player perception of a 'fair fight'," and "create behavior variation among bots" in terms of aggression, skill, teamwork, reaction times, and morale (Booth, 2004). The same work mentions simple but important from the standpoint of user perception AI features, such as treating a human player as the head (bots refer to human players "Sir" or "Commander") and congratulating players occasionally by sending a message "nice shot, sir" to a human player on a successful attack.

Orkin (2006) connects raising awareness of believability in game AI systems with general evolution of computer games: "in the early generations of shooters, such as *Shogo* (1998) players were happy if the A.I. noticed them at all and started attacking. ... Today, players expect more realism, to complement the realism of the physics and lighting in the environments."

The contribution of such human-like AI-controlled characters is likely to be especially valuable in case of believable cooperating opponents, as noted by Yannakakis and Hallam (2007). So we can analyze not only individual believable agents, but also whole teams of believable agents, which are a topic of special interest in the case of first-person shooters and military training virtual 3D worlds.

However, believability is not the only feature that makes AI-controlled characters fun to play with. A game should be challenging, so AI should possess reasonable skills or, in other words, to be *effective*.[4] Effectiveness of decision-making is a classical aim for AI design: developing virtual characters that can compete with human opponents is a demanding task for high variety of computer games. As already stated, the goals of believability and effectiveness are not always synonymous: a highly skillful agent is not always believable; a believable character can be a weak opponent.

A good example of a virtual environment where successful AI is completely identified with effective AI is RoboCup Simulation League (Kitano et al., 1998). Within this project, the participants create competing teams of virtual soccer players. A winning team should exhibit effective behavior, which does not have to be similar to strategies of human players in a real soccer match.

PRACTICAL CHALLENGES IN AI DEVELOPMENT

From the technical point of view, the approaches used to build virtual characters in practice are generally conservative. For example, Counter-Strike bots rely on preprogrammed rule-based scenarios (Booth, 2004), and Halo 2 AI is built on top of a hierarchical finite state machine (Isla, 2005). More advanced AI techniques, such as neural networks are primarily used when behavior learning is a significant part of gameplay, as in the case of Black & White and Creatures (Champandard, 2007).

During the last years, game AI technologies experienced significant evolutionary development. Hierarchical finite state machines have evolved into behavior trees (Knafla, 2011), successfully used in such games as Crysis (Pillosu, 2009) and Spore (Hecker, 2011). Existing technologies have matured, industry has developed specialized tools for AI authoring and debugging (Champandard, 2011); although, most game AI systems are based on handcrafted behavioral scripts.

The main problem with manual methods of designing AI behavior lies in their inability to address growing complexity. Complex behavior of AI agents leads to complex underlying algorithms and data structures. The solutions tend to suffer from poor scalability, and the consistency of decision-making rules is difficult to maintain. Some of these complexity issues can be overcome by following clear and consistent design principles (Isla, 2005)[5], but such recommendations seem to be tactical rather that strategic. Truly complex issues such as real-time adaptive learning or complex team behavior remain a serious challenge for well-established game AI methods in the game development industry.

A well-recognized alternative is to employ some variation of machine learning to create AI-controlled characters and to adjust their behavior patterns. This approach is not popular in today's commercial games due to various reasons, including (a) hard predictability of obtained behavior, which makes AI harder to control by game designers; (b) significant time that may be required to train an effective AI agent; (c) possible unreliability of trained AI, as it can get stuck in certain cases (Sánchez-Crespo Dalmau, 2005). Furthermore, machine learning often does not optimize AI in terms of skill level, so the developers are afraid that agents might learn inferior behavioral patterns (Spronck, Ponsen, Sprinkhuizen-Kuyper, & Postma, 2006).

In comparison to research projects, commercial video and computer games are usually developed under much stricter bounds. The code has to be highly efficient, time and memory constraints are challenging, and the development should be finished within a given time frame, under a specified budget. Thus, game developers do not always have a chance to experiment with cutting-edge AI research. Furthermore, AI agents in commercial games have to be robust and reliable, which normally makes the use of research technologies intolerably risky. Though, according to observations made by Champandard (2011), recent attempts to bridge the gap between academia and industry in the field of AI research are very promising. In this next section we address some of the potentially promising experimental approaches to AI development.

EXPERIMENTAL APPROACHES TO AI DEVELOPMENT

The development of believable and effective AI-controlled characters is a subject of numerous research projects. Many of them deal with isolated AI attributes, and the obtained systems are not always generalizable to full-scaled virtual worlds;

however, these experiments provide greater diversity in approaches to development of believable agents, and usually implement more advanced features, not yet available in released game titles. It should be mentioned that several recent projects are devoted to comprehensive AI research in currently available virtual worlds, thus bridging "academia-industry" gap, as Champandard (2011) noted. However, this needs to be balanced with the reality that experimental methods are still often not mature enough to form a solid ground for a commercial game's AI, as their robustness and reliability are not always guaranteed.

Testbeds

In order to develop AI-controlled characters inhabiting a virtual world, one first needs a virtual world. While certain researchers work with specialized worlds, designed specifically for the experiment, many projects rely on existing virtual environments. By utilizing ready-made engines, researchers can concentrate on pure AI development, and prevent possible criticism of producing a "toy example," not scalable for the needs of real systems. Naturally, the popularity of a certain testbed is determined by a variety of both technical and non-technical factors, such as complexity of the environment (and thus the possibility to test complex behavior patterns), ease of interface and programming, quality of documentation, availability of the virtual world (as an open source or for a reasonable price), general widespreadness of the environment and the presence of a community around it.

A good example of a testbed popular in the past is Quake 2. It was used in early experiments with learning schemes of human-like behavior (Thurau, Bauckhage, & Sagerer, 2004) and believable bots (Laird, 2002). Quake 2 implements a special interface that allows third-party developers to access internal data structures and thus program engine-agent interaction. However, this environment was characterized as being too restricted

for studying complex behavior (Laird, 2002). So the world of Quake 2 allows obtaining relevant results, but its capabilities are already exhausted with the current AI technologies.

Naturally, particular types of virtual environments are best suitable for different kinds of AI research. While military-style first-person shooters are best for developing arcade behavioral elements (shooting and dodging) and spatial reasoning, role-playing environments are best for computer-simulated social interactions, and real-time strategies are popular for creating team behavior and long-term goal-based planning modules. The most used testbeds of the present day include (but not limited to):

- **Quake 3 Arena:** Referenced in (Choi et al., 2007) as a testbed for a believable agent, built with the help of general-purpose cognitive architecture called ICARUS. Also used in experiments with neural network-based AI by Westra and Dignum (2009), and with genetic algorithm-based AI strategy optimization by Liaw, Wang, Tsai, Ko, & Hao (2013). Since the engine's source code is freely available now under GNU license, some researchers implement new algorithms directly in the code of existing game bots (El Rhalibi & Merabti, 2008).
- **Unreal Tournament:** Used as a testbed for creating human-like bots (Hirono & Thawonmas, 2009), to learn winning AI policies (Smith, Lee-Urban, & Munoz-Avila, 2007), and as a user-end system for a distributed interactive military simulator (Manojlovich, Prasithsangaree, Hughes, Chen, & Lewis, 2003). Unreal Tournament also lies in the foundation of a well-known America's Army recruiting simulation project (Zyda, et al., 2003). This engine is known for an extensive software development kit (shipped with the Unreal Tournament game) and a built-in programming language UnrealScript, allowing to

design own virtual worlds (Laird, 2002). Unreal engine's extension Gamebots (Adobbati, et al., 2001) is specifically developed for multi-agent research in 3D worlds. Currently Gamebots serves as a framework for several AI research projects (Hingston, 2009[6]; Lee & Gamard, 2003; Robertson & Good, 2005). Unreal engine is free for noncommercial use.

- **Second Life:** Since Second Life is an online virtual world, mostly inhabited by real people, AI-controlled characters are often used to analyze human population, and to establish contacts with humans. For example, research bot by Friedman et al. (2007) collects age data of avatars; Ijaz, Bogdanovych, and Simoff (2011) develop a conversational agent with improved abilities to understand its environment; Morie, Chance, Haynes, & Purohit (2012) experiment with AI-controlled knowledge-rich interactive storytelling characters. Designing AI with advanced spatial reasoning is still a new topic for Second Life, but there are research projects aimed at integration of existing cognitive architectures into Second Life's virtual world (Ranathunga, Cranefield, & Purvis, 2011). AI-controlled characters in Second Life are programmed with the built-in Linden Scripting Language. Basic Second Life accounts are free; additional capabilities are available for subscribed users.

- **Open Real-Time Strategy (ORTS) and Stratagus:** ORTS and Stratagus are open source engines, suitable for studying AI problems, applied to the domain of real-time strategy games. Real-time strategies are especially relevant for analyzing agent coordination (Lichocki, Krawiec, & Jaśkowski, 2009; van der Heijden, Bakkes, & Spronck, 2008) and strategic planning algorithms (Balla & Fern, 2009). Other directions include applying general AI methods (Hagelbäck & Johansson, 2009) and ex-

isting cognitive architectures (Wintermute, Xu, & Irizarry, 2007) to the domain of real-time strategies. Furthermore, real-time strategies serve as appropriate testbeds for developing and testing utility AI algorithms, e.g., pathfinding (Naveed, Kitchin, & Crampton, 2010).

- **StarCraft:** A popular game StarCraft became a notable testbed for evaluation of AI agents thanks to the open Broodwar API library *bwapi*[7] and the StarCraft AI Competition, first hosted by AIIDE Conference in 2010[8]. Participating AI systems are engaged in full-scaled StarCraft matches. The competition is, however, not aimed at creation of believable or fun characters; in this point it thus can be compared to RoboCup. Recently, two more competitions with similar rules (CIG and SSCAI) were launched[9].

- **RoboCup:** The RoboCup world (Kitano et al., 1998) serves for needs of Robot Soccer World Cup competition, evolved from a "robot soccer" game to a diverse set of competitions ranging from soccer to dance, among both physical and virtual (software) robots. Recent RoboCup challenges attracted hundreds of participating teams every year. As mentioned earlier, generally RoboCup leagues do not encourage higher believability of agents, only their effectiveness matters.

Believability Criteria

As discussed above, believability is an important property of AI-controlled characters. Computer-generated behavior should be reasonably "human-like" to provide feeling of realism, which contributes to general enjoyability of a game. In case of simulation and training applications (e.g., military training games), realism of the constructed virtual environment is one of the primary explicit design goals of simulation software.

Turing Test

Evaluating believability is not an easy task. One of the possible approaches to the problem is to adapt a well-known Turing test (Turing, 1950) to intelligent agents, behaving in a virtual world. Hingston (2009) describes this modified test as follows. A human player (judge) is engaged in a game against two opponents, taking place in a virtual world. One of these opponents is controlled by another human (confederate), while another is controlled by an AI system. The task of the judge is to identify the human among the opponents. The task of the AI system is to pretend to be human thus deceiving the judge. Hingston notes the following differences from the classic Turing test:

- All participants are independently playing against each other.
- The confederate simply tries to reach own goal (to win the game), and does not assist/ impede the judge.
- No natural language-related difficulties are involved.
- Human players and bots are supplied with different kinds of information: vision and sound for humans, data and events for bots.

A simplified version of this test suggests that the judge has to watch a game between two players, both of whose can be controllable by a human or an AI system. The task of the judge is to identify game participants. Such a test can be relatively easily passed by a conventional AI agent in case of simple games, due to the overall simplicity of gaming process. For example, a believable agent for Pong[10] is discussed in (Livingstone, 2006).

Complex game worlds demand more from AI-controlled players. Glende (2004) lists the following features that agents should possess in order to pass the Turing test:

- A reasonable combination of predictability and unpredictability in agent's decisions;
- Creativity in problem-solving;
- Clear personality;
- Internal intensions and autonomy in acting;
- The capability to plan and improvise;
- The ability to learn.

An experiment that involves evaluation of Quake 2 agents has been performed by Gorman, Thurau, Bauckhage, and Humphrys (2006). The idea of the study was to show a series of Quake 2 video clips (as seen by the player's first-person camera) to a number of people and to ask, whether they do believe that the active player is a human. In different clips, the game character was controlled by: (a) a real human player; (b) a popular Quake rule-based agent; (c) a specifically designed "imitation agent" that tried to reproduce human behavior using Bayesian motion modeling.

The results were positive for the imitation agent: it was misidentified as human in 69% of cases, while the conventional AI was mistaken as human only 36% of the time. The average experience level of evaluators was between "played first-person shooters monthly" and "played first-person shooters weekly." Sample evaluators' comments, quoted in (Gorman et al, 2006), indicate that quite simple clues were used to identify human players: "fires gun for no reason, so must be human," "stand and wait, AI wouldn't do this," "[performs] unnecessary jumping."

One should note that Quake 2 world is relatively uncomplicated (Laird, 2002). So we can expect that a more complex world would require much stronger AI capabilities to pass Turing test. Indeed, an open "believability competition" 2K BotPrize among Unreal Tournament bots, hosted by IEEE CIG Symposium in 2008, declared no winner. None of five competing systems was unable to deceive human judges[11] (Hingston, 2009). Moreover, all five participating human players were ranked by the judges as "more human" than any of the bots.

Still, after analyzing judges' comments, Hingston concludes with an optimistic prognosis: "the task is just a little beyond the current state of the art: neither so easy that we need not stretch ourselves to succeed, nor so hard that success cannot be imagined." Indeed, the recent 2K BotPrize held in 2012, has identified two bots that passed the Turing test successfully (Biever, 2012).

Automated Believability Tests

Direct Turing test involving human judges is not the only way to measure agents' believability. An alternative approach suggests employing automated algorithms: one can store action sequences, performed by human-controlled and AI-controlled characters in certain data structures, and analyze them for "believability attributes."

While this idea is certainly appealing, as it implies the use of objective numerical evaluation algorithms, automated analysis has notable drawbacks, contributing to higher popularity of Turing test-based schemes. First, game worlds are different, and thus may require designing distinct evaluation algorithms. Second, one can argue that automated tests may serve as indirect proofs of presence or absence of believable behavior, but the final decision can be made only by human judges.

Nevertheless, automated tests are used in some research projects, at least, as additional support for the claims of believability. Tencé and Buche (2008) describe a method to measure similarities between human-controlled and AI-controlled characters in Unreal Tournament game. The system calculates a "behavioral fingerprint" for each player in the form of a 20-dimensional numeric vector. Then a Principal Component Analysis is employed to visualize the vectors on a 2D plane. Tencé and Buche experimented with two different kinds of behavioral fingerprints: (1) a normalized vector of frequencies of velocity direction angle changes between two consecutive observation

points; (2) a normalized vector of frequencies of angles between player direction and velocity direction at given consecutive observation points (new observation point arrives every 125 milliseconds; the value of each angle is scaled to the range [0, 19]). The experiments showed a clear separation between the groups of human players and AI agents for both versions of behavioral vectors: each human-generated vector was closer to any other human-generated vector than to any of AI-generated vectors.

Kemmerling et al. (2009) used automated believability measure to improve the believability of the existing AI-controlled character. Through a number of surveys, they identified sets of human-like and non-human-like actions for the strategy game Diplomacy. A "believability calculator" that measures the believability of a given action sequence was set up. Then an additional functionality was added to the AI system to encourage human-like and discourage non-human-like actions. However, this method can be characterized as indirect: while the calculator shows the share of believable actions in AI behavior, it does not evaluate the overall believability of bot's playing style.

Riedl and Young (2005) proposed a semi-automatic believability evaluation procedure for the completely different domain of computer-aided story generation, where the task is to measure believability of characters that participate in the generated story. The evaluation procedure analyzes a tree-like QUEST model (Graesser, Lang, & Roberts, 1991) of the given story that incorporates story events and character goals as nodes, connected with links labeled with relationship types (five types are supported). Then specialized algorithms are used to generate random pairs of questions and answers, related to the story, and to rate the quality (coherence) of answers. Human experts are also asked to provide their rating of answers' quality. The idea is that for a well-structured, believable story human-supplied answer ratings should be close to machine-made guesses.

An interesting application of automated believability testing is discussed in the paper by Pao, Chen, and Chang (2010). The authors develop an algorithm that compares trajectories of Quake 2 characters with pre-recorded trajectories of human players and bots. The goal is to classify any given player as a human or an AI system, thus revealing game bots. Since game bots are prohibited in a number of online games (their use is treated as cheating), and their revelation requires efforts, the proposed automated procedure may have a commercial value.

Creating Believable Behavior

Most research projects follow a natural way of constructing human-like believable behavior by analyzing actual human behavior patterns and subsequently implementing them in AI system. Even hand-coded algorithms can implement specific behavioral patterns, considered as "human-like" by their creators (Booth, 2004). However, a greater interest is evoked by the methods that can automatically construct agents' knowledge by observing behavior of human players. Below we briefly introduce several projects devoted to believable AI creation (with the intention to illustrate typical ideas of how to obtain believable behavior, rather than to provide a thorough survey; furthermore, we do not consider a related but separate task of agent coordination, necessary to obtain believable teams of AI-controlled characters).

Choi et al. (2007) apply a general-purpose cognitive architecture ICARUS (Langley, Choi, & Rogers, 2005) to train an agent for Urban Combat—a modification of Quake 3 Arena game. ICARUS is specifically designed to assist reactive execution in physical environments and implements the following principles: (1) primacy of action and perception over cognition; (2) separation of categories from skills; (3) hierarchical structure of long-term memory; (4) correspondence between long-term and short-term structures (ICARUS, 2007). Initially the agent is given hand-coded

basic knowledge about the objectives and acting capabilities. Then the automated learning algorithm is executed every time whenever the agent has achieved a certain goal. Then this algorithm generates new behavioral skills that help to achieve the same goal with less effort, therefore, improving agent's performance. The experiments were conducted as a series of capture-the-flag games, where an agent has to find and pick up a flag, blocked by various obstacles. The authors make a conclusion that the agent exhibits reasonably human-like behavior by exploring the area, learning how to avoid obstacles, and utilizing obtained knowledge in other environments; however, no formal testing of believability (via Turing test or automated measurements) was performed.

Schrum, Karpov, and Miikkulainen (2011) describe UT^2—one of three top AI agents in the 2010 2K BotPrize competition among bots, acting in Unreal Tournament environment. Their AI system is based on a combination of evolved neural network and a database of traces of human behavior. Neural network is used for decision-making in battles (whether to chase an opponent, retreat, strafe, stand still, or pickup an item). It is first trained in a series of matches with Unreal Tournament built-in bots. Only three objectives were set during this training: maximize opponent's damage, minimize own damage, and minimize collisions with level geometry. The database of human replays has two applications. First, it is used to unstuck the bot in a human-like manner, if it cannot escape from the current level location. Second, it supports human-like navigation between the given level points: if the bot needs to proceed to a certain location, and the database contains a human-generated path to that point, the bot selects this ready path.

Interestingly, two other top AI agents were not based on learning by observation. The bot ICE-2010, described by Hirono and Thawonmas (2009), is based on a handcrafted finite-state machine with manually implemented "human-like" features, and the bot Conscious-Robots by

Arrabales and Muñoz (2010) relies on the functions of cognitive architecture CERA-CRANIUM (Arrabales, Ledezma, & Sanchis, 2009). This architecture can be viewed as a complex rule-based system, where individual rules "compete" in order to be applied in the current game context. Why does the latter approach produce believable behavior? The authors see the source of believability in human-likeness of decision making process: the rules are selected on the basis of bot's perceptions and understanding of the current game situation, supported by its long-term memory mechanisms.

In the recent 2K BotPrize competition held in 2012, the bots UT² and MirrorBot have successfully passed the Turing Test. The best-performed MirrorBot simply mimics opponents' behavior in case of no immediate threat, and this tactics proved to be sufficient for Unreal Tournament (Biever, 2012). The updated version of ICE-2010 has scored third, and the Conscious-Robots system did not participate. An earlier description of learning by observation-based Unreal Tournament bot is provided by Le Hy, Arrigoni, Bessière, and Lebeltel (2004). This decision-making system operates in the following way. A bot's internal state is represented as a vector of parameters. Each possible state has a number of outgoing transitions to the future probable states. Every outgoing transition (representing a bot's action) has an associated probability. Altogether, these probabilities form the behavioral pattern of the bot. Authors study both handcrafted probability distribution specifications (to obtain clearly shaped behavior—e.g., aggressive or cautious) and distributions obtained through learning by observation. The experiments prove the approach to be suitable for creating bots with good level of skill: a character, trained by an aggressive human player, demonstrates aggressive behavior and beats an average-skilled built-in AI agent. While the authors consider their approach as the way to construct believable bots, no believability testing was performed. However, they note that their method allows the game designer to translate own expertise easily to the AI system, contributing to the believability of the bot.

The application of case-based planning methods to the real-time strategy game WARGUS[12] is studied in (Ontañón, Mishra, Sugandh, & Ram, 2007). The database of cases is created on the fly by observing human expert behavior. The system watches human's atomic actions (such as "move," "build" or "attack") and allows the user to annotate behavior patterns by specifying intended goal of the pattern (chain of atomic actions), its preconditions and "alive conditions" that have to be satisfied while the pattern is being executed (in order to have a chance to be successful). Meanwhile, the system records the world's state at different time moments. This information is used for further action retrieval. At the end, the system builds a "plan tree"—a hierarchy of goals and subgoals that should be accomplished to win the game. During the game, AI agent constantly examines the current world's state to determine which subgoals can be achieved, and starts executing the corresponding behavioral patterns. The algorithm also implements certain techniques to adapt extracted behavioral sequence to the current world's state and to search for alternative ways of achieving failed subgoals. The experiments showed that this system performed significantly better than WARGUS' built-in AI agent. The authors evaluated two different human-supplied strategies independently, and then combined these strategies into a single knowledgebase. As expected, the later strategy was the best, as it was able to try a different approach for achieving the next subgoal, if the previous attempt has failed. Currently, the authors of this research project are working on automatic behavior optimization in order to improve AI's skill level (Mehta, Ontañón, & Ram, 2010). It should be mentioned that they also emphasize possible economic advantages of case-based reasoning approach, since behavior can be demonstrated rather than programmed.

We believe that these examples illustrate the following trend. Purely manual methods of behavior creation, primarily based on finite-state machines and behavior trees, are still popular, but they are often characterized as requiring too much effort, while the resulting computer-controlled agents still can be distinguished from humans by the observers. Behavior authoring is made easier by cognitive architectures, providing built-in reasoning mechanisms to support high-level decision making. This method, however, still needs manmade description of agent acting principles. Some of these principles often can be formulated in rather abstract terms, such as AI's high-level goals and beliefs. This capability of cognitive architectures provides a natural way to describe AI designer's intentions, thus contributing to complex, human-like behavior of obtained agents. Manual behavior authoring is minimized in learning by observation-based AI systems: agent's acting patterns are discovered automatically via machine learning methods. Currently, there are no generally preferred knowledge representation data structures and machine learning algorithms for the task of creating believable behavior.

Behavior Optimization

The projects surveyed in the last section primarily concentrate on believability of AI agents, while the problem of effectiveness is not considered as a primary aim. Since believability and effectiveness are not always connected, effective agents are often based on different principles than believable agents. In this context, it is interesting to compare 2K BotPrize believability competition among Unreal Tournament agents with StarCraft AI Competition that makes emphasis on effectiveness. As already mentioned, all three current top 2K BotPrize bots are based on different principles: (a) finite-state machine; (b) rule-based cognitive architecture; (c) neural network, trained on human-made behavioral traces. In contrast, the best current StarCraft bots rely on human-designed strategies,

most often implemented as finite-state machines, and on special *ad hoc* methods, such as "mimic opponent's behavior" (EIS, 2010).

Thus, a reasonable research goal would be to combine believability and effectiveness in order to obtain AI-controlled characters, yielding higher user satisfaction. One of possible approaches to tackle this problem is to optimize the behavior of an existing believable AI-controlled character, making it more effective in terms of skill level. A number of experimental projects are devoted to such behavior optimization. Though it should be mentioned that the task of optimizing *believable* agents is rarely addressed; more often researchers try to optimize a certain AI system without discussing its believability. Usually such experiments start with an agent having a hardcoded decision-making system that reflects the authors' abilities to design a winning strategy. Next, the agent's behavior is adjusted real-time or offline using automatic optimization methods. For example, having a number of applicable behavior patterns, it is possible to encourage the use of winning patterns, meanwhile discouraging inferior action sequences (often through reinforcement learning methods [Kaelbling, Littman, & Moore, 1996]). Since real-time adaptation and learning optimizes effectiveness rather than believability, the result is evaluated in terms of achieving game goals rather than in being "human-like."

Bonse, Kockelkorn, Smelik, Veelders, and Moerman (2004) extended the standard Quake 3 bot with a neural network that maps current game state parameters into a vector of weights of possible actions, and applied Q-learning algorithm to adjust these weights. The network was trained on a large number (100 000 – 200 000) of one-on-one games (the game continues until one of the opponents is killed). The results showed that the improved bot has a 65% chance to win in a match with the original Quake 3 AI agent. The project by Bonacina, Lanzi, and Loiacono (2008) continues this research by learning better dodging (i.e. hit-avoidance) behavior. In their experiments, a neural network-backed Quake 3 bot has to survive as long as possible in an empty room with an enemy computer-controlled bot equipped with a rocket launcher. Experiments show that the bot quickly learns dodging, which allows it to survive for more than 150 game tics, while the original bot has an average lifetime of 100 tics.

Cole, Louis, and Miles (2004) successfully applied genetic programming to the task of optimizing Counter-Strike built-in bot's behavior. A bot's playing style is defined with a set of parameters that affects weapon selection preferences and agressivity. The selection of parameters is not easy, as many non-obvious combinations can result in better performance, while a slight change in one of the parameters can have a negative impact on bot's effectiveness. The idea of the experiment was to employ genetic programming to automate parameter adjustment process. The authors have demonstrated that their approach can provide bots as effective as the ones designed by human experts. Moreover, genetic optimization algorithm found several different winning sets of parameters, and therefore produced a number of highly effective bots with distinct playing styles.

Research performed by Spronck et al. (2006) shows the possibility of applying a variation of reinforcement learning, called dynamic scripting, to a dynamic 3D role-playing game Neverwinter Nights. Generally, the method works according to the following scheme. When a system generates a new character, it compiles a "script" that defines its behavior from basic rules, stored in a database. Each rule has an associated numerical weight, adjusted in run-time with reinforcement learning algorithm. The weight adjustment function takes into account both the goals of individual agents and of the whole team (as agents do act in coordinated teams). Since the game had no alternative AI implementations, the authors have evaluated dynamic scripting by comparing it with straightforward rigid agent strategies ("offensive," "disabling," "defensive," etc.). Dynamic scripting clearly outperforms such static strategies. It worth noting that the authors used reinforcement learning

not only to find winning behavioral patterns, but also to match AI skills with the player's skills. For instance, if the computer team starts to beat the player too often, AI stops using rules having the highest weights (i.e. removes the most effective behavioral patterns).

The later example highlights two important facts: (1) it is possible to use reinforcement learning to adapt AI actions to human players rather than to search for a winning strategy; and (2) reinforcement learning can be applied to a set of already available behavioral patterns. The second observation makes us believe that human-like behavior can be combined with reinforcement learning-based optimization to achieve both believable and effective behavior. If all behavioral patterns in the knowledgebase are obtained through observation, the behavior should be believable. If the AI system uses effective patterns only (and adjusts its own strategies if necessary), the behavior also becomes effective.

In the subsequent research by Bakkes, Spronck, and van den Herik (2009, 2011) this idea of "adaptation plus effectiveness" is emphasized explicitly. The authors apply a variation of a case-based reasoning algorithm to obtain an adaptive and effective AI system for a real-time strategy game. The proposed solution extracts behavioral patterns of existing game players, and uses them to build a knowledgebase for case-based reasoning. During the game, the system selects the best performing actions, according to past observations. The authors developed an evaluation function that assesses the quality of player's current situation, thus giving the ability to judge the outcome of any chosen action.

BUILDING A BELIEVABLE AND EFFECTIVE AI AGENT: A CASE STUDY

The authors of this work used a 3D boxing video game environment to experiment with some of the topics discussed above, such as: (a) obtaining believable behavior through learning by observation and case-based reasoning; (b) believability evaluation with Turing tests and automated schemes; (c) optimizing AI behavior in terms of effectiveness by means of reinforcement learning (Mozgovoy & Umarov, 2010a,b). Since the boxing game world is relatively simple, our research can serve as an easily understandable project that binds together several core concepts, and thus serves as a useful case study.

We have designed and implemented an AI system for controlling virtual boxers, having the following goals in mind:

- Complex, non-repetitive behavior of AI agents;
- Distinct personalities of AI boxers, exhibiting a variety of skill levels and playing styles;
- Capability to design, edit, and adjust AI's behavior (for a game designer);
- "Train your own boxer" mode as a user-end feature.

The project included two stages. During the first stage, we implemented a learning-by-observation based AI system, capable of reproducing human behavior. We trained several AI-controlled boxers and verified their believability by means of Turing-based and automated believability tests. During the second stage, we employed reinforcement learning to optimize agents' effectiveness by encouraging repetition of the most successful behavioral patterns.

AI-Controlled Boxer's Memory Model

The above stated goals encouraged us to use a variation of finite-state machine that we call *acting graph* as a primary data structure of an AI-controlled boxer's knowledgebase (a similar solution was used by Le Hy et al., 2004). Normally, this graph is being constructed automatically during learning by observation phase. A human expert plays the game, and the computer system builds the acting graph on the fly.

The nodes of this graph correspond to game situations. A game situation is a unique description of the current state of the game world, represented with a set of numerical attributes, defined by the game designer. For the game of boxing such attributes include, in particular, the coordinates of both opponents, their directions (where opponents look), their body positions (standing, leaning, blocking, etc.), and health levels.

The edges of the graph represent the observed character's actions that modify game states. For example, a simple action "move left" connects two game situations that have a difference in player character's horizontal coordinate. Each edge also has an associated probability: while a certain game situation may have numerous outgoing actions, not all of them may be equally preferable (see Figure 1).

The acting graph possesses the following features that help us to achieve our goals:

1. The graph stores all behavioral patterns, demonstrated by human players. Unlike many knowledge representation mechanisms, such as neural networks, it does not suppress rare training samples (often treated as "noise"): every action sequence occurred during training sessions will be preserved in the graph. Thus an AI agent acquires all idiosyncratic elements of its trainer's style.

2. The acting graph can be visualized and manually edited by the game designer. One can remove unwanted or unintentional sections, create artificial acting sequences, and join separate graphs into a single knowledgebase. While this point might not seem major, it is an important factor for practical game developers, who are responsible for AI quality and prefer to have more control over system configuration.

3. Acting graph provides facilities for basic planning functions. For example, the game

designer might want to implement a heuristic ranking procedure that selects the best action from a set of admissible actions, produced by the case-based reasoning subsystem. Such a procedure can traverse a graph, discover that a certain action is always weak (e.g., it always leads to game states with lower health level of the character), and discard it. While long-term planning may not be needed for boxing, it is crucial for several other types of games.

Learning and Acting

In order to train an agent our system is set-up for watching a human expert actually play a match against a human- or computer-controlled opponent. Every time the observed player makes an action (including "do nothing" case), the system updates AI agent's knowledgebase. Most individual actions last 1-60 frames of animation, while the game runs at a constant speed of 60 frames per second. Thus, during a typical 15 minute learning session the system records around 4000 samples.

In AI acting mode, the system performs case-based reasoning: it identifies a node in the acting graph that matches the current game situation, and applies one of the actions, found in outgoing edges. This process involves more complicated techniques, required by heuristic nature of matching algorithm: perfect matches are rare, so the system needs to be able to relax matching conditions gradually until an approximate match is found. Since the details are not relevant here, let us just mention that the game designer is given an ability to specify a sequence of calls of matching algorithm, parameterizing each call with a set of relaxations. A relaxation may include either excluding a certain attribute from matching or specifying a range of admissible deviations for an attribute's value.

The readied agent has no built-in capability of distinguishing strong and weak actions; it repeats human-demonstrated behavioral patterns, even if they lead to inevitable defeat. Moreover, as experiments show, the agent, trained by a certain player, is less skillful than its trainer. It happens because the case-based reasoning system is imperfect: sometimes it fails to find the most appropriate actions that should be chosen according to the training session. Therefore, we decided to include an optional module that optimizes the agent's behavior with the help of reinforcement learning.

Without reinforcement learning enabled, the case-based reasoning module extracts the set of actions, applicable in the given game situation, and uses weighted random choice to select the next action (action frequency is used as a weight). Reinforcement learning procedure analyzes the outcome of the just applied action (we simply check whether our boxer got more or less damage than his opponent), and modifies the action weight accordingly. Successful actions get higher weights and higher probabilities of being chosen. A backpropagation routine distributes action reward among preceding actions.

It should be noted that even in such a seemingly reactive game as boxing a skillful AI can discover several distinct playing styles, for example, by choosing quick light jabs over slow straight arm punches or by giving preference to offensive rather than defensive behavior. Thus backpropagation can be considered as an instrument for behavior planning, not just as a method of giving preference to action with the best immediate effect.

Testing Believability

In order to test believability of our agent, we used a Turing test-based technique, similar to the one described in Hingston (2009). We recorded a number of one-minute game fragments between random opponents. Each opponent could be a human player; a boxer, controlled with our AI; or a boxer, controlled with a boxing engine's built-in AI system, based on a handcrafted finite-state machine[14].

Figure 1. A fragment of acting graph (rendered with Graphviz package[13])

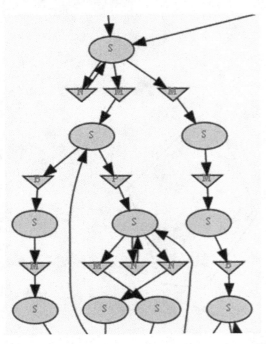

We asked six people with various gaming experience to watch the fragments and to guess the opponents (each boxer could be marked as "human" or "computer"). Each person was asked to analyze nine video clips. Our AI-controlled boxer was identified as human in 80.6% of cases. In contrast, the engine's built-in AI system was able to deceive the judges in only 14% of cases (see Table 1).

Table 1. Results of the Turing test

Scenario	Probability	σ	σ$_{mean}$
Built-in AI system identified as an AI agent	86.1%	1.07	0.44
Human player identified as a human	77.8%	0.75	0.30
Machine learning-based AI identified as a human	80.6%	0.69	0.28

Since we were also curious to try automated believability tests, we implemented a method, somewhat similar to the one described by Tencé and Buche (2008). Our algorithm calculates a "style similarity ratio" for the given pre-recorded action sequences, belonging to two boxers. For each action sequence we compute a vector of probabilities of each possible combination of two successive actions. A style similarity ratio is simply a dot product of these vectors. Using this algorithm, we calculated a matrix of similarity ratios between the following eleven boxers:

- Three boxers, controlled by the built-in AI system (AI1-AI3);
- Two boxers, controlled by two different human players (WEAK_H, AVG_H);
- Six AI-controlled boxers, trained by the same human players (WEAK1-WEAK3, AVG1-AVG3).

The analysis of the obtained matrix revealed two clearly separated clusters: the one with the built-in AI-controlled boxers and the one with all other boxers. Thereby, the automated test supported the earlier observation that AI agents, created through learning by observation, are closer (in terms of behavior style) to human-controlled boxers than to the boxers controlled by the built-in handcrafted AI system (see Figure 2[15]).

During these experiments, we made another important observation: behavior optimization through reinforcement learning does not reduce agent's believability. A believable agent remains believable even after adjustments, made by reinforcement learning. However, the style of such an agent resembles the style of its human trainer to a lesser extent. In our case, reinforcement learning introduces no new behavioral patterns: the boxer still uses the same human-supplied action sequences, only their weights, used by the weighted random choice procedure, are adjusted.

Figure 2. Visualized results of automated believability tests

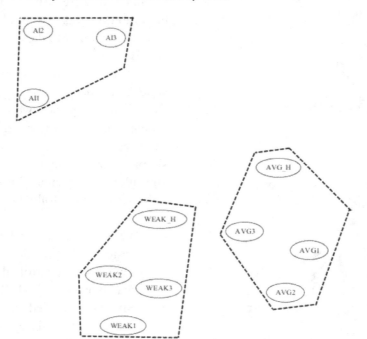

DISCUSSION

An obvious factor in the development of virtual worlds is their growing complexity. This growth concerns literally all aspects of virtual worlds—audiovisual presentation, ways of character-character interaction, physics, and world use scenarios. Generally, virtual worlds are designed to be realistic, fun and immersive. As we have seen, worlds are often inhabited by both human-controlled and computer-controlled characters. So it is natural to analyze, how this growing complexity affects AI systems, used in virtual worlds.

We have to admit that not all virtual worlds are tightly bound with AI-controlled characters. Worlds like World of Warcraft consider game bots as unwelcomed participants[16], and worlds like Second Life, being distant relatives of internet chatrooms, are primarily populated with humans, who are mostly interested in social interaction. But there is also a high variety of game genres, such as first-person shooters, real-time strategies, and

sport games, where AI systems are often present. Moreover, AI is often mentioned by researchers and developers among key fun factors that contribute to the overall success of a game.

In its turn, complex realistic virtual worlds need complex and realistic AI-controlled characters that are able to act believably and effectively. This trend is also widely recognized, so in recent years we have seen numerous novel approaches to AI design, and even "believability competitions" for game bots. Probably, the primary problem in AI development is scalability. Most current AI systems are still handcrafted (at least, partially), but growing complexity of virtual worlds entails the growing complexity and increasing volume of work, needed to create satisfactory decision making modules. Modern AI design instruments, such as behavior trees, are able to remedy the problem to some extent, but cannot solve it completely. Scripted, scenario-based decision making methods become insufficient, and more advanced approaches are on rise as topics of practical studies.

Among general approaches to believable AI development, we would highlight two: the use of learning by observation and the use of cognitive architectures. Most probably, they can be seen as complimentary to each other.

Learning by observation is a method of behavior creation by watching behavioral patterns of existing game characters, usually human-controlled. This idea is a variation of a well-known concept of machine learning, and can be used to acquire both believable and effective elements of behavior. As we have seen, learning by observation and case-based reasoning were indeed applied to a variety of game worlds.

Cognitive architectures are usually responsible for high-level reasoning and strategic decision making. Their adopters often attribute human-likeness of the obtained AI behavior to human-likeness of decision making processes implemented in cognitive architectures: typically they are based on psychophysiological models of reasoning, and this fact makes AI-controlled game characters believable.

One should also note that people are prone to the "ELIZA Effect" (Hofstadter, 1995): they often attribute human-likeness to computer systems that just exhibit simple human-like behavioral patterns. As the recent 2K BotPrize competition has shown, it is possible for an AI agent to pass the believability Turing test simply by mimicking human behavior. While game AI systems can certainly rely to some extent on "ELIZA Effect" to simulate human-likeness (Ahlquist & Novak, 2007), we would emphasize that a pure mimicry-based AI system has performed well in the situation where believability was the only goal; in real video games believability is just one of the factors of a successful AI, so probably it would be difficult to create intelligent game characters solely on such a basis.

However, every particular game world has own peculiarities and fine points, so it is probably impossible to suggest an ultimate approach. For example, in sport games strategic decision making is less important than quick and smart reaction to immediate actions of the opponent. In contrast, real-time strategies need careful goal-based, long-term planning. Another notable topic not covered in this chapter, is agent-agent coordination and cooperation. If a certain virtual world requires believable behavior of AI-controlled teams of characters, their creators face a new dimension of complexity. This topic is a subject of numerous studies (see, e.g., Panait & Luke, 2005; Chernova & Veloso, 2007; Ros, Veloso, de Mántaras, Sierra, & Arcos, 2007; Stone, Kaminka, Kraus, & Rosenschein, 2010).

CONCLUSION

As virtual worlds become more and more complex, the importance of high-quality AI solutions increases. While in relatively simple "shoot 'em up" games, traditional game AI algorithms work reasonably well, modern virtual worlds require more advanced approaches that can provide more realistic and effective behavior. Realism (or believability, human-likeness) can itself be a goal for an AI agent—especially in simulation and training applications, where believability is crucial. Effectiveness (in terms of achieving an agent's own goals) is also harder to achieve with traditional methods in complex environments, where a winning strategy might require hierarchical goal planning and real-time adjustment to human player's actions.

The problem of creating believable and effective AI agents is raised both by academic researchers and video game developers. However, current commercial games rarely implement AI algorithms that go beyond traditional finite state machines and rule-based systems. At the same time, research shows that believable agents should possess certain features, hardly achievable without methods that rely on observing and/or simulating human behavior.

A number of research projects prove that certain human behavior acquisition methods, such as learning by observation and imitation learning, are applicable to complex domains such as first-person shooters and real-time strategy games. There is evidence that these methods can be combined with automatic winning strategy-selecting algorithms to provide both believable and effective behavior, as shown, for example, in the AI system for a 3D boxing game described as the case study in this chapter and our earlier works (Mozgovoy & Umarov, 2010a, 2010b). Long-term planning and strategic thinking support can be obtained from general-purpose cognitive architectures, also successfully applied in the domain of computer game worlds (Wintermute, et al., 2007; Choi, et al., 2007).

We believe that further research in learning by observation, advanced reasoning methods, and agent-agent coordination will be extremely useful for constructing believable and effective AI agents, inhabiting complex, immersive virtual worlds.

ACKNOWLEDGMENT

This paper is based on: I. Umarov, M. Mozgovoy, P. C. Rogers. Believable and Effective AI Agents in Virtual Worlds: Current State and Future Perspectives. *International Journal of Gaming and Computer-Mediated Simulations*, 2012, vol. 4(2), p. 37-59.

REFERENCES

Adobbati, R., Marshall, A., Scholer, A., Tejada, S., Kaminka, G., Schaffer, S., & Sollitto, C. (2001). Gamebots: A 3D Virtual World Test-Bed For Multi-Agent Research. In *Proc. of 2nd Workshop on Infrastructure for Agents*, (pp. 47-52). Academic Press.

Ahlquist, J., & Novak, J. (2007). *Game Development Essentials: Game Artificial Intelligence*. Delmar Cengage Learning.

Arrabales, R., Ledezma, A., & Sanchis, A. (2009). CERA-CRANIUM: A Test Bed for Machine Consciousness Research. In *Proceedings of International Workshop on Machine Consciousness*. Academic Press.

Arrabales, R., & Muñoz, J. (2010). *The Awakening of Conscious Bots: Inside the Mind of the 2K BotPrize 2010 Winner*. Retrieved from http://aigamedev.com/open/articles/conscious-bot/

Bakkes, S., Spronck, P., & van den Herik, J. (2009). Rapid and Reliable Adaptation of Video Game AI. *IEEE Transactions on Computational Intelligence and AI in Games*, *1*(2), 93–104. doi:10.1109/TCIAIG.2009.2029084

Bakkes, S., Spronck, P., & van den Herik, J. (2011). A CBR-Inspired Approach to Rapid and Reliable Adaption of Video Game AI. In *Proc. of the 19th International Conference on Case-Based Reasoning*, (pp. 17-26). Academic Press.

Balla, R.-K., & Fern, A. (2009). UCT for Tactical Assault Planning in Real-Time Strategy Games. In *Proceedings of 21st International Joint Conference on Artificial Intelligence*, (pp. 40-45). Academic Press.

Bates, J. (1994). The Role of Emotion in Believable Characters. *Communications of the ACM*, *37*, 122–125. doi:10.1145/176789.176803

Bell, M. (2008). Toward a Definition of "Virtual Worlds". *Journal of Virtual Worlds Research*, *1*(1).

Biever, C. (2012, September). *Mimicry Beats Consciousness in Gaming's Turing Test*. Retrieved from http://www.newscientist.com/article/dn22305-mimicry-beats-consciousness-in-gamings-turing-test.html

Blizzard. (2010). *World of Warcraft Terms of Use*. Retrieved from http://us.blizzard.com/en-us/company/legal/wow_tou.html

Bonacina, S., Lanzi, P., & Loiacono, D. (2008). Evolving Dodging Behavior for OpenArena using Neuroevolution of Augmenting Topologies. In *Proceedings of PPSN'08 Workshop (Computational Intelligence and Games)*. PPSN.

Bonse, R., Kockelkorn, W., Smelik, R., Veelders, P., & Moerman, W. (2004). *Learning Agents in Quake III (Technical Report)*. University of Utrecht, Department of Computer Science.

Booth, M. (2004). The Official Counter-Strike Bot. In *Proceedings of Game Developers Conference'04*. Academic Press.

Champandard, A. (2007). Most Influental AI Games. *AIGameDev.com*. Retrieved from http://aigamedev.com/open/highlights/top-ai-games/

Champandard, A. (2011). *This Year in Game AI: Analysis, Trends from 2010 and Predictions for 2011*. Retrieved 02.10.2011, from http://aigamedev.com/open/editorial/2010-retrospective/

Chernova, S., & Veloso, M. (2007). Multiagent Collaborative Task Learning through Imitation. In *Proc. of the 4th International Symposium on Imitation in Animals and Artifacts*, (pp. 74-79). Academic Press.

Choi, D., Kim, H., & Kim, J. (1999). Toward the Construction of Fun Computer Games: Differences in the Views of Developers and Players. *Personal and Ubiquitous Computing*, *3*(3), 92–104.

Choi, D., Konik, T., Nejati, N., Park, C., & Langley, P. (2007). A Believable Agent for First-Person Perspective Games. In *Proc. of the 3rd Artificial Intelligence and Interactive Digital Entertainment International Conference*. Academic Press.

Cole, N., Louis, S., & Miles, C. (2004). Using a Genetic Algorithm to Tune First-Person Shooter Bots. In *Proc. of the International Congress on Evolutionary Computation*, (pp. 139-145). Academic Press.

Csikszentmihalyi, M. (1991). *Flow: The Psychology of Optimal Experience*. New York: Harper Perennial.

EIS. (2010). *Expressive Intelligence Studio: 2010 StarCraft AI Competition Results*. Retrieved 30.09.2011, from http://eis.ucsc.edu/StarCraftAICompetition#Results

El Rhalibi, A., & Merabti, M. (2008). A Hybrid Fuzzy ANN System for Agent Adaptation in a First Person Shooter. *International Journal of Computer Games Technology*, 1–18. doi:10.1155/2008/432365

Eyewitness: Complete AI Interviews. (2002, September 18). *PC Gamer*. Retrieved 30.09.2011 from http://tinyurl.com/eyewitness-2002-09-18

Friedman, D., Steed, A., & Slater, M. (2007). Spatial Social Behavior in Second Life. *Lecture Notes in Computer Science*, *4722*, 252–263. doi:10.1007/978-3-540-74997-4_23

Glende, A. (2004). Agent Design to Pass Computer Games. In *Proc. of the 42nd Annual ACM Southeast Regional Conference*, (pp. 414-415). ACM.

Gorman, B., Thurau, C., Bauckhage, C., & Humphrys, M. (2006). Believability Testing and Bayesian Imitation in Interactive Computer Games. *Lecture Notes in Computer Science*, *4095*, 655–666. doi:10.1007/11840541_54

Graesser, A., Lang, K., & Roberts, R. (1991). Question Answering in the Context of Stories. *Journal of Experimental Psychology. General*, *120*(3), 254–277. doi:10.1037/0096-3445.120.3.254

Hagelbäck, J., & Johansson, S. (2009). A Multiagent Potential Field-Based Bot for Real-Time Strategy Games. *International Journal of Computer Games Technology*, 1–10. doi:10.1155/2009/910819

Hecker, C. (2011). *My Liner Notes for Spore*. Retrieved 20.09.2011, from http://chrishecker. com/My_liner_notes_for_spore

Hingston, P. (2009). A Turing Test for Computer Game Bots. *IEEE Transactions on Computational Intelligence and AI in Games*, *1*(3), 169–186. doi:10.1109/TCIAIG.2009.2032534

Hirono, D., & Thawonmas, R. (2009). Implementation of a Human-Like Bot in a First Person Shooter: Second Place Bot at BotPrize 2008. In *Proc. of Asia Simulation Conference*. Academic Press.

Hofstadter, D. (1995). Preface 4: The Ineradicable Eliza Effect and Its Dangers. In *Fluid Concepts and Creative Analogies: Computer Models of the Fundamental Mechanisms of Thought*. New York: Basic Books.

ICARUS. (2007). *ICARUS Project*. Retrieved from http://cll.stanford.edu/research/ongoing/icarus/

Ijaz, K., Bogdanovych, A., & Simoff, S. (2011). Enhancing the believability of embodied conversational agents through environment-, self-and interaction-awareness. In *Proc. of Australasian Compuer Science Conference*. Academic Press.

Isla, D. (2005). Handling Complexity in the Halo 2 AI. In *Proceedings of Game Developers Conference'05*. Academic Press.

Jones, R. M., Laird, J. E., Nielsen, P. E., Coulter, K. J., Kenny, P., & Koss, F. (1999). Automated intelligent pilots for combat flight simulation. *AI Magazine*, *20*(1), 27–41.

Kaelbling, L., Littman, M., & Moore, A. (1996). Reinforcement Learning: A Survey. *Journal of Artificial Intelligence Research*, *4*, 237–285.

Kemmerling, M., Ackermann, N., Beume, N., Preuss, M., Uellenbeck, S., & Walz, W. (2009). Is Human-Like and Well Playing Contradictory for Diplomacy Bots?. In *Proceedings of IEEE Symposium on Computational Intelligence and Games*, (pp. 209-216). IEEE.

Kitano, H., Asada, M., Kuniyoshi, Y., Noda, I., Osawai, E., & Matsubara, H. (1998). RoboCup: A Challenge Problem for AI and Robotics. *Lecture Notes in Computer Science*, *1395*, 1–19. doi:10.1007/3-540-64473-3_46

Knafla, B. (2011). *Introduction to Behavior Trees*. Retrieved 15.09.2011, from http://bjoernknafla. com/introduction-to-behavior-trees

Laird, J. (2002). Research in Human-level AI using Computer Games. *Communications of the ACM*, *45*, 32–35. doi:10.1145/502269.502290

Langley, P., Choi, D., & Rogers, S. (2005). *Interleaving Learning, Problem-Solving, and Execution in the ICARUS Architecture (Technical Report)*. Computational Learning Laboratory, Stanford University.

Le Hy, R., Arrigoni, A., Bessière, P., & Lebeltel, O. (2004). Teaching Bayesian Behaviours to Video Game Characters. *Robotics and Autonomous Systems*, *47*, 177–185. doi:10.1016/j. robot.2004.03.012

Lee, F., & Gamard, S. (2003). Hide and Seek: Using Computational Cognitive Models to Develop and Test Autonomous Cognitive Agents for Complex Dynamic Tasks. In *Proc. of the 25th Annual Conference of the Cognitive Science Society*. Academic Press.

Liaw, C., Wang, W.-H., Tsai, C.-T., Ko, C.-H., & Hao, G. (2013). Evolving A Team In A First-Person Shooter Game By Using A Genetic Algorithm. *Applied Artificial Intelligence*, *27*(3), 199–212. doi:10.1080/08839514.2013.768883

Lichocki, P., Krawiec, K., & Jaśkowski, W. (2009). Evolving Teams of Cooperating Agents for Real-Time Strategy Game. *Lecture Notes in Computer Science, 5484,* 333–342. doi:10.1007/978-3-642-01129-0_37

Livingstone, D. (2006). Turing's Test and Believable AI in Games. *Computers in Entertainment, 4*(1), 6–18. doi:10.1145/1111293.1111303

Malone, T. (1981). What Makes Computer Games Fun? *Byte, 6*(12), 258–278.

Manojlovich, J., Prasithsangaree, P., Hughes, S., Chen, J., & Lewis, M. (2003). UTSAF: A Multi-agent-based Framework for Supporting Military-based Distributed Interactive Simulations in 3D Virtual Environments. In *Proc. of 2003 Simulation Conference.* Academic Press.

Mehta, M., Ontañón, S., & Ram, A. (2010). Meta-Level Behavior Adaptation in Real-Time Strategy Games. In *Proceedings of ICCBR 2010 Workshop on Case Based Reasoning for Computer Games.* ICCBR.

Milward, D. (2009). *List of Neverwinter Nights 2 NPCs.* Retrieved 03.10.2011, from http://www.sorcerers.net/Games/NWN2/Walkthrough/NPCList.php

Mitchell, D. (1995). *From MUDs to Virtual Worlds.* Microsoft Virtual Worlds Group.

Morie, J., Chance, E., Haynes, K., & Purohit, D. (2012). Storytelling with Storyteller Agents in Second Life. In *Proc. of International Conference on Cyberworlds,* (pp. 165-170). Academic Press.

Mozgovoy, M., & Umarov, I. (2010a). Building a Believable Agent for a 3D Boxing Simulation Game. In *Proc. of the 2nd International Conference on Computer Research and Development,* (pp. 46-50). Academic Press.

Mozgovoy, M., & Umarov, I. (2010b). Building a Believable and Effective Agent for a 3D Boxing Simulation Game. In *Proc. of the 3rd IEEE International Conference on Computer Science and Information Technology,* (pp. 14-18). IEEE.

Naveed, M., Kitchin, D., & Crampton, A. (2010). Monte-Carlo Planning for Pathfinding in Real-Time Strategy Games. In *Proceedings of PlanSIG Workshop,* (pp. 125-132). PlanSIG.

Ontañón, S., Mishra, K., Sugandh, N., & Ram, A. (2007). Case-based Planning and Execution for Real-time Strategy Games. *Lecture Notes in Computer Science, 4626,* 164–178. doi:10.1007/978-3-540-74141-1_12

Orkin, J. (2006). Three States and a Plan: the AI of FEAR. In *Proceedings of Game Developers Conference'06.* Academic Press.

Panait, L., & Luke, S. (2005). Cooperative Multi-Agent Learning: The State of the Art. *Autonomous Agents and Multi-Agent Systems, 11*(3), 387–434. doi:10.1007/s10458-005-2631-2

Pao, H.-K., Chen, K.-T., & Chang, H.-C. (2010). Game Bot Detection via Avatar Trajectory Analysis. *IEEE Transactions on Computational Intelligence and AI in Games, 2*(3), 162–175. doi:10.1109/TCIAIG.2010.2072506

Pillosu, R. (2009). *Coordinating Agents with Behavior Trees: Synchronizing Multiple Agents in CryEngine 2.* Retrieved from AIGameDev.com

Ranathunga, S., Cranefield, S., & Purvis, M. (2011). Interfacing a Cognitive Agent Platform with a Virtual World: a Case Study using Second Life. In *Proc. of the 10th International Conference on Autonomous Agents and Multiagent Systems,* (vol. 3, pp. 1181-1182). Academic Press.

Riedl, M., & Young, R. (2005). *An Objective Character Believability Evaluation Procedure for Multi-Agent Story Generation Systems* (pp. 278–291). Intelligent Virtual Agents. doi:10.1007/11550617_24

Robertson, J., & Good, J. (2005). Adventure Author: an Authoring Tool for 3D Virtual Reality Story Construction. In *Proceedings of AIED-05 Workshop on Narrative Learning Environments*, (pp. 63-69). Academic Press.

Ros, R., Veloso, M., de Mántaras, R., Sierra, C., & Arcos, J. (2007). Beyond Individualism: Modeling Team Playing Behavior. *Proc. of the National Conference on Artificial Intelligence*, 22(2), 1671-1674.

Sánchez-Crespo Dalmau, D. (2005, March). Postcard from GDC 2005: Tutorial — Machine Learning. *Gamasutra, 8*.

Schrum, J., Karpov, I., & Miikkulainen, R. (2011). UT^2: Human-like Behavior via Neuroevolution of Combat Behavior and Replay of Human Traces. In *Proc. of IEEE Conference on Computational Intelligence and Games*, (pp. 329-336). IEEE.

Smith, M., Lee-Urban, S., & Munoz-Avila, H. (2007). RETALIATE: Learning Winning Policies in First-person Shooter Games. In *Proc. of the National Conference on Artificial Intelligence*, (pp. 1801-1806). Academic Press.

Soni, B., & Hingston, P. (2008). Bots Trained to Play Like a Human are More Fun. In *Proceedings of IEEE International Joint Conference on Neural Networks*, (pp. 363-369). IEEE.

Spronck, P., Ponsen, M., Sprinkhuizen-Kuyper, I., & Postma, E. (2006). Adaptive Game AI with Dynamic Scripting. *Machine Learning, 63*, 217–248. doi:10.1007/s10994-006-6205-6

Stone, P., Kaminka, G., Kraus, S., & Rosenschein, J. (2010). Ad Hoc Autonomous Agent Teams: Collaboration without Pre-Coordination. In *Proc. of the 24th AAAI Conference on Artificial Intelligence*, (pp. 1504-1509). AAAI.

Sweetser, P., & Wyeth, P. (2005). *GameFlow: a Model for Evaluating Player Enjoyment in Games* (Vol. 3, p. 3). Computers in Entertainment.

Taatgen, N., van Oploo, M., Braaksma, J., & Niemantsverdriet, J. (2003). How to Construct a Believable Opponent using Cognitive Modeling in the Game of Set. In *Proc. of the 5th International Conference on Cognitive Modeling*, (pp. 201-206). Academic Press.

Tencé, F., & Buche, C. (2008). Automatable Evaluation Method Oriented toward Behaviour Believability for Video Games. In *Proceedings of International Conference on Intelligent Games and Simulation*, (pp. 39-43). Academic Press.

Thurau, C., Bauckhage, C., & Sagerer, G. (2004). Learning Human-like Movement Behavior for Computer Games. In *Proc. of the 8th International Conference on the Simulation of Adaptive Behavior (SAB'04)*. SAB.

Turing, A. (1950). Computing Machinery and Intelligence. *Mind, 59*, 433. doi:10.1093/mind/LIX.236.433

van der Heijden, M., Bakkes, S., & Spronck, P. (2008). Dynamic Formations in Real-Time Strategy Games. In *Proceedings of IEEE Symposium on Computational Intelligence and Games*, (pp. 47-54). IEEE.

Wang, H., Shen, C., & Ritterfeld, U. (2009). Enjoyment of Digital Games. In U. Ritterfeld, M. Cody, & P. Vorderer (Eds.), Serious Games: Mechanisms and Effects (pp. 25–47). Academic Press.

Westra, J., & Dignum, F. (2009). Evolutionary Neural Networks for Non-Player Characters in Quake III. In *Proceedings of IEEE Symposium on Computational Intelligence and Games*, (pp. 302-309). Academic Press.

Wintermute, S., Xu, J., & Irizarry, J. (2007). *SORTS Tech Report. Artificial Intelligence Lab.* University of Michigan.

Yannakakis, G., & Hallam, J. (2004). *Evolving Opponents for Interesting Interactive Computer Games* (Vol. 8, pp. 499–508). From Animals to Animats.

Yannakakis, G., & Hallam, J. (2005). A Generic Approach for Obtaining Higher Entertainment in Predator/Prey Computer Games. *Journal of Game Development*, *1*(3), 23–50.

Yannakakis, G., & Hallam, J. (2007). Towards Optimizing Entertainment in Computer Games. *Applied Artificial Intelligence*, *21*, 933–971. doi:10.1080/08839510701527580

Zyda, M., Hiles, J., Mayberry, A., Wardynski, C., Capps, M., & Osborn, B. et al. (2003). The MOVES Institute's Army Game Project: Entertainment R&D for Defense. *IEEE Computer Graphics and Applications*, *23*, 28–36. doi:10.1109/MCG.2003.1159611

ENDNOTES

[1] According to Encyclopedia Britannica, *realism* is "the accurate, detailed, unembellished depiction of nature or of contemporary life".

[2] Available at http://tankionline.com/en/game/

[3] However, Yannakakis and Hallam (2007) note the lack of evidence that human-like behavior should generate more enjoyment; instead, they connect user satisfaction with individual AI features (such as high skill level, diversity and adaptivity of behavior), not necessarily ensuring human-likeness. Although, a more recent study by Soni and Hingston (2008) shows that AI's human-likeness is indeed a notable fun factor.

[4] Effectiveness is important not only for AI-controlled opponents. Human players might expect reasonably skillful behavior also from their teammates and neutral characters.

[5] The author lists the following features of a reasonable AI architecture: customizability, simple and explicit ways to add hacks into the code, the capability to build new features on the basis of existing features.

[6] This project (2K BotPrize) is especially relevant for our discussion, as it aims to identify the most believable Unreal bots through open "believability competition".

[7] http://code.google.com/p/bwapi/

[8] http://eis.ucsc.edu/StarCraftAICompetition

[9] The list of ongoing competitions is available on the page http://code.google.com/p/bwapi/wiki/Competitions

[10] Pong is the simplest variation of 2D tennis, where each player controls a rectangular bat, moveable in vertical direction.

[11] The competition involved five judges; four of them were experienced computer game players.

[12] WARGUS is a Stratagus engine-based modification of Blizzard's commercial game Warcraft 2.

[13] Available at http://www.graphviz.org

[14] It should be mentioned that the game engine used in our experiments is a mature product that serves as a core of a commercial award-winning PlayStation / Xbox video game, and its built-in AI system was actually used in release version.

[15] The plot is visualized with *neato* tool (included into Graphviz package); dashed lines are drawn manually.

[16] This concerns user-created AI agents. There are a limited number of AI-controlled characters, developed by Blizzard, in the World of Warcraft.

Chapter 4
Face and Object Recognition Using Biological Features and Few Views

J.M.F. Rodrigues
University of the Algarve, Portugal

R. Lam
University of the Algarve, Portugal

K. Terzić
University of the Algarve, Portugal

J.M.H. du Buf
University of the Algarve, Portugal

ABSTRACT

In recent years, a large number of impressive face and object recognition algorithms have surfaced, both computational and biologically inspired. Only a few of these can detect face and object views. Empirical studies concerning face and object recognition suggest that faces and objects may be stored in our memory by a few canonical representations. In cortical area V1 exist double-opponent colour blobs, also simple, complex, and end-stopped cells that provide input for a multiscale line and edge representation, keypoints for dynamic feature routing, and saliency maps for Focus-of-Attention. All these combined allow us to segregate faces. Events of different facial views are stored in memory and combined in order to identify the view and recognise a face, including its expression. The authors show that with five 2D views and their cortical representations it is possible to determine the left-right and frontal-lateral-profile views, achieving view-invariant recognition. They also show that the same principle with eight views can be applied to 3D object recognition when they are mainly rotated about the vertical axis. Although object recognition is here explored as a special case of face recognition, it should be stressed that faces and general objects are processed in different ways in the cortex.

DOI: 10.4018/978-1-4666-6252-0.ch004

INTRODUCTION

One of the most important topics of image analysis is face detection and recognition. There are several reasons for this, such as the wide range of commercial vigilance and law-enforcement applications. Face recognition is also one of the most prominent capabilities of our visual system. A person's gender, ethnicity, age and emotions contribute to the recognition process. For instance, in court, a lot of credibility is attributed to identifications by eyewitnesses, although studies have shown that people are not always reliable when comparing faces with recollections (Smeets et al., 2010).

State-of-the-art recognition systems have reached a certain level of maturity, but their accuracy is still limited when imposed conditions are not perfect. View-invariant object recognition is still problematic (Pinto et al., 2010). For faces, all possible combinations of changes in illumination, pose and age, with artefacts like beards, moustaches and glasses, including different facial expressions and partial occlusions, may cause problems. The robustness of commercial systems is still far away from that of the human visual system, especially when dealing with different views. For this reason, despite the fact that the human visual system may not be 100% accurate, the development of models of visual perception and their application to real-world problems is important and, eventually, may lead to a significant breakthrough.

In this chapter we present a cortical model to recognise 3D faces from their 2D projections (Rodrigues et al., 2012a), by exploiting the aspect ratios but without using stereo disparity. We consider all common degrees of rotation like pan (from frontal to lateral and profile views) and tilt (the face looking up or down). We study the number of 2D feature templates required to represent all views. In the recognition process we first detect the view and then match the input face with view-based templates stored in memory. We also test the same model to elongated 3D objects,

i.e., 4-legged animals, because their shape and view can also be inferred from the aspect ratio if they are rotated about the vertical axis (pan). The rest of this chapter is organised as follows: we first present the state-of-the art in 3D face and object recognition. Then we discuss the cortical background of the model, before explaining the frameworks for 3D faces and 3D objects. Recognition results are presented and discussed in the next section, and we end this chapter with conclusions.

RECENT 3D FACE AND OBJECT RECOGNITION METHODS

Because of the limitations of 2D approaches and with the advent of 3D scanners, face-recognition research has expanded from 2D to 3D with a concurrent improvement in performance. There are many face-recognition methods in 2D and 3D, including facial expression recognition; for detailed surveys see Bowyer et al. (2006), Abate et al. (2007), Li & Jain (2011) and Sandbach et al. (2012). Rashad et al. (2009) presented a face-recognition system that overcomes the problem of changes in facial expressions in 3D range images by using a local variation detection and restoration method based on 2D principal component analysis. Ramirez-Valdez & Hasimoto-Beltran (2009) also considered facial expression in recognition. A 3D range image is modelled by the finite-element method with three simplified layers representing the skin, fatty tissue and the cranium. Muscular structures are superimposed in the 3D model for the synthesis of expressions. Their approach consists of three main steps: a denoising algorithm, which removes long peaks in the 3D face samples; automatic detection of control points, to detect particular landmarks such as eyes and mouth corners, nose tip, etc.; and registration of the 3D face model to each face with neutral expression in the training database. Berretti et al. (2010) took into account 3D geometrical information and encoded the relevant information into a compact graph representation. The nodes of the graph represent equal-width, iso-geodesic facial stripes. The edges between pairs of nodes are labelled by descriptors, and referred to as 3D weighted walkthroughs that capture the mutual relative spatial displacement between all node pairs in the corresponding stripes. Fadaifard et al. (2013) presented a 3D curvature scale-space representation for shape matching, and applied it to face recognition. The representation is obtained by evolving the surface curvatures according to the heat equation; this process yields a stack of increasingly smoothed surface curvatures that is useful for keypoint extraction and descriptor computations. The scale parameter is used for automatic scale selection, which is applied to 2D scale-invariant shape-matching applications.

There are also many object categorisation and recognition methods in 2D and 3D; see e.g. Galleguillos & Belongie (2010) and Weinland et al. (2011) for detailed surveys. Recognition of general 3D objects can be based on 2D projected images (Su et al., 2006), on 3D shape retrieval methods (Tangelder & Veltkamp, 2008), on multiresolution signatures (Lam & du Buf, 2011), and on feature extraction in combination with spatial clustering (Fenzi et al., 2012). Other approaches, like the one presented in this chapter, can be applied to both 3D objects and faces (Passalis et al., 2007). More recently, we explored 2D real-time object recognition based on cortical multiscale keypoints and SIFT descriptors (Terzić et al., 2013a; Terzić et al., 2013b).

All these methods produce interesting results, but none can approach the performance of our visual system which can easily recognise faces and objects independent of their view.

CORTICAL BACKGROUND

Face perception in humans is mediated by a distributed neural system which links multiple brain regions. The functional organisation of this system embodies a distinction between the representation of invariant aspects of faces, which is the basis for recognising persons. A core system, consisting of occipitotemporal regions in extrastriate visual cortex, mediates visual analysis of faces (Haxby et al., 2002). Faces are represented as locations in a multidimensional space, where the distances separating the representations are proportional to the degree of dissimilarity between the faces The structure of this face–space is tolerant to lighting and viewpoint transformations (Blank & Yove, 2011).

Invariant face and object detection, categorisation and recognition depend on a hierarchy of cortical stages that build invariance gradually (Grossberg et al., 2011), involving both bottom-up and top-down data streams in the so-called "what" and "where" subsystems (Deco & Rolls, 2004), including the integration of both subsystems (Farivar, 2009). In cortical area V1 there are simple and complex cells, which are tuned to different spatial frequencies (scales) and orientations, but also to stereo disparity (depth) because of neighbouring left-right hypercolumns (Hubel, 1995). These cells provide input for grouping cells which code line and edge information (Rodrigues & du Buf, 2009a) and attribute depth information (Rodrigues & du Buf, 2004; Rodrigues et al., 2012b). In V1 there are also double-opponent colour blobs (Tailor et al., 2000) and end-stopped cells which, together with sophisticated inhibition processes, allow to extract keypoints, i.e., singularities, vertices and points of high curvature (Heitger et al., 1992; Rodrigues & du Buf, 2006). Such keypoints can be applied to object recognition (Terzić et al., 2013a) and to optical flow (Farrajota et al., 2011).

On the basis of models of neural processing schemes, it is now possible to create a cortical architecture bootstrapped by global and local gist (Martins et al., 2009; Rodrigues & du Buf, 2011), with face and figure-ground segregation (Rodrigues & du Buf, 2006; Rodrigues & du Buf, 2009a; Farrajota et al., 2011), focus-of-attention (Rodrigues & du Buf, 2006; Martins et al., 2009), face/object categorisation and recognition (Rodrigues & du Buf, 2006; Rodrigues & du Buf, 2009a), including recognition of facial expressions (Sousa et al., 2010) and hand gestures (Farrajota et al., 2012).

Recent work (Kourtzi & Connor, 2011) has provided a more precise picture of how 2D and 3D object structure is encoded in intermediate and higher-level visual cortices. Nevertheless, the same authors stated that there are other studies which suggest that higher-level visual cortex represents categorical identity rather than spatial structure. Furthermore, cell responses to objects are surprisingly adaptive to changes in environmental factors, implying that learning through evolution, development, but also short-term experience in adulthood, may optimise the object code (Kourtzi & Connor, 2011).

In conclusion, there are several open questions related to the perception and recognition of objects and faces in the brain. One of those is which and how many templates we store of a person's face, and how those templates are related to create the notion of a 3D face in our brain. In the cortical hypercolumns in area V1, information from the left and right retinal projections is very close. As a consequence, dendritic fields of cells can receive input from both projections, and many simple and complex cells are tuned to disparity such that depth can be attributed to detected lines and edges, mainly vertical ones (du Buf et al., 2013). This could yield a sort of 3D wireframe representation, like the one used in computer graphics for the modelling of solid objects. This approach will not be applied here, but it is possible to combine disparity information with projected features.

In this chapter we focus mainly on a cortical model for face recognition and a specific case of object recognition – animals (asymmetric objects). The present model is based on a previous one (Rodrigues & du Buf, 2009b) which employs multiscale line/edge and keypoint representations based on V1 cells. That model was shown to give good results for frontal and frontal-to-3/4 views,

also with small occlusions. In the present chapter we go much further. We test faces with more degrees of rotation[1] (y-rotated $\pm 90°$, pan; x-rotated $\pm 10°$, tilt), the number of 2D templates needed to represent a 3D face, the relation between them, and the detected view (left-right and profile-lateral-frontal). We also apply the same model to 3D objects (animals) with other degrees of rotation (y-rotated $\pm 180°$, pan; x-rotated $\pm 10°$, tilt).

CORTICAL LINE, EDGE, AND KEYPOINT MODELS

There is extensive evidence that the visual input is processed at different spatial scales, and both psychophysical and computational studies have shown that different scales offer different qualities of information (Bar, 2004; Oliva & Torralba, 2006). Gabor quadrature filters provide a model of cortical simple cells (Rodrigues & du Buf, 2006). In the spatial domain (x, y) they consist of a real cosine and an imaginary sine, both with a Gaussian envelope. A receptive field (RF) is denoted by

$$G_{\lambda,\sigma,\theta,\varphi}(x,y) = \exp\left(-\frac{\tilde{x}^2 + \gamma\tilde{y}^2}{2\sigma^2}\right) \cdot \cos\left(\frac{2\pi\tilde{x}}{\lambda} + \varphi\right),$$

with $\tilde{x} = x\cos\theta + y\sin\theta$ and $\tilde{y} = y\cos\theta - x\sin\theta$, the aspect ratio $\gamma = 0.5$ and σ is the size of the RF. The spatial frequency is $1/\lambda$, λ being the wavelength. For the bandwidth σ/λ we use 0.56, which yields a half-response width of one octave. The angle θ determines the orientation (we use 8 orientations), and the phase φ the symmetry (0 or $-\pi/2$). Below, the scale of analysis will be given by λ expressed in pixels, where $\lambda = 1$ corresponds to 1 pixel. All tested images have 256×256 pixels.

Responses of even and odd simple cells, which correspond to real and imaginary parts of a Gabor kernel, are obtained by convolving the input image with the RFs, and are denoted by $R^E_{s,i}(x,y)$ and $R^O_{s,i}(x,y)$, s indicating the scale, i the orientation ($\theta_i = i\pi / N_\theta$) and N_θ the number of orientations (here 8) with $i = [0, N_\theta - 1]$. Responses of complex cells are then modelled by the modulus

$$C_{s,i}(x,y) = [\{R^E_{s,i}(x,y)\}^2 + \{R^O_{s,i}(x,y)\}^2]^{1/2}.$$

A basic scheme for line and edge (LE) detection is based on responses of simple cells: a positive (negative) line is detected where R^E shows a local maximum (minimum) and R^O shows a zero crossing. In the case of edges, the even and odd responses are swapped. This gives four possibilities for positive and negative events (polarity). An improved scheme (Rodrigues & du Buf, 2009a) consists of combining responses of simple and complex cells, i.e., simple cells serve to detect positions and event types, whereas complex cells are used to increase the confidence. Lateral and cross-orientation inhibitions are used to suppress spurious cell responses beyond line and edge terminations, and assemblies of grouping cells serve to improve event continuity in the case of curved events.

At each (x,y) in the multiscale line and edge event space, four gating LE cells code the 4 event types: positive line, negative line, positive edge and negative edge (Rodrigues & du Buf, 2009a). These are coded by different levels of gray, from white to black, in the 3rd row of Figure 1. It shows 3 scales of the face in the 2nd row, middle column. For the results presented in this chapter we used 20 scales with $\lambda = [4, 24]$ and $\Delta\lambda = 1$, scale $s = 1$ corresponding to $\lambda = 4$. With this LE information plus lowpass information available through special retinal ganglion cells (Gollisch & Meister, 2010), we can reconstruct in our visual system faces; for details and illustrations see Rodrigues and du Buf (2009a).

Keypoints are based on end-stopped cells (Rodrigues & du Buf, 2006). They provide important information because they code local image complexity. There are two types of end-stopped cells, single (S) and double (D). If $[\cdot]^+$ denotes the suppression of negative values, then

$$S_{s,i}(x,y) = [C_{s,i}(x + d\mathcal{S}_{s,i}, y - d\mathcal{C}_{s,i}) - C_{s,i}(x - d\mathcal{S}_{s,i}, y + d\mathcal{C}_{s,i})]^+$$

and

$$D_{s,i}(x,y) = [C_{s,i}(x,y) - \frac{1}{2}C_{s,i}(x + 2d\mathcal{S}_{s,i}, y - 2d\mathcal{C}_{s,i}) - \frac{1}{2}C_{s,i}(x - 2d\mathcal{S}_{s,i}, y + 2d\mathcal{C}_{s,i})]^+,$$

with $\mathcal{C}_i = \cos\theta_i$ and $\mathcal{S}_i = \sin\theta_i$. The distance d is scaled linearly with filter scale: $d = 0.6\lambda$. All end-stopped responses along straight lines and edges are suppressed, for which tangential (T) and radial (R) inhibition, $I_s = I^T_s + I^R_s$, are used (Rodrigues & du Buf, 2006). Keypoints are detected by the local maxima of $K_s(x,y)$ in x and y, where

$$K_s(x,y) = \max$$
$$\left\{\sum_{i=0}^{N_\theta-1} S_{s,i}(x,y) - gI_s(x,y), \sum_{i=0}^{N_\theta-1} D_{s,i}(x,y) - gI_s(x,y)\right\},$$

with $g \approx 1.0$. Keypoints are shown by the diamond symbols in the 4th row of Figure 1, at the same scales as the LE information in the 3rd row. For a detailed explanation with illustrations see Rodrigues and du Buf (2006).

The "what" and "where" subsystems are steered, top-down, on the basis of expected faces or objects and positions in the prefrontal cortex (Deco & Rolls, 2004). Our eyes are constantly moving in order to suppress static projections of blood vessels etc. in our retinae. During a fixation, stable information propagates from the retinae via the LGN to V1, where first features are extracted, and then, also during the next saccade, to higher

Figure 1. Top row: two expressions of the same face with possible rotation intervals. Second row: profile, lateral and frontal 2D views of the neutral face (y-rotated). Third row: multiscale line and edge coding at three scales $\lambda = \{4, 12, 24\}$ of the frontal face view on the 2nd row. Fourth row: detected keypoints at the same scales. The bottom row shows saliency maps of the 2D views on the 2nd row.

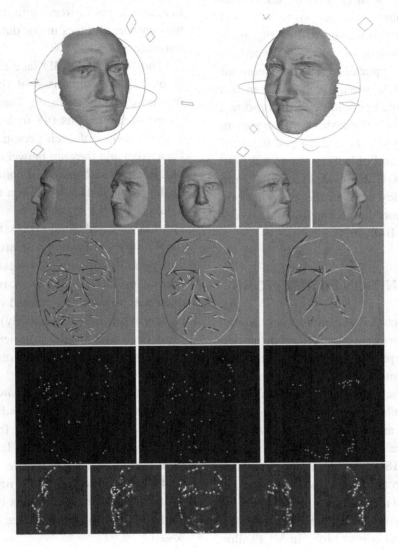

areas. Fixation points in regions where complex and therefore important information can be found are much more important than points in homogeneous regions. Focus-of-attention (FoA), for guiding the where system in parallel with the steering of our eyes, is thought to be driven by an attention component in prefrontal cortex because of overt attention: while strongly fixating our eyes to one point, we can direct mental attention to points in the neighbourhood (Parkhurst et al., 2002).

For modelling FoA we need a map, called saliency map S, which indicates the most important points to be analysed (fixated). We propose a simple scheme based on the multiscale keypoint representation, because keypoints code local image complexity. The activities of all keypoint cells at position (x, y) are summed over scales s by grouping cells, assuming that each keypoint has a certain Region-of-Interest (RoI). The size of this is coupled to the scale (size) of the underlying simple and complex cells. At positions where keypoints are stable over many scales, this summation map will show distinct peaks at the centres of faces, also at important facial and contour landmarks. This data stream is data-driven and bottom-up, and could be combined with top-down processing from the inferior-temporal cortex in order to actively probe the presence of faces (or facial landmarks) and objects in the visual field (Deco & Rolls, 2004). The bottom row of Figure 1 shows the saliency maps of the face views on the 2nd row. For more details and illustrations see Rodrigues and du Buf (2006).

FACE RECOGNITION FRAMEWORK

We humans can detect faces under many conditions, including poor lighting and at large distances. Colour is one of the primary attributes in detection, but it needs to be integrated with other attributes like keypoints for the detection of facial landmarks and their spatial relationships (Rodrigues & du Buf, 2006). There are several methods based on skin colour for face detection (Kakumanu et al., 2007). Agbinya and Silva (2005), although without a biological background, presented interesting results. Their method is now being implemented by using a biologically-inspired representation based on double-opponent colour blobs in V1 (Tailor et al., 2000), also combining other attributes to achieve accurate face segregation.

Face segregation is beyond the scope of this chapter. We consider faces that are already segregated, as in the "GavabDB" database (Moreno et al., 2004). The scheme presented below is a simplification, because in real vision the system starts with a first categorisation, for example on the basis of the colour of the hair and gender. After having a first gist, the system will dynamically select (in prefrontal cortex) a group of possible templates, optimising the recognition process by changing parameters. Here we skip categorisation and focus on recognition. For this reason we consider all faces in our database as possible templates.

The "GavabDB" 3D face database (Moreno et al., 2004) contains 549 three-dimensional meshes of facial surfaces. These meshes correspond to 61 persons (45 male and 16 female), with 9 meshes of each person. All persons are Caucasian and they are between 18 and 40 years old. Each mesh consists of connected 3D points of the facial surface without a texture map. The database provides systematic variations with respect to pose and facial expression. In particular, the 9 meshes of each person are: 2 frontal views with neutral expression; 2 x-rotated views ($\pm 30°$, looking up and looking down, respectively) with neutral expression; 2 y-rotated views ($\pm 90°$, left and right profiles, respectively) with neutral expression; and 3 frontal non-neutral expressions (laugh, smile and a random one chosen by the person).

Figure 1 shows on the top row two expressions of the same face with the possible rotation intervals. The second row shows, from left to right, five 2D views, i.e., left profile, left lateral, frontal, right lateral and right profile of the y-rotated neutral face. The following rows illustrate the multiscale feature extractions described in this section, but only at three of all scales, $\lambda = \{4, 12, 24\}$.

From the "GavabDB" database we randomly selected 10 persons. Of each person we took one 3D mesh with neutral expression to create five 2D views, using OpenGL with oblique diffuse lighting and Gouraud shading. Examples are shown on the 2nd row in Figure 1 and the top three rows in Figure 4. These are used as templates stored in memory: frontal, lateral ($\pm 45°$ y-rotated) and profile ($\pm 90°$ y-rotated); see also (Valentin et al., 1997). For testing and for each face, 10 images of each face were randomly selected, considering: a) neutral or different expressions, but discarding extreme ones; b) any degree of y-rotation (pan); c) a maximum x-rotation of $\pm 10°$ (tilt); and d) a maximum z-rotation of $\pm 2°$. Images with the same rotation angles as the templates were excluded.

For each face, the templates stored in prefrontal cortex are: the LE maps at 20 scales with events characterised by type and polarity (4: line/edge and positive/negative) for each view (5: frontal, lateral right/left and profile right/left), and the multiscale KP maps (at the same 20 scales as used for LE). The latter are used in conjunction with other processing schemes for dynamic routing to achieve normalisation of the pair to be matched, i.e., input face and template (Rodrigues & du Buf, 2009a,b).

Figure 2 shows on the first 2 rows part of the templates stored in memory, in the case of the frontal view shown in Figure 1: left to right, the multiscale KPs and LE maps at 5 of the 20 scales, equally spaced from fine to coarse scales on $\lambda \in [4, 24]$). The 3rd row shows examples of faces to be recognised. The fourth and fifth row show, for the leftmost image on the third row marked by a red quare, the multiscale KP and LE maps at the same scales as in the 1st row. The bottom row shows (at left) the summed KP maps with the accumulated keypoints (see below) marked in red. Also marked (in green) are the limits of the segregated face. On the right is the saliency map with the combined RoIs in white. The recognition model consists of the following steps:

1. **Segregate the face from the scene**: This step consists of extracting the region where there is a face, for instance using colour information as briefly explained above. For small faces and/or z-rotated faces, size- and z-pose normalisation can be achieved by dynamic routing; see details in Rodrigues & du Buf (2009b) or in Rodrigues et al. (2012a).

Here the faces are already segregated and normalised.

2. **Multiscale keypoint and line/edge detection**: For each input face we compute the keypoints, and lines and edges with their polarity. We use 20 scales $\lambda = [4, 24]$ with $\Delta \lambda = 1$. We apply all scales at 8 orientations, although there is evidence that face perception mainly relies on horizontal information at intermediate and high spatial frequencies (Goffaux et al., 2011).

3. **Determine the view of the input face**: We compute the accumulated keypoints or AKPs. The AKPs are computed as follows: at each (x, y) in the multiscale keypoint space, detected keypoints are first summed by grouping cells over all 20 scales, $mKP = \sum_{s} KP_{s}$. Then, by using two other grouping cells with large dendritic fields (DFs) the size of the segregated face, all existing mKP are summed over x and y, $AKP_x = \sum_{x} mKP*x$ and $AKP_y = \sum_{y} mKP*y$. The two AKPs yield a single central position with coordinates x and y: $(x, y)_{AKP} = (AKP_y / m\tilde{K}P, AKP_y / m\tilde{K}P)$ where $m\tilde{K}P = \sum_{DF} mKP$. The AKP position is marked in red in Figure 2 (bottom-left). From the mKP map we compute the minimum and maximum coordinates in x and y, denoted by $CKP_{min/max,x/y}$. These are the first and last position in x and y where mKP has at least a value of 2; they are marked in green in Figure 2 (bottom-left). This means that at least two keypoint cells must have responded at the same position. With this information we can compute the aspect ratio AR of the input face. Mathematically

$$AR = \frac{CKP_{max,x} - CKP_{min,x}}{CKP_{max,y} - CKP_{min,y}}.$$

Figure 2. Top two rows, left to right: fine to coarse scales of the KP and LE maps stored in memory in the case of the frontal view shown in Figure 1. Third row: examples of faces to be tested. Fourth and fifth rows: KP and LE maps of the face marked by a red square in the 3rd row. Bottom row: the AKP marked on red on the left and saliency map on the right.

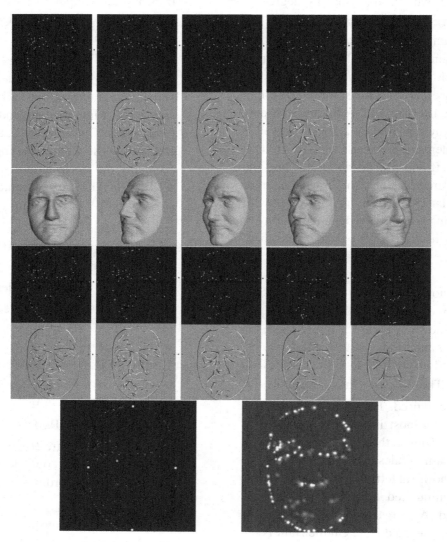

a.   Six gating cells are used to select the face view: frontal if $AR = \left]0.61, 1\right]$, frontal-lateral if $AR = \left]0.50, 0.61\right]$, lateral-frontal if $AR = \left]0.40, 0.50\right]$, lateral-profile if $AR = \left]0.33, 0.40\right]$, profile-lateral if $AR = \left]0.31, 0.33\right]$ and profile if $AR = \left]0, 0.31\right]$. These values were determined using the information from the templates, i.e., the AR s of the frontal, lateral and profile views were computed for each template and the average of all templates with the same view was calculated. The different levels of views were equally spaced between the anchor thresholds.

b.   Two gating cells are used to select the lateral side: a face is seen from the right if coordinate AKP_x is closer to $CKP_{max,x}$ or from the left if it is closer to $CKP_{min,x}$. The above processes may occur mainly in the dorsal where stream, i.e., the occipito-parietal area which exhibits object-selective responses and many 3D cues of shape, and can relay the information to cue- and view-invariant representations in the ventral what stream (Farivar, 2009).

4.   **Construction of saliency and symbolic representation maps**: For each input image we build the saliency map as explained above, and symbolic representation maps in which events (positions) are expanded by Gaussian cross-profiles (lines) and bipolar, Gaussian-truncated error function profiles (edges). The sizes of these profiles are coupled to the scale of the underlying simple and complex cells; see Rodrigues and du Buf (2009a) for details and illustrations.

5.   **Recognition process**: We assume that templates (views) of faces are stored in memory and that these have been built through experience. Each face template in memory is represented by 5 views times 20 scales times 4 types of events (line/edge, positive/negative), which involves 400 maps.

The recognition scheme compares representations of input images (in the database) with those of templates (in memory). Depending on the input face view selected in step (C), the two most similar views of the templates are selected and weighted. If the input face is classified as being frontal, the two selected templates are: the frontal and – depending on the detected face side, for instance the right one – the lateral-right template.

The weight of each template is determined as a function of the aspect ratio AR (see Table 1). If the input face is classified as being *Frontal R/L* or *Profile R/L*, then template view 1 (with weight A) is *Frontal* respectively *Profile R/L*, and template view 2 (with weight 1-A) in both cases is *Lateral R/L*. If the input face is *Frontal-Lateral R/L* or *Profile-Lateral R/L*, then template view 1 (weight B) is *Frontal* respectively *Profile R/L*, and template view 2 (weight 1-B) is in both cases *Lateral R/L*. Finally, if the input is *Lateral-Frontal R/L* or *Lateral-Profile R/L*, then template view 1 (weight B) in both cases is *Lateral R/L*, and template view 2 (weight 1-B) is *Frontal* respectively *Profile R/L*. Best results were achieved with A = 0.8 and B = 0.6.

At each scale (of the two selected template views), events in the 4 representation maps of the input image are compared with those in the corresponding maps of the templates, but only in regions where the saliency map of the input image is active. These are the white regions in Figure 2

Table 1. Weights applied to each template view as a function of the view assigned to the input image. Right is denoted by R and left by L.

input face	templ. view 1	weight	templ. view 2	weight	input face	templ. view 1	weight	templ. view 2	weight
Frontal R/L	Frontal	A	Lateral R/L	1-A	Profile R/L	Profile R/L	A	Lateral R/L	1-A
Frontal-Lateral R/L	Frontal	B	Lateral R/L	1-B	Profile-Lateral R/L	Profile R/L	B	Lateral R/L	1-B
Lateral-Frontal R/L	Lateral R/L	B	Frontal	1-B	Lateral-Profile R/L	Lateral R/L	B	Profile R/L	1-B

(bottom-right). Event co-occurrences are summed by grouping cells, which is a sort of event-type and scale-specific correlation. The outputs of the 4 event-type grouping cells are summed by another grouping cell (correlation over all event types). The global co-occurrence is determined by one more grouping cell which sums over all scales. A final grouping cell sums the results of the two views. The template (of the combined two views) with the maximum response is selected by non-maximum suppression.

The multiscale line/edge representation is exploited because this characterises facial features. Saliency maps which have been used for Focus-of-Attention are used to "gate" detected lines and edges in associated RoIs. This resembles the bottom-up data streams in the where (FoA) and what (line/edge) subsystems. However, it remains a simplification because processing is limited to cortical area V1, whereas in reality the two subsystems contain higher-level feature extractions in areas V2, V4, etc. (Hamker, 2005). The same way, top-down data streams are simplified by assuming that face templates held in memory are limited to lines, edges and keypoints, and 2D canonical views are limited to frontal, left/right lateral, and left/right profile.

OBJECT RECOGNITION FRAMEWORK

In Rodrigues & du Buf (2009b) we explained in detail how invariant object categorisation and recognition can be achieved by using a 2D model with a single view of a template and an object.

This process is called dynamic routing; see Rodrigues & du Buf (2009b) or Rodrigues et al. (2012b). Here we do not apply the principle of dynamic routing, because it is beyond the scope of this chapter and our aim is to show that a predefined number of views (8 for animal objects) is enough to recognise such 3D objects if they are rotated 360° around their vertical axis.

From the AIM@SHAPE (2008) database we selected 3D mesh models of eight animals; see Figure 3 (top) and Figure 4 (bottom). Of each model we created eight 2D views; see the two examples in Figure 3 (bottom). These are used as templates stored in memory: frontal, frontal-lateral (±45° y-rotated), profile (±90°), rear (180°) and lateral-rear (±135°). For testing and for each object, 12 images of each object were randomly selected, considering: a) any degree of y-rotation (pan); b) a maximum x-rotation of ±10° (tilt); and c) a maximum z-rotation of ±2°; see examples in Figure 4. Images with the same rotation angles as the templates were excluded.

The framework used for object recognition is the same as that for faces, but with the following modifications: In step (C-i) six gating cells are used to select the object view: frontal if AR=[0.0,0.6], frontal-lateral if AR=]0.6,0.8], lateral-frontal if AR=]0.8,0.9], lateral-profile if AR=]0.9,1.0], profile-lateral if AR=]1.0,1.1] and profile if AR>1.1. These values were determined using the information from the templates, i.e., the ARs of the frontal, lateral and profile views were computed for each template and the average of all templates with the same view was calculated (considering both frontal and rear views; see Figure 3, middle and bottom rows). The different AR levels of the views were equally spaced between the anchor thresholds.

In step (C-ii) two gating cells are used to select the lateral side: an object is seen from the right if coordinate AKP_x is closer to $CKP_{max,x}$ or from the left if it is closer to $CKP_{min,x}$. We must stress that this process only works for asymmetrical objects like animals, that all objects must be normalised in memory in the same way (in this case all animals with their heads to the left), and the reference side for the left/right view is relative to the rear view, opposite to the head, because normally the keypoint density is much larger there.

In the recognition scheme, as in the case of faces, we compared representations of input im-

Figure 3. Two examples of object templates (animals) from the AIM@SHAPE (2008) database

ages (in the database) with those of templates (in memory). Depending on the input view selected in step (C), the two most similar views of the templates are selected and weighted, but now in two pairs corresponding to the front and the rear of the object. We note that at this stage it is not yet possible to distinguish between the frontal and rear views. Therefore, the frontal and rear templates are first combined, and the correct view, frontal or rear, will be detected later. If the input object is classified as being "frontal" (AR=[0.0,0.6]), the two pairs of selected templates are the frontal

and – depending on the detected object side, for instance the right one – the frontal-lateral-right template (first pair), and the rear and rear-lateral-right template (second pair). The weight of each template is determined as a function of the aspect ratio AR, using the same views and weights (the same values of A and B as used for faces) per template. We used the same weights for both pairs.

At each scale, for each pair (front and rear), and in each of the two templates with the two selected views, events in the 4 representation maps of the input image are compared with those in the

Figure 4. Top two rows examples of other face templates, 3rd row tested faces, and bottom 3 rows examples of tested objects (animals)

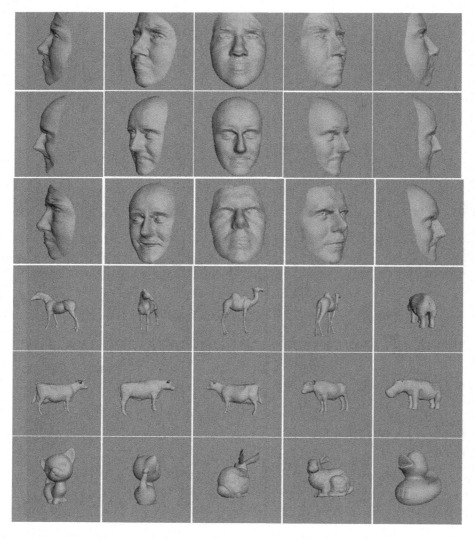

corresponding maps of the templates, but only in regions where the saliency map of the input image is active. Event co-occurrences are summed by grouping cells (event-type and scale-specific correlation). The outputs of the 4 event-type grouping cells are summed by another grouping cell. The global co-occurrence is determined by one more grouping cell which sums over all scales. A final grouping cell sums the results of the two views. The two templates for the front and for the rear (of the combined two views) with the maximum is selected by non-maximum suppression. The selection of the final template (recognition) and view (front vs. rear) of the object is also done by non-maximum suppression. In summary, in the first step we select the view of the object (left-right plus frontal-lateral-profile), and in the second step we check if the head of the animal (or a reference view of an object) is facing to the front or to the back.

RESULTS AND DISCUSSION

For testing the face framework we used 100 images, 10 views per person, with different expressions (including the neutral) and also with different degrees of rotation: x axis $\left[-10°, +10°\right]$, y axis $\left[-90°, +90°\right]$ and z axis $\left[-2°, +2°\right]$. Figure 4 shows representative examples of templates (two top rows) and test images (3rd row).

We tested the algorithm for: (a) The correct face side (left/right), which yielded a result of 99%. (b) The correct view must correspond to one of the three categories frontal, lateral or profile. For this we considered that an image returning frontal or frontal-lateral fits the frontal class, lateral-frontal and lateral-profile fit the lateral class, and profile and profile-lateral fit the profile class. The overall recognition rate was 93%, with the following misclassifications: 3% lateral were assigned to profile and 4% profile were assigned to lateral.

We also tested (c) different numbers of templates and different weights of the pairs of template views. The best result of 91% was achieved using the 5 views (templates) of each face, combined in two pairs in function of the input view (with A=0.8 and B=0.6). These two parameters fine-tune the model and should change from face to face in function of the initial gist, the gender and facial expression etc. This dynamic weighting remains to be implemented.

The model is based on the automatic detection of the template views to be applied, i.e., two views in function of the input. In this case the entire model was applied. But we also tested the model based on a single view. In this case step C (determine the view of the input face) was removed from the model. In a last test scenario with two predefined views, i.e., frontal & lateral or frontal & profile, only the right/left detection of step C was applied, with both views equally weighted. From the results we can conclude that using a single frontal view (56%) is not enough to recognise a face from different views. Nevertheless, using two views (frontal & lateral) plus the face side and 3 templates per face (frontal, lateral-right and -left), the recognition result (88%) approached the best result of 91%. As expected, this means that 5 templates give the best characterisation of the different face views, but if the view selection is undetermined or fuzzy, the most important templates to be used are the frontal and lateral ones.

It is possible to compare our results with those of other models which were tested on the GavabDB database. Moreno and Sanchez (2004), who created GavabDB, developed a feature-based model and reported a recognition rate of 78.0%. Celenk and Aljarrah (2006) projected the face scans to 2D range images and applied a PCA approach, achieving 92.0%. In their work only frontal projections of 60 persons were tested, the same projections as used by Li et al. (2009), who obtained a recognition rate of 94.7%. Li et al. (2009) also reported results from 4 other studies which explored the same database, the results ranging from 83.0% to 91.0%. Rashad et al. (2009) used 427 surface images of all 61 persons in the database, and achieved a recognition rate of 80.3%.

Although only based on 10 randomly selected persons from all 61 in the database, our best result of 91% is close to the best results achieved by the other groups, despite the fact that most only considered frontal views. In addition, our method is the only biologically-inspired one which can cope with different views of the same person.

For testing the model in case of objects (animals), we used the following eight models: camel, cow, cow2, horse, hippo, duck, bunny and kitten, with a total of 96 projections which included 12 views of each object with different degrees of rotation: x axis $\left[-10°, +10°\right]$, y axis $\left[-180°, +180°\right]$ and z axis $\left[-2°, +2°\right]$; see the examples in Figure 4, three bottom rows. We tested the algorithms for: (a) The correct object side (left/right), which yielded a result of 84%. (b) The correct view. Like faces, these must correspond to one of the three categories frontal/rear, lateral and profile. This test resulted in 90% correct views. (c) Identifying the frontal or rear view, which yielded a result of 82%. The overall recognition rate of views and objects was 83%.

The misclassifications of test (a) were mainly due to the duck, because being a toy the duck's head is much bigger than its rear. This implies a larger keypoint density of the head view relative to the rear view; please recall that the reference to determine the animal's side is the rear view due to the normally larger keypoint density. In test (b) many misclassifications were lateral views assigned to profile views for several animals. In test (c) the view of some animals as seen from opposite sides (front vs. rear) was misclassified. However, in overall recognition they were still correctly classified because the front and the rear views, considering the overall shape, are quite similar, for example in case of the camel. The object recognition framework cannot yet be compared with other frameworks, because we tested only eight objects/animals and with rotations mainly about the y axis. Nevertheless, Lam & du Buf (2011) achieved 92.5% with 40 objects, and in the SHREC contest of 2010, with 10,000 3D models, recognition rates were between 45 and 70% (Veltkamp et al., 2010).

TOWARDS REAL-TIME VIEW RECOGNITON USING KEYPOINTS

One of the big bottlenecks of the method (and of most biological methods) is the necessary CPU time. There are several ways to decrease this time, such as decreasing the number of scales or applying saliency maps with a higher threshold (fewer events per template). As mentioned before, multiscale keypoints are used for saliency maps and focus-of-attention, dynamic routing and view detection. They can also be used, before lines and edges are employed, to achieve a first categorisation (Rodrigues & du Buf, 2009b).

We can combine extracted cortical keypoints with any kind of descriptor to obtain categorisation. We tested one of the most well-known, SIFT (Lowe, 2004), i.e., we extract a SIFT descriptor at each cortical keypoint location. The width of the SIFT descriptor is set to 2λ. The SIFT descriptor is used to facilitate comparisons to similar work, but we are planning to explore more biologically plausible descriptors in the future. The *training* stage consists of extracting all keypoints and their descriptors from all template faces/objects, storing them in class-specific K-D trees to enable a fast nearest-neighbour search (Terzić et al., 2013a).

For each query face/object (*testing*), we extract keypoints and descriptors as before. For each descriptor $d_i \in \{ d_1 \ldots d_N \}$, we find the nearest neighbour (in descriptor space) $NN_C(d_i)$ in each class C and sum all distances per class. The winning class is the one which minimises the total distance. We note that we are grouping descriptors from labelled images per class, not per image.

Focusing attention on keypoints significantly reduces the number of required nearest-neighbour lookups. Most nearest-neighbour approaches extract descriptors on a densely sampled grid, which can lead to about 90,000 descriptors per image. Using Caltech 101, which has 101 categories, typically with 30 images used for training, categorising a single image requires about 2.5×10^{13} nearest-neighbour lookups. Hence, recognition is slow, despite using efficient nearest-neighbour lookups. Our keypoint extraction stage typically yields about 500 keypoints per image, reducing the number of lookups to about 7.5×10^8, a speedup of $30,000$ in the case of a full, exhaustive search! In practice, the use of K-D trees reduces the nearest-neighbour search to logarithmic time, so the speedup is smaller (roughly linear with the reduction of descriptors per image), but it is still significant. We pay for this speedup by a drop in classification rate, roughly from 65% to 50% when training with only 15 images per category, but this drop is acceptable for many applications. For more details about the implementation and results see Terzić et al. (2013a). In Terzić et al. (2013b) we show that the ("fast") cortical keypoint detector is competitive with state-of-the-art detectors and particularly well-suited for tasks such as object recognition. We show that by using these points we can achieve state-of-the-art categorization results in a fraction of the time required by competing algorithms.

This categorisation step should be integrated after the side and view have been detected and before face/object recognition, allowing the model to achieve real-time performance. However, due to the use of the SIFT descriptor, this implementation is not yet fully biological, and thus not yet integrated in the model presented in this chapter.

CONCLUSION

We presented a bio-inspired face-recognition model that can determine the side (left/right) and the view (frontal/lateral/profile) of a face to be recognised, as well as recognise faces from different views and with different expressions. Nevertheless, the presented model is a simplification, because in real vision the system starts with a first segregation and categorisation, for example on the basis of the colour of the hair and skin. After having a first gist (a group of possible face templates), the system dynamically selects the template views according to the view of the input face, and it can adapt the recognition process by changing parameters in relation to the gender and facial expression, etc. In view of the tremendous amount of data already involved in our simple experiments, the entire system has been developed in different modules which are being integrated with fast GPU processing.

The system achieves good results mainly because the line/edge representation at coarser scales provides a stable abstraction of facial features. This explains, at least partly, the generalisation that allows us to classify faces with different expressions and views. The problem of normalisation, which is not addressed here, can be solved by using a segregated face based on colour with detected keypoints and dynamic routing (Rodrigues & du Buf, 2006). Keypoints can be used to determine facial landmarks (eye, nose, mouth), which has already been implemented and tested, but only for frontal views (Rodrigues & du Buf, 2006). In this chapter we showed that keypoints can also be used to determine the view of the face. A complementary approach is to compute the disparity, and distances, angles and areas of fiducial points on the 3D surface. This procedure can also guarantee that templates in memory are really representative.

An interesting aspect for future research is the incorporation of age and biometric differences (e.g., gender, colour of the skin, age, birth marks, etc.), also expression classification already achieved by using multiscale lines and edges (Sousa et al., 2010). As for now, face recognition with extreme expressions or newly grown beards etc. remains a big challenge. Furthermore, occlusions caused by objects like sunglasses must be addressed in a systematic way.

We also showed that the same framework, with minor modifications, can be applied to 3D object recognition, although more tests need to be done and full 3D recognition can only be achieved by using more views (templates). The minimum number of views is still subject to research. Another open aspect is how objects are stored in memory: all animal views are defined by relating them to the same side, like all heads to the left as in this chapter. Instead, this could depend on the object type and be a function of one or several features, for instance keypoint density or focus-of-attention. It should be stressed that object recognition has been explored as a special case of face recognition because of the aspect ratios of 2D projections.

Using the same framework does not mean that faces and general objects cannot be processed in different ways in the visual cortex. Indeed, there are several indications that there are differences (Biederman & Kalocsai, 1997). The facts that faces are very important in our social behaviour, and that there are cells which only respond when a face is present in their receptive field, point at the existence of a special face-processing subsystem, part of which may overlap the circuitry for dealing with general objects. The main difference is that faces always have the same geometry, more or less, which was exploited in face detection on the basis of the multi-scale keypoint representation by assuming standard relations between eyes, nose and mouth (Rodrigues & du Buf, 2006). A similar geometry with standard relations between parts does not exist in case of general 3D objects and, unlike faces, most general 3D objects can be rotated arbitrarily. The latter requires storing many more feature templates in visual memory which cover all canonical views.

Despite the problems and possible solutions mentioned above, the results obtained are very encouraging. We expect significant improvements by implementing a dynamic system, in which successive tests are performed each time that more complete information is available, starting at coarse scales and adding then finer scales, such that all effort can be spent on scrutinising the images which have not yet been identified with absolute certainty. This process simulates the converging processing in the bottom-up and top-down data streams in the what and where subsystems of our visual system.

ACKNOWLEDGMENT

This work was supported by the Portuguese Foundation for Science and Technology (FCT), project PEst-OE/EEI/LA0009/2013, EU project NeuroDynamics, ICT-2009.2.1-270247 and FCT project SparseCoding EXPL/EEI-SII/1982/2013.

REFERENCES

Abate, A., Nappi, M., Riccio, D., & Sabatino, G. (2007). 2D and 3D face recognition: A survey. *Pattern Recognition Letters, 28*(14), 1885–1906. doi:10.1016/j.patrec.2006.12.018

Agbinya, J. I., & Silva, S. D. (2005). Face recognition programming on mobile handsets. In *Proc. 12th Int. Conf. on Telecommunications*. Cape Town, South Africa: Academic Press.

AIM@SHAPE. (2008). Retrieved from http://www.aimatshape.net

Bar, M. (2004). Visual objects in context. *Nature Reviews. Neuroscience, 5*, 619–629. doi:10.1038/nrn1476 PMID:15263892

Berretti, S., Del Bimbo, A., & Pala, P. (2010). 3D face recognition using iso-geodesic stripes. *IEEE Trans. PAMI, 32*(12), 2162–2177. doi:10.1109/TPAMI.2010.43

Biederman, I., & Kalocsai, P. (1997). Neurocomputational bases of object and face recognition. *Philosoph. Trans. R. Soc.: Biol. Sci., 352*, 1203–1219. doi:10.1098/rstb.1997.0103 PMID:9304687

Blank, I., & Yove, G. (2011). The structure of face–space is tolerant to lighting and viewpoint transformations. *Journal of Vision (Charlottesville, Va.), 11*(8), 1–13. doi:10.1167/11.8.15 PMID:21795412

Bowyer, K., Chang, K., & Flynn, P. (2006). A survey of approaches and challenges in 3D and multi-modal 3D + 2D face recognition. *Computer Vision and Image Understanding, 101*(1), 1–15. doi:10.1016/j.cviu.2005.05.005

Celenk, M., & Aljarrah, I. (2006). Internal shape-deformation invariant 3D surface matching using 2D principal component analysis. In *Proc. of SPIE-IS&T Electronic Imaging*, (vol. 6056, pp. 118-129). SPIE.

Deco, G., & Rolls, E. T. (2004). A neurodynamical cortical model of visual attention and invariant object recognition. *Vision Research*, *44*(6), 621–642. doi:10.1016/j.visres.2003.09.037 PMID:14693189

du Buf, J. M. H., Terzic, K., & Rodrigues, J. M. H. (2013). Phase-differencing in stereo vision: solving the localisation problem. In *Proc. 6th Int. Conf. on Bio-inspired Systems and Signal Processing*, (pp. 254-263). Academic Press.

Fadaifard, H., Wolberg, G., & Haralick, R. (2013). Multiscale 3D feature extraction and matching with an application to 3D face recognition. *Graphical Models*, *75*(4), 157–176. doi:10.1016/j.gmod.2013.01.002

Farivar, R. (2009). Dorsal-ventral integration in object recognition. *Brain Research. Brain Research Reviews*, *61*(2), 144–153. doi:10.1016/j.brainresrev.2009.05.006 PMID:19481571

Farrajota, M., Rodrigues, J. M. F., & du Buf, J. M. H. (2011). Optical flow by multi-scale annotated keypoints: A biological approach. In *Proc. Int. Conf. on Bio-inspired Systems and Signal Processing*, (pp. 307-315). Academic Press.

Farrajota, M., Saleiro, S., Terzic, K., & Rodrigues, J. M. H & du Buf, J.M.H (2012). Multi-scale cortical keypoints for realtime hand tracking and gesture recognition. In *Proc 1st Int. Workshop on Cognitive Assistive Systems: Closing the Action-Perception Loop, in conjunction with IEEE/RSJ Int. Conf. on Intelligent Robots and Systems*, (pp. 9-15). Academic Press.

Fenzi, M., Dragon, R., Leal-Taixé, L., Rosenhahn, B., & Ostermann, J. (2012). 3D Object recognition and pose estimation for multiple objects using multi-prioritized RANSAC and model updating. *Pattern Recognition, LNCS*, *7476*, 123–133. doi:10.1007/978-3-642-32717-9_13

Galleguillos, C., & Belongie, S. (2010). Context based object categorization: A critical survey. *Computer Vision and Image Understanding*, *114*(6), 712–722. doi:10.1016/j.cviu.2010.02.004

Goffaux, V. & van Zon, J,& Schiltz, C. (2011). The horizontal tuning of face perception relies on the processing of intermediate and high spatial frequencies. *Journal of Vision, 11*(10), 1-9.

Gollisch, T., & Meister, M. (2010). Eye smarter than scientists believed: neural computations in circuits of the retina. *Neuron*, *65*(2), 150–164. doi:10.1016/j.neuron.2009.12.009 PMID:20152123

Grossberg, S., Srinivasan, K., & Yazdanbakhsh, A. (2011). On the road to invariant object recognition: How cortical area V2 transforms absolute to relative disparity during 3D vision. *Neural Netw, 24*(7), 686-92.

Hamker, F. (2005). The reentry hypothesis: the putative interaction of the frontal eye field, ventrolateral prefrontal cortex, and areas V4, IT for attention and eye movement. *Cerebral Cortex*, *15*, 431–447. doi:10.1093/cercor/bhh146 PMID:15749987

Haxby, J., Hoffman, E., & Gobbini, M. (2002). Human neural systems for face recognition and social communication. *Biological Psychiatry*, *51*(1), 59–67. doi:10.1016/S0006-3223(01)01330-0 PMID:11801231

Heitger, F. et al. (1992). Simulation of neural contour mechanisms: from simple to end-stopped cells. *Vision Research*, *32*(5), 963–981. doi:10.1016/0042-6989(92)90039-L PMID:1604865

Hubel, D. H. (1995). *Eye, brain and vision*. Scientific American Library.

Kakumanu, P., Makrogiannis, S., & Bourbakis, N. (2007). A survey of skin-color modeling and detection methods. *Pattern Recognition*, *40*(3), 1106–1122. doi:10.1016/j.patcog.2006.06.010

Kourtzi, Z., & Connor, C. (2011). Neural representations for object perception: structure, category, and adaptive coding. *Annual Review of Neuroscience*, *34*, 45–67. doi:10.1146/annurev-neuro-060909-153218 PMID:21438683

Lam, R., & du Buf, J. M. H. (2011). Retrieval of 3D polygonal objects based on multiresolution signatures. In *Proc. Int. Symp. Visual Computing*, (LNCS) (vol. 6939, pp. 136–147). Berlin: Springer.

Li, S. Z., & Jain, A. K. (2011). *Handbook of Face Recognition*. London: Springer. doi:10.1007/978-0-85729-932-1

Li, X., Jia, T., & Zhang, H. (2009) Expression-insensitive 3D face recognition using sparse representation. In *Proc. IEEE Conf. on Computer Vision and Pattern Recognition* (pp. 2575-2582). IEEE.

Lowe, D. G. (2004). Distinctive image features from scale-invariant keypoints. *International Journal of Computer Vision*, *60*(2), 91–110. doi:10.1023/B:VISI.0000029664.99615.94

Martins, J. A., Rodrigues, J. M. F., & du Buf, J. M. H. (2009) Focus of attention and region segregation by low-level geometry. In *Proc. Int. Conf. on Computer Vision - Theory and Applications*, (vol. 2, pp. 267-272). Academic Press.

Moreno, A. B., & Sanchez, A. (2004) GavabDB: A 3D face database. In *Proc. 2nd COST275 Workshop on Biometrics on the Internet*, (pp. 77-85). Academic Press.

Oliva, A., & Torralba, A. (2006). Building the gist of a scene: the role of global image features in recognition. Progress in Brain Res. *Visual Perception*, *155*, 23–26.

Parkhurst, D., Law, K., & Niebur, E. (2002). Modelling the role of salience in the allocation of overt visual attention. *Vision Research*, *42*(1), 107–123. doi:10.1016/S0042-6989(01)00250-4 PMID:11804636

Passalis, G., Kakadiaris, I., & Theoharis, T. (2007). Intraclass retrieval of nonrigid 3D objects: application to face recognition. *IEEE Trans. PAMI*, *29*(2), 218–229. doi:10.1109/TPAMI.2007.37 PMID:17170476

Pinto, N., Barhomi, Y., Cox, D., & DiCarlo, J. (2010). Comparing state-of-the-art visual features on invariant object recognition tasks. In *Proc. IEEE Workshop on Applications of Computer Vision*, (pp. 463-470). IEEE.

Ramirez-Valdez, L., & Hasimoto-Beltran, R. (2009). 3D-facial expression synthesis and its application to face recognition systems. *J. of Applied Research and Technology*, *7*, 323–339.

Rashad, A., Hamdy, A., Saleh, M., & Eladawy, M. (2009). 3D face recognition using 2DPCA. Int. *J. of Computer Science and Network Security*, *9*(12), 149–155.

Rodrigues, J., & du Buf, J. M. H. (2004). Visual cortex frontend: integrating lines, edges, keypoints and disparity. In *Proc. Int. Conf. Image Anal. Recogn.* (LNCS) (Vol. 3211, pp. 664-671). Berlin: Springer.

Rodrigues, J., & du Buf, J. M. H. (2006). Multiscale keypoints in V1 and beyond: object segregation, scale selection, saliency maps and face detection. *Bio Systems*, *2*, 75–90. doi:10.1016/j.biosystems.2006.02.019 PMID:16870327

Rodrigues, J., & du Buf, J. M. H. (2009a). Multi-scale lines and edges in V1 and beyond: brightness, object categorization and recognition, and consciousness. *Bio Systems*, *95*, 206–226. doi:10.1016/j.biosystems.2008.10.006 PMID:19026712

Rodrigues, J., & du Buf, J. M. H. (2009b). A cortical framework for invariant object categorization and recognition. *Cognitive Processing*, *10*(3), 243–261. doi:10.1007/s10339-009-0262-2 PMID:19471984

Rodrigues, J. M. F., & du Buf, J. M. H. (2011). A cortical framework for scene categorization. In *Proc. Int. Conf. on Computer Vision, Imaging and Computer Graphics - Theory and Applications*, (pp. 364-371). Academic Press.

Rodrigues, J. M. F., Lam, R., & du Buf, J. M. H. (2012a). Cortical 3D face and object recognition using 2D projections. *International Journal of Creative Interfaces and Computer Graphics*, *3*(1), 45–62. doi:10.4018/jcicg.2012010104

Rodrigues, J. M. F., Martins, J., Lam, R., & du Buf, J. M. H. (2012b). Cortical multiscale line-edge disparity model. In *Proc. Int. Conf. on Image Analysis and Recognition* (LNCS) (vol. 7324, pp. 296-303). Berlin: Springer.

Sandbach, G., Zafeiriou, S., Pantic, M., & Yin, L. (2012). Static and dynamic 3D facial expression recognition: A comprehensive survey. *Image and Vision Computing*, *30*(10), 683–697. doi:10.1016/j.imavis.2012.06.005

Smeets, D., Claes, P., Vandermeulen, D., & Clement, J. (2010). Objective 3D face recognition: Evolution, approaches and challenges. *Forensic Science International*, *1-3*, 125–132. doi:10.1016/j.forsciint.2010.03.023 PMID:20395086

Sousa, R., Rodrigues, J. M. F., & du Buf, J. M. H. (2010) Recognition of facial expressions by cortical multi-scale line and edge coding. In *Proc. Int. Conf. on Image Analysis and Recognition*, (vol. 1, pp. 415-424). Academic Press.

Su, T., Lin, C., Lin, P., & Hu, J. (2006). Shape memorization and recognition of 3D objects using a similarity-based aspect-graph approach. In *Proc. IEEE Int. Conf. on Systems, Man, and Cybernetics*, (pp. 4920-4925). IEEE.

Tailor, D., Finkel, L., & Buchsbaum, G. (2000). Color-opponent receptive fields derived from independent component analysis of natural images. *Vision Research*, *40*(19), 2671–2676. doi:10.1016/S0042-6989(00)00105-X PMID:10958917

Tangelder, J., & Veltkamp, R. (2008). A survey of content based 3D shape retrieval methods. *Multimedia Tools and Applications*, *39*, 441–471. doi:10.1007/s11042-007-0181-0

Terzić, K., Rodrigues, J. M. F., & du Buf, J. M. H. (2013a). Real-Time object recognition based on cortical multi-scale keypoints. In J. Sanches, L. Micó, & J. Cardoso (Eds.), Pattern Recognition and Image Analysis SE - 37 (Vol. 7887, pp. 314–321). Berlin: Springer. doi:doi:10.1007/978-3-642-38628-2_37 doi:10.1007/978-3-642-38628-2_37

Terzić, K., Rodrigues, J. M. F., & du Buf, J. M. H. (2013b). Fast cortical keypoints for real-time object recognition. In *Proc. IEEE Int. Conf. on Image Processing*, (pp. 3372-3376). IEEE.

Valentin, D., Abdi, H., & Edelman, B. (1997). What represents a face? A computational approach for the integration of physiological and psychological data. *Perception*, *26*(10), 1271–1288. doi:10.1068/p261271 PMID:9604063

Veltkamp, R. C., Giezeman, G. J., Bast, H., Baumbach, T., Furuya, T., Giesen, J., et al. (2010) Shrec 2010 track: Large scale retrieval. In *Proc. Eurographics/ACM SIGGRAPH Symp. on 3D Object Retrieval* (pp. 63–69). ACM.

Weinland, D., Ronfard, R., & Boyer, E. (2011). A survey of vision-based methods for action representation, segmentation and recognition. *Computer Vision and Image Understanding*, *115*(2), 224–241. doi:10.1016/j.cviu.2010.10.002

ENDNOTES

[1]   y-rotated stands for rotated about the vertical y-axis. The x-axis is horizontal "in the plane of the paper," whereas the z-axis is "perpendicular to the paper."

Chapter 5
Improving Spatial Decision Making in Cloud Computing

Michele Argiolas
Università degli Studi di Cagliari, Italy

Maurizio Atzori
Università degli Studi di Cagliari, Italy

Nicoletta Dessì
Università degli Studi di Cagliari, Italy

Barbara Pes
Università degli Studi di Cagliari, Italy

ABSTRACT

The increasing capabilities of Internet have caused a qualitative change in the management of spatial information while recent advances in Web 2.0 technologies have enabled the integration of data and knowledge in intuitive thematic maps. This has wide-ranging indirect effects in supporting the ways stakeholders make a decision based on information coming from various distributed resources, but the real question is, What applications and technologies are in place to deal with these decisional environments? Aiming at giving an answer to this question, this chapter explores the feasibility of a computational environment that supports the Web-based exploration and the spatial analysis in real estate decisional processes. It relies on the concept of dataspace as a new scenario for accessing, integrating, and analyzing geo-spatial information regardless of its format and location. Built on top of a cloud environment, it is made up of specialized modules, each of which provides a well-defined service. Mash-ups integrate data from different resources on the Internet and provide the user with a flexible and easy-to-use way for geo-referencing data in the maps provided by Google Maps and Google Earth. Through an interactive process, the user arrives at some interesting maps, glimpses the most important facets of the decisional problem, and combines them to fashion a solution. Applicative experiments demonstrate the effectiveness of the computational environment proposed.

DOI: 10.4018/978-1-4666-6252-0.ch005

1. INTRODUCTION

To be effective in supporting decision making, computational tools should give the user a simple method to access and analyze data and directly link the data and analysis results to other computer applications such as word processing, spreadsheets etc. As well, the user should be allowed to extract (when this extraction is allowed) appropriate data from external databases and append to these local data either directly or from other databases. Data acquisition results in a very difficult task when data can soon become unmanageable or even unworkable since they are scattered in heterogeneous resources as authorities, agencies, municipal archives, government archives and so on. Data integration requires different structures and formats to be merged with full consideration of the data complexities and intricacies. It is also essential when undertaking this type of data integration that valuable information is not lost.

This integration is becoming a necessity for facing planning processes characterized by interactions between environmental and socio-economic systems which result in the possibility of diverse decision alternatives. This integration is the principal aim of our paper which explores how spatial analysis resources can be interfaced within decision making environments in a single framework, namely a *Spatial Decision Support System (SDSS)*.

Leveraging on recent research work (Dittrich & Salles, 2006; Dong & Halevy, 2007; Franklin et. al, 2005; Halevy et al., 2006), this paper adopts the concept of *dataspace* as a new integration paradigm characterized by a very loosely structured data model and geared towards the management of data coming from a diverse set of distributed resources. A dataspace consists of components (also called participants) and a set of relationships among them. Each participant knows the relationships to other participants and their source, i.e., if the participant is added by a user or automatically generated. As well, each participant contains information about the kind of data it contains, the data allocation, the storage format. Our basic philosophy is to integrate the dataspace participants (i.e. the distributed sources of information) within GIS services available in Internet (i.e. Google Earth and Google Maps). This results in a dataspace that creates a highly productive symbiosis between the computational environment and the user who can manipulate maps to rapidly gain insight about data.

Specifically, we investigate how application services can become innovative components of these emerging decisional supports in order to automatically offer functionalities that are not longer locked to a static infrastructure, as it happens in data warehousing systems or enterprise databases, but refer to computational resources made available through a computer network. We try to explore the features of a reference model for designing a flexible decisional environment by identifying its critical aspects, the limits of its applicability and its scope.

On the IT management side, we propose that the SDSS be hosted with the aid of cloud computing technology which enables to host and easily scale services up or down as needed. Leveraging on Software-as-a-Service (SaaS) philosophy (Mell & Grance, 2011), our SDSS focuses on providing mechanisms for: (1) abstract the complexity of integrating data in heterogeneous computing environments and (2) provide a decisional support with a high level of flexibility to the user needs. The level of flexibility is intrinsically linked to the way in which these mechanisms are able to integrate information, regardless of its format and location, and make complementary the different aspects of decision processes.

The main contribute of this paper focuses on proposing:

- A flexible service oriented data integration which gathers data from heterogeneous networked sources, interfaces business tools and added-values services offered by different providers, including Internet providers;

- The adoption of dataspace paradigm as a reference model for structuring information relevant to a particular organization, regardless of its format and location;
- A cloud-based architecture that merges the two in an acceptable manner.

To illustrate the potential benefits of our approach we present some applicative experiments in real estate domain which reveal the potential of a demonstrator we are implementing.

The paper is organized as follows. Section 2 discusses the key design requirements of the proposed SDSS. Section 3 presents the architecture that supports the SDSS and details the technical aspects of its implementation. Section 4 illustrates some applicative experiments in the real estate domain. Section 5 presents a review of the related work. Finally, section 6 gives conclusions.

2. SYSTEM REQUIREMENTS

This section presents the requirements we considered in modelling efficient decision making support.

First, data integration capabilities are one of the most imminent design requirements for efficiently gathering data from heterogeneous sources. The dataspace abstraction helps reasoning about data management, with different systems seen as related components in an evolving framework rather than isolated data sources, and where various (rather than a single) integration techniques address component specific needs. A dataspace would also facilitate leveraging past experience via mechanisms supporting the correlation and reuse of various data management system elements. Consequently, applying the dataspace abstraction to business environments could immediately benefit the development of a new generation of decisional support systems as well as improve the

organization of existing systems and resources. Basically, the dataspace acts as a container for data and a catalogue for acquiring information from web resources.

A second important design requirement is the provision of high-level services for data-intensive processing and mining. This is motivated by the need for a richer and more precise business information with the consequential demand for more dynamic computing techniques allowing versatile exploration of this information. Being the challenge to raise up the level at which information is filtered and integrated, services are needed to mining and processing the huge volume of data gathered from heterogeneous networked sources. These services will incorporate advanced graphic features, geo-spatial presentation and context aware visualization tools.

Finally, cloud computing must be seen as the paradigm needed to finally shift the processing component of the decision support system from the desktop to distributed resources by the mean of the following classes of services:

- Searching services intended to replace the functionalities offered by current data warehousing systems with a more simple, network based "pay and use" model;
- Cloud services that try to deliver information in a transparent way without targeting decision makers directly;
- Low-level services to provide functionality about the dataspace management, improvement, updating.

3. ARCHITECTURE

According to the above requirements, Figure 1 describes the cloud-based architecture we propose for supporting a Decision Support System (DSS). It is organized into four layers: a *Presentation layer*, a *Business layer*, a *Data Integration layer*, and a *Data layer*. Each layer handles specific tasks, has specific responsibilities to the other layers and uses a simple interface contract to describe its partner relationships.

In more detail, the *Presentation layer* supports user interactions. It exposes a user interface through which the user can access the functionality provided. It is responsible for transforming data in a format suitable for a web browser interface. Contextual application services allow results presentation on different types of devices, like mobile phones, PDA etc.

The *Business layer* contains the core business logic processing, i.e. the services supporting the decision processes. Its functionality is implemented by two classes of services: *DSS business services* providing operational guidance for dealing with decisional tasks and *external services* provided in the web including calculation models, statistical packages and simulation tools. Each service contributes a distinct activity for addressing the problems encountered in the various steps of the decision process. This layer is also responsible for transforming the high level user requirements to a set of low level parameters that can be passed to other business services.

One of the main advantages of the proposed architecture is the *Data Integration layer*, a middleware which is responsible for data integration by offering services the boundary conditions of which depend on each other. They cover the basic steps of the dataspace life cycle, i.e. *bootstrapping* (Das Sarma et al., 2008), *query process* and *incremental improvement*.

Bootstrapping aims to identify the data resources and integrate them. It is supported predominantly by standard model operators (Bernstein & Melnik, 2007; Hedeler et al., 2011) augmented with operations that infer high-level schematic correspondences from matches and that generate mappings from the correspondences (Hedeler et al., 2011). Operators are mechanisms to support the integration of heterogeneous data sources through different manipulation of schemas and the schematic correspondences that hold between them. Different integration strategies are possible. For example, one strategy merges the source schemas, one selects one of the source schema as integration schema etc.

The *query process* is carried on by a service-based distributed query processor (Lynden et al.,

Figure 1. The proposed architecture

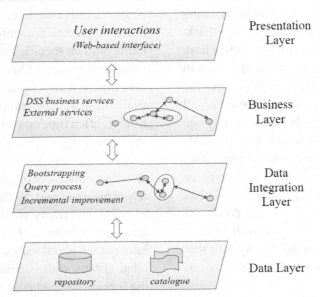

2009) that supports querying over data storage and analysis of resources that are made available as services. It allows the construction and execution of distributed query plans and provides seamless querying on the structured and unstructured data. Because much of the user interaction within the dataspace involves exploring the data, and users do not have a single schema to which they can pose queries, additional services allow the generation of subqueries and the query expansion by means of mapping selection operators (Bernstein & Melnik, 2007).

Incremental improvement is one of the main challenges of dataspace systems. It is accomplished by using different techniques to automatically match different schemas (Rahm & Bernstein, 2001) and carry on entity resolution (Cohen et al., 2003) between disparate data sources. This results in a set of potential matches, which can incrementally improve the performance of a dataspace. However, Jeffery et al. (2008) and Doan & Halevy (2005) have stressed that it is necessary to introduce human involvement at this stage and feedback from user could be of much benefit.

So far incremental improvement has focused on a single mechanism: the user feedback (Doan et al., 2001; Wu et al., 2004). Specifically, research carried out by Doan et al. (2001) and Wu et al. (2004) has tackled the problem by assisting the schema matching task with user feedback. Similarly, Sarawagi & Bhamidipaty (2002) have worked on an active learning based approach in which the feedback from the user is fed into the system to train suitable classifiers. However, all these approaches are primarily based on only one type of data integration task and their methods of selecting the potential matches for presenting to the user are heavily dependent on the type of classifiers used (Mirza et al., 2010). It has been argued (Mirza et al., 2010) that instead of different mechanisms that might work very well in their own capacities, there is a need of a system that combines them all and then makes the decisions

which could possibly serve the goal of providing improved query results for the final user.

The *Data Layer* persistently stores the dataspace components, i.e. the model-independent representation of schemas, the elicited matches, the schematic correspondences supported by the matches, the mappings derived from the latter, the user feedback collected and the corresponding query results. Components are stored in a repository whose primary scope is twofold:

- To provide a logically central repository for collection and storage of dataspace components;
- To provide a common decisional environment that facilitates information sharing between the various decision makers.

The repository works under the premise that major business missions and policies of an organisation are the driving force in the design of the decisional environment that evolves over time through organizational policies. The decisional environment involves accessing or gathering data from multiple sources, followed by data correlation, classification, review, and curation using domain specific tools and expertise. In practice, the decisional environment is less daunting when it is considered in the context of an iterative strategy based on gradual data integration while accumulating domain specific knowledge throughout the integration process. This strategy allows analysing information with "coarse granularity" that is made available in a single component that is refined via further, often time consuming, computations and expert review.

In a large scale scenario, a dataspace may consist of a vast number of participating components. Being aware of and dealing with data integration becomes extremely challenging and difficult: a catalogue facilitates this integration. It contains information about various components and their relationships, with associated mechanisms providing support for gradually extending this catalogue as the dataspace expands. In a catalogue, basic information about components includes: resource, name, location, size, creation date, owner, etc. Additionally, the catalogue stores resource schemas for components, statistic data, modification time and precision, possibility of executing queries, owner data, access politics and confidentiality support. Relationships within components are stored as metadata, query transformations, dependence graphs, and textual descriptions.

Besides storing and indexing components, the catalogue contains mechanisms for creating new relationships by modifying the existing ones (e.g. join or invert representation, join schemas and unified representation of several resources).

To orchestrate the flow activities presented in Figure 1 for specifying actions or for controlling service flows, a mash-up approach has been adopted. Specifically, a mash-up is a process that integrates data/content from different resources on the Internet in order to provide the user with a flexible and easy-of-use way for service composition on the web. Basically, a mash-up environment utilizes an open, heterogeneous set of tools to connect with each other, content, and tools into a single computational environment. Usually hosted on a web server, a mash-up application is rendered in a web browser, through which user interaction takes place. Mash-ups combine third-party data and content from more than one source to create a completely new application. Providers that promote free tools on the Internet and release their APIs for free make this process possible.

The mash-up gathers information from web sites that:

- Provide their information publicly in structured format (Google Maps and Google Earth are well known examples of this kind of web sites);
- Provides a possibility for outsiders to bring content into their web site, again using some structured web data transfer format.

Although our architecture is generic to support a standard executable language, such as BPEL (Louridas, 2008) for service coordination, we choose mash-ups for orchestrating the service flows in an "ad hoc" way. This is more suitable to the specific application scenario where the user is able to iteratively refine and modify the answer to a graphical query as well as formulate queries about the source of data. Most importantly, users can define new tasks properly and determine carefully what criteria should be employed in the evaluations and comparisons of alternative decisions. Mash-ups are conceived as a middleware that gets the data from proper layers. Additionally, the user interface is capable of assembling and composing mashed-up content.

4. APPLICATIVE EXPERIMENTS

Real Estate (RE) market is every day more and more influenced by global markets and, therefore, characterized by dynamics considerably faster than those observed just few years ago. Probably, the actual methods for market monitoring have to be enhanced in order to be able to perform some step closer to a real time analysis. Nowadays, in industrialized contexts, the existing market supply is almost entirely contained into considerable RE intermediation web-sites and represents a significant opportunity for improving the methodologies actually used to study market trends. Through data-mining and spatial econometrics techniques, it is now possible to estimate market supply with a modest use of time and human working resources. This analysis can give back a "sentiment" able to predict the upcoming objective results that will come from recorded trades.

During the last five years, we have witnessed a gradual process of "data structuration" of real estate supply; property advertise, previously published on local journal, are now reported with the corresponding picture and other extended information on RE brokerage web-sites (Trulia,

Idealista, etc). By exploiting this opportunity, the exposed methodology would be able to detect, with greater advance, the short-term real estate market trend. In contrast to the official reports on RE market transactions, the proposed decision support system can generate a real time knowledge of market supply, an important point of view for every average potential buyer.

This new opportunity takes place in a historical period wherein the correlation between the performance of the real estate market and the dynamics of the stock market often results demonstrated (Heaney & Sriananthakumar, 2012). In fact, during the last ten years, real estate market has shown, especially in the United States, a dynamic nature never seen so far and, consequently, a extraordinarily high level of risk to investors, often consisting of families performing the main investment of their lives. The recent subprime mortgage scandal is an example of how a housing bubble may directly approach the financial market and vice versa. On the other hand, the existing systems capable of monitoring the status of the housing market are extremely far from those, although improvable, available to analyze the financial market.

Just as in the commodities stock market we can follow conscientiously the latest report resulting from the production lines, the same approach can be applied to the property market supply, analyzing both the offer spatial distribution and consistence. It is also possible quantify the relationship between the supply and other parameters like the rents offered, the average income per capita or other macro-economic indicators.

Although is not an objective reference point, a real time market supply analysis can be an useful element to generate predictions related to market price, i.e. the hypothetical judgments of equivalence between a property and a certain amount of money in the given circumstances of time and place (Forte & De Rossi, 1974). This possibility can be an extremely powerful analysis tool both for those who are going to buy a home and for who is involved in administering the territory, in order, eventually, to reduce the impact of any anomalous trends of the market, by anticipating events with proper urban planning interventions.

4.1 Case of Study

The exposed case study is based on the definition of a web application able to assess the state of health of an urban housing market and, in general, to inform citizens about their actual capacity purchase/lease of a property. This assessment is clearly correlated with the medium prices in different market areas that compose a specific urban context.

The proposed application relies on the real estate listing elaboration regarding ten Italian municipalities[1], reported in the leading websites of real estate brokerage. Through the acquisition of such information and the subsequent insertion in a geo-database, it is possible to quantify medium offer values and provide a map that represents the relative spatial trend.

Obviously, the first aspect to study regards the sample density and the relative coverage of the whole urban centre's residential areas. In some cases, it was possible to mash-up some information taken from the approved urban plan and limit the study exclusively to effective residential zones. In other cases, we were forced to base the study on the hypothesis that, depending on the sample density, the residential zones cannot exceed 500 meters or one Km from any single residential property offer collected (Figure 2-left).

Once defined the spatial region object of study, the next step consists in removing any supply anomalies through a Morans I spatial regression analysis. This kind of spatial analysis is able to evidence the potential lack of spatial correlation between the collected listing prices. As shown in Figure 2 (right), offer values that generate an unexpected and isolated increase/decrease of supply values are highlighted and re-analyzed. Sometimes, the sudden change may correspond

Figure 2. Residential area definition: 500 meters and 1 km buffers (left). Rendering of spatial cluster and Morans I outliers analysis (right).

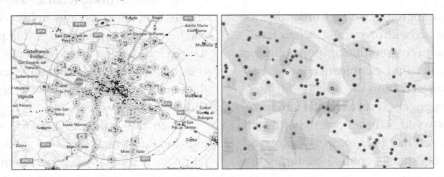

to an effective decrease of the urban quality level, in other cases it can be a sign of a residential property whose offer price is not in line with what is ordinarily expressed by the market. In these cases, the Real Estate appraisal principle of predictability requires us to exclude this offer price (outliers) from reference sample.

Once outliers are removed from the sample, it is possible to proceed with the creation of an interpolation surface of recorded medium values. Such surface creation can be performed as a function of two parameters: the number of neighbours to consider and the maximum radial distance used to retrieve references.

Using of a large number of neighbours or a consistent search radius tends, significantly, to reduce the specificities of the market in the urban

region by flattening the interpolation surface, especially where the market value references tend to change consistently. Conversely, a small number of properties reference neighbours or a limited search radius of interpolation tends to bring out such variations allowing inaccurate information to significantly affect the interpolation surface (Figure 3).

The ideal compromise between these two parameters is related both to the specific urban contest and to the sample dimension/density. Actually a correct definition of this interpolation surface needs the supervision of a professional appraiser who is familiar with the local real estate market. Once the proper interpolation surface has been defined, it can be clipped within the limits of the urban residential area.

Figure 3. Interpolation surfaces created respectively with 1,2,3,5,10,23 km radius

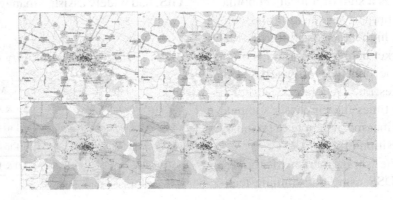

4.2 Measuring Home Affordability

Can I afford home purchase? Which urban district can be well-matched with my current income level? Frequently, when a common citizen ponders these questions, he can't find an objective answer, an answer disconnected from the opinion of interested market operators. Probably, the subprime mortgage crisis would not have occurred with such intensity if citizen had been properly informed about the housing market conditions during the sudden price growth we assists in US during 2003-2008. In fact, many economists have identified the main cause of recent global real estate market crisis in the poor diffusion of systems capable of monitoring the historical property values and in the scarce public awareness about the risks of real estate investments crisis (Bardhan, 2008; Shiller, 2008).

Using ordinary macro-economic criteria to assess home affordability can give a relevant answer to the former questions. The target of this case of study is providing this answer using Housing Affordability Index on an interactive web map (i.e. OSM or Google Map). To calculate Spatial Housing Affordability is necessary to know both the average property market values and the medium household income.

The Annual Demographia International Housing Affordability Survey[2] (2008) identifies five different categories of purchase accessibility in house property market. Generally, a high ratio between the price of a property and the average household income is a sign of a local economic unsustainability in property acquisition and, consequently, it will be higher the possibility of a real estate housing market bubble. This ratio is often measured taking in account the mortgage payment and the related interest rate. Generally, when home price exceeds four times the purchaser's annual average household income, it denotes a seriously unaffordable acquisition (Table 1).

Leveraging on the average market offer prices, acquired by the SDSS using data mining tech-niques, the user has just to declare two parameters: the average apartment retail area he is looking for and the amount of savings in his possession that can be currently used for a partial property payment. Once known these parameters, the system is able to calculate the minimum income required for a quite sustainable (HAI = 4) home purchase (Figure 4).

Given the ability to monitor market offerings in almost real time, this application is also particularly useful for any person involved in the territorial political administration. In accordance with the correlation between the housing market accessibility and the local population medium income, administrators can take any necessary corrective planning measures, which may facilitate the market to regain an adequate level of sustainability and, at the same time, prevent the occurrence of dangerous housing market bubbles.

5. RELATED WORK

As the computational basis for spatial decision support was then and still is today some form of GIS technology, research on SDSSs originated from two distinct sources, namely the GIS community and the DSS community.

Early SDSS implementations (Densham & Armstrong, 1987) were concerned with the integration between spatial databases and spatial processing routines. In the past two decades, the use of spatial information technologies, especially GIS, had widely assisted managers in their work.

Table 1. Housing affordability rating categories

Rating	Median Multiple
Severely Unaffordable	5.1 & Over
Seriously Unaffordable	4.1 to 5.0
Moderately Unaffordable	3.1 to 4.0
Affordable	3.0 & Under

(source: demographia.com)

Figure 4. Estimated household median income needed to buy a 75 m² apartment in Rome (left) and Bologna (right)

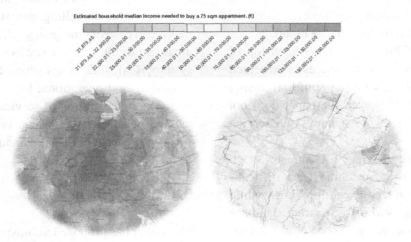

However, the sophisticated nature of GISs often excludes many potential stakeholders from getting benefit from the use of distributed spatial information (Rinner et al., 2008). Additionally, despite their huge capacities in storing and managing geographical data, GISs have some limits in solving most real-world spatial decision problems (Sugumaran & Sugumaran, 2007).

Recent advances in Internet technology offer opportunities that let us able to develop modern applications, usually referred to as Web 2.0 applications, starting from contents and functionality that are available on the web in form of open APIs or reusable services. This results in the use of state-of-the-art technology for the construction of a new generation of decision support tools (Bernstein & Melnik, 2007; Marchi & Argiolas, 2008; Sugumaran & Sugumaran, 2007; Vescoukis et al., 2012) that integrate plain data sources, public programmable APIs (like Google Maps) or any kind of available services providing support in decisional processes.

Numerous publications have investigated issues (e.g. data exchange, software, model sharing) of implementing SDSSs on the web and concluded that developments in web technologies will have

an huge impact on future SDSS development (Bharati & Chaudhury, 2004; Hall & Leahy, 2006; Sugumaran & Sugumaran, 2007; Sugumaran, & DeGroote, 2011; Wang & Cheng, 2006).

A review which summarizes research directions on web-based SDSSs is presented in (Rinner, 2003): it underlines the need for systematic studies and the adoption of architectures for chaining interoperable geo-processing services to build specific SDSS services. Rinner et al. (2008) underlines the importance of developing WebGIS applications based on publicly available free geo-spatial data and recommends Google Maps as an excellent candidate to construct the groundwork of any collaborative WebGIS development.

Concerning the deployment of databases onto the cloud, Aboulnaga et al. (2009) presents some of the challenges about the placement of VM's across physical machines, the partitioning of resources across VM's and dealing with dynamic workloads. These challenges are considered critical in moving data warehousing system towards the cloud.

In exploring limitation and opportunities of moving data management into the cloud, Abadi (2009) argues that current database systems are not yet particularly suited for moving into the cloud where ACID properties are difficult to guarantee. Being these properties not important for data warehousing, the migration of these systems will take advantage of moving into the cloud.

An attempt of building a DBMS on top of Amazon's S3 (Amazon web services) is presented in (Brantner et al., 2008) and some promising results are shown. However, the paper does not explore the possibilities of Amazon's EC2 service in detail.

About database efficiency, Ganapathi et al. (2009) proposes some machine learning techniques to predict query execution times while a technique using VM's to separate database instances is introduced in (Soror et al., 2008), which is relevant for example for multi-tenant hosting in the cloud.

As discussed in (Buyya et al., 2009), cloud computing is seen as the potential fifth utility besides electricity, water, gas and telephony. The paper defines cloud computing and provides an architecture for creating clouds with market-oriented resource allocation by leveraging technologies such as Virtual Machines.

Similar to our approach, Vigne et al. (2012) presents the advantages of an hybrid service and process repository as the foundation for a structured marketplace for arbitrary services which not only holds a flat list of services, but also exposes a generic set of uses cases. The paper stresses the difficulties in integrating several cloud services as computing resource vendors keep their own interfaces. For solving questions arising from these heterogeneous environments, the authors envision a marketplace, a set of resources or services, where consumers can select from a variety of available services to build complex applications.

With the aim to contribute a new architectural template for heterogeneous, distributed information systems, Vescoukis et al. (2012) proposes a flexible service oriented architecture for planning and decision support for an environmental information management. The architecture uses real time geospatial datasets and 3D presentations tools, integrated with added-value services for environmental modelling and support decision making in case of emergency. The paper presents a case study on a forest fire crisis management system. Real world maps support environmental modelling and operational logistic implementation. The orchestration of service flow is implemented in ad hoc way which is suitable to the specific scenario of disaster handling (i.e. fire).

6. CONCLUSION

This paper has proposed a dataspace as a new approach to support real estate evaluation that relies on web technologies and GIS for combining the spatial, environmental and economic information. Intelligent spatial decision analysis is carried on by the presentation of computational results using suitable outputs including diagrams, tables and reports, surfaces, geographic maps.

The dataspace allows appraisers to evaluate how much of the risk of investing in a property arises from the spatial characteristics of the specific property and how much of the risk arises from common confluences across others indicators, such as the levels of economic activities and the urban processes.

Most importantly, we tried to identify the nature of the technology needed to provide the basic functionality relevant to the spatial analysis in real estate domain. This resulted in a decision support system that assembles a set of functions which offer a prospect of new insights in spatial analysis. The next stage of our work is to incorporate new functionality and test the system with new real estate scenarios.

We are confident that the computational environment we presented will suggest new approaches for web-based exploration and spatial analysis in real estate evaluation.

ACKNOWLEDGMENT

This work has been funded in part by Regione Autonoma della Sardegna (R.A.S.), Project CRP-17615 DENIS: Dataspace Enhancing Next Internet in Sardinia.

REFERENCES

Abadi, D. (2009). Data Management in the Cloud: Limitations and Opportunities. Data Engineering.

Aboulnaga, A., Salem, K., Soror, A. A., Minhas, U. F., Kokosielis, P., & Kamath, S. (2009). *Deploying Database Appliances in the Cloud. IEEE Data Eng. Bull.*

Amazon web services. (n.d.). Retrieved from http://aws.amazon.com/http://aws.amazon.com/

Bardhan, R. (2008). Global Financial Integration and real estate security returns. *Real Estate Economics*, *36*, 285–381. doi:10.1111/j.1540-6229.2008.00214.x

Bernstein, P. A., & Melnik, S. (2007). Model management 2.0: manipulating richer mappings. In *Proceedings of the 2007 ACM SIGMOD international conference on Management of data*, (pp. 1-12). ACM.

Brantner, M., Florescu, D., Graf, D., Kossmann, D., & Kraska, T. (2008). Building a Database on S3. In Proceedings of ACM SIGMOD 2008. ACM.

Buyya, R., Yeo, C. S., Venugopal, S., Broberg, J., & Brandic, I. (2009). Cloud computing and emerging IT platforms: Vision, hype, and reality for delivering computing as the 5th utility. *Future Generation Computer Systems*, *25*(6). doi:10.1016/j.future.2008.12.001 PMID:21308003

Cohen, W. W., Kumar, P. R., & Fienberg, S. E. (2003). A comparison of string distance metrics for name matching tasks. In *Proceedings of IJCAI Workshop on Information Integration on the Web*, (pp. 73-78).

Das Sarma, A., Dong, X., & Halevy, A. Y. (2008). Bootstrapping pay-as-you-go data integration systems. In Proceedings of SIGMOD 2008. ACM.

Densham, P. J., & Armstrong, M. P. (1987). *A spatial Decision Support System for locational planning: Design implementation and operation*. Paper presented at the Eighth International Symposium on Computer-Assisted Cartography. Baltimore, MD.

Dittrich, J. P., & Salles, M. A. V. (2006). iDM: A unified and versatile data model for personal dataspace management. In Proceedings of VLDB 2006, (pp. 367–378). VLDB.

Doan, A., & Halevy, A. Y. (2005). Semantic integration research in the database community. *AI Magazine*, *26*, 83–94.

Doan, A. H., Domingos, P., & Halevy, A. Y. (2001). Reconciling schemas of disparate data sources: A machine learning approach. *SIGMOD Record*, *30*, 509–520. doi:10.1145/376284.375731

Dong, X., & Halevy, A. Y. (2007). Indexing dataspaces. In *Proceedings of SIGMOD Conference*, (pp. 43–54). ACM.

Forte, C., & De Rossi, B. (1974). *Principi di economia ed estimo*. Milano: Etas libri.

Franklin, M. J., Halevy, A. Y., & Maier, D. (2005). From databases to dataspaces: a new abstraction for information management. *SIGMOD Record*, *34*(4), 27–33. doi:10.1145/1107499.1107502

Ganapathi, A., Kuno, H., Dayal, U., Wiener, J. L., Fox, A., Jordan, M., & Patterson, D. (2009). Predicting Multiple Metrics for Queries: Better Decisions Enabled by Machine Learning. In *Proceedings of the 2009 IEEE International Conference on Data Engineering*. IEEE.

Halevy, A. Y., Franklin, M. J., & Maier, D. (2006). Principles of dataspace systems. In *Stijn Vansummeren* (pp. 1–9). ACM.

Heaney, R., & Srirananthakumar, S. (2012, September). Time-varying correlation between stock market returns and real estate returns. *Journal of Empirical Finance*, *19*(4), 583–594. doi:10.1016/j.jempfin.2012.03.006

Hedeler, C., Belhajjame, K., Paton, N. W., Fernandes, A. A. A., Embury, S. M., Mao, L., & Guo, C. (2011). Pay-As-You-Go Mapping Selection in Dataspaces. In Proceedings of SIGMOD 2011, (pp. 1279-1282). ACM.

Jeffery, S. R., Franklin, M. J., & Halevy, A. Y. (2008). Pay-as-you-go user feedback for dataspace systems. In *Proceedings of the ACM SIGMOD International Conference on Management of Data*, (pp. 847-860). ACM.

Louridas, P. (2008). Orchestrating web services with BPEL. *IEEE Software*, 85–87. doi:10.1109/MS.2008.42

Lynden, S., Mukherjee, A., Hume, A. C., Fernandes, A. A. A., Paton, N. W., Sakellariou, R., & Watson, P. (2009). The design and implementation of OGSA-DQP: A service-based distributed query processor. *Future Generation Computer Systems*, *25*(3), 224–236. doi:10.1016/j.future.2008.08.003

Marchi, G., & Argiolas, M. (2008). A GIS based technology for representing and analyzing real estate values. In *Proceedings of UDMS 2007*, (pp. 345-354). UDMS.

Mell, P., & Grance, T. (2011). *The NIST Definition of Cloud Computing*. NIST Special Publication 800-145.

Mirza, H. T., Chen, L., & Chen, G. (2010). Practicability of Dataspace Systems. *International Journal of Digital Content Technology and its Applications*, *4*(3), 233-243.

Rahm, E., & Bernstein, P. A. (2001). A survey of approaches to automatic schema matching. *The VLDB Journal*, *10*, 334–350. doi:10.1007/s007780100057

Rinner, C. (2003). Web-based Spatial Decision Support: Status and Research Directions. *Journal of Geographic Information and Decision Analysis*, *7*(1), 14–31.

Rinner, C., Keßler, C., & Andrulis, S. (2008). The Use of Web 2.0 Concepts to Support Deliberation in Spatial Decision-Making. *Computers, Environment and Urban Systems*, *32*(5), 386–395. doi:10.1016/j.compenvurbsys.2008.08.004

Sarawagi, S., & Bhamidipaty, A. (2002). Interactive deduplication using active learning. In *Proceedings of the eighth international conference on Knowledge discovery and data mining*, (pp. 269-278). Academic Press.

Shiller, R. J. (2008). *The Subprime Solution*. Princetown University Press.

Soror, A. A., Minhas, U. F., Aboulnaga, A., & Salem, K. Kokosielis, & P., Kamath, S. (2008). Automatic Virtual Machine Configuration for Database Workloads. In Proceedings of ACM SIGMOD 2008. ACM.

Sugumaran, R., & DeGroote, J. (2011). Spatial Decision Support Systems: Principles and Practices. Boca Raton, FL: CRC Press, Taylor & Francis.

Sugumaran, V., & Sugumaran, R. (2007). Web-based Spatial Decision Support Systems (Web-SDSS): Evolution, Architecture, Examples and Challenges. *Communications of the Association for Information Systems*, *19*, 40.

Vescoukis, V., Doulamis, N., & Karagiorgou, S. (2012). A service-oriented architecture for decision support systems in environmental crisis management. *Future Generation Computer Systems*, *28*, 593–604. doi:10.1016/j.future.2011.03.010

Vigne, R., Mangler, J., Schikuta, E., & Rinderle-Ma, S. (2012). A structured marketplace for arbitrary services. *Future Generation Computer Systems*, *28*, 48–57. doi:10.1016/j.future.2011.05.024

Wang, L., & Cheng, Q. (2006). Web-Based Collaborative Decision Support Services: Concept, Challenges and Application. In *Proceedings of the ISPRS Symposium*. ISPRS.

Wu, W., Yu, C., Doan, A. H., & Meng, W. (2004). An interactive clustering based approach to integrating source query interfaces on the deep web. In *Proceedings of the ACM SIGMOD 2004*, (pp. 95-106). ACM.

ENDNOTES

[1] Bologna, Cagliari, Firenze, Genova, Milano, Napoli, Palermo, Roma, Torino, Venezia.
[2] www.demographia.com

Chapter 6
Further Development of an Application Framework for Computational Chemistry (AFCC) Applied to New Drug Discovery

J. Tindle
University of Sunderland – St. Peter's Campus, UK

R.L. Warrender
University of Sunderland – St. Peter's Campus, UK

M. Gray
University of Sunderland – City Campus, UK

K. Ginty
University of Sunderland – St. Peter's Campus, UK

P.K.D. Dawson
University of Sunderland – City Campus, UK

ABSTRACT

This chapter describes the performance of a compute cluster applied to solve Three Dimensional (3D) molecular modelling problems. The primary goal of this work is to identify new potential drugs. The chapter focuses upon the following issues: computational chemistry, computational efficiency, task scheduling, and the analysis of system performance. The philosophy of design for an Application Framework for Computational Chemistry (AFCC) is described. Eighteen months after the release of the original chapter, the authors have examined a series of changes adopted which have led to improved system performance. Various experiments have been carried out to optimise the performance of a cluster computer, the results analysed, and the statistics produced are discussed in the chapter.

DOI: 10.4018/978-1-4666-6252-0.ch006

1. INTRODUCTION

Computational methods have been developed that allow researchers to carry out comprehensive investigation of molecules and their reactions. Molecular modelling allows the researcher to observe biological reactions and the associated dynamics providing highly accurate descriptions of the relevant interatomic forces. In most cases it is computationally expensive to solve the high level quantum chemistry models.

Chemists are now able to investigate the properties of chemical structures at the molecular level. The aim of the research described in this paper is to discover new drugs that target particular cells and cure diseases at the cellular or genetic level.

This paper describes the performance of a compute cluster applied to solve a large number of molecular models. The paper considers factors such as the computational chemistry and molecular modelling, computational efficiency, task scheduling and the analysis of cluster system performance. The updated design of an application framework for computational chemistry (AFCC) research is discussed (Tindle, Gray, Warrender, Ginty & Dawson, 2012).

The University of Sunderland installed and commissioned a general purpose high performance compute cluster in the Computing department. This development is based upon Microsoft High Performance Computing HPC Servers and the Compute Cluster Pack ("What is Microsofts High Performance Computing HPC Server," 2014; "Microsoft Compute Cluster Pack," 2014). The design of the cluster computer was completed by University of Sunderland (UoS) and Dell engineers (Ginty, Tindle, & Tindle, 2009; "Eco-Friendly Super Computing," 2014), refer to Appendix 1. A more detailed description of the cluster system hardware and software configuration may be found in the paper by Ginty (2009). The UoS cluster computer has been used in areas such as 3D computer graphics (CG) modelling projects (Tindle, Ginty & Tindle, 2009), as well as crash analysis simulation using finite element modelling software. Staff employed within the departments of Computing and Pharmacy collaborated upon this research.

2. MOLECULAR MODELLING

Molecular modelling software allows the user to select atoms from the periodic table and to place them in a three dimensional workspace. In most modelling systems it is possible to build a three dimensional molecular structure by using a colour graphics user interface (GUI), refer to Figure 1. The initial position of the atoms is normally determined by the user calling upon common sense and experience. In all cases the actual position that the atoms assume in the real world is determined by the Laws of Physics. Computational chemistry is a general name for computer based algorithms that may be used to solve this type of problem. There are numerous algorithms that may be deployed and normally this involves computing the minimum value of an energy function to find the optimum solution.

For complex structures in many cases the rate of convergence is relatively slow and it is therefore often necessary to employ high performance computing methods to produce solutions in a reasonable period of time.

2.1 Model Convergence Time

There are three principle factors that influence the time required to produce an acceptable solution.

- The initial position of the atoms selected by the user. This initial set of atomic positions is the seed for the numerical solver algorithm embedded in Gaussian 09.
- The number of heavy atoms in the model of the molecular structure.

Figure 1. Molecular modelling workspace

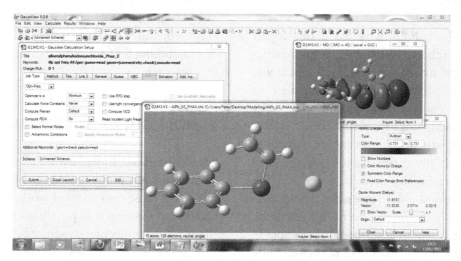

- The basis set and the method deployed, for example, the molecular mechanics protocol UFF which is intrinsically fast or the ab initio method MP4 that is relatively slow (Vinter, David, & Saunders, 1987; Sastryl, Johnson, Goldberg, Martinez, Leiding, & Owens, 2007).

A system that accurately models the Schrodinger Equation will normally require a long time to produce a good solution whereas more approximate methods produce solutions more rapidly.

$$T \text{ is proportional to } K * A^n$$

where

- T is the time to produce a solution
- K is a constant that is associated with method in use
- A is the number of heavy (non-hydrogen) atoms
- n is a scalar value of 4

When large numbers of atoms are involved in a model the time taken to generate a solution can be very long.

3. NEW DRUG DISCOVERY

By using HPC methods and computational chemistry it is possible for the user to create a set of new potential drugs. The output data produced by the solver algorithms allows the user to evaluate each potential candidate and select the best for production and further testing. In this scenario it is only necessary to manufacture and test the best candidate molecular structures and the data associated with poor models may be discarded or archived. By evaluating a large number of the most promising models and selecting only the most promising cases it is possible to minimise production and testing costs.

The cost of developing a new drug can run into hundreds of millions or even several billion dollars. The traditional process will usually take ten or more years and result in the synthesis, purification and biological evaluation of ten thousand or more new compounds in order to produce a single viable clinical candidate.

In order to reduce the costs implicit within the above, the pharmaceutical industry has invested heavily in computational approaches to drug discovery. These approaches often rationalise existing biological data to make informed choices as to the next series of compounds to make, so called Pharmacophore or Quantitative Structure Activity Relationship (QSAR) approaches. Alternatively, where good quality structural information is available regarding the intended biological target molecule, usually a particular enzyme, receptor protein or strand of DNA/RNA, a research team can embark upon a programme of so called Rational Drug Design.

Rational Drug Design comes in several subtypes, the details of which are beyond the scope of this paper. However, they all operate by defining a region of space within the target biomolecule within which the drug candidate must fit. The usual analogy for this is that we are trying to find a specific key (the drug candidate) that fits a particular lock (the drug target). Thus the drug candidate must be the correct size and shape to snugly fit within the available space in order to maximise the potential for interactions between drug and target without being too big to fit at all.

Along with the relatively crude considerations that must be made with regards to a complementary shape between lock and key we must also consider the complementarity or otherwise between the surface electrostatic potentials of the two molecules. All molecules whether natural or synthetic are made from atoms and these atoms are made in turn from three components: protons, neutrons and electrons. The protons which are positively charged and neutrons which are electrically neutral form a dense nucleus within the heart of each atom which is surrounded by a swarm of negatively charged electrons. However, when we put atoms together to make molecules certain atoms attract more of the electron density towards themselves on average than others. This leads to the surface of typical molecules being electron rich and electrostatically negative in some areas and electron deficient or electrostatically positive in others.

If we were to find molecules with the correct shape to fit to our binding site but would place regions of high electron density in contact with one another, Coulomb's Law dictates that the two molecules would repel and thus binding would not be able to take place. Similarly, repulsion would take place between molecules with a significant degree of electrostatically positive contact. Productive binding can thus only take place when the drug and drug target display regions of opposite charge on the electrostatic surfaces that would be in contact with one another when the drug docks into the target binding site.

Many programmes have been developed that are able to assign surface electrostatic potentials of molecules based upon a qualitative knowledge of the properties of their constituent atoms and then attempt to dock them together, and many new compounds in the clinic have been designed with the aid of these techniques. However, the ability of the computer to assign these charges and other properties of the molecules in question is entirely dictated by parameter sets stored within the computer.

In reality, it is known that when two molecules come into contact with one another they perturb the electron distribution within one another. This interplay between the electrostatic potentials of the two molecules in many instances is rather subtle but in some cases can lead to unexpected effects when the two molecules are allowed to bind to one another in real life. Moreover, many drugs that have long been on the market, such as aspirin and penicillin, operate by causing a chemical reaction between themselves and their target molecules alongside the initial binding event. These effects are much more difficult to anticipate and are often impossible to predict using the standard software in the industry based upon the traditional parameterised molecular mechanics (MM) approaches.

Problems such as reactivity and mutual polarisability that occur when two molecules come into intimate contact are however able to be tackled using Quantum Mechanics (QM). Quantum mechanical programmes such as Gaussian operate by finding approximate solutions to the Schrodinger Equation for collections of atoms and molecules using only physical constants such as the masses of subatomic particles and the speed of light. This means that there are no limitations or biases in these calculations from pre-determined parameter sets and the true nature of the interactions and reactions between molecules becomes realisable.

However QM methods are highly computationally resource intensive to the extent that while programmes for carrying out such calculations have been available for many years their implementation in biologically relevant problems such as drug design has not been feasible until recently due to the size and complexity of these molecules. Even now full QM approaches are not deemed to be cost effective for medium or large biological molecules and thus hybrid, or so called QM/MM approaches, have been developed. In a typical QM/MM calculation the drug or natural ligand to be studied is treated quantum mechanically, as are the parts of the target molecule which make up the binding site. The rest of the target molecule is treated using more traditional MM methods.

3.1 Parallel Processing

To identify a new potential drug a large number of jobs must be evaluated. This results in many hundreds of or even thousands of jobs being presented to the compute cluster for processing. Each job takes a finite time from perhaps a few hours up to many days

3.1.1 Compute Cluster Multiprocessing (CCM)

If all the resources of the compute cluster are focused upon single job individual solutions are usually produced very rapidly. This method is termed compute cluster multiprocessing CCM. However, the operation of splitting the task between nodes results in an increased communication overhead and normally a reduced level of efficiency.

3.1.2 Symmetric Multiprocessing (SMP)

An alternative approach is to suffer the longer time delay incurred and allocate a single job to each Compute Node for processing. The authors selected symmetric multiprocessing SMP for this work. The SMP approach works in conjunction with a job scheduler so that many jobs can run in parallel. The use of the scheduler ensures that there is no delay between the allocations of new jobs to Compute Nodes. SMP techniques that optimise the use of CPU cores and available RAM have been employed to ensure that CPU usage of 100% is normally achieved for long periods at each Compute Node (Warrender, Tindle, & Nelson, 2013).

4. COMPUTATIONAL CHEMISTRY AND GAUSSIAN

Professor John Pople designed the first version of the Gaussian computer program to make his computational techniques easily accessible to researchers. The use of Gaussian makes possible the theoretical study of molecules, their properties, and how they act together in chemical reactions. The Gaussian program has been continuously developed by many researchers and today it is a software product that is used by thousands of chemists. Professor John Pople was awarded the Nobel Prize in chemistry in 1998 for his pioneering contributions in developing computational methods. Researchers can use Gaussian 09 to conduct research into the following topics ("Gaussian 09 Reference Manual," 2014).

- Investigate the structures of molecules and their reactions
- Predict and interpret spectra
- Predict optical spectra, including hyperfine spectra

- Investigate thermo chemistry and excited state processes
- Study solvent effects upon structures, reactions and spectroscopic properties
- Model NMR properties of molecules.

In the past chemists used standard laboratory methods to undertake research, for example by using chemical compounds, solvents, test tubes and heat sources. It is now possible to complete much of this practical research work by using powerful computers and computational chemistry software. The application of computation chemistry has many advantages mainly by helping to reduce the need for access to expensive laboratory time, test equipment and chemicals.

From experience the authors have found that it takes about five minutes to manually prepare a single Gaussian 09 job to be sent to the scheduler prior to execution on the cluster computer. The manually preparation of jobs for execution is a standard approach often adopted by many research groups. This approach is most appropriate where a relatively small number of jobs are being processed by the scheduler, for example less than one hundred jobs.

The authors of this paper are working with a group of six research chemists working upon drug development. These researchers have produced large number of jobs in batches of various sizes for execution on the cluster computer. A single batch contains typically between one hundred and five hundred Gaussian 09 jobs. It is anticipated that the total number of jobs that will eventually be processed on the cluster will be of the order ten thousand for any given development. To date more than six thousand jobs have been completed. In this paper the initial two hundred and seventy six jobs have been analysed to determine the performance characteristics of the cluster computer. The development of the AFCC allows a large batch of jobs, for example more than 500 jobs, to be easily submitted to the cluster normally within a few minutes thereby saving valuable time.

By using the computational chemistry techniques researchers are able to carry out a series of experiments on a particular molecular structure (compound or solvent) in a manner similar to that employed in a conventional laboratory facility. AFCC currently employs a scheme where 'the human is in the loop'.

In a typical scenario the researcher inspects the output results obtained for chemical structure of interest and determines the direction of future experimentation. A range of factors is taken into account. The most important factor is usually the molecular structure, which can be inspected and manipulated in three dimensions by using the GaussView GUI. By inspecting the results it is also possible to interrogate the bonds between atoms, electron transition states, spectra and photo luminescence effects when a compound is mixed in a solution.

In AFCC there is no limit to the number of experimental steps that may be deployed. To date the number of successive experiments that have been made on a single compound is between two and six. A naming and numbering system has been devised to ensure that data sets are clearly grouped together to assist in the organisation and analysis of results.

At present it has proven to be impossible to embed an intelligent search algorithm within the AFCC to direct a series of experiments. The authors have been informed that for the current type of research work being undertaken at the UoS, the intermediate results of the last experiment must be evaluated by a chemist or researcher to determine the direction of the next experiment.

A group based in Australia (Brain & Addicoat, 2010) have developed a framework that enables a genetic algorithm (GA) to direct a series of experiments using Gaussian 09. The authors have investigated the possible application of an intelligent search algorithm embedded (particle swarm optimisation – PSO) within the AFCC (Namasivayam & Günther, 2007). However it has not been possible to identify an appropriate fitness function for the reason outlined above. In addition a typical GA requires a large number of iterations and associated potential solution evaluations. As the average Gaussian 09 job run time is about fifteen hours at this time the authors do not consider it feasible to apply an intelligent search algorithm for the range of experiments currently being investigated.

A team based in Illinois (United States) have employed multi-objective genetic algorithms to optimise semi empirical chemistry models based on excited state photodynamics for materials applications (e.g., LCD and LED), pharmaceuticals and chemical manufacturing (Sastryl et al., 2007).

4.1 GaussView

GaussView provides features for studying large molecular systems, such as importing molecules from input files, modifying structural features and setting up calculations in Gaussian 09, as well as viewing and plotting the final results. In addition GaussView can also import many other structure exchange formats.

GaussView allows the user to build a 3D molecular structure by using a colour graphics user interface. A file (.gjf) is produced by GaussView that may be sent to the input of the Gaussian solver program ("GaussView 5 Reference Table Contents," 2014).

4.2 Gaussian 09

Gaussian 09 is designed to model a broad range of molecular systems under a variety of conditions. All computations performed start from the basic laws of quantum mechanics. Theoretical chemists can use Gaussian 09 to carry out basic research in established and emerging areas of interest.

Experimental chemists can use it to study molecules and reactions of potential interest, including both stable structures and compounds that are difficult or impossible to observe experi-

mentally such as short-lived intermediates and transition-state structures.

Gaussian 09 can also predict energies, molecular structures, vibrational frequencies and numerous molecular properties for systems as solids, in solution and the gas phase. In addition it can model structures in both their ground state and excited states. Furthermore research chemists can apply these fundamental results to their own investigations, to explore chemical phenomena such as reaction mechanisms and electronic transitions.

The Gaussian package is a suite of programs and the 32-bit multicore version of Gaussian 09 has been installed on all of the Cluster Compute Nodes ("Gaussian 09 Reference Manual," 2014). The package includes a number of utility programs. These programs may be deployed to convert binary data in plain readable text or into a 3D visualisation of the molecular structures being investigated.

Gaussian 09 takes as an input the (.gjf) file produced by GaussView and runs the analyser to produce a solution to the problem. A typical command line for the solver is given below.

G09.exe input_file.gjf output_file.out
Checkpoint file: output_file.chk

An output text file (.out) is created that can be that can be read and inspected by a human – however these files are very large and detailed making manual analysis difficult. In addition, a checkpoint file (.chk) is also produced that may be processed by a computer to produce further detailed information.

5. APPLICATION FRAMEWORK FOR COMPUTATIONAL CHEMISTRY (AFCC)

During initial testing jobs were manually submitted to the scheduler and the time taken to load each job was typically between five and nine minutes. However it rapidly became apparent that for a very large number of jobs it would be necessary to develop a more efficient system to complete six main tasks.

1. To prepare batches of Gaussian files (.gjf) so they could run efficiently on the cluster computer
2. To submit batches of (.gjf) files to the scheduler under program control
3. To run the G09 program on a Compute Node, also to setup the local environment and transfer I/O files
4. To archive the set of files associated with each job so that they can be indexed, dated and searched
5. To analyse and extract specific textual data from the output files (.out) under program control

6. To prepare a batch of input files so that they may be resubmitted to the scheduler program along with the previously generated (.chk) files.

A set of C Sharp (C#) programs have been developed to satisfy these goals. The system that has been developed has been given the name an Application Framework for Computational Chemistry (AFCC), refer to Figure2. To date more than six thousand separate jobs have been processed using the AFCC.

Sudholta and Buyya1 have also developed an application framework for molecular modelling (Sudholta, Baldridgea, Abramson, Enticott, Garicm Kondric, & Nguyen, 2005; Buyyal & Murshed, 2002; Buyyal, Branson, Giddy, &

Figure 2. Application Framework for Computational Chemistry (AFCC)

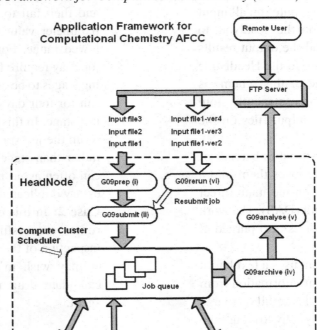

Abramson, 2003) and both systems are based upon grid computing methods.

G09prep (1): This program is used to modify the input file so that it is compatible with the compute cluster requirements by defining various input/output data paths and the size of RAM for program execution.

G09submit (2): This program is used to submit a job to the job scheduler. The parameters passed to this module determine where the input file is stored and the final location of the output file. This C# program code constructs the various UNC paths required by the system.

G09local (3): This program is used to set up environmental variables on a Compute Node and to invoke the g09 executable. The program g09.exe is installed on all Compute Nodes. All input and output files reside in a storage area associated with the cluster HeadNode. During a compute run all input files are pulled down from the HeadNode to the Compute Nodes and the output results files are pushed back up to the HeadNode filestore. An advantage of this scheme is that there is no need to permanently store any Gaussian input or output files on the Compute Nodes.

G09archive (4): This program takes batches of Gaussian job files and moves them into a central archive created on the main direct attached disk storage unit (DAS). The work space on the Head Node is also purged at the end of a batch run.

G09analyse (5): This program uses a text based search to extract relevant information from the output file. As these files are all very large this program significantly helps to reduce the time taken to extract relevant information from the large set of large files, for example, a hundred files each of size about 20MB.

G09analyse has virtually eliminated the need to manually load a large file into a text editor and search for specific information. Experience has shown that manual searching can be a very difficult and time-consuming process. Current research work is focused upon adding new features to the analysis module; refer to Section 7 for more detailed information.

At the end of a batch run all jobs are archived in an indexed central storage area and work areas on the cluster purged to release space on disk drives. An FTP server has also been installed so that remote users may download the results produced by the Gaussian program.

G09rerun (6): This module is used to prepare and resubmit a job to the cluster. The module G09rerun is a modified version of G09prep. Normally there are two reasons why it is necessary to resubmit a job to the cluster.

- **Case 1:** A job may run for a long time and then fail to complete because a parameter value is not within an allowed range. For example, a typical job may require five or more processing stages to be completed. A job may run for four days and then fail at the last stage. In this case it is possible to rerun the job starting from stage four rather than stage one. This approach can often avoid many days of unnecessary duplicated processing.

- **Case 2:** In this case a job may have run to successful completion. After inspection of the results the researcher may wish to determine how the candidate drug reacts with another agent.

In both of the above cases the new information required to restart and control the analysis process is embedded in a modified version of the (gjf) input

Table 1. Overall batch processing results

Comment	
Total number of jobs submitted	276
Total number of jobs successfully completed	247
Efficiency = job completed/ jobs submitted * 100	89%
Jobs that failed	11%
Average job time	15.6 hours
Maximum job time	>60 hours

file. In addition the (chk) checkpoint file (created during the first run) must also be sent to the G09 scheduler to enable the analysis to restart from an intermediate stage. The role of module G09rerun in the (AFCC) framework is shown in Figure 2.

It is possible to use the rerun process a number of times to investigate the properties of the candidate drug. This approach helps to facilitate incremental drug development and minimise the time required to run a series of interrelated jobs.

In the AFCC the initial path taken by a typical G09 job is shown by grey arrows whereas a job that is resubmitted follows a path described by the white arrows, refer to Figure 2.

FTP Server - this server has been installed on the cluster to enable researchers working remotely to upload jobs and to download the results obtained from use of the AFCC.

6. RESULTS

Jobs were submitted to the cluster computer and various different batch sizes have been processed. The overall efficiency of the cluster computer and the batch process being employed is given in Table 1. The data set (Series1) was analysed to produce the information shown in Figures 3 and 4. A graph showing the execution time against the job number is shown in Figure 3. By inspecting the graph it can be seen that the maximum job time is greater than 60 hours. The average time has been calculated to be 15.6 hours. Figure 4 shows a plot of job time frequency versus job time with a bin size of 2 hours.

A total of 276 jobs were submitted for processing and 89% were successfully completed. A total of 11% failed to run successfully. Further analysis of the failed jobs produced the results in Table 2.

Figure 3. Job time (hours) versus job number

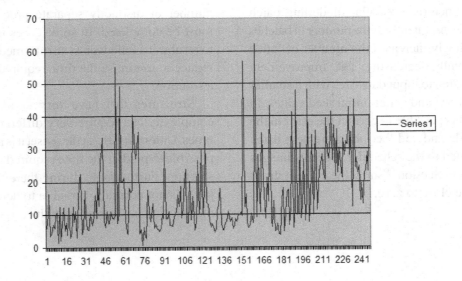

Table 2. Analysis of failed jobs

Comment	Percentage
Total number of jobs that failed to converge in a reasonable time. In these cases the run time was typically more than three days.	5%
Total number of jobs that failed because an error was detected in the input file. In these cases the run time was typically less than 4 seconds.	4%
A small number of Compute Nodes crashed during program execution.	2%
Failed jobs total	11%

Figure 4. Job time frequency versus job time (hours)

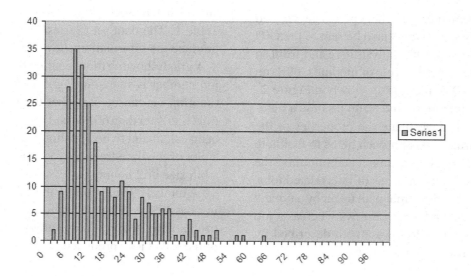

As time progresses the authors are gaining more experience of molecular modelling batch processing. Consequently as the number of batches processed slowly increases the number of failed jobs is gradually decreasing. This improvement can be attributed to input data files with a smaller number of errors and better initial seed values. In most cases it is possible to correct the error in the input data file and add the job to the next batch to be submitted to the scheduler. Recent changes documented in Section 7 show the current drop-out rate to be close to zero.

To solve a molecular modelling problem a number of distinctly separate processing steps must be completed. In some cases it is possible to resubmit a failed job at an intermediate stage to reduce to minimise the time required to produce a solution.

Structures that have very similar levels of complexity can require very different execution times. Unfortunately, at the outset it is not normally possible to predict the time required to produce a solution. Furthermore during the execution of a job it is not normally possible to determine how much longer is required to produce a good solution even when processing the last stage, for example stage four or five. As a result it is difficult to decide upon the best criteria for termination of the solver. The authors normally terminate a process if a solution is not found within five days.

6.1 Job Execution Time Variation

Further tests were carried out to determine if there was any variation in the time taken to solve a job by submitting three different jobs many times to the scheduler. The jobs selected for this test were of short duration, refer to Table 3. These test files were copied twenty times, renamed to avoid duplication and three different groups sent to the scheduler. The initial seed values were not modified for this test.

In Table 3 the standard deviation is expressed as a percentage of the average runtime. The results presented show that there is no significant variation in the time taken for the cluster to process a particular job. Any variation in the time taken to complete a job could be attributed to network congestion at the time when the output files are written to the Head Node disk store. The authors concluded that the network congestion does not adversely influence the job run time to any great extent.

6.2 Job Execution Time Using Different Computer Systems

A series of tests were carried out to compare the performance of the Compute Nodes with other machines that could have been employed. The results obtained from this test are shown in Table 4.

The relative processing times for the machines list in Table 4 is given the column R. These values are rounded and normalised after taking the clock frequency into account. By inspecting Table 4 it can be seen that computational performance of a Compute Node is much better than that of Workstations 1 or 2. It was found that the time taken to run a job is roughly proportional to the number of CPU cores deployed. The results were not markedly influenced by the amount of RAM allocated for the job.

Table 3. Run time repeatability

Test Name	Average Run Time hours	Number of runs	Standard Deviation %	Output File Size MByte approx.
Test01	0.67	20	<0.1	20
Test02	2.58	20	<0.1	20
Test03	3.00	20	<0.1	20

Table 4. A Comparison of run times for different computers

Machine	CPU	CPUs	Cores	Clock GHz	Ram GB	R
Compute Node	Dual core Xeon	2	4	2.66	8	1
Workstation1	Dual core	1	2	2.66	4	2
Workstation2	Single core	1	1	1.0	1	4

Further work has also been carried out by the authors to evaluate the use of Virtual Machines (VMs) in High Performance Clusters (Warrender, Tindle, Nelson, 2013). In certain circumstances, VMs can result in increased performance of a cluster.

6.3 Job Execution Time using Various RAM Sizes

Further tests were carried out on a Compute Node to determine how the number of CPU cores and the amount of RAM allocated for job execution influenced the run time. The authors carried out experiments to determine the parameter setting that would maximise the processing efficiency.

6.3.1 A Typical Long Job (>20 hours)

Figure 5 again shows how the job run time varies as the amount of allocated RAM is varied. In this case the run time was greater than 20 hours. The results show that the best performance is obtained when the amount of RAM is set to 1400MByte. In this state the total amount of RAM in use is about 550MB for operating systems plus 1400MB for Gaussian 09, which is just less than the recommended value of 2GB for a 32-bit system.

6.3.2 Varying the number of CPU Cores

Figure 6 show the job execution time in hours versus the number of CPU cores selected to execute the job in a Compute Node. The benefit of employing a multi-core processor with support for symmetric multiprocessing for molecular modelling is clearly demonstrated by this data.

7. ITERATIVE PROCESSING

In the last eighteen months various improvements have been made which will be described in this section. In the current arrangement all jobs are initially processed using a low resolution solver running on a desktop PC. The advantage of this approach is that a good initial seeds are rapidly produced that may be sent to the input of the AFCC. In addition, all jobs with incorrect structures are removed from the batch and therefore only valid structures are sent to the AFCC for processing. In a typical analysis there could be between three and five stages of processing to produce the final result.

As described the offline process (proc1) used to produce an initial seed for the AFCC (out1 become in2). The first process in the AFCC (proc2) produces the output data (out2). At this

Figure 5. Run time (hours) versus Ram size (MByte)

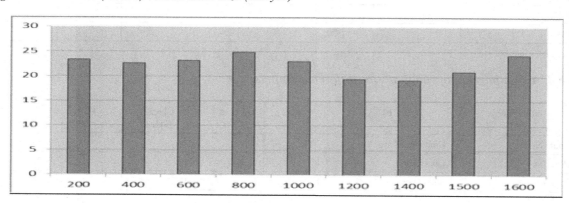

Figure 6. Job execution time (Hours) versus number of CPU cores

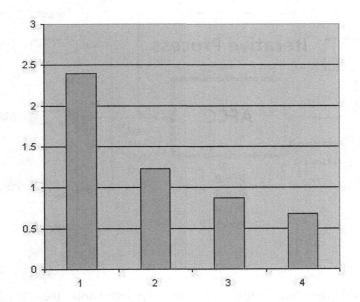

stage the chemist inspects the output data and decides upon further processing with the aim of producing, for example, a new drug or a sensory molecule to indicate the presence of a pathogen or disease, or even to detect an illegal drug in a sample. The decision relating to the direction of the next path to follow is based upon numerical analysis of the output data. For example, further processes could involve mixing the candidate drug or molecular structure with a solvent and/or other molecules, such as drug targets. For molecules designed for sensing applications computational tasks monitoring colour, fluorescence or other spectroscopic changes can then be set in motion.

At present the authors are investigating how to implement the various iterative processing stages automatically within the AFCC without the need for human intervention either by a chemist of or system manager. This task will probably require the creation of a new dedicated scripting language. To complete this development the authors are working towards identifying all of the various numerical tests, experimental processes and possible pathways involved in creating a new drug candidate. Figure 7 illustrates the AFCC iterative process under development in a simplified form.

In the recent past the bottleneck associated with computational chemistry at the University of Sunderland was mostly associated with job processing. The AFCC has successfully addressed this problem. However, when a good sized batch job is submitted to the AFCC a large amount of numerical data is produced, for example, one thousand jobs typically produces 20 Giga Byte of output data for analysis. For this reason the authors are now primarily focusing their efforts upon the creation of new code to help automate output data analysis.

In order to facilitate the development of an automated system, the authors have focused their attention upon the G09rerun program, see Figure 2 (vi). G09rerun is similar to the G09prep program but utilises the presence of a checkpoint file (.chk) file produced from a single run. The checkpoint file contains useful information that may be used in subsequent calculations – for example the geometry of the molecule. For the re-run to be used the input file (.gjf) supplied must contain both a section that describes the corresponding check-

Figure 7. AFCC iterative processes

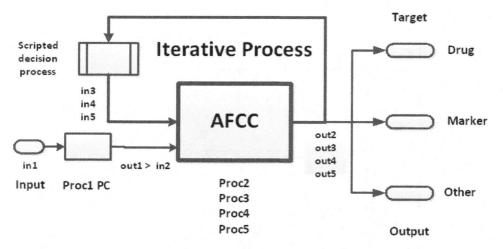

point file (.chk) and request in the route section of a Gaussian job the parameters it wishes to use from the checkpoint file.

The authors found that by carrying out an offline low level minimisation that the following benefits accrued.

1. Generating an initial geometry produced a good seed which reduced the time required to find a high level solution on the cluster.
2. The good initial seed generally eliminated the jobs that failed to converge on the cluster.
3. Jobs that were incorrectly defined were detected and corrected prior to be being submitted to the cluster.

This largely addresses the problems highlighted above in Table 2. In the current scheme the number of failed jobs is normally zero which substantially improves the efficiency of the cluster.

In addition, by selecting a different solver with increasingly higher levels of accuracy during each stage of processing it is possible to reduce the overall processing time.

To test the revised AFCC scheme the authors processed three identical batches using different methods. In batches one to three solvers with increasing levels of accuracy were employed. The

times required to solve these batches is shown in Figure 8.

- Batch 1 was not subjected to any initial pre-processing.
- Batch 2 was subjected to a medium level of pre-processing.
- Batch 3 was subjected to a medium-high level of pre-processing.

Initially optimisation and frequency calculations were carried out on each batch using the cluster with the basis set uhf/6-31(d). As can be seen from Figure 8 Batch 1 required the longest processing time whereas Batch 3 the shortest.

It should be noted that Batch 1 time represents the time to process the successful 68 jobs. In addition, a total of 25 plus a further 16 jobs required to be resubmitted due to problems associated with molecular symmetry within this set of modules.

8. CONCLUSION

Prior to the use of AFCC on the cluster computer a single much less powerful machine was employed to process molecular modelling jobs. In all cases jobs were manually submitted for processing with-

Figure 8. Batch processing times in minutes

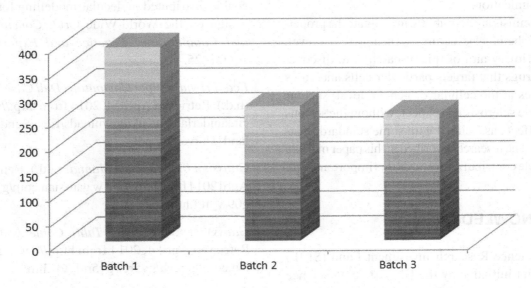

Overall time consumed by the cluster for each batch

out using a task scheduler. The typical run time for a single job was between one and two weeks.

By using the cluster computer it is now possible to produce overnight (average run time 15.6 hours) results that would have previously required a run time of more than forty weeks or more.

The AFCC framework developed by the authors has been proven to be reliable providing support for the following operations within a molecular modelling job: prepare, submit, run, archive, analyse and iterative processes (rerun).

The massive computational speedup of the cluster computer (USCC) has now been realised via the AFCC enabling researchers to significantly reduce the cycle time required to design, model and evaluate molecular structures for drug development.

Symmetric multiprocessing SMP methods have been successfully applied using a cluster computer in the domain of Computational Chemistry to efficiently and successfully solve a large number of molecular modelling problems.

The use of the AFCC framework has proved to be successful and researchers are now able to prepare and schedule large numbers of molecular modelling jobs for the cluster within a short period of time (a few minutes). The total time required to process a large batch, take for example a batch of one thousand jobs will be typically around fifteen days. A batch of this size produces a large amount of output data in the form of plaintext as well as typically one thousand check files (.chk) with a total size of the order 20GByte. In the future it is planned that a large number of batches of this size will be submitted for processing.

The authors are currently working to develop and improve the performance of the G09 analysis and G09rerun modules. The primary goal in this respect is to eliminate the need for a chemist to manually inspect output data and decide upon the next stage of processing. Hopefully the new automated approach described in section 7 and shown in Figure 7 will thereby help to reduce the total analysis time required to produce new candidate drugs.

The authors argue that the AFCC framework may be adapted and applied successfully particularly in other domains where the number of jobs is relatively large (>100) and the analysis time is greater than the time associated with network communication.

Chemists are now able to investigate the properties of chemical structures at the molecular level. The primary aim of this research is to discover new drugs that targets particular cells and cures diseases at the cellular or genetic level, such as multiple sclerosis and cancer, without the serious side effects associated with some standard treatments. The research described in this paper makes a valuable contribution towards this important goal.

ACKNOWLEDGMENT

The Science Research Investment Fund (SRIF) is a joint initiative by the UK Office of Science and Technology (OST) and the Department for Education and Skills (DfES). The purpose of SRIF is to contribute to higher education institutions' (HEIs) long-term sustainable research strategies and address past under-investment in research infrastructure. The University of Sunderland Cluster Computer was purchased with the support of the SRIF III fund – see Appendix 1.

REFERENCES

Brain, Z., & Addicoat, M. (2010). Using meta-genetic algorithms to tune parameters of genetic algorithms to find lowest energy molecular conformers. In *Proceedings of the Alife XII Conference* (pp. 378-385). Odense, Denmark: The MIT Press.

Buyya1, R., & Murshed, M. (2002) GridSim: A toolkit for the modeling and simulation of distributed resource management and scheduling for Grid computing. *Concurrency and Computation: Practice and Experience, 14*(13-15), 1175–1220.

Buyya1, R., Branson, K., Giddy, J., & Abramson, D. (2003). The virtual laboratory: A toolset to enable distributed molecular modelling for drug design on the World-Wide Grid. *Concurrency and Computation: Practice and Experience, 15*(1)1–25.

Eco_Friendly Super Computing, Dell Case Study. (n.d.). Retrieved April, 4, 2014 from http://www.cit.sunderland.ac.uk/downloads/files/Sunderland_University.pdf

Gaussian 09 Reference Manual (n.d.). Retrieved April 2014 from http://www.gaussian.com/g_tech/g09w_ref.htm

GaussView 5 Reference Table Contents. (n.d.). Retrieved April 4, 2014 from http://www.gaussian.com/g_tech/gv5ref/gv5ref_toc.htm

Ginty, K., Tindle, J., & Tindle, S. J. (2009). Cluster systems – An open-access design solution. In *Proceedings of International Conference on Systems Engineering (ICSE).* Coventry University.

Microsoft Compute Cluster Pack. (n.d.). Retrieved April 4, 2014 from http://msdn.microsoft.com/en-us/library/cc136762%28v=vs.85%29.aspx

Namasivayam, V., & Günther, R. (2007). A Fast Flexible Molecular Docking Program Based on Swarm Intelligence. *Journalism, 70*(6), 475–484. Chemical Biology and Drug Design PMID:17986206

Sastry1, K., Johnson, D. D., Thompson, A. L., Goldberg, D. E., Martinez, T. J., Leiding, J., & Owens, J. (2007). Optimization of Semiempirical Quantum Chemistry Methods via Multiobjective Genetic Algorithms: Accurate Photodynamics for Larger Molecules and Longer Time Scales. *Materials and Manufacturing Processes, 22*(5), 553–561.

Sudholta, W., Baldridgea, K. K., Abramson, D., Enticott, C., Garic, S., Kondric, C., & Nguyen, D. (2005). Application of grid computing to parameter sweeps and optimizations in molecular modelling. *Future Generation Computer Systems*, *21*(1), 27–35. doi:10.1016/j.future.2004.09.010

Tindle, J., Ginty, K., & Tindle, S. J. (2009) Rendering 3D Computer Graphics on a Parallel Computer. In *Proceedings of International Conference on Systems Engineering (ICSE)*. Coventry University.

Tindle, J., Gray, M., Warrender, R. L., Ginty, K., & Dawson, P. K. D. (2012). Application Framework for Computational Chemistry (AFCC) Applied to New Drug Discovery. *International Journal of Grid and High Performance Computing*, *4*(2), 46–62. doi:10.4018/jghpc.2012040104

Vinter, J. G., Davis, A., & Saunders, M. R. (1987). Strategic approaches to drug design. An integrated software framework for molecular modelling. *Journal of Computer-Aided Molecular Design*, *1*(1), 31–51. doi:10.1007/BF01680556 PMID:3505586

Warrender, R. L., Tindle, J., & Nelson, D. (2013). Job Scheduling in a High Performance Computing Environment. In *Proceedings of International Conference on High Performance Computing & Simulation (HPCS2013)*. Helsinki, Finland: HPCS.

Warrender, R. L., Tindle, J., & Nelson, D. (2013). Evaluating The Use of Virtual Machines in High Performance Clusters. *International Journal of Advanced Computer Technology*, *2*(5), 25–30.

What is Microsoft's High Performance Computing HPC Server?. (n.d.). Retrieved April 4, 2014 from http://www.microsoft.com/hpc/en/us/product/cluster-computing.aspx

APPENDIX: UOS CLUSTER COMPUTER OUTLINE SPECIFICATION

UoS Cluster Computer Head and Compute Nodes

- Number of compute nodes: 40
- Head nodes (Linux/Windows): 2
- Compute nodes based upon Dell Server type 2950
- Head node boots Win2008 Server HPC version (64bit)
- Central processor unit Xeon 5100 64bit, 2.66GHz,
- Number of CPU processor per node: 2
- Number of CPU cores per node: 4
- Total number of compute cores in the cluster: 160
- RAM per node: 8Gbyte, per CPU core: 2Gbyte
- Network bandwidth Gigabit Ethernet 1Gbps
- Networks - Data, IPC and IPMI

Main Switch Unit

- Main switch type Cisco 6509
- Number of line cards: 3
- Line card type 48 port 10/100/1000Mbps
- Total number of 1Gbps ports: 144

Central Data Storage

- Central storage 15 * 500Gbyte disk, 8 Linux and 7 Windows
- Total central storage on Dell MD1000 DAS: 7.5Tbyte
- Bandwidth 2 * 12Gbps

Operating Systems

- All compute nodes support dual boot
- Scali Manage provides support for managing the cluster, monitoring performance and control of services
- Control via Linux Parallel Shell or Windows Grid Administrator

Chapter 7
Research on Letter and Word Frequency and Mathematical Modeling of Frequency Distributions in the Modern Bulgarian Language

Tihomir Trifonov
St. Cyril and St. Methodius University of Veliko Tarnovo, Bulgaria

Tsvetanka Georgieva-Trifonova
St. Cyril and St. Methodius University of Veliko Tarnovo, Bulgaria

ABSTRACT

The purpose of this chapter is to present current research on the modern Bulgarian language. It is one of the oldest European languages. An information system for the management of the electronic archive with texts in Bulgarian language is described. It provides the possibility for processing the collected text information. The detailed and comprehensive researches on the letter and the word frequency in the modern Bulgarian language from varied sources (fiction, scientific and popular science literature, press, legal texts, government bulletins, etc.) are performed, and the obtained results are represented. The index of coincidence of the Bulgarian language as a whole and for the individual sources is computed. The results can be utilized by different specialists – computer scientists, linguists, cryptanalysts, and others. Furthermore, with mathematical modeling, the authors found the letter and word frequency distributions and their models and they estimated their standard deviations by documents.

INTRODUCTION

The frequencies of the letters in the text have often been studied for use in the cryptography (Lee, 1999; Lewand, 2000; Tilborg, 2000). Although the modern ciphers work on bits instead on letters, the values of the frequencies for a given language are still an important tool for the cryptanalysts (Computer news, 1999; Quaresma, 2008). More recent analyses show that the letter frequency and the word frequency are distinguishable by the

DOI: 10.4018/978-1-4666-6252-0.ch007

author and by the subject of the examined text. The frequencies of the letters, the bigrams, the trigrams, the words, the lengths of the words and the sentences can be calculated for the particular authors and utilized for confirmation or disproof of the authorship of texts, even for authors whose styles are not so divergent.

The results from researches on the frequencies of the letters and the words in the text are also performed for solving the problems related to keyboard layouts (Anson et al., 2001; Burrell, 2009; Piepgrass, 2006; Skordev, 2007; Stefanov & Birdanova, 1997; Functional Multilingual Extensions to European Keyboard Layouts, 2008).

The accurate relative frequencies of the letters can be gleaned by analyzing a large amount of representative text. The availabilities of modern technologies and tools for computer calculation, as well as for collection and storage of large amount of text corpora, facilitate the accomplishment of such computations. The applications for databases related to the domain of text mining (Barsegyan, Kupriyanov, Stepanenko, & Holod, 2008; Berry, 2003; Plantevit, Charnois, Klema, Rigotti, & Cremilleux, 2009; Xue & Zhou, 2009) acquire an increasing interest. In these types of applications the frequencies of the words occurring in the texts have significant importance.

The present research is motivated by the lack of detailed and comprehensive results from computations of the frequencies of the letters and the words in the Bulgarian language. In this paper, a realized information system for maintaining and processing texts in Bulgarian language is represented. The results from the accomplished researches on the frequencies of the letters and the words in the modern Bulgarian language are given from various sources (fiction, scientific and popular scientific literature, newspapers, legal texts, governmental bulletins and other genres). The relative frequencies of the letters, the bigrams, the trigrams, the words, the lengths of the words, the first and the last letters of the words, the words with equal lengths, the average length of the words

are computed, as well as the index of coincidence. Moreover, we found the frequency distributions of the length of the distinct words, the length of the words, the letters, the words, the first and the last letters of words, the bigrams, the trigrams and we estimated their standard deviations by documents.

The rest of the paper is organized as follows. Section 2 contains historical notes for the Bulgarian alphabet and a survey of the existing researches on the frequencies of the letters and the words in the Bulgarian language. In Section 3, a realized information system for maintaining an electronic archive with texts in Bulgarian language is described. In Section 4, the obtained results for the frequencies of the letters and the words in the modern Bulgarian language are represented. In Section 5, the letter and word frequency distributions in the modern Bulgarian language are examined. The results from the computed standard deviations of the letter and word frequencies are summarized in Section 6. The additional results included in Section 7 are evaluating the entropy of the text and the average length of the letter representations in Morse code.

RESEARCHES ON THE FREQUENCIES OF THE LETTERS AND THE WORDS IN THE BULGARIAN LANGUAGE

The frequency of the occurring the letters, the bigrams, the trigrams, the first and the last letters of the words, the average length of the words, the frequencies of the words reflect the way by which the people use their own language and determine unique characteristics of this language.

Detailed and comprehensive researches on the frequencies of the letters and the words in the English language are already published. The relative frequencies of the letters in the English alphabet are represented in (Lewand, 2000). The first twelve most frequent letters in the English alphabet comprise about 80% of the total used letters. LetterFrequency.org (LetterFrequency, 2010) provides detailed information on frequencies of the letters and the words in the English language obtained from various sources (press reporting, religious texts, scientific texts and general fiction). The represented results show differences especially for the general fiction with the position of the letters 'h' and 'i'. Besides the frequencies of the letters in the English language, in (Lee, 1999) the frequencies of the space and others non-alphabetic characters such as digits, punctuation, etc., are computed.

As has been mentioned before, this paper aims to provide detailed and extensive researches on the frequencies of the letters and the words in the modern Bulgarian language. In the present section, a historical information is included, about the origin and the development of the Bulgarian alphabet, as well as a survey of the calculations for the frequencies of the letters and the words in the Bulgarian language performed until now.

Origin and Development of the Bulgarian Language

The modern Bulgarian alphabet (Curta, 2006; Grudev, 1999; Mirchev, 1963) is a modernized version of the Cyrillic alphabet, developed in the 9th century A.D. The basis of the early Cyrillic is founded on the Glagolhic alphabet from the 9th century in which some letters are borrowed from the Greek alphabet. The Saints brothers Cyril and Methodius, monks from Thessalonica, are the creators of the Glagolhic alphabet. This alphabet has significant importance not only for the Slavonic nations, but for entire Europe, because by its usage the dissemination of the Christian culture becomes comprehensible for these nations languages (Paul, 1985). Non fortuitously the device on the highest Bulgarian award after the creation of the Third Bulgarian state "St. St. Equal to the Apostles Cyril and Methodius" is "Light from the East – Ex Oriente Lux". The early Cyrillic is developed from Saint Clement from Ohrid, a follower of the Saint Cyril and Saint Methodius, as well as others their followers which are worked at Preslav school in the north-eastern Bulgaria.

The modern languages based on the Cyrillic (Encyclopedia Britannica, 2009), use alphabet, obtained by removing some superfluous letters. The Bulgarian alphabet consists of 30 letters, the Russian has 32 letters (33, with inclusion of the soft sign), the Serbian has 30 letters, the Ukrainian – 32 (33). The modern Cyrillic is adapted for many non-Slavonic languages, in some cases with addition of the special letters. The languages utilizing Cyrillic are six Slavonic languages – Bulgarian, Russian, Ukrainian, Belarusian, Serbian, Macedonian; one Persian language – Tadjik; three Turkic languages – Kazakh, Uzbek, Kyrgyz; one Altaic language – Mongolian.

Today the nations writing by using Cyrillic alphabet are more than 60 nations living in seven countries – Bulgaria, Macedonia, Russia, Ukraine, Belarus, Serbia and Mongolia, composing about 10% from the population on the Earth. Together with the Latin and the Arabian alphabets, the Cyrillic is one of the three most used alphabets, and with the Latin alphabet – one of two alphabets of the world, on whose basis new nations build their scripts.

With the membership of Bulgaria to the European Union on 1 January 2007, Cyrillic alphabet became the third official alphabet of the European Union, along with Latin and Greek.

Frequencies of the Letters and the Words in the Bulgarian Language

Penkov, Obretenov, Sendov, Kirpikova, & Joukanov (1962) provide information about the arrangement of the Bulgarian letters by descending order of their frequencies in a fragment of the novel „Under the yoke". Table 1 shows the letters frequency obtained from the published data in (Penkov et al., 1962). The values are done in percentages. The authors are examined a frag-

Table 1. Frequencies (in %) of the letters in a fragment from the novel "Under the yoke" (Penkov et al., 1962)

а	12.99	е	9.22	к	3.76	п	3.03	ф	0.12	щ	0.61
б	1.82	ж	0.61	л	3.03	р	4.61	х	0.85	ъ + ь	1.94
в	4.25	з	2.18	м	2.43	с	4.49	ц	0.49		
г	1.70	и	8.37	н	6.43	т	7.16	ч	1.33	ю	0.12
д	3.64	й	0.73	о	9.22	у	1.70	ш	1.09	я	2.06

ment containing 131050 letters and the spaces between words.

In (Skordev, 2007) the electronic issue of the novel „Under the yoke" is used (Vazov, 1999) and the frequencies of the letters in the entire novel are found. The obtained results are shown in Table 2.

In the rubric "The frequency of the letters in texts in Bulgarian and English language" of the paper (Stefanov & Birdanova, 1997) the results in percentage are given from examinations of the authors on the frequencies of the letters in some Bulgarian texts (Table 3).

The problems related to the usage of the Cyrillic alphabet in the electronic communication are discussed in (Functional Multilingual Extensions to European Keyboard Layouts, 2008). The possibilities for improving the keyboard layout and proposing a new standard for keyboard layout are considered. The results from the study of the ANABELA (Association for the National Bulgarian Electronic Archive) are obtained on two text corpora – the first is from the 50 million running words general corpus of the Bulgarian language, the second is from a 1 million running words corpus of texts from the register of state administration. Table 4 and Table 5 show the first 20 letters according to their frequencies in both corpora. Table 6 contains the first 20 most frequent occurring bigrams.

On (BulTreeBank Group, 2010) Bulgarian texts are available. They are collected from Internet and contain more than 72000000 running words, from which 15% of the texts belong to the fiction, 78% come from newspapers and about 7% are

Table 2. Frequencies (in %) of the letters in the entire novel "Under the yoke" (Skordev, 2007)

а	12.52	е	9.09	к	3.76	п	2.80	ф	0.17	щ	0.64
б	1.81	ж	0.73	л	3.15	р	4.50	х	0.91	ъ	1.88
в	4.38	з	2.28	м	2.51	с	4.60	ц	0.52	ь	0.01
г	1.84	и	8.04	н	6.15	т	7.10	ч	1.53	ю	0.13
д	3.63	й	0.85	о	9.21	у	1.77	ш	1.25	я	2.20

Table 3. Frequencies (in %) of the letters in Bulgarian texts (Stefanov & Birdanova, 1997)

а	11.60	е	9.21	к	2.99	п	3.05	ф	0.37	щ	0.43
б	1.65	ж	0.77	л	3.57	р	5.42	х	0.67	ъ	1.71
в	4.71	з	2.36	м	2.68	с	5.02	ц	0.75	ь	0.01
г	1.19	и	8.82	н	8.09	т	7.38	ч	1.44	ю	0.11
д	3.11	й	0.32	о	8.75	у	1.54	ш	0.42	я	1.86

Table 4. The letters, ordered by their frequencies in the corpus from 50 million words (Functional Multilingual Extensions to European Keyboard Layouts, 2008)

а	и	е	о	т	н	р	с	в	д	к	л	п	м	з	я	ъ	б	г	у

Table 5. The letters, ordered by their frequencies in the corpus from 1 million words (Functional Multilingual Extensions to European Keyboard Layouts, 2008)

а	е	о	и	т	н	р	с	в	д	л	п	к	м	з	я	ъ	г	б	у

Table 6. Bigrams, ordered by their frequencies (Functional Multilingual Extensions to European Keyboard Layouts, 2008)

на	та	то	ни	ат	ст	ра	те	ва	ен
ит	от	пр	ре	но	ан	за	по	да	не

form legal texts, government bulletins and other genres. Besides, a list with the first 100000 most frequent words in the archive are accessible, 27 from which are shown on Table 7.

A demo version of the system developed by Ognyan Chernokozhev and Atanas Kiryakov morphological analyzer is accessible. The system recognizes the word forms of more than 110000 Bulgarian lexemes and assigns to them the appropriate morphosyntactic characteristics.

The XML-based software system CLaRK for management, storage and extraction of the text documents is proposed in (Simov et al., 2001). The main purpose of this system is to support the linguists in their work during building the text corpora.

The performed survey indicates the necessity of the detailed and comprehensive researches on the frequencies of the letters and the words in the Bulgarian language, what already exist for the English and other languages. In this paper, we have made deepening and expanding the research presented in (Trifonov & Georgieva, 2012). The frequency distributions of the length of the distinct words, the length of the words, the letters, the words, the first and the last letters of words, the bigrams, the trigrams are found, as well as their standard deviations by documents are estimated.

Table 7. Words, ordered by their frequencies (BulTreeBank Group, 2010)

на	и	в	да	се	за	от	с	не	че	ще	си	са	по	това
като	а	но	до	които	му	той	към	след	през	го				
който	има	може	само	при	беше	или	още	те	бе	ако				
трябва	много	няма	което	бъде	ли	която	България	един						

115

INFORMATION SYSTEM FOR MAINTAINING AND PROCESSING THE TEXTS OF BULGARIAN LANGUAGE

In the present section, the architecture of the developed client/server system is described, as well as the services included in its realization. The structure of the created database, which stores the needed information, is represented. A client application ADP (*access data project*) (Pearson, 2004), whose purpose is to provide possibilities for insertion, edition and searching the data, is proposed.

Architecture of the System

The architecture of the developed client/server system is based on the two-layer information model (Figure1).

The layer for data processing is realized by using the database management system. For the present system we use Microsoft SQL Server, which allows efficient storage of large databases and provides functionality for accessing the data (Bieniek et al., 2006; Garcia-Molina, Ullman, & Widom, 2002; Gruber, 2001; Houlette, 2001; Kroenke, 2003; Microsoft Corporation, 2001; Microsoft Corporation, 2008).

The client part consists of an ADP application, providing a convenient interface for insertion, updating and searching the data.

Database on SQL Server for Data Storage

The database is realized by means of the database management system Microsoft SQL Server. The relevant relational tables are shown in Figure 2.

The structure of the database is defined to provide the best efficiency of the most frequently used operations – insertion, updating, searching the data.

The LetterWordFreqDB database serves for storage and processing the data for the text documents. Information on the topic of the document, the year of publishing, the category (genre), the author(s), the text contained in the document, the location of the file with the document is maintained. For each document the possibility for storage the computed frequencies of the letters and the words in it, is provided.

The basic functions of the database include:

- Addition of a new document in the database;
- Editing of the data in the documents;
- Deletion of documents from the database;

Figure 1. Architecture of the system

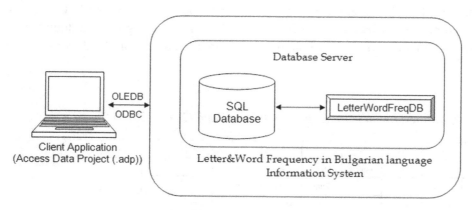

Figure 2. Relational model of the database LetterWordFreqDB

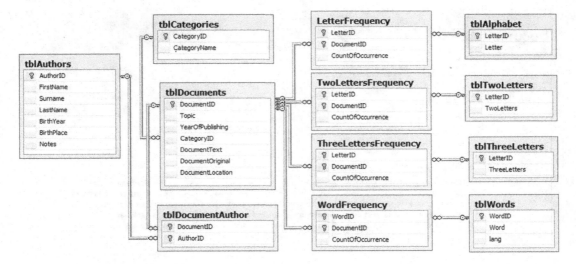

- Browsing the data in the documents;
- Searching the documents by applying different criteria;
- Computing the frequencies of the letters, the bigrams, the trigrams, the words in one or more documents;
- Encrypting and decrypting the text in a chosen document with the Vigenere cipher (Tilborg, 2000).

The LetterWordFreqDB database of SQL Server contains the created views for extracting the data from several related tables, as well as the stored procedures for computing the frequencies of the letters and the words in the documents; obtaining the information about the documents published in a fixed year or period; the documents from a chosen category; the documents from a given author. The stored procedures provide a better performance of the client/server system because they decrease the exchange of data between the client and the server. Besides the stored procedures can accept parameters and therefore they can be executed from multiple client applications by applying different input data.

Client Application ADP for Insertion and Searching of the Data

Microsoft Access allows the establishment of a connection between the current database and tables from other databases of Microsoft SQL Server and other data sources. ADP is connected with a database of SQL Server and provides an access to the objects created in that database (such as tables, views, stored procedures, triggers, etc.). The data are stored in the database of SQL Server. ADP does not contain any data and tables, but it can be used for easy creation of forms, reports, or macros. As a result of that, the end user has the opportunity for insertion, editing, and deletion of the data by means of a comfortable interface.

Forms for insertion and updating the data are realized. Their purpose is to facilitate actualization of the information. The form for insertion of the data about the documents and computing the frequencies of the letters and the words in them is shown in Figure 3.

Besides this, the application allows the execution of different queries, which perform finding the specific information, corresponding to the given

Figure 3. Form for insertion of the data for text documents

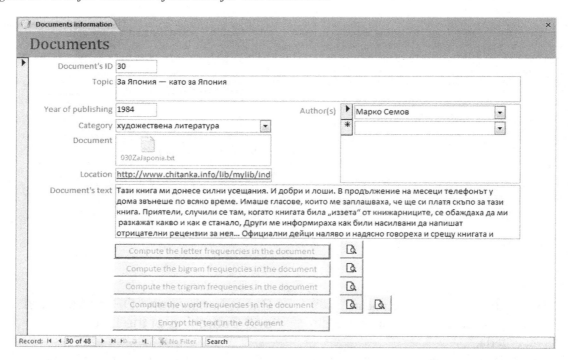

searching criteria. Each user can search by filling in text boxes and/or list boxes which correspond to the listed characteristics of the documents stored in the database. The results from each query are presented in a format convenient for the end user. The forms and the reports are implemented with the record sources – views and stored procedures designed for:

- Extracting the data about documents from a chosen category and/or year (or period) of publishing;
- Extracting the data about documents from a chosen author and/or year (or period) of publishing;
- Computing the frequencies of the letters from the Bulgarian alphabet in a given document or chosen documents (by category, author, and/or year (or period) of publishing);

- Computing the frequencies of the bigrams from the Bulgarian alphabet in a given document or chosen documents;
- Computing the frequencies of the trigrams from the Bulgarian alphabet in a given document or chosen documents;
- Computing the frequencies of pairs of identical letters from the Bulgarian alphabet in the documents;
- Computing the frequencies of the words from the Bulgarian alphabet in a given document or chosen documents;
- Computing the frequencies of the words with the same lengths;
- Computing the frequency of the serial letter from the beginning or from the end of the words in the documents;
- Computing the frequencies of the lengths of the words in the documents;
- Computing the frequencies of the letters immediately following the letter 'a';

- Computing the frequencies of the letters immediately preceding the letter 'a';
- Extracting the data about percentage proportion of the words in Cyrillic alphabet and Latin alphabet in the documents;
- Extracting the data about percentage proportion of the words from the different categories of the documents;
- Encrypting the text in a chosen document with the Vigenere cipher (Figure 4);
- Decrypting the text with the Vigenere cipher (Figure 5).

RELATIVE FREQUENCIES OF THE LETTERS AND THE WORDS IN THE MODERN BULGARIAN LANGUAGE

In this section, detailed and comprehensive results from the usage of the realized information system for computing the frequencies of the letters and the words in the collected documents are represented. The calculations are performed on the Bulgarian

texts containing more than 1090497 running words, for which 37.14% of the words are found in the texts that belong to fiction, 30.15% come from scientific and popular scientific literature, 13.08% are from newspapers and about 19.63% are from legal texts, government bulletins and other genres.

Relative Frequencies of the Letters, Bigrams, Trigrams in the Modern Bulgarian Language

The relative frequencies of the letters in the Bulgarian language for all documents are shown on Table 8, where the letters are arranged in alphabetical order.

Figure 6 also illustrates the relative frequencies of the letters in the Bulgarian language for all documents, but the letters are arranged according to their frequency in the texts.

From the obtained results it becomes clear that like the English alphabet the first twelve most frequent letters in the Bulgarian alphabet comprise about 80% of the total used letters.

Figure 4. Encrypting the text in a chosen document with the Vigenere cipher

119

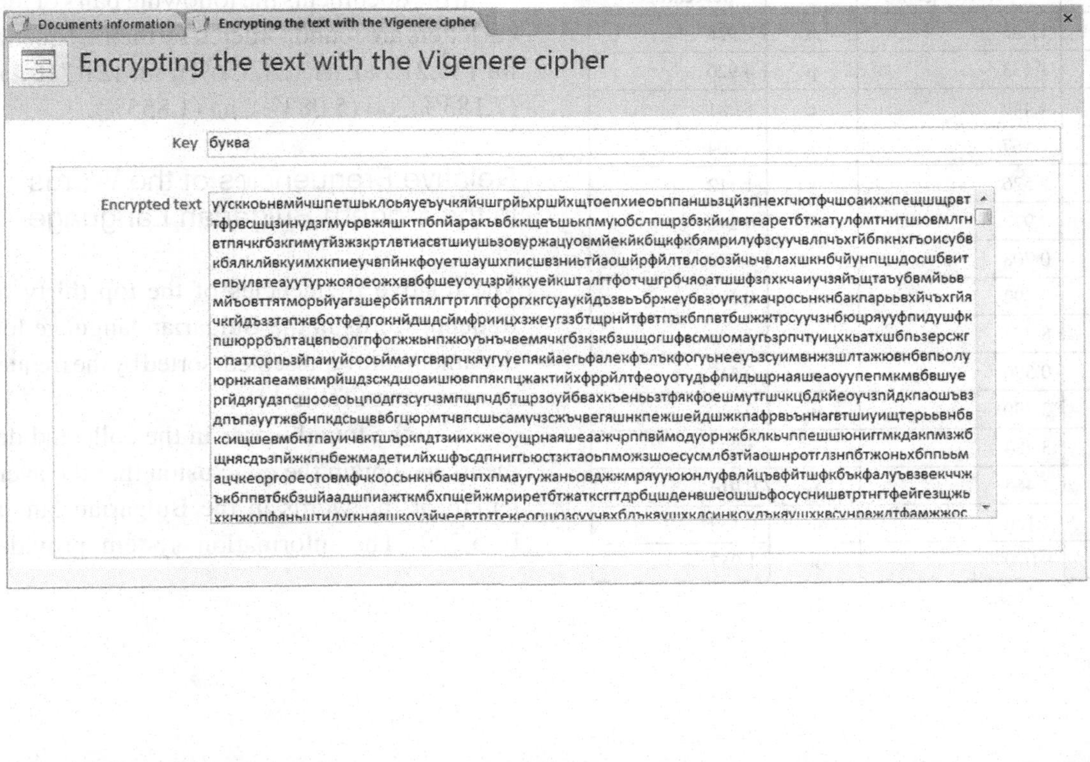

Figure 5. Decrypting the text with the Vigenere cipher

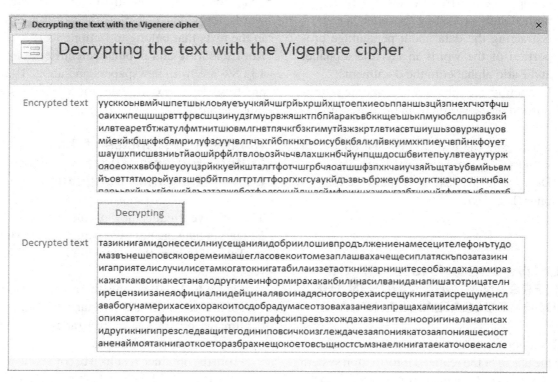

Table 8. Relative frequencies of the letters in the texts

Letter	Frequency (in percentages)	Letter	Frequency (in percentages)
а	12.323	п	2.928
б	1.533	р	4.920
в	4.449	с	5.081
г	1.567	т	7.604
д	3.526	у	1.312
е	8.972	ф	0.210
ж	0.708	х	0.655
з	2.292	ц	0.595
и	8.875	ч	1.338
й	0.590	ш	0.615
к	3.390	щ	0.612
л	3.284	ъ	1.832
м	2.465	ь	0.014
н	7.136	ю	0.138
о	9.079	я	1.957

The relative frequencies of the top thirty most frequent bigrams and trigrams in the Bulgarian language for all documents are presented in Table 9 and Table 10.

In the documents the following pairs of identical letters are found, ordered by their frequencies: нн (36.212%), тт (24.556%), ии (21.718%), ее (7.183%), оо (5.083%), дд (1.855%).

Relative Frequencies of the Words in the Modern Bulgarian Language

The relative frequencies of the top thirty most frequent words in the Bulgarian language for all documents are represented, sorted by the frequency of occurring (Table 11).

From the found words in the collected documents we obtain the conclusion that the average length of the words in the Bulgarian language is 5.209. The information system provides a

Figure 6. Relative frequencies of the letters in the texts, sorted by their frequencies in descending order

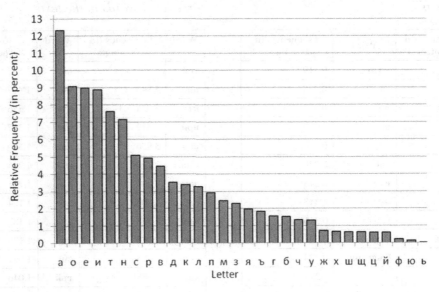

possibility for computing the frequencies of the words with the same lengths. The most frequent two letter words, three letter words and four letter words and their relative frequencies are shown in Table 12, Table 13 and Table 14.

The realized information system allows computing the frequency of the serial letter from the beginning or from the end of the words in the documents. Table 15 and Table 16 contain the

Table 9. Relative frequencies of the most frequent bigrams in the texts

Bigram	Frequency (in percentages)	Bigram	Frequency (in percentages)
на	2.990	от	1.196
то	2.015	за	1.192
та	1.830	ия	1.166
ни	1.705	не	1.149
ст	1.649	по	1.134
ат	1.612	да	1.083
ра	1.482	ко	1.077
ва	1.469	ов	0.970
те	1.453	ка	0.955
ен	1.336	ри	0.894
но	1.269	ед	0.886
ка	1.267	ет	0.883
пр	1.251	ос	0.878
от	1.232	ти	0.873
по	1.200	ли	0.760

Table 10. Relative frequencies of the most frequent trigrams in the texts

Trigram	Frequency (in percentages)	Trigram	Frequency (in percentages)
ите	1.091	ава	0.364
ата	0.984	при	0.359
пре	0.611	ане	0.352
ето	0.548	ани	0.348
ени	0.546	раз	0.344
ост	0.492	тел	0.341
ото	0.464	ият	0.327
ред	0.425	ния	0.326
кат	0.395	ски	0.317
ств	0.393	ато	0.317
про	0.392	нит	0.313
нат	0.381	ван	0.303
ста	0.372	ран	0.299
ние	0.370	ест	0.269
ова	0.366	ава	0.364

Table 11. Relative frequencies of the most frequent words in the texts

Word	Frequency (in percentages)	Word	Frequency (in percentages)
на	5.190	като	0.519
и	3.627	са	0.478
да	2.600	но	0.407
в	2.333	а	0.390
се	2.031	до	0.327
за	1.851	той	0.320
от	1.790	или	0.318
е	1.509	му	0.318
не	1.178	които	0.316
с	1.133	година	0.297
че	0.974	България	0.274
си	0.771	към	0.274
по	0.626	ми	0.267
това	0.586	го	0.262
ще	0.579	при	0.246

Table 13. Relative frequencies of the most frequent three letter words in the texts

Word	Frequency (in percentages)	Word	Frequency (in percentages)
той	5.871	бил	1.583
или	5.845	под	1.477
към	5.024	тук	1.356
при	4.512	нас	1.337
ако	3.956	пак	1.330
има	3.270	път	1.236
още	2.994	две	1.231
със	2.804	нея	1.194
във	2.348	там	1.187
ние	2.088	над	1.120
съм	2.075	сме	1.051
как	1.888	тъй	1.046
все	1.879	ден	1.036
без	1.869	бях	0.989
тях	1.746	два	0.921

Table 12. Relative frequencies of the most frequent two letter words in the texts

Word	Frequency (in percentages)	Word	Frequency (in percentages)
на	23.639	ми	1.218
да	11.841	го	1.195
се	9.248	те	0.943
за	8.428	аз	0.881
от	8.155	ли	0.824
не	5.365	тя	0.746
че	4.434	бе	0.720
си	3.512	ти	0.666
по	2.850	ме	0.615
ще	2.639	ни	0.598
са	2.179	ги	0.558
но	1.852	им	0.553
до	1.491	би	0.478
му	1.448	то	0.411

Table 14. Relative frequencies of the most frequent four letter words in the texts

Word	Frequency (in percentages)	Word	Frequency (in percentages)
това	5.974	бъде	1.422
като	5.294	вече	1.300
само	2.356	него	1.251
след	2.234	едно	1.077
през	2.227	нещо	1.065
беше	2.225	пред	0.986
може	2.201	сега	0.954
така	2.175	бяха	0.953
този	2.046	днес	0.913
един	2.034	били	0.817
една	1.945	дори	0.812
тази	1.733	също	0.797
каза	1.589	част	0.712
няма	1.549	защо	0.705
тези	1.487	нищо	0.678

Table 15. The top ten frequent letters, which occur at the beginning of words

Letter	Frequency (in percentages)	Letter	Frequency (in percentages)
с	12.178	д	6.622
н	11.636	о	5.580
п	10.180	к	5.568
и	7.212	т	4.976
в	6.654	з	4.106

Table 16. The top ten frequent letters, which occur at the end of words

Letter	Frequency (in percentages)	Letter	Frequency (in percentages)
а	27.502	я	3.975
е	16.271	в	3.234
и	15.367	н	2.385
о	12.508	с	1.968
т	6.056	м	1.634

Table 17. Relative frequencies of the most frequent lengths of the words in the texts

Length of word	Frequency (in percentages)	Length of word	Frequency (in percentages)
2	22.015	7	8.673
6	10.346	8	7.516
5	9.952	9	5.546
4	9.835	3	5.460
1	9.430	10	4.036

Table 18. Relative frequencies of the most frequent length of the different words in the texts

Length of word	Frequency (in percentages)	Length of word	Frequency (in percentages)
7	15.439	10	8.876
8	14.479	11	6.026
6	14.019	4	5.725
9	11.774	12	4.275
5	10.370	3	2.301

lists with the top ten most frequent letters, which occur at the beginning and ate the end of words.

The calculations of the frequencies of the lengths of the words in the examined texts indicate that the most used words are the two letter words (Table 17).

Besides, the set of the words, found in the collected documents is explored and it is established that the most frequent length of the different words is 7 (Table 18).

Index of Coincidence

The index of coincidence, invented by William Friedman, is applied for analyzing the text containing natural language as well as for cryptanalysis (Stinson, 2006). Moreover this index support establishing whether two texts are written in the same language or in different languages using the same alphabet, because the count of the coinci-dences for texts in the same languages is distinctly higher than the texts in the different languages.

The expected value for the index of coincidence can be computed from the relative frequencies of the letters f_i ($i=1,...,c$) on the corresponding language:

$$IC_{expected} = \frac{\sum_{i=1}^{c} f_i^2}{1/c}$$

where c is the number of the letters in the alphabet.

According our computations the value for the index of coincidence for the letters in the Bulgarian language is 1.93389. For comparison this index for Russian language is 1.76.

We can expect that for an arbitrary string of Bulgarian language its index of coincidence will be approximately equal to this obtained value.

Figure 7 represents the computed indexes of coincidence by the different categories of texts

Figure 7. Index of coincidence by categories

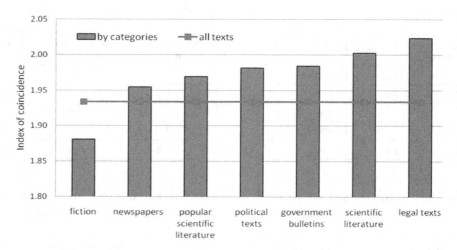

sources. The obtained results show that texts, belonging to the fiction, have the lowest value of the index of coincidence 1.88091, and these belonging to the scientific literature and legal texts have the highest values: 2.00328 and 2.02419, respectively. Obviously, this fact is caused by the greater formalization and specialization to the scientific and legal sources. The proposed considerations can be used in the algorithms for text mining and authorization of documents, books, papers, etc.

FREQUENCY DISTRIBUTIONS OF THE LETTERS AND THE WORDS IN THE MODERN BULGARIAN LANGUAGE

Mathematical Models for the Frequencies of the Letters and the Words

We examined the frequency distributions of the length of the distinct words; the length of the words; the letters; the words; the first and the last letters of words; the bigrams; the trigrams. For this purpose, the following mathematical models for frequency distributions have been studied and implemented.

Frequency Distribution of the Length of the Distinct Words

In (Smith, 2012) the following approach to predicting the number of the distinct words with length N is proposed:

$$W_N = L^{Np^N} - 1, \qquad (1)$$

where L is the number of the letters in the alphabet; p is a parameter.

Gamma Distribution

In (Sigurd, Eeg-Olofsson, & Weijer, 2004) the following formula is proposed for approximating the frequencies of the word and the sentence lengths:

$$f_N = aN^b c^N, \qquad (2)$$

where f_N is the frequency of the words with length N; a, b and c are parameters.

This formula is a variant of the so-called gamma distribution and reflects both the fact that the number of possible words increases with the word length, and the fact that there is a trend to longer words to be avoided, perhaps because they are uneconomical.

Zipf Distribution

Zipf's law (Zipf, 1932) connects the rank of a word in a text with its relative frequency on the text as follows: given a text T, Zipf's law states that the relative frequency of a word is inversely proportional to the word rank obtained by sorting the words according to their frequency in descending order. If R is the number of the distinct words in T, then the relative frequency f_r of a word with rank r in T can be approximated by the following formula:

$$f_r = \frac{1}{r \ln(1.78R)} \tag{3}$$

In (Zipf, 1949) a generalization of Zipf's law is given, whereby there is a relation between the frequency of occurrence of an event and its rank obtained by sorting the events according to their frequency of occurrence in descending order. This relation is represented by the following equation:

$$f_r = \frac{a}{r^b}, \tag{4}$$

where f_r is a frequency of an event of rank r; a and b are parameters.

Geometric Series Distribution

In (Sigurd, 1968) a distribution based on geometric series for frequencies of the phonemes is suggested in the form:

$$f_r = ab^r, \tag{5}$$

where f_r is a frequency for rank r; a and b are parameters of the text.

Yule Distribution

Yule distribution (Tambovtsev & Martindale, 2007) is proposed for the frequencies of the phonemes and it is represented by the following formula:

$$f_r = \frac{a}{r^b} c^r, \tag{6}$$

where f_r is a frequency for rank r; a, b and c are parameters.

We have applied discussed above distributions represented by the formulas (1) - (6) on the data about the frequencies and the ranks of the letters, the words and the word lengths to computing the predicted values of the corresponding frequencies. Besides, we have calculated the values of the determination coefficient R^2 for each model, defined by the following way: Let a dataset is given with n observed values y_i, $i = 1, ..., n$. By f_i are denoted the predicted values obtained from the corresponding model and

$$\bar{y} = \frac{1}{n} \sum_{i=1}^{n} y_i$$

is the average of the observed values. Then the coefficient of determination is calculated by the formula:

$$R^2 = 1 - \frac{SS_{err}}{SS_{tot}},$$

where

$$SS_{err} = \sum_{i=1}^{n} (y_i - f_i)^2$$

is the sum of the error squares;

$$SS_{tot} = \sum_{i=1}^{n} (y_i - \overline{y})^2$$

is the total sum of the squares. The determination coefficient provides information on the extent to which the predicted values obtained from the model correspond to the observed values.

Results

We have applied two approaches to computing the approximation of the frequencies of the length of the distinct words. The first method comprises of implementing Equation (1). The parameter p is computed to minimize the chi-squared error between the data and the distribution. Moreover, we have produced the frequency distribution of the lengths of the distinct word based on the gamma distribution according to Formula (2).

Our research on the word frequency distribution is based on Zipf's law according to Formulas (3) and (4), as well as geometric series distribution represented by Formula (5).

We have found frequency distributions of the word lengths, the letters, the first letters of the words, the last letters of the words, the bigrams, the trigrams. For this purpose, we have applied Zipf's law according to Formula (4), geometric series distribution according to Formula (5) and Yule distribution according to Formula (6).

The obtained results are summarized in Tables 19-26. The values of parameters *a*, *b* and *c* are chosen such as to minimize the sum of the squared

differences between observed and predicted values SS_{err}.

Frequency Distribution of the Length of the Distinct Words

The computed values of the parameters and the determination coefficients of the frequency distribution of the lengths of the distinct words are represented in Table 19.

Figure 8 provides the graphical view of the observed and predicted frequencies of the different word lengths in correspondence with both of the considered distributions.

Frequency Distribution of the Word Length

The word frequencies according to their length are shown in Figure 9*a*. To facilitate finding an approximation of the frequencies of the word lengths, the word lengths are sorted according to their frequencies in descending order and by this way their ranks are obtained. Figure 9*b* shows the word frequencies according to the ranks of the word lengths.

Table 20 contains the obtained results from the computations of the parameter values and the determination coefficient for the frequency distribution of the ranks of the word lengths.

Figure 10 is a graphical view of the frequencies of the ranks of the word lengths derived from the collected texts and the predicted values according to the three considered distributions.

Table 19. Distributions, parameters and computed determination coefficients for the frequency data of the length of the distinct words

Distribution	Parameters	Determination coefficient
a) Frequency distribution of the length of the distinct words (1)	$p = 0.875$	$R^2 = 0.99179$
b) Gamma distribution (2)	$a = 0.011$ $b = 7.1$ $c = 0.39$	$R^2 = 0.98003$

Figure 8. Observed and predicted frequencies of the length of the distinct words acording to: a) Frequency distribution of the length of the distinct words (1); b) Gamma distribution (2)

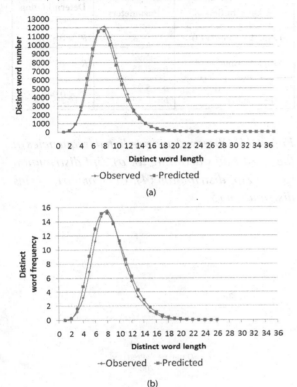

(a)

(b)

Figure 9. Frequencies of the word lengths

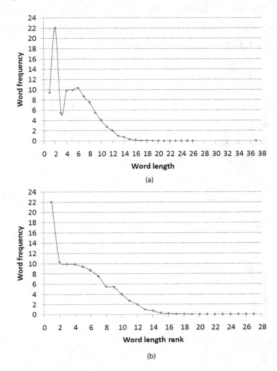

(a)

(b)

Similarly, we have found the ranks of the word, the letters, the first letters of the words, the last letters of the words, bigrams, trigrams, i.e. by sorting according to their frequencies in descending order. The used distributions, the calculated parameter values and the computed determination coefficients for the frequencies of the ranks are summarized in Tables 21-26. Figures 11–16 provide a graphical representation of the observed and the predicted frequencies according to the relevant distributions.

Frequency Distribution of the Words

See Table 21 and Figure 11.

Table 20. Distributions, parameters and computed determination coefficients for the frequencies of the word length ranks

Distribution	Parameters	Determination coefficient
a) Zipf distribution (4)	$a = 22.85$ $b = 0.85$	$R^2 = 0.8583$
b) Geometric series distribution (5)	$a = 22.53$ $b = 0.82$	$R^2 = 0.9198$
c) Yule distribution (6)	$a = 22.91$ $b = 0.28$ $c = 0.88$	$R^2 = 0.93015$

Figure 10. Observed and predicted frequencies of the word length ranks acording to: a) Zipf distribution (4); b) Geometric series distribution (5); c) Yule distribution (6)

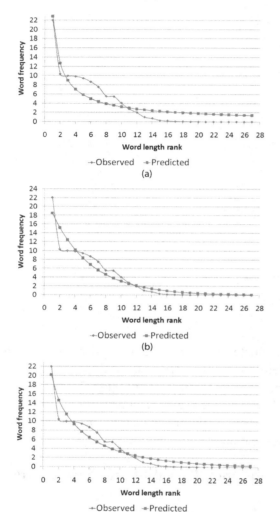

(a)

(b)

(c)

Table 21. Distributions, parameters and computed determination coefficients for the word rank frequencies

Distribution	Parameters	Determination coefficient
a) Zipf distribution (3)	&	$R^2 = 0.8390$
b) Zipf distribution (4)	$a = 5.92$ $b = 0.85$	$R^2 = 0.9595$
c) Geometric series ditribution (5)	$a = 5.23$ $b = 0.85$	$R^2 = 0.9462$

Figure 11. Observed and predicted frequencies of the word ranks acording to: a) Zipf distribution (3); b) Zipf distribution (4); c) Geometric series distribution (5)

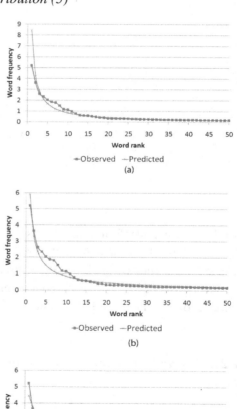

(a)

(b)

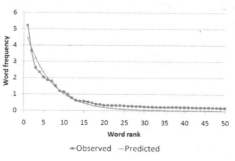

(c)

Frequency Distribution of the Letters

See Table 22 and Figure 12.

Frequency Distribution of the First Letters of the Words

See Table 23 and Figure 13.

Table 22. Distributions, parameters and computed determination coefficients for the letter rank frequencies

Distribution	Parameters	Determination coefficient
a) Zipf distribution (4)	$a = 14.57$ $b = 0.64$	$R^2 = 0.8354$
b) Geometric series distribution (5)	$a = 12.98$ $b = 0.89$	$R^2 = 0.9853$
c) Yule distribution (6)	$a = 13.29$ $b = 0.02$ $c = 0.89$	$R^2 = 0.9857$

Table 23. Distributions, parameters and computed determination coefficients for the rank-frequencies of the first letters of the words

Distribution	Parameters	Determination coefficient
a) Zipf distribution (4)	$a = 15.22$ $b = 0.65$	$R^2 = 0.8227$
b) Geometric series distribution (5)	$a = 14.16$ $b = 0.88$	$R^2 = 0.98414$
c) Yule distribution (6)	$a = 14.32$ $b = 0.004$ $c = 0.88$	$R^2 = 0.98396$

Figure 12. Observed and predicted frequencies of the letter ranks acording to: a) Zipf distribution (4); b) Geometric series distribution (5); c) Yule distribution (6)

Figure 13. Observed and predicted rank-frequencies of the first letters of the words acording to: a) Zipf distribution (4); b) Geometric series distribution (5); c) Yule distribution (6)

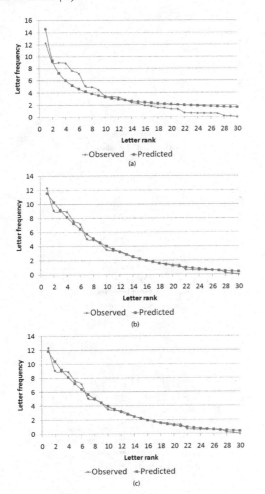

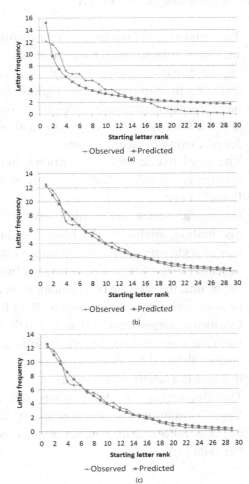

Frequency Distribution of the Last Letters of the Words

See Table 24 and Figure 14.

Frequency Distribution of the Bigrams

See Table 25 and Figure 15.

Frequency Distribution of the Trigrams

When applying Yule distribution with $c = 1.00$, we obtain Zipf distribution, shown in Figure 16a.

The following conclusions can be drawn from the found frequency distributions:

- The frequencies of the length of the distinct words are approximated more precisely using the distribution given by Equation (1);
- Yule distribution provides the highest value of the determination coefficient in comparison with the other two used methods for predicting the word lengths;
- The word frequencies are predicted most accurately by using Zipf's law, given by Equation (4);
- Geometric series distribution and Yule distribution, applied to the letter frequencies provide very similar predictions of the observed frequencies. As can be seen from the results, the relevant determination coefficients have very close values (0.9853 for Geometric series distribution and 0.9857 for Yule distribution). Similar results are also established for the frequencies of the first and last letters of the words.
- The frequencies of the bigrams follow Yule distribution, the frequencies of the trigrams follow Zipf's law represented by Formula (4).

Table 24. Distributions, parameters and computed determination coefficients for the rank-frequencies of the last letters of the words

Distribution	Parameters	Determination coefficient
a) Zipf distribution (4)	$a = 29.78$ $b = 1.02$	$R^2 = 0.91811$
b) Geometric series distribution (5)	$a = 37.00$ $b = 0.72$	$R^2 = 0.9793$
c) Yule distribution (6)	$a = 34.83$ $b = 0.20$ $c = 0.78$	$R^2 = 0.97996$

Figure 14. Observed and predicted rank-frequencies of the last letters of the words acording to: a) Zipf distribution (4); b) Geometric series distribution (5); c) Yule distribution (6)

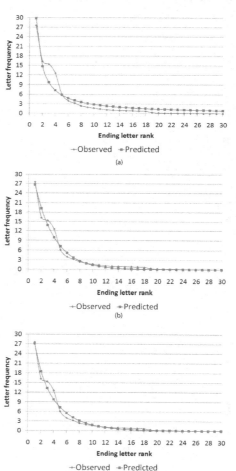

Table 25. Distributions, parameters and computed determination coefficients for the frequencies of the bigram ranks

Distribution	Parameters	Determination coefficient
a) Zipf distribution (4)	$a = 3.91$ $b = 0.6$	$R^2 = 0.8329$
b) Geometric series ditribution (5)	$a = 1.73$ $b = 0.98$	$R^2 = 0.9443$
c) Yule distribution (6)	$a = 2.75$ $b = 0.27$ $c = 0.99$	$R^2 = 0.9931$

Table 26. Letters, their occurrences and structures according to their presentations in Morse code

Distributions	Parameters	Determination coefficient
a) Zipf distribution (4)	$a = 1.46$ $b = 0.58$	$R^2 = 0.87375$
b) Geometric series distribution (5)	$a = 1.46$ $b = 0.58$	$R^2 = 0.76763$
c) Yule distribution (6)	$a = 1.46$ $b = 0.58$ $c = 1.00$	$R^2 = 0.87375$

Figure 15. Observed and predicted frequencies of the bigram ranks acording to: a) Zipf distribution (4); b) Geometric series distribution (5); c) Yule distribution (6)

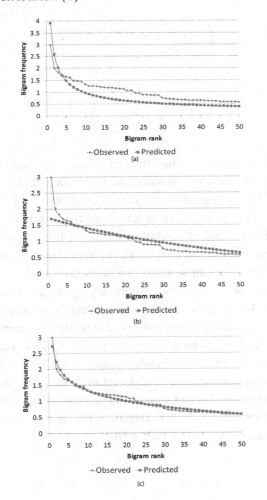

Figure 16. Observed and predicted frequencies of the trigram ranks acording to: a) Zipf distribution (4); b) Geometric series distribution (5); c) Yule distribution (6)

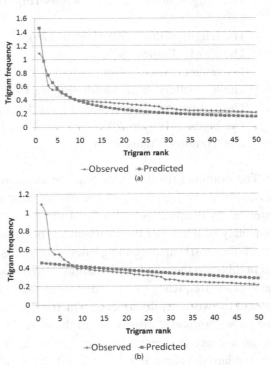

STANDARD DEVIATION OF LETTER AND WORD FREQUENCIES BY DOCUMENTS

In this section, the frequency distributions of the letters, the words and their lengths by documents are considered. Table 27 provides some summary

Table 27. Summary data for the words in the texts

Characteristic	Value
Number of the distinct words	77863
Number of the words that occur at least twice	1050791
Number of the words that occur in at least two documents	1011908
Number of the words that occur in at least half of the documents	852597

data for the words in Bulgarian language that are contained in the collected documents.

We have computed the average and the standard deviation by documents of the frequencies of:

- The length of the distinct words (Figure 17*a*);
- The length of the words (Figure 17*b*);
- The words (Figure 18*a*);
- The letters (Figure 18*b*);
- The first letters of the words (Figure 19*a*);
- The last letters of the words (Figure 19*b*);
- The bigrams (Figure 20*a*);
- The trigrams (Figure 20*b*).

The obtained results show that the standard deviation of the frequency of the most frequent letter 'a' by documents is 4.49% of the average frequency of that letter by documents. The same letter is the most frequent ending letter of the words, but in this case the standard deviation is 9.78% of the average frequency of the letter 'a' as the last letter of the words by documents, which is 27.9%. The most common starting letter of the words 'c' has an average frequency by documents 12.2%, the standard deviation is 1.26%, i.e. 10.35% of it.

The standard deviation of the most frequent word in the texts 'на' is 40.83% of the average frequency of this word by documents. Furthermore, this word is the bigram with highest frequency, but considered as a bigram has standard deviation that is 14.13% of the average frequency by docu-

Figure 17. Average value and standard deviation by documents of the frequencies of (a) the distinct words according to their lengths and (b) the words according to their lengths

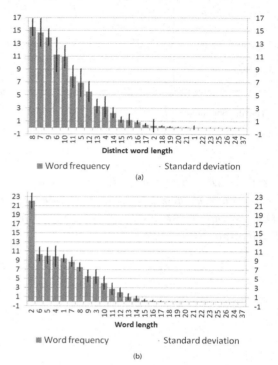

ments. The trigrams with the highest frequency of all texts is 'ите', its standard deviation is 25.03% of the average frequency by documents.

The most common length of the words is 2 with a standard deviation 7.72% of the average frequency by documents; the most frequent length of the different words is 8 with a standard deviation 9.49% of average frequency by documents.

A comparison of the average and the standard deviation of the frequencies of the different letters is realized, which are respectively 3.333% and 3.276%. The most distinguishing values have the average and the standard deviation of the frequencies of the distinct words, the percentage of their difference is 95.864. Detailed data about other results are given in Table 28.

Figure 18. Average value and standard deviation by documents of the frequencies of (a) the first 25 most frequent words and (b) the letters

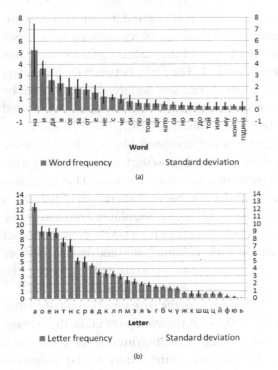

Figure 19. Average value and standard deviation by documents of the frequencies of (a) the first letters of the words and (b) the last letters of the words

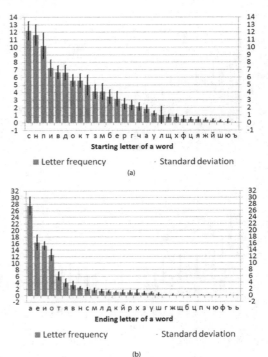

ADDITIONAL RESULTS

This section presents the results of estimating the entropy of the text, using the collected texts in Bulgarian language. Besides, it is considered the issue of the average length of the presentation of the letters in these texts in Morse code.

Estimation of Text Entropy

The number of the possible words of length N can be estimated by the conditional entropies H_N of order N in the following way proposed in (Smith, 2012):

$$W_N = 2^{N H_N}$$

Consequently, for the entropy of order N we obtain:

$$H_N = \frac{\log_2 W_N}{N},$$

where N is the length of the words; W_N is the number of the distinct words of length N.

We apply this formula to the number of the different words according to their lengths in Bulgarian language and we evaluate the higher order entropies as shown in Table 29. The used data about the words in English and German language are taken from (Smith, 2012).

Figure 20. Average value and standard deviation by documents of the frequencies of (a) the first 25 most frequent bigrams and (b) the first 25 most frequent trigrams

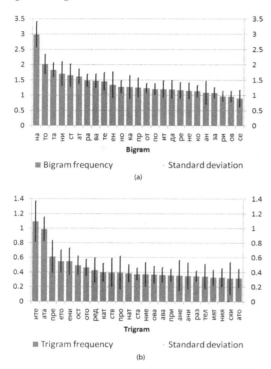

(a)

(b)

Figure 21 provides a graphical view of the computed values of the predicted higher order entropies of Bulgarian, English and German language.

Average Length of the Letter Presentations in Morse Code

Each character is structured into units. The minimum signal duration is represented by 1 – one dot; the length of the dash is equal to three units duration – 111. The pause between the characters in the letter is one unit duration and is denoted by 0 (zero); the pause between the letters in the word – three units duration (000). Table 30 shows the corresponding structures obtained by the Morse code representations of the letters in the Bulgarian alphabet (the column *Structure*). This table also contains the number of occurrences of the letters in the collected texts (the column *Frequency*), the number of characters for a single presentation of each letter (the column *Units*) and the total number of characters for all occurrences of each letter (the column *Total = Frequency.Units*).

The average of the structured length of a letter is 10.433333, i.e. the average of units; the average of the letter representation in correspondence with the frequencies of the letters in the Bulgarian alphabet is $Total/Frequency = 8.755552$. Consequently, the words derived from random grouping of letters, have an average length that is 19.1624% longer than the average length of normal Bulgarian words.

Table 28. Average, standard deviation of the frequencies and the percent of their difference

	Average Value of the Frequencies	Standard Deviation of the Frequencies	Percent of the Difference
Distinct word lengths	3.704	5.178	28.475
Word lengths	3.704	5.291	30.006
Words	0.001	0.031	95.864
Letters	3.333	3.276	1.736
First letters of the words	3.448	3.527	2.243
Last letters of the words	3.333	6.336	47.394
Bigrams	0.125	0.283	55.611
Trigrams	0.012	0.037	68.337

Figure 21. Predicted high order entropies of Bulgarian, English and German language

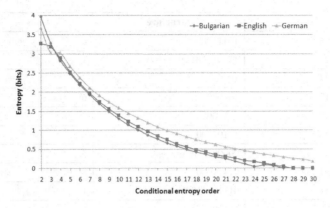

Table 29. High order entropies estimated by using the number of the distinct words with corresponding lengths

Order	Bulgarian words	Predicted entropy	English words	Predicted entropy	German words	Predicted entropy
2	242	3.96	93	3.27	164	3.68
3	932	3.29	754	3.19	546	3.03
4	2487	2.82	3027	2.89	4323	3.02
5	5381	2.48	6110	2.52	10486	2.67
6	8746	2.18	10083	2.22	19092	2.37
7	11447	1.93	14424	1.97	27574	2.11
8	12096	1.70	16624	1.75	38933	1.91
9	10855	1.49	16551	1.56	52212	1.74
10	8483	1.31	14888	1.39	60596	1.59
11	6125	1.14	12008	1.23	63115	1.45
12	4320	1.01	8873	1.09	59232	1.32
13	2592	0.87	6113	0.97	49708	1.20
14	1763	0.77	3820	0.85	39908	1.09
15	959	0.66	2323	0.75	30678	0.99
16	644	0.58	1235	0.64	22897	0.91
17	335	0.49	707	0.56	16978	0.83
18	189	0.42	413	0.48	11883	0.75
19	116	0.36	245	0.42	8158	0.68
20	57	0.29	135	0.35	5584	0.62
21	37	0.25	84	0.30	3684	0.56
22	15	0.18	50	0.26	2398	0.51
23	6	0.11	23	0.20	1557	0.46
24	2	0.04	16	0.17	974	0.41
25	4	0.08	9	0.13	633	0.37
26	3	0.06	4	0.08	386	0.33
27	0	0.00	2	0.04	237	0.29
28	0	0.00	1	0.00	128	0.25
29	0	0.00	0	0.00	95	0.23
30	0	0.00	0	0.00	44	0.18

Table 30. Letters, their occurrences and structures according to their presentations in Morse code

Letter	Frequency	Structure	Units	Total
а	765946	10111000	8	6127568
о	564327	11101110111000	14	7900578
е	557664	1000	4	2230656
и	551617	101000	6	3309702
т	472619	111000	6	2835714
н	443546	11101000	8	3548368
с	315838	00000	5	1579190
р	305824	01110000	8	2446592
в	276534	01110111000	11	3041874
д	219183	11100000	8	1753464
к	210701	11100111000	11	2317711
л	204110	011100000	9	1836990
п	181993	011101110000	12	2183916
м	153246	1110111000	10	1532460
з	142444	111011100000	12	1709328
я	121624	011100111000	12	1459488
ъ	113859	111000111000	12	1366308
г	97425	11101110000	11	1071675
б	95267	111010101000	12	1143204
ч	83186	111011101110000	15	1247790
у	81555	00111000	8	652440
ж	44037	000111000	9	396333
х	40713	000000	6	244278
ш	38231	111011101110111000	18	688158
щ	38059	111011100111000	15	570885
ц	36971	111001110000	12	443652
й	36649	011101110111000	15	549735
ф	13050	001110000	9	117450
ю	8599	001110111000	12	103188
ь	875	111001110111000	15	13125
Total:	6215692			54421820
Average:			10. 433333	

The same kind of computations are implemented for other languages (Pierpont, 1998) and the following results are obtained for the average length of the character presentations: English – 9.076, German – 8.640, French – 8.694, Spanish – 8.286.

CONCLUSION

In this paper, the automated system is proposed. It explores a client/server based approach to managing the information on texts in the Bulgarian language. The created database contains information about different characteristics of the documents and it is realized on Microsoft SQL Server. The interface is developed by means that allow the establishment of a connection with the database of the ADP project. This gives users the possibility of easily accessing detailed information about collected documents.

The realized system allows computing the frequencies of occurring letters, the bigrams, the trigrams, the words in a chosen document or a set of collected documents.

This paper examines the frequency distributions of the lengths of the distinct words, the word lengths, the letters, the words, the first and the last letters of the words, the bigrams, the trigrams. The standard deviations of the letter and the word frequencies by documents are estimated. Some mathematical models for letter and word frequencies are proposed and examined. The entropy of the stored texts in Bulgarian language is estimated and the average length of the presentation of the letters in these texts in Morse code is considered.

Our future work includes calculating the frequency of the space and other non-alphabetic characters, some phrase, as well as development of the application for mining the constraint-based association rules in the text of the documents, which allows performing the association analysis of the different words from their contents. The improved application will be also utilized for the purposes of the cryptanalysis and the authentication of the text documents in Bulgarian language.

REFERENCES

Anson, D., Eck, C. L., King, J., Mooney, R., Sansom, C., Wilkerson, B., & Wychulis, D. (2001). *Efficacy of alternate keyboard configurations: Dvorak vs. Reverse-QWERTY*. Retrieved March 27, 2013, from http://atri.misericordia.edu/Papers/Dvorak.php

Barsegyan, A. A., Kupriyanov, M. S., Stepanenko, V. V., & Holod, I. I. (2008). *Technologies for data analysis: data mining, visual mining, text mining, OLAP*. Sankt-Peterburg, Russia: BHV-Peterburg.

Berry, M. W. (2003). *Survey of text mining: clustering, classification, and retrieval*. Springer.

Bieniek, D., Dyess, R., Hotek, M., Loria, J., Machanic, A., Soto, A., & Wiernik, A. (2006). *Microsoft SQL Server 2005 implementation and maintenance – training kit*. Microsoft Press.

BulTreeBank Group. (2010). *Available linguistic resources for Bulgarian*. Retrieved March 27, 2013, from http://www.bultreebank.org/Resources.html

Burrell, M. (2009). *Serbian Dvorak*. Retrieved March 27, 2013, from http://www.csd.uwo.ca/~mburrel/software/serbian-dvorak

Computer news. (1999). *Computer linguistics*. Retrieved March 27, 2013, from http://kv.minsk.by/index1999262201.htm

Curta, F. (2006). Southeastern Europe in the Middle Ages, 500-1250. Cambridge University Press.

Encyclopedia Britannica. (2009). *Cyrillic alphabet. Encyclopedia Britannica 2009 Student and Home Edition*. Chicago: Encyclopedia Britannica.

Functional Multilingual Extensions to European Keyboard Layouts. (2008). *The Bulgarian alphabet and keyboard in the context of EU communications*. Retrieved March 27, 2013, from http://www.csc.fi/english/pages/meek/The-Bulgarian-Alphabet-and-Keyboard

Garcia-Molina, H., Ullman, J. D., & Widom, J. (2002). *Database systems: The complete book*. Moscow, Russia: Williams.

Gruber, M. (2001). *Mastering SQL*. Sofia, Bulgaria: SoftPress.

Grudev, I. (1999). *The first Slavonic-Bulgarian alphabet – The Cyrillic*. Retrieved June 03, 2010, from http://www.fortunecity.com/victorian/coldwater/293/pyr_k.htm

Houlette, F. (2001). *SQL: A beginner's guide*. Sofia, Bulgaria: SoftPress.

Kroenke, D. M. (2003). *Database processing*. Moscow, Russia: Piter.

Lee, E. S. (1999). *Essays about computer security*. University of Cambridge Computer Laboratory.

LetterFrequency. (2010). *Letter & Word Frequency in English / Other Language Frequencies*. Retrieved March 27, 2013, from http://www.letterfrequency.org

Lewand, R. E. (2000). *Cryptological mathematics*. The Mathematical Association of America.

Microsoft Corporation. (2001). *MCSE training: Microsoft SQL Server 2000 – design and implementing databases*. Sofia, Bulgaria: SoftPress.

Microsoft Corporation. (2008). *Transact SQL*. Retrieved March 27, 2013, from http://www.microsoft.com/sql

Mirchev, K. (1963). Konstantin-Cyril, the creator of the Old-Bulgarian literary language. *Journal "Bulgarian Language", 13*(3).

Paul, J., II. (1985). *Encyclical epistle slavorum apostoli of the supreme pontiff John Paul II to the bishops, priests and religious families and to all the Christian faithful in commemoration of the eleventh centenary of the evangelizing work of SAINTS CYRIL AND METHODIUS*. Retrieved March 27, 2013, from http://www.vatican.va/holy_father/john_paul_ii/encyclicals/documents/hf_jp-ii_enc_19850602_slavorum-apostoli_en.html

Pearson, W. (2004). *MS Access for the business environment: stored procedures from the MS Access client*. Retrieved March 27, 2013, from http://www.databasejournal.com/features/msaccess/article.php/3363511

Penkov, B., Obretenov, A., Sendov, B., Kirpikova, T., & Joukanov, T. (1962). Frequencies of letters in written Bulgarian. *Acad. bulgare Sci., 15*, 243-244.

Piepgrass, D. (2006). *The Asset Keyboard*. Retrieved March 27, 2013, from http://millikeys.sourceforge.net/asset

Pierpont, W. G. (1998). *The Art & Skill of Radio-Telegraphy* (2nd rev. ed.). Retrieved March 27, 2013, from http://www.zerobeat.net/tasrt/c28.htm

Plantevit, M., Charnois, T., Klema, J., Rigotti, C., & Cremilleux, B. (2009). Combining sequence and itemset mining to discover named entities in biomedical texts: a new type of pattern. *International Journal of Data Mining. Modelling and Management, 1*(2), 119–148.

Quaresma, P. (2008). *Frequency analysis of the Portuguese language*. Centre for Informatics and Systems of University of Coimbra, TR 2008/003, ISSN 0874-338X.

Sigurd, B. (1968). Rank-frequency distributions for phonemes. *Phonetica, 18*, 1–15. doi:10.1159/000258595

Sigurd, B., Eeg-Olofsson, M., & Weijer, J. (2004). Word length, sentence length and frequency-Zipf revisited. *Studia Linguistica, 58*(1), 37–52. doi:10.1111/j.0039-3193.2004.00109.x

Simov, K., Peev, Z., Kouylekov, M., Simov, A., Dimitrov, M., & Kiryakov, A. (2001). CLaRK – An XML-based system for corpora development. In *Proceedings of the Conference on Corpus Linguistics* (pp. 558-560). Academic Press.

Skordev, D. (2007). *Some consideration in relation with the Bulgarian keyboard layouts*. Retrieved March 27, 2013, from http://www.fmi.uni-sofia.bg/fmi/logic/skordev/bg_layouts0.htm

Smith, R. (2012). Distinct word length frequencies: distributions and symbol entropies. *Glottometrics*, *23*, 7–22.

Stefanov, B., & Birdanova, V. (1997). Hygienic-ergonomic evaluation of the computer keyboard layouts. *Computer*, *2*, 56–62.

Stinson, D. (2006). *Cryptography: theory and practice*. CRC Press.

Tambovtsev, Y., & Martindale, C. (2007). Phoneme Frequencies Follow a Yule Distribution. *SKASE Journal of Theoretical Linguistics*, *4*(2), 1–11.

Tilborg, H. C. A. (2000). *Fundamentals of cryptology*. Kluwer Academy Publisher.

Trifonov, T., & Georgieva-Trifonova, T. (2012). Research on letter and word frequency in the modern Bulgarian language. *International Journal of Knowledge-Based Organizations*, *2*(3), 74–90. doi:10.4018/ijkbo.2012070105

Vazov, I. (1999). Under the yoke. *Slovoto*. Retrieved March 27, 2013, from http://www.slovo.bg/showwork.php3?AuID=14&WorkID=5778&Level=1

Xue, X.-B., & Zhou, Z.-H. (2009). Distributional features for text categorization. *IEEE Transactions on Knowledge and Data Engineering*, *21*(3), 428–442. doi:10.1109/TKDE.2008.166

Zipf, G. K. (1932). *Selective Studies and the Principle of Relative Frequency in Language*. Cambridge: Harvard University Press.MA doi:10.4159/harvard.9780674434929

Zipf, G. K. (1949). *Human Behavior and the Principle of Least Effort*. Cambridge, MA: Addison-Wesley Press.

Chapter 8
Vague Correlation Coefficient of Interval Vague Sets and its Applications to Topsis in MADM Problems

John Robinson P.
Bishop Heber College (Autonomous), India

Henry Amirtharaj E. C.
Bishop Heber College (Autonomous), India

ABSTRACT

Various attempts are made by researchers on the study of vagueness of data through Intuitionistic Fuzzy sets and Vague sets, and also it is shown that Vague sets are Intuitionistic Fuzzy sets. However, there are algebraic and graphical differences between Vague sets and Intuitionistic Fuzzy sets. In this chapter, an attempt is made to define the correlation coefficient of Interval Vague sets lying in the interval [0,1], and a new method for computing the correlation coefficient of interval Vague sets lying in the interval [-1,1] using α-cuts over the vague degrees through statistical confidence intervals is also presented by an example. The new method proposed in this work produces a correlation coefficient in the form of an interval. The proposed method produces a correlation coefficient in the form of an interval from a trapezoidal shaped fuzzy number derived from the vague degrees. This chapter also aims to develop a new method based on the Technique for Order Preference by Similarity to Ideal Solution (TOPSIS) to solve MADM problems for Interval Vague Sets (IVSs). A TOPSIS algorithm is constructed on the basis of the concepts of the relative-closeness coefficient computed from the correlation coefficient of IVSs. This novel method also identifies the positive and negative ideal solutions using the correlation coefficient of IVSs. A numerical illustration explains the proposed algorithms and comparisons are made with some existing methods.

DOI: 10.4018/978-1-4666-6252-0.ch008

INTRODUCTION

Various attempts are made by researchers on the study of data vagueness through intuitionistic fuzzy sets and Vague Sets (VSs). Gau & Buehrer, (1994) introduced the concept of vague sets, and it was shown that vague sets are indeed intuitionistic fuzzy sets (Bustince & Burillo, 1996). But Lu & Ng, (2005, 2009) based their research on the algebraic and graphical differences between vague sets and intuitionistic fuzzy sets. Combining interval-valued fuzzy sets and vague sets, Zhi-feng et al., (2001) introduced the concept of Interval Vague Sets (IVSs). Gau & Buehrer, (1994), Li & Rao, (2001), Liu, P.D., (2009) and Liu, P.D., & Guan, (2008; 2009) have detailed the essential operations of vague sets and interval vague sets. Interval vague set is one of the higher order fuzzy sets and is being applied in various fields. The notion of truth membership function, false membership function and uncertainty function in interval vague sets describes the objective world more realistically and practically. Interval vague sets reflect people's understanding in three aspects comprehensively: Support degree, Negative degree and Uncertainty degree.

In this work, an attempt is made initially to define the correlation coefficient of interval vague sets lying in the interval [0,1]. An another attempt is made to compute the correlation coefficient of interval vague sets lying in the interval [-1,1] using α-cuts over the vague degrees through statistical confidence intervals, producing a correlation coefficient in the form of an interval. Many of the previously defined correlation coefficient for imprecise data lie in the interval [0,1], except for a very few authors who tried to make it fall in the interval [-1,1]. The correlation coefficient of interval vague sets is defined on the usual interval [0,1] and then a new computational method is proposed which allows the correlation coefficient of interval vague sets to fall in the interval [-1,1]. The novelty of this approach is that the correlation coefficient of interval vague sets is obtained in

the form of an interval rather than a single point measure. Statistical confidence intervals and α-cuts are used to construct a kind of trapezoidal fuzzy number derived from the vague degrees.

Of the numerous approaches available for Decision Support Systems (DSS), one most prevalent is the Technique for Order Preference by Similarity to Ideal Solution (TOPSIS), first developed by Hwang & Yoon, (1981). TOPSIS is a logical decision-making approach, dealing with the problem of choosing a solution from a set of candidate alternatives characterized in terms of some attributes. The merit of the TOPSIS method suggested by Hwang & Yoon, (1981) is that it deals with both quantitative and qualitative assessments in the process evaluation with less computation. It is based upon the concept that the chosen alternative should have the shortest distance from the positive ideal solution and the farthest from the negative ideal solution. In the TOPSIS process, the performance ratings and the weights of the criteria are given as crisp values. In fuzzy TOPSIS, attribute values are represented by fuzzy numbers. Janic, (2003) stated that the TOPSIS method embraces seven steps which are:

1. Construction of normalized decision matrix;
2. Construction of weighted-normalized decision matrix;
3. Determining positive ideal and negative ideal solution;
4. Calculating the separation measure of each alternative from the ideal one;
5. Calculating the relative distance of each alternative to the ideal and negative ideal solution;
6. Ranking alternatives in descending order with respect to relative distance to the ideal solution;
7. Identifying the preferable alternative as the closest to the ideal solution.

In many applications, ranking of IVSs plays a very important role in the decision making processes. Liu, P. D., (2009) presented a novel method of TOPSIS using a new type of score and precise function for choosing positive and negative ideal solutions in contrast to the score and accuracy functions defined by Chen & Tan, (1994), Hong & Choi, (2000), Wang, J., et al., (2006) and Xu, (2007). However, Nayagam et al, (2011) proved the insufficiency of many of the score functions proposed in literature, and proposed a novel method of accuracy function for MADM problems under Interval Valued IFS environment. In most of the previous TOPSIS techniques presented in literature, different forms of score and accuracy functions were used to identify positive and negative ideal solutions. In this work, a novel method is presented where the correlation coefficient of IVSs is used to identify positive and negative ideal solutions and for ranking alternatives based on the closeness coefficient. Comparison is made between the proposed method and existing methods proposed by Chen & Tan, (1994), Xu, (2007), Hong & Choi, (2000) and Liu, P. D., (2009).

CORRELATION COEFFICIENT OF VAGUE SETS

Definition 1: (Vague Set)

A vague set A in a universe of discourse U is characterized by a truth membership function, t_A, and a false membership function, f_A, as follows:
$t_A : U \rightarrow [0,1]$, $\qquad f_A : U \rightarrow [0,1]$ and $t_A(u) + f_A(u) \leq 1$, where $t_A(u)$ is a lower bound on the grade of membership of u derived from the evidence for u, and $f_A(u)$ is a lower bound on the grade of membership of the negation of u derived from the evidence against u.

Suppose $U = \{u_1, u_2, ..., u_n\}$. A vague set A of the universe of discourse U can be represented as:

$$A = \sum_{i=1}^{n} [t(u_i), \ 1 - f(u_i)] \ / \ u_i,$$
$$0 \leq t(u_i) \leq 1 - f(u_i) \leq 1, \quad i = 1, 2, ..., n.$$

In other words, the grade of membership of u_i is bound to a subinterval $\left[t_A(u_i), \ 1 - f_A(u_i) \right]$ of $[0,1]$.

Let $X = \{x_1, x_2, ..., x_n\}$ be the finite universal set and $A, B \in VS(X)$ be given by

$$A = \left\{ \left\langle x, \left[t_A(x), 1 - f_A(x) \right] \right\rangle \ / \ x \in X \right\},$$

$$B = \left\{ \left\langle x, \left[t_B(x), 1 - f_B(x) \right] \right\rangle \ / \ x \in X \right\}.$$

And the length of the vague values are given by

$$\pi_A(x) = 1 - t_A(x) - f_A(x)$$
$$\pi_B(x) = 1 - t_B(x) - f_B(x).$$

Robinson & Amirtharaj, (2011a; 2011b; 2012a; 2012b) defined the correlation coefficient of vague sets and some higher order intuitionistic fuzzy sets. The correlation coefficient of vague sets is defined as follows:

For each $A \in VS(X)$, the informational vague energy of A is defined as:

$$E_{VS}(A) = \frac{1}{n} \sum_{i=1}^{n} \left[t_A^2(x_i) + \left(1 - f_A(x_i) \right)^2 + \pi_A^2(x_i) \right],$$
$$(1)$$

And for each $B \in VS(X)$, the informational vague energy of B is defined as:

$$E_{VS}(B) = \frac{1}{n} \sum_{i=1}^{n} \left[t_B^2(x_i) + \left(1 - f_B(x_i) \right)^2 + \pi_B^2(x_i) \right],$$
$$(2)$$

The correlation of A and B is given by the formula:

$$C_{VS}(A, B) = \frac{1}{n} \sum_{i=1}^{n} \begin{bmatrix} t_A(x_i) t_B(x_i) + (1 - f_A(x_i)) \\ (1 - f_B(x_i)) + \pi_A(x_i) \pi_B(x_i) \end{bmatrix},$$

(3)

Furthermore, the correlation coefficient of A and B is defined by the formula:

$$K_{VS}(A, B) = \frac{C_{VS}(A, B)}{\sqrt{E_{VS}(A) \cdot E_{VS}(B)}}.$$

(4)

where $0 \le K_{VS}(A, B) \le 1$.

Proposition 1: For $A, B \in$ VS(X), the following are true:

$$0 \le C_{VS}(A, B) \le 1,$$

$$C_{VS}(A, B) = C_{VS}(B, A),$$

$$K_{VS}(A, B) = K_{VS}(B, A),$$

The following theorems are true for the correlation coefficient of vague sets (Robinson & Amirtharaj, 2011a)

Theorem 1: For $A, B \in$ VS(X), then
$$0 \le K_{VS}(A, B) \le 1.$$
Theorem 2: $K_{VS}(A, B) = 1 \Leftrightarrow A = B$.
Theorem 3: $C_{VS}(A, B) = 0 \Leftrightarrow A$ and B are non-fuzzy sets and satisfy the condition $t_A(x_i) + t_B(x_i) = 1$ or $f_A(x_i) + f_B(x_i) = 1$ or $\pi_A(x_i) + \pi_B(x_i) = 1$, $\forall x_i \in$ X.
Theorem 4: $C_{VS}(A, A) = 1 \Leftrightarrow A$ is a non-fuzzy set.

INTERVAL VAGUE SETS

Because of the uncertainty and complexity of the decision, the values of $t_A(x)$ and $f_A(x)$ are difficult to express by exact real number values. The interval values are more flexible than the real number values and extending $t_A(x)$ and $f_A(x)$ from real number values to an interval value, an interval vague set is obtained. Obviously this set is much stronger to express uncertain data or vague data. The interval vague value is denoted as $\tilde{x} = <\tilde{t}_x, \tilde{f}_x>$, where $\tilde{t}_x = [t_x^-, t_x^+] \subseteq [0,1]$, $\tilde{f}_x = [f_x^-, f_x^+] \subseteq [0,1]$, $t_x^+ + f_x^+ \le 1$ and also the following equation is satisfied:

$$\tilde{\pi}_A(x) = [1,1] - \tilde{t}_A(x) - \tilde{f}_A(x) = [1 - t_A^+(x) - f_A^+(x), 1 - t_A^-(x) - f_A^-(x)]$$

(6)

Operations of Interval Vague Sets

Some basic operations of interval vague sets were discussed by Gau & Buehrer, (1994) and Li & Rao, (2001). Consider the following two interval vague values:

$$\tilde{x} = \langle \tilde{t}_x, \tilde{f}_x \rangle = \langle [t_x^-, t_x^+], [f_x^-, f_x^+] \rangle$$

$$\tilde{y} = \langle \tilde{t}_y, \tilde{f}_y \rangle = \langle [t_y^-, t_y^+], [f_y^-, f_y^+] \rangle$$

where $\tilde{t}_x, \tilde{f}_x, \tilde{t}_y, \tilde{f}_y \subseteq [0,1]$ and $t_x^+ + f_x^+ \le 1$, $t_y^+ + f_y^+ \le 1$.

The following operational rules and relations can be observed for an interval vague set shown in Box 1.

Box 1.

$$\tilde{\tilde{x}} = \left\langle \tilde{f}_x, \tilde{t}_x \right\rangle$$
$$= \left\langle [f_x^-, f_x^+], [t_x^-, t_x^+] \right\rangle \tag{7}$$

$$\tilde{x} + \tilde{y} = \left\langle \tilde{t}_x + \tilde{t}_y - \tilde{t}_x \tilde{t}_y, \tilde{f}_x \tilde{f}_y \right\rangle$$
$$= \left\langle [t_x^- + t_y^- - t_x^- t_y^-, t_x^+ + t_y^+ - t_x^+ t_y^+], [f_x^- f_y^-, f_x^+ f_y^+] \right\rangle \tag{8}$$

$$\tilde{x} \times \tilde{y} = \left\langle \tilde{t}_x \tilde{t}_y, \tilde{f}_x + \tilde{f}_y - \tilde{f}_x \tilde{f}_y \right\rangle$$
$$= \left\langle [t_x^- t_y^-, t_x^+ t_y^+], [f_x^- + f_y^- - f_x^- f_y^-, f_x^+ + f_y^+ - f_x^+ f_y^+] \right\rangle \tag{9}$$

$$\lambda \times \tilde{x} = \left\langle [1 - (1 - t_x^-)^\lambda, 1 - (1 - t_x^+)^\lambda], [(f_x^-)^\lambda, (f_x^+)^\lambda] \right\rangle, \lambda \geq 0. \tag{10}$$

The resultant of all the above operations is interval vague values. According to the operational rules, the following relations are observed:

$$\tilde{x} + \tilde{y} = \tilde{y} + \tilde{x}$$

$$\tilde{x} \times \tilde{y} = \tilde{y} \times \tilde{x}$$

$$\lambda(\tilde{x} + \tilde{y}) = \lambda \tilde{x} + \lambda \tilde{y}$$

$$\lambda_1 \tilde{x} + \lambda_2 \tilde{x} = (\lambda_1 + \lambda_2)\tilde{x}, \quad \lambda_1, \lambda_2 \geq 0.$$

CORRELATION COEFFICIENT OF INTERVAL VAGUE SETS

Reviewing the Park et al., (2009) method of correlation coefficient for Interval Valued Intuitionistic Fuzzy Sets (IVIFSs), a new type of correlation coefficient is defined for IVSs as follows:

Suppose X is a domain of n elements, A and B are interval vague sets,

$$A = \left\{ \left\langle [t_A^-(x), t_A^+(x)], [f_A^-(x), f_A^+(x)] \right\rangle / x \in X \right\},$$
$$B = \left\{ \left\langle [t_B^-(x), t_B^+(x)], [f_B^-(x), f_B^+(x)] \right\rangle / x \in X \right\}$$

and the vague degrees are given by:

$$\pi_A^-(x) = 1 - t_A^+(x) - f_A^+(x),$$
$$\pi_A^+(x) = 1 - t_A^-(x) - f_A^-(x),$$
$$\pi_B^-(x) = 1 - t_B^+(x) - f_B^+(x),$$
$$\pi_B^+(x) = 1 - t_B^-(x) - f_B^-(x).$$

These measures are also called hesitation degree or uncertain degree or the length of the vague value. Let IVS(X) be the set of all interval vague sets.

In the following, a new method to calculate the correlation coefficient of Interval Vague Sets (IVSs) is proposed. For each $A \in$ IVS(X), the informational vague energy of A is defined as follows in Box 2.

Theorem 5: For all $A, B \in$ IVS(X), the correlation coefficient satisfies:

i. $K_{IVS}(A, B) = K_{IVS}(B, A)$.
ii. $0 \leq K_{IVS}(A, B) \leq 1$.
iii. $A = B$ iff $K_{IVS}(A, B) = 1$.

Proof:

i. The proof is obvious and straightforward.
ii. Using Schwarz inequality, the proof in Box 3 can be obtained.

Box 2.

$$E_{IVS}(A) = \frac{1}{2}\sum_{i=1}^{n}\left\{\begin{array}{l}\left(t_A^-(x_i)\right)^2 + \left(t_A^+(x_i)\right)^2 + \left(1 - f_A^-(x_i)\right)^2 \\ + \left(1 - f_A^+(x_i)\right)^2 + \left(\pi_A^-(x_i)\right)^2 + \left(\pi_A^+(x_i)\right)^2\end{array}\right\} \quad (11)$$

And for each $B \in \text{IVS}(X)$, the informational vague energy of B is defined as follows:

$$E_{IVS}(B) = \frac{1}{2}\sum_{i=1}^{n}\left\{\begin{array}{l}\left(t_B^-(x_i)\right)^2 + \left(t_B^+(x_i)\right)^2 + \left(1 - f_B^-(x_i)\right)^2 \\ + \left(1 - f_B^+(x_i)\right)^2 + \left(\pi_B^-(x_i)\right)^2 + \left(\pi_B^+(x_i)\right)^2\end{array}\right\} \quad (12)$$

The correlation of A and B is defined as follows:

$$C_{IVS}(A,B) = \frac{1}{2}\sum_{i=1}^{n}\left\{\begin{array}{l}\left(t_A^-(x_i).t_B^-(x_i)\right) + \left(t_A^+(x_i).t_B^+(x_i)\right) + \left(1 - f_A^-(x_i)\right)\left(1 - f_B^-(x_i)\right) + \\ \left(1 - f_A^+(x_i)\right)\left(1 - f_B^+(x_i)\right) + \left(\pi_A^-(x_i).\pi_B^-(x_i)\right) + \left(\pi_A^+(x_i).\pi_B^+(x_i)\right)\end{array}\right\} \quad (13)$$

Furthermore, the correlation coefficient of A and B is defined by the relation:

$$K_{IVS}(A,\ B) = \frac{C_{IVS}(A,\ B)}{\sqrt{E_{IVS}(A)\ .\ E_{IVS}(B)}} \quad (14)$$

The notations shown in Box 4 are used for further computations.

Thus $0 \le K_{IVS}(A, B) \le 1$.

iii. The proof of the sufficiency part is trivial. It is only needed to prove the necessity. Now, $K_{IVS}(A, B) = 1$ if and only if

$$t_A^-(x_i) + t_A^+(x_i) + \left(1 - f_A^-(x_i)\right)$$
$$+ \left(1 - f_A^+(x_i)\right) + \pi_A^-(x_i) + \pi_A^+(x_i) =$$
$$k\left[\begin{array}{l}t_A^-(x_i) + t_A^+(x_i) + \left(1 - f_A^-(x_i)\right) \\ + \left(1 - f_A^+(x_i)\right) + \pi_A^-(x_i) + \pi_A^+(x_i)\end{array}\right],$$

for some $k > 0$. Since,

$$t_A^+(x_i) + f_A^+(x_i) + \pi_A^-(x_i) = 1,$$
$$t_A^-(x_i) + f_A^-(x_i) + \pi_A^+(x_i) = 1,$$
$$t_B^+(x_i) + f_B^+(x_i) + \pi_B^-(x_i) = 1,$$
$$t_B^-(x_i) + f_B^-(x_i) + \pi_B^+(x_i) = 1.$$

it should be $k = 1$, i.e., $A = B$.

Numerical Example for Correlation Coefficient of Interval Vague Sets

Consider the two interval vague sets A and B as given in Table 1.

The informational vague energy (equations (11) and (12)), the correlation of A and B (equation (13)) and the correlation coefficient of A and B (equation (14)) are calculated as follows:

Box 3.

$$K_{IVS}\left(A,\ B\right) =$$

$$\left[\sum_{i=1}^{n} \begin{array}{l} [t_A^-(x_i)t_B^-(x_i) + t_A^+(x_i)t_B^+(x_i) + (1-f_A^-(x_i))(1-f_B^-(x_i)) + \\ (1-f_A^+(x_i))(1-f_B^+(x_i)) + \pi_A^-(x_i)\pi_B^-(x_i) + \pi_A^+(x_i)\pi_B^+(x_i)] \end{array}\right] \times$$

$$\left[\sum_{i=1}^{n} \begin{array}{l} [(t_A^-(x_i))^2 +(t_A^+(x_i))^2 + (1-f_A^-(x_i))^2 + \\ (1-f_A^+(x_i))^2 + (\pi_A^-(x_i))^2 + (\pi_A^+(x_i))^2] \end{array}\right]^{-1/2} \times$$

$$\left[\sum_{i=1}^{n} \begin{array}{l} [(t_B^-(x_i))^2 +(t_B^+(x_i))^2 + (1-f_B^-(x_i))^2 + \\ (1-f_B^+(x_i))^2 + (\pi_B^-(x_i))^2 + (\pi_B^+(x_i))^2] \end{array}\right]^{-1/2}$$

$$\leq \left\{ \left(\sum_{i=1}^{n} [t_A^-(x_i)]^2 \cdot \sum_{i=1}^{n} [t_B^-(x_i)]^2\right)^{1/2} + \right.$$

$$\left(\sum_{i=1}^{n} [t_A^+(x_i)]^2 \cdot \sum_{i=1}^{n} [t_B^+(x_i)]^2\right)^{1/2} +$$

$$\left(\sum_{i=1}^{n} [1-f_A^-(x_i)]^2 \cdot \sum_{i=1}^{n} [1-f_B^-(x_i)]^2\right)^{1/2} +$$

$$\left(\sum_{i=1}^{n} [\pi_A^-(x_i)]^2 \cdot \sum_{i=1}^{n} [\pi_B^-(x_i)]^2\right)^{1/2} +$$

$$\left. \left(\sum_{i=1}^{n} [\pi_A^+(x_i)]^2 \cdot \sum_{i=1}^{n} [\pi_B^+(x_i)]^2\right)^{1/2} \right\} \times$$

$$\left\{ \left(\sum_{i=1}^{n} [t_A^-(x_i)]^2 + \sum_{i=1}^{n} [t_A^+(x_i)]^2 + \sum_{i=1}^{n} [1-f_A^-(x_i)]^2 \right.\right.$$

$$\left. +\sum_{i=1}^{n} [1-f_A^+(x_i)]^2 + \sum_{i=1}^{n} [\pi_A^-(x_i)]^2 + \sum_{i=1}^{n} [\pi_A^+(x_i)]^2\right) \times \left(\sum_{i=1}^{n} [t_B^-(x_i)]^2 + \sum_{i=1}^{n} [t_B^+(x_i)]^2\right.$$

$$\left.\left. + \sum_{i=1}^{n} [1-f_B^-(x_i)]^2 + \sum_{i=1}^{n} [1-f_B^+(x_i)]^2 + \sum_{i=1}^{n} [\pi_B^-(x_i)]^2 + \sum_{i=1}^{n} [\pi_B^+(x_i)]^2\right) \right\}^{-1/2}.$$

$E_{IVS}\left(A\right) =$ 14.8225, $E_{IVS}\left(B\right) =$ 14.5900, $C_{IVS}\left(A,B\right) =$ 14.3965, $K_{IVS}\left(A,B\right) = 0.9789$.

The correlation coefficient derived by the above method for interval vague sets is observed to be a crisp value and lies in the interval [0,1]. In this chapter a new method is proposed to derive the correlation coefficient lying in the interval [-1,1].

Box 4.

$$a = \sum_{i=1}^{n} \; [t_A^-(x_i)]^2 \; , \qquad b = \sum_{i=1}^{n} \; [t_B^-(x_i)]^2 \; , \qquad c = \sum_{i=1}^{n} \; [t_A^+(x_i)]^2 \; , \qquad d = \sum_{i=1}^{n} \; [t_B^+(x_i)]^2$$

$$e = \sum_{i=1}^{n} \; [1 - f_A^-(x_i)]^2 \; , \qquad f = \sum_{i=1}^{n} \; [1 - f_B^-(x_i)]^2 \; , \qquad g = \sum_{i=1}^{n} \; [1 - f_A^+(x_i)]^2 \; , \qquad h = \sum_{i=1}^{n} \; [1 - f_B^+(x_i)]^2$$

$$i = \sum_{i=1}^{n} \; [\pi_A^-(x_i)]^2 \; , \qquad j = \sum_{i=1}^{n} \; [\pi_B^-(x_i)]^2 \; , \qquad k = \sum_{i=1}^{n} \; [\pi_A^+(x_i)]^2 \; , \qquad l = \sum_{i=1}^{n} \; [\pi_B^+(x_i)]^2$$

(15)

Then the above inequality is represented as follows:

$$K_{IVS}(A, \; B) \le \frac{\sqrt{ab} + \sqrt{cd} + \sqrt{ef} + \sqrt{gh} + \sqrt{ij} + \sqrt{kl}}{\sqrt{(a + c + e + g + i + k)}\sqrt{(b + d + f + h + j + l)}} \qquad (16)$$

Then since $0 \le K_{IVS}(A, B)$,

$$K^2_{IVS}(A, \; B) \; \le \; \frac{\left(\sqrt{ab} + \sqrt{cd} + \sqrt{ef} + \sqrt{gh} + \sqrt{ij} + \sqrt{kl}\right)^2}{(a + c + e + g + i + k)(b + d + f + h + j + l)}$$

$$= 1 - \left\{\left(\sqrt{ad} - \sqrt{bc}\right)^2 + \left(\sqrt{af} - \sqrt{be}\right)^2 + \left(\sqrt{ah} - \sqrt{bg}\right)^2 + \left(\sqrt{aj} - \sqrt{bi}\right)^2 + \left(\sqrt{al} - \sqrt{bk}\right)^2 + \left(\sqrt{cf} - \sqrt{de}\right)^2 \right.$$

$$+ \left(\sqrt{ch} - \sqrt{dg}\right)^2 + \left(\sqrt{cj} - \sqrt{di}\right)^2 + \left(\sqrt{cl} - \sqrt{dk}\right)^2 + \left(\sqrt{eh} - \sqrt{fg}\right)^2 + \left(\sqrt{ej} - \sqrt{fi}\right)^2 + \left(\sqrt{el} - \sqrt{fk}\right)^2$$

$$+ \left. \left(\sqrt{gj} - \sqrt{hi}\right)^2 + \left(\sqrt{gl} - \sqrt{hk}\right)^2 + \left(\sqrt{il} - \sqrt{jk}\right)^2 \right\} \times \left\{\left(a + c + e + g + i + k\right)\left(b + d + f + h + j + l\right)\right\}^{-1} \le \; 1$$

Table 1. Evaluation data given by two examiners A and B.

Q.No:	INTERVAL VAGUE SET A ($[t_A^-, t_A^+], [f_A^-, f_A^+]$)	INTERVAL VAGUE SET B ($[t_B^-, t_B^+], [f_B^-, f_B^+]$)
1	([0.4, 0.6], [0.2, 0.3])	([0.3, 0.6], [0.1, 0.2])
2	([0.3, 0.5], [0.2, 0.4])	([0.4, 0.6], [0.2, 0.3])
3	([0.5, 0.7], [0.1, 0.2])	([0.3, 0.6], [0.3,0.35])
4	([0.6, 0.7], [0.1, 0.2])	([0.5, 0.8], [0.1, 0.17])
5	([0.5, 0.6], [0.2, 0.3])	([0.5, 0.6], [0.2, 0.3])
6	([0.4, 0.6],[0.2, 0.3])	([0.4, 0.6], [0.1, 0.2])
7	([0.4, 0.5], [0.3, 0.4])	([0.3, 0.5], [0.3, 0.4])
8	([0.3, 0.5], [0.2, 0.3])	([0.2, 0.6], [0.3, 0.35])
9	([0.4, 0.5], [0.3, 0.4])	([0.2, 0.5], [0.3, 0.4])
10	([0.5, 0.6], [0.2, 0.3])	([0.4, 0.6], [0.3, 0.37])
11	([0.3, 0.6], [0.1, 0.2])	([0.2, 0.5], [0.2, 0.3])
12	([0.5, 0.6], [0.2, 0.3])	([0.5, 0.8], [0.1, 0.15])
13	([0.6, 0.7], [0.1, 0.2])	([0.5, 0.7], [0.2, 0.27])
14	([0.7, 0.75], [0.1, 0.2])	([0.5, 0.7], [0.1, 0.2])
15	([0.6, 0.7], [0.1, 0.2])	([0.2, 0.4], [0.1, 0.2])

STATISTICAL CONFIDENCE INTERVALS FOR FUZZY DATA

Basic Concepts of Statistical Confidence Intervals

Wu, H.C., (2009) proposed a new method to compute the fuzzy confidence intervals. Let X be a random variable having distribution with parameters $\theta_1,...,\theta_n$. Let $\widetilde{X}$ be a fuzzy random variable. Then $\widetilde{X}_\alpha^{\,L}$ and $\widetilde{X}_\alpha^{\,U}$ are random variables (Lower and Upper) for all $\alpha \in [0,1]$. Then $\widetilde{X}$ has the same distribution as X with fuzzy parameters $\widetilde{\theta}_1,...,\widetilde{\theta}_n$ if $\widetilde{X}_\alpha^{\,L}$ has the parameters $\left(\widetilde{\theta}_1\right)_\alpha^L,...,\left(\widetilde{\theta}_n\right)_\alpha^L$ and $\widetilde{X}_\alpha^{\,U}$ has the parameters $\left(\widetilde{\theta}_1\right)_\alpha^U,...,\left(\widetilde{\theta}_n\right)_\alpha^U$.

Let $X_1,...,X_n$ be independent and identically distributed random variables. Let $L(X)$ and $U(X)$ be two statistics such that $L(X) \geq U(X)$, where $X = (X_1,...,X_n)$. If the random interval $[L(X),\ U(X)]$ satisfies $P_\theta\{L(X) \geq \theta \geq U(X)\} = 1-\alpha$, then $[L(X),U(X)]$ is a confidence interval for θ with confidence coefficient $1-\alpha$, where $x = (x_1,...,x_n)$ and each x_i is the observed value of X_i for $i = 1,2,...,n$. Let $\widetilde{X}_1,...,\widetilde{X}_n$ be independent and identically distributed fuzzy random variables with fuzzy parameter $\widetilde{\theta}$. Let $\widetilde{x}_i$ be the observed values of $\widetilde{X}_i$ for $i = 1,2,...,n$ where each $\widetilde{x}_i$ is a canonical fuzzy number. The $X_{1\alpha}^{\,L},...,X_{n\alpha}^{\,L}$ and $X_{1\alpha}^{\,U},...,X_{n\alpha}^{\,U}$ are independent and identically distributed random variables. Therefore it can be written as $\widetilde{X}_\alpha^{\,L} = \left(X_{1\alpha}^{\,L},...,X_{n\alpha}^{\,L}\right)$ and $\widetilde{X}_\alpha^{\,U} = \left(X_{1\alpha}^{\,U},...,X_{n\alpha}^{\,U}\right)$. From these two groups of observed values, a confidence interval $\left[L\left(\widetilde{X}_\alpha^{\,L}\right), U\left(\widetilde{X}_\alpha^{\,L}\right)\right]$ can be constructed for $\widetilde{\theta}_\alpha^{\,L}$ with confidence coefficient $1-\alpha$ and a confi-

dence interval $\left[L\left(\widetilde{X}_\alpha^{\,U}\right), U\left(\widetilde{X}_\alpha^{\,U}\right)\right]$ for $\widetilde{\theta}_\alpha^{\,U}$ with confidence coefficient $1-\alpha$.

Proposition 2: Let $\widetilde{A}$ be a fuzzy subset of R with membership function $\mu_{\widetilde{A}}$ and the α-level set $\widetilde{A}_\alpha = \{r\ /\ \mu_{\widetilde{A}}(r) \geq \alpha\}$ for $\alpha \in [0,1]$. Then the membership function of A can be represented by $\mu_{\widetilde{A}}(r) = \sup\limits_{0 \geq \alpha \geq 1} \alpha.1_{A_\alpha}(r)$, where $1_{\widetilde{A}_\alpha}(r)$ is an indicator function of $\widetilde{A}_\alpha$ such that

$$1_{\widetilde{A}_\alpha}(r) = \begin{cases} 1 & r \in \widetilde{A}_\alpha \\ 0 & r \notin \widetilde{A}_\alpha \end{cases}$$

Hence $\widetilde{A}$ is a fuzzy subset of R with membership function defined by $\mu_{\widetilde{A}}(r) = \sup\limits_{0 \geq \alpha \geq 1} \alpha.1_{A_\alpha}(r)$. This is known as the Resolution Identity

Proposition 3: An upper semi-continuous function assumes maximum over a compact set, while a lower semi-continuous function assumes minimum over a compact set.

Proposition 4: Let $\left\{A_\alpha\right\}$, where $A_\alpha = \left\{[\eta_1(\alpha),\eta_2(\alpha)]\ /\ 0 \geq \alpha \geq 1\right\}$ be a family of closed intervals in R, where the function η_1 and η_2 are continuous on $[0,1]$. Suppose that $\widetilde{A}$ is a fuzzy subset of R induced by the family $\left\{A_\alpha\right\}$ with the membership function defined by $\mu_{\widetilde{A}}(r) = \sup\limits_{0 \geq \alpha \geq 1} \alpha.1_{A_\alpha}(r)$.

Then the α-level set $\widetilde{A}_\alpha$ of $\widetilde{A}$ is given by:

$$\widetilde{A}_\alpha = \{r\ /\ \mu_{\widetilde{A}}(r) \geq \alpha\} = \left\{r\ /\ \sup\limits_{0 \geq t \geq 1} t.1_{A_t}(r) \geq \alpha\right\} = \left[\min\limits_{\alpha \geq t \geq 1}\eta_1(t), \max\limits_{\alpha \geq t \geq 1}\eta_2(t)\right]$$

Proposition 5: Let $\left\{A_\alpha\right\}$, as in *Proposition* 4 be a family of closed intervals in R. Suppose that $A_1 \neq \phi$, η_1 and η_2 are bounded and continuous on [0,1]. Then the fuzzy subset $\widetilde{A}$ induced by the family $\left\{A_\alpha\right\}$ as shown in $\mu_{\widetilde{A}}(r) = \sup\limits_{0 \geq \alpha \geq 1} \alpha.1_{A_\alpha}(r)$ turns into a fuzzy number.

Definition 2: (Canonical fuzzy number)

Let $\widetilde{a}$ be a fuzzy number. Then $\widetilde{a}_\alpha = \left[\widetilde{a}_\alpha^{\,L}, \widetilde{a}_\alpha^{\,U}\right]$.

It can be seen that $\widetilde{a}$ is a canonical fuzzy number, if $\eta_1(\alpha) = \widetilde{a}_\alpha^{\,L}$ and $\eta_2(\alpha) = \widetilde{a}_\alpha^{\,U}$ are continuous on [0,1]. If the membership function of $\widetilde{a}$ is strictly increasing on the interval $\left[\widetilde{a}_0^{\,L}, \widetilde{a}_1^{\,L}\right]$ and strictly decreasing on the interval $\left[\widetilde{a}_1^{\,U}, \widetilde{a}_0^{\,U}\right]$, then it is easy to see that $\eta_1(\alpha) = \widetilde{a}_\alpha^{\,L}$ and $\eta_2(\alpha) = \widetilde{a}_\alpha^{\,U}$ are continuous on [0,1]. i.e., $\widetilde{a}$ is a canonical fuzzy number.

Now by *Proposition* 4 two fuzzy subsets $\widetilde{L}(\widetilde{x})$ and $\widetilde{U}(\widetilde{x})$ can be induced with membership functions defined by $\mu_{\widetilde{L}(\widetilde{x})}(r) = \sup\limits_{0 \geq \alpha \geq 1} \alpha.1_{A_\alpha^{\,L}}(r)$ and $\mu_{\widetilde{U}(\widetilde{x})}(r) = \sup\limits_{0 \geq \alpha \geq 1} \alpha.1_{A_\alpha^{\,U}}(r)$, where $A_\alpha^{\,L} = \left[l^L(\alpha), u^L(\alpha)\right]$, $A_\alpha^{\,U} = \left[l^U(\alpha), u^U(\alpha)\right]$. Where in turn

$$l^L(\alpha) = \min\left\{L(\widetilde{x}_\alpha^{\,L}), L(\widetilde{x}_\alpha^{\,U})\right\},$$

$$u^L(\alpha) = \max\left\{L(\widetilde{x}_\alpha^{\,L}), L(\widetilde{x}_\alpha^{\,U})\right\}$$

and

$$l^U(\alpha) = \min\left\{U(\widetilde{x}_\alpha^{\,L}), U(\widetilde{x}_\alpha^{\,U})\right\}$$

$$u^U(\alpha) = \max\left\{U(\widetilde{x}_\alpha^{\,L}), U(\widetilde{x}_\alpha^{\,U})\right\}.$$

By *Proposition* 5 it is seen that $\widetilde{L}(\widetilde{x})$ and $\widetilde{U}(\widetilde{x})$ are fuzzy numbers and have α-level sets. Finally $\left[L\left(\widetilde{X}_\alpha^{\,U}\right), U\left(\widetilde{X}_\alpha^{\,U}\right)\right]$ is a fuzzy confidence interval for the fuzzy parameter $\widetilde{\theta}$ with confidence coefficient $1 - \alpha$, since the end points of the interval are fuzzy numbers.

Numerical Example for Fuzzy Confidence Interval

Consider the system with fuzzy probabilities (Buckley et al., 2004; Buckley & Jovers, 2006), where i customers arrive during time interval t. Suppose the system during N time periods is observed and find that there have been n_i times that i customers have arrived for service, $i=0,1,2,\ldots$ Let $p(i)$ be the probability that i customers arrive during time period t, $i=0,1,2,\ldots$ then a point estimate of $p(i)$ is simply n_i / N. However to show the uncertainty in this estimate, a confidence interval for $p(i)$ can also be computed. Hence the $(1 - \beta)$ 100% confidence intervals for $p(i)$, for all $0.01 \leq \beta < 1$ is denoted by $[p(i)_1(\beta), p(i)_2(\beta)]$. Starting at 0.01 is arbitrary, and one can choose to begin at 0.001 or 0.005. Then $[n_i / N, n_i / N]$ is the 0% confidence interval for $p(i)$. Now, placing these confidence intervals, one on the top of the other, a triangular shaped fuzzy number $p(i)$ whose α-cuts are confidence intervals, can be formed. This kind of representation gives more information on the point estimate. Then using the α-cuts $p(i)[\alpha] = [p(i)_1(\alpha), p(i)_2(\alpha)]$, can be formed for $0.01 \leq \alpha \leq 1$. Suppose $N=500$, $n_i = 100$, then a $(1-\beta)100\%$ confidence interval for $p(1)$ is given by:

$$\left[0.2 - Z_{\beta/2}\sqrt{\frac{0.2(1 - 0.2)}{500}}, 0.2 + Z_{\beta/2}\sqrt{\frac{0.2(1 - 0.2)}{500}}\right] \tag{17}$$

where $Z_{\beta/2}$ is defined by $\int_{-\infty}^{Z_{\beta/2}} N(0,1)dx = 1 - \beta / 2$.

$N(0,1)$ denotes normal density with mean zero and unit variance. However in the rest of the chapter trapezoidal shaped fuzzy numbers obtained from the vague estimates of the interval vague values will be used from *Table* 1.

VAGUE MEASURES FOR THE CORRELATION COEFFICIENT OF IVSs

Correlation Coefficient of IVS through α-Cuts

In most of the previous works, the fuzzy correlation coefficient is derived to be a crisp value, and also lying in the interval [0,1] (Yu, 1993; Wang & Li, 1999; Chiang & Lin, 1999; Hong & Hwang, 1995; Gerstenkorn & Manko, 1991; Bustince & Burillo, 1995). Hung & Wu, (2002) introduced the concept of positively and negatively correlated results for intuitionistic fuzzy sets. Kao & Liu, (2002) introduced the fuzzy measures for the correlation coefficient of fuzzy numbers to lie in the interval [-1,1]. In this chapter an attempt is made to present the correlation coefficient as an interval lying in the range [-1,1]. Statistical confidence intervals are used for this purpose. The vague degrees of the vague values from *Table* 1 are computed and treated as point estimates for confidence intervals. Using these point estimates, vague confidence intervals are evaluated and α-cuts are used to make these confidence intervals look like a trapezoidal fuzzy number. Given a sample of *n*-independent pairs of observations $(X_1,Y_1),(X_2,Y_2),...,(X_n,Y_n)$, the correlation coefficient $\rho_{X,Y}$ between X and Y is calculated using the formula:

$$\rho_{X,Y} = \frac{\sum_{i=1}^{n}(X_i - \overline{X})(Y_i - \overline{Y})}{\sqrt{\sum_{i=1}^{n}(X_i - \overline{X})^2 \sum_{i=1}^{n}(Y_i - \overline{Y})^2}} \quad (18)$$

$$\overline{X} = \sum_{i=1}^{n}\frac{X_i}{n} \quad ; \quad \overline{Y} = \sum_{i=1}^{n}\frac{Y_i}{n}$$

are sample means of X and Y. When all observations are fuzzy, equation (18) becomes what was given by Kao & Liu, (2002):

$$\tilde{\rho}_{X,Y} = \frac{\sum_{i=1}^{n}\left(\widetilde{X}_i - \sum_{i=1}^{n}\frac{\widetilde{X}_i}{n}\right)\left(\widetilde{Y}_i - \sum_{i=1}^{n}\frac{\widetilde{Y}_i}{n}\right)}{\sqrt{\sum_{i=1}^{n}\left(\widetilde{X}_i - \sum_{i=1}^{n}\frac{\widetilde{X}_i}{n}\right)^2 \sum_{i=1}^{n}\left(\widetilde{Y}_i - \sum_{i=1}^{n}\frac{\widetilde{Y}_i}{n}\right)^2}} \quad (19)$$

Since it is difficult to derive membership function for $\tilde{\rho}_{X,Y}$ directly, the Zadeh's extension principle (1978), which is given as follows, is used:

$$\mu_{\tilde{\rho}_{X,Y}}(\rho) = \sup_{X,Y} \min\left\{\mu_{\widetilde{X}_i}(x_i), \mu_{\widetilde{Y}_i}(y_i)\forall i \, / \, \rho = \rho_{X,Y}\right\} \quad (20)$$

Numerical Example

In this section, a new method is proposed to derive the correlation coefficient of interval vague sets in the form of an interval, falling in the range [-1,1]. Fix N to be 500 and $\beta/2$ are the α-cut values 0.0,0.1,0.2,...,1.0. Hence using Buckley et al., (2004) method, a trapezoidal shaped fuzzy number is derived as the confidence interval for the vague degrees as seen in *Table* 2 and *Table* 3 from the interval vague values of *Table* 1. The trapezoidal fuzzy number for the vague degree (0.1,0.4) whose vague number is ([0.4,0.6][0.2,0.3]) from *Table* 2 is clearly shown in *Figure* 1. Similarly the trapezoidal fuzzy number for the

vague degree (0.2,0.6) whose vague number is ([0.3,0.6][0.1,0.2]) from Table 1 is clearly shown in Figure 2. The values obtained at each α-level for different vague values in Tables 2 and 3 con-

Table 2. Trapezoidal fuzzy numbers of the confidence intervals from vague degrees of IVS A

Interval vague set IVS A	Vague degree			Left and Right Spreads of the Vague Degrees					
				α=1.0	α=0.8	α=0.6	α=0.4	α=0.2	α=0.0
([0.4,0.6][0.2,0.3])	(0.1,0.4)	L	0.1	0.097317	0.094633	0.09195	0.089267	0.086584
		R	0.4	0.404382	0.408764	0.413145	0.417527	0.421909
([0.3,0.5][0.2,0.4])	(0.1,0.5)	L	0.1	0.097317	0.094633	0.09195	0.089267	0.086584
		R	0.5	0.504472	0.508944	0.513416	0.517889	0.522361
([0.5,0.7][0.1,0.2])	(0.1,0.4)	L	0.1	0.097317	0.094633	0.09195	0.089267	0.086584
		R	0.4	0.404382	0.408764	0.413145	0.417527	0.421909
([0.6,0.7][0.1,0.2])	(0.1,0.3)	L	0.1	0.097317	0.094633	0.09195	0.089267	0.086584
		R	0.3	0.304099	0.308198	0.312296	0.316395	0.320494
([0.5,0.6][0.2,0.3])	(0.1,0.3)	L	0.1	0.097317	0.094633	0.09195	0.089267	0.086584
		R	0.3	0.304099	0.308198	0.312296	0.316395	0.320494
([0.4,0.6][0.2,0.3])	(0.1,0.4)	L	0.1	0.097317	0.094633	0.09195	0.089267	0.086584
		R	0.4	0.404382	0.408764	0.413145	0.417527	0.421909
([0.4,0.5][0.3,0.4])	(0.1,0.3)	L	0.1	0.097317	0.094633	0.09195	0.089267	0.086584
		R	0.3	0.304099	0.308198	0.312296	0.316395	0.320494
([0.3,0.5][0.2,0.3])	(0.2,0.5)	L	0.2	0.196422	0.192845	0.189267	0.185689	0.182111
		R	0.5	0.504472	0.508944	0.513416	0.517889	0.522361
([0.4,0.5][0.3,0.4])	(0.1,0.3)	L	0.1	0.097317	0.094633	0.09195	0.089267	0.086584
		R	0.3	0.304099	0.308198	0.312296	0.316395	0.320494
([0.5,0.6][0.2,0.3])	(0.1,0.3)	L	0.1	0.097317	0.094633	0.09195	0.089267	0.086584
		R	0.3	0.304099	0.308198	0.312296	0.316395	0.320494
([0.3,0.6][0.1,0.2])	(0.2,0.6)	L	0.2	0.196422	0.192845	0.189267	0.185689	0.182111
		R	0.6	0.604382	0.608764	0.613145	0.617527	0.621909
([0.5,0.6][0.2,0.3])	(0.1,0.3)	L	0.1	0.097317	0.094633	0.09195	0.089267	0.086584
		R	0.3	0.304099	0.308198	0.312296	0.316395	0.320494
([0.6,0.7][0.1,0.2])	(0.1,0.3)	L	0.1	0.097317	0.094633	0.09195	0.089267	0.086584
		R	0.3	0.304099	0.308198	0.312296	0.316395	0.320494
([0.7,0.75][0.1,0.2])	0.05,0.2)	L	0.05	0.048051	0.046101	0.044152	0.042203	0.040253
		R	0.2	0.203578	0.207155	0.210733	0.214311	0.217889
([0.6,0.7][0.1,0.2])	(0.1,0.3)	L	0.1	0.097317	0.094633	0.09195	0.089267	0.086584
		R	0.3	0.304099	0.308198	0.312296	0.316395	0.320494

L – Left spread ; R – Right spread.

Table 3. Trapezoidal fuzzy numbers of the confidence intervals from vague degrees of IVS B

Interval vague set IVS B	Vague degree		α=1.0	Left and Right Spreads of the Vague Degrees				
				α=0.8	α=0.6	α=0.4	α=0.2	α=0.0
([0.3,0.6][0.1,0.2])	(0.2,0.6)	L	0.2	0.196422	0.192845	0.189267	0.185689	0.182111
		R	0.6	0.604382	0.608764	0.613145	0.617527	0.621909
([0.4,0.6][0.2,0.3])	(0.1,0.4)	L	0.1	0.097317	0.094633	0.09195	0.089267	0.086584
		R	0.4	0.404382	0.408764	0.413145	0.417527	0.421909
([0.3,0.6][0.3,0.35])	(0.05,0.4)	L	0.05	0.048051	0.046101	0.044152	0.042203	0.040253
		R	0.4	0.404382	0.408764	0.413145	0.417527	0.421909
([0.5,0.8][0.1,0.17])	(0.03,0.4)	L	0.03	0.028474	0.026948	0.025423	0.023897	0.022371
		R	0.4	0.404382	0.408764	0.413145	0.417527	0.421909
([0.5,0.6][0.2,0.3])	(0.1,0.3)	L	0.1	0.097317	0.094633	0.09195	0.089267	0.086584
		R	0.3	0.304099	0.308198	0.312296	0.316395	0.320494
([0.4,0.6][0.1,0.2])	(0.2,0.5)	L	0.2	0.196422	0.192845	0.189267	0.185689	0.182111
		R	0.5	0.504472	0.508944	0.513416	0.517889	0.522361
([0.3,0.5][0.3,0.4])	(0.1,0.4)	L	0.1	0.097317	0.094633	0.09195	0.089267	0.086584
		R	0.4	0.404382	0.408764	0.413145	0.417527	0.421909
([0.2,0.6][0.3,0.35])	(0.05,0.5)	L	0.05	0.048051	0.046101	0.044152	0.042203	0.040253
		R	0.5	0.504472	0.508944	0.513416	0.517889	0.522361
([0.2,0.5][0.3,0.4])	(0.1,0.5)	L	0.1	0.097317	0.094633	0.09195	0.089267	0.086584
		R	0.5	0.504472	0.508944	0.513416	0.517889	0.522361
([0.4,0.6][0.3,0.37])	(0.03,0.3)	L	0.03	0.028474	0.026948	0.025423	0.023897	0.022371
		R	0.3	0.304099	0.308198	0.312296	0.316395	0.320494
([0.2,0.5][0.2,0.3])	(0.2,0.6)	L	0.2	0.196422	0.192845	0.189267	0.185689	0.182111
		R	0.6	0.604382	0.608764	0.613145	0.617527	0.621909
([0.5,0.8][0.1,0.15])	(0.05,0.4)	L	0.05	0.048051	0.046101	0.044152	0.042203	0.040253
		R	0.4	0.404382	0.408764	0.413145	0.417527	0.421909
([0.5,0.7][0.2,0.27])	(0.03,0.3)	L	0.03	0.028474	0.026948	0.025423	0.023897	0.022371
		R	0.3	0.304099	0.308198	0.312296	0.316395	0.320494
([0.5,0.7][0.1,0.2])	(0.1,0.4)	L	0.1	0.097317	0.094633	0.09195	0.089267	0.086584
		R	0.4	0.404382	0.408764	0.413145	0.417527	0.421909
([0.2,0.4][0.1,0.2])	(0.4,0.7)	L	0.4	0.395618	0.391236	0.386855	0.382473	0.378091
		R	0.7	0.704099	0.708198	0.712296	0.716395	0.720494

L – Left spread ; R – Right spread.

stitutes a confidence interval, and placing these confidence intervals one on the top of the other, a trapezoidal shaped fuzzy number is obtained as seen in Figures 1 and 2. The Correlation coefficient obtained at different α-levels computed using the formula $\tilde{\rho}_{A,B}$, (equation (20)) is also seen to be a trapezoidal fuzzy number from *Table* 4 and *Figure* 3, and lies in the interval [-1,1].

Figure 1.Trapezoidal fuzzy number as confidence interval for the vague value ([0.4, 0.6][0.2, 0.3])

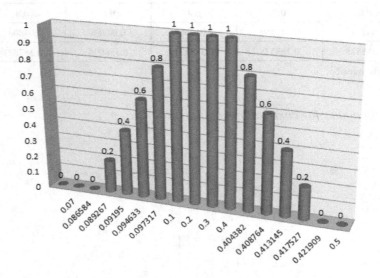

Figure 2.Trapezoidal fuzzy number as confidence interval for the vague value ({0.3, 0.6][0.1, 0.2])

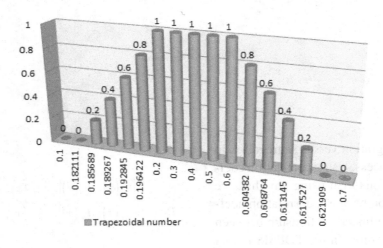

APPLICATION OF CORRELATION COEFFICIENT OF INTERVAL VAGUE SETS IN TOPSIS

In this work, TOPSIS is used to confirm the order of the evaluation objects with regard to the positive and negative ideal solutions of the multi-attribute problems. A novel TOPSIS algorithm is presented where correlation coefficient is utilized to identify the positive and negative ideal solutions as well as ranking of the best alternatives. In most of the previous TOPSIS works in literature, different forms of distance and similarity functions are used to calculate the closeness coefficient. If near things are related, then distant things, although less related, are related too and in different ways

Table 4. Correlation coefficient of the Trapezoidal fuzzy numbers at different α-levels

α-levels	0.0	0.2	0.4	0.6	0.8	1.0
L	0.047241	0.047455	0.047661	0.04786	0.048082	0.048235
R	0.388828	0.388578	0.388327	0.388074	0.387821	0.387567

L – Left spread ; R – Right spread.

Figure 3.Trapezoidal number for correlation coefficient

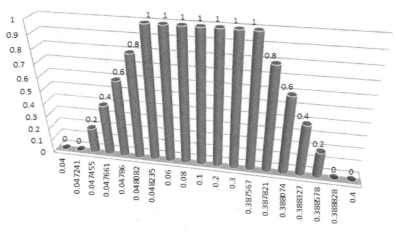

■ Correlation coefficient

reflecting their integration versus segregation in the data analysis process. Using correlation coefficient is advantageous than using any distance or similarity function because, correlation coefficient preserves the linear relationship between the variables under study. In the TOPSIS model of Liu, P. D., (2009) score function was used to identify positive and negative ideal solutions. In the proposed TOPSIS algorithm, correlation coefficient of IVSs is utilized instead of score and accuracy functions to identify the positive and negative ideal solutions (Table 5).

Definition 3 (Zhou & Wu, 2006; Wang, 2006):

Suppose A and B are interval vague sets

$$A = \left\{ \left\langle \left[t_A^-(x),\ t_A^+(x) \right],\ \left[f_A^-(x),\ f_A^+(x) \right] \right\rangle \ / \ x \in X \right\},$$

$$B = \left\{ \left\langle \left[t_B^-(x),\ t_B^+(x) \right],\ \left[f_B^-(x),\ f_B^+(x) \right] \right\rangle \ / \ x \in X \right\}.$$

Then the distance between the interval vague sets A and B is defined as follows.

$$d(A,B) = \frac{1}{4n} \sum_{i=1}^{n} \begin{pmatrix} \left| t_A^-(x_i) - t_B^-(x_i) \right| + \left| t_A^+(x_i) - t_B^+(x_i) \right| + \\ \left| f_A^-(x_i) - f_B^-(x_i) \right| + \left| f_A^+(x_i) - f_B^+(x_i) \right| + \\ \left| \pi_A^-(x_i) - \pi_B^-(x_i) \right| + \left| \pi_A^+(x_i) - \pi_B^+(x_i) \right| \end{pmatrix}$$

(21)

Table 5. The decision factors involved in the proposed TOPSIS method

Decision Factors	Formulation
Decision Alternatives	$A = \left\{ A_1, A_2, ..., A_n \right\}$
Attribute Set of Interval Vague Values	$C = \left\{ C_1, C_2, ..., C_n \right\}$
Individual Interval Vague Value	$\tilde{\phi}_{ij} = \left\langle \tilde{t}_{ij}, \tilde{f}_{ij} \right\rangle, \; t_{ij}^+ + f_{ij}^+ \le 1$
Decision Alternative satisfying the Attribute	$\tilde{t}_{ij} = \left[t_{ij}^-, t_{ij}^+ \right] \subseteq \left[0, 1 \right]$
Decision Alternative not satisfying the Attribute	$\tilde{f}_{ij} = \left[f_{ij}^-, f_{ij}^+ \right] \subseteq \left[0, 1 \right]$
Attribute Weights	$W = \left(\tilde{w}_1, \tilde{w}_2, ..., \tilde{w}_n \right), \; \tilde{w}_j = \left\langle \tilde{t}_{wj}, \tilde{f}_{wj} \right\rangle,$ $t_{wj}^+ + f_{wj}^+ \le 1$
Truth Membership of Attribute Weights	$\tilde{t}_{wj} = \left[t_{wj}^-, t_{wj}^+ \right] \subseteq \left[0, 1 \right]$
False Membership of Attribute Weights	$\tilde{f}_{wj} = \left[f_{wj}^-, f_{wj}^+ \right] \subseteq \left[0, 1 \right]$
Decision Matrix	$\tilde{B} = \left(\tilde{\phi}_{ij} \right)_{m \times n}$
Weighted Decision Matrix	$B = \left(b_{ij} \right)_{m \times n}$

The weighted attribute value for the decision matrix $\tilde{B} = \left(\tilde{\phi}_{ij} \right)_{m \times n}$ of each interval vague value $\tilde{\phi}_{ij}$ is given as follows:

$$b_{ij} = \tilde{w}_j \tilde{\phi}_{ij} \qquad (22)$$

$$= \left\langle \tilde{t}_{b_{ij}}, \tilde{f}_{b_{ij}} \right\rangle$$

$$= \left\langle \left[t_{b_{ij}}^-, t_{b_{ij}}^+ \right], \left[f_{b_{ij}}^-, f_{b_{ij}}^+ \right] \right\rangle,$$

where,

$$\tilde{t}_{bij} = \left[t_{ij}^- t_{wj}^-, t_{ij}^+ t_{wj}^+ \right], \qquad (23)$$

$$\tilde{f}_{bij} = \left[f_{ij}^- + f_{wj}^- - f_{ij}^- f_{wj}^-, f_{ij}^+ + f_{wj}^+ - f_{ij}^+ f_{wj}^+ \right], \qquad (24)$$

The positive ideal solution is the best solution that is assumed (V^+). Each indicator value is the best value of the optional schemes.

The interval vague set positive ideal solution V^+ is given as:

$$\max\_i = \max_i \left(k_{ij} \right)$$

$$V^+ = \left\langle [t^-_{V^+_j}, t^+_{V^+_j}], [f^-_{V^+_j}, f^+_{V^+_j}] \right\rangle$$

$$= \left\langle [t^-_{b^{\max}_{ij}}, t^+_{b^{\max}_{ij}}], [f^-_{b^{\max}_{ij}}, f^+_{b^{\max}_{ij}}] \right\rangle, \qquad (25)$$

where $b^{\max}_{ij}$ refers to the b_{ij} corresponding to the maximum value obtained from the correlation coefficient k_{ij} between each b_{ij} and $\tilde{r}^+ = \big([1,1], [0,0] \big)$.

The negative ideal solution is another worst solution that is assumed (V^-). Each indicator value is the worst value of the optional projects.

The interval vague set negative ideal solution V^- is given as:

$$\min\_i = \min_i \left(k_{ij} \right)$$

$$V^- = \left\langle [t^-_{V^-_j}, t^+_{V^-_j}], [f^-_{V^-_j}, f^+_{V^-_j}] \right\rangle$$

$$= \left\langle [t^-_{b^{\min}_{ij}}, t^+_{b^{\min}_{ij}}], [f^-_{b^{\min}_{ij}}, f^+_{b^{\min}_{ij}}] \right\rangle, \qquad (26)$$

where $b^{\min}_{ij}$ refers to the b_{ij} corresponding to the minimum value obtained from the correlation coefficient k_{ij} between each b_{ij} and $\tilde{r}^+ = \big([1,1], [0,0] \big)$.

V^+ and V^- are compared with each interval vague value in the original project set. The correlation coefficient is used to confirm the order of the alternatives.

Model 1: The TOPSIS Algorithm with Correlation Coefficient of IVSs for both Ideal Solutions and Closeness Coefficient

Step 1: Calculate the weighted attribute value $b_{ij} = \widetilde{w}_j \widetilde{\phi_{ij}}$ of each interval vague value given in the decision matrix $\widetilde{B} = \left(\widetilde{\phi_{ij}} \right)_{m \times n}$.

Step 2: Calculate the Correlation coefficient k_{ij} between the individual interval vague values and the perfect positive vague value $\tilde{r}^+ = \big([1,1], [0,0] \big)$, and form the corresponding correlation coefficient matrix $K = \left(k_{ij} \right)_{m \times n}$:

$$k_{ij} = k_{IVS}(b_{ij}, \tilde{r}^+) = \frac{C_{IVS}(b_{ij}, \tilde{r}^+)}{\sqrt{E_{IVS}(b_{ij}) . E_{IVS}(\tilde{r}^+)}} \qquad (27)$$

Step 3: Confirm the positive ideal solution V^+ and the negative ideal solution V^- of the evaluation object based on the calculated Correlation coefficient k_{ij}.

Step 4: Calculate the correlation coefficient between each value b_{ij} and the positive ideal solution, as follows:

$$k^+_i(b_{ij}, V^+) = \frac{C_{IVS}(b_{ij}, V^+)}{\sqrt{E_{IVS}(b_{ij}) . E_{IVS}(V^+)}} \qquad (28)$$

Step 5: Calculate the correlation coefficient between each value b_{ij} and the negative ideal solution, as follows:

$$k_i^-(b_{ij}, V^-) = \frac{C_{IVS}(b_{ij}, V^-)}{\sqrt{E_{IVS}(b_{ij}) . E_{IVS}(V^-)}} \qquad (29)$$

Step 6: Confirm the relative adjacent degree and rank the alternatives based on the highest degree. The relative adjacent degree of the evaluation object and the ideal solution is:

$$D_i = \frac{K_i^-}{K_i^+ + K_i^-} \quad i = 1, 2, ..., m \qquad (30)$$

where $K_i^- = 1 - k_i^-$ and $K_i^+ = 1 - k_i^+$.

(With regard to the relative adjacency relationship in analyzing how linearly the objects are interrelated, requires the computational property $K_i^- = 1 - k_i^-$ and $K_i^+ = 1 - k_i^+$, with respect to the maximum value 1)

Model 2: The TOPSIS Algorithm with Correlation Coefficient of IVSs for Ideal Solutions and Distance Function for Closeness Coefficient

Step 1: Calculate the weighted attribute value $b_{ij} = \widetilde{w}_j \widetilde{\phi}_{ij}$ of each interval vague value given in the decision matrix $\widetilde{B} = \left(\widetilde{\phi}_{ij}\right)_{m \times n}$.

Step 2: Calculate the Correlation coefficient k_{ij} between the individual interval vague values and the perfect positive vague value $\widetilde{r}^+ = \big([1,1],[0,0]\big)$, and form the corresponding correlation coefficient matrix $K = \left(k_{ij}\right)_{m \times n}$:

$$k_{ij} = k_{IVS}(b_{ij}, \widetilde{r}^+) = \frac{C_{IVS}(b_{ij}, \widetilde{r}^+)}{\sqrt{E_{IVS}(b_{ij}) . E_{IVS}(\widetilde{r}^+)}}$$

Step 3: Confirm the positive ideal solution V^+ and the negative ideal solution V^- of the evaluation object based on the calculated correlation coefficient k_{ij}.

Step 4: Calculate the distance between each value b_{ij} and the positive ideal solution, as shown as follows.

$$d_i^+ = \frac{1}{4n} \sum_{j=1}^{n} \left(\begin{array}{l} \left|t_{b_{ij}}^- - t_{V_j^+}^-\right| + \left|t_{b_{ij}}^+ - t_{V_j^+}^+\right| + \left|f_{b_{ij}}^- - f_{V_j^+}^-\right| + \\ \left|f_{b_{ij}}^+ - f_{V_j^+}^+\right| + \left|\pi_{b_{ij}}^- - \pi_{V_j^+}^-\right| + \left|\pi_{b_{ij}}^+ - \pi_{V_j^+}^+\right| \end{array} \right)$$

$$(31)$$

Step 5: Calculate the distance between each value b_{ij} and the negative ideal solution, as shown as follows.

$$d_i^- = \frac{1}{4n} \sum_{j=1}^{n} \left(\begin{array}{l} \left|t_{b_{ij}}^- - t_{V_j^-}^-\right| + \left|t_{b_{ij}}^+ - t_{V_j^-}^+\right| + \left|f_{b_{ij}}^- - f_{V_j^-}^-\right| + \\ \left|f_{b_{ij}}^+ - f_{V_j^-}^+\right| + \left|\pi_{b_{ij}}^- - \pi_{V_j^-}^-\right| + \left|\pi_{b_{ij}}^+ - \pi_{V_j^-}^+\right| \end{array} \right)$$

$$(32)$$

Step 6: Confirm the relative adjacent degree and rank alternatives based on the highest degree. The relative adjacent degree of the evaluation object and the ideal solution is:

$$A_i = \frac{d_i^-}{d_i^+ + d_i^-} \quad i = 1, 2, ..., m \qquad (33)$$

NUMERICAL ILLUSTRATION

A company intends to select a person for the department manager position. Four aspects of the candidate are evaluated by experts, which are as follows:

C_1: Moral quality
C_2: Professional ability
C_3: Creative ability

C$_4$: Knowledge range

The experts provide evaluation data and weights to each aspect and they are all denoted by an interval vague value, namely, the interval number of the support degree given, and the interval number of the object degree, also given. The evaluation data and attribute weight are shown as follows. The order of the 5 candidates must be confirmed. The evaluation data of different candidates given by experts are shown in Box 5.

Algorithm Using MODEL-1

Step 1: Calculate the weighted $\tilde{b}_{ij}$ as in equations (22) to (24) from the decision matrix $\widetilde{B}$

$$\tilde{b}_{ij} = \widetilde{w}_j \widetilde{\phi}_{ij}$$

$$= \left\langle \tilde{t}_{b_{ij}}, \tilde{f}_{b_{ij}} \right\rangle$$

$$= \left\langle \left[t_{bij}^-, t_{bij}^+ \right], \left[f_{bij}^-, f_{bij}^+ \right] \right\rangle,$$

where, $\tilde{t}_{b_{ij}} = \left\langle \left[t_{ij}^- t_{wj}^-, t_{ij}^+ t_{wj}^+ \right] \right\rangle,$

$\tilde{f}_{b_{ij}} = \left\langle \left[f_{ij}^- + f_{wj}^- - f_{ij}^- f_{wj}^-, f_{ij}^+ + f_{wj}^+ - f_{ij}^+ + f_{wj}^+ \right] \right\rangle,$

$$\tilde{t}_{b_{11}} = \left(\left[t_{11}^- t_{w1}^-, t_{11}^+ t_{w1}^+ \right] \right)$$

$$= \left(\left[(0.65)(0.3), (0.72)(0.4) \right] \right)$$

$$= \left(\left[0.195, 0.288 \right] \right)$$

Similarly the other values can be calculated and are given as follows:
Therefore, see Box 6.

Step 2: Calculate the Correlation coefficient k_{ij} between the individual interval vague values b_{ij} of the matrix B and the perfect positive vague value $\tilde{r}^+ = \left([1,1], [0,0] \right)$:

Consider the interval vague value

$$b_{11} = \left([0.195, 0.288], [0.610, 0.704] \right).$$

$$E_{IVS}(b_{11}, b_{11}) = 0.5134, \quad E_{IVS}(\tilde{r}^+, \tilde{r}^+) = 1,$$
$$C_{IVS}(b_{11}, \tilde{r}^+) = 0.2415, \quad k_{IVS}(b_{11}, \tilde{r}^+) = 0.3370.$$

Hence $k_{11} = 0.3370$.
Similarly the correlation coefficient for all the other entries can be calculated (see Box 7).

Box 5.

$$\widetilde{B} = \begin{pmatrix} ([0.65, 0.72], [0.22, 0.27]) & ([0.52, 0.63], [0.16, 0.32]) & ([0.62, 0.71], [0.23, 0.28]) & ([0.32, 0.43], [0.21, 0.29]) \\ ([0.46, 0.52], [0.34, 0.41]) & ([0.73, 0.81], [0.12, 0.18]) & ([0.56, 0.61], [0.25, 0.29]) & ([0.41, 0.51], [0.24, 0.38]) \\ ([0.52, 0.60], [0.33, 0.40]) & ([0.33, 0.45], [0.26, 0.41]) & ([0.62, 0.76], [0.13, 0.21]) & ([0.53, 0.62], [0.27, 0.31]) \\ ([0.44, 0.53], [0.30, 0.45]) & ([0.38, 0.50], [0.27, 0.35]) & ([0.43, 0.64], [0.24, 0.32]) & ([0.61, 0.72], [0.17, 0.21]) \\ ([0.51, 0.58], [0.35, 0.40]) & ([0.64, 0.80], [0.13, 0.19]) & ([0.38, 0.58], [0.22, 0.38]) & ([0.58, 0.65], [0.23, 0.31]) \end{pmatrix}$$

The attribute weight given by the experts as follows:

$$W = \left\{ \left([0.3, 0.4], [0.5, 0.6] \right), \left([0.6.0.7].[0.1.0.2] \right), \left([0.6.0.7].[0.2.0.3] \right), \left([0.3.0.4].[0.5.0.6] \right) \right\}$$

Box 6.

$$
B = \begin{pmatrix}
([0.195,0.288],[0.610,0.708]) & ([0.312,0.441],[0.244,0.456]) \\
([0.138,0.208],[0.670,0.764]) & ([0.438,0.567],[0.208,0.344]) \\
([0.156,0.240],[0.665,0.760]) & ([0.198,0.315],[0.334,0.528]) \\
([0.132,0.212],[0.650,0.780]) & ([0.228,0.350],[0.343,0.480]) \\
([0.153,0.232],[0.675,0.760]) & ([0.384,0.560],[0.217,0.352])
\end{pmatrix}
$$

$$
\begin{array}{cc}
([0.372,0.497],[0.384,0.496]) & ([0.096,0.172],[0.605,0.716]) \\
([0.336,0.427],[0.400,0.503]) & ([0.123,0.204],[0.620,0.752]) \\
([0.372,0.532],[0.304,0.447]) & ([0.159,0.248],[0.635,0.724])
\end{array}
$$

(The positive ideal solution is boxed and the negative ideal solution underlined)

Step 3: Confirm the ideal solution and the negative solution of the evaluation object. The vague set ideal solution V^+ and the negative ideal solution V^- are shown as shown below.

$$\max\_i = \max_i\left(k_{ij}\right)$$

$$V^+ = \left\langle \left[t^-_{V^+_j}, t^+_{V^+_j}\right], \left[f^-_{V^+_j}, f^+_{V^+_j}\right] \right\rangle$$

$$= \left\langle [t^-_{b^{\max}_{ij}}, t^+_{b^{\max}_{ij}}], [f^-_{b^{\max}_{ij}}, f^+_{b^{\max}_{ij}}] \right\rangle,$$

$$V^+ = \left\{ \left[\begin{matrix}0.195,\\0.288\end{matrix}\right], \left[\begin{matrix}0.610,\\0.704\end{matrix}\right], \left[\begin{matrix}0.438,\\0.567\end{matrix}\right], \left[\begin{matrix}0.208,\\0.344\end{matrix}\right], \right.$$
$$\left. \left[\begin{matrix}0.372,\\0.532\end{matrix}\right], \left[\begin{matrix}0.304,\\0.447\end{matrix}\right], \left[\begin{matrix}0.183,\\0.288\end{matrix}\right], \left[\begin{matrix}0.585,\\0.684\end{matrix}\right] \right\}$$

$$\min\_i = \min_i\left(k_{ij}\right)$$

$$V^- = \left\langle \left[t^-_{V^-_j}, t^+_{V^-_j}\right], \left[f^-_{V^-_j}, f^+_{V^-_j}\right] \right\rangle$$

Box 7.

$$
K_{ij} = \begin{pmatrix}
k_{11} & k_{12} & k_{13} & k_{14} \\
k_{21} & k_{22} & k_{23} & k_{24} \\
k_{31} & k_{32} & k_{33} & k_{34} \\
k_{41} & k_{42} & k_{43} & k_{44} \\
k_{51} & k_{52} & k_{53} & k_{54}
\end{pmatrix} = \begin{pmatrix}
\boxed{0.3370} & 0.6079 & 0.6717 & \underline{0.1877} \\
0.2299 & \boxed{0.7905} & 0.6098 & 0.2230 \\
0.2629 & \underline{0.4127} & \boxed{0.7063} & 0.2799 \\
\underline{0.2277} & 0.4766 & 0.5517 & \boxed{0.3362} \\
0.2549 & 0.7468 & \underline{0.4902} & 0.3002
\end{pmatrix}
$$

$$= \left\langle [t^-_{b^{min}_{ij}}, t^+_{b^{min}_{ij}}], [f^-_{b^{min}_{ij}}, f^+_{b^{min}_{ij}}] \right\rangle,$$

$$V^- = \left\{ \left(\begin{bmatrix} 0.132, \\ 0.212 \end{bmatrix}, \begin{bmatrix} 0.650, \\ 0.780 \end{bmatrix} \right), \left(\begin{bmatrix} 0.198, \\ 0.315 \end{bmatrix}, \begin{bmatrix} 0.334, \\ 0.528 \end{bmatrix} \right), \right.$$
$$\left. \left(\begin{bmatrix} 0.228, \\ 0.406 \end{bmatrix}, \begin{bmatrix} 0.376, \\ 0.566 \end{bmatrix} \right), \left(\begin{bmatrix} 0.096, \\ 0.172 \end{bmatrix}, \begin{bmatrix} 0.605, \\ 0.716 \end{bmatrix} \right) \right\}$$

Step 4: Calculate the correlation coefficient between each interval vague value of the matrix B and the positive ideal solution,

$$E_{IVS}(b_{ij}, b_{ij}) =$$
$$\frac{1}{2} \sum_{j=1}^{n} \left(\begin{array}{c} (t^-_{b_{ij}})^2 + (t^+_{b_{ij}})^2 + (1 - f^-_{b_{ij}})^2 \\ + (1 - f^+_{b_{ij}})^2 + (\pi^-_{b_{ij}})^2 + (\pi^+_{b_{ij}})^2 \end{array} \right)$$

$$E_{IVS}(V^+, V^+) =$$
$$\frac{1}{2} \sum_{j=1}^{n} \left(\begin{array}{c} (t^-_{V^+_j})^2 + (t^+_{V^+_j})^2 + (1 - f^-_{V^+_j})^2 \\ + (1 - f^+_{V^+_j})^2 + (\pi^-_{V^+_j})^2 + (\pi^+_{V^+_j})^2 \end{array} \right)$$

$$C_{IVS}(b_{ij}, V^+) =$$
$$\frac{1}{2} \sum_{j=1}^{n} \left(\begin{array}{c} (t^-_{b_{ij}} t^-_{V^+_j}) + (t^+_{b_{ij}} t^+_{V^+_j}) + (1 - f^-_{b_{ij}})(1 - f^-_{V^+_j}) \\ + (1 - f^+_{b_{ij}})(1 - f^+_{V^+_j}) + (\pi^-_{b_{ij}} \pi^-_{V^+_j}) + (\pi^+_{b_{ij}} \pi^+_{V^+_j}) \end{array} \right)$$

$$k^+_i = k_{IVS}(b_{ij}, V^+) = \frac{C_{IVS}(b_{ij}, V^+)}{\sqrt{E_{IVS}(b_{ij}, b_{ij}). E_{IVS}(V^+, V^+)}}$$

Where, $\tilde{\pi}^-_{b_{ij}}(x) = 1 - t^+_{b_{ij}}(x) - f^+_{b_{ij}}(x)$,

$\tilde{\pi}^+_{b_{ij}}(x) = 1 - t^-_{b_{ij}}(x) - f^-_{b_{ij}}(x)$.

The entries of b_{1j} in the matrix B and the positive and negative ideal solutions taken in the order $t^-, t^+, f^-, f^+, \pi^-, \pi^+$ are given as follows:
The entries of b_{1j} in the matrix B

0.195	0.288	0.610	0.704	0.004	0.195
0.312	0.441	0.244	0.456	0.103	0.444
0.372	0.497	0.384	0.496	0.007	0.244
0.096	0.172	0.605	0.716	0.112	0.299

The entries of positive ideal solution V^+

0.195	0.288	0.610	0.704	0.004	0.195
0.438	0.567	0.208	0.344	0.089	0.354
0.372	0.532	0.304	0.447	0.021	0.324
0.183	0.288	0.585	0.684	0.028	0.232

Calculating the correlation coefficient between the entries of b_{1j} and the positive ideal solution, the values can be obtained as follows:

$E_{IVS}(b_{1j}, b_{1j}) = 1.8257,$
$E_{IVS}(V^+, V^+) = 1.8174,$
$C_{IVS}(b_{1j}, V^+) = 1.7984$

$$k^+_1 = k_{IVS}(b_{1j}, V^+) =$$
$$\frac{C_{IVS}(b_{1j}, V^+)}{\sqrt{E_{IVS}(b_{1j}, b_{1j}). E_{IVS}(V^+, V^+)}} = 0.9873$$

Similarly all the correlation coefficients can be calculated, and given as follows:

$k^+_2 = k_{IVS}(b_{2j}, V^+) = 0.9887,$
$k^+_3 = k_{IVS}(b_{3j}, V^+) = 0.9725,$
$k^+_4 = k_{IVS}(b_{4j}, V^+) = 0.9737,$

$k_5^+ = k_{IVS}(b_{5j}, V^+) = 0.9892.$

$K_1^+ = 0.0127, \quad K_2^+ = 0.0113, \quad K_3^+ = 0.0275,$
$K_4^+ = 0.0263, K_5^+ = 0.0108.$

where $K_i^+ = 1 - k_i^+.$

Step 5: Calculate the correlation coefficient between each interval vague value of the matrix B and the negative ideal solution,

$$E_{IVS}(b_{ij}, b_{ij}) =$$
$$\frac{1}{2} \sum_{j=1}^{n} \left[\begin{array}{c} (t_{b_{ij}}^-)^2 + (t_{b_{ij}}^+)^2 + (1 - f_{b_{ij}}^-)^2 + \\ (1 - f_{b_{ij}}^+)^2 + (\pi_{b_{ij}}^-)^2 + (\pi_{b_{ij}}^+)^2 \end{array} \right]$$

$$E_{IVS}(V^-, V^-) =$$
$$\frac{1}{2} \sum_{j=1}^{n} \left[\begin{array}{c} (t_{V_j^-}^-)^2 + (t_{V_j^-}^+)^2 + (1 - f_{V_j^-}^-)^2 \\ + (1 - f_{V_j^-}^+)^2 + (\pi_{V_j^-}^-)^2 + (\pi_{V_j^-}^+)^2 \end{array} \right]$$

$$C_{IVS}(b_{ij}, V^-) =$$
$$\frac{1}{2} \sum_{j=1}^{n} \left[\begin{array}{c} (t_{b_{ij}}^- t_{V_j^-}^-) + (t_{b_{ij}}^+ t_{V_j^-}^+) + (1 - f_{b_{ij}}^-)(1 - f_{V_j^-}^-) + \\ (1 - f_{b_{ij}}^+)(1 - f_{V_j^-}^+) + (\pi_{b_{ij}}^- \pi_{V_j^-}^-) + (\pi_{b_{ij}}^+ \pi_{V_j^-}^+) \end{array} \right]$$

$$k_i^- = k_{IVS}(b_{ij}, V^-) = \frac{C_{IVS}(b_{ij}, V^-)}{\sqrt{E_{IVS}(b_{ij}, b_{ij}) \cdot E_{IVS}(V^-, V^-)}}.$$

The entries of b_{1j} in the matrix B

0.195	0.288	0.610	0.704	0.004	0.195
0.312	0.441	0.244	0.456	0.103	0.444
0.372	0.497	0.384	0.496	0.007	0.244
0.096	0.172	0.605	0.716	0.112	0.299

The entries of negative ideal solution V^-

0.132	0.212	0.650	0.780	0.008	0.218
0.198	0.315	0.334	0.528	0.157	0.468
0.228	0.406	0.376	0.566	0.028	0.396
0.096	0.172	0.605	0.716	0.112	0.299

Calculating the correlation coefficient between the entries of b_{1j} and the negative ideal solution, the values are obtained as follows:

$E_{IVS}(b_{1j}, b_{1j}) = 1.8257,$
$E_{IVS}(V^-, V^-) = 1.8843,$
$C_{IVS}(b_{1j}, V^-) = 1.8248$

$$k_1^- = k_{IVS}(b_{1j}, V^-) = \frac{C_{IVS}(b_{1j}, V^-)}{\sqrt{E_{IVS}(b_{1j}, b_{1j}) \cdot E_{IVS}(V^-, V^-)}} = 0.9838$$

Similarly all the correlation coefficients can be calculated, and given as follows:

$k_2^- = k_{IVS}(b_{2j}, V^-) = 0.9689,$
$k_3^- = k_{IVS}(b_{3j}, V^-) = 0.9879,$
$k_4^- = k_{IVS}(b_{4j}, V^-) = 0.9937,$

$k_5^- = k_{IVS}(b_{5j}, V^-) = 0.9725.$

$K_1^- = 0.0162, \quad K_2^- = 0.0311, \quad K_3^- = 0.0121,$
$K_4^- = 0.0063, K_5^- = 0.0275.$

Where $K_i^- = 1 - k_i^-.$

Step 6: Confirm the relative adjacent degree and rank alternatives based on the highest degree. The relative adjacent degree of the evaluation object and the ideal solution are:

$$A_i = \frac{K_i^-}{K_i^+ + K_i^-} \quad i = 1, 2, \ldots, m$$

$$A_1 = \frac{K_1^-}{K_1^+ + K_1^-} = 0.5605,$$

$$A_2 = \frac{K_2^-}{K_2^+ + K_2^-} = 0.7335,$$

$$A_3 = \frac{K_3^-}{K_3^+ + K_3^-} = 0.3055,$$

$$A_4 = \frac{K_4^-}{K_4^+ + K_4^-} = 0.1932,$$

$$A_5 = \frac{K_5^-}{K_5^+ + K_5^-} = 0.7180.$$

Ranking alternatives based on the relative adjacent degree, it follows that:

$$A_2 > A_5 > A_1 > A_3 > A_4.$$

Hence A_2 is the best alternative.

Algorithm using Model 2

Step 1 to Step 4 of the numerical illustration for Model-2 is same as that of the numerical illustration for Model-1, which is clear from the algorithm given for both models.

Step 4: Calculate the distance between each interval vague value of the matrix B and the positive ideal solution, shown in Box 12.

$$d_i^+ = \frac{1}{4n} \sum_{j=1}^{n} \left(\begin{vmatrix} t_{b_{ij}}^- - t_{V_j^+}^- \end{vmatrix} + \begin{vmatrix} t_{b_{ij}}^+ - t_{V_j^+}^+ \end{vmatrix} + \begin{vmatrix} f_{b_{ij}}^- - f_{V_j^+}^- \end{vmatrix} + \\ \begin{vmatrix} f_{b_{ij}}^+ - f_{V_j^+}^+ \end{vmatrix} + \begin{vmatrix} \pi_{b_{ij}}^- - \pi_{V_j^+}^- \end{vmatrix} + \begin{vmatrix} \pi_{b_{ij}}^+ - \pi_{V_j^+}^+ \end{vmatrix} \right)$$

$$d_1^+ = d_1^+(b_{1j}, V^+) = 0.0730,$$
$$d_2^+ = d_2^+(b_{2j}, V^+) = 0.0606,$$
$$d_3^+ = d_3^+(b_{3j}, V^+) = 0.1244,$$

$$d_4^+ = d_4^+(b_{4j}, V^+) = 0.0955,$$
$$d_5^+ = d_5^+(b_{5j}, V^+) = 0.0704.$$

Step 5: Calculate the distance between each interval vague value of the matrix B and the negative ideal solution shown in Box 13.

$$d_i^- = \frac{1}{4n} \sum_{j=1}^{n} \left(\begin{vmatrix} t_{b_{ij}}^- - t_{V_j^-}^- \end{vmatrix} + \begin{vmatrix} t_{b_{ij}}^+ - t_{V_j^-}^+ \end{vmatrix} + \begin{vmatrix} f_{b_{ij}}^- - f_{V_j^-}^- \end{vmatrix} + \\ \begin{vmatrix} f_{b_{ij}}^+ - f_{V_j^-}^+ \end{vmatrix} + \begin{vmatrix} \pi_{b_{ij}}^- - \pi_{V_j^-}^- \end{vmatrix} + \begin{vmatrix} \pi_{b_{ij}}^+ - \pi_{V_j^-}^+ \end{vmatrix} \right)$$

$$d_1^- = d_1^-(b_{1j}, V^-) = 0.0784,$$
$$d_2^- = d_2^-(b_{2j}, V^-) = 0.1054,$$
$$d_3^- = d_3^-(b_{3j}, V^-) = 0.0643,$$
$$d_4^- = d_4^-(b_{4j}, V^-) = 0.0473,$$
$$d_5^- = d_5^-(b_{5j}, V^-) = 0.0901.$$

Step 6: Confirm the relative adjacent degree and rank alternatives based on the highest degree. The relative adjacent degree of the evaluation object and the ideal solution are:

$$A_i = \frac{d_i^-}{d_i^+ + d_i^-} \quad i = 1, 2, \ldots, m$$

$$A_1 = \frac{d_1^-}{d_1^+ + d_1^-} = 0.5178,$$

$$A_2 = \frac{d_2^-}{d_2^+ + d_2^-} = 0.6349,$$

$$A_3 = \frac{d_3^-}{d_3^+ + d_3^-} = 0.3407,$$

$$A_4 = \frac{d_4^{-}}{d_4^{+} + d_4^{-}} = 0.3312,$$

$$A_5 = \frac{d_5^{-}}{d_5^{+} + d_5^{-}} = 0.5614.$$

Ranking the alternatives based on the relative adjacent degree, it follows that:

$$A_2 > A_5 > A_1 > A_3 > A_4.$$

Hence A_2 is the best alternative.

COMPARISON OF PROPOSED TOPSIS WITH EXISTING METHODS

The proposed TOPSIS algorithm is compared with the previous methods of score and accuracy functions and presented as follows:

Definition 4 (Chen & Tan, 1994): Let $A = \left\langle \left[t_{ij}^{-}, t_{ij}^{+} \right], \left[f_{ij}^{-}, f_{ij}^{+} \right] \right\rangle$ be an interval vague value. Then the score function for the interval vague value A is defined as:

$$S_{ij} = \frac{t_{ij}^{-} + t_{ij}^{+}}{2} - \frac{f_{ij}^{-} + f_{ij}^{+}}{2} \tag{34}$$

Definition 5 (Hong & Choi, 2000): Let $A = \left\langle \left[t_{ij}^{-}, t_{ij}^{+} \right], \left[f_{ij}^{-}, f_{ij}^{+} \right] \right\rangle$ be an interval vague value. Then the score function for the interval vague value A is defined as:

$$H_{ij} = \frac{t_{ij}^{-} + t_{ij}^{+}}{2} + \frac{f_{ij}^{-} + f_{ij}^{+}}{2} \tag{35}$$

Xu, (2007e) also defined a same kind of function for IVIFSs and named it accuracy function which is given as follows:

Definition 6 (Xu, 2007): Let $A = \left\langle [a,b], [c,d] \right\rangle$ be an interval valued intuitionistic fuzzy number. Then the accuracy function for the interval valued intuitionistic fuzzy number A is defined as follows:

$$H(A) = \frac{a + b + c + d}{2} \tag{36}$$

Definition 7 (Liu, P.D., 2009): Let $A = \left\langle \left[t_{ij}^{-}, t_{ij}^{+} \right], \left[f_{ij}^{-}, f_{ij}^{+} \right] \right\rangle$ be an interval vague value. Then the score function for the interval vague value A is defined as follows:

$$\begin{aligned} L_{ij} &= \left(t_{ij}^{*} + t_{ij}^{*}.\pi_{ij}^{*} \right) - \left(f_{ij}^{*} + f_{ij}^{*}.\pi_{ij}^{*} \right) \\ &= \left(t_{ij}^{*} - f_{ij}^{*} \right)\left(1 + \pi_{ij}^{*} \right) \end{aligned} \tag{37}$$

where,

$$t_{ij}^{*} = \frac{t_{ij}^{-} + t_{ij}^{+}}{2}, \quad f_{ij}^{*} = \frac{f_{ij}^{-} + f_{ij}^{+}}{2}, \quad \pi_{ij}^{*} = \frac{\pi_{ij}^{-} + \pi_{ij}^{+}}{2}.$$

Nayagam et al, (2011) proved the invalidity of the Chen & Tan, (1994), Hong & Choi, (2000) and the Xu, (2007e) score and accuracy functions and suggested a novel and reasonable accuracy function which claims the comparability of all interval valued intuitionistic fuzzy numbers. Their accuracy function is as follows:

Definition 8 (Nayagam et al, 2011): Let $A = \left\langle [a,b], [c,d] \right\rangle$ be an interval valued intuitionistic fuzzy number. Then the accuracy function for the interval valued intuitionistic fuzzy number A is defined as follows:

$$L(A) = \frac{a + b - d(1 - b) - c(1 - a)}{2} \tag{38}$$

The distance function used in Liu, P.D., (2009) is utilized for all the comparison methods to calculate the closeness coefficient.

Comparison with the Score Function of Chen and Tan (1994)

The TOPSIS Algorithm with the Score Function of Chen & Tan, (1994) for the same numerical illustration is given as follows:

Step 1: Calculate the weighted attribute value of each interval vague value as in equations (22) to (24).

Step 2: Calculate the Score function S_{ij} for each individual Interval vague values using equation (34).

Step 3: Confirm the positive and the negative ideal solutions as given in equations (25) and (26) of the evaluation object based on the calculated Score function S_{ij}.

Step 4: Calculate the distance between each value b_{ij} and the positive ideal solution, as follows:

$$d_i^+ = \frac{1}{4n}\sum_{j=1}^n \left(\begin{array}{l} \left|t_{b_{ij}}^- - t_{V_j^+}^-\right| + \left|t_{b_{ij}}^+ - t_{V_j^+}^+\right| + \left|f_{b_{ij}}^- - f_{V_j^+}^-\right| + \\ \left|f_{b_{ij}}^+ - f_{V_j^+}^+\right| + \left|\pi_{b_{ij}}^- - \pi_{V_j^+}^-\right| + \left|\pi_{b_{ij}}^+ - \pi_{V_j^+}^+\right| \end{array} \right)$$

Step 5: Calculate the distance between each value b_{ij} and the negative ideal solution, as shown below:

$$d_i^- = \frac{1}{4n}\sum_{j=1}^n \left(\begin{array}{l} \left|t_{b_{ij}}^- - t_{V_j^-}^-\right| + \left|t_{b_{ij}}^+ - t_{V_j^-}^+\right| + \left|f_{b_{ij}}^- - f_{V_j^-}^-\right| + \\ \left|f_{b_{ij}}^+ - f_{V_j^-}^+\right| + \left|\pi_{b_{ij}}^- - \pi_{V_j^-}^-\right| + \left|\pi_{b_{ij}}^+ - \pi_{V_j^-}^+\right| \end{array} \right)$$

Step 6: Confirm the relative adjacent degree and rank alternatives based on the highest degree. The relative adjacent degree of the evaluation object and the ideal solution is:

$$A_i = \frac{d_i^-}{d_i^+ + d_i^-} \quad i = 1, 2, ..., m$$

Solution to the Same Illustration

Calculate the Score function S_{ij} for each individual interval vague values (see Box 8).

Confirm the ideal solution and the negative solution of the evaluation object using the above Score function value obtained from Step 2. The vague set ideal solution V^+ and the negative ideal solution V^- is shown as follows:

$$V^+ =$$
$$\left\{ \left(\left[\begin{array}{c}0.195, \\ 0.288\end{array}\right], \left[\begin{array}{c}0.610, \\ 0.704\end{array}\right] \right), \left(\left[0.438, 0.567\right], \left[0.208, 0.344\right] \right), \right.$$
$$\left. \left(\left[0.372, 0.532\right], \left[0.304, 0.447\right] \right), \left(\left[\begin{array}{c}0.183, \\ 0.288\end{array}\right], \left[\begin{array}{c}0.585, \\ 0.684\end{array}\right] \right) \right\}$$

$$V^- =$$
$$\left\{ \left(\left[\begin{array}{c}0.138, \\ 0.208\end{array}\right], \left[\begin{array}{c}0.670, \\ 0.764\end{array}\right] \right), \left(\left[\begin{array}{c}0.198, \\ 0.315\end{array}\right], \left[\begin{array}{c}0.334, \\ 0.528\end{array}\right] \right), \right.$$
$$\left. \left(\left[\begin{array}{c}0.228, \\ 0.406\end{array}\right], \left[\begin{array}{c}0.376, \\ 0.566\end{array}\right] \right), \left(\left[\begin{array}{c}0.096, \\ 0.172\end{array}\right], \left[\begin{array}{c}0.605, \\ 0.716\end{array}\right] \right) \right\}$$

Calculate the distance between each value b_{ij} and the positive ideal solution, as follows:

$$d_1^+ = d_1^+(b_{1j}, V^+) = 0.0730,$$
$$d_2^+ = d_2^+(b_{2j}, V^+) = 0.0669,$$
$$d_3^+ = d_3^+(b_{3j}, V^+) = 0.0866,$$

$$d_4^+ = d_4^+(b_{4j}, V^+) = 0.0955,$$
$$d_5^+ = d_5^+(b_{5j}, V^+) = 0.0704,$$

Calculate the distance between each value b_{ij} and the negative ideal solution, as follows:

Box 8.

$$S_{ij} = \begin{pmatrix} s_{11} & s_{12} & s_{13} & s_{14} \\ s_{21} & s_{22} & s_{23} & s_{24} \\ s_{31} & s_{32} & s_{33} & s_{34} \\ s_{41} & s_{42} & s_{43} & s_{44} \\ s_{51} & s_{52} & s_{53} & s_{54} \end{pmatrix} = \begin{pmatrix} \boxed{-0.4175} & 0.0265 & -0.0055 & \underline{-0.5265} \\ -0.5440 & \boxed{0.2265} & -0.0700 & -0.5225 \\ -0.5145 & \underline{-0.1745} & \boxed{0.0765} & -0.4760 \\ -0.5430 & -0.1225 & -0.1050 & \boxed{-0.3990} \\ -0.5250 & 0.1875 & \underline{-0.1540} & -0.4525 \end{pmatrix}$$

$d_1^- = d_1^-(b_{1j}, V^-) = 0.0779,$

$d_2^- = d_2^-(b_{2j}, V^-) = 0.1006,$

$d_3^- = d_3^-(b_{3j}, V^-) = 0.0621,$

$d_4^- = d_4^-(b_{4j}, V^-) = 0.0530,$

$d_5^- = d_5^-(b_{5j}, V^-) = 0.0874,$

Confirm the relative adjacent degree and rank alternatives based on the highest degree. The relative adjacent degree of the evaluation object and the ideal solution are:

$$A_i = \frac{d_i^-}{d_i^+ + d_i^-} \quad i = 1, 2, \ldots, m$$

$A_1 = 0.5162, \quad A_2 = 0.6006, \quad A_3 = 0.4176,$

$A_4 = 0.3569, A_5 = 0.5538.$

$A_2 > A_5 > A_1 > A_3 > A_4.$

Hence A_2 is the best alternative.

Comparison with the Score Function of Hong and Choi (2000)

The TOPSIS Algorithm with the Score Function of Hong & Choi, (2000) for the same numerical illustration is given as follows:

Step 1: Calculate the weighted attribute value of each interval vague value as in equations (22) to (24).

Step 2: Calculate the Score function H_{ij} of Hong & Choi, (2000) for each individual Interval vague values from equation (35).

Step 3: Confirm the positive and the negative ideal solutions as given in equations (25) and (26) of the evaluation object based on the calculated Score function H_{ij}.

Step 4: Calculate the distance between each value b_{ij} and the positive ideal solution, as shown as follows:

$$d_i^+ = \frac{1}{4n} \sum_{j=1}^{n} \left(\begin{array}{l} \left| t_{b_{ij}}^- - t_{V_j^+}^- \right| + \left| t_{b_{ij}}^+ - t_{V_j^+}^+ \right| + \left| f_{b_{ij}}^- - f_{V_j^+}^- \right| + \\ \left| f_{b_{ij}}^+ - f_{V_j^+}^+ \right| + \left| \pi_{b_{ij}}^- - \pi_{V_j^+}^- \right| + \left| \pi_{b_{ij}}^+ - \pi_{V_j^+}^+ \right| \end{array} \right)$$

Step 5: Calculate the distance between each value b_{ij} and the negative ideal solution, as follows:

$$d_i^- = \frac{1}{4n} \sum_{j=1}^{n} \left(\begin{array}{l} \left| t_{b_{ij}}^- - t_{V_j^-}^- \right| + \left| t_{b_{ij}}^+ - t_{V_j^-}^+ \right| + \left| f_{b_{ij}}^- - f_{V_j^-}^- \right| + \\ \left| f_{b_{ij}}^+ - f_{V_j^-}^+ \right| + \left| \pi_{b_{ij}}^- - \pi_{V_j^-}^- \right| + \left| \pi_{b_{ij}}^+ - \pi_{V_j^-}^+ \right| \end{array} \right)$$

Step 6: Confirm the relative adjacent degree and rank alternatives based on the highest degree. The relative adjacent degree of the evaluation object and the ideal solution are:

$$A_i = \frac{d_i^-}{d_i^+ + d_i^-} \quad i = 1, 2, ..., m$$

Solution to the Same Illustration

Calculate the Score function S_{ij} for each individual Interval vague values (Box 9).

Confirm the ideal solution and the negative solution of the evaluation object using the above Score function value obtained from Step 2. The vague set ideal solution V^+ and the negative ideal solution V^- is shown as follows.

$$V^+ = \left\{ \left(\begin{bmatrix} 0.156, \\ 0.240 \end{bmatrix}, \begin{bmatrix} 0.665, \\ 0.760 \end{bmatrix} \right), \left(\begin{bmatrix} 0.438, \\ 0.567 \end{bmatrix}, \begin{bmatrix} 0.208, \\ 0.344 \end{bmatrix} \right), \right.$$
$$\left. \left(\begin{bmatrix} 0.372, \\ 0.532 \end{bmatrix}, \begin{bmatrix} 0.304, \\ 0.447 \end{bmatrix} \right), \left(\begin{bmatrix} 0.174, \\ 0.260 \end{bmatrix}, \begin{bmatrix} 0.615, \\ 0.724 \end{bmatrix} \right) \right\}$$

$$V^- = \left\{ \left(\begin{bmatrix} 0.132, \\ 0.212 \end{bmatrix}, \begin{bmatrix} 0.650, \\ 0.780 \end{bmatrix} \right), \left(\begin{bmatrix} 0.198, \\ 0.315 \end{bmatrix}, \begin{bmatrix} 0.334, \\ 0.528 \end{bmatrix} \right), \right.$$
$$\left. \left(\begin{bmatrix} 0.228, \\ 0.406 \end{bmatrix}, \begin{bmatrix} 0.376, \\ 0.566 \end{bmatrix} \right), \left(\begin{bmatrix} 0.096, \\ 0.172 \end{bmatrix}, \begin{bmatrix} 0.605, \\ 0.716 \end{bmatrix} \right) \right\}$$

Calculate the distance between each value b_{ij} and the positive ideal solution as follows:

$$d_1^+ = d_1^+(b_{1j}, V^+) = 0.0684,$$

$$d_2^+ = d_2^+(b_{2j}, V^+) = 0.0391,$$

$$d_3^+ = d_3^+(b_{3j}, V^+) = 0.0816,$$

$$d_4^+ = d_4^+(b_{4j}, V^+) = 0.0909,$$

$$d_5^+ = d_5^+(b_{5j}, V^+) = 0.0454,$$

Calculate the distance between each value b_{ij} and the negative ideal solution as follows:

$$d_1^- = d_1^-(b_{1j}, V^-) = 0.0777,$$

$$d_2^- = d_2^-(b_{2j}, V^-) = 0.1064,$$

$$d_3^- = d_3^-(b_{3j}, V^-) = 0.0642,$$

$$d_4^- = d_4^-(b_{4j}, V^-) = 0.0472,$$

$$d_5^- = d_5^-(b_{5j}, V^-) = 0.0901,$$

Confirm the relative adjacent degree and rank alternatives based on the highest degree. The relative adjacent degree of the evaluation object and the ideal solution is:

Box 9.

$$H_{ij} = \begin{pmatrix} h_{11} & h_{12} & h_{13} & h_{14} \\ h_{21} & h_{22} & h_{23} & h_{24} \\ h_{31} & h_{32} & h_{33} & h_{34} \\ h_{41} & h_{42} & h_{43} & h_{44} \\ h_{51} & h_{52} & h_{53} & h_{54} \end{pmatrix} = \begin{pmatrix} 0.9005 & 0.7265 & 0.8475 & \underline{0.7945} \\ 0.8900 & \boxed{0.7785} & 0.8215 & 0.8495 \\ \boxed{0.9105} & \underline{0.6875} & \boxed{0.8275} & 0.8830 \\ \underline{0.8870} & 0.7005 & 0.8110 & 0.8700 \\ 0.9100 & 0.7565 & \underline{0.7880} & \boxed{0.8865} \end{pmatrix}$$

$$A_i = \frac{d_i^-}{d_i^+ + d_i^-} \quad i = 1, 2, \dots, m$$

$$d_i^- = \frac{1}{4n} \sum_{j=1}^{n} \left(\begin{array}{c} \left| t_{b_{ij}}^- - t_{V_j^-}^- \right| + \left| t_{b_{ij}}^+ - t_{V_j^-}^+ \right| + \left| f_{b_{ij}}^- - f_{V_j^-}^- \right| + \\ \left| f_{b_{ij}}^+ - f_{V_j^-}^+ \right| + \left| \pi_{b_{ij}}^- - \pi_{V_j^-}^- \right| + \left| \pi_{b_{ij}}^+ - \pi_{V_j^-}^+ \right| \end{array} \right)$$

$A_1 = 0.5318, \quad A_2 = 0.7313, \quad A_3 = 0.4403,$

$A_4 = 0.3418, \; A_5 = 0.6649.$

Ranking the alternatives based on the relative adjacent degree, it follows that:

$$A_2 > A_5 > A_1 > A_3 > A_4.$$

Hence A_2 is the best alternative.

Comparison with the Score Function of Liu, P.D. (2009)

The TOPSIS Algorithm with the Score Function of Liu, P.D., (2009) for the same numerical illustration is given as follows:

Step 1: Calculate the weighted attribute value of each interval vague value as in equations (22) to (24).

Step 2: Calculate the Score function L_{ij} of Liu, P.D., (2009) for each individual Interval vague values from equation (37).

Step 3: Confirm the positive and the negative ideal solutions as given in equations (25) and (26) of the evaluation object based on the calculated Score function L_{ij}.

Step 4: Calculate the distance between each value b_{ij} and the positive ideal solution, as follows.

$$d_i^+ = \frac{1}{4n} \sum_{j=1}^{n} \left(\begin{array}{c} \left| t_{b_{ij}}^- - t_{V_j^+}^- \right| + \left| t_{b_{ij}}^+ - t_{V_j^+}^+ \right| + \left| f_{b_{ij}}^- - f_{V_j^+}^- \right| + \\ \left| f_{b_{ij}}^+ - f_{V_j^+}^+ \right| + \left| \pi_{b_{ij}}^- - \pi_{V_j^+}^- \right| + \left| \pi_{b_{ij}}^+ - \pi_{V_j^+}^+ \right| \end{array} \right)$$

Step 5: Calculate the distance between each value b_{ij} and the negative ideal solution, as follows.

Step 6: Confirm the relative adjacent degree and rank alternatives based on the highest degree. The relative adjacent degree of the evaluation object and the ideal solution is:

$$A_i = \frac{d_i^-}{d_i^+ + d_i^-} \quad i = 1, 2, \dots, m$$

Solution to the Same Illustration

Calculate the Score function S_{ij} for each individual Interval vague values (Box 10).

Confirm the positive and the negative ideal solutions of the evaluation object using the above Score function value obtained from Step 2. The vague set ideal solution V^+ and the negative ideal solution V^- is shown as follows:

$$V^+ = \left\{ \left(\begin{bmatrix} 0.195, \\ 0.288 \end{bmatrix}, \begin{bmatrix} 0.610, \\ 0.708 \end{bmatrix} \right) \left(\begin{bmatrix} 0.438, \\ 0.567 \end{bmatrix}, \begin{bmatrix} 0.208, \\ 0.344 \end{bmatrix} \right), \right.$$
$$\left. \left(\begin{bmatrix} 0.372, \\ 0.532 \end{bmatrix}, \begin{bmatrix} 0.304, \\ 0.447 \end{bmatrix} \right) \left(\begin{bmatrix} 0.183, \\ 0.288 \end{bmatrix}, \begin{bmatrix} 0.585, \\ 0.684 \end{bmatrix} \right) \right\}$$

$$V^- = \left\{ \left(\begin{bmatrix} 0.153, \\ 0.232 \end{bmatrix}, \begin{bmatrix} 0.675, \\ 0.760 \end{bmatrix} \right) \left(\begin{bmatrix} 0.198, \\ 0.315 \end{bmatrix}, \begin{bmatrix} 0.334, \\ 0.528 \end{bmatrix} \right), \right.$$
$$\left. \left(\begin{bmatrix} 0.258, \\ 0.448 \end{bmatrix}, \begin{bmatrix} 0.392, \\ 0.524 \end{bmatrix} \right) \left(\begin{bmatrix} 0.096, \\ 0.172 \end{bmatrix}, \begin{bmatrix} 0.605, \\ 0.716 \end{bmatrix} \right) \right\}$$

Calculate the distance between each value b_{ij} and the positive ideal solution as follows:

Box 10.

$$
L_{ij} = \begin{pmatrix} l_{11} & l_{12} & l_{13} & l_{14} \\ l_{21} & l_{22} & l_{23} & l_{24} \\ l_{31} & l_{32} & l_{33} & l_{34} \\ l_{41} & l_{42} & l_{43} & l_{44} \\ l_{51} & l_{52} & l_{53} & l_{54} \end{pmatrix} = \begin{pmatrix} \boxed{-0.4599} & 0.0337 & -0.0062 & \underline{-0.6347} \\ -0.6038 & \boxed{0.2766} & -0.0817 & -0.6273 \\ -0.5605 & \underline{-0.2290} & \boxed{0.0899} & -0.5317 \\ -0.6044 & -0.1592 & \underline{-0.1248} & \boxed{-0.4508} \\ \underline{-0.6195} & 0.2256 & 0.1866 & -0.5038 \end{pmatrix}
$$

$d_1^+ = d_1^+(b_{1j}, V^+) = 0.0730,$

$d_2^+ = d_2^+(b_{2j}, V^+) = 0.0669,$

$d_3^+ = d_3^+(b_{3j}, V^+) = 0.0866,$

$d_4^+ = d_4^+(b_{4j}, V^+) = 0.0955,$

$d_5^+ = d_5^+(b_{5j}, V^+) = 0.0704,$

Calculate the distance between each value b_{ij} and the negative ideal solution as follows:

$d_1^- = d_1^-(b_{1j}, V^-) = 0.0635,$

$d_2^- = d_2^-(b_{2j}, V^-) = 0.0977,$

$d_3^- = d_3^-(b_{3j}, V^-) = 0.0491,$

$d_4^- = d_4^-(b_{4j}, V^-) = 0.0445,$

$d_5^- = d_5^-(b_{5j}, V^-) = 0.0929,$

Confirm the relative adjacent degree and rank alternatives based on the highest degree. The rela-tive adjacent degree of the evaluation object and the ideal solution is:

$$
A_i = \frac{d_i^-}{d_i^+ + d_i^-}
$$

$i = 1, 2, ..., m$

$A_1 = 0.4652, \quad A_2 = 0.5935, \quad A_3 = 0.3618,$
$A_4 = 0.3178, A_5 = 0.5689.$

Ranking alternatives based on the relative adjacent degree, it follows that:

$A_2 > A_5 > A_1 > A_3 > A_4.$

Hence A_2 is the best alternative.

Comparison with the Accuracy Function of Nayagam et al. (2011)

Proceeding with the same TOPSIS algorithm and using the Accuracy function of Nayagam et al., (2011) to identify the positive and negative ideal solutions, the same numerical results as in Chen & Tan, (1994) numerical illustration are obtained. The Score function $L(A)$ for each individual Interval vague values is given as shown in Box 11.

Box 11.

$$L(A) = \begin{pmatrix} L_{11} & L_{12} & L_{13} & L_{14} \\ L_{21} & L_{22} & L_{23} & L_{24} \\ L_{31} & L_{32} & L_{33} & L_{34} \\ L_{41} & L_{42} & L_{43} & L_{44} \\ L_{51} & L_{52} & L_{53} & L_{54} \end{pmatrix} = \begin{pmatrix} \boxed{-0.2561} & 0.0751 & 0.1892 & \underline{-0.4359} \\ \underline{-0.4183} & \boxed{0.3696} & 0.1046 & -0.4077 \\ -0.3714 & \underline{-0.0583} & \boxed{0.2519} & -0.3357 \\ -0.4174 & -0.0006 & 0.0629 & \boxed{-0.2469} \\ -0.3852 & 0.3277 & \underline{0.0037} & -0.3049 \end{pmatrix}$$

The ranking of the alternatives is given as follows:

$$A_2 > A_5 > A_1 > A_3 > A_4.$$

Where, the best alternative is A_2.

DISCUSSION

From the numerical illustrations and comparisons made above, it can be observed that the final decision on the ranking of alternatives remains the same in all the TOPSIS methods. The proposed method differs from existing methods in identifying positive and negative ideal solutions. *Table*-6 presents the details of the final order of ranking of alternatives. It is seen from the proposed model that correlation coefficient can also be used as a tool for identifying the positive and negative ideal solutions in TOPSIS methods. The positive and negative ideal solutions identified by using correlation coefficient differ from the positive and negative ideal solutions identified by using existing score and accuracy functions. For the positive ideal solution, computed through correlation coefficient, it is seen that its entries contain all the other entries of that particular attribute for all the five alternatives. For the negative ideal solution, computed through correlation coefficient, it is observed that its entries are contained in all the other entries of that particular attribute for all the five alternatives. This is an indication for a better ideal solution for any decision making system. Hence the proposed method of TOPSIS with correlation coefficient for identifying the ideal solutions is a better tool when compared with existing methods in literature.

CONCLUSION

As the decision making is fuzzy and uncertain, the interval vague set's ability to express the fuzziness and uncertainty is stronger. It is easier to express decision information using the interval vague values. In this work, a new method was proposed to derive the correlation coefficient of IVSs lying in the interval [-1,1], using the concept of Buckley et al., (2004) fuzzy confidence intervals. The vague degrees of the interval vague values were used to construct the fuzzy confidence intervals, and thereby giving a trapezoidal shaped number, from which the correlation coefficient was calculated. The resulting correlation coefficient was obtained in the form of an interval. The proposed method of the correlation coefficient of interval vague sets is also used as a tool to rank alternatives in MADM problems under vague fuzzy environment.

This work also explored the multi-attribute decision making problem based on interval vague sets for TOPSIS. First, based on the operation rules of the interval vague sets, weighted operations to the interval vague attribute value are introduced. Then the positive and negative ideal solutions are confirmed on the basis of the correlation coefficient of IVSs instead of score functions used in literature. The relative adjacent degree is calculated in the TOPSIS algorithm using the same correlation coefficient of IVSs, and according to the calculated relative adjacent degree, the order of the alternatives is confirmed. Two different

TOPSIS algorithms are proposed, Model-1 is the TOPSIS algorithm with correlation coefficient of IVSs for both ideal solutions and closeness coefficient and Model-2 is the TOPSIS algorithm with correlation coefficient of IVSs for ideal solutions and distance function for closeness coefficient. The numerical illustration proves the practicality of the proposed TOPSIS model. A detailed comparison is made with the existing methods of score and accuracy functions to identify positive and negative ideal solutions. The comparison study reveals the advantage of using correlation coefficient over the score and accuracy functions in identifying ideal solutions. The final ranking of the alternatives remains the same throughout all the methods as clearly presented in *Table*-6.

Table 6. Comparison table

Topsis Methods	Ranking of Alternatives
7. Proposed MODEL-1 (TOPSIS with correlation coefficient of IVSs for Ideal solutions & Closeness coefficient)	$A_2 > A_5 > A_1 > A_3 > A_4.$ The best alternative is A_2.
8. Proposed MODEL-2 (TOPSIS with correlation coefficient of IVSs for Ideal solutions & Distance function for Closeness coefficient)	$A_2 > A_5 > A_1 > A_3 > A_4.$ The best alternative is A_2.
9. Chen & Tan, (1994) Method of Score Function for Ideal Solutions	$A_2 > A_5 > A_1 > A_3 > A_4.$ The best alternative is A_2.
10. Hong & Choi, (2000) Method of Score Function for Ideal Solutions	$A_2 > A_5 > A_1 > A_3 > A_4.$ The best alternative is A_2.
11. Liu, P.D., (2009) Method of Score Function for Ideal Solutions	$A_2 > A_5 > A_1 > A_3 > A_4.$ The best alternative is A_2.
12. Nayagam et al., (2011) Method of Accuracy Function for Ideal Solutions	$A_2 > A_5 > A_1 > A_3 > A_4.$ The best alternative is A_2.

REFERENCES

Atanassov, K. (1986). Intuitionistic fuzzy sets. *Fuzzy Sets and Systems*, *20*, 87–96. doi:10.1016/S0165-0114(86)80034-3

Atanassov, K. (1989). More on intuitionistic fuzzy sets. *Fuzzy Sets and Systems*, *33*, 37–46. doi:10.1016/0165-0114(89)90215-7

Atanassov, K. (1994). Operators over interval-valued intuitionistic fuzzy sets. *Fuzzy Sets and Systems*, *64*, 159–174. doi:10.1016/0165-0114(94)90331-X

Atanassov, K., & Gargov, G. (1989). Interval-valued intuitionistic fuzzy sets. *Fuzzy Sets and Systems*, *31*, 343–349. doi:10.1016/0165-0114(89)90205-4

Buckley, J. J., & Jovers, L. J. (2006). *Simulating Continuous Fuzzy Systems, Studies in Fuzziness and Soft Computing* (Vol. 188). Springer-Verlag Berlin Heidelberg.

Buckley, J. J., Reilly, K., & Zhang, X. (2004). Fuzzy probabilities for web planning. *Soft Computing*, *8*, 464–476. doi:10.1007/s00500-003-0305-z

Bustince, H., & Burillo, P. (1995). Correlation of interval-valued intuitionistic fuzzy sets. *Fuzzy Sets and Systems*, *74*, 237–244. doi:10.1016/0165-0114(94)00343-6

Bustince, H., & Burillo, P. (1996). Vague sets are intuitionistic fuzzy sets. *Fuzzy Sets and Systems*, *79*, 403–405. doi:10.1016/0165-0114(95)00154-9

Chen, S. M., & Tan, J. M. (1994). Handling multicriteria fuzzy decision making problems based on vague sets. *Fuzzy Sets and Systems*, *67*, 163–172. doi:10.1016/0165-0114(94)90084-1

Chiang, D. A., & Lin, N. P. (1999). Correlation of fuzzy sets. *Fuzzy Sets and Systems*, *102*, 221–226. doi:10.1016/S0165-0114(97)00127-9

Gau, W. L., & Buehrer, D. J. (1994). Vague sets, IEEE Transactions on Systems, *Man and Cybernetics. Part A*, *23*, 610–614.

Gerstenkorn, T., & Manko, J. (1991). Correlation of intuitionistic fuzzy sets. *Fuzzy Sets and Systems*, *44*, 39–43. doi:10.1016/0165-0114(91)90031-K

Hong, D. H., & Choi, D. H. (2000). Multicriteria fuzzy decision making problems based on vague set theory. *Fuzzy Sets and Systems*, *114*, 103–113. doi:10.1016/S0165-0114(98)00271-1

Hong, D. H., & Hwang, S. W. (1995). Correlation of intuitionistic fuzzy sets in probability spaces. *Fuzzy Sets and Systems*, *75*, 77–81. doi:10.1016/0165-0114(94)00330-A

Hung, W. L., & Wu, J. W. (2002). Correlation of intuitionistic fuzzy sets by centroid method. *Information Sciences*, *144*, 219–225. doi:10.1016/S0020-0255(02)00181-0

Hwang, C. L., & Yoon, K. (1981). *Multiple Attributes Decision Making Methods and Applications*. Berlin, Heidelberg: Springer. doi:10.1007/978-3-642-48318-9

Janic, M. (2003). Multicriteria evaluation of high-speed rail, trans rapid maglev and air passenger transport in Europe. *Trans Plan Technol.*, *26*(6), 491–512. doi:10.1080/03081060320000167373

Kao, C., & Liu, S. T. (2002). Fuzzy measures for correlation coefficient of fuzzy numbers. *Fuzzy Sets and Systems*, *128*, 267–275. doi:10.1016/S0165-0114(01)00199-3

Li, F., & Rao, Y. (2001). Weighted multi-criteria decision making based on vague sets. *Computer Science*, *28*(7), 60–65.

Liu, P. D. (2009). Multi-Attribute decision-making method research based on interval vague set and TOPSIS method, *Technological and Economic Development of Economy. Baltic Journal of Sustainability.*, *15*(3), 453–463.

Liu, P. D., & Guan, Z. L. (2008). Research on group decision making based on the vague set and hybrid aggregation operators. *Journal of Wuhan University of Technology*, *30*(10), 152–155.

Liu, P. D., & Guan, Z. L. (2009). An approach for multiple attribute decision-making based on Vague sets. *Journal of Harbin Engineering University, 30*(1), 106–110.

Lu, A., & Ng, W. (2005). Lecture Notes in Computer Science: Vol. 3716. *Vague sets or intuitionistic fuzzy sets for handling vague data: Which one is better* (pp. 401–416). Springer.

Lu, A., & Ng, W. (2009). Maintaining consistency of vague databases using data dependencies. *Data & Knowledge Engineering, 68*(7), 622–641. doi:10.1016/j.datak.2009.02.007

Nayagam, L. G., Muralikrishnan, S., & Sivaraman, G. (2011). Multi-Criteria Decision Making based on Interval-Valued Intuitionistic Fuzzy Sets. *Expert Systems with Applications, 38*, 1464–1467. doi:10.1016/j.eswa.2010.07.055

Park, D. G., Kwun, Y. C., Park, J. H., & Park, I. Y. (2009). Correlation coefficient of interval-valued intuitionistic fuzzy sets and its application to multiple attribute group decision making problems. *Mathematical and Computer Modelling, 50*, 1279–1293. doi:10.1016/j.mcm.2009.06.010

Robinson, J. P., & Amirtharaj, E. C. H. (2011a). A short primer on the Correlation coefficient of Vague sets. *International Journal of Fuzzy System Applications, 1*(2), 55–69. doi:10.4018/ijfsa.2011040105

Robinson, J. P., & Amirtharaj, E. C. H. (2011b). Extended TOPSIS with correlation coefficient of Triangular Intuitionistic fuzzy sets for Multiple Attribute Group Decision Making. *International Journal of Decision Support System Technology, 3*(3), 15–40. doi:10.4018/jdsst.2011070102

Robinson, J. P., & Amirtharaj, E. C. H. (2012a). Vague Correlation coefficient of Interval Vague sets. *International Journal of Fuzzy System Applications, 2*(1), 18–34. doi:10.4018/ijfsa.2012010102

Robinson, J. P., & Amirtharaj, E. C. H. (2012b). A Search for the Correlation coefficient of Triangular and Trapezoidal intuitionistic Fuzzy sets for Multiple Attribute Group Decision Making. Communications in Computer and Information Science, 283, 333-342.

Robinson, J. P., & Amirtharaj, E. C. H. (in press). Efficient Multiple Attribute Group Decision Making models with Correlation coefficient of Vague sets. *International Journal of Operations Research and Information Systems*.

Wang, G., & Li, X. (1999). Correlation of information energy of interval valued fuzzy numbers. *Fuzzy Sets and Systems, 103*, 169–175. doi:10.1016/S0165-0114(97)00303-5

Wang, J., Zhang, J., & Liu, S.-Y. (2006). A new score function for Fuzzy MCDM based on Vague set theory. *International Journal of Computational Cognition, 4*(1), 44–48.

Wang, J. Q. (2006). Multi-criteria interval intuitionistic fuzzy decision making approach with incomplete certain information. *Control and Decision, 11*, 1253–1256.

Wu, H. C. (2009). Statistical confidence intervals for fuzzy data. *Expert Systems with Applications, 36*, 2670–2676. doi:10.1016/j.eswa.2008.01.022

Xu, Z. S. (2007). Methods for aggregating interval-valued intuitionistic fuzzy information and their application to decision making. *Control and Decision, 22*(2), 215–219.

Yu, C. (1993). Correlation of fuzzy numbers. *Fuzzy Sets and Systems, 55*, 303–307. doi:10.1016/0165-0114(93)90256-H

Zadeh, L. A. (1978). Fuzzy sets as a basis for a theory of possibility. *Fuzzy Sets and Systems, 1*, 3–28. doi:10.1016/0165-0114(78)90029-5

Zeng, W., & Li, H. (2007). Correlation Coefficient of Intuitionistic Fuzzy sets. *Journal of Industrial Engineering International, 3*, 33–40.

Zhi-feng, Ma., Cheng, Z.H., Xiaomei, Z. (2001). Interval valued vague decision systems and an approach for its rule generation. *Acta Electronica Sinica, 29*(5), 585–589.

Zhou, Z., & Wu, Q. Z. (2006). Multi-criteria decision making based on interval valued vague sets. *Transactions of Beijing Institute of Technology, 8,* 693–696.

Chapter 9
Decomposition Theorem of Generalized Interval–Valued Intuitionistic Fuzzy Sets

Amal Kumar Adak
Vidyasagar University, India

Monoranjan Bhowmik
VTT College, India

Madhumangal Pal
Vidyasagar University, India

ABSTRACT

In this chapter, the authors establish decomposition theorems of Generalized Interval-Valued Intuitionistic Fuzzy Sets (GIVIFS) by use of cut sets of generalized interval-valued intuitionistic fuzzy sets. First, new definitions of eight kinds of cut sets generalized interval-valued intuitionistic fuzzy sets are introduced. Second, based on these new cut sets, the decomposition generalized interval-valued intuitionistic fuzzy sets are established. The authors show that each kind of cut sets corresponds to two kinds of decomposition theorems. These results provide a fundamental theory for the research of generalized interval-valued intuitionistic fuzzy sets.

1. INTRODUCTION

In 1965, Zadeh introduced the concept of fuzzy subsets. Latter many authors defined different directions of fuzzy subsets. Atanassov introduced the concept of intuitionistic fuzzy sets (IFSs), which is more generalization of fuzzy subsets and as well as IVFSs. Several authors present a number of results using IFSs. Gargov and Atanassov (1989)

introduced the interval-valued intuitionistic fuzzy sets (IVIFSs). They have shown several properties on IVIFSs and shown some applications of IVIFSs. Mondal and Samanta (2002) introduced another concept of IFSs called generalized IFSs. Bhowmik and Pal (2009, 2010) defined generalized interval-valued intuitionistic fuzzy set (GIVIFS) and presented various properties of it.

DOI: 10.4018/978-1-4666-6252-0.ch009

J. Li and H. Li (2008) discussed on the cut-sets of fuzzy sets and reveals the relationship between the fuzzy sets and classical sets. Decomposition theorem can be obtained based on the cut-sets. X. Yuan, H. Xing Li, K. Sun (2011) described by neighborhood relation of the fuzzy point and fuzzy set, which has many applications in fuzzy topology and fuzzy algebra.

The organization of this article is as follows. In Section 2, some basic properties of GIVIFS are redefined. In Section 3, different types of interval cut-sets of GIVIFS are defined and some properties of these cut-sets are given. In Section 4, three decomposition theorems on interval cut-sets of GIVIFSs are gained. Finally, in Section 5, a conclusion of this paper is given.

2. PRELIMINARIES

In this section, we recalled some preliminaries and the definition of IVIFS and GIVIFS.

Definition 2.1: An IVIFS A over X (universe of discourse) is an object having the form $A = \{\langle x, M_A(x), N_A(x) \rangle \mid x \in X\}$, where $M_A(x): X \to [I]$ and $N_A(x): X \to [I]$. The intervals $M_A(x)$ and $N_A(x)$ denote the intervals of the degree of membership and degree of non-membership of the element x to the set A, where $M_A(x) = [M_{AL}(x), M_{AU}(x)]$ and $N_A(x) = [N_{AL}(x), N_{AU}(x)]$, for all $x \in X$, with the condition $0 \leq M_{AU}(x) + N_{AU}(x) \leq 1$.

For simplicity, we denote $A = \{\langle x, [A^-(x), A^+(x)], [B^-(x), B^+(x)] \rangle \mid x \in X\}$.

Definition 2.2: If the IVIFS $A = \{\langle x, MA(x), NA(x) \rangle \mid x \in X\}$, satisfying the condition $MAU(x) \wedge NAU(x) \leq 0.5$ for all $x \in X$ then A is called generalized interval-valued intuitionistic fuzzy set (GIVIFS). The condition $M_{AU}(x) \wedge N_{AU}(x) \leq 0.5$ is called generalized interval-valued intuitionistic fuzzy condition (GIV-IFC). The maximum value of MAU(x) and $N_{AU}(x)$ is 1.0, therefore GIVIFC imply that $0 \leq M_{AU}(x) + N_{AU}(x) \leq 1.5$.

It may be noted that all IVIFS are GIVIFS but the converse is not true.

Let F(X) be the set of all GIVIFSs defined on X.

2.1. Some Operations on GIVIFSs

In [2], Bhowmik and Pal defined some relational operations on GIVIFSs. Let A and B be two GIVIFSs on X, where

$$A = \{\langle [M_{AL}(x), M_{AU}], [N_{AL}(x), N_{AU}(x)]: x \in X \rangle\}$$

and

$$B = \{\langle [M_{BL}(x), M_{BU}], [N_{BL}(x), N_{BU}(x)]: x \in X \rangle\}.$$

Then,

1. $A \subseteq B$ iff $\{(M_{AU}(x) \leq M_{BU}(x)$ and $M_{AL}(x) \leq M_{BL}(x))\}$ and

$\{(N_{AU}(x) \geq N_{BU}(x)$ and $N_{AL}(x) \geq N_{BL}(x))\}$, for all $x \in X$.

2. $A \cap B = \{\langle [\min\{M_{AL}(x), M_{BL}(x)\}, \min\{M_{AU}(x), M_{BU}(x)\}],$

$[\max\{N_{AL}(x), N_{BL}(x)\}, \max\{N_{AU}(x), N_{BU}(x)\}]\rangle: x \in X\}$.

3. $A \cup B = \{\langle [\max\{M_{AL}(x), M_{BL}(x)\}, \max\{M_{AU}(x), M_{BU}(x)\}],$

$[\min\{N_{AL}(x), N_{BL}(x)\}, \min\{N_{AU}(x), N_{BU}(x)\}]\rangle: x \in X\}$.

3. INTERVAL CUT-SETS ON GIVIFS AND SOME RESULTS

In [8], Wang and Jin has introduced some kinds of cut-sets for interval-valued fuzzy sets based on fuzzy interval and interval-valued fuzzy sets. Here we define some types of interval cut-sets for GIVIFS.

Definition 3.1: Let A be a GIVIFS and $\alpha = [\alpha 1, \alpha 2]$, $\beta = [\beta 1, \beta 2] \in [I]$, satisfying the condition $0 \le \alpha 2 \wedge \beta 2 \le 0.5$. Then different types of interval cut-sets on GIVIFS A are defined in Box 1, where $A^{(i,j)}{}_{[\alpha 1, \alpha 2], [\beta 1, \beta 2]}$ is the (i, j)th $([\alpha_1, \alpha_2], [\beta_1, \beta_2])$ interval cut-set of GIVIFS A.

Note: If α and β does not satisfy GIVIFC, then cut-sets will be empty.

In the following we discussed some propositions for GIVIFS and interval cut-sets of GIVIFSs.

Definition 3.2: Let X be a nonempty set, A be a GIVIFS on F(X) and $\alpha, \beta \in [I]$, where $\alpha = [\alpha 1, \alpha 2]$, $\beta = [\beta 1, \beta 2]$ satisfying the condition $0 \le \alpha 2 \wedge \beta 2 \le 0.5$. We define it in Box 2.

Proposition 3.1: Let X be a nonempty set, A is a GIVIFS and $\alpha = [\alpha 1, \alpha 2]$, $\beta = [\beta 1, \beta 2] \in [I]$, satisfying the condition $0 \le \alpha 2 \wedge \beta 2 \le 0.5$ then

$$A_{[\alpha_1, \alpha_2], [\beta_1, \beta_2]}{}^{(i,j)} = (A^-)^i{}_{\alpha_1, \beta_1} \cap (A^+)^j{}_{\alpha_2, \beta_2} \quad i,j=1,2$$
$$A_{[\alpha_1, \alpha_2], [\beta_1, \beta_2]}{}^{(i,j)} = (A^-)^i{}_{\alpha_1, \beta_1} \cap (A^+)^j{}_{\alpha_2, \beta_2} \quad i,j=3,4.$$

Proof: Here, we prove only for i = 1, j = 1 and $\alpha = [\alpha_1, \alpha_2]$, $\beta = [\beta_1, \beta_2] \in [I]$ and other proves are similar.

$$A_{[\alpha_1, \alpha_2], [\beta_1, \beta_2]}{}^{(1,1)} = (A^-)^1{}_{\alpha_1, \beta_1} \cap (A^+)^1{}_{\alpha_2, \beta_2}$$

Let

$$x \in A_{[\alpha_1, \alpha_2], [\beta_1, \beta_2]}{}^{(1,1)}$$

$$\Leftrightarrow \left\{ x \in X : \left\langle \begin{matrix} x, [A^-(x) \ge \alpha_1, A^+(x) \ge \alpha_2], \\ [B^-(x) \ge \beta_1, B^+(x) \ge \beta_2] \end{matrix} \right\rangle \right\}$$

$$\Leftrightarrow \left\{ \left\langle \begin{matrix} x, [A^-(x) \ge \alpha_1, A^+(x)], \\ [B^-(x) \ge \beta_1, B^+(x)] \end{matrix} \right\rangle \middle| x \in X \right\}$$

$$and \left\{ x \in X : \left\langle \begin{matrix} x, [A^-(x), \\ A^+(x) \ge \alpha_2], \\ [B^-(x), B^+(x) \ge \beta_2] \end{matrix} \right\rangle \right\}$$

$$\Leftrightarrow x \in (A^-)^1{}_{\alpha_1, \beta_1} \cap (A^+)^1{}_{\alpha_2, \beta_2}.$$
Therefore, $A_{[\alpha_1, \alpha_2], [\beta_1, \beta_2]}{}^{(1,1)} = (A^-)^1{}_{\alpha_1, \beta_1} \cap (A^+)^1{}_{\alpha_2, \beta_2}.$

Box 1.

$$A_{\alpha, \beta}{}^{(1,1)} = A_{[\alpha_1, \alpha_2], [\beta_1, \beta_2]}{}^{(1,1)} = \left\{ \left\langle x, [A^-(x) \ge \alpha_1, A^+(x) \ge \alpha_2], [B^-(x) \ge \beta_1, B^+(x) \ge \beta_2] \right\rangle \middle| x \in X \right\}$$

$$A_{\alpha, \beta}{}^{(1,2)} = A_{[\alpha_1, \alpha_2], [\beta_1, \beta_2]}{}^{(1,2)} = \left\{ \left\langle x, [A^-(x) \ge \alpha_1, A^+(x) > \alpha_2], [B^-(x) \ge \beta_1, B^+(x) > \beta_2] \right\rangle \middle| x \in X \right\}$$

$$A_{\alpha, \beta}{}^{(2,1)} = A_{[\alpha_1, \alpha_2], [\beta_1, \beta_2]}{}^{(2,1)} = \left\{ \left\langle x, [A^-(x) > \alpha_1, A^+(x) \ge \alpha_2], [B^-(x) > \beta_1, B^+(x) \ge \beta_2] \right\rangle \middle| x \in X \right\}$$

$$A_{\alpha, \beta}{}^{(2,2)} = A_{[\alpha_1, \alpha_2], [\beta_1, \beta_2]}{}^{(2,2)} = \left\{ \left\langle x, [A^-(x) > \alpha_1, A^+(x) > \alpha_2], [B^-(x) > \beta_1, B^+(x) > \beta_2] \right\rangle \middle| x \in X \right\}$$

$$A_{\alpha, \beta}{}^{(3,3)} = A_{[\alpha_1, \alpha_2], [\beta_1, \beta_2]}{}^{(3,3)} = \left\{ \left\langle x, [A^-(x) \le \alpha_1, A^+(x) \le \alpha_2], [B^-(x) \le \beta_1, B^+(x) \le \beta_2] \right\rangle \middle| x \in X \right\}$$

$$A_{\alpha, \beta}{}^{(3,4)} = A_{[\alpha_1, \alpha_2], [\beta_1, \beta_2]}{}^{(3,4)} = \left\{ \left\langle x, [A^-(x) \le \alpha_1, A^+(x) < \alpha_2], [B^-(x) \le \beta_1, B^+(x) < \beta_2] \right\rangle \middle| x \in X \right\}$$

$$A_{\alpha, \beta}{}^{(4,3)} = A_{[\alpha_1, \alpha_2], [\beta_1, \beta_2]}{}^{(4,3)} = \left\{ \left\langle x, [A^-(x) < \alpha_1, A^+(x) \le \alpha_2], [B^-(x) < \beta_1, B^+(x) \le \beta_2] \right\rangle \middle| x \in X \right\}$$

$$A_{\alpha, \beta}{}^{(4,4)} = A_{[\alpha_1, \alpha_2], [\beta_1, \beta_2]}{}^{(4,4)} = \left\{ \left\langle x, [A^-(x) < \alpha_1, A^+(x) < \alpha_2], [B^-(x) < \beta_1, B^+(x) < \beta_2] \right\rangle \middle| x \in X \right\},$$

Box 2.

$$(A^-)^1_{\alpha_1,\beta_1} = \left\{ \left\langle x, [A^-(x) \geq \alpha_1, A^+(x)], [B^-(x) \geq \beta_1, B^+(x)] \right\rangle \middle| x \in X \right\}$$

$$(A^-)^2_{\alpha_1,\beta_1} = \left\{ \left\langle x, [A^-(x) > \alpha_1, A^+(x)], [B^-(x) > \beta_1, B^+(x)] \right\rangle \middle| x \in X \right\}$$

$$(A^+)^1_{\alpha_2,\beta_2} = \left\{ \left\langle x, [A^-(x), A^+(x) \geq \alpha_2], [B^-(x), B^+(x) \geq \beta_2] \right\rangle \middle| x \in X \right\}$$

$$(A^+)^2_{\alpha_2,\beta_2} = \left\{ \left\langle x, [A^-(x), A^+(x) > \alpha_2], [B^-(x), B^+(x) > \beta_2] \right\rangle \middle| x \in X \right\}$$

$$(A^-)^3_{\alpha_1,\beta_1} = \left\{ \left\langle x, [A^-(x) \leq \alpha_1, A^+(x)], [B^-(x) \leq \beta_1, B^+(x)] \right\rangle \middle| x \in X \right\}$$

$$(A^-)^4_{\alpha_1,\beta_1} = \left\{ \left\langle x, [A^-(x) < \alpha_1, A^+(x)], [B^-(x) < \beta_1, B^+(x)] \right\rangle \middle| x \in X \right\}$$

$$(A^+)^3_{\alpha_2,\beta_2} = \left\{ \left\langle x, [A^-(x), A^+(x) \leq \alpha_2], [B^-(x), B^+(x) \leq \beta_2] \right\rangle \middle| x \in X \right\}$$

$$(A^+)^4_{\alpha_2,\beta_2} = \left\{ \left\langle x, [A^-(x), A^+(x) < \alpha_2], [B^-(x), B^+(x) < \beta_2] \right\rangle \middle| x \in X \right\}.$$

Proposition 3.2: Let $A \in F(X)$ and $A^{(i,j)}_{\alpha,\beta}$ be the (i, j) th interval cut-set of GIVIFS A, where $\alpha = [\alpha_1, \alpha_2]$, $\beta = [\beta_1, \beta_2]$ satisfying the condition. Then,

$$A^{(2,2)}_{[\alpha_1,\alpha_2],[\beta_1,\beta_2]} \subset A^{(1,2)}_{[\alpha_1,\alpha_2],[\beta_1,\beta_2]} \subset A^{(1,1)}_{[\alpha_1,\alpha_2],[\beta_1,\beta_2]}$$

$$A^{(2,2)}_{[\alpha_1,\alpha_2],[\beta_1,\beta_2]} \subset A^{(2,1)}_{[\alpha_1,\alpha_2],[\beta_1,\beta_2]} \subset A^{(1,1)}_{[\alpha_1,\alpha_2],[\beta_1,\beta_2]}$$

$$A^{(4,4)}_{[\alpha_1,\alpha_2],[\beta_1,\beta_2]} \subset A^{(3,4)}_{[\alpha_1,\alpha_2],[\beta_1,\beta_2]} \subset A^{(3,3)}_{[\alpha_1,\alpha_2],[\beta_1,\beta_2]}.$$

$$A^{(4,4)}_{[\alpha_1,\alpha_2],[\beta_1,\beta_2]} \subset A^{(4,3)}_{[\alpha_1,\alpha_2],[\beta_1,\beta_2]} \subset A^{(3,3)}_{[\alpha_1,\alpha_2],[\beta_1,\beta_2]}$$

Proof: We prove

$$A^{(2,2)}_{[\alpha_1,\alpha_2],[\beta_1,\beta_2]} \subset A^{(1,2)}_{[\alpha_1,\alpha_2],[\beta_1,\beta_2]} \subset A^{(1,1)}_{[\alpha_1,\alpha_2],[\beta_1,\beta_2]}$$

and other proofs are similar.
Let,

$x \in A^{(2,2)}_{[\alpha_1,\alpha_2],[\beta_1,\beta_2]}$

$\Rightarrow \{x \in X \mid \{\langle x, [A^-(x) > \alpha_1, A^+(x) > \alpha_2], [B^-(x) > \beta_1, B^+(x) > \beta_2] \rangle\}$

$\subset \{x \in X \mid \{\langle x, [A^-(x) \geq \alpha_1, A^+(x) > \alpha_2], [B^-(x) \geq \beta_1, B^+(x) > \beta_2] \rangle\} = A^{(1,2)}_{\alpha,\beta}$

$\subset \{x \in X \mid \{\langle x, [A^-(x) \geq \alpha_1, A^+(x) \geq \alpha_2], [B^-(x) \geq \beta_1, B^+(x) \geq \beta_2] \rangle\} = A^{(1,1)}_{\alpha,\beta}$

So, $A^{(2,2)}_{[\alpha_1,\alpha_2],[\beta_1,\beta_2]} \subset A^{(1,2)}_{[\alpha_1,\alpha_2],[\beta_1,\beta_2]} \subset A^{(1,1)}_{[\alpha_1,\alpha_2],[\beta_1,\beta_2]}.$

Definition 3.3: Let A be an GIVIFS on F(X), and $\alpha = [\alpha_1, \alpha_2]$, $\beta = [\beta_1, \beta_2] \in [I]$ and $0 \leq \alpha2 \wedge \beta2 \leq 0.5$ then (i, j)-th (α, β) interval cut-set of GIVIFS on A is $A^{(i,j)}_{\alpha,\beta}$.

Then the complements of different interval cut-set on A are given below:

$(A^{(1,1)}_{[\alpha1,\alpha2],[\beta1,\beta2]})^c = \{\langle x, [A^-(x) \not\geq \alpha_1, A^+(x) \not\geq \alpha_2], [B^-(x) \not\geq \beta_1, B^+(x) \not\geq \beta_2] \rangle \mid x \in X\}$

$(A^{(1,2)}_{[\alpha1,\alpha2],[\beta1,\beta2]})^c = \{\langle x, [A^-(x) \not\geq \alpha_1, A^+(x) \not> \alpha_2], [B^-(x) \not\geq \beta_1, B^+(x) \not> \beta_2] \rangle \mid x \in X\}$

$(A^{(2,1)}_{[\alpha1,\alpha2],[\beta1,\beta2]})^c = \{\langle x, [A^-(x) \not> \alpha_1, A^+(x) \not\geq \alpha_2],$
$[B^-(x) \not> \beta_1, B^+(x) \not\geq \beta_2]\rangle \mid x \in X\}$

$(A^{(2,2)}_{[\alpha1,\alpha2],[\beta1,\beta2]})^c = \{\langle x, [A^-(x) \not> \alpha_1, A^+(x) \not> \alpha_2],$
$[B^-(x) \not> \beta_1, B^+(x) \not> \beta_2]\rangle \mid x \in X\}.$

From the definition of complements it is easy to observe the following results:

$$\left(A^{(1,1)}_{[\alpha_1,\alpha_2],[\beta_1,\beta_2]}\right)^c = A^{(4,4)}_{[\alpha_1,\alpha_2],[\beta_1,\beta_2]}$$

$$\left(A^{(1,2)}_{[\alpha_1,\alpha_2],[\beta_1,\beta_2]}\right)^c = A^{(4,3)}_{[\alpha_1,\alpha_2],[\beta_1,\beta_2]}$$

$$\left(A^{(2,1)}_{[\alpha_1,\alpha_2],[\beta_1,\beta_2]}\right)^c = A^{(3,4)}_{[\alpha_1,\alpha_2],[\beta_1,\beta_2]}$$

$$\left(A^{(2,2)}_{[\alpha_1,\alpha_2],[\beta_1,\beta_2]}\right)^c = A^{(3,3)}_{[\alpha_1,\alpha_2],[\beta_1,\beta_2]}$$

Definition 3.4: For $\alpha = [\alpha1, \alpha2], \beta = [\beta1, \beta2] \in$ [I] satisfying the condition $0 \leq \alpha2 \wedge \beta2 \leq$ 0.5 and $A \in F(X)$, we define two interval Cartesian products, which convert each GIVIFS to special type of GIVIFS i.e. $(\alpha,\beta).A$, and $(\alpha, \beta) * A \in$ GIVIFS defined for each $x \in X$ as follows:

$(\alpha, \beta).A = \{x \in X: [\alpha_1 \wedge A^-(x), \alpha_2 \wedge A^+(x)], [\beta_1 \vee B^-(x), \beta_2 \vee B^+(x)]\}$

and

$(\alpha, \beta) * A = \{x \in X: [\alpha_1 \vee A^-(x), \alpha_2 \vee A^+(x)], [\beta_1 \wedge B^-(x), \beta_2 \wedge B^+(x)]\},$

where two fundamental operators $\vee$ and $\wedge$ are defined for all x, y $\in$ [0, 1] such that

(i) $x \vee y = \max(x, y)$ and (ii) $x \wedge y = \min(x, y)$.

Proposition 3.3: For A, B $\in$ F(X) and $\alpha, \beta, \alpha1, \beta1, \alpha2, \beta2 \in$ [I] then

(a) For $\alpha_1 \leq \alpha_2, \beta_1 \leq \beta_2$, (i) $(\alpha_1, \beta_1).A \subseteq (\alpha_2, \beta_2).A$ (ii) $(\alpha_1, \beta_1) * A \subseteq (\alpha_2, \beta_2) * A$.

(b) For A $\subseteq$ B, (i) $(\alpha, \beta).A \subseteq (\alpha, \beta).B$ (ii) $(\alpha, \beta) * A \subseteq (\alpha, \beta) * B$.

Proof: The prove are straight forward.

4. DECOMPOSITION ON INTERVAL CUT-SET OF GIVIFS

The principal role of interval cut-set of GIVIFSs is their capability to represent GIVIFSs. The representation of an arbitrary GIVIFS A in terms of interval Cartesian product, which are defined in terms of interval cut-set of GIVIFS of A, is usually referred to as a decomposition theorem.

In this section, we give three decomposition theorems of GIVIFSs as follows:

Theorem 4.1: Let A be an GIVIFS on F(X), then for $\alpha = [\alpha1, \alpha2], \beta = [\beta1, \beta2] \in$ [I] satisfying the condition $0 \leq \alpha2 \wedge \beta2 \leq 0.5$,

$$A = \bigcup_{\alpha,\beta} (\alpha, \beta).A^{(1,j)}_{\alpha,\beta}, j = 1, 2.$$

$\alpha,\beta \in$ [I]

Proof: To prove this theorem we assume that the set A has n elements of the form

$A = \{\langle xi, ai, bi \rangle\}$, where i = 1, 2, $\cdots$, n and ai = $[a_{1i}, a2i], b = [b_{1i}, b_{2i}], \alpha = [\alpha_1, \alpha_2], \beta = [\beta_1, \beta_2] \in$ [I].

Now $\bigcup$ $(\alpha, \beta).A(1,j) \alpha,\beta$

$\alpha,\beta \in [I]$

$= \{ \langle xi, [\max \{\alpha_1 \wedge a_{1i}\}, \max \{\alpha_2 \wedge a_{2i}\}][\min \{\beta_1 \vee b_{1i}\}, \min \{\beta_2 \vee b_{2i}\}] \rangle \}$

$\alpha_1, \alpha_2, \beta_1, \beta_2$

Here two cases may arise. Case-(i): ai < α, bi < β and case-(ii): ai ≥ α, bi ≥ β

Case-(i): When a < α, b < β then A(1,j)
[α1,α2],[β1,β2]= ϕ and therefore ([α_1, α_2],
[β_1, β_2]).$A^{(1,j)}$ [α1,α2],[β1,β2]= ϕ.

Case-(ii): When $a_i \geq \alpha$, $b_i \geq \beta$ then we have

$A(1,j)[\alpha1,\alpha2],[\beta1,\beta2] = \{ \langle x_i, [a_{1i}, a_{2i}], [b_{1i}, b_{2i}] \rangle \}$
$([\alpha_1, \alpha_2], [\beta_1, \beta_2]).A^{(1,j)}[\alpha1,\alpha2],[\beta1,\beta2]$

$= \{ \langle x, [\max \{\alpha_1 \wedge a_{1i}\}, \max \{\alpha_2 \wedge a_{2i}\}], [\min \{\beta_1 \vee b_{1i}\}, \min\{\beta_2 \vee b_{2i}\}] \rangle \}$

α1, α2, β1, β2

$= \{ \langle xi, [a_{1i}, a_{2i}], [b_{1i}, b_{2i}] \rangle \}.$

From Case-(i) and Case-(ii) we have

$\bigcup$ $(\alpha, \beta).A(1,j)\alpha,\beta = \bigcup$ $(\alpha, \beta).A^{(1,j)}_{\alpha,\beta} \bigcup$ $(\alpha, \beta).A^{(1,j)}_{\alpha,\beta}$

$\alpha,\beta \in [I]$ ± <ai, ² <bi ai ≥ ai, ² ≥ bi

$= \{ \langle xi, [a_{1i}, a_{2i}], [b_{1i}, b_{2i}] \rangle \}$

$= A.$

Therefore for every $x_i \in X$.

$A = \bigcup$ $(\alpha, \beta).A(1,j)\alpha,\beta, j = 1, 2.$

$\alpha,\beta \in [I]$

Theorem 4.2: Let A be an GIVIFS on F(X), then
for α = [α1, α2], β = [β1, β2] ∈ [I] and 0 ≤
α2 ∧ β2 ≤ 0.5,

$A = (\cap(\alpha, \beta) * A^{(4,i)}_{\alpha,\beta})^c, i = 3, 4.$

$\alpha,\beta \in [I]$

Suppose H be a mapping from [I] to P(X),
where P(X) is the crisp set, H: [I] → P(X), for
every α, β ∈ [I]. We have H(α, β) ∈ P(X). Obviously interval cut-set of interval-valued intuitionistic fuzzy set, Aα,β ∈ P(X), it means that mapping H indeed exits. Based on Theorem 1,
Theorem 2, we have the following theorem in
general. For A ∈ GIVIFS, we have

Theorem 4.3: (1) If $A^{(1,2)}_{\alpha,\beta} \subseteq H(\alpha, \beta) \subseteq A^{(1,1)}_{\alpha,\beta}$
then

$A = \bigcup$ $(\alpha, \beta).H(\alpha, \beta)$

$\alpha,\beta \in [I]$

and if $A^{(4,4)}_{\alpha,\beta} \subseteq H(\alpha, \beta) \subseteq A^{(4,3)}_{\alpha,\beta}$ then

$A = (\bigcup$ $(\alpha, \beta) * H(\alpha, \beta)^c)^c.$

$\alpha,\beta \in [I]$

5. CONCLUSION

In this article, we first introduce some kinds of
cut sets for GIVIFSs and give their some interesting properties respectively. Next, we obtain
decomposition theorems of GIVIFSs based on
these cut sets and their properties. This concept of

decomposition theorem can be applied for solving fuzzy system of linear equations.

ACKNOWLEDGMENT

The authors are very grateful and would like to express their sincere thanks to anonymous referee and editor for their valuable comments.

REFERENCES

Atanassov, K., & Gargov, G. (1989). Interval-valued intuitionistic fuzzy sets. *Fuzzy Sets and Systems*, *31*(1), 343–349. doi:10.1016/0165-0114(89)90205-4

Bhowmik, M., & Pal, M. (2009). Partition of generalized interval-valued intuitionistic fuzzy sets and some properties. *International Journal of Applied Mathematical Analysis and Applications*, *4*(1), 1–10.

Bhowmik, M., & Pal, M. (2010). Generalized interval-valued intuitionistic fuzzy sets. *The Journal of Fuzzy Mathematics*, *18*(2), 357–371.

Huang, H. (2013). Some properties on the cut sets of intuitionistic fuzzy sets. *Annals of Fuzzy Mathematics and Informatics*, *5*(3), 475–481.

Li, J., & Li, H. (2008). The cut sets, decomposition theorems and representation theorems on R-fuzzy sets. *International Journal of Information and systems sciences*, *6*(1), 61-71.

Mondal, T. K., & Samanta, S. K. (2002). Generalized intuitionistic fuzzy sets. *The Journal of Fuzzy Mathematics*, *10*(4), 839–862.

Panigrahi, M., & Nanda, S. (2006). A comparison between intuitionistic fuzzy sets and generalized intuitionistic fuzzy sets. *The Journal of Fuzzy Mathematics*, *14*(2), 407–421.

Sharma, P. K. (2011). (α,β) cut for intuitionistic fuzzy groups. *International Mathematical Forum*, *6*(53), 2605–2614.

(1965). Yuan, X. (1997). New cut sets and their applications. *Fuzzy Systems and Mathematics*, *11,* 37-43.

Yuan, X., Li, H., Xing, & Sun, K. (2011). The cut sets, decomposition theorems and representation theorems on intuitionistic fuzzy sets and interval valued fuzzy sets. *Science China Information Sciences*, *54*(1), 91-110.

Zadeh, L.A. (1965) Fuzzy sets. *Information and Control, 8,* 338–353. doi:10.1016/S0019-9958(65)90241-X

Chapter 10
A Generalized Graph Strict Strong Coloring Algorithm:
Application on Graph Distribution

Meriem Bensouyad
University Constantine 2, Algeria

Mourad Bouzenada
University Constantine 2, Algeria

Nousseiba Guidoum
University Constantine 2, Algeria

Djamel-Eddine Saïdouni
University Constantine 2, Algeria

ABSTRACT

This chapter examines the graph coloring problem. A graph strict strong coloring algorithm has been proposed for trees in Haddad and Kheddouci (2009). In this chapter, the authors recall the heuristic-based algorithm for general graphs named GGSSCA (for Generalized Graph Strict Strong Coloring Algorithm) proposed in Bouzenada, Bensouyad, Guidoum, Reghioua, and Saidouni (2012). The complexity of this algorithm is polynomial with considering the number of vertices. Later, in Guidoum, Bensouyad, and Saidouni (2013), GGSSCA was applied to solve the graph distribution problem.

1. INTRODUCTION

The graph coloring is a combinatorial optimization problem. The coloring process is done according to some properties. Let G be a given graph, a proper vertex coloring of a graph is a vertex coloring such that no two adjacent vertices have

the same color. The minimum number of colors among all proper colorings of G is its chromatic number χ(G). It is well known that the k-coloring problem for general graphs is NP-complete and the calculation of the chromatic number is NP-hard (Klotz, 2002).

A plenty variety of graph coloring is presented in Chen, Gyarfas, and Schelp (1998). Some others

DOI: 10.4018/978-1-4666-6252-0.ch010

colorings deal with edges of graphs (Caragiannisa, Kaklamanisa, & Persianob, 2002), others with lists (Albertson, Grossman, & Haas, 2000). In addition too, solutions for coloring both vertices and edges of graphs have been proposed (Borodin, Kostochka, & Woodall, 1998). Often, graph coloring and dominance problems are correlated. Several relations between the chromatic number and some dominance parameters are presented in Chellali and Volkmann (2004).

In Zverovich (2006), a notion of graph strong coloring has been introduced. It defines a dominance relation between graph vertices and color classes. Strong coloring problem has been shown as NP-complete. After that, in Haddad and Kheddouci (2009), authors defined a strict strong *k*-coloring (*k*-SSColoring) of graphs, which is a strong k-coloring with a non-empty constraint on color classes (Figure 1). The new coloring parameters define the dominance property.

An exact polynomial time of graph strict strong coloring algorithm for trees has been proposed.

The Graph Strict Strong Coloring Problem (GSSCP) consists to find the minimum number of colors which check the dominance property for each vertex. In fact, finding exact solutions for general graphs are NP-complete (Haddad & Kheddouci, 2009).

As an application of such coloring process, we can cite broadcasting (Haddad, Dekar, & Kheddouci, 2008), data dissemination, gossiping and graph distribution (Guidoum et al., 2013). This latter is introduced to deal with state space explosion problem which is a fundamental obstacle in formal verification of concurrent systems. The graph distribution problem will be detailed later.

In this chapter, we illustrate that heuristic based algorithms may be a good approach to solve graph strict strong coloring problem for general graphs. Especially, we focus on the GGSSCA algorithm (for Generalized Graph Strict Strong Coloring Algorithm) which has a polynomial complexity with respect to the number of vertices (Bouzenada et al., 2012).

In the other hand, we also show that coloring concept can be useful to solve the graph distribution problem by means of the SSCGDA algorithm (for Strict Strong Coloring based-Graph Distribution Algorithm) proposed in Guidoum et al., (2013).

The chapter is organized as follows: Section 2 gives some preliminary notations and definitions related to graph coloring. In Section 3, the GGSSCA is described. Section 4 presents GGSSCA's experimental results. In section 5, GGSSCA is applied on trees and results are compared with those of the exact algorithm.

In section 6, GGSSCA is adapted to solve the graph distribution problem. Specifically, in this section, the graph distribution problem is introduced then the relation between graph distribution and graph strict strong coloring is shown. Next, the GGSSCA application named SSCGDA (for Strict Strong Coloring based Graph Distribution Algorithm) is illustrated. Finally, various experimental results related to SSCGDA are presented.

Figure 1. Example of graph strict strong coloring (adapted from Haddad & Kheddouci, 2009)

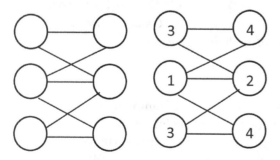

Non colored graph.

Strict strong colored graph using 4 colors.

2. PRELIMINARY DEFENITIONS

In this chapter, we mean by graph a simple undirected loopless graph with no isolated vertices.

Let $G = (V, E)$ be a graph such that $V = \{v1, v2... vn\}$ is a finite set of vertices and $E \subseteq V \times V$ is a finite set of edges.

Two vertices u and v are neighbors or adjacent if $(u, v) \in E$. For any $u \in V$, let $N(u) = \{v \in V$ such that $(u, v) \in E\}$ be the set of adjacent vertices of u. Let $deg(u) = |N(u)|$ be the degree of the vertex u. A subset of vertex $S \subseteq V$ is said stable or independent if and only if for any vertices u and v of S, $(u, v) \notin E$. In other words, elements of S are not adjacent vertices.

For $u \in V$ and $Y \subseteq V$. $u \sim Y$ means that u is adjacent to all vertices of Y.

A proper vertex coloring of a graph is a vertex coloring such that no two adjacent vertices have the same color. A proper coloring C using at most k colors is called a proper k-coloring, it is a function $C: V \rightarrow \{1... k\}$ such that $C(u) \neq C(v)$ for any $(u, v) \in E$ (Klotz, 2002). $C(v)$ is called the color of v. The vertices having the same color constitute a color class.

Since each color class is an independent set of G, a coloring may also be seen as a partition of V into independent sets $(C1, C2 ... Ck)$ where $Ci = \{x \in V$ such that $C(x) = i\}$ (Dharwadker, 2006).

A graph is k-colorable if it has a proper k-coloring. The chromatic number $\chi(G)$ is the minimum number of colors required for coloring G.

A strong coloring is a graph coloring such that for each vertex v, there is a color class Ci such that v is adjacent to every vertex of Ci. A graph is strongly k-colorable if it has a strong k-coloring (Zverovich, 2006).

A strict strong k-coloring (k-SSColoring) of a graph is a strong k-coloring such that there is non-empty color class. More formally, the k-SSColoring of G is a proper k-coloring $\{C_1, C_2 ... C_k\}$ of G such that for every vertex $u \in V$, there

exists $i \in \{1, 2... k\}$ where u is adjacent to every vertex of C_i and $C_i \neq \varnothing$ (i.e., $u \sim C_i$) (Haddad & Kheddouci, 2009). The strict strong chromatic number $\chi_{ss}(G)$ is defined as the minimum number of colors among all strict strong colorings (Haddad & Kheddouci, 2009).

It is easy to see that $\chi(G) \leq \chi_{ss}(G) \leq |V|$.

In addition to proper coloring, the SSColoring respects a new constraint which is the dominance property. This latter increases the chromatic number $\chi(G)$. Note that, for a complete graph G, all vertices are neighbors, in such case, each vertex will be colored with a unique color. Then $\chi(G)$ is equal to $|V|$, consequently $\chi_{ss}(G)=|V|$.

The graph strict strong coloring problem (GSSCP) can be seen either as a decision or as an optimization problem: The decision formulation of the ''k strict strong coloring problem'' (k-SSCP) for a graph G and an integer k such that $k \leq |V|$ consists in answering the question ''is G k-strict strong colorable?''.

The optimization formulation of the GSSCP for a graph G consists to find $\chi_{ss}(G)$. The k-strict strong coloring problem of connected graphs is NP-complete, for $k \geq 4$ (Haddad & Kheddouci, 2009).

3. GENERALIZED GRAPH STRICT STRONG COLORING ALGORITHM (GGSSCA)

This section presents the heuristic based graph strict strong coloring algorithm for general graphs called GGSSCA. This algorithm calculates the chromatic number preserving the proper coloring property and the dominance property (Bouzenada et al., 2012).

3.1 The Algorithm

See Box 1.

Box 1. The Generalized Graph Strict Strong Coloring Algorithm (GGSSCA)

Input: A graph G = (V, E)
Output: A number of colors k
Initialization:
Satisfied: A variable which memorizes the set of vertices having the dominance property. Initially this variable is empty.
Colored: A variable which memorizes the set of colored vertices. Initially this variable is empty.
k: Integer initialized to 0.
$D \subseteq V \times Integer$: Is a set containing a degree of vertex at a given calculation step.
C: A variable which memorizes the set of coloring classes indexed by k.
Begin
 Step1: // *Ensuring the dominance property*
Repeat
 D: $= U\{(u, deg(u) - |N(u) \cap Satisfied|\}$...($\alpha$)
  $_{u \in (V - Colored)}$

Select (u, n) such that **u** is a vertex with a maximal number **n** in the set **D**............(β)
$k := k + 1$;
$C[k] := \{u\}$; //*Attribute a new color to vertex u*.......................................(γ)
Colored: = Colored $\cup$ $\{u\}$;
Satisfied: = Satisfied $\cup$ N (u);
Until (Satisfied = V)
 Step2: // *Proper coloring*
This step colors optimally all not yet colored vertices by means of a proper coloring algorithm (Klotz, 2002).
The constructive RLF method has been used to complete our coloring process as follows:
Y:=(V − Colored); //*None colored vertices.*
While (Y $\neq$ $\emptyset$) **do**
$k := k + 1$;
B:= $\emptyset$; //*Set of vertices.*
Choose a vertex v $\in$ Y of maximal degree deg (v);
$C[k] := C[k] \cup \{v\}$;
B:= B $\cup$ N (v);
Y:= Y- ($\{v\}$ $\cup$ N (v));
While (Y $\neq$ $\emptyset$) **do**
Choose v $\in$ Y of maximal degree;
$C[k] := C[k] \cup \{v\}$;
B:= B $\cup$ N (v);
Y:= Y- ($\{v\}$ $\cup$ N (v));
End While
Y:= B;
End While
End

3.2 Explanation

To explain the algorithm, let us consider the example of none colored graph of Figure 2.

The first step ensures the dominance property. At the end of this step, each vertex must be adjacent to at least one non empty color class.

The line (α) calculates the degree of each none colored vertex without considering its satisfied neighbors. Note that, a vertex is said to be satisfied if and only if it checks the dominance property. After that, the vertex u with a greater calculated degree is selected (line β) and used for creating a new color class Ck (line γ). The color of this vertex is k (u is added to the set *Colored*). So, its neighbors $N(u)$ dominate the color k and they are considered satisfied ($N(u)$ is added to the set *Satisfied*). The process is repeated until all vertices become elements of the set *Satisfied*. The result of this first step on the previous example is shown in Figure 3. Three coloring classes are obtained and all vertices are satisfied (marked vertices).

As a result of the first step, each none colored vertex is adjacent to at least one colored vertex.

Figure 2. None colored graph

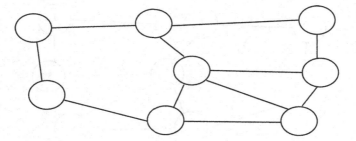

Figure 3. The result of step 1

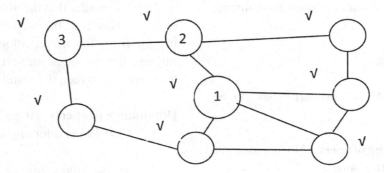

To complete the coloring process, it remains only to color properly the not yet colored vertices using a proper coloring algorithm. For example the reader may find such algorithms in Klotz (2002). This coloring process constitutes the second step of the algorithm. The constructive RLF method (Leighton, 1979) has been applied for completing the coloring process. It is more effective and yielding good results.

The RLF method (Figure 4) constructs successively the classes of colors. Let *Y* be the set of not yet colored vertices which can be included in the independent set *C[k]* and let *B* be the set of uncolored vertices which cannot be included in *C[k]* due to the fact that they are adjacent to at least one vertex in *C[k]*. The process is repeated until all vertices become colored (Figure 5). As

Figure 4. The result of the first iteration of RLF algorithm

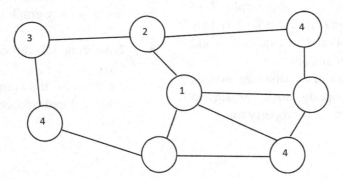

Figure 5. The result of step 2

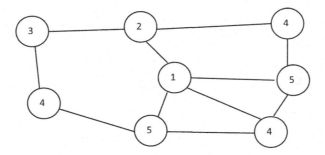

it can be seen, five colors are used for coloring this graph.

3.3 Correctness

To assess GGSSCA, two properties should be checked:

1. **Proper coloring property:** No two adjacent vertices have the same color.
2. **Dominance property:** Each vertex is adjacent to at least one non empty color class elements.

Proof.

3.3.1 Proper Coloring Property

For proving this property, let us assume that two adjacent vertices u and v have the same color, it means that $(u, v) \in E$ with u and v elements of Ck, then $|Ck| \geq 2$.

In the first step, at each iteration the line (γ) ensures the attribution of a unique color k to the selected vertex (line (β)). So, $|Ck| = 1$. This contradicts the assumption. Consequently, u and v may not be both elements of Ck.

In this case, the result of the first step ensures the proper coloring property. So, it remains to verify that step 2 ensures this property too.

Let us consider that the assumption is a result of step 2. However, this step uses a proper coloring algorithm for not yet colored vertices, which implies that two adjacent vertices may not have the same color, then the result.

Dominance property: At each iteration, in step 1, Ck= {v} and for any u ∈ N(v), u ~ Ck.

The process is repeated until ($\bigcup_{v \in V} N\left(v\right) = V$), which implies that, at the end of step 1, for any $u \in V$, it exists a non-empty color class Ck such that $u \sim Ck$. Then, the first step ensures the dominance property.

The second step calculates the proper coloring for all not yet colored vertices using new colors. Consequently, the dominance property remains verified.

3.4 Complexity

Following the complexity computing (Karp, 1972), the algorithm GGSSCA performs the SSColoring of any graph in $O\ (|V|^2)$.

*   Satisfying all vertices is within $O\ (|V|)$ (step1).
*   At line (α), the computation of D for all none colored vertices is done in $O\ (|V|)$ time.

4. EXPERIMENTS AND RESULTS

In this section, we discuss the obtained results after applying GGSSCA on a Benchmark of 15 graphs (http://mat.gsia.cmu.edu/COLOR/instances.html), namely the DIMACS graphs whose chromatic numbers are known.

As expected, for each graph, its strict strong chromatic number computed by the GGSSCA algorithm is in general greater than the chromatic number proposed in DIMACS data base (Section 2).

In Table 1, the meaning of parameter names is as follows:

- $|V|$ denotes the number of vertices (the graph order),
- $|E|$ denotes the number of edges (the graph size),
- χ is the chromatic number,
- k is the computed strict strong chromatic number,

T-exec: The average execution run-time (in milliseconds) corresponds to 10 runs.

Observe that the execution time depends on the number of vertices and edges. In addition, the computed strict strong chromatic number becomes more near to $\chi(G)$ when the connectivity between vertices increases (see the last two cases).

5. GGSSCA VERSUS EXACT ALGORITHM FOR TREES

As trees are particular graphs, this section compares GGSSCA with the exact algorithm defined for trees and proposed in Haddad and Kheddouci (2009).

In Haddad and Kheddouci (2009), several kinds of vertices and structures, such as base vertex, bridge, b-locality and pseudo b-locality, have been defined for trees. The purpose is the decomposition of trees and by the way coloring them with an exact and appropriate number of colors. However, GGSSCA considers all vertices similar. The application of the algorithm for a tree will choose vertices having maximum number of none satisfied neighbors and color them with dominated color. None colored vertices are colored by means of a proper coloring algorithm.

Table 2 compares the obtained results.

Let r be the root of the tree. An induction proof on the tree's depth d (the maximal distance between the leaves and the root r) has been used. Vnb denotes the number of vertices. χ_{ss} and k are the

Table 1. Results on DIMACS graphs

Graph	$|V|$	$|E|$	X	$k \approx \chi_{ss}$	(T-Exec)(ms)
queen5.5	25	160	5	8	27
queen6 .6	36	290	7	13	41
queen7_7	49	476	7	15	65
queen8_8	64	728	9	17	56
Huck	74	301	11	20	49
queen9_9	81	2112	10	19	85
David	87	406	11	12	52
games120	120	638	9	24	68
miles250	128	387	8	39	59
miles500	128	1170	20	32	128
miles750	128	2113	31	40	206
anna	138	493	11	18	83
myciel7	191	2360	8	16	159
fpsol2.i.1	496	11654	65	66	1033
Inithx.i.1	864	18707	54	56	3359

Table 2. Comparison table

D	Vnb	χ_{ss}	K
1	2	2	2
	> 2	2	3
≥ 2	≥ 2	N	N

strict strong chromatic number calculated by the exact and the GGSSCA algorithms respectively.

In all cases $\chi_{ss} = k$ except in the case of *d = 1* with *Vnb > 2*. In this case *k = 3* and $\chi_{ss} = 2$.

This result may be explained as follows:

The first dominated color is for the root. This guarantees the dominance property of the leaves. The second dominated color is given to one of the leaves for satisfying the root. At this step, all vertices become satisfied and none colored vertices will be colored with the third same color (leaves are not adjacent).

5.1 Induction Proof on the Tree Depth

For d = 2

The strict strong chromatic number obtained by the application of GGSSCA to a tree is always equal to DC + 1 where DC is the number of dominated colors obtained by step one. These colors are attributed as follows:

- The root is colored by one color ensuring dominance property for vertices of level 1 in the tree.
- Each none leaf vertex at level 1 is colored by one new color. Then each new colored vertex dominates its leaves.
- All leaves are colored by the same color because they are not connected.

Concluding that, the strict strong chromatic number given by GGSSCA is DC + 1. This number is equal to the not leaf vertices plus one, which is the strict strong chromatic number given by the exact algorithm for trees (Haddad & Kheddouci, 2009).

Induction Step: Suppose that k = χ_{ss} for d = n, and prove that k = χ_{ss} for d = n+1.

Extending the depth d from n to n + 1, new vertices connected to leaves of depth n should be added. Then, according to GGSSCA, $k_{(d=n+1)} = k_{(d=n)} + $ |new parents|.

In Haddad and Kheddouci (2009), the exact algorithm gives $\chi_{ss\,(d=n+1)} = \chi_{ss\,(d=n)} + $ |new base vertices|, where new base vertices correspond to new parents in the GGSSCA. Then $\chi_{ss} = k$ for d = n+1.

For that, the $\chi_{ss} = k$ for any tree of depth greater or equal than two.

6. GRAPH DISTRIBUTION BASED ON STRICT STRONG COLORING

As application of coloring approaches, in this section, we show that the coloring concept, especially SSColoring, may be useful to solve a classical problem called the graph distribution problem.

The graph distribution is introduced to deal with applications using large scale graphs used in formal verification, parallel computing, communication protocols, distributed algorithms, and industrial case studies...

In this chapter, we take for instance the formal verification process of concurrent systems which suffers frequently from the state space explosion problem (Bérard et al., 2001; Clarke, Grumberg, & Peled, 1999; Valmari, 1998). This latter occurs when the graphs, modeling finite state systems, became too large and complex. In this case, the formal verification process becomes more and more slowly and may not be terminated.

Such problem may be overcome by distributing state space among several workstations (workers) which communicate through a message in a network.

Note that, the graph distribution is a well known optimization problem. It has been formulated as an NP-complete problem (Bixby, Kennedy & Kremer, 1993).

To have a good distribution, several factors should be taken into account. The most important of them are the workload balancing (i.e. no unemployed or overloaded workers) and the minimization of the distribution cost (i.e. edges to be cut).

In this section, the heuristic based on coloring concept and dominance relation in graphs called SSCGDA is presented to find a good distribution within a reasonable time. This basic solution is improved in two steps: the initialization and optimization step. It is based on GGSSCA presented in section 3. Particularly, its first step which insures the dominance property is used to make the initial distribution. After that, another process will be started to build the final and optimal distribution.

The goal of the approach is, given a graph G as input and a number of workers W, to find the better distribution of G which respects the balancing constraint (i.e. holds good load balancing), and minimizes the communication costs (i.e. edges between states on different parts).

6.1 State Space Distribution Concepts

Before introducing the approach, some basic definitions and concepts are given to be used later.

State space representation of system's behavior is described as follow:

- All the states, the system can be in, are represented as vertices of a graph.
- A transition, that can change the system from one state to another, is represented by an edge from one node to another. Note that, edges may be unidirectional or bi-directional.

A distribution of state space graph on W network nodes (parts, workers) is a partition of its set of vertices into W pair-wise disjoint subsets $(V = \bigcup_{i=1}^{w} V_i$ and $V_i \cap V_j = \emptyset$ for all $1 \leq i, j \leq W)$ which respect some constraints and minimize an objective function. We denote by E_{ij} the cross

(external) edges (i.e. the set of edges between the vertices assigned to worker i and he vertices assigned to worker j). Then, the elements of the sets E_{ii} are internal (local) edges.

For goals discussed above, an efficient distribution should have:

- A minimal number of cross (external) edges E_{ij}, in other words, as many internal (local) edges E_{ii} as possible. We express this factor by the rate $\ddot{o}(\%)$ which is equal to the number of internal edges divided by the total number of edges.

Rate of internal edges:

$$\ddot{o}(\%) = 100 * \sum_{i=1}^{w} \frac{|E_{ii}|}{|E|}$$

- Balance, i.e., more-or-less the same number of vertices on each part. To determine this, we establish the notion of standard deviation of the number of nodes, denoted by $\tilde{A}_V$ and defined as follows:

$$\sigma_V = \sqrt{\frac{1}{w} \sum_{i=1}^{w} \left(|V_i| - \text{avg} \right)^2}$$

Such that, the average load (*avg*) is the total number of vertices divided by the number of parts (*W*), since the sets of vertices assigned to different parts are disjoint:

$$\text{avg} = \frac{|V|}{W}.$$

6.2 Graph Distribution vs. Graph Strict Strong Coloring

After proposing GGSSCA, authors have observed that the SSColoring has an adapted behavior for solving the graph distribution problem which is completely different from the problem of graph coloring. This latter concept is used to make an initial distribution of given graph. Precisely, the first phase of GGSSCA presented in section 3 is applied. At the end of this step, the dominated colors number (i.e. called *DC* is equal to *k* in step 1 of GGSSCA) is given and each vertex of the graph is adjacent to at least one non empty color class (*C[k]* in step 1). The number *DC* is used to identify the number of parts of initial distribution such that each color presents one of the parts. The vertex colored with dominated color is considered as a center of a new part and its neighbors (i.e. which dominate this color class) are put with it on the same part.

However, this process may leads to joint constructive parts (i.e. parts have elements in common: the same vertex can dominate more than one color class respecting definition of SSColoring presented in (Haddad & Kheddouci, 2009)). This contradicts the definition of graph distribution which aims to obtain *W* (constant defined number) pair-wise disjoint subsets. For this raison, another process must be defined to reorganize the initial parts and obtain *DC* independent parts (See subsection 6.3.1: *The initial distribution construction process*).

6.3 Strict Strong Coloring Based-Graph Distribution Algorithm (SSCGDA)

This approach is divided into two parts: an initialization and an optimization processes.

In the initialization process, the strict strong coloring is done to make the initial distribution of none distributed graph. Particularly, the first phase of GGSSCA which gives the initial number of parts is used. Then, the *initial distribution construction process* is called to reorganize the initial distribution.

In the following step (optimization process), the *grouping* (*splitting*) *process* will be used to fusion (split) initial parts if its number (*DC* in the

Box 2) is upper (less) than the required number of parts (constant number: *W*). The global graph distribution method is given by Box 2.

As an example, let us consider a distributed system with 4 workers. For the graph of Figure 6, the first phase of GGSSCA leads to the initial distribution showed in Figure 7.

As it will be clarified in the sequel, the number of parts obtained initially is equal to eight (*DC* = 8), since the number of workers is equal to four (*W*=4), the second phase of the algorithm groups the parts as showed in Figure 8.

However, for the graph of Figure 9, *DC* is equal to two (see Figure 10). In this case, the second phase of the algorithm splits the obtained parts and leads to the distributed graph of Figure 11.

Subsections 6.3.1 and 6.3.2 explain the two steps of the algorithm.

6.3.1 Initialization Process

The initial distribution construction is based on the strict strong coloring principle. After applying the first phase of GGSSCA, we obtain the number of parts of initial distribution (*DC*) and get centers for all parts such that the part center is defined as a colored vertex with dominated color (*Centers*: set of colored vertices, considered as parts centers, equal to *Colored* in step 1) (see section 3).

The *initial distribution construction process* (See Box 3) is used for constructing the initial pair-wise disjoint parts (*DC* parts).

Each part (V_i) initially contains exactly one center which is a colored vertex ($u \in Centers$). Then, the neighbors $N(u)$ will be added to V_i with elimination of each neighbor which is already associated to another parts $\{v \in N(u) / Belong(v)\}$. Finally, this process ensures that all obtained parts are independents.

To more explain the algorithm of the initial distribution construction, let us consider the previous examples.

Box 2. The global graph distribution algorithm

Input: Graph $G = (V, E)$.
W: the number of workers.
Output: π_w distribution (partition) of graph G into W sub-graphs (parts).
Initialization:
DC: The number of dominated colors obtained after executing the first step of GGSSCA.
Centers: is the set of colored vertices with dominated colors, obtained by GGSSCA.
Begin
Step 1: *Initialization process*
Centers: = GGSSCA.step1 (G);
DC:=|*Centers*|;
Initial distribution construction process (); // Builds π_{DC} of G; .... (α)
Step2: *Optimization process*
If $(DC > W)$ **Then**
Grouping process (); .... (β)
Else
If $(DC < W)$ **Then**
Splitting process (); .... (γ)
 End if
End if
End

Figure 6. None distributed graph

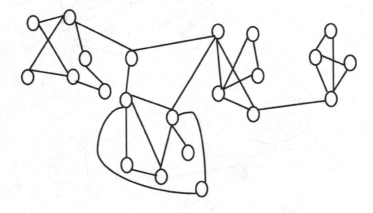

Figure 7. The result of the 'initial distribution construction process'

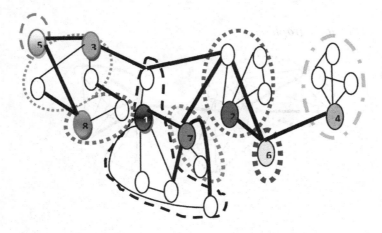

Figure 8. The result of the 'grouping process'

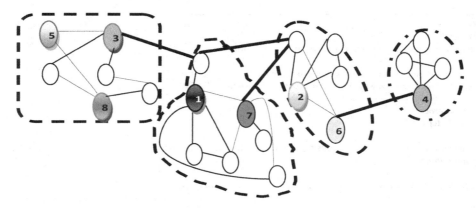

Figure 9. None distributed graph

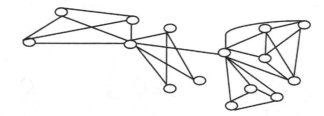

Figure 10. The initial distribution

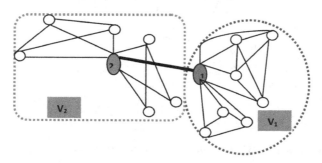

Figure 11. The final distributed graph

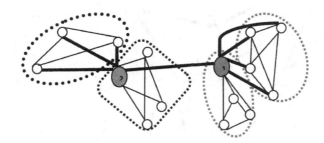

Box 3. The initial distribution construction process (line α)

Input: Graph $G= (V, E)$.
DC: the initial number of parts obtained by GGSSCA.
Centers: is the set of colored vertices with dominated colors, obtained by GGSSCA, considered as parts centers in this algorithm.
Output: Partition π_{DC} of G / | π_{DC} |$=DC$.
Initialization:
$\pi_{DC} = \{V_1, V_2, ... V_{DC}\}$: such that for all $V_i \in \pi_{DC}$, V_i is an independent part. Initially $V_i = \{u \mid u \in Centers\}$.
Belong (v): is a boolean function equal to true when the vertex v already belongs to one part.
Belong (v) = true if $v \in V_i$ / $i \in \{1..DC\}$.
Conflicting _vertices $_u$: is the set of neighbors of u which already belong to one part.
i: integer initialized to 0.
Begin
While ($i<DC$)

$$Conflicting \_vertices_u = \left\{ v \in N\left(u\right) / u \in V_i \ \text{ and } \ Belong\left(v\right)\right\};$$

$$V_i = V_i \bigcup (N(u) - Conflicting\ vertices_u);$$
End while
End

Figures 12 and 13 illustrate the result of the first step of GGSSCA on the graphs of Figure 6 and 9 respectively.

After that, the *initial distribution construction process* is done and the results are as shown in Figures 7 and 10.

6.3.2 Optimization Process

In this step, the choice between *grouping* and *splitting processes* is made according to the number DC of dominated colors. This latter represents the number of parts obtained at the end of the initialization process.

If W is less than DC there is a *grouping* else there is a *splitting process*.

α Grouping process

The *grouping process* is described in Box 4. The algorithm has a main loop which terminates when the current number of parts is equal to W. At each iteration, the algorithm selects two parts V_i and V_j to be merged. First, it selects the part (V_i)

Figure 12. The result of step 1 of GGSSCA: 8 color classes are obtained

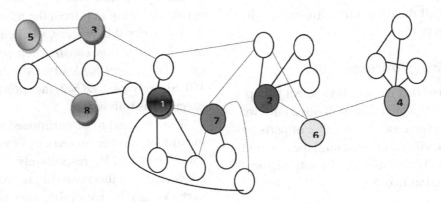

Figure 13. The result of step 1 of GGSSCA: 2 color classes are obtained

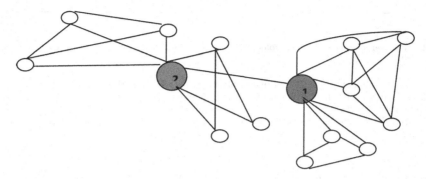

Box 4. The grouping process

Input: π_{DC} initial distribution of G with DC parts.
W: number of workers.
Output: π_w distribution of G on W workers.
Begin
$\pi = \pi_{DC}$; // π is a distribution variable used for computing the final distribution.
Repeat
Select V_i which has the minimum number of local edges $|E_{ii}|$;
Select V_j which has the maximum number of cross (external) edges $|E_{ij}|$;
Merge V_i and V_j into one part;
$|\pi| = |\pi|-1$;
Until $(|\pi| = W)$
$\pi_w = \pi$;
End

which has the lower local connections $|E_{ii}|$ in π. Then, it searches the most connected neighbor part of V_i in the partition π. This second part (V_j) will be grouped with the first one (V_i) for constructing one relaxed balanced part (Figure 14).

After complete execution of the *grouping process*, 4 relaxed balanced parts are created with only four cross transitions ($|E_{ij}|=4$) compared to the number of all the connections ($|E|=31$). The result is shown in Figure 8.

6.3.2.1 β Splitting Process

The main idea of this process is to select the appropriate part (V_i) which will be divided into two new parts. This increases the number of parts by 1. This process will be repeated until the required number of parts W is obtained. The splitting process is presented in Box 5.

At each iteration, the algorithm selects the part (V_i) having the maximum number of vertices (for obtaining a relaxed balanced between different parts). Then, it searches in V_i the vertices which have a strong connection in order to keep them in the new and same part ($V_{|\pi+1|}$). Finally, the distribution will be updated by adding the new part $V_{|\pi+1|}$ and removing all vertices existing in it from the main part (V_i).

To clarify this process, as already noted, the *initial distribution construction process* on the graph, of Figure 9, has lead to two parts (see Figure 10). Since $W=4 > DC=2$, the *splitting process* is executed as follows:

The first part to be partitioned which has the maximum number of vertices (8 vertices) is V_1. The elements of $V_{1.1}$ respectively $V_{1.2}$ are strongly connected. For this raison, V_1 is divided into two parts ($V_{1.1}$ and $V_{1.2}$) reserving workload balancing.

Figure 14. The result of the first and second iteration of the 'grouping process' on the graph of Figure 6

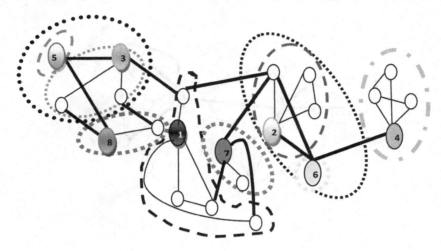

Box 5. The splitting process

Input: π_{DC} initial distribution of G.
W: number of workers.
Output: π_w distribution of G with W parts.
Begin
$\pi = \pi_{DC}$; // π is a distribution variable used for computing the final distribution.
Repeat
Select V_i which has the maximum number of nodes;
Compute the connectivity between nodes in V_i;
Put the vertices, strongly connected, in the same partition $V_i\pi_{I+1}$;
Remove all vertices existing in $V_i\pi_{I+1}$ from V_i;
$|\pi| = |\pi| + 1$;
Until ($|\pi| = W$)
$\pi_w = \pi$;
End

Similarly, the part V_2 is partitioned into two new parts ($V_{2.2}$, $V_{2.1}$). Accordingly, the required number ($W=4$) is obtained (Figure 15)

6.4 Experiments on SSCGDA

In order to illustrate the performance of the presented approach, we consider measurements given before.

The experiment consists of the distributing state space of the systems and the computation of given measurements.

As examples, 3 well known classic case studies in system models have been selected.

These models include: dining philosophers system (http://ccl.northwestern.edu/netlogo/models/ DiningPhilosophers), Peterson solution for mutual exclusion (http://sumo.lip6.fr/Peterson_model. html) and shared memory system (Dijkstra, 1965). All these models were parameterized by the number of participating processes.

The specification and the graph generation (state space generation) of these systems are performed under the platform FrameKit6 (http:// www.lip6.fr/framekit; http://coloane.lip6.fr).

The obtained results are shown in Table 3 where:

Figure 15. The result of the 'splitting process' on the graph of Figure 9

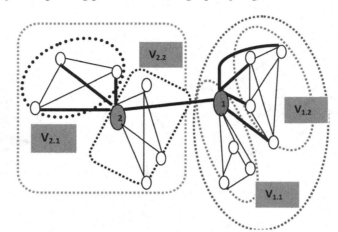

Table 3. Results of SSCGDA on the 3 selected systems

Graph	|V|	|E|	DC	W	avg	$\tilde{A}_v$	Æ	(T-Exec)(s)
Philosophers	729	3402	127	10	72	17,99	55,8%	0,446
				20	36	11,04	46,2%	0,413
				30	24	10,41	0,41%	0,384
				40	18	6,74	0,38%	0,352
				50	14	5.29	35,9%	0,327
Shared memory	8019	52974	432	20	400	176,70	65,7%	26,529
				40	200	102,55	56,8%	27,241
				60	133	76,76	50,6%	26,314
				80	100	60,94	46,5%	25,130
				100	80	47,86	42,4%	23,015
Peterson	20754	62262	4669	20	1037	387,80	91,2%	1896,802
				40	518	225,98	87,07%	2025,680
				60	345	131,12	84,6%	1838,278
				80	259	121,70	81,9%	1882,383
				100	207	102,88	80,2%	1837,855

\|V\| denotes the number of vertices,
\|E\| denotes the number of edges,
W is the required number of parts (workers),

$\acute{o}_V$ is the standard deviation of vertices on each part. It is important to note that the standard derivation is calculated after removing the outlier points. Outliers are extreme (exceptional) values that stand out from the other values of a data set. If not removed, these extreme values can skew the conclusions that might be drawn from the data in question. To identify and remove these outlying values, a statistical test, called Grubbs (Grubbs, 1950; Grubbs, 1969), has been applied on data set (the workload of each part of the partition).

$\ddot{o}$ is the fraction of the number of local connections divided by the number of all connections.

DC is the number of dominated colors obtained by GGSSCA, T-exec is the average execution runtime (in seconds) taken using 10 runs.

According to the results reported on Table 3, the performance depends enormously on the number of workers W.

The rate of internal edges is very good when the number of workers decreases (see Peterson graph with W=20, the rate of local connections is over 91%). In opposition, the standard derivation reduces when the number of workers W increases.

This result is obvious in the case of one worker and the rate of internal edges will be 100%. Remember that the main target of this approach is to favor local edges in detriment of workload balancing.

In the other hand, the quality of the rate depends also on the number of dominated colors obtained by application of GGSSCA. The rate is improved when the number of colors grows.

For the computing time, it depends on the number of vertices, edges and also the obtained number of dominated colors. This latter, may affect extremely the execution time. E.g. for Peterson graph with W = 20, the computing time is over 1800 seconds. This result is due to the obtained number of dominated colors which is very large (4669). At each iteration of the grouping process, the number of parts is decreased by one. So, this process will be executed (4669-W) times. Consequently, the execution time increases enormously. Ignoring that case, the proposed approach is fast.

To more show the quality of the approach (SSCGDA), it is compared to the hash function (MD5) based algorithm (Bouneb & Saïdouni, 2009) (i.e. one of the approaches used for distributing the state space, using a hash function based on the function of encoding MD5 -Message Digest algorithm 5-: cryptographic hash function that produces a 128-bit, it has been employed in a wide variety of security application).

Table 4 recapitulates the obtained results.

As remarked, SSCGDA gives an excellent rate of local edges compared to all the edges, especially in the case of Peterson graph. Also, it presents a good balance compared to the hash function (MD5) based algorithm.

As a conclusion, the obtained results showed that SSCGDA is very powerful in terms of the workload balancing and the minimization of cross (external) edges.

Table 4. Comparative results of SSCGDA and MD5 based algorithm

W=20	|V|	|E|	avg	Method	σ_V	φ
Philosophers	729	3402	36	MD5	18,92	6%
				SSCGDA	11,04	46,2%
Shared memory	8019	52974	400	MD5	201,26	7%
				SSCGDA	176,70	65,7%
Peterson	20754	62262	1037	MD5	519	7%
				SSCGDA	387,80	91,2%

6.5 Worker's Number Effect

The reliability of the presented approach depends on the behavior of the systems and the choice of the number of workers. After several runs on multiple graphs with different nature, the algorithm gives a good rate when the number of workers (W) is near or equal to the number of distinguished parts of a graph representing the state space system.

To illustrate this observation, let us consider the graph called add32 (http://www2.research. att.com/~yifanhu/GALLERY/GRAPHS/PDF/

Hamm@add32.pdf) showed in Figure 16 which is taken from Chris Walshaw's database (http:// staffweb.cms.gre.ac.uk/~wc06/partition/).

This latter contains graphs of different nature and get from multiple sources. The chosen graph has a particular nature (i.e. its kind is circuit simulation problem) with observed and distinguished parts.

Table 5 presents different obtained results with different values of workers number (W).

By observing the Figure 16 of the graph to be distributed, the required number of workers (W =

Table 5. Results of SSCGDA on add32 graph

Graph	|V|	|E|	DC	W	Avg	$\tilde{A}_v$	$\mathcal{A}$
Add32	4960	9462	1478	10	496	132.04	99%
				30	156.285	13.42	97%
				50	99.2	47.43	94%
				70	71.857	42.36	93%
				90	55.11	32.98	91%

Figure 16. Add32 graph

30) can be estimated. This number gives optimal results of both rate of internal edges and balancing workload. Moreover, the approach may be very useful when systems have particular behaviors (example trees) with distinguished parts.

7. CONCLUSION

In this chapter, we recalled two approaches: first, we have presented a heuristic-based strict strong coloring algorithm for general graphs called GGSSCA. Moreover, this heuristic was adapted to solve the graph distribution problem.

The GGSSCA was the first heuristic that gives an SScoloring for general graphs with a polynomial complexity respecting the number of vertices. The algorithm has been experimented on a Benchmark graph data base DIMACS. The obtained results showed that GGSSCA is very useful for coloring graphs. A comparison of GGSSCA with the exact algorithm developed for trees in Haddad and Kheddouci (2009) has shown that the strict strong chromatic numbers computed respectively by the two algorithms are similar for trees with depth greater or equal than two.

In the other side, we have also presented the approach based on graph strict strong coloring algorithm, named SSCGDA, to solve the graph distribution problem. It is important to note that it was the first time when coloring concept is used to solve this problem. Through different experiments, the SSCGDA proves its efficiency and demonstrates that it may be very useful when systems have particular behavior representation graphs.

REFERENCES

Albertson, M. O., Grossman, S., & Haas, R. (2000). Partial list colorings. *Discrete Mathematics, 214*(1-3), 235–240. doi:10.1016/S0012-365X(99)00315-5

Bérard, B., Bidoit, M., Finkel, A., Laroussinie, F., Petit, A., Petrucci, L., & Schnoebelen, Ph. (2001). *Systems and Software Verification: Model-Checking Techniques and Tools*. Springer. doi:10.1007/978-3-662-04558-9

Bixby, R., & Kennedy, K. & Kremer, U. (1993). *Automatic data layout using 0-1 integer programming* (Tech. Rep. CRPC-TR93349-S). Houston, TX: Rice University, Center for Research on Parallel Computation.

Borodin, O. V., Kostochka, A. V., & Woodall, D. R. (1998). Total colourings of planar graphs with large girth. *European Journal of Combinatorics, 19*(1), 19–24. doi:10.1006/eujc.1997.0152

Bouneb, Z., & Saïdouni, D. (2009). Parallel state space construction for a model checking based on maximality semantics. In *Proceedings of the 2nd Mediterranean Conference on Intelligent Systems and Automation* (Vol. 1107, pp. 7-12). Zarzis, Tunisia: Academic Press. doi:10.1063/1.3106517.

Bouzenada, M., Bensouyad, M., Guidoum, N., Reghioua, A., & Saïdouni, D. (2012). A Generalized Graph Strict Strong Coloring Algorithm. *International Journal of Applied Metaheuristic Computing, 3*(1), 24–33. doi:10.4018/jamc.2012010103

Caragiannisa, I., Kaklamanisa, C., & Persianob, P. (2002). Edge coloring of bipartite graphs with constraints. *Theoretical Computer Science, 270*(1-2), 361–399. doi:10.1016/S0304-3975(00)00400-X

Chellali, M., & Volkmann, L. (2004). Relations between the lower domination parameters and the chromatic number of a graph. *Discrete Mathematics, 274*(1-3), 1–8. doi:10.1016/S0012-365X(03)00093-1

Chen, G., Gyarfas, A., & Schelp, R. (1998). Vertex colorings with a distance restriction. *Discrete Mathematics, 191*(1-3), 65–82. doi:10.1016/S0012- 365X(98)00094-6

Clarke, E., Grumberg, O., & Peled, D. (1999). *Model Checking*. Cambridge, MA: The MIT Press.

Dharwadker, A. (2006). The independent set algorithm. Retrieved from http://www.dharwadker.org/independent_set.

Dijkstra, E. W. (1965). Solution of a problem in concurrent programming control. *CACM, 8*(9), 569. doi:10.1145/365559.365617

Grubbs, F. E. (1950). Sample criteria for testing outlying observations. *Annals of Mathematical Statistics, 21*, 27–58. doi:10.1214/aoms/1177729885

Grubbs, F. E. (1969). Procedures for detecting outlying observations in samples. *Technometrics, 11*(1), 1–21. doi:10.1080/00401706.1969.10490657

Guidoum, N., Bensouyad, M., & Saïdouni, D. (2013). The strict strong coloring based graph distribution algorithm. [IJAMC]. *International Journal of Applied Metaheuristic Computing, 4*(1). doi:10.4018/jamc.2013010104

Haddad, M., Dekar, L., & Kheddouci, H. (2008). A distributed strict strong coloring algorithm for broadcast applications in ad hoc networks. In *Proceedings of the 8th International Conference on New Technologies in Distributed Systems*. Lyon, France: Academic Press.

Haddad, M., & Kheddouci, H. (2009). A strict strong coloring of trees. *Information Processing Letters, 109*(18), 1047–1054. doi:10.1016/j.ipl.2009.06.012

Karp, R. M. (1972). Reducibility among combinatorial problems. In *Proceedings of the Symposium on the Complexity of Computer Computations* (pp. 85-103). Academic Press.

Klotz, W. (2002). *Graph coloring algorithms* (Tech. Rep. No. 5). Clausthal, Germany: Clausthal University of Technology.

Leighton, F. (1979). A graph coloring algorithm for large scheduling problems. *Journal of Research of the National Bureau of Standards, 84*, 489–505. doi:10.6028/jres.084.024

Orzan, S., van de Pol, J., & Valero Espada, M. (2005). A state space distribution policy based on abstract interpretation. *Electronic Notes in Theoretical Computer Science, 128*(3), 35–45. doi:10.1016/j.entcs.2004.10.017

Valmari, A. (1998). The State Explosion Problem. Lectures on Petri Nets I: Basic Models, 1491, 429–528.

Zverovich, I. E. (2006). A new kind of graph coloring. *Journal of Algorithms, 58*(2), 118–133. doi:10.1016/j.jalgor.2005.0

Chapter 11
Precordial Vibrations:
Seismocardiography – Techniques and Applications

Mikko Paukkunen
Aalto University, Finland

Matti Linnavuo
Aalto University, Finland

ABSTRACT

In the era of medicine, the heart and cardiovascular system has become one of the standard observation targets. Palpation and auscultation in the precordial area is performed as part of the regular physical examination to detect possible cardiovascular and pulmonary problems. However, due to the large number of people suffering from cardiovascular problems, labor-intensive methods such as auscultation might be inefficient in preventive cardiovascular condition screening. Seismocardiography (SCG) could have the potential to be a part of the solution to this problem. SCG is one of many modalities of cardiac-induced vibration measurements, and it has been shown to be of use in detecting coronary artery disease and assessing myocardial contractility. Lately, due to advances in sensor technologies, the SCG measurement is being developed by introducing three-dimensional measurements. Three-dimensional approach is considered to yield more information about the cardiovascular system than any single uniaxial approach. In conclusion, SCG seems to have the potential to offer a complementary view to cardiovascular function and a cost-effective method for screening of cardiovascular diseases. SCG is explored in this chapter.

1. INTRODUCTION

In living person, the function of the heart and cardiovascular system can easily be monitored by listening and palpating the vibrations transmitted to the chest. This fact has apparently been known during the whole history of the mankind. In the era of medicine, the heart and cardiovascular system has become one of the standard observation targets (Agress et al., 1964). Palpation and auscultation in precordial area is performed as part of the regular physical examination to detect possible cardiovascular and pulmonary problems. However, due to the large number of people suf-

DOI: 10.4018/978-1-4666-6252-0.ch011

fering from cardiovascular problems (Lawes, Hoorn, & Rodgers, 2008; Young, 2004), labor- and skill-intensive methods such as auscultation might be inefficient in preventive cardiovascular condition screening. To address this problem, in addition to promoting a healthy lifestyle, developing efficient cardiovascular screening techniques could be beneficial.

The cardiovascular system palpation is a well-established technique (Kurtz, 1990), but it has not reached the interpretation and diagnostic level of heart sound examination and analysis. The stethoscope, on the other hand, is a standard auscultation instrument, but 90% of the vibrational energy encountered in the body lies in the infrasonic region (DIMOND, 1964). Thus, to take advantage of the majority of the vibrational energy produced by myocardial activity, infrasonic measurement methods could be used as a part of the solution to the growing need of cardiovascular monitoring. The current state of microelectronics and signal processing technologies provide new opportunities to develop these techniques as non-invasive cardiac diagnostic and monitoring tools (Tavakolian, Ngai, Blaber, & Kaminska, 2011).

Ballistocardiography (BCG) which was first reported by Gordon (Gordon, 1877) is an old yet rare infrasonic measurement method. In BCG, the vibrations of the entire body are registered and it has been shown to reflect the functions of the cardiovascular system (Mandelbaum & Mandelbaum, 1953; Starr & Wood, 1961) . Therefore, BCG could be a solution to the need of cost-effective assessing of the cardiovascular function. In seismocardiography (SCG), on the other hand, the vibrations are measured locally. SCG has also been proposed to be a valuable tool (Tavakolian et al., 2011). This fundamental difference in the measurement loci of BCG and SCG might lead to BCG being more prone to inter-subject differences due to different structure of subjects' bodies. Thus, in terms of cardiac event detection, SCG could be more accurate because there is less distance between the heart and the sensor. SCG and BCG are, however, two of many modalities of cardiac induced vibration measurements (Giovangrandi, Inan, Wiard, Etemadi, & Kovacs, 2011) and should not be thought of as exclusive but rather complementary methods due to their different nature.

1.1 Precordial Vibrations: Seismocardiography

Any recording that records the vibration of the precordium can be named a precordial vibration (PCV) measurement. PCV measurements include displacement, velocity, and acceleration measurements of the precordium. Lately, one particular modality of PCV recordings, namely seismocardiography (SCG), has received a considerable amount of interest. This revived interest in an old technique is probably due to advances in sensor technology which makes SCG more potential to both clinical and telemonitoring applications.

Diverse nomenclature for naming the modalities of SCG has existed since the field has emerged. Even some of the first works in the field of SCG recording have used divergent nomenclature. Mounsey et al (Mounsey, 1957) called their technique precordial ballistocardiography (P-BCG) while Bozhenko et al (Bozhenko, 1961) and Baevsky et al (Baevsky, Egorov, & Kazarian, 1964) called their technique SCG. Lately, there have been some attempts to classify the signals in a structured way (Tavakolian et al., 2011), but no unanimous agreement has been reached. Fairly recent examples of this can be found in the literature (Neary, MacQuarrie, Jamnik, Gledhill, & Busse, 2011; Tavakolian, Vaseghi, & Kaminska, 2008) where SCG recordings are referred to as BCG, which seems to contradict the current practice proposed in Tavakolian et al (Tavakolian et al., 2011). Another example is the work of Trefny et al (Stork & Trefny, 2010) where a chair BCG measurement is referred to as an SCG measurement. Also, the nomenclature used to describe BCG waveforms has been used to describe SCG recordings (McKay, Gregson, McKay, & Militzer, 1999; Neary et al., 2011), which further adds to the confusion. Zanetti et al (D. Salerno & Zanetti, 1990) named the SCG waveforms regarding to cardiac events, and the tradition has been since continued in at least some of the current research (Paukkunen, Linnavuo, Haukilehto, & Sepponen, 2012; Tavakolian et al., 2011). The modern 3D-SCG measurements have complicated the nomenclature by displaying new axes of measurement. The superior-inferior axis has been called sternal acceleration ballistocardiography (SAB) (McKay et al., 1999), SCG y axis (Dinh, Choi, & Ko, 2011; Paukkunen et al., 2012), and BCG z axis (Vogt, MacQuarrie, & Neary, 2012). The dorso-ventral axis has been traditionally called SCG (D. Salerno & Zanetti, 1990; Tavakolian et al., 2011), SCG z axis (Dinh et al., 2011; Paukkunen et al., 2012), and BCG x axis (Vogt et al., 2012). The sinistro-dexter axis has been called SCG x axis (Dinh et al., 2011; Paukkunen et al., 2012) and BCG y axis (Vogt et al., 2012). To propose a more unified method of classification, below is the authors' view on how the SCG measurement methods could be classified.

The cardiac signals can be divided into two categories using the human hearing range: infrasonic (< 20 Hz) and sonic (20 - 20000 Hz). Examples for measurement methods for infrasonic and sonic categories are ballistocardiography (BCG) and phonocardiography (PCG), respectively. According to Tavakolian et al (Tavakolian et al., 2011), the infrasonic signals can be further divided into two categories: circulatory reaction recordings and precordial vibration recordings. The circulatory reaction recordings include BCG and quantitative BCG (Q-BCG), for example. BCG and Q-BCG are methods where the movement of the entire subject is measured either in the supine (Starr, Rawson, Schroeder, & Joseph, 1939) or sitting position (Trefný et al., 2011). The precordial vibration recordings refer to measurements where the sensor is attached to the precordium and local vibrations due to cardiovascular function are recorded. PCV measurements include techniques such as SCG

(D. Salerno & Zanetti, 1990), sternal acceleration SAB (McKay et al., 1999), P-BCG (Mounsey, 1957), and cardiac micro accelerations (CMA) (Giorgis et al., 2008). The division between circulatory reaction recordings and precordial vibration recordings and division of the PCV category is shown in more detail in Figure 1.

To continue the work of Tavakolian et al (Tavakolian et al., 2011), the SCG category is further divided into single-axis measurements: superior-inferior (SI-SCG), dorso-ventral SCG (DV-SCG), and sinistro-dexter SCG (SD-SCG) (see Figure 1). The most prevalent axis is the dorso-ventral axis SCG which is traditionally called simply SCG, while the superior-inferior and sinistro-dexter axes have received less attention (McKay et al., 1999; Paukkunen, Linnavuo, & Sepponen, 2013). The authors' suggest that researchers clearly state the axis of measurement using the above mentioned nomenclature. Lately, due to, for example, advances in sensor technology, three-dimensional approaches (3D-SCG), which integrate the SI-, DV, and SD-SCG signals, have begun to emerge (Dinh, 2011; Pandia, Inan, Kovacs, & Giovangrandi, 2012; Paukkunen et al., 2012). Multi-axial approaches are expected to yield more information than uniaxial approaches (De Ridder, Migeotte, Neyt, Pattyn, & Prisk, 2011; McKay et al., 1999; Paukkunen et al., 2012).

1.2 SCG Events Related to Myocardial Activity

The cardiac cycle can be divided into seven phases: atrial systole (AS), isovolumetric contraction (IVC), rapid ejection, reduced ejection, isovolumetric relaxation (IVR), rapid filling (RF), reduced filling or diastasis (Berne & Levy, 1977; Klabunde, 2005). All of these phases have been shown to be detectable from the DV-SCG signal, as described below.

Several points in the DV-SCG have been shown to occur simultaneously with specific events of the cardiac cycle. Some of these events are peak of atrial systole (AS) (Crow, Hannan, Jacobs,

Figure 1. The proposed division of PCV measurement techniques. The following abbreviations are used: SCG = seismocardiography, SI = superior-inferior, DV = dorso-ventral, SD = sinistro-dexter.

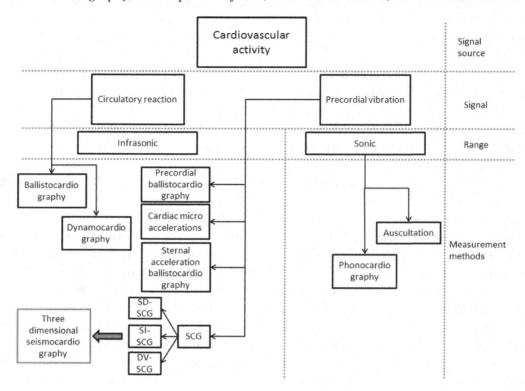

Hedquist, & Salerno, 1994), mitral valve closure (MC) (Akhbardeh et al., 2009; Crow et al., 1994), IVC (Akhbardeh et al., 2009), aortic valve opening (AO) (Akhbardeh et al., 2009; Crow et al., 1994; Gurev et al., 2012), peak of rapid systolic ejection (RE) (Akhbardeh et al., 2009; Crow et al., 1994; Gurev et al., 2012), aortic valve closure (AC) (Akhbardeh et al., 2009; Crow et al., 1994; Gurev et al., 2012), mitral valve opening (MO) (Akhbardeh et al., 2009; Crow et al., 1994), and rapid filling (Akhbardeh et al., 2009; Crow et al., 1994). Also, points called isotonic contraction (ITC) and isovolumic movement (IM) were identified by Crow et al (Crow et al., 1994). The ITC point Crow et al named IM has also been named maximum acceleration or SCG-min (MA) corresponding to maximum acceleration of blood in the aorta (Gurev et al., 2012). The pre-ejection period (PEP) is annotated according to Tavakolian

et al (Tavakolian et al., 2012a) as the time interval from ECG R wave to DV-SCG AO wave. Figure 2 shows the DV-SCG signal from Paukkunen et al (Paukkunen et al., 2012) where the selected points of the signals are annotated regarding the cardiac cycle. The SI-SCG signal has MA and RE annotated according to the preliminary observations of Paukkunen et al (Paukkunen et al., 2013).

1.3 Measurement Techniques

During the history of PCV measurement, the signal has been measured with several methods. Lately, the most prevalent methods have been the accelerometer-based techniques. While the size and cost of accelerometers has come down, the achieved signal quality is increasingly better.

Mounsey's measurements (Mounsey, 1957) were made with an electrochemical accelerom-

Figure 2. Average waveform from a subject in supine position from the in vivo tests in Paukkunen et al (Paukkunen et al., 2012). The black line is the SD-SCG, the red the SI-SCG, the blue the DV SCG, and the green the ECG. The DV-SCG signal's AC point is annotated according to Zanetti et al (Zanetti, Poliac, & Crow, 1991). The following abbreviations are used: AS = atrial systole, MC = mitral valve closure, IVM = isovolumic movement, AO = aortic valve opening, ITC = isotonic contraction, MA = point of maximum acceleration, IVC = isovolumetric contraction, RE = peak of rapid ejection, AC = aortic valve closure, MO = mitral valve clousure, RF = rapid filling, PEP = pre-ejection period. The PEP is annotated according to Tavakolian et al (Tavakolian et al., 2012a).

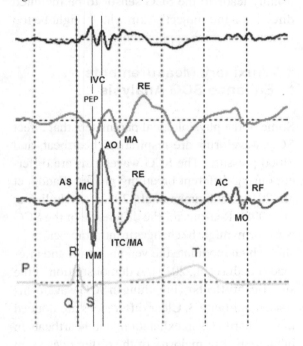

eter with flat frequency response in the range 0 to 3000 Hz and linear response from 0 to 0.015 g and above (ELLIOTT, PACKARD, & KYRAZIS, 1954). The accelerometer was based on electrical changes at the surfaces of contact of mercury-sulfuric acid interface (ELLIOTT et al., 1954). Zanetti's approach used a bulky piezoelectric accelerometer weighing almost one kilogram

(D. Salerno & Zanetti, 1990). The accelerometer had linear response between 0.3 and 800 Hz with sensitivity of 1.0V/g (D. Salerno & Zanetti, 1990). The current state-of-the-art 3D-SCG systems use lightweight accelerometers based on micro electro mechanical systems (MEMS) technology, for example. Paukkunen et al (Paukkunen et al., 2012) described a system where the 3D-SCG was realized using three orthogonally mounted high-sensitivity (2 V/g) single-axis accelerometers with flat frequency response in the range of 0 to 47 Hz. Use of miniature accelerometers with surface area of approximately $0.25\ cm^2$ is presented in the research of Pandia et al (Pandia et al., 2012) and Dinh et al (Dinh et al., 2011).

1.4 Applications

SCG is a non-invasive and easy-to-perform measurement. SCG can also be implemented at a fairly low cost. Thus, SCG might be a potential tool for several applications such as screening different cardiovascular diseases and long-term monitoring of rehabilitation. Several applications have been developed for both clinical and telemonitoring assessments, as described in the following paragraphs.

Although SCG in general has not been accepted as a diagnostic tool, it has been shown to have potential in multiple clinical applications. These applications include diagnosis of different heart diseases, aiding other clinical procedures, and deriving auxiliary attributes of physiological function. Since, at the moment, the DV-SCG is the most prevalent axis of SCG measurements, the majority of applications are for DV-SCG. However, due to the recent advances in 3D-SCG sensing the amount of applications for other axes is expected to be rising. One example of this phenomenon is the application of SI-SCG to the assessment of stroke volume (McKay et al., 1999). A recent example is the authors' most recent work (Paukkunen et al., 2013).

As discussed in the section 1.3, DV-SCG has shown to be a potential tool to assess the timing of different events in the cardiac cycle (Crow et al., 1994; Gurev et al., 2012; Tavakolian, Blaber, Ngai, & Kaminska, 2010). Using these events, myocardial contractility might be possible to assess accurately (Tavakolian et al., 2012a). In Figures 2 and 4, the time interval (R-AO or PEP) used to assess myocardial contractility is depicted. Another application of the cardiac timings is aiding the timing of diastolic timed vibrations (Tavakolian et al., 2013; Tavakolian et al., 2012b). SCG has also been proposed to be capable of providing enough information to compute heart rate variability estimates (Ramos-Castro et al., 2012). A more complex application of cardiac timings and SCG waveform amplitudes is the computing of respiratory information from the SCG signal as proposed by Pandia et al (Pandia et al., 2012)

SCG has also been shown to be potential in diagnosing heart diseases. In one study (Wilson, Bamrah, Lindsay, Schwaiger, & Morganroth, 1993), it was shown that SCG was significantly more sensitive than ECG for detecting physiologically and anatomically significant coronary artery disease. The application of DV-SCG to the detection of ischemia was proposed by Salerno et al (D. M. Salerno et al., 1991; D. M. Salerno & Zanetti, 1991). The proposal was enhanced by recording DV-SCG signal during balloon angioplasty and coronary angiography and evaluating the changes in the SCG signal.

Due to the non-invasiveness and ease-of-use SCG has potential to be used in variety of clinical on-site monitoring in noisy environment and tele-monitoring applications. SCG is proposed to function as a feasible method when monitoring cardiac activity during magnetic resonance imaging (MRI) method (Jerosch-Herold et al., 1999; Naemura & Iseki, 2003). SCG has been used, for example, in sleep studies (Baevsky, Bogomolov, Funtova, Slepchenkova, & Chernikova, 2011; Castiglioni et al., 2012). In the works of Dehkordi et al (P. K. Dehkordi, Marzencki, Tavakolian, Kaminska, &

Kaminska, 2011; P. Dehkordi, Marzencki, Tavakolian, Kaminska, & Kaminska, 2012), SCG signal recorded from the suprasternal notch was used to respiratory parameters to detect apnea. Also, wearable (Castiglioni, Faini, Parati, & Di Rienzo, 2007; Castiglioni et al., 2011; Di Rienzo et al., 2011) and even ambulatory (Di Rienzo, Meriggi, Vaini, Castiglioni, & Rizzo, 2012) monitoring applications have been proposed. Since SCG is very prone to movement induced noise, both the signal acquisition and processing methods have to be enhanced. A current challenge in SCG instrumentation, in comparison to BCG, for example, is that SCG needs a sensor to have good mechanical contact to the subject's body. This requirement usually leads to the SCG sensor to be mounted directly on the subject's skin which might be too invasive for some applications.

1.5 Auxiliary Measurements to Enhance SCG Analysis

Some of the physiological parameters that affect SCG waveforms are respiration, heartbeat, and blood pressure. The SCG waveforms are different during different breathing phases (Pandia et al., 2012; Paukkunen et al., 2012; Tavakolian et al., 2008). Reasons for the difference of the SCG waveforms might be changes in intra-thoracic pressure which modulate the venous return and after load (Pandia et al., 2012). A demonstration of the significant effects of breathing in SCG waveforms is seen in Figure 3. Clear differences are noticed in the heartbeats in exhalation, and heartbeats in inhalation. The majority of the differences seem to be amplitude and timing differences.

ECG is the most used auxiliary measurement in SCG studies. In most cases, ECG's R wave serves as a timing reference. Using the R wave, heartbeats can be detected and the acquired SCG time traces can be averaged. ECG can also be used in deriving reference heart rate and PEP according to Tavakolian et al (Tavakolian et al., 2012a). Figure 4 shows both averaged waveforms and all heart-

Figure 3. Heartbeats and their averages superimposed on the same figure. On the left, the subject is holding one's breath in the inhalation phase. On the right, the subjects is holding one's breath in the exhalation phase. The black lines depict the SD-SCG, the red the SI-SCG, the blue the DV-SCG, the green the ECG, and the cyan the PPG. The magenta lines superimposed on top of the waveforms depict the averages of the corresponding signal (Paukkunen et al., 2012).

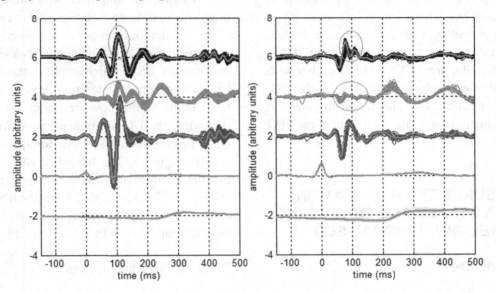

Figure 4. Heartbeats and their averages superimposed on the same figure. The black lines depict the SD-SCG, the red the SI-SCG, the blue the DV-SCG, the green the ECG, and the cyan the PPG. The magenta lines superimposed on top of the waveforms depict the averages of the corresponding signal (Paukkunen et al., 2012).

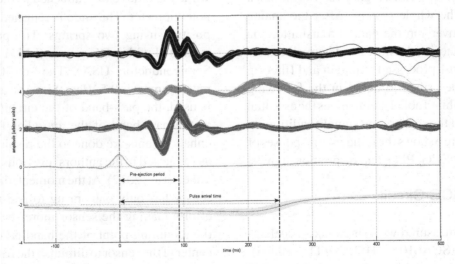

beats superimposed on the same figure together with IVC and PEP time intervals. Superimposing the heartbeats is an effective way to visualize the beat-to-beat variation of SCG signals.

Blood pressure is an important parameter in SCG studies since it might significantly affect the SCG waveforms. Blood pressure related parameters such as pulse arrival time (PAT) can be derived when ECG is used together with photoplethysmography (PPG). Also, with PPG, changes in peripheral systolic blood pressure can be approximated using the amplitude of the PPG waveform.

2. MEASUREMENT REALIZATION CASE: A SYSTEM FOR DETECTION OF THREE-DIMENSIONAL SCG

2.1 Hardware

2.1.1 Overall System Parameters

The analog part of the instrumentation consists of 3D-SCG, ECG, PPG, respiration sensors, and gain and filtering circuits. Figure 5 shows the block diagram of the whole system. After the analog to digital conversion the data is transmitted via a USB-interface to the host PC where all data is stored and post-processed. All gain and filtering circuitry is described in detail in the following paragraphs while Table 1 summarizes the essential parameters of the sensors and signal conditioning circuits. Figure 6 shows the frequency responses of the 3D-SCG, ECG, PPG, and respiration signals.

2.1.2 3D-SCG Circuit

Each axis is measured with single-axis acceleration sensors (SCA610-C21H1A, VTI, Finland), that have a sensitivity of 2 V/g and true DC response. The three acceleration sensors were mounted orthogonally to form a 3D sensor. The accelerometers used in this study were individu-

ally measured at Murata Electronics' laboratories to verify their frequency and phase response. In the tests, all the accelerometers showed the -3dB point at 47 Hz.

All signals are amplified with circuits having identical topologies (see Figure 7). The output of the acceleration sensor is processed using an instrumentation amplifier stage (INA337, Texas Instruments, USA) which amplifies the difference between the raw acceleration sensor signal and its baseline value. Low frequency components (including the DC component) are extracted using a single-pole passive RC low-pass filter as seen in Figure 7. The reference voltage for the instrumentation amplifier is a bandgap voltage reference (LM4120AIM-2.5, National Semiconductor, USA). The gain and passband of the SCG circuitry can be seen in Table 1 and Figure 8.

2.1.3 Respiration Circuit

The respiration signal is measured with a 10-cm long 10-kΩ slide potentiometer (EVAJQLR15B14, Panasonic, Japan) attached to the subject with a non-stretching band. One end of the band is fixed while the other end is attached to the slide of the potentiometer. The slide is returned to its initial position using two springs. The potentiometer is excited with a DC source (LM317L, National Semiconductor, USA). The sensitivity of the measurement is 0.5 V/cm. Since no amplification is used, the pass-band of the circuit is the same as the pass-band of the anti-alias filters. Some enhancements are done to the respiration sensor as suggested in the authors' previous work (Paukkunen et al., 2012). At the moment, the respiration sensor has only one spring to resist respiration efforts making the sensor more sensitive. Also, the mounting point of the band is moved to the center of the sensor to diminish the friction caused by the band moving against the sensor structure. The current design of the respiration sensor is depicted in Figure 9. The frequency response of the respiration measurement is shown in Figure 6.

Figure 5. The block diagram of the entire system

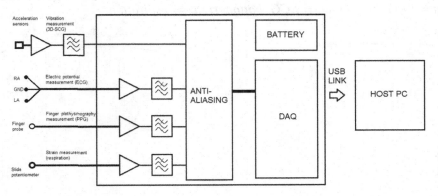

Table 1. Technical parameters of the measurement equipment used in this study

Measurement	Gain (dB)	Rated Sensor Sensitivity	High-Pass Cutoff Frequency (Hz)	Low-Pass Cutoff Frequency (Hz)
SD-SCG	24	2 V/g	0.12	95
SI-SCG	24	2 V/g	0.12	95
DV-SCG	24	2 V/g	0.12	95
ECG	60	N/A	0.4	70
PPG	165	N/A	0.15	65
Respiration	0	0.5 V/cm	0	95

2.1.4 ECG Circuit

The ECG signal is measured with three lead wires using a basic unshielded commercial cable and electrodes (Blue Sensor L, Ambu®, Denmark). The ECG signal is amplified in two stages. First, an instrumentation amplifier (INA326, Texas Instruments, USA) followed by a single-pole RC low-pass filter is used for auxiliary amplification. After the first stage, an operational amplifier (OPA2335, Texas Instruments, USA) amplifies the difference between the signal from the first stage and a reference voltage source (LM4120AIM-1.8, National Semiconductor, USA). To provide high-pass filtering, the signal from the instrumentation amplifier stage is fed back to the reference voltage pin of the instrumentation amplifier via an operational amplifier coupled as an integrator (OPA2335, Texas Instruments, USA). The non-inverting input of the integrator is coupled to the same reference voltage source as the second stage. The gain and passband of the ECG circuit can be seen in Table 1 and Figure 6. The ECG circuit diagram is shown in Figure 10.

2.1.5 PPG Circuit

The PPG sensor is a commercial PPG finger probe (Oxytip+, GE Healthcare Finland, Finland). The PPG measurement is made using visible red light excited with a DC source (LM317L, National Semiconductor, USA). The output of the finger probe's photodiode is first amplified with an operational amplifier (OPA337, Texas Instruments, USA) coupled as a transimpedance amplifier. After the first stage, the signal is amplified similarly to the 3D-SCG signals, as described earlier. The pass-band of the PPG circuit including the anti-

Figure 6. Frequency response of the gain and filtering circuits including the anti-alias stage. Top left = SCG, top right = PPG, bottom left = ECG, bottom right = respiration.

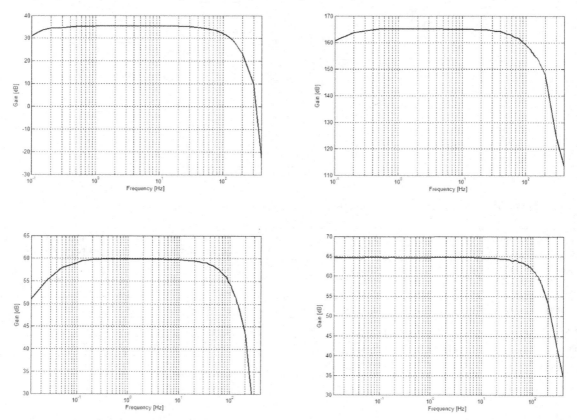

Figure 7. The implementation of the 3D-SCG circuitry

Figure 8. The circuit diagram of the SCG gain circuit

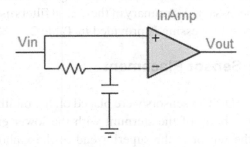

Figure 10. The circuit diagram of the ECG gain circuit

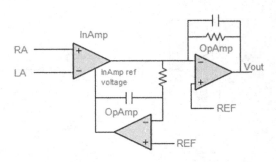

aliasing filters is from 0.15 Hz to 65 Hz. The gain of the PPG circuit is 165 dB. To keep the design simple, no synchronous demodulation scheme is used. However, an impermeable band is placed on the finger probe to protect from ambient light fluctuations. The circuit diagram of the PPG gain configuration is shown in Figure 11.

2.1.6 Anti-Aliasing and Analog to Digital Conversion

After the amplification stage, the 3D-SCG signals, ECG, respiration, and PPG signals pass through identical 8th-order Bessel low-pass filters, all of which have a rated cut-off frequency of 100 Hz and attenuation of at least 96 dB at 800 Hz. The Bessel filter was chosen for its constant group delay. The filters are implemented using quad operational amplifiers (AD8630, Analog Devices, USA) connected in the Sallen-Key to-

pology. Figure 12 shows the circuit diagram of the anti-aliasing stage. All signals are sampled with a commercial 16-bit simultaneous sampling DAQ (USB-1608FS, Measurement Computing Corporation, USA). The sampling rate is 2000 samples/second.

2.2 Software

The DAQ is connected to the host PC with a USB link. The host PC runs a custom virtual instrumentation program (LabVIEW® 2009 9.0 32-bit, National Instruments, USA) that visualizes the signals online and stores them for further analyzing. Although the emphasis of the analysis is on the post-processing phase, the monitoring option of the software allows the investigator to detect noise and beat-to-beat variation of the signals. All post-processing of the data is done

Figure 9. 3D-model of the enhanced respiration sensor

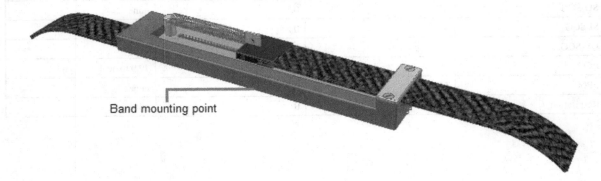

Figure 11. The circuit diagram of the PPG gain circuit

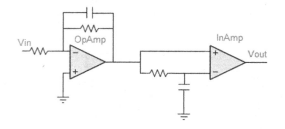

in the MATLAB® (R2010b, MathWorks, USA) environment.

A common way to investigate SCG signals for anomalies is to use an average computed from a relatively long period of time. Such a period could last, for example, two minutes. To produce the averages, the ECG signal's R wave is used as the reference point. The window for the averages is from 150 ms before the peak of the R wave to 500 ms after the peak. To remove baseline wandering, all signals except the respiration signal are high-pass filtered with a cut-off frequency of 0.5 Hz. To remove undesirable frequencies, the 3D-SCG, ECG, PPG, and respiration signals are lowpass filtered with cut-off frequencies of 47 Hz, 70 Hz, 40 Hz, and 5 Hz, respectively. The ECG signal is also notch filtered from 49.9 Hz to 50.1 Hz to avoid line noise. Adaptive filtering is often used when consistent error sources are present. As none were detected, any adaptive filtering was deemed unnecessary. A summary of the digital filters used in post-processing is provided in Table 2.

2.3 Sensor Placement

The 3D-SCG sensors were placed on the midline of the body of the sternum with the lower end of the sensor at the superior end of the xiphoid process. Double-sided adhesive tape was used to secure the contact to the skin. The ECG electrodes were attached to the volar side of the wrists just proximal to the hand and the medial side of the right ankle just proximal to the medial malleolus while avoiding bone and thick muscle. This placement of electrodes produces the so-called bipolar limb lead I registration. Prior to attaching the electrodes the skin was wiped with a cleansing wipe to ensure proper contact. The PPG signal was recorded from the right index finger. The respiration sensor was placed approximately two finger-breadths caudad to the xiphoid process. The band was tightened so that it didn't feel uncomfortable or interfere with breathing but tight enough to ensure adequate registration of inspiration and expiration in the supine position. Figure 13 depicts the orientation of the axes used in the 3D-SCG detection.

Table 2. Digital filtering parameters used in the study

Measurement	High-Pass Cutoff Frequency (Hz)	Low-Pass Cutoff Frequency (Hz)	Additional Stopbands
SD-SCG	47	0.5	none
SI-SCG	47	0.5	none
DV-SCG	47	0.5	none
ECG	70	0.5	49.9 to 50.1
PPG	50	0.5	none
Respiration	5	0	none

Figure 12. The circuit diagram of the anti-aliasing stage

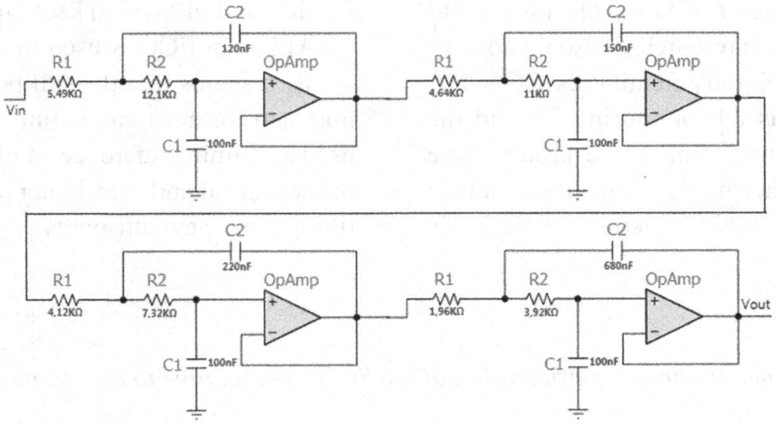

2.4 Signal Analysis

In the DV-SCG signal, points of mitral valve closure (MC), aortic valve opening (AO), maximum acceleration of blood in the aorta (MA), onset of rapid ejection of blood into the aorta (RE), aortic valve closure (AC), and mitral valve opening (MO) can be detected (Crow et al., 1994; Gurev et al., 2012). To the best of the authors' knowledge, there have been no reports on the cardiac event based nomenclature of the 3D-SCG signal's SD- and SI-axes. Thus, to achieve preliminary information about the usability of the SD- and SI-SCG signals, the signals are annotated by visual detection based on the events in the DV-SCG.

2.5 In Vivo Measurements

Measurements of six healthy volunteers with no known heart diseases (five male, one female) were made to demonstrate the functioning of the system. The age of the subjects ranged from 25 to 58 years (average 39.8 years, SD 12.86), with an average weight of 72.2 kg (SD 13.8, range 53 – 90 kg), an average height of 1.71m (SD 0.04, range 1.65 – 1.78 m), and an average body mass index (BMI) of 24.4 kg/m^2 (SD 3.6, range 19.5 – 28.4 kg/m^2).

The recordings were made with the subjects lying supine on a bed with an approximately 10-cm thick mattress. The study protocol consisted of three approximately 10-minute long recordings for each subject. All the electrodes were replaced and sensors removed and then reattached between each recording. Each recording began with a five-minute baseline recording under spontaneous quiet respiration conditions after which the subject was informed to take a deep breath and hold it for as long as it was comfortable. After expiration, the subjects were allowed to recover for about one minute before the second deep inspiration and breath holding. After another one-minute recovery the subject was instructed to exhale deeply and then hold his/her breath for as long as it was comfortable. This exhalation procedure was repeated after a one-minute recovery, completing the ten minute recording session.

3. AREAS FOR FUTURE RESEARCH

3.1 Physiological Interpretation of the SCG Waveforms

For SCG to be introduced into routine clinical practice, a major part of the research must focus on basic research of the SCG. At the moment, to the best of authors' knowledge, the observations made from the cause of SCG waveforms are still not conclusive. Basic research is also mandatory to effectively exploit the potential of SCG in any application such as telemonitoring. To aid the physiological interpretation some groups have used ECHO or other modern imaging methods (Akhbardeh et al., 2009; Tavakolian et al., 2010;

Zanetti et al., 1991). This kind of work is essential for the field of SCG to keep moving forward.

Although ECG is used in almost every SCG study, it seems that the full potential of ECG is not used. In most cases, only ECG's R wave is used as a timing reference. With the use of ECG's phases (atrial and ventricular de- and repolarization), some new attributes could be found from

Figure 13. Sensor positioning and orientation of the SCG axes relative to the sternum

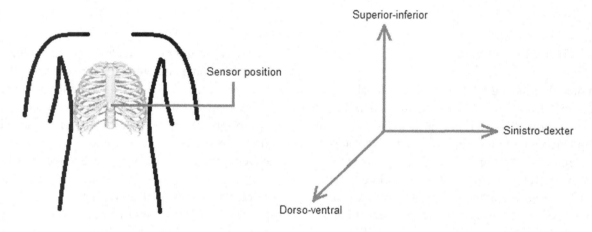

Figure 14. An example of preliminary ECG enhanced SCG annotation. The black line is the SD-SCG, the red the SI-SCG, the blue the DV SCG, and the green the ECG.

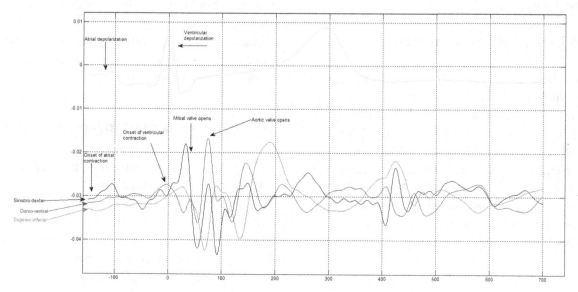

the SCG signal. In Figure 14, a hypothesis of such waveform annotation is depicted.

While the SD-SCG and SI-SCG signal waveforms are yet to be thoroughly characterized and annotated, they seem to exhibit consistent waveforms (see Figures 3, 4, and 15). The SD-SCG and SI-SCG are most probably due to the same cardiac events as the DV-SCG waveforms. Thus, more emphasis should be given on the analysis of all three SCG axes. While, DV-SCG might be superior in some cases, some data has also been demonstrated in favor of SI-SCG also (McKay et al., 1999; Paukkunen et al., 2013). The different axes should be viewed rather more complementary than exclusive. In addition to examining the waveforms as distinct measurements three-dimensional vector SCG (V-SCG) could provide unforeseen insight into myocardial activities. Precordial vibration is by definition a vector quantity changing from person to person so there is no reason to expect that venturing into 3D-SCG analysis wouldn't be worthwhile.

4. CONCLUSION

In this chapter, SCG's history, state-of-the-art, applications and physiological interpretation were described. Also, an in-depth view of the implementation of a current SCG research system was given. While measurement techniques for SCG are very feasible, some issues in SCG analysis still remain. Especially the physiological interpretation of the signal needs more research. SCG seems to have the potential to offer a complementary view to cardiovascular function and a cost-effective method for screening of cardiovascular diseases.

Figure 15. Average waveform from a subject in supine position from the in vivo tests in Paukkunen et al (Paukkunen et al., 2012). The black line is the SD-SCG, the red the SI-SCG, the blue the DV SCG, and the green the ECG. The DV-SCG signal's AC point is annotated according to Zanetti et al (Zanetti et al., 1991). SD- and SI-SCG are annotated according to the DV-SCG. The following abbreviations are used: MC = mitral valve closure, AO = aortic valve opening, MA = point of maximum acceleration, RE = peak of rapid ejection, AC = aortic valve closure, MO = mitral valve closure.

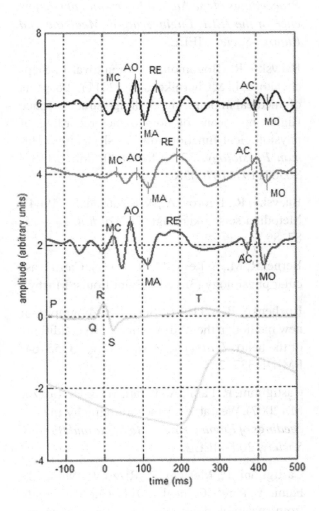

REFERENCES

Agress, C. M., Wegner, S., Bleifer, D. J., Lindsey, A., Van Houten, J., Schroyer, K., & Estrin, H. M. (1964). The common origin of precordial vibrations. *The American Journal of Cardiology, 13*(2), 226–231. doi:10.1016/0002-9149(64)90177-8 PMID:14122011

Akhbardeh, A., Tavakolian, K., Gurev, V., Lee, T., New, W., Kaminska, B., & Trayanova, N. (2009). Comparative analysis of three different modalities for characterization of the seismocardiogram. In *Proceedings of the Annual International Conference of the IEEE Engineering in Medicine and Biology Society*. IEEE.

Baevsky, R., Bogomolov, V., Funtova, I., Slepchenkova, I., & Chernikova, A. (2011). Prospects of medical monitoring of long-duration space flights by means of non-contact recording of physiological functions during sleep time. *Human Physiology, 37*(7), 816–820. doi:10.1134/S036211971107005X

Baevsky, R., Egorov, A., & Kazarian, L. (1964). Metodika seismokardiografii. *Kardiologiia, 18*, 87–89.

Berne, R. M., & Levy, M. N. (1977). Cardiovascular physiology (3rd ed.). Saint Louis: Mosby.

Bozhenko, B. S. (1961). Seismocardiography--a new method in the study of functional conditions of the heart. *Terapevticheskii Arkhiv, 33*, 55–64. PMID:13872234

Castiglioni, P., Faini, A., Parati, G., & Di Rienzo, M. (2007). Wearable seismocardiography. In *Proceedings of Engineering in Medicine and Biology Society, 2007*. IEEE.

Castiglioni, P., Meriggi, P., Rizzo, F., Vaini, E., Faini, A., Parati, G., et al. (2011). Cardiac sounds from a wearable device for sternal seismocardiography. In *Proceedings of Engineering in Medicine and Biology Society*. IEEE.

Castiglioni, P., Meriggi, P., Rizzo, F., Vaini, E., Faini, A., Parati, G., & Di Rienzo, M. (2012). Seismocardiography while sleeping at high altitude. In *Proceedings of Engineering in Medicine and Biology Society* (EMBC). IEEE.

Crow, R. S., Hannan, P., Jacobs, D., Hedquist, L., & Salerno, D. M. (1994). Relationship between seismocardiogram and echocardiogram for events in the cardiac cycle. *American Journal of Noninvasive Cardiology, 8*(1), 39–46.

De Ridder, S., Migeotte, P. F., Neyt, X., Pattyn, N., & Prisk, G. (2011). Three-dimensional ballistocardiography in microgravity: A review of past research. In *Proceedings of Engineering in Medicine and Biology Society*. IEEE.

Dehkordi, P., Marzencki, M., Tavakolian, K., Kaminska, M., & Kaminska, B. (2012). Monitoring torso acceleration for estimating the respiratory flow and efforts for sleep apnea detection. In *Proceedings of Engineering in Medicine and Biology Society* (EMBC). IEEE.

Dehkordi, P. K., Marzencki, M., Tavakolian, K., Kaminska, M., & Kaminska, B. (2011). Validation of respiratory signal derived from suprasternal notch acceleration for sleep apnea detection. In *Proceedings of Engineering in Medicine and Biology Society*. IEEE.

Di Rienzo, M., Meriggi, P., Rizzo, F., Vaini, E., Faini, A., Merati, G., et al. (2011). A wearable system for the seismocardiogram assessment in daily life conditions. In *Proceedings of Engineering in Medicine and Biology Society*. IEEE.

Di Rienzo, M., Meriggi, P., Vaini, E., Castiglioni, P., & Rizzo, F. (2012). 24h seismocardiogram monitoring in ambulant subjects. In *Proceedings of Engineering in Medicine and Biology Society (EMBC), 2012 Annual International Conference of the IEEE*. San Diego, CA: IEEE.

Dimond, E. G. (1964). Precordial vibrations clinical clues from palpation. *Circulation*, *30*(2), 284–300. doi:10.1161/01.CIR.30.2.284 PMID:14205557

Dinh, A. (2011). Design of a seismocardiography using tri-axial accelerometer embedded with electrocardiogram. In *Proceedings of the World Congress on Engineering and Computer Science 2011*. Academic Press.

Dinh, A., Choi, Y., & Ko, S. B. (2011). A heart rate sensor based on seismocardiography for vital sign monitoring systems. In *Proceedings of Electrical and Computer Engineering* (CCECE). IEEE.

Elliott, R. V., Packard, R. G., & Kyrazis, D. T. (1954). Acceleration ballistocardiography: Design, construction, and application of a new instrument. *Circulation*, *9*(2), 281–291. doi:10.1161/01.CIR.9.2.281 PMID:13127190

Giorgis, L., Hernandez, A. I., Amblard, A., Senhadji, L., Cazeau, S., Jauvert, G., & Donal, E. (2008). Analysis of cardiac micro-acceleration signals for the estimation of systolic and diastolic time intervals in cardiac resynchronization therapy. *Computers in Cardiology*, *2008*, 393–396.

Giovangrandi, L., Inan, O. T., Wiard, R. M., Etemadi, M., & Kovacs, G. (2011). Ballistocardiography—A method worth revisiting. In *Proceedings of the 30th Annual International Conference of the IEEE Engineering in Medicine and Biology Society*, (pp. 4279-4282). IEEE.

Gordon, J. (1877). Certain molar movements of the human body produced by the circulation of the blood. *Journal of Anatomy and Physiology*, *11*(3), 533–536. PMID:17231163

Gurev, V., Tavakolian, K., Constantino, J., Kaminska, B., Blaber, A. P., & Trayanova, N. A. (2012). Mechanisms underlying the isovolumic and ejection peaks in seismocardiogram morphology. *Journal of Medical and Biological Engineering*, *32*(2), 103–110. doi:10.5405/jmbe.847 PMID:23105942

Jerosch-Herold, M., Zanetti, J., Merkle, H., Poliac, L., Huang, H., & Mansoor, A. et al. (1999). The seismocardiogram as magnetic-field-compatible alternative to the electrocardiogram for cardiac stress monitoring. *International Journal of Cardiac Imaging*, *15*(6), 523–531. doi:10.1023/A:1006364518204 PMID:10768746

Klabunde, R. (2005). *Cardiovascular physiology concepts*. LWW.

Kurtz, K. J. (1990). Bruits and hums of the head and neck. In H. K. Walker, W. D. Hall, & J. W. Hurst (Eds.), *Clinical methods: The history, physical, and laboratory examinations* (3rd ed.). Boston: Butterworth Publishers, a division of Reed Publishing.

Lawes, C. M. M., Hoorn, S. V., & Rodgers, A. (2008). Global burden of blood-pressure-related disease, 2001. *Lancet*, *371*(9623), 1513–1518. doi:10.1016/S0140-6736(08)60655-8 PMID:18456100

Mandelbaum, H., & Mandelbaum, R. A. (1953). Studies utilizing the portable electromagnetic ballistocardiograph: IV. the clinical significance of serial ballistocardiograms following acute myocardial infarction. *Circulation*, *7*(6), 663–673. doi:10.1161/01.CIR.7.6.910 PMID:13051833

McKay, W. P. S., Gregson, P. H., McKay, B. W. S., & Militzer, J. (1999). Sternal acceleration ballistocardiography and arterial pressure wave analysis to determine stroke volume. *Clinical and Investigative Medicine. Medecine Clinique et Experimentale*, *22*(1), 4–14. PMID:10079990

Mounsey, P. (1957). Praecordial ballistocardiography. *British Heart Journal*, *19*(2), 259. doi:10.1136/hrt.19.2.259 PMID:13413014

Naemura, K., & Iseki, H. (2003). Vibration isolation for seismocardiogram measurement in the OpenMRI-guided operating theater. *JSME International Journal Series C*, *46*(4), 1426–1433. doi:10.1299/jsmec.46.1426

Neary, J., MacQuarrie, D., Jamnik, V., Gledhill, S., & Busse, E. (2011). Assessment of mechanical cardiac function in elite athletes. *Open Sports Medicine Journal, 5,* 26–37. doi:10.2174/1874387001105010026

Pandia, K., Inan, O. T., Kovacs, G. T. A., & Giovangrandi, L. (2012). Extracting respiratory information from seismocardiogram signals acquired on the chest using a miniature accelerometer. *Physiological Measurement, 33*(10), 1643–1660. doi:10.1088/0967-3334/33/10/1643 PMID:22986375

Paukkunen, M., Linnavuo, M., Haukilehto, H., & Sepponen, R. (2012). A system for detection of three-dimensional precordial vibrations. [IJMTIE]. *International Journal of Measurement Technologies and Instrumentation Engineering, 2*(1), 52–66. doi:10.4018/ijmtie.2012010104

Paukkunen, M., Linnavuo, M., & Sepponen, R. (2013). A portable measurement system for the superior-inferior axis of the seismocardiogram. *Journal of Bioengineering & Biomedical Science, 3*(1). doi: doi:10.4172/2155-9538.1000123

Ramos-Castro, J., Moreno, J., Miranda-Vidal, H., Garcia-Gonzalez, M., Fernández-Chimeno, M., Rodas, G., & Capdevila, L. (2012). Heart rate variability analysis using a seismocardiogram signal. In *Proceedings of Engineering in Medicine and Biology Society (EMBC), 2012 Annual International Conference of the IEEE,* (pp. 5642-5645). IEEE.

Salerno, D., & Zanetti, J. (1990). Seismocardiography: A new technique for recording cardiac vibrations. concept, method, and initial observations. *Journal of Cardiovascular Technology, 9*(2), 111–118.

Salerno, D. M., & Zanetti, J. (1991). Seismocardiography for monitoring changes in left ventricular function during ischemia. *Chest, 100*(4), 991–993. doi:10.1378/chest.100.4.991 PMID:1914618

Salerno, D. M., Zanetti, J. M., Green, L. A., Mooney, M. R., Madison, J. D., & Van Tassel, R. A. (1991). Seismocardiographic changes associated with obstruction of coronary blood flow during balloon angioplasty. *The American Journal of Cardiology, 68*(2), 201–207. doi:10.1016/0002-9149(91)90744-6 PMID:2063782

Starr, I., Rawson, A., Schroeder, H., & Joseph, N. (1939). Studies on the estimation of cardiac ouptut in man, and of abnormalities in cardiac function, from the heart's recoil and the blood's impacts, the ballistocardiogram. *American Journal of Physiology: Legacy Content, 127*(1), 1-28.

Starr, I., & Wood, F. C. (1961). Twenty-year studies with the ballistocardiograph: The relation between the amplitude of the first record of "healthy" adults and eventual mortality and morbidity from heart disease. *Circulation, 23*(5), 714–732. doi:10.1161/01.CIR.23.5.714

Stork, M., & Trefny, Z. (2010). *Quantitative seismocardiography system with separate QRS detection.* Academic Press.

Tavakolian, K., Blaber, A. P., Ngai, B., & Kaminska, B. (2010). Estimation of hemodynamic parameters from seismocardiogram. In *Proceedings of the Computing in Cardiology,* (pp. 1055-1058). Academic Press.

Tavakolian, K., Khosrow-Khavar, F., Kajbafzadeh, B., Marzencki, M., Blaber, A., Kaminska, B., & Menon, C. (2013). Precordial acceleration signals improve the performance of diastolic timed vibrations. *Medical Engineering & Physics, 35*(8), 1133–1140. doi:10.1016/j.medengphy.2012.12.001 PMID:23291107

Tavakolian, K., Khosrow-Khavar, F., Kajbafzadeh, B., Marzencki, M., Rohani, S., Kaminska, B., & Menon, C. (2012b). Seismocardiographic adjustment of diastolic timed vibrations. In *Proceedings of Engineering in Medicine and Biology Society (EMBC), 2012 Annual International Conference of the IEEE,* (pp. 3797-3800). IEEE.

Tavakolian, K., Ngai, B., Blaber, A. P., & Kaminska, B. (2011). Infrasonic cardiac signals: Complementary windows to cardiovascular dynamics. In *Proceedings of Engineering in Medicine and Biology Society*. IEEE.

Tavakolian, K., Portacio, G., Tamddondoust, N. R., Jahns, G., Ngai, B., Dumont, G. A., & Blaber, A. P. (2012a). Myocardial contractility: A seismocardiography approach. In *Proceedings of Engineering in Medicine and Biology Society (EMBC), 2012 Annual International Conference of the IEEE*, (pp. 3801-3804). IEEE.

Tavakolian, K., Vaseghi, A., & Kaminska, B. (2008). Improvement of ballistocardiogram processing by inclusion of respiration information. *Physiological Measurement, 29,* 771–781. doi:10.1088/0967-3334/29/7/006 PMID:18560054

Trefný, Z., Svačinka, J., Kittnar, O., Slavíček, J., Trefný, M., Filatova, E., . . . Loučka, M. (2011). Quantitative ballistocardiography (Q-BCG) for measurement of cardiovascular dynamics. *Academia Scientiarum Bohemoslovaca, 60*(4), 617.

Vogt, E., MacQuarrie, D., & Neary, J. P. (2012). Using ballistocardiography to measure cardiac performance: A brief review of its history and future significance. *Clinical Physiology and Functional Imaging*. doi:10.1111/j.1475-097X.2012.01150.x PMID:23031061

Wilson, R. A., Bamrah, V. S., Lindsay, J., Schwaiger, M., & Morganroth, J. (1993). Diagnostic accuracy of seismocardiography compared with electrocardiography for the anatomic and physiologic diagnosis of coronary artery disease during exercise testing. *The American Journal of Cardiology, 71*(7), 536–545. doi:10.1016/0002-9149(93)90508-A PMID:8438739

Young, J. B. (2004). The global epidemiology of heart failure. *The Medical Clinics of North America, 88*(5), 1135–1143. doi:10.1016/j.mcna.2004.06.001 PMID:15331310

Zanetti, J., Poliac, M., & Crow, R. (1991). Seismocardiography: Waveform identification and noise analysis. *Proceedings of the Computers in Cardiology, 1991,* 49–52. doi:10.1109/CIC.1991.169042

ADDITIONAL READING

Tavakolian, K. (2010). *Characterization and Analysis of Seismocardiogram for Estimation of Hemodynamic Parameters*. (PhD thesis). Simon Fraser University.

KEY TERMS AND DEFINITIONS

3D-SCG: Three-dimensional seismocardiography.

AC: Aortic valve closure.

AO: Aortic valve opening.

AS: Atrial systole.

BCG: Ballistocardiography.

CMA: Cardiac micro accelerations.

DAQ: Data acquisition.

DC: Direct current.

ECG: Electrocardiography.

ECHO: Echocardiography.

IM: Isovolumic movement.

ITC: Isotonic contraction.

IVC: Isovolumetric contraction.

IVR: Isovolumetric relaxation.

MA: Maximum acceleration.

MC: Mitral valve closure.

MEMS: Micro electo-mechanical system.

MO: Mitral valve opening.

MRI: Magnetic resonance imaging.
P-BCG: Precordial ballistocardiography.
PAT: Pulse arrival time.
PC: Personal computer.
PCG: Phonocardiography.
PCV: Precordial vibrations.
PEP: Pre-ejection period.
PPG: Photoplethysmography.
Q-BCG: Quantitative ballistocardiography.

R Wave: Peak of ventricular depolarization in ECG signal.
RC: Resistor-capacitor.
RE: Rapid ejection.
RF: Rapid filling.
SAB: Sternal acceleration ballistocardiography.
SCG: Seismocardiography.
USB: Universal Serial Bus.

Chapter 12
Nanostructures Cluster Models in Solution:
Extension to C, BC₂N, and BN Fullerenes, Tubes, and Cones

Francisco Torrens
Universitat de València, Spain

Gloria Castellano
Universidad Católica de Valencia, Spain

ABSTRACT

The existence of Single-Wall C-Nanocones (SWNCs), especially nanohorns (SWNHs), and BC_2N/Boron Nitride (BN) analogues in cluster form is discussed in solution in this chapter. Theories are developed based on models bundlet and droplet describing size-distribution function. The phenomena present unified explanation in bundlet in which free energy of $(BC_2N/BN-)$SWNCs involved in cluster is combined from two parts: volume one proportional to the number of molecules n in cluster and surface one, to $n^{1/2}$. Bundlet enables describing distribution function of $(BC_2N/BN-)$SWNC clusters by size. From geometrical differences bundlet $[(BC_2N/BN-)$SWNCs] and droplet $(C_{60}/B_{15}C_{30}N_{15}/B_{30}N_{30})$ predict dissimilar behaviours. Various disclination $(BC_2N/BN-)$SWNCs are studied via energetic and structural analyses. Several $(BC_2N/BN-)$SWNC's ends are studied that are different because of closing structure and arrangement type. Packing efficiencies and interaction-energy parameters of $(BC_2N/BN-)$SWNCs/SWNHs are intermediate between $C_{60}/B_{15}C_{30}N_{15}/B_{30}N_{30}$ and $(BC_2N/BN-)$Single-Wall C-Nanotube (SWNT) clusters: in-between behaviour is expected; however, properties of $(BC_2N/BN-)$SWNCs, especially $(BC_2N/BN-)$SWNHs, are calculated closer to $(BC_2N/BN-)$SWNTs. Structural asymmetry in different $(BC_2N/BN-)$SWNCs characterized by cone angle distinguishes properties of types: P2. BC_2N/BN, especially species isoelectronic with C-analogues may be stable.

DOI: 10.4018/978-1-4666-6252-0.ch012

INTRODUCTION

Nanoparticles (NPs) interest arose from the shape-dependent physical properties of nanoscale materials (Faraday, 1857; Murphy *et al.* 2010). Single-wall C-nanocones (SWNCs) were used to study the nucleation/growth of curved C-nanostructures (NSs) suggesting pentagon role. When a pentagonal defect is introduced into an $C_{graphite}$ sheet ($C_{graphene}$) *via* extraction of a 60° sector from the piece a cone leaf is formed. The presence of pentagons in an SWNC apex is analogue of single-wall C-nanotube (SWNT) tip topology. Balaban *et al.* (1994), Klein (2002) and Klein and Balaban (2006) analyzed the eight classes of positive-curvature graphitic nanocones, and Klein (1992), Misra *et al.* (2009ab), Balaban & Klein (2009) and Klein & Balaban (2011) examined the Clar theory for conjugated C-NSs. The SWNT ends predicted electronic states related to topological defects in $C_{graphite}$ lattice (Tamura & Tsukada, 1995). Kim *et al.* (1999) observed resonant peaks in the density of states in SWNTs and Carroll *et al.* (1997), in multiple-wall C-nanotubes (MWNTs).

Krishnan *et al.* (1997) observed SWNCs with discrete opening angles θ of *ca.* 19, 39, 60, 85 and 113° in C-sample generated by hydrocarbon pyrolysis. Observation was explained by a cone wall model composed of wrapped $C_{graphene}$ sheets, where geometrical requirement for seamless connection naturally accounted for semi-discrete character and absolute angles θ. Total disclinations are multiples of 60° corresponding to number ($P \geq 0$) of pentagons in SWNC apices. Considering $C_{graphene}$-sheet symmetry and Euler theorem five SWNC types are obtained from continuous $C_{graphene}$ sheet matching to $P = 1$–5. Angle results $\theta = \sin(\theta/2) = 1 - P/6$, leading to flat discs and caped SWNTs corresponding to $P = 0, 6$, respectively; most abundant SWNC with $P = 5$ ($\theta \approx 19°$) is single-wall C-nanohorn (SWNH). Several configurations exist for given SWNC angle depending on pentagon arrangement. According to *isolated pentagon rule* (IPR) configurations containing isolated pentagons lead to isomers that are more stable than those including grouped ones (Kroto, 1987); Han & Jaffe (1998) derived another rules from *ab initio* calculations. Covalent SWNCs functionalization with NH_4^+ improved solubility (Tagmatarchis *et al.*, 2006), which was achieved by skeleton (Cioffi *et al.*, 2006, 2007; Pagona *et al.*, 2007b)/cone-end (Pagona *et al.*, 2006a) functionalization and supramolecular π–π stacking interactions (Pagona *et al.*, 2006b, 2007a; Zhu *et al.*, 2003) with pyrenes/porphyrins. An MNDO calculation of BN substitutions in C_{60} showed that analogous one gave $B_{30}N_{30}$ (Xia *et al.*, 1992). Atom substitution in $C_{diamond}$ by alternating B/N atoms provided BN-cubic (Silaghi-Dumitrescu *et al.*, 1993). BN-hexagonal (h) resembles $C_{graphite}$ since it consists of fused planar six-membered B_3N_3 rings; however, interlayer B–N interactions exist. Hamilton *et al.* (1993, 1995) and Loiseau *et al.* (1996) visualized BN nanotubes. Rubio *et al.* (1994) proposed BN-h. Bourgeois *et al.* (1999, 2000) and Terauchi *et al.* (2000) observed BN nanocones, and Mota *et al.* (2003) and Machado *et al.* (2003abc, 2004, 2005) calculated them; most abundant ones presented 240/300° disclinations. Thesing *et al.* (2006) computed BN/AlN nanotube junction. Calculations of BC_2N tubules (Miyamoto *et al.*, 1994) and $C_{graphite}$-like onion/nanotube production using layered materials [*e.g.*, WS_2 (Tenne *et al.*, 1992), MoS_2 (Margulis *et al.*, 1993), BC_2N, BC_3 (Weng-Sieh *et al.*, 1995), BN (Chopra *et al.*, 1995)] allowed structures with oxidation resistance and low thermal/electronic conductivities. The NSs of pyrolytically grown $B_xC_yN_z$ were studied: concentration profiles along/across tubes revealed that B, C and N are separated into C/BN domains; compound provides materials that are useful as robust nanocomposites (NCs) and semiconductor devices enhanced towards oxidation (Kohler-Redlich *et al.*, 1999; Madden, 2009; Terrones *et al.*, 1996). Kallus *et al.* (2010) examined dense periodic packings (Betke & Henk, 2000; Chen *et al.*, 2010) of tetrahedra and Baker & Kudrolli (2010), those of Platonic solids.

In earlier publications SWNT (Torrens & Castellano, 2005, 2007abcd, 2011) and (BC_2N/BN-)SWNC (Torrens & Castellano, 2010, 2012, 2013ab) *bundlet* cluster model was presented. A wide class of phenomena accompanying solution behaviour is analyzed from a unique point of view taking into account cluster formation. Different structures with delocalized electrons in models droplet/bundlet are examined. Based on droplet model (BC_2N/BN-)SWNCs bundlet is examined. The aim of the present report is to perform a comparative study of C, BC_2N and BN fullerenes, nanotubes, cones and horns. The following section describes computational methods. Next sections review inorganic fullerene-like NPs/tubes, chelate/co-operativity effects in metal/protein–ligand bindings, tuning spin state in Fe^{II} complexes based on pentadentate ligand bztpen, organic photochemistry to make NPs, NPs to direct organic chemistry, superconductor vortices on move, molecular motor laboratory, motors in core of molecular biology deoxyribonucleic acid (DNA) genes, atomic/magnetic force microscopies, functional CdSe/ZnS NPs capped with thiols, photophysics, photochemistry, sensors, nanomaterials toxicology, developing of *nano*-quantitative structure–activity relationships (QSARs), advances and challenges. Next, results are presented/discussed. The last section summarizes our conclusions.

COMPUTATIONAL METHOD

Solubility mechanism is based on SWNC cluster formation. Aggregation changes thermodynamic parameters, which displays phase equilibrium and changes solubility. *Bundlet* is valid when characteristic SWNC number in cluster $n \gg 1$. In saturated SWNC solution, chemical potentials

per SWNC for dissolved substance, crystal and clusters match. Cluster free energy contains two parts: volume one proportional to number of SWNCs n in cluster and surface one, to $n^{1/2}$ (Bezmel'nitsyn *et al.*, 1998; Gasser *et al.*, 2001; Haluska *et al.*, 2006; Neu *et al.*, 2002; Notman *et al.*, 2006). Model assumes that clusters present bundlet shape and Gibbs energy G_n for n-sized cluster results:

$$G_n = G_1 n - G_2 n^{1/2} \qquad (1)$$

where $G_{1/2}$ are responsible for contribution to Gibbs energy of molecules, placed inside volume and on surface of cluster. Chemical potential μ_n of cluster of size n is:

$$\mu_n = G_n + T \ln C_n \qquad (2)$$

where T is absolute temperature. With (1) it results:

$$\mu_n = G_1 n - G_2 n^{1/2} + T \ln C_n \qquad (3)$$

where $G_{1/2}$ are expressed in temperature units. In saturated SWNC solution, cluster-size distribution function is determined *via* equilibrium condition, linking clusters of specified size with solid phase, which corresponds to equality between chemical potentials for SWNCs incorporated into clusters of any size and crystal, resulting in expression for distribution function in saturated solution:

$$f(n) = g_n \exp\left(\frac{-An + Bn^{1/2}}{T}\right) \qquad (4)$$

where A is equilibrium difference between SWNC interaction energies with its surroundings in solid phase and cluster volume, B, similar difference for SWNCs located on cluster surface and g_n statistical weight of cluster of size n. One neglects $g_n (n,T)$ dependences in comparison with exponential (4). Normalization for distribution function (4):

$$\sum_{n=1}^{\infty} f(n)n = C \tag{5}$$

requires $A > 0$, and C is solubility in relative units. As $n \gg 1$, normalization (5) results:

$$C = \bar{g}_n \int_{n=1}^{\infty} n \exp\left|\frac{-An + Bn^{1/2}}{T}\right| dn =$$
$$C_0 \int_{n=1}^{\infty} n \exp\left|\frac{-An + Bn^{1/2}}{T}\right| dn \tag{6}$$

where $\bar{g}_n$ is cluster statistical weight averaged over n that makes major contribution to integral (6), and C_0, SWNC molar fraction. The $A/B/C_0$ were taken from C_{60} in hexane/toluene/CS_2 ($A = 320K$, $B = 970K$, $C_0 = 5 \cdot 10^{-8}$). For (poly)(BN), A/B were renormalized with regard to $B_{30}N_{30}/C_{60}$ energies ($A = 350K$, $B = 1062K$). Correction takes into account packing efficiencies of C_{60}/SWNTs/ SWNCs:

$$A' = \frac{\eta_{cyl}}{\eta_{sph}} A \text{ and } B' = \frac{\eta_{cyl}}{\eta_{sph}} B \text{ (SWNTs)}$$
$$A' = \frac{\eta_{con}}{\eta_{sph}} A \text{ and } B' = \frac{\eta_{con}}{\eta_{sph}} B \text{ (SWNCs)} \tag{7}$$

where $\eta_{cyl} = \pi/2(3)^{1/2}$ is cylinder packing efficiency in space (equal to that of circles on plane), $\eta_{sph} = \pi/3(2)^{1/2}$, that of spheres (face-centred cubic, FCC) and η_{con}, that of cones. As $\eta_{sph} < \eta_{con} < \eta_{cyl}$, SWNC behaviour is expected to be intermediate between that of spherical fullerenes and cylindrical SWNTs. Dependences of cluster-size distribution function on concentration and temperature lead to those of thermodynamic and kinetic parameters, characterizing SWNCs. For an unsaturated solution, distribution function is determined by clusters equilibrium condition. From Equation (3) one can obtain distribution function *vs.* concentration:

$$f_n(C) = \lambda^n \exp\left(\frac{-An + Bn^{1/2}}{T}\right) \tag{8}$$

where λ depends on concentration and is determined by normalization condition:

$$C = C_0 \int_{n=1}^{\infty} n\lambda^n \exp\left|\frac{-An + Bn^{1/2}}{T}\right| dn \tag{9}$$

where C_0 defines absolute concentration; $C_0 = 10^{-4} \text{mol} \cdot L^{-1}$ is found by requiring saturation in Equation (9). The formation energy of a cluster of n SWNCs is:

$$E_n = n(An - Bn^{1/2}) \tag{10}$$

Using the cluster-size distribution function, one obtains a formula governing the thermal effect of SWNCs solution per mole of dissolved substance:

$$H = \frac{\sum_{n=1}^{\infty} E_n f_n(C)}{\sum_{n=1}^{\infty} n f_n(C)} N_A =$$
$$\frac{\sum_{n=1}^{\infty} n(An - Bn^{1/2})\lambda^n \exp\left[\left(-An + Bn^{1/2}\right)/T\right]}{\sum_{n=1}^{\infty} n\lambda \exp\left[\left(-An + Bn^{1/2}\right)/T\right]} N_A \tag{11}$$

where N_A is Avogadro number and λ^ν depends on the solution total concentration by normalization condition (9). The solute diffusion coefficient results:

$$D = D_0 \frac{\int_{n=1}^{\infty} n^{3/2} \lambda^{n-1} \exp\left[\left(-An + Bn^{1/2}\right)/T\right] dn}{\int_{n=1}^{\infty} n^2 \lambda^{n-1} \exp\left[\left(-An + Bn^{1/2}\right)/T\right] dn} \tag{12}$$

where D_0 is diffusion coefficient of a unit, which was taken equal to C_{60} in toluene $D_0 = 10^{-9} \text{m}^2 \cdot \text{s}^{-1}$. Equations (1)–(12) are modelled in a home-built program available from authors. A *droplet* cluster model of C_{60} is proposed following modified Equations (1')–(12'):

$$G_n = G_1 n - G_2 n^{2/3} \quad (1')$$

$$\mu_n = G_1 n - G_2 n^{2/3} + T \ln C_n \quad (3')$$

$$f(n) = g_n \exp\left(\frac{-An + Bn^{2/3}}{T}\right) \quad (4')$$

$$C = \bar{g}_n \int_{n=1}^{\infty} n \exp\left(\frac{-An + Bn^{2/3}}{T}\right) dn =$$
$$C_0 \int_{n=1}^{\infty} n \exp\left(\frac{-An + Bn^{2/3}}{T}\right) dn \quad (6')$$

$$f^n(C) = \lambda^n \exp\left(\frac{-An + Bn^{2/3}}{T}\right) \quad (8')$$

$$C = C_o \int_{n=1}^{\infty} n \lambda^n \exp\left(\frac{-An + Bn^{2/3}}{T}\right) dn \quad (9')$$

$$E_n = n(An - Bn^{2/3}) \quad (10')$$

$$H = \frac{\sum_{n=1}^{\infty} E_n f_n(C)}{\sum_{n=1}^{\infty} n f_n(C)} N_A =$$
$$\frac{\sum_{n=1}^{\infty} n(An - Bn^{2/3}) \lambda^n \exp\left[\left(-An + Bn^{2/3}\right)/T\right]}{\sum_{n=1}^{\infty} n \lambda^n \exp\left[\left(-An + Bn^{2/3}\right)/T\right]} N_A \quad (11)$$

$$D = D_0 \frac{\int_{n=1}^{\infty} n^{5/3} \lambda^{n-1} \exp\left[\left(-An + Bn^{2/3}\right)/T\right] dn}{\int_{n=1}^{\infty} n^2 \lambda^{n-1} \exp\left[\left(-An + Bn^{2/3}\right)/T\right] dn} \quad (12')$$

Modelling Mass Transfer Rate During Biocoagulation–Flocculation of Coal-Rich Wastewater

Jimoda *et al.* (2013) developed a mathematical model for destabilized particle transfer during biocoagulation-flocculation of turbid drinking water from the relative motion of destabilized particles towards the reference particle. Conservation of mass of destabilized particles in the system was accomplished by identifying the simplifying assumptions, defining appropriate initial and boundary conditions. The following assumptions will be made: homogeneous system is assumed, unidimensional mass (particle) transfer occurs, the process is isothermal, the initial suspended particles (turbidity) concentration in the system is uniform and external resistance to particle transport is neglected. Consider a collection of Brownian spherical particles with radius R_j, diffusing in the vicinity of a target sphere with radius R_i centred at origin. Frequency of *j*-spheres collisions on target sphere is found *via* a stationary diffusion model as follows: imagine that every *j*-sphere that hits target sphere is removed from bulk solution while simultaneously a new *j*-sphere is added to bulk far away from target. Continuity equation for *j*-spheres number concentration C_j is:

Time rate of change of reference particle
=influx of mass into the reference sphere particle
-outflux of mass from the reference sphere particle
$$(13)$$

Time rate of change of mass of the floc=
$$\frac{\partial(C) 4\pi r^2}{\partial t} \quad (14)$$

Influx of mass into the floc=J4πr² $\quad (15)$

Outflux of mass from the floc$= \left(J + \dfrac{\partial J}{\partial r}\right)4\pi r^2$

$$\text{(16)}$$

Combining Equations (13)–(16) gives:

$$\frac{\partial(C)4\pi r^2}{\partial t} = J4r^2 - \left(J + \frac{\partial J}{\partial r}\right)4\pi r^2 \qquad (17)$$

Simplifying Equation (17):

$$\frac{\partial(C)4\pi r^2}{\partial t} = -\frac{\partial J}{\partial r}4\pi r^2 \qquad (18)$$

Dividing Equation (18) by 4π gives:

$$\frac{r^2\partial C_j}{\partial t} = -r^2\frac{\partial J}{\partial r} \qquad (19)$$

Recalling first Fick's law:

$$J = -D\frac{\partial C_j}{\partial r} \qquad (20)$$

Substituting Equation (20) into Equation (19) gives:

$$\frac{r^2\partial C_j}{\partial t} = r^2\frac{\partial}{\partial r}D\frac{\partial C_j}{\partial r}$$
$$\frac{\partial c_j}{\partial t} = \frac{\partial}{\partial r}\frac{\partial C_j}{\partial r} \qquad (21)$$

Equation (21) is partial differential equation that describes the rate of mass (destabilized particle) transfer during biocoagulation/flocculation of coal-rich wastewater. However,

$$D = \frac{K_r}{8\pi R_p} \qquad (22)$$

Menkiti & Onukwuli (2010) obtained Equation (22) from von Smoluchowski rate constant expression where $R_p = 2a$ = particle diameter, D = particle diffusion coefficient, J = flux of particle across unit area per time, a = particle radius, C_j = concentration of spherical particle j and K_R = von Smoluchowski rate constant for coagulation/flocculation. Initial condition is:

$$C_j(t = 0, r) = C_{j0} \qquad (23)$$

Boundary conditions are:

$$C_j(r = 0, t) = C_{e0} \qquad (24)$$

$$C_j(r = a, t) = C_{e0} \qquad (25)$$

where C_{e0} = concentration of particles in system in equilibrium with surface one at both boundaries.

C_0 = initial suspended particle concentration value of coal-rich effluent

$$\text{(26)}$$

From Equation (21), let $C_j r^2 = U$; therefore, Equation (21) becomes:

$$\frac{\partial C_j}{\partial t} = \frac{\partial}{\partial r}D\frac{\partial C_j}{\partial r} = \frac{\partial U}{\partial t} = \frac{\partial}{\partial r}D\frac{\partial U}{\partial r} \qquad (27)$$

Then define the following dimensionless parameters, dimensionless space variable:

$$\eta = \frac{r}{R}$$

dimensionless time variable:

$$\tau = \frac{Dt}{R^2}$$

Now introduce dimensionless concentration function:

$$U^* = \frac{U_t - U_e}{U_0 - U_e} \qquad (28)$$

Then the dimensionless function changes the initial and boundary conditions to:

$$U^*(\tau = 0, \eta) = 1 \qquad (29)$$

$$U^*(\tau, 0) = 0 \qquad (30)$$

$$U^*(\tau, 1) = 1 \qquad (31)$$

Substituting dimensionless variables into Equation (27) gives:

$$\frac{\partial U^*}{\partial \tau} = \frac{\partial^2 U^*}{\partial \eta^2} \qquad (32)$$

Equation (32), dimensionless, predicts rate of suspended particle transfer at different conditions.

Chelate and Co-Operativity Effects in Metal–Ligand and Protein–Ligand Bindings

Thermodynamics of complexes formed by metal cation and ligands parallels protein–ligands binding. Chelate/co-operativity effects concepts are useful to analyze relations between the two fields. Chelate effect, which is apparent in complexes increased stability, occurs when two/more co-ordinating donor atoms belong to the same ligand molecule (Schwarzenbach, 1952), whereas co-operativity effect occurs when both/more donor atoms belong to different molecules (Weber, 1975). Homotropic (equal donor atoms)/heterotropic (different donor atoms) chelate effects are observed, as homo/heterotropic co-operativity

effects exist. Analogy leads to choice of standard states, equilibrium constants and energy scale by which both effects are measured. Equilibrium constants suitable to establish common scale are calculated as ratio of operational equilibrium constants, each must be expressed in homogeneous reciprocal concentration units. Chelate effect comprehends co-operativity effect (*cf.* Table 1). Two chelation equilibrium constants K_ε and K_η ($K_{\varepsilon'}$ and $K_{\eta'}$ for heterotropic chelate effect) are proposed to evaluate chelate effect, and one equilibrium constant K_γ ($K_{\gamma'}$), to evaluate co-operativity effect. Relations $K_\eta = K_\varepsilon K_\gamma$ and $K_{\eta'} = K_{\varepsilon'} K_{\gamma'}$ hold. Consistent energy scale is obtained.

$$\Delta\mu_\gamma = -RT \ln K_\gamma$$

$$\Delta\mu_{\gamma'} = -RT \ln K_{\gamma'}, \text{ etc.} \qquad (33)$$

where $\Delta\mu$ indicates chemical-potential change (Schellman, 1975). On energy scale, co-operativity effect comes out to be in range $8 > \Delta\mu_\gamma > -6 \text{kJ} \cdot \text{mol}^{-1}$ for both metal–ligand and macromolecule–ligand bindings; chelate effect amounts to $-29 > \Delta\mu_\eta > -151 \text{kJ} \cdot \text{mol}^{-1}$ for Cu^{II} complexes bound by polyamines.

Inorganic Fullerene-Like Nanoparticles and Inorganic Nanotubes: AFM of LDMs

After C_{60} discovery and fullerene-chemistry advent considerable attention was directed towards associated cylindric/polyhedral forms of $C_{graphite}$; however, observations of such closed structures were limited to C-system. Tenne group reported formation of equivalent stable structures in layered semiconductor WS_2. After heating thin W films in $H_2S_{(g)}$, transmission electron microscopy revealed variety of concentric polyhedral/cylindrical structures growing from amorphous W matrix. They verified structures closed nature by

Table 1. Equilibrium constants for the evaluation of two-donor chelate and co-operativity effects

Effect	Co-operativity	Homotropic	$K_\gamma = \beta_{MA_2}^{1/2}\beta_{MA}^{-1}$
		Heterotropic	$K_{\gamma'} = \beta_{MAB}^{1/2}\left(\beta_{MA}\beta_{MB}\right)^{-1/2}$
	Chelate	Homotropic	$K_\varepsilon = K_{ML}\beta_{MA_2}^{-1/2}$
		Heterotropic	$K_{\varepsilon'} = K_{ML}\beta_{MAB}^{-1/2}$
		Homotropic	$K_\eta = K_{ML}\beta_{MA}^{-1}$
		Heterotropic	$K_{\eta'} = K_{ML}\left(\beta_{MA}\beta_{MB}\right)^{-1/2}$

M = metal or macromolecule, A, B = monodentate ligands, L = bidentate chelating ligand,

β = cumulative formation constants (*e.g.*, $\beta_{MA_2} = \left[MA_2\right]\left[M\right]^{-1}\left[A\right]^{-2}$).

[] indicate concentrations.

The constants K_γ, $K_{\gamma'}$, K_e, $K_{e'}$ are not corrected for statistical effects.

electron diffraction and lattice imaging. As with C-system, complete closure of WS$_2$ layers requires structural-defects presence or atoms arrangement in polyhedra other than planar hexagonal geometry. They informed nested fullerene-like structures. Layered-compounds NPs (*e.g.*, MoS$_2$, WS$_2$) presenting hollow closed-cage structures and known as inorganic fullerene-like (IF) and nanotubes (INTs) are synthesized in macroscopic amounts. They show tribological properties and serve as solid-state additives to different lubrication fluids. Metallic films incorporating IF NPs were prepared *via* wet and physical vapour deposition methods. Incorporation of NPs endows such coatings self-lubricating behaviour, *i.e.*, low friction and wear, which is desirable for applications variety. Adini *et al.* (2011) reviewed materials synthesis of IF/INT phases and applications to medical devices/drug delivery. Inorganic-compounds NPs with layered two-dimensional (2D) structures (*e.g.*, C$_{graphite}$, MoS$_2$) are unstable in planar form and fold on themselves forming seamless hollow structures (*e.g.*, multiwall nanotubes, fullerene-like NPs). Tenne & Redlich (2010) discussed developments in the field and applications for such nanophases, *e.g.*, solid lubricants, ultra-strong NCs catalysts, *etc.* C$_{graphene}$ properties renewed interest in inorganic, 2D materials with unique electronic/optical attributes. Transition metal dichalcogenides (TMDCs) are layered materials with strong in-plane bonding and weak out-of-plane interactions enabling exfoliation into 2D layers of single-unit-cell thickness. Advances in nanomaterials characterization and device fabrication opened up opportunities for 2D layers of thin TMDCs in nano/optoelectronics. The TMDCs, *e.g.*, MoS$_2$, MoSe$_2$, WS$_2$ and WSe$_2$ present sizeable bandgaps that change from indirect to direct in single layers allowing applications (*e.g.*, transistors, photodetectors, electroluminescent devices). Wang *et al.* (2012) reviewed TMDCs development, methods for preparing atomically thin layers, electronic/optical properties and prospects for advances.

The atomic force microscope (AFM) was invented by Binning *et al.* (1986) based on ideas from Binning and Rohrer. With AFM one can obtain images of physical objects and biologic/chemical entities (viruses/bacteria, atoms/molecules). Settlement of AFMs achieve a share of nanometres. Using AFM one can study two-objects interaction: (1) to measure friction, elasticity and adhesion forces and (2) move individual atoms precipitate/remove them with surface (Hartmann, 1985). The AFM revealed DNA double helix (Bruker, 2013). Low-dimensional materials (LDMs), *e.g.*, graphene, are composed of a single or a few layers of atoms. To resolve LDMs structure requires an instrument with sub-Ångstrom resolution (a regime where AFM excels). Going beyond simple topography measurements, a host of mechanical and electrical characterization techniques exists that rely on AFM cantilever being able to *feel* literally the mechanical and electrical properties of the material. Bertolazzi *et al.* (2013) described several applications where AFM is used to probe the mechanical and electrical properties of rapidly emerging LDMs. Monolayers structurally similar to graphene with different atoms behave as semiconductors (MoS_2) and insulators (BN). C-lattice in graphene presents strong, highly directional bonds. The high bond energy means that defects are rare and do not propagate easily *via* the lattice as occurs with dislocations in metals. As a result both modulus and strain-to-failure for graphene are high. Monolayer MoS_2 presents a lower modulus comparable to stainless steel yet shows a breaking strength 30 times higher than stainless steel. As with graphene the strength of monolayer MoS_2 is close to the theoretical intrinsic strength of its constituent chemical bonds, indicating a high degree of molecular perfection. Directional bonds give LDMs their layered nature with unique frictional properties on layers surface. They used force curves to test the elasticity and strength of MoS_2 membranes stretched over circular holes in

a SiO_2 support. Its mechanical properties make MoS_2 an excellent candidate material for incorporation into flexible and robust electronic devices, *e.g.*, molecular sensors and actuators (Bertolazzi *et al.*, 2011).

Tuning Spin State in Fe^{II} Complexes Based on Pentadentate Ligand bztpen

Ortega-Villar *et al.* (2005) synthesized mononuclear diamagnetic compound {Fe(bztpen)[N(CN)$_2$]} (PF$_6$)CH$_3$OH [bztpen = *N*-benzyl-*N*,*N*',*N*'-tris(2-pyridylmethyl)ethylenediamine] and studied crystal structure. Complex is precursor of dinuclear, –N≡C–N–C≡N-bridged Fe^{II} complexes with generic formula {[Fe(bztpen)]$_2$[μ-N(CN)$_2$]} (PF$_6$)$_3$·nH$_2$O (n = 1 or 0) that they characterized in solid/solution. In all three complexes Fe atoms present distorted [FeN$_6$] octahedral co-ordination defined by bztpen and terminal/bridging –N≡C–N–C≡N–. In solid, complexes (n = 0, 1) are molecular isomers that differ by position of phenyl ring in *Z/E* {Fe(bztpen)[N(CN)$_2$]}$^+$ halves. Depending on texture, complex n = 1 exhibits paramagnetic behaviour or incomplete spin transition (ST) at 1 atm. Complex n = 0 undergoes gradual two-step ST with no hysteresis in solid. Both steps are 100K wide centred at 200/350K with a plateau of 80K separating transitions. They determined crystal structure of complex n = 0 in 50K steps in 90–400K that provides insight into structural behaviour and ST nature. Dis/order transitions occur in bridge –N≡C–N–C≡N– and PF$_6^-$ with ST suggesting that transitions trigger two-step character. In solution, complexes (n = 0, 1) display continuous STs. Electrochemical studies of complexes (n = 0, 1) showed voltammograms typical of dimeric systems with metals electronic coupling *via* –N≡C–N–C≡N–. In this laboratory Coronado *et al.* (2007) reported bistable ST NPs showing magnetic thermal hysteresis near room temperature (RT). Prins *et al.* (2011) informed RT electrical addressing of bistable ST molecular system.

Organic Photochemistry to Make NPs and NPs to Direct Organic Chemistry

Stamplecoskie & Scaiano (2010) discovered method for preparing Ag NPs of various sizes/ morphologies (*e.g.*, dodecahedra, nanorods, nanoplates); they described photochemical synthesis of citrate-stabilized spherical Ag NPs, which can in turn be used to prepare multiple NSs with predict/controllable size/morphology *via* irradiation with narrow-band light-emitting diodes (LEDs); they described common mechanism for Ag NP-types formation. Variations in morphology resulted in spectroscopic changes. Shukla *et al.* (2005) reported chain-amplified photochemical reaction initiated by electron transfer from excited sensitizer to *N*-methoxypyridinium (NMP) salts, which leads to N–O bond cleavage. Abstraction of H by methoxy radical MeO$^\bullet$ from alcohol HC(R_1R_2OH) yields α-hydroxy radical $^\bullet$C(R_1R_2OH) that reduces another NMP and propagates chain, which amplification is enhanced in water presence (Shukla *et al.*, 2006). Kinetic studies of 4-cyano-*N*-methoxypyridinium (CMP) salt reaction, with benzhydrol (BH), showed that rate constant for CMP reduction by diphenyl ketyl radical [$^\bullet$C(Ph$_2$OH), 1.1×10^6L·mol^{-1}s^{-1}] increases by more than one order of magnitude in water presence, which results of coupling electron to proton transfer from $^\bullet$C(Ph$_2$OH) to water, which decreases endothermicity. Unfortunately increase in rate constant, for one of two propagation steps, is accompanied by increase in rate constant(s) of competing termination reaction(s) of $^\bullet$C(Ph$_2$OH). Enhancement in chain amplification results of increase in ratio propagation to termination rate constants of MeO$^\bullet$ reactions. Main chain-terminating

reactions of MeO$^\bullet$ are D-abstraction from solvent, CD$_3$CN, and reaction with sensitizer, thioxanthone. Effect of increase in ratios of propagation rate constant of MeO$^\bullet$ (H-abstraction from BH), to those of both termination reactions, is larger than unfavourable water effect on $^\bullet$C(Ph$_2$OH) reactions. Chain-amplification rise depends on reactants concentration; at 0.037M of both, quantum yield increases from 16 to 45 in <1% water. 4-Phenyl-*N*-methoxypyridinium (PMP) reaction with 4-methoxybenzyl alcohol does not proceed *via* chain amplification because of endothermicity for electron transfer from $^\bullet$C(HArOH) to PMP; however, chain amplification could be induced by water addition where at 10% water quantum yield of 5 was obtained. Water-induced, proton-coupled electron transfer increases rate constant for PMP reduction from negligible to dominant level.

Scaiano *et al.* (2012) reported that Norrish type-I photocleavage is source of reducing free radicals, which are used to convert soluble metal cations into atomic state that proceed to form NPs. Proton-coupled electron transfer (PCeT) is tool to interpret mechanism for metal-cation reduction, which involves multisite PCeT with proton/electron having separate receiving substrates. Bueno-Alejo *et al.* (2012) informed nanosecond laser ablation synthesis for spherical Au NPs of 4nm in 5s (532nm, 0.66J·cm^{-2}) where protecting agent can be selected in protocol, which avoids repeated sample irradiation and undesired exposure of capping agent during ablation. The method takes synthesis advantage of clean unprotected polymorph/ disperse Au NSs using H$_2$O$_2$ as reducing agent. Laser drop technique provides tool for delivering controlled doses to small drops, which undergo assisted fall into capping agent solution/suspension, yielding monodisperse custom-derivatized composite materials *via* simple technique. Au-NPs photoexcitation in their plasmon transition 530nm allows carrying high-energy reactions at RT. For dicumyl peroxide (activation energy of

34.3kcal·mol^{-1}) reaction occurs in <1min under 532nm laser excitation. Results suggest that per-oxide is exposed to temperatures of 500°C, for submicrosecond times, and guides which organic-reactions type benefits from plasmon-mediated energy delivery (Fasciani *et al.*, 2011). Plasmon excitation (532nm) of Au NPs in resazurin/hy-droxylamine presence leads to its efficient photo-catalytic reduction to resorufin. In laser excitation under laser-drop conditions, process is complete following 8ns laser pulse at 532nm. Bueno Alejo (2011) proved that excitation with LED sources at 530nm is simple/cost-efficient way to promote plasmon-assisted reactions; they proposed that catalytic reaction is thermally activated by Au NP and takes advantage of high temperatures achievable under plasmon excitation.

Stamplecoskie *et al.* (2011) showed that in visible (VIS) light exposure of Ag NPs-containing films, enhanced field around Ag NPs in thin film containing azo free-radical initiator (2,2'-azo-bis-isobutyronitrile, AIBN) and triacrylate selectively cross-links triacrylate within plasmonic region around NPs. Cross-linked polymer is lesser soluble than precursor and behaves as solubility switch. After film is developed with ethanol, polymer-encapsulated NPs are preserved on surface. Poly-mer structure of 8–10nm, which encapsulates NPs, maps/preserves plasmon-field morphology in Ag NP-controlled NSs. Stamplecoskie *et al.* (2012) obtained hierarchy of lithographic-type imaging generating 3μm lines, incorporating subdiffraction limit features *via* two-step reaction. Photochemi-cally generated ketyl radicals were used to make Ag NPs-defined lines. Excitation of NP-surface plasmons was used to generate localized heat, which causes polymerization selectively on excited-NPs surfaces. Generated nylon-6 polymer serves as solubility switch used to retain features on substrate selectively; they used various imaging techniques to establish nylon-shells nature. Heat generated by plasmon excitation is exploited to generate negative-type lithographic features with dimensions below diffraction limit.

Carl Zeiss Microscopy (2013) obtained an im-age of double bowtie plasmonic device made in Au on glass by high-resolution microscopy. Fujishima and Honda discovered (1972) photocatalytic split-ting of water on TiO$_2$ electrode under influence of ultraviolet (UV) light (Fujishima *et al.*, 2000). Efforts were devoted to TiO$_2$ material, which led to applications in fields ranging from photovoltaics/catalisys to photoelectronics/sensors, which can be divided into *energy* and *green* categories, in which TiO$_2$ of different modifications are used (Gratzel, 2001). Photodegradation was used in waste/water treatment of all methods, *e.g.*, froth flotation coagulation, *etc.*; it offers prospects for overall treatment of dyestuff effluent. Shanthi & Priya (2012) carried out photodegradation of aniline blue/crystal violet dyes from aqueous solutions of binary mixture, *via* TiO$_2$ as photo-catalyst. Performing photodegradation varying experimental parameters they found optimum conditions required for maximum degradation; they performed dye photodegradation *via* different energy sources (*e.g.*, solar, microwave, MW); they performed degradations at temperatures 25, 35 and 45°C to calculate rate constant and activation parameters. Both sources are equivalent in causing degradation except time/photocatalyst dose; time is lesser for MW than for solar radiation but pho-tocatalyst dose is higher for MW. Results will help to design effluent treatment plants in industries.

Superconductor Vortices on Move: A Molecular Motor Laboratory

Abrikosov (1957) studied magnetic properties of bulk superconductors for which Ginzburg–Landau (GL) theory parameter $\chi > 1/2^{1/2}$ (superconduc-tors type-2, SCT2); he explained SCT2-alloys behaviour in magnetic field. Mkrtchyan & Shmidt (1972) calculated free energy of SCT2 vortex in superconductor interacting with hollow cylindri-cal channel of radius $r << \delta_0$ parallel to it (δ_0 is penetration depth); capture of only single vortex by channel is energetically favourable. Pinning force is computed: $f_p = H_{cm}^2 \xi(T)/2$, where H_{cm} is critical thermodynamic field strength. Buzdin (1993) discussed formation possibility of multiple-quanta vortices on columnar defects (CDs) produced by ion irradiation. Upper-critical field for localized superconductivity near CDs depends nonmonotonously on their radius. Takezawa & Fukushima (1994) examined insulating-inclusion effectiveness in SCT2 as pinning centre. With regard to single-quantum vortex, they investigated dependence of minimum pinning potential U_p on radius R of cylindrical insulating inclusion solving GL equations numerically. The U_p is defined by free-energy difference between vortex inside and infinitely distant. The $U_p < 0$ for all Rs and is shallow for $R < \xi(T)$ (coherence length). Depth of U_p increases rapidly with increasing R up to penetration depth $\lambda(T)$ and there U_p saturates. The U_p for $R \geq \lambda(T)$ is much deeper than for $R \leq \xi(T)$; *i.e.*, even for single vortex insulating inclusion with $R \geq \lambda(T)$ it gives stronger attractive interaction with vortex and works as more effective pinning centre than with $R \leq \xi(T)$. Numerically solving two-dimensional GL equations, Takezawa & Fukushima (1997) evaluated optimal size of insulating inclusion for pinning single-quantum vortex in SCT2. Although it was believed that optimal size of pinning centre is twice coherence length, they found that in case of low magnetic fields and pinning centre density prismatic insulating inclusion, with square cross-section of side length equal to penetration depth, gives strongest pinning force to vortex. Teresawa *et al.* (1998) investigated experimentally effects of CDs with splayed configurations on flux pinning/creep; they introduced parallel/splayed CDs into $La_{2-x}Sr_xCuO_4$ specimens by high-energy heavy-ion irradiation; they observed enhancement of flux pinning and critical current density J_c because of splayed CDs: (1) At $T < 15K$ and $H = 0.1T$, effective pinning potential U_0 of specimen with splayed CDs was larger than with parallel CDs; (2) at $15K \leq T \leq 30K$ and $H = 0.1T$, U_0 of specimen with splayed CDs was smaller than with parallel CDs.

Harada *et al.* (1996) investigated matching microscopic mechanism in SCT2, which manifested as peaks production in critical current at specific values of applied magnetic field, with Lorentz microscopy to allow vortices observation in Nb thin film presenting regular array of artificial defects; they observed vortices forming regular lattices at matching magnetic field, multiples and fractions. Dynamic observation revealed that vortices are most difficult to move at matching field whereas excess ones move easily. Linke (2002) edited a special issue on ratchets/Brownian motors. Linke *et al.* (2006) reported that liquids perform self-propelled motion when they are placed in contact with hot surfaces with asymmetric topology; they observed pumping effect when liquid is in Leidenfrost (film boiling) regime for many liquids over wide temperature range; they showed that liquid motion is driven by viscous force exerted by vapour flow between solid and liquid.

Molecular Motors in the Core of Molecular Biology Deoxyribonucleic-Acid Genes

Ternary complexes of DNA-dependent ribonucleic acid (RNA) polymerase (RNAP), with its DNA template and nascent transcript, are transcription intermediates (Uptain *et al.*, 1997). Unusual biochemical reactions were discovered that affect RNAP progression in ternary complexes *via* various transcription units, which are signalled intrinsically by nucleic-acid sequences/RNAP or extrinsically by protein/regulatory factors that affect processes, *e.g.*, promoter proximal/distal pausing in prokaryotes/eukaryotes, and regulate gene-expression. In eukaryotes at least two factors are related to cellular transformation and cancers. Models for ternary-complexes structure and mechanism by which they move along DNA provide explanations for biochemical reactions, which predict that RNAP moves along DNA without dissociation/termination constant possibility; furthermore, RNAP moves in discontinuous/inchworm-like manner. Direct predictions were confirmed; however, one feature of RNA chain elongation is that DNA sequence determines whether RNAP moves discontinuous/monotonically. In at least two cases RNAP/DNA block to elongation encounter induces specifically discontinuous synthesis mode, which provide insights into RNA chain elongation and understanding bioregulatory systems at molecular level. Research advances, in structure/function of RNAP II elongation complex, enlightened mechanisms governing elongation of eukaryotic messenger (m)RNA synthesis (Rugar *et al.*, 1990). Elongation regulation features by DNA/RNA binding transcriptional activators were illuminated; action mechanisms of elongation factors that suppress pausing/premature arrest transcribing RNAP II were defined, and elongation factors implicated in human disease were identified. Reines *et al.* (1999) biochemical/genetic studies shed light on structure/function of RNAP II elongation complex and transcription factors that control it. Elongation factors were identified and action mechanisms characterized; insights into elongation-factors bioroles were gained from genetic studies of mRNA-synthesis regulation in yeast, and links between RNAP II elongation machinery and DNA-repair/recombination pathways emerged.

Chain elongation of RNA is processive/accurate, which is regulated by numerous intrinsic/extrinsic signals. Bar-Nahum *et al.* (2005) described mechanism that governs RNAP movement and response to regulatory inputs (*e.g.*, pauses, terminators, elongation). *Escherichia coli* RNAP moves by complex Brownian ratchet mechanism that acts before phosphodiester bond formation. Incoming substrate and flexible F-bridge domain of catalytic centre serve as separate ratchet devices, which function in concert to drive forward translocation. Adjacent G-loop domain controls F-bridge motion keeping balance between elongation-complex productive and inactive states, which is critical for cell viability since it determines transcription rate, processivity and fidelity.

From Atomic Force Microscopy to Magnetic Force Microscopy

Magnetic force microscopy (MFM) was invented by Martin & Wickramasinghe (1987) equipped with sharp magnetic tip, which is sensitive to spatial derivatives of stray fields from sample that depends on magnetization divergence. Scanning samples surface and measuring long-range magnetostatic force between both ferromagnetic tip and sample *vs.* position, domain-walls, Bloch-lines and ripple-structures image could be observed (Rugar *et al.*, 1990). In order to separate topography/magnetic signals, tip–sample separations are relatively large so that only long-range magnetostatic forces dominate. Traditional MFM presents magnetic-domain resolution >50nm that limits applications in NSs characterization; high-resolution MFM invented by Swiss Probe reaches resolution <10nm, which compares with scanning electron microscopy with polarization analysis (SEMPA). Probing short-range magnetic exchange interactions magnetic exchange force microscopy (MExFM), it is possible to reach atomic resolution and detect spin configurations (Kaiser *et al.*, 2007).

Functional CdSe and /ZnS NPs Capped with Thiols: Photophysics/Chemistry and Sensors

Murphy & Coffer (2002). published a quantum dots (QDs) primer. Wuister *et al.* (2004) prepared luminescent CdSe/CdTe QDs in hot solvent of capping molecules [trioctylphosphine (TOP)/trioctylphosphine oxide (TOPO)/hexadecylamine (HDA) for CdSe, TOP/dodecylamine (DDA) for CdTe]; they investigated exchange influence of capping molecules with different thiols types [amino ethanethiol, (3-mercaptopropyl)trimethoxysilane, hexanethiol, 2-propenethiol and 4-mercaptophenol] for CdSe/CdTe QDs; they observed difference: capping exchange with thiols results in increased luminescence efficiency for

CdTe QDs but induces quenching of excitonic emission of CdSe QDs; they explained difference between the two types of II-VI QDs by difference in energy of valence band top. Lower energetic position of valence band for CdSe results in hole trapping of photogenerated hole on thiol, quenching luminescence. For CdTe valence band is situated at higher energies with respect to redox level of most thiols inhibiting hole trapping and maintaining high luminescence efficiency. One method to render CdSe/ZnS core–shell QDs water soluble is to functionalize surface with carboxylate groups *via* heterobifunctional ligands, *e.g.*, 3-mercaptopropionic acid, where thiolic end binds onto outer ZnS shell; however, ligand exchanges starting with TOPO-capped QDs lead to quantum-yields loss and colloids poor stability in water. Pong *et al.* (2008) used computations to understand binding nature between alkyl thiols and ZnS wurtzite surfaces; guided by computations they modified ligand exchange and increased 3-mercaptopropionic-acid reactivity toward ZnS surface in $CHCl_3$. Functionalization reaction required mild conditions and led to QD NPs that were individually dispersed in water with colloidal stability. Photoluminescence performance of QDs was preserved.

Aguilera-Sigalat *et al.* (2011) reported that while alkyl-thiols addition reduces fluorescence (FL) of CdSe core QDs(-C), it enhances emission of FL amine-capped CdSe/ZnS core–shell QDs(-CS). Aguilera-Sigalat *et al.* (2012b) synthesized highly FL organic/water-soluble CdSe/ZnS QD-CS with thiol ligands chemisorbed on QD surface by amine-ligands replacement by alkyl thiols under mild conditions. The QDs exhibited greater photostability than initial amine capped QD-CS. Aguilera-Sigalat *et al.* (2012a) prepared supramolecular system based on ketoprofen-functionalized CdSe/ZnS NPs and pyrene (Py)-modified β-*cyclo*dextrin (CD_7), and used it for molecular sensing of different analytes; they reported strategy for individual recovery of all components of sensing assay.

The Py fluorophores of Py-functionalized CdSe QD(@Py), and alkylpyrene (R–Py)/Py, undergo fast degradation in aerated $CHCl_3$ under UV-A ($316 < \lambda < 400$nm) illumination. Steady-state FL of irradiated $CHCl_3$ solutions of QD@Py showed formation of new bands red-shifted compared to Py (Aguilera-Sigalat *et al.*, 2012c). Similar behaviour is observed for Py/R–Py. Column chromatography of Py photolysate in $CHCl_3$ allowed isolating photoproducts arising from Py degradation and obtaining structural information of photoproducts responsible for emission bands. Most predominant photoproducts were originating from Py reaction with $^\bullet CHCl_2$. Phototransformation of QD@Py/R–Py involves R detachment from aromatic ring induced by $^\bullet CHCl_2$ and R oxidation at benzylic position was detected. By contrast, Py's showed photostability in aerated CH_2Cl_2. Transient absorption showed formation of $^3Py/Py^{+\bullet}$ for all Py's in halogenated solvents. Yield of $Py^{+\bullet}$ for Py is higher than QD@Py/R–Py. The $Py^{+\bullet}$ was longer-lived in CH_2Cl_2 than $CHCl_3$. Reason for Py photostabilty in CH_2Cl_2 is different reactivity of $^\bullet CH_2Cl/^\bullet CHCl_2$ towards Py/O_2. Use of CH_2Cl_2 is alternative to $CHCl_3$ when solubility properties of halogenated solvents are needed to dissolve FL-probe Py. Wadhavane *et al.* (2012) characterized highly FL organogels (QD–organogel), prepared combining pseudopeptidic macrocycle and different types of CdSe QDs, using optical/microscopic techniques. Presence of QDs not only does not disrupt supramolecular organization of internal fibrillar net of organogel but also decreases gelator critical concentration needed to form stable/thermoreversible organogels. Regarding QDs photophysical properties they observed different trends depending on presence of ZnS inorganic shell around CdSe core. While QD-CS preserve photophysical properties in organogel, they observed high/moderate rise of FL intensity and lifetime for QD-C embedded in organogel. Luminescent organogels based on QDs present applications as hybrid materials.

Kumar & Wei (2013) reviewed QDs for nano–bioapplications as technological platform of future. The QDs are versatile inorganic probes with unique photophysical properties, *e.g.*, narrow and size-dependent FL with broad absorption spectra, strong FL intensity and excellent anti-photobleaching. The QDs were used in diverse bioapplications in different domains, *e.g.*, cell labelling, genomic detection, optical sensors, nanosensors, quantum mechanics-based drug delivery systems and biomedical imaging. Nanotechnology presents the potential to revolutionize medicine and many other seemingly unrelated subjects, *e.g.*, electronics, textiles and energy production.

Nanomaterials Toxicology: Toward Development of *Nano-QSARs*. Advances and Challenges

Shevchenko *et al.* (2003) analyzed nanoworld structural diversity/origin; they considered different problem aspects (*e.g.*, nonequilibrium, coherence, hierarchical structure, fragmentariness, generalized symmetry); they treated NP structure inhomogeneity and nanoworld structural diversity as self-organization result of nonequilibrium nonlinear multivariant system. Engineered-nanomaterials proliferation presented dilemma to regulators regarding hazard identification. International Life Sciences Institute Research Foundation/Risk Science Institute convened expert working group, to develop screening strategy for hazard identification of engineered nanomaterials. Working group report presented *elements* of screening strategy rather than detailed testing protocol (Oberdörster *et al.*, 2005). Based on limited-data evaluation, the account presented broad data gathering strategy applicable to hazard identification in risk-assessment development for nanomaterials. They included oral, dermal, inhalation and injection exposure routes recognizing that depending on use patterns nanomaterials exposure may occur by any route. Toxicity-screening elements are: physicochemical characteristics and

in vitro/vivo assays. (1) Likelihood exists that NPs bioactivity will depend on physicochemical parameters not considered in toxicity screening. Physicochemical properties in understanding toxic effects of test materials include particle size/size distribution, agglomeration state, shape, crystal structure, chemical composition, surface area, chemistry and charge, and porosity. (2) *In vitro* techniques allow specific biomechanistic pathways to be isolated/tested under controlled conditions in ways that are not feasible in *in vivo* tests. They suggested tests for portal-of-entry toxicity for lungs, skin and mucosal membranes, and target organ toxicity for endothelium, blood, spleen, liver, nervous system, heart and kidney; they considered non-cellular assessment of NP durability, protein interactions, complement activation and pro-oxidant activity. (3) They proposed Tier-1 *in vivo* assays for pulmonary, oral, skin and injection exposures, and Tier-2 evaluations for pulmonary exposures. Tier-1 evaluations include inflammation, oxidative-stress and cell-proliferation markers in portal-of-entry and selected remote organs/tissues. Tier-2 evaluations for pulmonary exposures comprise: (a) deposition, translocation and toxicokinetics/biopersistence studies, (b) multiple-exposures effects, (c) potential effects on reproductive system, placenta and foetus, (d) alternative animal models and (e) mechanistic studies.

Leszczynski & Shukla (2009) edited a monograph on practical computational chemistry. Puzyn *et al.* (2009) highlighted achievements/challenges relating to QSAR application in risk assessment of nanometre-sized materials; they discussed advances in *classical*-QSAR context; they reviewed possible ways for structural characterization of nanocompounds; they evaluated toxicological data applicability for developing QSARs; they presented models; they highlighted need to develop interpretative nanosystems descriptors; they suggested that because of molecular-structures variability and different toxicity mechanisms, NPs individual classes should be modelled separately.

Table 2. Numbers of pentagons (P) and cones, angles and covering efficiencies in graphene hexagonal network

P [a]	Disclination Angle [°]	Cone Angle [°]	Solid Angle [sr]	No. of Cones	Solid-Angle-Covering Efficiency	Sphere-Covering Efficiency
0	**0**	180.00	6.28319	2	1.00000	0.90690
1	60	112.89	2.81002	4	0.89446	0.81118
2	120	83.62	1.59998	7	0.89125	0.80828
3	180	60.00	0.84179	14	0.93782	0.85051
4	240	38.94	0.35934	34	0.97225	0.88173
5	300	19.19	0.08788	142	0.99306	0.90060
6	360	0.00	0.00000	∞	1.00000	0.90690
12	720	360.00	12.56637	1	1.00000	0.90690

[a] $P = 0$ (disc), 1–5 (cone), 5 (horn), 6 (tube), 12 (sphere).

$C_{graphene}$-related research grew at spectacular pace in wide disciplines range while more and more scientists are considering health/ecosystem risks. Work/challenges were reviewed from metals and small molecules to human health and ecosystem (Hu & Zhou, 2013). Current goal is to reduce gaps between expanding material applications and studies on human health/ecosystem risks *via* correct assay methods, valid administration procedures, long-term tests and meaningful data. Nel *et al.* (2013) edited special issue on environmental health/safety considerations for nanotechnology (nano-EHS).

Calculation Results and Discussion

Table 2 lists the number of pentagons P, disclination angles D_θ, cone apex angles θ, solid angles Ω, number of cones in a sphere and solid-angle/sphere-covering efficiencies in an $C_{graphene}$-h net. A given disclination, *e.g.*, 300° ($P = 5$), is built by extraction of one segment generating one distinct cone type (horn). Cone angle decays as number of pentagons increases from flat discs ($P = 0$) to cones ($P = 1$–5, *e.g.*, SWNHs $P = 5$) to tubes ($P = 6$). Solid angle results: $\Omega = 2\pi[1-\cos(\theta/2)]$; maximum corresponds to sphere ($P = 12$): $\Omega_{sph} = 4\pi$. Solid-angle-covering efficiency discards

uncomplete SWNCs; sphere-covering efficiency corrects it by packing efficiency of parallel cylinders η_{cyl}: both drop as number of pentagons increases from discs ($P = 0$) to cones ($P = 1$–5).

Packing efficiencies η, correction factors and parameters $A'/B'/C_0$ determining molecule interaction energy (*cf.* Table 3) show that $\eta_{sph} < \eta_{con} < \eta_{cyl}$, and cone parameters result in-between spheres ($P = 12$) and cylinders ($P = 6$); *e.g.*, SWNH ($P = 5$) parameters are closest to $P = 6$.

Table 4 lists the packing parameters *closeness*, dimension D and efficiency η of equal objects for atom clusters with short-range interaction (Betke & Henk, 2000; Conway & Torquato, 2006; Jiao & Torquato, 2011).

For closest/not closest/extremely low packings, packing efficiency η variations *vs.* packing dimension D show many superimposed points. On going from $D = 2$ to 3, $\eta_{extremely\,low}$ decays quicker than $\eta_{not\,closest/closest}$. For all cases packings with lower dimension show best fits. Fits result:

$$\eta_{closest} = 1.00 + 0.0344\,D - 0.0400D^2 \qquad (34)$$

$$\eta_{notclosest} = 1.00 + 0.0125D - 0.0463D^2,$$
$$n = 16, r = 0.833, s = 0.093, F = 14.8$$
$$(35)$$

Table 3. Packing-efficiencies and parameters determining molecule interaction energy. $C_0 = 5 \cdot 10^{-8}$ (molar fraction)

Molecule	No. of Pentagons[a]	Packing Efficiency	η-Correction Factor	A' [K]	B' [K]
SWNC η-correction[b]	0	0.90690	1.22474	392	1188
	1	0.81118	1.09548	351	1063
	2	0.80828	1.09156	349	1059
	3	0.85051	1.14859	368	1114
	4	0.88173	1.19075	381	1155
	5	0.90060	1.21624	389	1180
SWNT η-correction[c]	6	0.90690	1.22474	392	1188
C_{60}-face-centred cubic[d]	12	0.74048	1.00000	320	970

[a] $P = 0$ (disc), 1–5 (cone), 5 (horn), 6 (tube), 12 (sphere).
[b] SWNC: single-wall carbon nanocone.
[c] SWNT: single-wall carbon nanotube.
[d] For $T > 260K$.

where n is the number of points, r, correlation coefficient, s, standard deviation and F, Fischer ratio. Results are improved if data for tetrahedra I-IV and truncated tetrahedron I are suppressed:

$$\eta_{notclosest} = 1.00 + 0.0192D - 0.0497D^2$$
$$n = 11, r = 0.942, s = 0.054, F = 31.3 \quad (36)$$

For extremely low packing:

$$\eta_{extremely\ low} = 1.00 - 0.317D \quad (37)$$

Parabolic nature of models (34)–(36) suggests that linearization would be achieved, if reciprocal packing dimension D^{-1} is used as abscissa instead of D. For closest, not closest and extremely low packings, η vs. D^{-1} shows many superimposed points. The $\eta_{extremely\ low}$ raises quicker than $\eta_{not\ closest}$ than $\eta_{closest}$. Again packing objects with lower packing dimension D present best fits that result:

$$\eta_{closest} = 0.408 + 0.999D^{-1} \quad (38)$$

$$\eta_{not\ closest} = 0.182 + 1.31D^{-1}$$
$$n = 15, r = 0.780, s = 0.093, F = 20.2,$$
$$MAPE = 9.10\%, AEV = 0.3916 \quad (39)$$

where mean absolute percentage error (MAPE) is 9.10% and approximation error variance (AEV), 0.3916. Results are bettered if data for tetrahedra I-IV and truncated tetrahedron I are excluded:

$$\eta_{not\ closest} = 0.152 + 1.38D^{-1}$$
$$n = 10, r = 0.918, s = 0.054, F = 42.9 \quad (40)$$
$$MAPE = 6.38\%, AEV = 0.2366$$

and AEV decays by 40%. For extremely low packing:

$$\eta_{extremely\ low} = -0.589 + 1.91D^{-1} \quad (41)$$

The rising rate of packing efficiency η vs. D^{-1} increases from closest to not closest to extremely low packing efficiencies. Linear models (37)–(41) perform better for extrapolations than quadratic models (34)–(36). Property-*closeness* inclusion allows performing linear fit for $\eta_{closest}/\eta_{not\ closest}$:

Table 4. Objects, closeness, packing dimensions D and efficiencies η for equal objects

Objects	Closeness	D	Packing efficiency
Low-density sphere (LDS) I	Extremely low	3	0.042
Low-density sphere (LDS) II	Extremely low	3	0.045
Low-density sphere (LDS) III	Extremely low	3	0.056
Tetrahedron I	Not closest	3	$18/49 \approx 0.36735$
Sphere simple cubic (SC)	Not closest	3	$\dfrac{\pi}{6} \approx 0.52360$
Sphere random *loose* (RL)	Not closest	3	0.601 ± 0.005
Sphere random close (RC)	Not closest	3	0.6366 ± 0.0005
Tetrahedron II	Not closest	3	$2/3 \approx 0.66667$
Sphere body-centred cubic (BCC)	Not closest	3	$\dfrac{\pi\sqrt{3}}{8} \approx 0.68017$
Truncated tetrahedron I	Not closest	3	$207/304 \approx 0.68092$
Tetrahedron III	Not closest	3	$17/24 \approx 0.70833$
Tetrahedron IV	Not closest	3	$\dfrac{139 + 40\sqrt{10}}{369} \approx 0.71949$
Sphere (FCC alias cubic closest packing, CCP or hexagonal closest packing, HCP)	Closest	3	$\dfrac{\pi}{3\sqrt{2}} \approx 0.74048$
Tetrahedron V	–	3	0.7786
Tetrahedron VI	–	3	0.7820
Truncated icosahedron	–	3	0.78499
Snub cube	–	3	0.78770
Snub dodecahedron	–	3	0.78864
Rhombic icosidodecahedron	–	3	0.80471
Tetrahedron VII	–	3	0.8226
Truncated icosidodecahedron	–	3	0.82721
Icosahedron	–	3	0.83636
Truncated cubeoctahedron	–	3	$\dfrac{99}{992}\sqrt{66} - \dfrac{231}{1984}\sqrt{33} + \dfrac{2835}{992}\sqrt{2} - \dfrac{6615}{1984} \approx 0.84937$
Tetrahedron VIII	–	3	0.85027
Tetrahedron IX	–	3	$100/117 \approx 0.85470$
Tetrahedron X	–	3	$4000/4671 \approx 0.85635$
Icosidodecahedron	–	3	0.86472
Rhombic cubeoctahedron	–	3	$\dfrac{16\sqrt{2} - 20}{3} \approx 0.87581$

continued on following page

Table 4. Continued

Objects	Closeness	D	Packing efficiency
Truncated dodecahedron	–	3	0.89779
Dodecahedron	–	3	0.90451
Cubeoctahedron	–	3	$45/49 \approx 0.91837$
Octahedron	–	3	$18/19 \approx 0.94737$
Truncated tetrahedron II	–	3	$23/24 \approx 0.95833$
Truncated cube	–	3	$\dfrac{9}{5 + 3\sqrt{2}} \approx 0.97375$
Truncated tetrahedron III	–	3	$207/208 \approx 0.99519$
Cube	Closest	3	1.0
Truncated octahedron	Closest	3	1.0
Cylinder in space as square packing (SP) of circles on a plane	Not closest	2	$\dfrac{\pi}{4} \approx 0.78540$
Cone ($P = 2$)	Not closest	2	0.80828
Cone ($P = 1$)	Not closest	2	0.81118
Cone ($P = 3$)	Not closest	2	0.85051
Cone ($P = 4$)	Not closest	2	0.88173
Cone ($P = 5$, horn)	Not closest	2	0.90060
Cylinder (as hexagonal packing of circles on a plane)	Closest	2	$\dfrac{\pi}{2\sqrt{3}} \approx 0.90690$

$$\eta = 0.180 + 0.0976 closeness + 1.31D^{-1}$$
$$n = 12, r = 0.924, s = 0.053, F = 26.5,$$
$$MAPE = 5.17\%, AEV = 0.1453$$

$$(42)$$

and AEV drops by 63%. One more time the packing objects with lower packing dimension show the best fit. The quadratic-term inclusion allows the best model:

$$\eta = 1.00 + 0.0102D + 0.0381 closeness D - 0.0455D^2$$
$$n = 18, r = 0.847, s = 0.089, F = 11.9$$

$$(43)$$

Results are improved if the data for tetrahedra I-IV and truncated tetrahedron I are neglected:

$$\eta = 1.00 + 0.0151D + 0.0402 closeness D - 0.0481D^2$$
$$n = 13, r = 0.946, s = 0.051, F = 25.6,$$
$$MAPE = 4.34\%, AEV = 0.1050$$

$$(44)$$

and AEV decreases by 73%. Once more the packing objects with lower packing dimension present the best fit. Quadratic models (43) and (44) perform better than linear model (39) for intrapolation. Predictions for packing objects with lower packing dimension show an improvement; *e.g.*, for sphere (C_{60}) and cylinder (SWNT) the results are quite good.

The disclination angles D_θ, numbers of 2-membered rings (2MR), squares S and pentagons P, and cone apex angles θ in a poly(BN) hexagonal net (*cf.* Table 5) show that a given disclination, *e.g.*, 240°, can be built by extraction of one segment generating one distinct cone type (2MR = S = P = 0); however, the same disclination can be derived by extraction of two separated segments of 120° each (S = 1, P = 2) or four unconnected segments of 60° each (S = 0, P = 4). The cone angles decay as numbers of 2MR, squares or pentagons increase from flat discs (D_θ = 0°, 2MR = S = P = 0) to cones (D_θ = 60–300°, 2MR = 0–1, S = 0–2, P = 0–5) to tubes (D_θ = 360°, 2MR = 0, S = 0–3, P = 0–6). The structures observed in BN cones are attributed to lower energy of squares compared with pentagons; indeed B–N present higher stability than B–B than N–N bonds, *e.g.*,

line defect D_θ = 300°, 2MR = S = P = 0 would consist of B–B bonds.

The equilibrium difference between Gibbs free energies of interaction of an SWNC with its surroundings, in solid phase and cluster volume/ on surface (*cf.* Figure 1), shows that results for $B_{15}C_{30}N_{15}/B_{30}N_{30}$ collapse on C_{60}, and (BC$_2$N/ BN-)SWNC/SWNT on SWNT. On going from C_{60} (droplet) to SWNT (*bundlet*), minimum is less marked (68% of C_{60}), which causes lesser number of units in (BC$_2$N/BN-)SWNT/SWNCs ($n_{min} \approx 2$) than in $C_{60}/B_{15}C_{30}N_{15}/B_{30}N_{30}$ clusters (≈ 8); moreover abscissa is longer in $C_{60}/B_{15}C_{30}N_{15}/ B_{30}N_{30}$ ($n_{abs} \approx 28$) than in (BC$_2$N/BN-)SWNT/ SWNCs (≈ 9). When going from C_{60} to $B_{15}C_{30}N_{15}$ to $B_{30}N_{30}$ (or from SWNT to BC$_2$N- to BN-SWNT

Table 5. Angles, numbers of 2-membered rings (2MR), squares S and pentagons P in a poly(BN) hexagonal network

Disclination Angle [°]	2MR	S	P	Cone Angle [°]
0	0	0	0	180.00
60	0	0	1	112.89
120	0	1	0	83.62
120	0	0	2 in opposed ends of an edge	83.62
120	0	0	2 neighbours	83.62
120	0	0	2 isolated by a hexagon	83.62
180	0	0	3 in line	60.00
180	0	0	3 in an arrangement such that each ring has 2 pentagons as nearest neighbours	60.00
180	0	0	3 isolated by a hexagon	60.00
180	0	1	1	60.00
240	0	0	0; 2 2-co-ordinated atoms at the apex	38.94
240	0	0	4 isolated by 2 hexagons	38.94
240	0	0	4 neighbours sharing 2 3-co-ordinated atoms at the apex	38.94
240	0	1	2	38.94
240	0	2	0	38.94
240	1	0	0	38.94
300	0	0	0; line defect consisting of like bonds	19.19
300	0	0	5	19.19
360	0	0	6	0.00
360	0	3	0	0.00
720	0	0	12	360.00

Figure 1. $C_{60}/B_{15}C_{30}N_{15}/B_{30}N_{30}-(BC_2N/BN-)SWNT-SWNH$ interaction energy with surroundings in cluster volume/surface

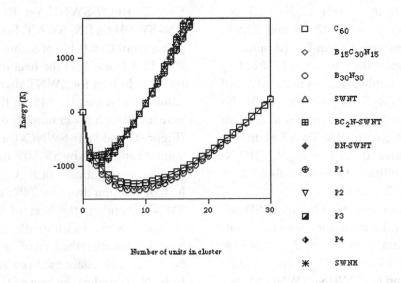

or from SWNCs to BC_2N- to BN-SWNCs), minimum is increasingly emphasized (4.6% and 9.5%, respectively) while it contains the same number of units. In SWNCs/BC_2N-SWNCs/BN-SWNCs (bundlet), minima result 61–67% of $C_{60}/B_{15}C_{30}N_{15}/B_{30}N_{30}$, similar to those in ($BC_2N$/BN-)SWNT.

Solubility of SWNC *vs.* temperature (*cf.* Figure 2) shows that (BC_2N/BN-)SWNC/SWNT data collapse on SWNT. Solubility decays with temperature because of cluster formation. At $T \approx$ 260K, C_{60}-crystal presents an orientation disorder phase transition from FCC to simple cubic (SC). Solubility decays are less marked for (BC_2N/BN-)

Figure 2. Temperature dependence of solubility of $C_{60}/B_{15}C_{30}N_{15}/B_{30}N_{30}-(BC_2N/BN-)SWNT/SWNH$

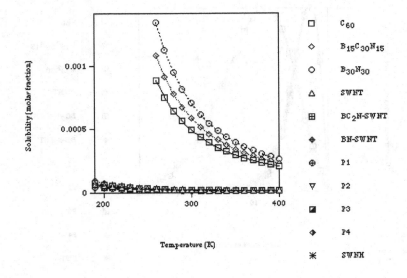

SWNT/SWNCs in agreement with lesser numbers of units in clusters (Figure 1). In particular at T = 260K on going from C_{60} to $B_{15}C_{30}N_{15}$ to $B_{30}N_{30}$ (droplet) solubility rises by 22.8% and 52.5%, respectively. When going from C_{60} (droplet) to SWNT (bundlet) solubility decays to 2.6% of C_{60}; SWNCs (bundlet) solubility drops to 2.0–2.5% of C_{60}. On going from $B_{15}C_{30}N_{15}$ (droplet) to BC_2-SWNT (bundlet) solubility decreases to 2.4% of $B_{15}C_{30}N_{15}$; from $B_{30}N_{30}$ to BN-SWNT (bundlet) solubility diminishes to 2.2% of $B_{30}N_{30}$; $BC_2N/$BN-SWNCs solubilities decay to 1.8–2.3% of $B_{15}C_{30}N_{15}$ and 1.6–2.1% of $B_{30}N_{30}$.

Cluster distribution function by size in SWNC solution in CS_2, calculated for saturation concentration at solvent temperature T = 298.15K (*cf.* Figure 3), shows that $B_{15}C_{30}N_{15}/B_{30}N_{30}$ data collapse on C_{60}, and ($BC_2N/$BN-)SWNC/SWNT on SWNT. On going from $C_{60}/B_{15}C_{30}N_{15}/B_{30}N_{30}$ (droplet) to ($BC_2N/$BN-)SWNT/SWNCs (bundlet), maximum cluster size decays from $n_{max} \approx 8$ to ≈ 2 and distribution is narrowed in agreement with lesser number of units in clusters (Figure 1).

The concentration dependence of the heat of solution in toluene, benzene and CS_2 calculated

at solvent temperature T = 298.15K (*cf.* Figure 4) shows that the results for SWNH collapse on SWNT, BC_2N-SWNH on BC_2N-SWNT, and BN–SWNH on BN–SWNT. For C_{60} (droplet), on going from $C < 0.1\%$ of saturated ($<n> \approx 1$) to $C = 15\%$ ($<n> \approx 7$) the heat of solution decays by 73%. In turn for SWNT (bundlet) the heat of solution increases by 54% in the same range in agreement with lesser number of units in clusters (Figures 1 and 3). In SWNCs (bundlet) the heat of solution augments by 55–80% in accordance with smaller aggregations. In $B_{15}C_{30}N_{15}$ (droplet) the heat of solution drops by 74%; in turn for BC_2N-SWNT (bundlet) the heat of solution rises by 49% in agreement with smaller clusters. In BC_2N-SWNCs (bundlet) the heat of solution enlarges by 50–63% in accordance with smaller aggregations. In $B_{30}N_{30}$ (droplet) the heat of solution decays by 73%; in turn for BN-SWNT (bundlet) the heat of solution increases by 44% in agreement with smaller clusters. In BN-SWNCs (bundlet) the heat of solution enlarges by 45–57% in accordance with smaller aggregations. The discrepancy between the various experimental data of the heat of solution of fullerenes, poly($BC_2N/$BN) and ($BC_2N/$BN-)

Figure 3. Cluster distribution saturated in CS_2 at 298.15K of $C_{60}/B_{15}C_{30}N_{15}/B_{30}N_{30}$–($BC_2N/$BN-)SWNT/SWNH

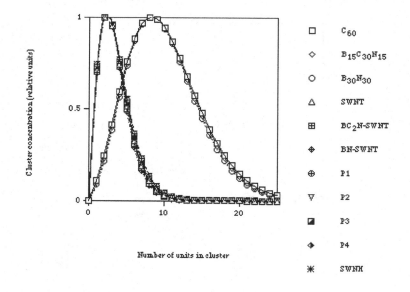

Figure 4. Heat of solution vs. concentration of $C_{60}/B_{15}C_{30}N_{15}/B_{30}N_{30}$—$(BC_2N/BN$-$)SWNT/SWNC$ in toluene/benzene/CS_2 at 298.15K

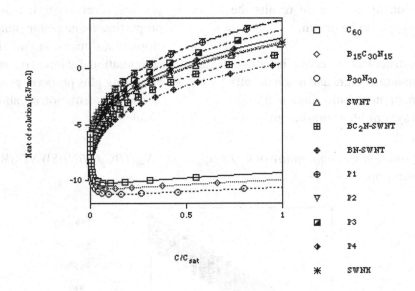

SWNT/SWNCs may be ascribed to the sharp concentration dependence of the heat of solution. The effect of different number of pentagons P on concentration dependence shows that the results for SWNC P2 collapse on P1, and SWNH on SWNT. The heat of solution varies: P2 $\approx$ P1 > P3 > P4 > SWNH $\approx$ SWNT >> C_{60}.

The temperature dependence of the heat of solution in toluene, benzene and CS_2 calculated for the saturation concentration (*cf.* Figure 5) shows that the results for SWNH collapse on SWNT, BC_2N-SWNH on BC_2N-SWNT, and BN-SWNH on BN-SWNT. The data of C_{60}, *etc.* are plotted for $T > 260$K after FCC/SC transition. For C_{60} (droplet) on going from $T = 260$K to $T = 400$K the heat of solution increases 2.7kJ·mol⁻¹. For SWNT and SWNCs (bundlet) the heat of solution augments 10.4 and 10.4–10.9kJ·mol⁻¹, respectively, in the same range. For $B_{15}C_{30}N_{15}$ (droplet) the heat of solution rises 2.5kJ·mol⁻¹. For BC_2N-SWNT and BC_2N-SWNCs (bundlet) the heat of solution augments 10.2 and 10.2–10.7kJ·mol⁻¹. For $B_{30}N_{30}$ (droplet) heat of solution enlarges 2.3kJ·mol⁻¹. For BN-SWNT and BN-SWNCs (bundlet) heat of solution rises 9.9 and 10.0–10.5kJ·mol⁻¹.

Diffusion coefficient *vs.* concentration in toluene at $T = 298.15$K (*cf.* Figure 6) shows that SWNH data collapse on SWNT, BC_2N-SWNH on BC_2N-SWNT and BN-SWNH on BN-SWNT. Cluster formation in solution close to saturation decreases diffusion coefficients by 56%, 69% and 69–71% for C_{60}, SWNT and SWNCs, respectively, as compared with $(C_{60})_1$. For SWNT (bundlet) diffusion coefficient drops by 29% and for SWNCs (bundlet) diffusion coefficients, by 29–33% with regard to C_{60} (droplet). Cluster formation close to saturation diminishes diffusion coefficients by 56%, 68% and 68–70% for $B_{15}C_{30}N_{15}$, BC_2N-SWNT and BC_2N-SWNCs as compared with $(B_{15}C_{30}N_{15})_1$. For BC_2N-SWNT (bundlet) diffusion coefficient decays by 28% and for BC_2N-SWNCs (bundlet), by 28–31% with regard to $B_{15}C_{30}N_{15}$ (droplet). Cluster formation close to saturation decreases diffusion coefficients by 56%, 67% and 67–69% for $B_{30}N_{30}$, BN-SWNT and BN-SWNCs as compared with $(B_{30}N_{30})_1$. For BN-SWNT (bundlet) diffusion coefficient decays by 26% and for BN-SWNCs (bundlet), by 26–29% with regard to $B_{30}N_{30}$ (droplet).

CONCLUSION

From the discussion of the present results the following conclusions can be drawn.

1. Nanoworld structural diversity is consequence of quantum nature and result of self-organization of nonequilibrium nonlinear multivariant system. Structural inhomogeneity is fundamental. Packing structures were deduced fitting voids between close-packed spheres; several criteria reduced analysis to properties manageable quantity: packing closeness, dimension and efficiency. Non-computationally intensive approach, object clustering plus property prediction allowed assessing calculation reliability and solving problem.

Figure 5. Heat of solution vs. temperature of C_{60}/$B_{15}C_{30}N_{15}$/$B_{30}N_{30}$–$(BC_2N/BN-)SWNT/SWNC$ in toluene/benzene/CS$_2$ for saturation

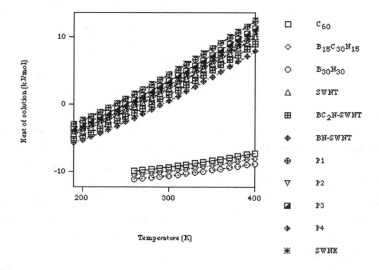

Figure 6. Diffusion coefficient vs. concentration of C_{60}/$B_{15}C_{30}N_{15}$/$B_{30}N_{30}$–$(BC_2N/BN-)SWNT/SWNC$ in toluene at 298.15K

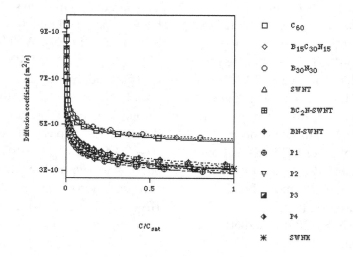

2. The packing efficiencies and interaction-energy parameters of nanocones are intermediate between C_{60} and tubes: an in-between behaviour was expected; however, cones result closer to tubes. The tube-like behaviour is observed in cones, which properties are calculated closer to tubes. The packing efficiency and interaction-energy parameters of horns are closest to tubes: most tube-like behaviour is observed and properties are calculated closest to tubes. Large structural asymmetry in different types of cones characterized by the number of pentagons (1–5) distinguished the calculated properties, especially for cones with two pentagons P2; *e.g.*, the heat of solution varied: P2 $\approx$ P1 > P3 > P4 > SWNH $\approx$ SWNT >> C_{60}.

3. BC_2N and BN will be stable especially species that are isoelectronic with C-analogues. Specific morphologies were observed for tube ends that result from B–N units. The chemical strain that 60° disclinations introduce in $B_{30}N_{30}$ governs its structural difference with C-tubes.

4. Some systems are dominated by isolated-pentagon-rule structures while others, by non-isolated-pentagon-rule ones. Further work will explore similar nanostructure nature: (a) way of bypassing weak homonuclear bonding exists in closed B_xN_x, involving replacement of 5-membered rings by 4-membered B_2N_2 annuli ensuring perfect heteroatom alternation and (b) BN/AlN tubes/heterojunctions. C-structures are more controllable while heterostructures present richer behaviour especially for transtition-metal compounds, which show lubricant/electronic applications.

ACKNOWLEDGMENT

The authors want to dedicate this manuscript to Dr. Luis Serrano-Andrés, who was greatly interested in this research and would have loved to see its conclusion. One of us, F. T., thanks support from the Spanish Ministerio de Economía y Competitividad (Project No. BFU2013-41648-P) and EU ERDF.

REFERENCES

Abrikosov, A. A. (1957). On the magnetic properties of superconductors of the second group. [English Translation]. *Soviet Physics, JETP, 5,* 1174–1182.

Adini, A. R., Redlich, M., & Tenne, R. (2011). Medical applications of inorganic fullerene-like nanoparticles. *Journal of Materials Chemistry, 21,* 15121–15131. doi:10.1039/c1jm11799h

Aguilera-Sigalat, J., Casas-Solvas, J. M., Morant-Miñana, M. C., Vargas-Berenguel, A., Galian, R. E., & Pérez-Prieto, J. (2012a). Quantum dot/ *cyclo*dextrin supramolecular systems based on efficient molecular recognition and their use for sensing. *Chemical Communications, 48,* 2573–2575. doi:10.1039/c1cc15312a PMID:22080219

Aguilera-Sigalat, J., Rocton, S., Galian, R. E., & Pérez-Prieto, J. (2011). Fluorescence enhancement of amine-capped CdSe/ZnS quantum dots by thiol addition. *Canadian Journal of Chemistry, 89,* 359–363. doi:10.1139/V10-160

Aguilera-Sigalat, J., Rocton, S., Sánchez-Royo, J. F., Galian, R. E., & Pérez-Prieto, J. (2012b). Highly fluorescent and photostable organic- and water-soluble CdSe/ZnS core–shell quantum dots capped with thiols. *RSC Advances, 2,* 1632–1638. doi:10.1039/c1ra01005k

Aguilera-Sigalat, J., Sanchez-SanMartín, J., Agudelo-Morales, C. E., Zaballos, E., Galian, R. E., & Pérez-Prieto, J. (2012c). Further insight into the photostability of the pyrene fluorophore in halogenated solvents. *ChemPhysChem, 13*, 835–844. doi:10.1002/cphc.201100843 PMID:22271708

Baker, J., & Kudrolli, A. (2010). Maximum and minimum stable random packings of Platonic solids. *Physical Review E: Statistical, Nonlinear, and Soft Matter Physics, 82*, 061304-1–5. doi:10.1103/PhysRevE.82.061304

Balaban, A. T., & Klein, D. J. (2009). Claromatic carbon nanostructures. *The Journal of Physical Chemistry C, 113*, 19123–19133. doi:10.1021/jp9082618

Balaban, A. T., Klein, D. J., & Liu, X. (1994). Graphitic cones. *Carbon, 32*, 357–359. doi:10.1016/0008-6223(94)90203-8

Bar-Nahum, G., Epshtein, V., Ruckenstein, A. E., Rafikov, R., Mustaev, A., & Nudler, E. (2005). A ratchet mechanism of transcription elongation and its control. *Cell, 120*, 183–193. doi:10.1016/j.cell.2004.11.045 PMID:15680325

Bertolazzi, S., Brivio, J., & Kis, A. (2011). Stretching and breaking of ultrathin MoS_2. *ACS Nano, 5*, 9703–9709. doi:10.1021/nn203879f PMID:22087740

Bertolazzi, S., Brivio, J., Radenovic, A., Kis, A., Wilson, H., Prisbrey, L., … Proksch, R. (2013). Exploring flatland: AFM of mechanical and electrical properties of graphene, MoS_2 and other low-dimensional materials. *Microscopy and Analysis, (5)*, 21-24.

Betke, U., & Henk, M. (2000). Densest lattice packings of 3-polytopes. *Computational Geometry, 16*, 157–186. doi:10.1016/S0925-7721(00)00007-9

Bezmel'nitsyn, V. N., Eletskii, A. V., & Okun', M. V. (1998). Fullerenes in solutions. *Physics–Uspekhi, 41*, 1091–1114.

Binning, G., Quate, C. F., & Gerber, C. (1986). Atomic force microscope. *Physical Review Letters, 56*, 930–933. doi:10.1103/PhysRevLett.56.930 PMID:10033323

Bourgeois, L., Bando, Y., Han, W. Q., & Sato, T. (2000). Structure of boron nitride nanoscale cones: Ordered stacking of 240° and 300° disclinations. *Physical Review B: Condensed Matter and Materials Physics, 61*, 7686–7691. doi:10.1103/PhysRevB.61.7686

Bourgeois, L., Bando, Y., Shinozaki, S., Kurashima, K., & Sato, T. (1999). Boron nitride cones: Structure determination by transmission electron microscopy. *Acta Crystallographica. Section A, Foundations of Crystallography, 55*, 168–177. doi:10.1107/S0108767398008642 PMID:10927246

Bruker. (2013). Atomic force microscopy reveals DNA double helix. *Microscopy and Analysis, (3)*.

Bueno-Alejo, C. J., D'Alfonso, C., Pacioni, N. L., González-Béjar, M., Grenier, M., & Lanzalunga, O. et al. (2012). Ultraclean derivatized monodisperse gold nanoparticles through laser drop ablation customization of polymorph gold nanostructures. *Langmuir, 28*, 8183–8189. doi:10.1021/la3010689 PMID:22591001

Bueno Alejo, C. J., Fasciani, C., Grenier, M., Netto-Ferreira, J. C., & Scaiano, J. C. (2011). Reduction of resazurin to resorufin catalyzed by gold nanoparticles: Dramatic reaction acceleration by laser or LED plasmon excitation. *Catalysis Science & Technology, 1*, 1506–1511. doi:10.1039/c1cy00236h

Buzdin, A. I. (1993). Multiple-quanta vortices at columnar defects. *Physical Review B: Condensed Matter and Materials Physics, 47*, 11416–11419. doi:10.1103/PhysRevB.47.11416 PMID:10005280

Carl Zeiss Microscopy. (2013). *Cover story. Microscopy and Analysis Directory.*

Carroll, D. L., Redlich, P., Ajayan, P. M., Charlier, J.-C., Blase, X., de Vita, A., & Car, R. (1997). Electronic structure and localized states at carbon nanotube tips. *Physical Review Letters*, *78*, 2811–2814. doi:10.1103/PhysRevLett.78.2811

Chen, E. R., Engel, M., & Glotzer, S. C. (2010). Dense crystalline dimer packings of regular tetrahedra. *Discrete & Computational Geometry*, *44*, 253–280. doi:10.1007/s00454-010-9273-0

Chopra, N. G., Luyken, R. J., Cherrey, K., Crespi, V. H., Cohen, M. L., Louie, S. G., & Zettl, A. (1995). Boron nitride nanotubes. *Science*, *269*, 966–967. doi:10.1126/science.269.5226.966 PMID:17807732

Cioffi, C., Campidelli, S., Brunetti, F. G., Meneghetti, M., & Prato, M. (2006). Functionalisation of carbon nanohorns. *Chemical Communications*, *2006*, 2129–2131. doi:10.1039/b601176d PMID:16703130

Cioffi, C., Campidelli, S., Sooambar, C., Marcaccio, M., Marcolongo, G., & Meneghetti, M. et al. (2007). Synthesis, characterization, and photoinduced electron transfer in functionalized single wall carbon nanohorns. *Journal of the American Chemical Society*, *129*, 3938–3945. doi:10.1021/ja068007p PMID:17343379

Conway, J. H., & Torquato, S. (2006). Packing, tiling, and covering with tetrahedra. *Proceedings of the National Academy of Sciences of the United States of America*, *103*, 10612–10617. doi:10.1073/pnas.0601389103 PMID:16818891

Coronado, E., Galán-Mascarós, J. R., Monrabal-Capilla, M., García-Martínez, J., & Pardo-Ibáñez, P. (2007). Bistable spin-crossover nanoparticles showing magnetic thermal hysteresis near room temperature. *Advanced Materials*, *19*, 1359–1361. doi:10.1002/adma.200700559

Faraday, M. (1857). The Bakerian Lecture: Experimental relations of gold (and other metals) to light. *Philosophical Transactions of the Royal Society of London*, *147*, 145–181. doi:10.1098/rstl.1857.0011

Fasciani, C., Bueno Alejo, C. J., Grenier, M., Netto-Ferreira, J. C., & Scaiano, J. C. (2011). High-temperature organic reactions at room temperature using plasmon excitation: Decomposition of dicumyl peroxide. *Organic Letters*, *13*, 204–207. doi:10.1021/ol1026427 PMID:21142017

Fujishima, A., Rao, T. N., & Tryk, D. A. (2000). Titanium dioxide photocatalysis. *Journal of Photochemistry and Photobiology A Chemistry*, *1*, 1–21. doi:10.1016/S1389-5567(00)00002-2

Gasser, U., Weeks, E. R., Schofield, A., Pusey, P. N., & Weitz, D. A. (2001). Real-space imaging of nucleation and growth in colloidal crystallization. *Science*, *292*, 258–262. doi:10.1126/science.1058457 PMID:11303095

Gratzel, M. (2001). Photoelectrochemical cells. *Nature*, *414*, 338–344. doi:10.1038/35104607 PMID:11713540

Haluska, C. K., Riske, K. A., Marchi-Artzner, V., Lehn, J.-M., Lipowsky, R., & Dimova, R. (2006). Time scales of membrane fusion revealed by direct imaging of vesicle fusion with high temporal resolution. *Proceedings of the National Academy of Sciences of the United States of America*, *103*, 15841–15846. doi:10.1073/pnas.0602766103 PMID:17043227

Hamilton, E. J. M., Dolan, S. E., Mann, C. M., Colijn, H. O., McDonald, C. A., & Shore, S. G. (1993). Preparation of amorphous boron nitride and its conversion to a turbostratic, tubular form. *Science*, *260*, 659–661. doi:10.1126/science.260.5108.659 PMID:17812224

Hamilton, E. J. M., Dolan, S. E., Mann, C. M., Colijn, H. O., & Shore, S. G. (1995). Preparation of amorphous boron nitride from the reaction of haloborazines with alkali metals and formation of a novel tubular morphology by thermal annealing. *Chemistry of Materials, 7*, 111–117. doi:10.1021/cm00049a017

Han, J., & Jaffe, R. (1998). Energetics and geometries of carbon nanocone tips. *The Journal of Chemical Physics, 108*, 2817–2823. doi:10.1063/1.475672

Harada, K., Kamimura, O., Kasai, H., Matsuda, T., Tonomura, A., & Moshchalkov, V. V. (1996). Direct observation of vortex dynamics in superconducting films with regular arrays of defects. *Science, 274*, 1167–1170. doi:10.1126/science.274.5290.1167 PMID:8895460

Hartmann, U. (1985). *Theory of noncontact force microscopy: Scanning tunneling microscopy III. Theory of STM and related scanning techniques* (R. Wiensendanger, & J. H. Guntherodt, Eds.). Berlin: Springer.

Hu, X., & Zhou, Q. (2013). Health and ecosystem risks of graphene. *Chemical Reviews, 113*, 3815–3835. doi:10.1021/cr300045n PMID:23327673

Jiao, Y., & Torquato, S. (2011). Communication: A packing of truncated tetrahedra that nearly fills all of space and its melting properties. *The Journal of Chemical Physics, 135*, 151101–1–4. doi:10.1063/1.3653938 PMID:22029288

Jimoda, L. A., Oke, E. O., & Salam, K. K. (2013). Modelling of mass transfer rate during biocoagulation-flocculation of coal-rich wastewater. *Journal of Scientific Research Reports, 2*, 376–390. doi:10.9734/JSRR/2013/3492

Kaiser, U., Schwarz, A., & Wiesendanger, R. (2007). Magnetic exchange force microscopy with atomic resolution. *Nature, 446*, 522–525. doi:10.1038/nature05617 PMID:17392782

Kallus, Y., Elser, V., & Gravel, S. (2010). Gravel, Dense periodic packings of tetrahedra with small repeating units. *Discrete & Computational Geometry, 44*, 245–252. doi:10.1007/s00454-010-9254-3

Kim, P., Odom, T. W., Huang, J.-L., & Lieber, C. M. (1999). Electronic density of states of atomically resolved single-walled carbon nanotubes: Van Hove singularities and end states. *Physical Review Letters, 82*, 1225–1228. doi:10.1103/PhysRevLett.82.1225

Klein, D. J. (1992). Aromaticity via Kekule structures and conjugated circuits. *Journal of Chemical Education, 69*, 691–694. doi:10.1021/ed069p691

Klein, D. J. (2002). Topo-combinatoric categorization of quasi-local graphitic defects. *Physical Chemistry Chemical Physics, 4*, 2099–2110. doi:10.1039/b110618j

Klein, D. J., & Balaban, A. T. (2006). The eight classes of positive-curvature graphitic nanocones. *Journal of Chemical Information and Modeling, 46*, 307–320. doi:10.1021/ci0503356 PMID:16426066

Klein, D. J., & Balaban, A. T. (2011). Clarology for conjugated carbon nano-structures: Molecules, polymers, graphene, defected graphene, fractal benzenoids, fullerenes, nano-tubes, nano-cones, nano-tori, etc. *Open Organic Chemistry Journal, 5*(Suppl. 1-M3), 27-61.

Kohler-Redlich, P., Terrones, M., Manteca-Diego, C., Hsu, W. K., Terrones, H., & Rühle, M. et al. (1999). Stable BC_2N nanostructures: Low-temperature production of segregated C/BN layered materials. *Chemical Physics Letters, 310*, 459–465. doi:10.1016/S0009-2614(99)00845-3

Krishnan, A., Dujardin, E., Treacy, M. M. J., Hugdahl, J., Lynum, S., & Ebbesen, T. W. (1997). Photoisomerization in dendrimers by harvesting of low-energy photons. *Nature, 388*, 451–454. doi:10.1038/41284

Kroto, H. W. (1987). The stability of the fullerenes C_n, with $n = 24, 28, 32, 36, 50, 60$ and 70. *Nature*, *329*, 529–531. doi:10.1038/329529a0

Kumar, D. N. T., & Wei, Q. (2013). Analysis of quantum dots for nano–bio applications as the technological platform of the future. *Research Journal of Biotechnology*, *8*(5), 78–82.

Leszczynski, J., & Shukla, M. K. (Eds.). (2009). *Practical aspects of computational chemistry*. Berlin: Springer.

Linke, H. (Ed.). (2002). Special issue on Ratchets and Brownian Motors: Basics, Experiments and Applications. *Applied Physics. A, Materials Science & Processing*, *75*, 167–354. doi:10.1007/s003390201401

Linke, H., Alemán, B. J., Melling, L. D., Taormina, M. J., Francis, M. J., & Dow-Hygelund, C. C. et al. (2006). Self-propelled Leidenfrost droplets. *Physical Review Letters*, *96*, 154502–1–4. doi:10.1103/PhysRevLett.96.154502 PMID:16712160

Loiseau, A., Willaime, F., Demoncy, N., Hug, G., & Pascard, H. (1996). Boron nitride nanotubes with reduced numbers of layers synthesized by arc discharge. *Physical Review Letters*, *76*, 4737–4740. doi:10.1103/PhysRevLett.76.4737 PMID:10061368

Machado, M., Mota, R., & Piquini, P. (2003a). Electronic properties of BN nanocones under electric fields. *Microelectronics Journal*, *34*, 545–547. doi:10.1016/S0026-2692(03)00044-2

Machado, M., Piquini, P., & Mota, R. (2003b). Energetics and electronic properties of BN nanocones with pentagonal rings at their apexes. *The European Physical Journal D*, *23*, 91–93. doi:10.1140/epjd/e2003-00040-x

Machado, M., Piquini, P., & Mota, R. (2003c). Electronic properties of selected BN nanocones. *Materials Characterization*, *50*, 179–182. doi:10.1016/S1044-5803(03)00085-8

Machado, M., Piquini, P., & Mota, R. (2004). Charge distributions in BN nanocones: Electric field and tip termination effects. *Chemical Physics Letters*, *392*, 428–432. doi:10.1016/j.cplett.2004.05.088

Machado, M., Piquini, P., & Mota, R. (2005). The influence of the tip structure and the electric field on BN nanocones. *Nanotechnology*, *16*, 302–306. doi:10.1088/0957-4484/16/2/022 PMID:21727440

Madden, J. D. W. (2009). Stiffer than steel. *Science*, *323*, 1571–1572. doi:10.1126/science.1171169 PMID:19299609

Margulis, L., Salitra, G., Tenne, R., & Talianker, M. (1993). Nested fullerene-like structures. *Nature*, *365*, 113–114. doi:10.1038/365113b0 PMID:8371754

Martin, Y., & Wickramasinghe, H. K. (1987). Magnetic imaging by *force microscopy* with 1000Å resolution. *Applied Physics Letters*, *50*, 1455–1457. doi:10.1063/1.97800

Menkiti, M. C., & Onukwuli, O. D. (2010). Coag-flocculation studies of *Moringa oleifera* coagulant (MOC) in brewery effluent: Nephelometric approach. *Journal of American Science*, *6*(12), 788–806.

Misra, A., Klein, D. J., & Morikawa, T. (2009a). Clar theory for molecular benzenoids. *The Journal of Physical Chemistry A*, *113*, 1151–1158. doi:10.1021/jp8038797 PMID:19132846

Misra, A., Schmalz, T. G., & Klein, D. J. (2009b). Clar theory for radical benzenoids. *Journal of Chemical Information and Modeling*, *49*, 2670–2676. doi:10.1021/ci900321e PMID:19916509

Miyamoto, Y., Rubio, A., Cohen, M. L., & Louie, S. G. (1994). Chiral tubules of hexagonal BC_2N. *Physical Review B: Condensed Matter and Materials Physics*, *50*, 4976–4979. doi:10.1103/PhysRevB.50.4976 PMID:9976827

Mkrtchyan, G. S., & Shmidt, V. V. (1972). Interaction between a cavity and a vortex in a superconductor of the second kind. [English Translation]. *Soviet Physics, JETP, 34*, 195–197.

Mota, R., Machado, M., & Piquini, P. (2003). Structural and electronic properties of 240° nanocones. *Physica Status Solidi, 0*(c), 799–802. doi:10.1002/pssc.200306216

Murphy, C. J., & Coffer, J. L. (2002). Quantum dots: A primer. *Applied Spectroscopy, 56*, 16A–27A. doi:10.1366/0003702021954214

Murphy, C. J., Thompson, L. B., Alkilany, A. M., Sisco, P. N., Boulos, S. P., & Sivapalan, S. T. et al. (2010). The many faces of gold nanorods. *Journal of Physical Chemistry Letters, 1*, 2867–2875. doi:10.1021/jz100992x

Nel, A., Zhao, Y., & Mädler, L. (2013). Environmental health and safety considerations for nanotechnology. *Accounts of Chemical Research, 46*, 605–606. doi:10.1021/ar400005v PMID:23964654

Neu, J. C., Cañizo, J. A., & Bonilla, L. L. (2002). Three eras of micellization. *Physical Review E, 66*, 61406-1-9.

Notman, R., Noro, M., O'Malley, B., & Anwar, J. (2006). Molecular basis for dimethylsulfoxide (DMSO) action on lipid membranes. *Journal of the American Chemical Society, 128*, 13982–13983. doi:10.1021/ja063363t PMID:17061853

Oberdörster, G., Maynard, A., Donaldson, K., Castranova, V., Fitzpatrick, J., Ausman, K., … Yang, H. (2005). A report from the ILSI Research Foundation/Risk Science Institute Nanomaterial Toxicity Screening Working Group. *Particle and Fibre Toxicology, 2*, 8-1-35.

Ortega-Villar, N., Thompson, A. L., Muñoz, M. C., Ugalde-Saldívar, V. M., Goeta, A. E., Moreno-Esparza, R., & Real, J. A. (2005). Solid- and solution-state studies of the novel μ-dicyanamide-bridged dinuclear spin-crossover system {[(Fe(bztpen)]$_2$[μ-N(CN)$_2$]}(PF$_6$)$_3$·nH$_2$O. *Chemistry (Weinheim an der Bergstrasse, Germany), 11*, 5721–5734. doi:10.1002/chem.200500171 PMID:16028299

Pagona, G., Fan, J., Maigne, A., Yudasaka, M., Iijima, S., & Tagmatarchis, N. (2007a). Aqueous carbon nanohorn–pyrene–porphyrin nanoensembles: Controlling charge-transfer interactions. *Diamond and Related Materials, 16*, 1150–1153. doi:10.1016/j.diamond.2006.11.071

Pagona, G., Fan, J., Tagmatarchis, N., Yudasaka, M., & Iijima, S. (2006a). Cone-end functionalization of carbon nanohorns. *Chemistry of Materials, 18*, 3918–3920. doi:10.1021/cm0604864

Pagona, G., Sandanayaka, A. S. D., Araki, Y., Fan, J., Tagmatarchis, N., & Charalambidis, G. et al. (2007b). Covalent functionalization of carbon nanohorns with porphyrins: Nanohybrid formation and photoinduced electron and energy transfer. *Advances in Functionalized Materials, 17*, 1705–1711. doi:10.1002/adfm.200700039

Pagona, G., Sandanayaka, A. S. D., Araki, Y., Fan, J., Tagmatarchis, N., & Yudasaka, M. et al. (2006b). Electronic interplay on illuminated aqueous carbon nanohorn–porphyrin ensembles. *The Journal of Physical Chemistry B, 110*, 20729–20732. doi:10.1021/jp064685m PMID:17048875

Pong, B. K., Trout, B. L., & Lee, J. Y. (2008). Modified ligand-exchange for efficient solubilization of CdSe/ZnS quantum dots in water: A procedure guided by computational studies. *Langmuir, 24*, 5270–5276. doi:10.1021/la703431j PMID:18412382

Prins, F., Monrabal-Capilla, M., Osorio, E. A., Coronado, E., & van der Zant, H. S. J. (2011). Room-temperature electrical addressing of a bistable spin-crossover molecular system. *Advanced Materials*, *23*, 1545–1549. doi:10.1002/adma.201003821 PMID:21449059

Puzyn, T., Leszczynska, D., & Leszczynski, J. (2009). Toward the development of *nano-QSARs*: Advances and challenges. *Small*, *5*, 2494–2509. doi:10.1002/smll.200900179 PMID:19787675

Reines, D., Conaway, R. C., & Conaway, J. W. (1999). Mechanism and regulation of transcriptional elongation by RNA polymerase II. *Current Opinion in Cell Biology*, *11*, 342–346. doi:10.1016/S0955-0674(99)80047-7 PMID:10395562

Rubio, A., Corkill, J. L., & Cohen, M. L. (1994). Theory of graphitic boron nitride nanotubes. *Physical Review B: Condensed Matter and Materials Physics*, *49*, 5081–5084. doi:10.1103/PhysRevB.49.5081 PMID:10011453

Rugar, D., Mamin, H. J., Guethner, P., Lambert, S. E., Stern, J. E., McFadyen, I., & Yogi, T. (1990). Magnetic force microscopy: General principles and application to longitudinal recording media. *Journal of Applied Physics*, *68*, 1169–1183. doi:10.1063/1.346713

Scaiano, J. C., Stamplecoskie, K. G., & Hallett-Tapley, G. L. (2012). Photochemical Norrish type I reaction as a tool for metal nanoparticle synthesis: Importance of proton coupled electron transfer. *Chemical Communications*, *48*, 4798–4808. doi:10.1039/c2cc30615h PMID:22498952

Schellman, J. A. (1975). Macromolecular binding. *Biopolymers*, *14*, 999–1018. doi:10.1002/bip.1975.360140509

Schwarzenbach, G. (1952). Der chelateffekt. *Helvetica Chimica Acta*, *35*, 2344–2359. doi:10.1002/hlca.19520350721

Shanthi, S., & Priya, K. S. (2012). Photo degradation of dyes from their aqueous solutions of their binary mixture, using TiO_2 as the oxidant with different sources of energy. *Journal of Chemistry & Chemical Engineering*, *6*, 951–955.

Shevchenko, V. Y., Madison, A. E., & Shudegov, V. E. (2003). The structural diversity of the nanoworld. *Glass Physics and Chemistry*, *29*, 577–582. doi:10.1023/B:GPAC.0000007934.93203.f3

Shilatifard, A., Conaway, J. W., & Conaway, R. C. (1997). Mechanism and regulation of transcriptional elongation and termination by RNA polymerase II. *Current Opinion in Genetics & Development*, *7*, 199–204. doi:10.1016/S0959-437X(97)80129-3 PMID:9115429

Shukla, D., Ahearn, W. G., & Farid, S. (2005). Chain amplification in photoreactions of *N*-alkoxypyridinium salts with alcohols: Mechanism and kinetics. *The Journal of Organic Chemistry*, *70*, 6809–6819. doi:10.1021/jo050726j PMID:16095300

Shukla, D., Ahearn, W. G., & Farid, S. (2006). Enhancement of chain amplification in photoreactions of *N*-methoxypyridinium salts with alcohols. *Photochemistry and Photobiology*, *82*, 146–151. doi:10.1562/2005-06-28-RA-594 PMID:16178662

Silaghi-Dumitrescu, I., Haiduc, I., & Sowerby, D. B. (1993). Fully inorganic (carbon-free) fullerenes? The boron-nitrogen case. *Inorganic Chemistry*, *32*, 3755–3758. doi:10.1021/ic00069a034

Stamplecoskie, K. G., Fasciani, C., & Scaiano, J. C. (2012). Dual-stage lithography from a light-driven, plasmon-assisted process: A hierarchical approach to subwavelength features. *Langmuir*, *28*, 10957–10961. doi:10.1021/la301728r PMID:22803690

Stamplecoskie, K. G., Pacioni, N. L., Larson, D., & Scaiano, J. C. (2011). Plasmon-mediated photopolymerization maps plasmon fields for silver nanoparticles. *Journal of the American Chemical Society, 133,* 9160–9163. doi:10.1021/ja201139z PMID:21615121

Stamplecoskie, K. G., & Scaiano, J. C. (2010). Light emitting diode irradiation can control the morphology and optical properties of silver nanoparticles. *Journal of the American Chemical Society, 132,* 1825–1827. doi:10.1021/ja910010b PMID:20102152

Tagmatarchis, N., Maigne, A., Yudasaka, M., & Iijima, S. (2006). Functionalization of carbon nanohorns with azomethine ylides: Towards solubility enhancement and electron-transfer processes. *Small, 2,* 490–494. doi:10.1002/smll.200500393 PMID:17193072

Takezawa, N., & Fukushima, K. (1994). Optimal size of a cylindrical insulating inclusion acting as a pinning center for magnetic flux in superconductors. *Physica. C, Superconductivity, 228,* 149–159. doi:10.1016/0921-4534(94)90186-4

Takezawa, N., & Fukushima, K. (1997). Optimal size of an insulating inclusion acting as a pinning center for magnetic flux in superconductors: Calculation of pinning force. *Physica. C, Superconductivity, 290,* 31–37. doi:10.1016/S0921-4534(97)01574-8

Tamura, R., & Tsukada, M. (1995). Electronic states of the cap structure in the carbon nanotube. *Physical Review B: Condensed Matter and Materials Physics, 52,* 6015–6026. doi:10.1103/PhysRevB.52.6015 PMID:9981793

Tenne, R., Margulis, L., Genut, M., & Hodes, G. (1992). Polyhedral and cylindrical structures of tungsten disulphide. *Nature, 360,* 444–446. doi:10.1038/360444a0

Tenne, R., & Redlich, M. (2010). Recent progress in the research of inorganic fullerene-like nanoparticles and inorganic nanotubes. *Chemical Society Reviews, 39,* 1423–1434. doi:10.1039/b901466g PMID:20419198

Terauchi, M., Tanaka, M., Suzuki, K., Ogino, A., & Kimura, K. (2000). Production of zigzag-type BN nanotubes and BN cones by thermal annealing. *Chemical Physics Letters, 324,* 359–364. doi:10.1016/S0009-2614(00)00637-0

Teresawa, M., Takezawa, N., Fukushima, K., Mitamura, T., Fan, X., & Tsubakino, H. et al. (1998). Flux pinning and flux creep in $La_{2-x}Sr_xCuO_4$ with splayed columnar defects. *Physica. C, Superconductivity, 296,* 57–64. doi:10.1016/S0921-4534(97)01822-4

Terrones, M., Benito, A. M., Manteca-Diego, C., Hsu, W. K., Osman, O. I., & Hare, J. P. et al. (1996). Pyrolytically grown $B_xC_yN_z$ nanomaterials: Nanofibres and nanotubes. *Chemical Physics Letters, 257,* 576–582. doi:10.1016/0009-2614(96)00594-5

Thesing, L. A., Piquini, P., & Kar, T. (2006). Theoretical investigation on the stability and properties of III-nitride nanotubes: BN-AlN junction. *Nanotechnology, 17,* 1637–1641. doi:10.1088/0957-4484/17/6/016

Torrens, F., & Castellano, G. (2005). Cluster origin of the solubility of single-wall carbon nanotubes. *Computing Letters, 1,* 331–336. doi:10.1163/157404005776611303

Torrens, F., & Castellano, G. (2007a). Cluster nature of the solvation features of single-wall carbon nanotubes. *Current Research in Nanotechnology, 1,* 1–29.

Torrens, F., & Castellano, G. (2007b). Effect of packing on the cluster nature of C nanotubes: An information entropy analysis. *Microelectronics Journal, 38,* 1109–1122. doi:10.1016/j.mejo.2006.04.004

Torrens, F., & Castellano, G. (2007c). Cluster origin of the transfer phenomena of single-wall carbon nanotubes. *Journal of Computational and Theoretical Nanoscience, 4*, 588–603.

Torrens, F., & Castellano, G. (2007d). Asymptotic analysis of coagulation–fragmentation equations of carbon nanotube clusters. *Nanoscale Research Letters, 2*, 337–349. doi:10.1007/s11671-007-9070-8

Torrens, F., & Castellano, G. (2010). Cluster nature of the solvent features of single-wall carbon nanohorns. *International Journal of Quantum Chemistry, 110*, 563–570. doi:10.1002/qua.22054

Torrens, F., & Castellano, G. (2011). (Co-)solvent selection for single-wall carbon nanotubes: *Best* solvents, acids, superacids and guest–host inclusion complexes. *Nanoscale, 3*, 2494–2510. doi:10.1039/c0nr00922a PMID:21331393

Torrens, F., & Castellano, G. (2012). *Bundlet* model for single-wall carbon nanotubes, nanocones and nanohorns. *International Journal of Chemoinformatics and Chemical Engineering, 2*(1), 48–98. doi:10.4018/IJCCE.2012010105

Torrens, F., & Castellano, G. (2013a). Solvent features of cluster single-wall C, BC_2N and BN nanotubes, cones and horns. *Microelectronic Engineering, 108*, 127–133. doi:10.1016/j.mee.2013.02.046

Torrens, F., & Castellano, G. (2013b). Bundlet model of single-wall carbon, BC_2N and BN nanotubes, cones and horns in organic solvents. *Journal of Nanomaterials & Molecular Nanotechnology, 2*, 1000107-1-9.

Uptain, S. M., Kane, C. M., & Chamberlin, M. J. (1997). Basic mechanisms of transcript elongation and its regulation. *Annual Review of Biochemistry, 66*, 117–172. doi:10.1146/annurev.biochem.66.1.117 PMID:9242904

Wadhavane, P. D., Galian, R. E., Izquierdo, M. A., Aguilera-Sigalat, J., Galindo, F., & Schmidt, L. et al. (2012). Photoluminiscence enhancement of CdSe quantum dots: A case of organogel–nanoparticle symbiosis. *Journal of the American Chemical Society, 134*, 20554–20563. doi:10.1021/ja310508r PMID:23214451

Wang, Q. H., Kalantar-Zadeh, K., Kis, A., Coleman, J. N., & Strano, M. S. (2012). Electronics and optoelectronics of two-dimensional transition metal dichalcogenides. *Nature Nanotechnology, 7*, 699–712. doi:10.1038/nnano.2012.193 PMID:23132225

Weber, G. (1975). Energetics of ligand binding to proteins. *Advances in Protein Chemistry, 29*, 1–83. doi:10.1016/S0065-3233(08)60410-6 PMID:1136898

Weng-Sieh, Z., Cherrey, K., Chopra, N. G., Blase, X., Miyamoto, Y., & Rubio, A. et al. (1995). Synthesis of $B_xC_yN_z$ nanotubules. *Physical Review B: Condensed Matter and Materials Physics, 51*, 11229–11232. doi:10.1103/PhysRevB.51.11229 PMID:9977849

Wuister, S. F., de Mello Donegá, C., & Meijerink, A. (2004). Influence of thiol capping on the exciton liminiscence and decay kinetics of CdTe and CdSe quantum dots. *The Journal of Physical Chemistry B, 108*, 17393–17397. doi:10.1021/jp047078c

Xia, X., Jelski, D. A., Bowser, J. R., & George, T. F. (1992). MNDO study of boron-nitrogen analogues of buckminsterfullerene. *Journal of the American Chemical Society, 114*, 6493–6496. doi:10.1021/ja00042a032

Zhu, J., Kase, D., Shiba, K., Kasuya, D., Yudasaka, M., & Iijima, S. (2003). Binary nanomaterials based on nanocarbons: A case for probing carbon nanohorns' biorecognition properties. *Nano Letters, 3*, 1033–1036. doi:10.1021/nl034266q

Chapter 13
An Integrated Design for a CNC Machine

Amro Shafik
University of Toronto, Canada

Salah Haridy
Northeastern University, USA

ABSTRACT

Computer Numerical Control (CNC) is a technology that converts coded instructions and numerical data into sequential actions that describe the motion of machine axes or the behavior of an end effector. Nowadays, CNC technology has been introduced to different stages of production, such as rapid prototyping, machining and finishing processes, testing, packaging, and warehousing. The main objective of this chapter is to introduce a methodology for design and implementation of a simple and low-cost educational CNC prototype. The machine consists of three independent axes driven by stepper motors through an open-loop control system. Output pulses from the parallel port of Personal Computer (PC) are used to drive the stepper motors after processing by an interface card. A flexible, responsive, and real-time Visual C# program is developed to control the motion of the machine axes. The integrated design proposed in this chapter can provide engineers and students in academic institutions with a simple foundation to efficiently build a CNC machine based on the available resources. Moreover, the proposed prototype can be used for educational purposes, demonstrations, and future research.

INTRODUCTION

Over the last 50 years, computer numerical control (CNC) technology has been one of the major developments in manufacturing (Nanfara et al., 1995). This led to a conspicuous impact in manufacturing processes. The implementation of numerical control (NC) has been developed from simple automatic positioning machines controlled by instruction on punched tape or floppy disk to computerized numerical control in which a microcomputer is used to perform all the numerical control tasks (Tseng et al., 1989). The rapid advancement in NC machine technology has been accelerated by dramatic increases in machine programming and computational control (Kolluri & Tseng, 1989). These advances have provided the manufacturing industry with a new

DOI: 10.4018/978-1-4666-6252-0.ch013

and greater degree of freedom in designing and manufacturing different industrial products.

Xie et al. (2012) reviewed the concept, development status and trend of the NC machining simulation technology. Moreover, Xie et al. (2012) emphatically introduced the key technologies of the NC machining simulation technology including the geometric modeling technology, NC code translation, entity collision detection and the material removal process simulation.

Due to this new freedom, along with other related enhancements, significant changes in manufacturing methodologies have been adopted such as the use of computer aided manufacturing and flexible manufacturing systems. The part program for a product manufactured by CNC machines is a very important stage in the manufacturing process. Therefore, many techniques have been developed to generate CNC part programs, for example using developed software and computer aided design/manufacturing (CAD/CAM) systems (Mansour, 2002; Choy & Chan, 2003). Wang et al. (2011) reported the implementation and preliminary evaluation of an intelligent CNC lathe based on the assessment of existing strategy of intelligent machine tool design. Cui et al. (2012) investigated a framework of an error compensation software system. This software system is able to realize software error compensation via NC programs reconstructing. Computer vision has been recently used in many applications in the field of production engineering. These applications include lace cutting, defect analysis, sheet metal cutting, reverse engineering (Huang & Motavalli, 1994), tool wear assessment (Kurada & Bradley, 1997), feature recognition (Tuttle et al., 1998) and stress homogeneity (Chen et al. 2013). Satishkumar and Asokan (2008) outlined the development of an optimization strategy to determine the optimum cutting parameters for CNC multitool drilling system. Chen and Lee (2011) used the grey relational analysis to find the optimal values of parameters of the servo drives and the controller of a five-axis CNC tool

grinder in order to improve precision of grinding and accuracy of end mills. Wang (2011) proposed a new CNC system for ultrasonic vibration drilling based on the in-depth study of embedded systems technology and characteristics of the ultrasonic vibration drilling process. Naithani and Chauhan (2012) reviewed the literature regarding 'machining parameter optimization' for turning operation in CNC machines.

Due to the development of machine design and drive technology, modern CNC machines can be described to an increasingly extent as a characteristic example of complex mechatronic systems. A distinguishing feature of a mechatronic system is the achievement of system functionality through intensive integration of electrical and information (software) sub-functions on a mechanical carrier (Reinhart & Weissenberger, 1999). El Ouafi et al. (2000) presented a new approach to improve the accuracy of multi-axis CNC machines through software compensation of geometric, thermal and dynamic errors. Larson and Cheng (2000) developed a Web-based interactive cam design package which initially developed as a teaching and learning tool for educational use in an undergraduate Computer-Aided Mechanism Design course. Balic et al. (2006) proposed a computer-aided, intelligent and genetic algorithm (GA) based programming system for CNC cutting tools selection, tool sequences planning and optimization of cutting conditions. Álvares et al. (2008) described the implementation of an integrated web-based CAD/CAPP/CAM system for the remote design and manufacture of feature-based cylindrical parts and provided some examples illustrating the remote design, process planning, and manufacture of parts in a CNC turning center. Mokhtar et al. (2009) discussed the machining precedence of interactive and non-interactive STEP-NC features. Ülker et al. (2009) introduced a 'system software' based on a new artificial intelligence (AI) tool, called artificial immune systems (AIS). It is implemented using C programming language on a PC and can be used as an integrated module of a CNC machine tool. Du and Yan (2012) designed a multi-agent system for process planning in STEP-NC based manufacturing, in order to realize the STEP-NC-oriented CNC machining and achieve the optimal performance.

Bi et al. (2011) proposed some useful geometric modeling techniques in the CNC simulation field. Afzeri et al. (2011) introduced the methodology of machining technology for direct remote operation of networked milling machine. Chen et al. (2011) developed a systematic scheme to determine the acceleration and deceleration time of a three-axis CNC milling machine. Zhang et al. (2011) proposed a new data model for computer numerical control (CNC). This model provides rich information for CNC machine tools. Recently, Sato (2012) developed a mathematical model of a CNC rotary table driven by a worm gear. Tan et al. (2012) described the application of an expert system to develop the carbide cutting tools selection system for a CNC lathe machine. Zhang and Song (2012) proposed a real-time Non-uniform rational B-spline (NURBS) interpolator with feedrate optimization for CNC machining tools. This NURBS interpolator helps to make the real-time feedrate meet the CNC command subject to the system dynamics. Zhang et al. (2013) developed a dependence-aware task scheduling (DATS), considering the specific characteristics of CNC system tasks, to ensure the execution of the key preceding task by postponing the execution of the subsequent task with higher priority. Marvizadeh and Choobineh (2013) formulated an integer program to obtain the minimum number of setups for CNC punch presses. Huo and Poo (2013) discussed some of the factors that can affect the accuracy of the contour generated by CNC machines. Zhang et al. (2013) presented a multi-axis modified generalized predictive control approach, in order to improve the motion smoothness and contouring precision for multi-axis high-speed CNC machine tools.

Along with the dramatic advancement in technology and aggressive marketing competition,

CNC technology has attracted much research and scientific work because of its widespread applications in different manufacturing processes. The academic institutes play a vital role in providing students and engineers with a solid foundation of CNC technology research and knowledge. Due to the restrictions on some resources such as the budget, space, and operating cost, the capital-invest system such as CNC machines are infeasible or hardly available for many academic institutes. One possible alternative for the lack of hands-on system is the development of educational schemes for building CNC machines based on the available resources. Such schemes can serve as an effective and convenient tool for both research and instructions. Moreover, these educational schemes stand as a flexible integrated system for studying design strategies, manufacturing techniques, interface systems and programming development (Tseng et al., 1989). Valvo et al. (2012) presented an effective simulator for a CNC milling machine. It can be installed on a common PC and is able to control a CNC machine, read part programs and send instructions to the CNC machine for the cutting process. Haridy et al. (2012) proposed an educational scheme for designing a CNC drilling machine. This scheme provides academic institutions with a simple foundation to efficiently build a CNC machine based on the available resources.

In view of these facts, an educational scheme is proposed in this article to design and built a three-axis CNC drilling machine. A flexible and responsive visual C # program was developed to serve the machine. The design scheme for the CNC drilling machine derives from the need for introducing new features, especially for the educational environment. Using the parallel port output after processing by an interface card as a controller in addition to the economical and flexible design are unique features of the proposed scheme. The CNC machine and software are designed as versatile educational tools. A Visual C # program is developed to control the motion of the stepper motors. Visual C # is a simple, modern, object-oriented, and type-safe programming language derived from C and C++. It combines the high productivity of Microsoft Visual Basic and the raw power of C++. Finally, a user-friendly flexible and responsive software layout is used as an input for the desired positions of the holes. This improves the positional accuracy of the machine.

EXPERIMENTAL SETUP

The construction of the CNC drilling machine can be summarized as follows:

- Construct the basic frame.
- Provide the machine with stepper motors for driving the tables in the three axes and direct current (DC) servo motor for driving the spindle.
- Design the interface electronic card.
- Connect the interface electronic card to the PC parallel port.
- Code a computer program to control the machine from the PC.

THE MECHANICAL DESIGN

The mechanical design of the machine involves the conceptualization of the overall configuration of the machine, drafting, and design analysis to satisfy geometrical and force constraints. After the design process, the manufacture of parts is carried out, subject to a process planning schedule. The assembly of the machine is then performed. The parts are simple in design and easy to assemble. The machine is designed to perform drilling for PCB and relatively soft materials such as plastics. The maximum cutter diameter is 6 mm. The movements are limited to 300 mm in the X, 400 in the Y and 200 mm in the Z direction. Specifications of the machine are summarized in Table 1.

The basic components of the mechanical part are

- Basic frame: is the main frame or structure that holds all components together. It can be made out of a number of different materials. The basic frame must be able to carry Z-axis and spindle, stand without buckling, and be in regular shapes (e.g., rectangular, cylinders…)
- Linear guides: provide a smooth guiding surface on which the movable elements slide. Linear guides must be regular without any surface roundness, and be made of a material that has a high surface finish, good abrasion resistance characteristics and long lifetime (e.g., Chromium).
- Lead screws and bearing: stepper motors are connected to lead screws that are attached to the movable elements of the X, Y and Z axes. Lead screw is the most expensive component of a CNC router system. Lead screw must have a very small deflection not more than several microns (i.e., approximately zero deflection) and be made of a hard material (e.g., steel) to overcome the nut resistance (i.e., lead screws must be harder than nut so that the erosion is most likely to occur in the nut rather than the screw). Thrust ball bearings

Table 1. Mechanical specifications

Item	Specification
Maximum movement	X - 300 mm 300 mm Y - 400 mm 400mm Z - 200 mm 200 mm
Spindle speed	2000 rpm
Maximum feed	180 mm/min
Maximum depth of cut	10 mm
Stepper motors	1.8 degree/step
Axes reduction ratio	5:13
Maximum diameter of cutter	6 mm
Tool holder	Chuck
Workpiece	Printed circuit board (PCB) and plastics

Figure 1. Solid model of the CNC drilling machine

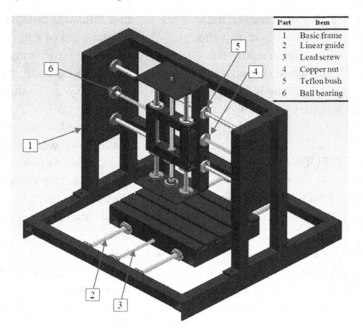

Part	Item
1	Basic frame
2	Linear guide
3	Lead screw
4	Copper nut
5	Teflon bush
6	Ball bearing

are adopted to support the high axial loads and cope efficiently with the movement of the lead screws.

- Bushes and nuts: Teflon bushes are used to provide a flexible and easy motion for the tables along the chromium guides. Copper nuts are used to drive the tables along the lead screws. Copper is a self-lubricant metal, consequently it provides more flexibility and less resistance to the lead screws during the movement.

Figure 1 represents a solid model of the CNC drilling machine while Figure 2 shows the assembly of the X-axis table.

A finite element analysis (FEA) is conducted to check the buckling of Y-frame columns. The total weight of the Z table including the spindle is estimated at 150 N. Hence, the force applied to one column = 150/2 = 75 N. The FEA is applied using Von Misses stress analysis method

with a cantilever mounting assumption for the columns. The results indicate that the design is safe as indicated in Figure 3. Moreover, the stiffness of the machine in x, y and z directions has been determined. The values of the stiffness in x, y and z directions have been found to be 52.36, 39.27 and 78.54 MPa, respectively. These values reflect a reasonable resistance of the structure against deformation.

Figure 2. The assembly of X-axis table

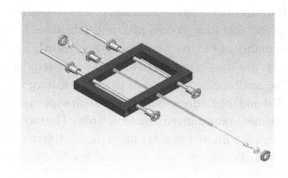

Figure 3. Finite element analysis for Y-frame columns

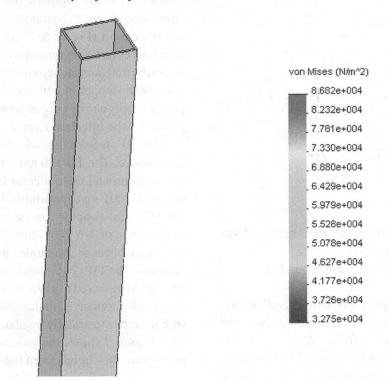

von Mises (N/m^2)

8.682e+004
8.232e+004
7.781e+004
7.330e+004
6.880e+004
6.429e+004
5.979e+004
5.528e+004
5.078e+004
4.627e+004
4.177e+004
3.726e+004
3.275e+004

THE ELECTRICAL AND INTERFACE DESIGN

Unlike many common DC motors which need little more than a battery to operate, stepper motors are unique in that their coils need to be energized and de-energized in a specific order. The personal computer (PC) parallel port output pulses are used to drive these motors after processing by an interface card (Figure 4).

A PC printer port is an inexpensive and yet powerful platform for implementing projects deal-ing with the control of real world peripherals. It can be a very useful I/O channel for connecting circuits to PC. PC parallel port is a 25 pin D-shaped female connector in the back of the computer. It is normally used for connecting computer to printer, but many other types of hardware for that port is available today. The pins of standard Female D-Type connector can be classified as follows

- 8 output pins accessed via the DATA Port.
- 5 input pins (one inverted) accessed via the STATUS Port.

Figure 4. Flow chart of the control system

| **Parallel Port Outputs** | → | **Interface Card** | → | **Stepper Motors** |

Figure 5. Block diagram of the interface card

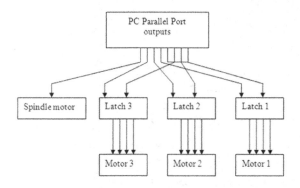

- 4 output pins (three inverted) accessed via the CONTROL Port.
- The remaining 8 pins are grounded.

To output any sequence from the parallel port, the signals must be sent in the required sequence that enables the latch (S74LS37N) in order to transfer this sequence to the stepper driving circuit. A total of three motors can be controlled using addressable data latches in hardware (Figure 5). Also, a buffer can be used for increasing the inputs to eight pins. The motor type used in this system is unipolar, as it is easier to drive. Bipolar motors will not work with this driver circuit, as they need an H-bridge circuit for each coil. It would not be

impossible to use bipolars, but much of the circuitry would need to be modified or replaced. The driving circuit (Figure 6) is really nothing more than four common-emitter Darlington transistors driven by the translator circuit via isolating inverters. 6-Volt stepper motors are used; therefore PC power supply can be used to provide the sufficient power for the interface circuit.

TIP120's is used in place of the TIP110's pictured above. The TIP120 has a built-in clamping diode (to protect the collector from HV spikes), so the 1N4001's can be omitted if TIP120 is used. TIL117 opto-coupler can be used for isolation in the place of 1/6 7407, but they are not really necessary because the diodes provide the safety required. The TIP120 comes in a TO-220 package and can be mounted to a heat sink. The metal tab is electrically connected to the collector, so the heat sink must be electrically insulated from the metal tabs. Figure 7 shows the interface card used for processing the signals from the PC parallel port.

THE PROGRAM IMPLEMENTATION

As aforementioned, the coils of stepper motors need to be energized and de-energized in a specific order. The personal computer (PC) parallel port

Figure 6. Driving circuit of the stepper motor

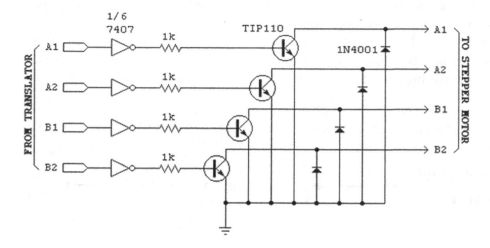

Figure 7. Interface card

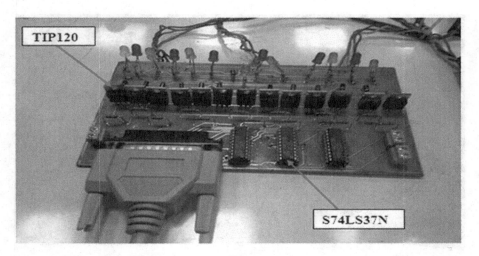

output pulses are used to drive these motors after processing by an interface card (Figure 4). Visual C # program is developed to control the motion of the stepper motors. C# (pronounced C sharp) is a new language introduced by Microsoft in 2001. It is the first component-oriented language in the C and C++ languages family. It's a simple, modern, object-oriented, and type-safe programming language derived from C and C++. It combines the high productivity of Microsoft Visual Basic and the raw power of C++. The basic function of the control program is to convert the output pulses from the parallel port to a rotational motion of the stepper motors through the interface card, and as a result, to a linear motion in X, Y, and Z directions. Three similar half-step stepper motors of 1.8 degree/step are used (i.e., the stepper motor undergoes a rotation of 1.8° for each pulse received). Hence, a revolution of 360° is performed by 200 pulses. The number of revolutions of the stepper motor is reduced by a pulley system with a reduction ratio of 5:13. Therefore, any axis revolution equals to 5/13 of the revolution of the stepper motor. In order to convert the axe revolution into a linear motion, the revolution of the ball screw is multiplied by its pitch size (1.75 mm). Finally, a user friendly flexible and responsive software layout was developed. In this layout, the Cartesian coordinates of the holes are the inputs. Based on the above discussion, the equation used for converting the number of pulses into distances is

No. of pulses = [200× distance] / [1.75 × (5/13)]

The direction of the motion is controlled by the sequence of the sent pulses. For example, if {"0001","0010","0100","1000"} is used for generating a movement in a specific direction, {"1000","0100","0010","0001"} will be used for inverting this movement in the opposite direction.

At last, the three parts (mechanical design, electrical and interface design, and program implementation) are integrated to produce an economical, reliable, and flexible CNC drilling machine (Figure 8).

COST AND ACCURACY COMPARISON

In this section, the accuracy and the cost of the developed CNC machine are compared with those of some commercial CNC systems (Table

Figure 8. CNC drilling machine

2). These commercial CNC systems were chosen based on the degree of the similarity in specifications (e.g., working zone, working speed and axis travel range) with the developed CNC machine. Table 2 indicates the reasonable accuracy and cost of the developed CNC machine compared with the other commercial CNC systems. The whole machine can be built for about $ 1000 with a position accuracy of accuracy 0.003 mm. The developed CNC machine has few transmission elements; consequently its reliability is considerably high. The machine is controlled by an open loop interface system using the PC parallel port. Visual C # can be effectively used for providing justifiable, responsive, and flexible control for the CNC drilling machine. This opens the door for future applications of different programming languages in the CNC technology. The CNC machine can provide a series of arrays to be done with specific increments by one command. Moreover, it has a reference or zero point whose coordinates can be easily defined by the program. These advantages make the educational scheme proposed in this article attractive and economical, especially for the educational and instructional environments.

CONCLUSION

This article presents a systematic integrated design scheme for a CNC drilling machine. The proposed scheme explores the rationale and the procedure of designing, manufacturing and controlling a 3-axes CNC drilling machine. The developed CNC machine can be used for PCB drilling and small diameter holes. The developed CNC machine has a reasonable accuracy and cost compared with similar commercial CNC systems in the marketplace.

Table 2. Cost and accuracy comparison

Manufacturer	Model	Accuracy (mm)	Cost (US $)
Xinyu Machinery (P&G Industrial)	DM17CNC	0.015	2000 - 3000
Nanjing Diding Numerical Control Technology	DL - 1212	0.010	
Shenzhen Zhouyu Intelligent Technology	TXC10005	0.020	
Beili Industry	KC1 - MACH	0.010	
The developed CNC machine		0.003	800-1000

The design proposed in this article can be used for different applications, especially for research and educational purposes. This design can be employed to improve the theoretical knowledge and practical skills of the students and validate research in manufacturing. It lays a foundation for basic research in CNC technology.

FUTURE WORK

For future works, some modifications can be carried out for improving the design of the CNC drilling machine to increase its performance and to introduce different helpful educational modules. These modifications can be divided into two main directions. The first one is concerning the hardware development, such as adding a small-size tool magazine and attaching an automatic tool changer (ATC) unit, adding a flow-controlled coolant system, and adding force and temperature sensors for detecting forces on each axis and for measuring the cutting temperature, respectively. The second direction is regarding the software and controller development. Based on the implanted sensors, the control system can be changed to be of closed-loop type instead of open-loop. In addition, adaptive control can be introduced to automatically update the feed rate, depth of cut, and the coolant flow rate according to the measured forces and the cutting temperature. Nonlinear control algorithms can also be applied to compensate the nonlinearities in the system, which result from frictions, impact backlash, and vibrations.

The goal is to have, eventually, a fully-integrated CNC vertical machining center (VMC) with a challenging price, size, accuracy, and quality, to be used for education and research purposes. The machine will be a scale model of the real industrial VMCs including its main modules and parts. The students can study these different modules, produce parts, and study the effect of changing machining parameters, such as feed rate and depth of cut, on the resulting forces on machining axes and the cutting temperature. They will also be able to tune the nonlinear controller gains and parameters and investigate how this affects the dimensional accuracy and surface quality of the product. All these studies can be done using the updated form of the software package which needs to have a user-friendly graphical user interface (GUI). Furthermore, the researchers can develop novel intelligent and nonlinear control algorithms and use the final proposed design of our CNC machine as an experimental test setup.

REFERENCES

Álvares, A. J., Ferreira, J. C. E., & Lorenzo, R. M. (2008). An integrated web-based CAD/CAPP/CAM system for the remote design and manufacture of feature-based cylindrical parts. *Journal of Intelligent Manufacturing*, *19*(6), 643–659. doi:10.1007/s10845-008-0117-1

Balic, J., Kovacic, M., & Vaupotic, B. (2006). Intelligent Programming of CNC Turning Operations using Genetic Algorithm. *Journal of Intelligent Manufacturing*, *17*(3), 331–340. doi:10.1007/s10845-005-0001-1

Bi, H. X., Li, S. J. & Zhang, Y. R. (2011). The geometric modeling of pieces in virtual milling simulation. *Advanced Materials Research*, *291*, 2262-2265.

Chen, J., & Lee, B. (2011). Parameter optimization of a five-axis tool grinder using Grey Relational analysis. Key Engineering Materials, 458, 246-251.

Chen, J. H., Yeh, S. S., & Sun, J. T. (2011). An S-curve acceleration/deceleration design for CNC machine tools using quintic feedrate function. *Computer-Aided Design and Applications*, *8*(4), 583-592.

Chen, Y., Lochegnies, D., Defontaine, R., Anton, J., Aben, H. & Langlais, R. (2013). Measuring the 2D residual surface stress mapping in tempered glass under the cooling jets: The influence of process parameters on the stress homogeneity and isotropy. *Strain, 49*(1), 60-67.

Choy, H. S., & Chan, K. W. (2003). A corner-looping based tool path for pocket milling. *Computer Aided Design, 35*(2), 155–166. doi:10.1016/S0010-4485(02)00049-0

Cui, G., Lu, Y., Li, J., Gao, D. & Yao, Y. (2012). Geometric error compensation software system for CNC machine tools based on NC program reconstructing. *International Journal of Advanced Manufacturing Technology, 63*(1-4), 169-180.

Du, J. & Yan, X. (2012). Multi-agent system for process planning in STEP-NC based manufacturing. *Research Journal of Applied Sciences, Engineering and Technology, 4*(20), 3865-3871.

El Ouafi, A., Guillot, M., & Bedrouni, A. (2000). Accuracy enhancement of multi-axis CNC machines through on-line neurocompensation. *Journal of Intelligent Manufacturing, 11*(6), 535-545.

Haridy, S., Wu, Z., & Shafik, A. (2012). An educational scheme for a CNC drilling machine. *International Journal of Manufacturing, Materials, and Mechanical Engineering, 2*(2), 1–11. doi:10.4018/ijmmme.2012040101

Huang, C. N., & Motavalli, S. (1994). Reverse engineering of planar parts using machine vision. *Computers & Industrial Engineering, 26*(2), 369–379. doi:10.1016/0360-8352(94)90070-1

Kolluri, S. P., & Tseng, A. A. (1989). Simulation of CNC Controller Features in Graphics-Based Programming. *Computers in Industry, 11*(2), 135–146. doi:10.1016/0166-3615(89)90101-2

Kurada, S., & Bradley, C. (1997). A machine vision system for tool wear assessment. *Tribology International, 30*(4), 295–304. doi:10.1016/S0301-679X(96)00058-8

Larson, j., & Cheng, H. H. (2000). Object-oriented cam design through the internet. *Journal of Intelligent Manufacturing, 11*(6), 515-534.

Mansour, S. (2002). Automatic generation of part programs for milling sculptured surfaces. *Journal of Materials Processing Technology, 127*(1), 31-39.

Marvizadeh, S. Z. & Choobineh, F. F. (2013). Reducing the number of setups for CNC punch presses. *Omega, 41*(2), 226-235.

Naithani, B., & Chauhan, S. (2012). Mathematical modelling approach for determining optimal machining parameters in turning with computer numerical control (CNC) machines. *International Journal of Computer Aided Engineering and Technology, 4*(5), 403–419. doi:10.1504/IJCAET.2012.048838

Mokhtar, A., Xu, X., & Lazcanotegui, I. (2009). Dealing with feature interactions for prismatic parts in STEP-NC. *Journal of Intelligent Manufacturing, 20*(4), 431–445. doi:10.1007/s10845-008-0144-y

Nanfara, F., Uccello, T., & Murphy, D. (1995). *The CNC Workbook: An Introduction to Computer Numerical Control.* Addison-Wesley Publishing Company.

Precision contouring control of machine tools. (2013). *The* International Journal of Advanced Manufacturing Technology, *64*(1-4), 319–333.

Reinhart, G., & Weissenberger, M. (1999). Multi-body simulation of machine tools as mechatronic systems for optimization of motion dynamics in the design process. In *Proceedings of Advanced Intelligent Mechatronics,* (pp. 605-610). IEEE.

Sato, R. (2012). Mathematical Model of a CNC Rotary Table Driven by a Worm Gear. [IJIMR]. *International Journal of Intelligent Mechatronics and Robotics*, 2(4), 27–40. doi:10.4018/ijimr.2012100103

(2008). Selection of optimal conditions for CNC multitool drilling system using non-traditional techniques. *International Journal of Machining and Machinability of Materials*, 3(1), 190–207. Satishkumar, S.Asokan, P.

Sutjipto, A. G. E., Muhida, R., & Konneh, M. (2011). Virtual simulation and remote desktop interface for CNC milling operation. *Advanced Materials Research*, 264, 1643-1647.

Tan, C. F., Singh, R. S., & Kher, V. K. (2012). An expert carbide cutting tools selection system for CNC Lathe machine. *International Review of Mechanical Engineering*, 6(7), 1402-1405.

Tseng, A. A., Kolluri, S. P., & Radhakrishnan, P. (1989). A CNC machining system for education. *Journal of Manufacturing Systems*, 8(3), 207–214. doi:10.1016/0278-6125(89)90042-3

Tuttle, R., Little, G., Corney, J., & Clark, D. E. R. (1998). Feature recognition for NC part programming. *Computers in Industry*, 35(3), 275–289. doi:10.1016/S0166-3615(97)00089-4

Ülker, E., Turanalp, M. E., & Halkaci, H. S. (2009). An artificial immune system approach to CNC tool path generation. *Journal of Intelligent Manufacturing*, 20(1), 67–77. doi:10.1007/s10845-008-0104-6

Valvo, E. L., Licari, R., & Adornetto, A. (2012). CNC milling machine simulation in engineering education. *International Journal of Online Engineering*, 8(2), 33-38.

Wang, B. F. (2011). Research and development of embedded CNC system for drilling based on ARM. *Advanced Materials Research*, 291, 2733-2736.

Wang, C. S., Wiegers, T. & Vergeest, J. S. (2011). An implementation of intelligent CNC machine tools. *Applied Mechanics and Materials*, 44, 557-561.

Xie, X., Xu, A. F., Lu, X. C., & Wang, B. (2012). Research of the numerical control machining simulation. *Advanced Materials Research*, 546, 767-771.

Zhang, C., Li, D., Lai, Y., & Tu, Y.(2013). Dependence-Aware task scheduling for resource-constrained CNC systems. *Advances in Information Sciences and Service Sciences*, 5, 607–615.

Zhang, L. B., You, Y. P., & Yang, X. F. (2013). A control strategy with motion smoothness and machining precision for multi-axis coordinated motion CNC machine tools. *International Journal of Advanced Manufacturing Technology*, 64(1-4), 335-348.

Zhang, X. T., & Song, Z. (2012). An iterative feedrate optimization method for real-time NURBS interpolator. *International Journal of Advanced Manufacturing Technology*, 62, 1273-1280.

Zhang, Y., Rauch, M., Xie, H., Zhao, Y., Xu, X., & Liu, Y. (2011). Machining simulation - A technical review and a proposed concept model. *International Journal of Internet Manufacturing and Services*, 3, 59-75.

Chapter 14
Computer–Aided Ceramic Design:
Its Viability for Building User–Centered Design

Folasayo Enoch Olalere
Universiti Malaysia Kelantan (UMK), Malaysia

Ab Aziz Bin Shuaib
Universiti Malaysia Kelantan (UMK), Malaysia

ABSTRACT

This chapter investigates the knowledge regarding how user-centered design can be achieved during ceramic product development with the aid of computer-aided ceramic design. The chapter gives the general overview of ceramics, computer-aided design, and its application in ceramic product development. It also illuminates on product emotion, its influence on consumers' behaviour, and how it can be integrated into new products. With reference to desire emotion, the chapter elaborates on the determining factors and the resulting appraisal that will elicit the desire emotion. Furthermore, it analyses the systematic approach in building user-centred design in new products. Based on this understanding, a study is described where a newly developed mug design and a multi-functional ceramic pot were tested to know emotive responses of people towards the products. The results from the study show some interesting findings by demonstrating the theories in practice and also reveal the viability of computer-aided design as a tool for building user-centered design.

INTRODUCTION

According to Chapman (2009), an approach to sustainable user-centred design reduces the consumption and waste of natural resources by increasing the resilience of relationships estab-

lished between consumer and product. With the arrival of economical development and technical progress, consumption demand has transformed from quantitative consumption to perceptual consumption. Therefore, despite the importance of technology capability, technology is not only

DOI: 10.4018/978-1-4666-6252-0.ch014

what it takes to captivate customers (Boatwright & Cagan, 2010), products are meant to satisfy some functional requirements such as; aspiration, cultural, social and emotional needs. This is because; consumer needs products that don't just do the right thing but also make them feels the right ways. They want to use products that should be functional at a physical level, usable at a psychological level and should be attractive at a subjective and emotional level.

The concept of emotion in products has existed many decades ago. In 1970s, Professor Mitsuo Nagamachi developed Kansei engineering which focuses on the development or improvement of products and services by translating customer's psychological feelings and needs into product parameters. Kansei Engineering parametrically links customer's emotional responses (i.e. physical and psychological) to a product or service with their properties and characteristics. In consequence, products can be designed to bring forward the intended feeling. This was also the subject of Pieter Desmet's research project where he tried to unravel the relationship between product and emotion. Along with his research, he also developed a Product-Emotion measuring instrument (PrEmo) with which emotion towards a product can be measured.

Research by Boatwright and Cagan (2010) revealed that people pay for products that address their emotional needs in all types of businesses. Therefore, product emotion is critical to the long-term success of any product that customers interact with directly or indirectly. In other words, engaging emotion as a partner to technology will deliver the next market place products that will captivate customers. In the present world of competitive and saturated market, corporations need to seek ways of engaging consumers in order to maintain their production rates. Thus, an emotive connection between product and user is imperative to the success or failure of a product (Overbeeke *et al.*, 1999). This is because, emotion in its various forms is a strong driving factor for a consumer

want; therefore, consumers needs to be captivated to desire, wanting new things even before the old had been invalidated.

Although, collaborations between manufacturers and supplies are becoming increasingly more usual, it is still far from common for the customer to be considered as a fundamental participant in the collaborative design chain (Camarinha-Matos *et al.*, 1999). The different types of customers that will filter the product throughout its life cycle are stakeholders in the process and should be given preferences from the very earliest design stages. In the light of this, this book chapter investigates the knowledge regarding how user-centre design can be achieved during ceramic product development with the aid of computer aided ceramic design. The chapter gives the general overview of ceramics, computer-aided design and its application in ceramic product development. It also illuminates on product emotion, its influence on consumers' behaviour and how it can be integrated into new product. With reference to desire emotion, the chapter elaborates on the determining factors and the resulting appraisal that will elicits the desire emotion. Furthermore, it analysed the systematic approach in building user-centred design in new product. Based on this understanding, a study was performed where a newly developed mug design and a multi-functional ceramic pot were tested to know emotive responses of people towards the products. The result from the study shows some interesting findings by demonstrating the theories in practice and also reveals the viability of computer aided design as tool for building user centered design.

CERAMICS OVERVIEW

Ceramics is the art and science of making useful products for man from inorganic, non-metallic materials by the action of heat and subsequent cooling (CTIOA, 2011). It can also be defined as heat-resistant, non-metallic, inorganic solids that are generally made up of compounds from metallic and non-metallic elements. Although different types of ceramics can have very different properties, in general ceramics are corrosion-resistant and hard, but brittle. Most ceramics are also good insulators and can withstand high temperatures. These properties have led to their use in virtually every aspect of modern life.

The two main categories of ceramics are traditional and advanced ceramics. Traditional ceramics are produced from materials that are obtained from common, naturally occurring raw materials such as clay minerals and quartz sand (Encyclopaedia Britannica, 2012). Traditional ceramics include objects made from clay and cements that have been hardened by heating at high temperatures. These include dishes, crockery, flowerpots and roof and wall tiles. Advanced ceramics includes carbides, oxides, nitrides and many other materials including the mixed oxide ceramics that can act as superconductors. Advanced ceramics requires modern processing techniques, and the development of these techniques has led to advances in medicines and engineering. Figure 1 and Figure 2 illustrates the difference and relationship between traditional and advance ceramics;

The overlapping relationship between traditional and advance ceramics results in the three classifications of ceramic product. These include; artistic ceramics, consumer ceramic products and engineering ceramics.

Artistic ceramics are creative ceramic pieces which are aesthetically pleasing; they focus more on the aesthetic values and less on functionality. They are concerned with the beauty, art and the perception of the final output product and the objectives is to create new concept and direction. Some of the factors that are considered in artistic ceramics production are perception, culture and product emotion of the customer. Examples of artistic ceramics include pottery wares, sculptural piece etc. Consumer products in ceramics are ceramic products produced meanly for personal or household use. The products focus on both the functionality and aesthetic values and the objectives are to solve problems, meet need and also create new innovations. The product includes some house hold utensils and fittings such as sanitary wares, kitchen wares, table wares, etc.

Engineering ceramics is the science and technology of creating objects from inorganic, non-metallic materials. This is done either by the action of heat, or at lower temperature using precipitation reactions from high purity chemical solutions. The term includes the purification of raw materials, the study and production of the

Figure 1. Illustration of the differences between traditional and advanced ceramic

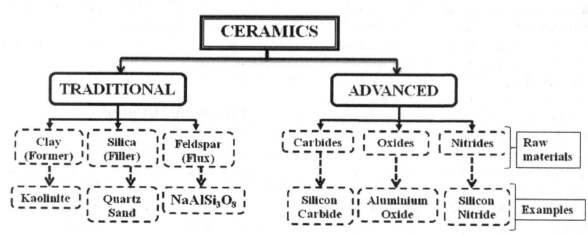

Figure 2. Overlapping relationship between traditional and advanced ceramics

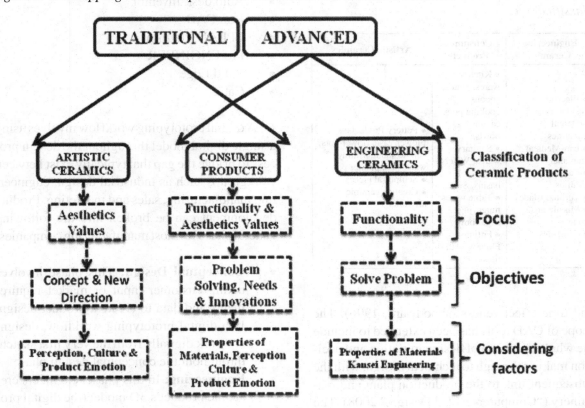

chemical compounds concerned, their formation into components and the study of their structure, composition and properties. Wide range of industries uses the applications of engineering ceramics, these include; mining, aerospace, medicine, refinery, food and chemical industries, packaging science, electronics, industrial and transmission electricity and guided light wave transmission (Kingery et al., 2006). Table 1 highlights examples of ceramic products in each classification.

COMPUTER AIDED DESIGN

Computer Aided design (CAD) also known as Computer Aided Design and Drafting (CADD) is the use of computer technology for the process of design and design documentation (Autodesk, 2013a). It is a computer application developed as a form of automation that help designers prepare drawings, specifications, parts lists and other design related elements using special graphics and calculation intensive computer pragrams. This technology is used for a wide variety of products in such fields as architecture, engineering and industrial design (Jackie, 2013). Some of the CAD software used by designers include; AutoCAD, Solid Works, Solid Edge, EPLAN Platform, Autodesk Inventor etc.

The use of computer aided tools has impacted significantly in the execution of technological innovation in almost all spheres of industrial design products development. Computer aided designs (CAD) in ceramics production has been expressed through conceptualization of ideas to realization of processes in the production of ceramics prototypes that utilize drawing seed, quality production, quick modifications, production innovation, cost

Table 1. Examples of ceramic products in each classification

Engineering Ceramics	Consumer Products	Artistic Ceramics
• Electric Insulators • Dental Ceramics • Bio-Medical Implants • Furnace Linings • Turbine Blades • Missile nose cone • Crucibles	• Kitchen wares: plates, spoons, cooking pots, casseroles, bowls. • Sanitary wares: Water closets, basins, Sinks. • Table wares: mugs, jug, sugar bowl. • Fittings: Floor & wall tiles.	• Pottery Products: Flower vase, flower pots, candle stand, ashtray, water jars, planter pots. • Sculptural pieces. • Creative ceramic artworks

and time effectiveness (Woodward, 1996). The scope of CAD tools has been extended to include the whole spectrum of design initiation and decision making through to technical design, with the subsequent link to the production plant and machinery ("Computer- Aided Design," 2008). The chart below illustrates the application of CAD as tools in ceramic product development (Figure 3).

Digital Prototyping

Digital prototyping helps product developers to design, iterate, optimize, validate and visualize their products digitally throughtout the product development process (Autodesk, 2013b). Companies often adopt digital prototyping with the goal of improving communication between product development stakeholders, getting products to market faster and facilitating product innovation. Some of the CAD softwares used by designers for digital prototyping includes;

- AutoCAD
- Siemens NX CAD
- Auto desk Algo
- Solid works

- Auto desk Inventor
- Iron CAD
- EPLAN Platform
- Pro ENGINEER
- Solid Edge
- Catia

A digital prototyping workflow involves using a single digital model throughout the design process to bridge the gap that typically exist between workgroups such as industrial design, engineering, manufacturing, sales and marketing. Product development can be broken into the following general phases at most manufacturing companies;

- **Conceptual Design:** This phase involves taking customer input or market requirements and data to create a product design. In a digital prototyping workflow, designers work digitally from the very first sketch, throughout the conceptual design phase.
- **Engineering:** In this phase, engineers create the product's 3D model (the digital prototype), integrating design data developed during the conceptual design phase. At this phase, the digital prototype is a fully real-

Figure 3. Application of CAD tools in ceramic product development

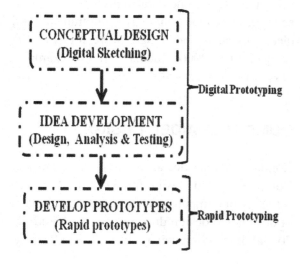

istic digital model of the complete product. Engineers test and validate the digital prototype throughout their design process to make the best possible design decision and avoid costly mistakes. Using the digital prototype, engineers can

- Perform integrated calculations and stress, deflection and motion simulations to validate designs.
- Test how moving parts will work and interact.
- Evaluate different solutions to motion problems.
- Test how the design functions under real-world constraints.
- Conducts stress analysis to analyze material selection and displacement.
- Verify the strength of a part.

- **Manufacturing:** This input helps engineers and manufacturing experts work together on the digital prototype throughout the design process to ensure that the product can be produced cost effectively. Manufacturing teams can see the product exactly as its intended, and provide input on manufacturability.

- **Customer Involvement:** Rather than waiting for a physical prototype to be complete, companies that use digital prototyping bring customers into the product development process early. They show customers realistic renderings and animations of the product's digital prototype so they'll know what the product looks like and how it will function. This early customer involvement helps companies get sign-off up front, so they don't waste time designing, engineering and manufacturing a product that doesn't fulfil the customer's expectations.

- **Marketing:** Using 3D CAD data from the digital prototype, companies can create realistic visualizations, renderings, and animations to market products in prints, on the web, in catalogues, or in television commercials.

Rapid Prototyping

Rapid prototyping is the automatic construction/fabrication of physical objects directly from computer aided design (CAD) data sources. Rapid prototyping is often the best manufacturing process available for small production runs and complicated objects. Most prototypes require from three to seventy-two hours to build, depending on the size and complexity of the object (Williams, 1998). This may seem slow, but it is much faster than the weeks or months required to make a prototype by traditional means such as machining. These dramatic time savings allow manufacturers to bring products to market faster and more cheaply. According to Steven (1995), in 1994, Pratt & Whitney were able to achieved cost reduction and time savings of 70 to 90 percent by incorporating rapid prototyping into their investment casting process.

There are different rapid prototyping techniques, each with unique strengths. However, because RP technologies are being increasingly used in non-prototyping applications, the techniques are often collectively referred to as solid free-form fabrication; computer automated manufacturing, or layered manufacturing (William, 1998). These systems add and bond materials in layers to form objects. With this additive technologies, object can be form with any geometric complexity or intricacy without the need for elaborate machine setup of final assembly (Venuvinod & Ma, 2004). Also, rapid prototyping systems reduce the construction of complex objects to a manageable straight forward and relatively fast process. This has result in their used by engineers as a way to reduce time to market in manufacturing, to better understand and communicate product designs, and to make rapid tooling to manufacture those products. Surgeons, architects, artist and individuals from many other disciplines also routinely use the technology. Table 2 illustrates the different prototyping technologies and their base materials.

PRODUCT EMOTION AND ITS INFLUENCE ON CONSUMERS' BEHAVIOUR

According to Carlson (1997), emotions differ from moods in term of time and physiological effects; emotions elicit a sharp change with a physiological change while moods are longer and less intense. Oxford English Dictionary (1999) defines emotion as an intense feeling contrasted with reason. Consumer behavior has assumed a hierarchy of effects where cognitive activity is followed by emotional evaluation in the formation of an attitude, which ultimately results in behavior (Elliott, 1998). According to Wrigley (2009), the emotional attachment between user and product is one of complex behavior and multifaceted reasoning, powerful enough to provoke and motivate consumers to select and purchase one product over the choice of another.

Table 2. Prototyping technologies and their base materials

Prototyping Technologies	Base Materials
Selective Laser Sintering (SLS)	Thermoplastic & metal powders
Direct Metal Laser Sintering (DMLS)	Alloy metals
Fused Deposition Modeling (FDM)	Thermoplastic, eutectic metals
Stereolithography (SLA)	Photopolymer
Laminated Object Manufacturing (LOM)	Paper
Electron Beam Melting (EBM)	Titanium alloys
3D Printing (3DP)	High performance composite

The influence of emotion in relation to products is evident in product; purchase, use, why people desire something and why attractive things work better. The psychological impact of product attributes on consumer's behavior was also confirmed by Norman in his explanation of the discovery by Kurosu & Kashimura (1995) that 'attractive things work better.' Norman (2004, p77) states: "Negative emotions kick in when there is a lack of understanding, when people feel frustrated and out of control; first uneasiness, then irritation, and if the lack of control and understanding persists, even anger." Whereas "when we are happy our though process expand, becoming more creative, more imaginative. That is, attractive things make you feel good, therefore if the user feels happy from the appearance, they are more likely to find solutions to the problem they encounter" (Norman, 2004), and thus, they appear to work better.

However, every group of user experiences different emotions towards a given product; this is as a result of different appraisal (Desmet, 2002). An appraisal is a judgment of the significance of a product to our concerns. It is non-intellectual because it is automatic and unconscious (Desmet, 2002). Human concerns are 'desired end-states' and every emotion hides a concern (Luke, 2009). According to Frijda (1994), concerns can be described as points of reference in the appraisal process. Therefore, all emotions are preceded and elicited by an appraisal (Roseman & Smith, 2001). As identified by Desmet (2002), there are four main product concerns that determine the nature of emotion that will be elicited by customer's appraisal (Figure 4). These are attitudes, goals, standard and knowledge & expectation. However, Desmet (2002) stated that knowledge & expectations is not a concern type but is relative to the appraisal of novelty (creativity).

1. **Attitudes**: Are dispositional likes (or dislikes) for certain objects or attributes of objects. They are our tastes for things. Therefore, a product that matches costumer's

Figure 4. Product concern that determines the nature of emotion

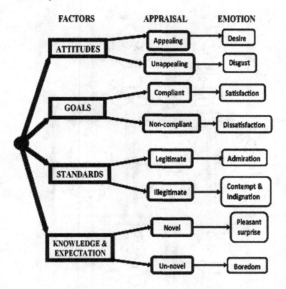

attitudes will be appraised as appealing and will result in an emotion such as desire. Whereas, a product that is incompatible with attitudes will be appraised as unappealing thereby resulting in an emotion such as disgust (Desmet, 2002).

2. **Goals**: Are some things we want or wish to obtain. It is how we would like things to be so therefore, a product that satisfies a goal will be appraised as motive compliant and this lead to emotion such as satisfaction. While a product that act like a barrier to a goal will be appraised as non-complaint and will result in an emotion such as dissatisfaction (Desmet, 2002).

3. **Standards:** Are our beliefs, norms, or conventions of how we think things should be. Therefore, a product that meet customer's standard is legitimate and this result in an emotion such as admiration while a product that conflict with customer's standard is illegitimate, resulting in an emotion such as contempt and indignation (Desmet, 2002).

4. **Knowledge and expectation**: Is our reference to which we know is fact. This is developed throughout our life from experience and education. Therefore, a product that obeys customer's knowledge or an expectation is appraised as un-novel and results in an emotion such as boredom, while a product that deviates from our knowledge or an expectation is appraised as novel, resulting in an emotion such as pleasant surprise (Desmet, 2002).

Therefore, the four product concern identified by Desmet results in 8 emotion experience which includes four (4) pleasant emotions (desire, satisfaction, admiration, pleasant surprise) and four (4) unpleasant emotions (disgust, dissatisfaction, contempt, boredom). However, the complete Desmet's model comprises of 14 emotions, 7 pleasant and 7 unpleasant. He refined 347 emotions down to 14 through several studies. The aim was to realize a manageable set of emotions that where distinct and relative to the context (Luke, 2009). With the 14 emotions, Desmet creates an emotion measuring tool, PrEmo (Figure 5), which is specifically for measure emotions elicited for a product appearance.

Also, Mittal (1988) developed characteristics of emotion into a model of "Affective Choice Mode". This model applies to the purchase of expressive products, and suggests that emotion-based choice is holistic self-focused and unable to be verbalized. Elliott (1998) explained holistic choice as choice that consumers are unable to separate out the individual attributes but form an overall impression. However, choice is self-focused in that emotional judgments of expressive products involve the judge directly. According to Zajonc (1980), emotional judgments are made almost instantaneously and reflect basic subjective feelings which may not have verbal descriptors. Therefore, emotion relies much more on non-verbal channels of communication.

Figure 5. The PrEmo interface (Desmet, 2003b)

Engaging Consumers through Elements of Desire

Desire is a sense of longing for a something or hoping for an outcome. The same sense is expressed by emotions such as craving or hankering. Desire can also be defined as the human appetite for a given object of attention. For example, desire for a product can be stimulated by advertising or showcasing the product attractively; which attempts to give buyers a sense of lack or wanting. Thus, Hobbes (1588–1679) asserted that human desire is the fundamental motivation of all human action, and the essence of desire is the readiness to approach or bring about situations of satisfaction

(Frijda, 1986). Desire can be brought about in three different ways; desire of consequence, desire of presence and the desire of identity (Desmet, 2002).

Desire of Consequence

This focus on the anticipated event of using the product which may fulfill a goal and the appraisal is motive compliance (Luke, 2009). According to Desmet (2003a), we never buy a product without having some motive to invest our resources, therefore, products can be regarded as instrument because we belief they can help us accomplish our goals. Goals refer to the states of affairs that we want to obtain; it is described by Ortony *et al.*,

(1988) as how we would like things to be. Our goals are the points of reference in the appraisal of motive compliance (Desmet, 2003a); thus, a product that facilitates goal achievement will be appraised as motive compliant, and therefore elicit emotion like satisfaction (Figure 6). For example, if wearing a particular pair of elegant shoes will have the consequence of being attractive; then, a person that has a goal to be attractive will appraise this particular pair of shoes as motive compliant and experience satisfactory emotion, thus, will desire to buy (Desmet, 2003a).

Desire of Presence

This is the focus of the object itself, this matches an attitude of aesthetics, and the appraisal is appealingness (Desmet, 2002). As products are physical objects, they look, feel, smell, taste and sound in a particular way. Each of these perceivable characteristics can be both delight and offend our senses (Desmet, 2003a). Therefore, Desmet opines that products can be appraised in terms of their appealingness and the concerns that are the points of reference in the appraisal of appealingness are attitudes. According to Ortony *et al.,* (1988), our

attitudes are our dispositional likings (or disliking) for certain objects or attributes of objects. Attitudes can be in respect to aspect or features of products (color or material) and can also be in respect to product styles. However, some attitudes are innate while some are learned. Thus a product that corresponds with our attitudes is appraised as appealing and will elicit emotions like fascination (Figure 7). In some cases, attitudes are embedded with personal meaning, for example, one can have a dispositional liking for a dress because it was a gift from someone special.

Desire of Identity

This is the focus of the products personality which matches a self ideal standard and therefore appraised to be legitimate. According to Desmet (2002), it is seen as a social desire through a personal identification with the product. Our standards are how we believe things should be and how people should act (Ortony *et al,* 1988), thus, standards are human concerns relevant to product emotions. Most standards are socially learned and represent the beliefs in terms of which moral and other kinds of judgmental evaluations are made

Figure 6. Illustration of emotion elicited through desire of consequence

Figure 7. Illustration of emotion elicited through desire of presence

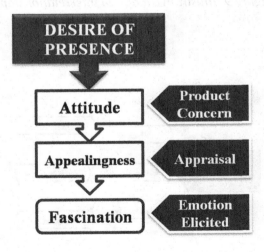

(Desmet, 2003a, p. 9). Products are embedded in our social environment; they are designed; used and owned by people. Therefore, since we cannot separate our view on products from our judgments of the people we associate them with, we tend to apply our social standards and norms, and appraise products in terms of legitimacy (Desmet, 2003a). Thus, products that meet our standards are appraised as legitimate and this elicit emotion like admiration (Desmet, 2002) (Figure 8). As stated by Desmet (2002), we can also 'resonate' with products as if they were somehow people; for example, "This Jeep is as relaxed as I would like to be myself."

Figure 8. Illustration of emotion elicited through desire of identity

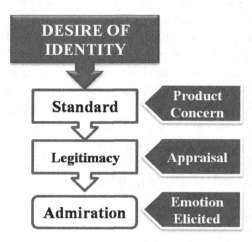

INTERRELATIONSHIP BETWEEN NORMAN'S THREE LEVELS OF DESIGN AND EMOTIONAL DESIRE

Norman (2004) breaks down emotional responses into three levels of design which are; visceral design, behavioral design and reflective design. According to Luke (2009), the three levels come from; within our instincts, visceral, from use, behavioral, reflective and from outside influence & aspiration. Each of the three levels of design is as important as the other, however, they requires dif-

ferent approach by the designer (Norman, 2004). The three ways buy which desire can be brought about are believed to be related to Norman's three levels of design as shown in Figure 9 below.

Visceral Design

Visceral design evokes our inner instincts and human drives. It's a foundation level of product emotions. The principles underlying visceral design are wired in, consistent across people and cul-

Figure 9. Illustrative diagram interrelationship between Norman's three levels of design and emotional desire

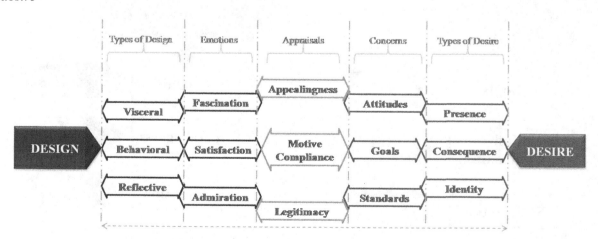

tures (Norman, 2004). According to Luke (2009), when something triggers an emotion at a visceral level, it has an immediate unknowing impact to a person. At visceral level, physical features (look, feel, etc) dominate (Norman, 2004). Therefore, attractiveness is a visceral level phenomenon where the response is entirely to the surface look of an object (Norman, 2004). For example, when a consumer takes one look at something and says 'I want it', before asking 'what does it do' and 'how much it cost' (Luke, 2009). Thus, it can be deduced that the attractiveness/fascination is as a result of the appealing appraisal which originates from product concern known as attitude. Hence, a visceral design will bring about a type of emotional desire known as 'desire of presence'.

Behavioral Design

Behavioral level is entirely about the use and performance of the product; appearance is less relevant. However, the appearance in context of the use is a contributing factor (Luke, 2009). Behavioral design addresses four main components; function, understandability; usability and physical feel. The function comes first while understandability focuses on establishing a proper conceptual model. However, a product that does what is required and is understandable may still not be usable. Therefore, usability needs to be put into consideration; it is the critical test of a product to know how the product will perform and how comfortable it feels to use. Physical feels also matters because we are biological creatures that interact between our sensory systems and the environment; therefore, they are critical to our behavioral assessment of a product. Behavioral design that addresses these four components will elicit a satisfactory emotion. This is because, it will fulfill a goal (product concern) and will therefore be appraised as motive compliant. Thus, a behavioral designed product will bring about emotional 'desire of consequence'.

Reflective Design

Reflective design points to our culture, meaning of a product or its use (Norman, 2004). It's how we see the products reflecting our self-image and aspirations to others (Luke, 2009). This is due to products playing an important role in the statements they make to others. According to Luke (2009), the reflective level is similar to Jordan (2002) Ideo-pleasure, which is where one appreciates the aesthetics, or the quality or perhaps the extent to which a product enhance life and respects the environment. However, reflective level product is about long-term customer experience and interaction. Reflective design elicit admiration emotion; this is because, the product matches self ideal standard and is therefore appraised to be legitimate. Thus, reflective level product will bring about emotional desire known has 'desire of identity'.

BUILDING USER-CENTERED DESIGN IN NEW PRODUCT

According to Venuvinod and Ma (2004), product development is a creative process and also an iterative process. An interesting view confirmed by Norman (2006) shows that a company that want success and guaranteed good design must approach the design in a structured iterative way. As each design concept is developed, it needs to be evaluated preferably with the aid of a prototype so that opportunities for improvement are identified. This cycle needs to be repeated until a satisfactory final design is reached. Figure 10 illustrate the modern product development cycle.

Norman (2004, p83) states that good behavioural design has to be fundamental part of the design process from the very start. It cannot be adopted once the product has been completed; therefore, user-centred design needs to be intrinsic to the development process (Mc Donagh Philip & Lebbon, 2000).

Figure 10. Modern product development

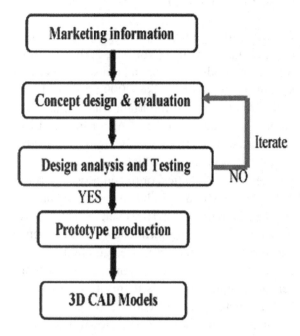

In order to achieve this, product emotion must be integrated into the conceptual design and evaluation stage of the development cycle. This is the stage where designers are expected to develop or improve products and services by translating customer's psychological feelings and needs into product design parameters which will bring forward the intended feelings. In order to identify consumer's psychological feelings and conceptualized product that will bring the intended feelings to them, designers has to do feasibility study on the targeted consumer by investigating their culture, perception and emotion. With the knowledge of these, designers can sketch and draft out the concept putting in mind their aim and objectives which include functionality, problem solving, needs and innovations etc.

Application of CAD in Building User-Centred Design

The scope of computer aided design (CAD) has been extended to include the spectrum from design initiation and decision making through to techni-

cal design, with subsequent link to the production plant and machinery ("Computer-Aided Design," 2008). Therefore, in other to enhance and reduce the time and cost in building user-centred design, CAD tools can be applied at the creating stage of the development process. According to Crossley (2003), the creating stage is the stage where designers define problems and create relevant ideas. To get these idea in an iterative prototypes, CAD tools can be employed as they enables iteration, quick modification, drawing speed, good rendering etc of visual prototypes. The use of CAD application at this stage will also help to link up with the other stages of development process easily and it can also be use to generate a rapid prototypes if the need for physical models arises.

Using 3D CAD data (digital prototypes), designers can create realistic visualizations, renderings and animations of their product ideas as this will help to gauge the emotive response behaviour of users. Also, early customer/user involvement will help companies not to waste time designing, engineering and manufacturing a product that doesn't fulfil the customer's expectations. Figure 11 demonstrates how designers can use computer aided design to know the impression and emotive response of users/customer so it can guide them in building user centred design in consumer ceramics product.

HOW CAN DESIGNERS APPLY THIS KNOWLEDGE?

The process of executing the user-centred design strategy begins by identifying emotions that consumers seek and ends with a product that meets those desires and this advance the connection of the company with the customer while extending the brand and reputation of the company within current and potential customers (Boatwright & Cagan, 2010). But if a company wants to achieve great design they need "someone with vision" to guide the process towards their goal using a

Figure 11. Building user-centred design from customers' impression

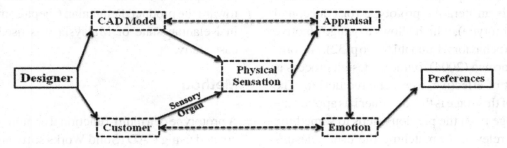

structured approach (Luke, 2009, p. 40). The approach described by Crossley (2003) in his paper "Building Emotions in Designs" can be adopted by designers. Crossley (2003) break his PDD[1] approach into a route of five overlapping stages, which are: Immersing, Storytelling, Observing, Creating and Communicating. From these stages, designers can gain an insight into the user's attitudes, aspiration and values.

Immersing

This is where designers immersed themselves into the user's lives, looking into their environments so as to gain clue about their value systems. According to Crossley (2003), "understanding people and their life context includes the knowledge, attitudes, aspirations and values that determine how people interpret the objects, situations and interactions they meet in their day-to-day activities." Thus, context immersing will help designers to identify and understand their users' belief system; because, the environments that people craft round themselves are rich with information, about personalities, values and lifestyles (Crossley, 2003, p. 38). Norman (2004, p. 225) also said that our possessions reflect our personalities. Therefore the essence of this stage is for designer to get clues regarding anticipated behaviors of users (Crossley, 2003 p. 38).

Storytelling

After understanding the anticipated behaviors of users, designers at this stage need to build empathy and understand users' past experiences. According to Crossley (2003), "empathic stance orients us as designers to other people's experience and meaning making, which is communicated to us through narrative." Thus, user needs to tell designers their experiences through stories. This is important because, to design relationships with products, designers need to understand fully people's relationship with object, other people, environment etc (Crossley, 2003, p. 39).

Observing

This is the third stage where designers watch customer using products so as to find out what they do with the product, what frustrate them and what gives them satisfaction (Crossley, 2003 p. 40). From this, designers will understand from a variety of angles and perspectives how they use products; thereby give insight on how they can enhance the behavioral level of design.

Creating

Here, designers need to focus on defining the essence of the problem and creating relevant ideas. These ideas would be in visual methods that both the designer and people can understand. A suitable method is an iterative prototype (or conceptual rough prototype), which allows to gauge emotive response behaviors (Lundahl, 2006 p. 32). According to Norman (2004), iterative design process is the heart of effective, user-centered design. The benefit of this stage is that designer has applied the knowledge from the previous steps to something suitably relevant to matching the user's desires and belief system.

Communicating

As the designer has immersed into the user space, the findings gathered should also be presented for others to take in. Therefore, it is suitable to present the findings in a visual manner. One method Crossley suggests is to use a promotional video as this can, capture the desired experience; bring visions to life, enabling them to communicate complex ideas and feelings in a more effective way. The benefit of this is to make sure the empathy is understood by all.

STUDY ONE

In order to test the viability of CAD in achieving user-centred design, a study was performed where a CAD-model of a multi-functional ceramic pot was created and a questionnaire with the image (CAD-model) and eight emotions was given to

participants so as to know their emotional response toward the product. Pengkalan Chepa community in Kelantan state of Malaysia was used as the case study.

Method

A prototype of a multi-functional ceramic pot was created using CAD (Solid Works software). This pot is multi-functional because it can be used as cooking pot and steamer simultaneously (Figure 12). In order to make the prototype user-centred design and also to know the emotional response of people towards the product, a questionnaire was given to a group of participants. This questionnaire consists of the previously mentioned eight (8) emotions (desire, satisfaction, admiration, pleasant surprise, disgust, dissatisfaction, contempt and boredom) and the image of the ceramic pot. Participants were asked to rate each of the emotions 0, 1, or 2 against the product (ceramic pot). These ratings referred to the following:

0: I do not feel this emotion (low emotion)
1: I feel some of this emotion (medium emotion)
2: I do feel this emotion (high emotion)

The participants were asked to rate all of the emotions, to be impartial and to leave a comment for the product. Twenty people participated and are randomly sampled within Pengkalan Chepa community.

Figure 12. Images of the multi-functional ceramic pot

Result

To analyse the result of the study, the following chart (Figure 13) was produced plotting the number of people that felt each level of emotion (high, medium, and low) towards the product against the eight emotions. Also, a chart (Figure 14) was plotted to show the emotional rating of participants. This was achieved by plotting the mean value of emotion against the eight emotions. Lastly, a pie chart was produced to compare the pleasant and unpleasant emotion elicited.

Discussion

Overall, the results produced some interesting findings such as; lack of participant with high boredom and contempt emotion. Generally, the study was able to demonstrate the theories in practice and to discover insight into product tested.

Emotion Elicited

The highest mean value for the product is pleasant surprise (Figure 14). This constant is apparent due to the conditions of pleasant surprise (Desmet, 2002). That is, the product deviates from their knowledge or expectation and is therefore appraised as novel, resulting in a pleasant surprise. This also reflects in participants comments such as; "it seems to be a new innovation", and "I'm seeing this kind of pot for the first time".

It was also noticed that satisfaction and admiration have the same mean value; this implies that the product elicited the same rate of emotional satisfaction and admiration. Also, boredom emotion has the lowest mean value. This is relative to pleasant surprise that has the highest mean value. This also revealed that the product is new to most of the participants.

Pleasant vs. Unpleasant Emotions

The overall emotions used were 8; 4 pleasant emotions (desire, satisfaction, admiration and pleasant surprise) and 4 unpleasant emotions (disgust, dissatisfaction, contempt and boredom). With respect to the overall emotions elicited by participants towards the product, 74% were pleasant emotions while 26% were unpleasant emotion (Figure 15). Dissatisfaction has the highest mean value among unpleasant emotion. This implies that the product

Figure 13. Chart of number of people that felt each level of emotion, against the 8 emotion

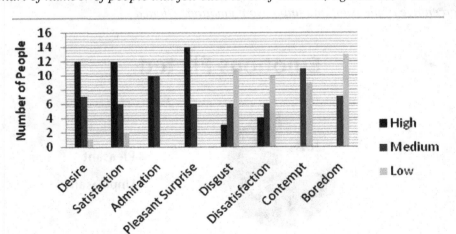

Figure 14. Emotional rating of participants towards the product

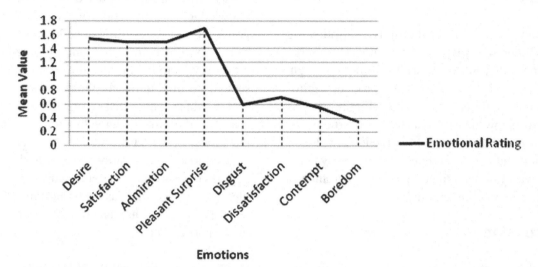

does not satisfy some participants' goal, it was therefore appraised as non-motive compliant and this result in emotional dissatisfaction. This reflected in some participants comment such as; "it looks new but I prefer steel pot and steamer".

Since the highest percentage of the emotional response was pleasant toward the product, therefore it's a confirmation that user-centred design as being successfully integrated into the product.

STUDY TWO

To further test the theory in practice, another study was performed on two ceramic mugs to know the level of desire emotions they will elicit. The first mug (Product A) is a common design of ceramic mug with handle while the second mug (Product B) is a handle-free, double sided mug (Figure 16). The students of the Faculty of Creative Technologies

Figure 15. Percentage of pleasant and unpleasant emotions elicited

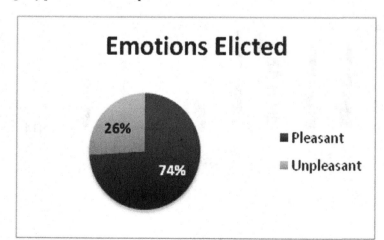

and Heritage of the Universiti Malaysia Kelantan (UMK) were the respondents for this case study. Seventy one (71) students participated with age range 18-24, and the three emotions of desire (fascination, satisfaction and admiration) where used for the study.

Method

A questionnaire with the picture of product A & B and the three emotions (fascination, satisfaction and admiration) was given to a group of participants (71 students). They were asked to rate each of the emotions 0, 1, or 2 against the products (A & B). These rating refer to the following;

2: High Emotion
1: Medium Emotion
0: Low Emotion

The participants were asked to rate all of the emotions based on how they feel about the products and to be impartial.

Result

To analyze the result of the study, the following charts (Figure 17a & 17b) were produced plotting the number of people that felt each level of emotion (high, medium and low) against the three emotions (fascination, satisfaction and admiration). Also a graph (Figure 18) was plotted to show the emotional rating of the products. This was achieved by plotting the mean value against the three emotions. The graph reveals the emotion with highest and lowest mean value of emotion and also shows the difference in emotional rating of the two products.

Discussion

The graph plotted (Figure 17) shows that fascination elicited by product B has the overall highest mean value while that of product B has the lowest mean value. This constant is apparent due to the conditions of fascination explained by Desmet (2002). That is, more respondents have dispositional likings (attitudes) for product B; therefore appraised the product as appealing and this result in the fascination emotion elicited. In the order way round, product-A, due to its common design elicited low level of fascination.

From the three emotions, satisfaction has the highest mean value in product A and the lowest mean value in product B. According to Luke (2009), satisfactory emotions are elicited after a period of product use; therefore, since product B is a new design which has not been used by respon-

Figure 16. Ceramic mugs (Product A & B) used for the study

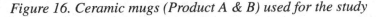

Figure 17. (a) Emotional response towards product A (b) "Emotional response towards product B

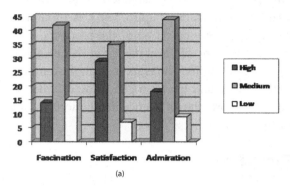

(a)

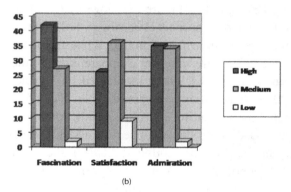

(b)

dents, they have low satisfaction emotions towards the product. However, Product A is an old design which has been used often by respondents; thus, based on product experience it was appraised has motive complaint and elicits satisfaction emotion.

The second highest mean value is admiration emotion elicited by product B. This is as a result of respondents' product aspiration (Luke, 2009); therefore, they admire the product on a first encounter. Since, fascination is the highest emotion elicited by product B; based on Norman's level of design, it can be concluded that product B is more of visceral level design.

CONCLUSION

Overall, the result from the two studies demonstrates the theories in practice and also shows insight to products tested. The studies practically revealed that computer aided design is a viable tool for building user-centered design. It shows that designers can apply computer aided design to gauge the emotive response of intended user even before producing the physical prototype; explore design alternatives; verify suitability of design and also evaluate design to identify possible faults. Thus, early customer involvement will help companies not to waste time and money designing, engineering and manufacturing a product that doesn't fulfill customers' expectation. This is because, designing for greatness based on misguided vision will lead to failure (Luke, 2009).

Figure 18. Emotional rating of the products

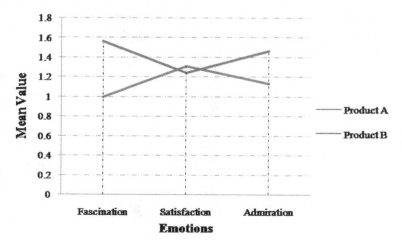

REFERENCES

Ashley, S. (1995). Rapid prototyping is coming of age. *Mechanical Engineering (New York, N.Y.)*, 63.

Autodesk. (2013a). *CAD software defined*. Retrieved January 10, 2013 from http://usa.autodesk.com/adsk/servlet/item?siteID=123112&id=17690382

Autodesk. (2013b). *Digital prototyping*. Retrieved January 10, 2013 from http://usa.autodesk.com/digital-prototyping/

Boatwright, P., & Cagan, J. (2010). *Product emotion: The way to captive customers*. Academic Press.

Camarinha-Matos, L. M., & Afsarmanesh, H. (1999). The virtual enterprise concept. In *Proceedings of the IFIP TC5WG5.3/PRODNET Working Conference on Infrastructures for Virtual Enterprises: Networking Industrial Enterprises* (Vol. 153, pp. 3-4). Academic Press.

Carlson, R. (1997). *Experienced cognition*. Mahwah, NJ: Lawrence Erlbaum.

Chapman, J. (2009). Design for emotionally durability. *Design Issues, 25*(4), 29–35. doi:10.1162/desi.2009.25.4.29

Crossly, L. (2003). Building emotions in design, PDD group. *The Design Journal, 6*(3), 35–45. doi:10.2752/146069203789355264

CTIOA. (2011). *Ceramic tile and stone standards*. Retrieved November 28, 2011, from http://www.ctioa.org

Design, C.-A. (2008) In *The Columbia Encyclopedia* (6th ed.). Retrieved February 26, 2009, from http://www.encyclopedia.com/1E1-ComputerAD.html

Desmet, P. (2002). *Designing emotions*. Delft, The Netherlands: Delft University Press.

Desmet, P. M. A. (2003a). A multilayered model of product emotions. *The Design Journal, 6*(2), 4–13. doi:10.2752/146069203789355480

Desmet, P. M. A. (2003b). Measuring emotion: development and application of an instrument to measure emotional responses to products. In M. Blythe, K. Overbeeke, A. F. Monk, & P. Wright (Eds.), *Funology: From Usability to Enjoyment* (pp. 111–123). Dordrecht: Kluwer Academic Publishers.

Elliott, R. (1998). A model of emotion-driven choice. *Journal of Marketing Management, 14*, 95-108.

Encyclopædia Britannica. (2012). *Traditional ceramics*. Retrieved May 1, 2012, from http://www.britannica.com/EBchecked/topic/601792/traditional -ceramics

Frijda, N. H. (1994). Varieties of affect: emotions and episodes, moods, and sentiments. In P. Ekman & R.J. Davidson (Eds.), The nature of emotion, fundamental questions (pp. 59-67). Oxford, UK: Oxford University Press.

Jackie, C. (2013). *What is CAD?*. Retrieved January 10, 2013, from http://architecture.about.com/od/software/g/CAD.htm

Jordan, P. (2002). *Designing pleasurable products: An introduction to the new human factors*. London: Taylor & Francis.

Kingery, W. D., Bowen, H. K., & Uhlmann, D. R. (2006). *Introduction of ceramics* (2nd ed.). New York, NY: Wiley-Interscience.

Kurosu, M. & Kashimura, K. (1995). *Apparent usability vs. inherent usablity: experimental analysis on the determinants of the apparent usability*. Academic Press.

Lucinda, C., & Martin, N. (1999). *Oxford English Dictionary* (4th ed.). Oxford, UK: Oxford University Press.

Luke, W. (2009). *The structure, influence and application of emotion in product design.* Leicester, UK: De Montfort University.

Lundahl, D. (2006). A holistic approach to product development. *Food Technology*, 28–33.

McDonagh-Philip, D., & Lebbon, C. (2000). The emotional domain in product design. *The Design Journal*, *3*(1), 31–43. doi:10.2752/146069200789393562

Mittal, B. (1988). The role of affective choice mode in the consumer purchase of expressive products. *Journal of Economic Psychology*, *9*, 499–524. doi:10.1016/0167-4870(88)90016-5

Norman, D. (2004). *Emotion design: Why we love (or hate) everyday things.* New York, NY: Basic Books.

Norman, D. (2006, August 19). *A discussion with Don Norman on what makes great design prt1: Icon-o-Cast by Lunar Design* [Podcast]. Retrieved from http://phobos.apple.com/ WebObjects/MZStore.woa/wa/viewPodcast?id=78 230141&s=143444

Ortony, A., Clore, G. L., & Collins, A. (1988). *The cognitive structure of emotions.* Cambridge: Cambridge University Press. doi:10.1017/CBO9780511571299

Overbeeke, C. J., & Hekkert, P. (Eds.). (1999). *Proceedings of the first international conference on Design and Emotion.* Delft: Department of Industrial Design.

Roseman, I. J., & Smith, G. A. (2001). Appraisal theory: Overview, assumptions, varieties, controversies. In K. R. Scherer, A. Schorr, & T. Johnstone (Eds.), *Appraisal processes in emotion: Theory, methods, research (Series in affective science)* (pp. 3–19). New York, NY: Oxford University Press.

Venuvinod, P. K., & Ma, W. (2004). *Rapid prototyping: Laser-based & other technologies.* Boston, MA: Kluwer Academic. doi:10.1007/978-1-4757-6361-4

William, P. (1998). *Rapid Prototyping Primer.* Retrieved January 10, 2013, from http://www.me.psu.edu/lamancusa/rapidpro/primer/chapter2.htm

Woodward, C. (1996). *Computer aided industrial design for ceramics and glass industries.* Finland: Dest Artes Oy.

Wrigley, C., Popovic, V. Chamorro-Koc, & Marianella. (2009). A methodological approach to visceral hedonic rhetoric. In Proceedings of the International Association of Societies of Design Research Conference 2009. COEX.

Zajonc, R. (1980). Feeling and thinking: Preferences need no inferences. *The American Psychologist*, *35*, 151–175. doi:10.1037/0003-066X.35.2.151

ENDNOTES

[1]   PDD is a product design consultancy in London.

Chapter 15
Clean and Green Energy Technologies, Sustainable Development, and Environment

Abdeen Mustafa Omer
Energy Research Institute (ERI), UK

ABSTRACT

The move towards a low-carbon world, driven partly by climate science and partly by the business opportunities it offers, will need the promotion of environmentally friendly alternatives, if an acceptable stabilisation level of atmospheric carbon dioxide is to be achieved. This requires the harnessing and use of natural resources that produce no air pollution or greenhouse gases and provide comfortable coexistence of humans, livestock, and plants. This chapter presents a comprehensive review of energy sources, and the development of sustainable technologies to explore these energy sources. It also includes potential renewable energy technologies, efficient energy systems, energy savings techniques, and other mitigation measures necessary to reduce climate changes. The chapter concludes with the technical status of the Ground Source Heat Pumps (GSHP) technology. The purpose of this chapter, however, is to examine the means of reduction of energy consumption in buildings, identify GSHPs as an environmentally friendly technology able to provide efficient utilisation of energy in the buildings sector, promote using GSHPs applications as an optimum means of heating and cooling, and to present typical applications and recent advances of the DX GSHPs.

1. INTRODUCTION

Over millions of years ago, plants have covered the earth converting the energy of sunlight into living plants and animals, some of which was buried in the depths of the earth to produce deposits of coal, oil and natural gas (Lin, and Chang, 2013; Glaas, and Juhola, 2013; Gerald, 2012). The past few decades, however, have experienced many valuable uses for these complex chemical substances and manufacturing from them plastics, textiles, fertiliser and the various end products of the petrochemical industry. Indeed, each decade sees increasing uses for these products. Coal, oil and gas, which will certainly be of great value to future generations, as they are to ours, are however

DOI: 10.4018/978-1-4666-6252-0.ch015

non-renewable natural resources. The rapid depletion of these non-renewable fossil resources need not continue. This is particularly true now as it is, or soon will be, technically and economically feasible to supply all of man's needs from the most abundant energy source of all, the sun. The sunlight is not only inexhaustible, but, moreover, it is the only energy source, which is completely non-polluting (Bendewald, and Zhai, 2013).

Industry's use of fossil fuels has been largely blamed for warming the climate. When coal, gas and oil are burnt, they release harmful gases, which trap heat in the atmosphere and cause global warming. However, there had been an ongoing debate on this subject, as scientists have struggled to distinguish between changes, which are human induced, and those, which could be put down to natural climate variability. Notably, human activities that emit carbon dioxide (CO_2), the most significant contributor to potential climate change, occur primarily from fossil fuel production. Consequently, efforts to control CO_2 emissions could have serious, negative consequences for economic growth, employment, investment, trade and the standard of living of individuals everywhere.

2. ENERGY SOURCES AND USE

Scientifically, it is difficult to predict the relationship between global temperature and greenhouse gas (GHG) concentrations. The climate system contains many processes that will change if warming occurs. Critical processes include heat transfer by winds and tides, the hydrological cycle involving evaporation, precipitation, runoff and groundwater and the formation of clouds, snow, and ice, all of which display enormous natural variability. The equipment and infrastructure for energy supply and use are designed with long lifetimes, and the premature turnover of capital stock involves significant costs. Economic benefits occur if capital stock is replaced with

more efficient equipment in step with its normal replacement cycle. Likewise, if opportunities to reduce future emissions are taken in a timely manner, they should be less costly. Such a flexible approach would allow society to take account of evolving scientific and technological knowledge, while gaining experience in designing policies to address climate change (Morrow, 2012).

The World Summit on Sustainable Development in Johannesburg in 2002 (Morrow, 2012) committed itself to ''encourage and promote the development of renewable energy sources to accelerate the shift towards sustainable consumption and production''. Accordingly, it aimed at breaking the link between resource use and productivity. This can be achieved by the following:

- Trying to ensure economic growth does not cause environmental pollution.
- Improving resource efficiency.
- Examining the whole life-cycle of a product.
- Enabling consumers to receive more information on products and services.
- Examining how taxes, voluntary agreements, subsidies, regulation and information campaigns, can best stimulate innovation and investment to provide cleaner technology.

The energy conservation scenarios include rational use of energy policies in all economy sectors and the use of combined heat and power systems, which are able to add to energy savings from the autonomous power plants. Electricity from renewable energy sources is by definition the environmental green product. Hence, a renewable energy certificate system, as recommended by the World Summit, is an essential basis for all policy systems, independent of the renewable energy support scheme. It is, therefore, important that all parties involved support the renewable energy certificate system in place if it is to work as planned. Moreover, existing renewable energy technologies (RETs) could play a significant mitigating role, but the economic and political climate will have to change first. It is now universally accepted that climate change is real. It is happening now, and GHGs produced by human activities are significantly contributing to it. The predicted global temperature increase of between 1.5 and 4.5ºC could lead to potentially catastrophic environmental impacts (Cantrell, and Wepfer, 1984). These include sea level rise, increased frequency of extreme weather events, floods, droughts, disease migration from various places and possible stalling of the Gulf Stream. This has led scientists to argue that climate change issues are not ones that politicians can afford to ignore, and policy makers tend to agree (ASHRAE, 2005). However, reaching international agreements on climate change policies is no trivial task as the difficulty in ratifying the Kyoto Protocol and reaching agreement at Copenhagen have proved.

Therefore, the use of renewable energy sources and the rational use of energy, in general, are the fundamental inputs for any responsible energy policy. However, the energy sector is encountering difficulties because increased production and consumption levels entail higher levels of pollution and eventually climate change, with possibly disastrous consequences. At the same time, it is important to secure energy at an acceptable cost in order to avoid negative impacts on economic growth. To date, renewable energy contributes only as much as 20% of the global energy supplies worldwide (ASHRAE, 2005). Over two thirds of this comes from biomass use, mostly in developing countries, and some of this is unsustainable. However, the potential for energy from sustainable technologies is huge. On the technological side, renewables have an obvious role to play. In general, there is no problem in terms of the technical potential of renewables to deliver energy. Moreover, there are very good opportunities for the RETs to play an important role in reducing emissions of the GHGs into the atmosphere, certainly far more

than have been exploited so far. However, there are still some technical issues to address in order to cope with the intermittency of some renewables, particularly wind and solar. Nevertheless, the biggest problem with relying on renewables to deliver the necessary cuts in the GHG emissions is more to do with politics and policy issues than with technical ones (Kavanaugh, and Rafferty, 1997). For example, the single most important step governments could take to promote and increase the use of renewables is to improve access for renewables to the energy market. This access to the market needs to be under favourable conditions and, possibly, under favourable economic rates as well. One move that could help, or at least justify, better market access would be to acknowledge that there are environmental costs associated with other energy supply options and that these costs are not currently internalised within the market price of electricity or fuels. This could make a significant difference, particularly if appropriate subsidies were applied to renewable energy in recognition of the environmental benefits it offers. Similarly, cutting energy consumption through end-use efficiency is absolutely essential. This suggests that issues of end-use consumption of energy will have to come into the discussion in the foreseeable future.

However, the RETs have the benefit of being environmentally benign when developed in a sensitive and appropriate way with the full involvement of local communities. In addition, they are diverse, secure, locally based and abundant. In spite of the enormous potential and the multiple benefits, the contribution from renewable energy still lags behind the ambitious claims for it due to the initially high development costs, concerns about local impacts, lack of research funding and poor institutional and economic arrangements (UN, 2003; UNFCCC, 2009). Hence, an approach is needed to integrate renewable energies in a way that meets the rising demand in a cost-effective way.

3. ROLE OF ENERGY EFFICIENCY SYSTEM

The prospects for development in power engineering are, at present, closely related to ecological problems. Power engineering has harmful effects on the environment, as it discharges toxic gases into atmosphere and also oil-contaminated and saline waters into rivers, as well as polluting the soil with ash and slag and having adverse effects on living things on account of electromagnetic fields and so on. Thus there is an urgent need for new approaches to provide an ecologically safe strategy. Substantial economic and ecological effects for thermal power projects (TPPs) can be achieved by improvement, upgrading the efficiency of the existing equipment, reduction of electricity loss, saving of fuel, and optimisation of its operating conditions and service life leading to improved access for rural and urban low-income areas in developing countries through energy efficiency and renewable energies.

Sustainable energy is a prerequisite for development. Energy-based living standards in developing countries, however, are clearly below standards in developed countries. Low levels of access to affordable and environmentally sound energy in both rural and urban low-income areas are therefore a predominant issue in developing countries. In recent years many programmes for development aid or technical assistance have been focusing on improving access to sustainable energy, many of them with impressive results. Apart from success stories, however, experience also shows that positive appraisals of many projects evaporate after completion and vanishing of the implementation expert team. Altogether, the diffusion of sustainable technologies such as energy efficiency and renewable energy for cooking, heating, lighting, electrical appliances and building insulation in developing countries has been slow. Energy efficiency and renewable

energy programmes could be more sustainable and pilot studies more effective and pulse releasing if the entire policy and implementation process was considered and redesigned from the outset (Rees, 1999). New financing and implementation processes, which allow reallocating financial resources and thus enabling countries themselves to achieve a sustainable energy infrastructure, are also needed. The links between the energy policy framework, financing and implementation of renewable energy and energy efficiency projects have to be strengthened and as well as efforts made to increase people's knowledge through training.

3.1 Energy Use in Buildings

Buildings consume energy mainly for cooling, heating and lighting. The energy consumption was based on the assumption that the building operates within ASHRAE-thermal comfort zone during the cooling and heating periods (Bos, My, Vu, and Bulatao, 1994). Most of the buildings incorporate energy efficient passive cooling, solar control, photovoltaic, lighting and day lighting, and integrated energy systems. It is well known that thermal mass with night ventilation can reduce the maximum indoor temperature in buildings in summer (Duchin, 1995). Hence, comfort temperatures may be achieved by proper application of passive cooling systems. However, energy can also be saved if an air conditioning unit is used (Givoni, 1998). The reason for this is that in summer, heavy external walls delay the heat transfer from the outside into the inside spaces. Moreover, if the building has a lot of internal mass the increase in the air temperature is slow. This is because the penetrating heat raises the air temperature as well as the temperature of the heavy thermal mass. The result is a slow heating of the building in summer as the maximal inside temperature is reached only during the late hours when the outside air temperature is already low.

The heat flowing from the inside heavy walls could be reduced with good ventilation in the evening and night. The capacity to store energy also helps in winter, since energy can be stored in walls from one sunny winter day to the next cloudy one. However, the admission of daylight into buildings alone does not guarantee that the design will be energy efficient in terms of lighting. In fact, the design for increased daylight can often raise concerns relating to visual comfort (glare) and thermal comfort (increased solar gain in the summer and heat losses in the winter from larger apertures). Such issues will clearly need to be addressed in the design of the window openings, blinds, shading devices, heating system, etc. In order for a building to benefit from daylight energy terms, it is a prerequisite that lights are switched off when sufficient daylight is available. The nature of the switching regime; manual or automated, centralised or local, switched, stepped or dimmed, will determine the energy performance. Simple techniques can be implemented to increase the probability that lights are switched off (ASHRAE, 2003). These include:

- Making switches conspicuous and switching banks of lights independently.
- Loading switches appropriately in relation to the lights.
- Switching banks of lights parallel to the main window wall.

There are also a number of methods, which help reduce the lighting energy use, which, in turn, relate to the type of occupancy pattern of the building. The light switching options include:

- Centralised timed off (or stepped)/manual on.
- Photoelectric off (or stepped)/manual on.
- Photoelectric and on (or stepped), photoelectric dimming.
- Occupant sensor (stepped) on/off (movement or noise sensor).

3.2 Energy Conservation

Likewise, energy savings from the avoidance of air conditioning can be very substantial. Whilst day-lighting strategies need to be integrated with artificial lighting systems in order to become beneficial in terms of energy use, reductions in overall energy consumption levels by employment of a sustained programme of energy consumption strategies and measures would have considerable benefits within the buildings sector. It would perhaps be better to support a climate sensitive design approach that encompasses some elements of the pure conservation strategy together with strategies, which work with the local ambient conditions making use of energy technology systems, such as solar energy, where feasible. In practice, low energy environments are achieved through a combination of measures that include:

- The application of environmental regulations and policy.
- The application of environmental science and best practice.
- Mathematical modelling and simulation.
- Environmental design and engineering.
- Construction and commissioning.
- Management and modifications of environments in use.

While the overriding intention of passive solar energy design of buildings is to achieve a reduction in purchased energy consumption, the attainment of significant savings is in doubt. The non-realisation of potential energy benefits is mainly due to the neglect of the consideration of post-occupancy user and management behaviour by energy scientists and designers alike. Calculating energy inputs in agricultural production is more difficult in comparison to the industry sector due to the high number of factors affecting agricultural production, as Table 1 shows. However, considerable studies have been conducted in different countries on energy use in agriculture

Table 1. Energy equivalent of inputs and outputs

Energy Source	Unit	Equivalent Energy (MJ)
Input		
1. Human labour	h	2.3
2. Animal labour		
Horse	h	10.10
Mule	h	4.04
Donkey	h	4.04
Cattle	h	5.05
Water buffalo	h	7.58
3. Electricity	kWh	11.93
4. Diesel	Litre	56.31
5. Chemicals fertilisers		
Nitrogen	kg	64.4
P_2O_5	kg	11.96
K_2O	kg	6.7
6. Seed		
Cereals and pulses	kg	25
Oil seed	kg	3.6
Tuber	kg	14.7
Total input	kg	43.3
Output		
7. Major products		
Cereal and pulses	kg	14.7
Sugar beet	kg	5.04
Tobacco	kg	0.8
Cotton	kg	11.8
Oil seed	kg	25
Fruits	kg	1.9
Vegetables	kg	0.8
Water melon	kg	1.9
Onion	kg	1.6
Potatoes	kg	3.6
Olive	kg	11.8
Tea	kg	0.8
8. By products		
Husk	kg	13.8
Straw	kg	12.5
Cob	kg	18.0
Seed cotton	kg	25.0
Total output	kg	**149.04**

(Kammerud, Ceballos, Curtis, Place, and Anderson, 1984; Shaviv, 1989; Singh, 2000) in order to quantify the influence of these factors.

4. RENEWABLE ENERGY TECHNOLOGIES

Sustainable energy is the energy that, in its production or consumption, has minimal negative impacts on human health and the healthy functioning of vital ecological systems, including the global environment (CAEEDAC, 2000; Yaldiz, Ozturk, and Zeren, 1993). It is an accepted fact that renewable energy is a sustainable form of energy, which has attracted more attention during recent years. Increasing environmental interest, as well as economic consideration of fossil fuel consumption and high emphasis of sustainable development for the future helped to bring the great potential of renewable energy into focus. Nearly a fifth of all global power is generated by renewable energy sources, according to a book published by the OECD/IEA (Dutt, 1982). ''Renewables for power generation: status and prospects'' claims that, at approximately 20%, renewables are the second largest power source after coal (39%) and ahead

of nuclear (17%), natural gas (17%) and oil (8%) respectively. From 1973-2000 renewables grew at 9.3% a year and it is predicted that this will increase by 10.4% a year to 2010. Wind power grew fastest at 52% and will multiply seven times by 2020, overtaking biopower and hence help reducing greenhouse gases, GHGs, emissions to the environment.

Table 2 shows some applications of different renewable energy sources. The challenge is to match leadership in the GHG reduction and production of renewable energy with developing a major research and manufacturing capacity in environmental technologies (wind, solar, fuel cells, etc.). More than 50% of the world's area is classified as arid, representing the rural and desert part, which lack electricity and water networks. The inhabitants of such areas obtain water from borehole wells by means of water pumps, which are mostly driven by diesel engines. The diesel motors are associated with maintenance problems, high running cost, and environmental pollution. Alternative methods are pumping by photovoltaic (PV) or wind systems. At present, renewable sources of energy are regional and site specific. It has to be integrated in the regional development plans (Baruah, 1995).

Table 2. Sources of renewable energy

Energy Source	Technology	Size
Solar energy	Domestic solar water heaters Solar water heating for large demands PV roofs: grid connected systems generating electric energy	Small Medium-large Medium-large
Wind energy	Wind turbines (grid connected)	Medium-large
Hydraulic energy	Hydro plants in derivation schemes Hydro plants in existing water distribution networks	Medium-small Medium-small
Biomass	High efficiency wood boilers CHP plants fed by agricultural wastes or energy crops	Small Medium
Animal manure	CHP plants fed by biogas	Small
CHP	High efficiency lighting High efficiency electric Householders appliances High efficiency boilers Plants coupled with refrigerating absorption machines	Wide Wide Wide Small-medium Medium-large

4.1 Solar Energy

The availability of data on solar radiation is a critical problem. Even in developed countries, very few weather stations have been recording detailed solar radiation data for a period of time long enough to have statistical significance. Solar radiation arriving on earth is the most fundamental renewable energy source in nature. It powers the bio-system, the ocean and atmospheric current system and affects the global climate. Reliable radiation information is needed to provide input data in modelling solar energy devices and a good database is required in the work of energy planners, engineers, and agricultural scientists. In general, it is not easy to design solar energy conversion systems when they have to be installed in remote locations. First, in most cases, solar radiation measurements are not available for these sites. Second, the radiation nature of solar radiation makes the computation of the size of such systems difficult. While solar energy data are recognised as very important, their acquisition is by no means straightforward. The measurement of solar radiation requires the use of costly equipment such as pyrheliometers and pyranometers. Consequently, adequate facilities are often not available in developing countries to mount viable monitoring programmes. This is partly due to the equipment cost as well as the cost of technical manpower. Several attempts have, however, been made to estimate solar radiation through the use of meteorological and other physical parameter in order to avoid the use of expensive network of measuring instruments (Sivkov, 1964).

Two of the most essential natural resources for all life on the earth and for man's survival are sunlight and water. Sunlight is the driving force behind many of the RETs. The worldwide potential for utilising this resource, both directly by means of the solar technologies and indirectly by means of biofuels, wind and hydro technologies, is vast. During the last decade interest has been refocused on renewable energy sources due to the increasing prices and fore-seeable exhaustion of presently used commercial energy sources. The most promising solar energy technology are related to thermal systems; industrial solar water heaters, solar cookers, solar dryers for peanut crops, solar stills, solar driven cold stores to store fruits and vegetables, solar collectors, solar water desalination, solar ovens, and solar commercial bakers. Solar PV system: solar PV for lighting, solar refrigeration to store vaccines for human and animal use, solar PV for water pumping, solar PV for battery chargers, solar PV for communication network, microwave, receiver stations, radio systems in airports, VHF and beacon radio systems in airports, and educational solar TV posts in villages. Solar pumps are most cost effective for low power requirement (up to 5 kW) in remote places. Applications include domestic and livestock drinking water supplies, for which the demand is constant throughout the year, and irrigation. However, the suitability of solar pumping for irrigation, though possible, is uncertain because the demand may vary greatly with seasons. Solar systems may be able to provide trickle irrigation for fruit farming, but not usually the large volumes of water needed for wheat growing (Thakur, and Mistra, 1993; Wu, and Boggess, 1999).

The hydraulic energy required to deliver a volume of water is given by the formula:

$$E_w = \rho_w \, g \, V \, H \qquad (1)$$

where E_w is the required hydraulic energy (kWh day^{-1}); ρ_w is the water density (kg m^{-3}); g is the gravitational acceleration (ms^{-2}); V is the required volume of water (m^3 day^{-1}); and H is the head of water (m).

The solar array power required is given by:

$$P_{sa} = E_w \, / \, E_{sr} \, \eta \, F \qquad (2)$$

where: P_{sa} is the solar array power (kW$_p$); E_{sr} is the average daily solar radiation (kWhm^{-2} day^{-1});

F is the array mismatch factor; and η is the daily subsystem efficiency.

Substituting Eq. (1) in Eq. (2), the following equation is obtained for the amount of water that can be pumped:

$$V = P_{sa} E_{sr} \eta F / \rho_w g H \qquad (3)$$

$P_{sa} = 1.6\ kW_p$, $F = 0.85$, $\eta = 40\%$.

A further increase of PV depends on the ability to improve the durability, performance and the local manufacturing capabilities of PV.

4.2 Biomass Utilisation

The data required to perform the trade-off analysis simulation of bio-energy resources can be classified according to the divisions given in Table 3, namely the overall system or individual plants, and the existing situation or future development. The effective economical utilisations of these resources are shown in Table 4, but their use is hindered by many problems such as those related to harvesting, collection, and transportation, besides the photosanitary control regulations. Biomass energy is experiencing a surge in interest stemming from a combination of factors, e.g., greater recognition of its current role and future potential contribution as a modern fuel, global environmental benefits, its development and entrepreneurial opportunities, etc. (OECD/IEA, 2004; Duffie, and Beckman, 1980). Possible routes of biomass energy development are shown in Table 5. However, biomass usage and application can generally be divided into the following three categories.

1. Biomass energy for petroleum substitution driven by the following factors.
    a. Oil price increase.
    b. Balance of payment problems, and economic crisis.
    c. Fuel-wood plantations and residue utilisation.
    d. Wood based heat and electricity.
    e. Liquid fuels from biomass.
    f. Producer gas technology.
2. Biomass energy for domestic needs driven by:
    a. Population increase.
    b. Urbanisation.
    c. Agricultural expansion.
    d. Fuel-wood crisis.
    e. Ecological crisis.
    f. Fuel-wood plantations, agro-forestry.
    g. Community forestry, and residue utilisation.
    h. Improved stoves, and improved charcoal production.

Table 3. Classifications of data requirements

Criteria	Plant Data	System Data
Existing data	Size Life Cost (fixed and variation operation and maintenance) Forced outage Maintenance Efficiency Fuel Emissions	Peak load Load shape Capital costs Fuel costs Depreciation Rate of return Taxes
Future data	All of above, plus Capital costs Construction trajectory Date in service	System lead growth Fuel price growth Fuel import limits Inflation

Table 4. Effective biomass resource utilisation

Subject	Tools	Constraints
Utilisation and land clearance for agriculture expansion	• Stumpage fees • Control • Extension • Conversion • Technology	• Policy • Fuel-wood planning • Lack of extension • Institutional
Utilisation of agricultural residues	• Briquetting • Carbonisation • Carbonisation and briquetting • Fermentation • Gasification	• Capital • Pricing • Policy and legislation • Social acceptability

Table 5. Agricultural residues routes for development

Source	Process	Product	End Use
Agricultural residues	Direct Processing Processing Carbonisation Fermentation	Combustion Briquettes Carbonisation (small scale) Briquettes Carbonised Biogas	Rural poor Urban household Industrial use Industrial use Limited household use Rural household (self sufficiency) Urban fuel Energy services Household, and industry
Agricultural, and animal residues	Direct Briquettes Carbonisation Carbonisation Fermentation	Combustion Direct combustion Carbonised Briquettes Biogas	(Save or less efficiency as wood) (Similar end use devices or improved) Use Briquettes use Use

3. Biomass energy for development driven by:
    a. Electrification.
    b. Irrigation and water supply.
    c. Economic and social development.
    d. Fuel-wood plantations.
    e. Community forestry.
    f. Agro-forestry.
    g. Briquettes.
    h. Producer gas technology.

The use of biomass through direct combustion has long been, and still is, the most common mode of biomass utilisation (Table 5). Examples for dry (thermo-chemical) conversion processes are charcoal making from wood (slow pyrolysis), gasification of forest and agricultural residues (fast pyrolysis – this is still in demonstration phase), and of course, direct combustion in stoves, furnaces, etc. Wet processes require substantial amount of water to be mixed with the biomass. Biomass technologies include:

•   Carbonisation and briquetting.
•   Improved stoves.
•   Biogas.
•   Improved charcoal.
•   Gasification.

4.2.1 Briquetting and Carbonisation

Briquetting is the formation of a charcoal (an energy-dense solid fuel source) from otherwise wasted agricultural and forestry residues. One of the disadvantages of wood fuel is that it is bulky with a low energy density and therefore requires transport. Briquette formation allows for a more energy-dense fuel to be delivered, thus reducing the transportation cost and making the resource more competitive. It also adds some uniformity, which makes the fuel more compatible with systems that are sensitive to the specific fuel input. Charcoal stoves are very familiar to African societies. As for the stove technology, the present charcoal stove can be used, and can be improved upon for better efficiency. This energy term will be of particular interest to both urban and rural households and all the income groups due to its simplicity, convenience, and lower air polluting characteristics. However, the market price of the fuel together with that of its end-use technology may not enhance its early high market penetration especially in the urban low income and rural households.

Charcoal is produced by slow heating wood (carbonisation) in airtight ovens or retorts, in chambers with various gases, or in kilns supplied with limited and controlled amounts of air. The charcoal yield decreased gradually from 42.6 to 30.7% for the hazelnut shell and from 35.6 to 22.7% for the beech wood with an increase of temperature from 550 to 1,150 K while the charcoal yield from the lignin content decreases sharply from 42.5 to 21.7% until it was at 850 K during the carbonisation procedures (Sivkov, 1964). The charcoal yield decreases as the temperature increases, while the ignition temperature of charcoal increases as the carbonisation temperature increases. The charcoal briquettes that are sold on the commercial market are typically made from a binder and filler.

4.2.2 Improved Cook Stoves

Traditional wood stoves are commonly used in many rural areas. These can be classified into four types: three stone, metal cylindrical shaped, metal tripod and clay type. Indeed, improvements of traditional cookers and ovens to raise the efficiency of fuel saving can secure rural energy availability, where woody fuels have become

scarce. However, planting fast growing trees to provide a constant fuel supply should also be considered. The rural development is essential and economically important since it will eventually lead to a better standard of living, people's settlement, and self-sufficiency.

4.2.3 Biogas technology

Biogas technology cannot only provide fuel, but is also important for comprehensive utilisation of biomass forestry, animal husbandry, fishery, agricultural economy, protecting the environment, realising agricultural recycling as well as improving the sanitary conditions, in rural areas. However, the introduction of biogas technology on a wide scale has implications for macro planning such as the allocation of government investment and effects on the balance of payments. Hence, factors that determine the rate of acceptance of biogas plants, such as credit facilities and technical backup services, are likely to have to be planned as part of general macro-policy, as do the allocation of research and development funds (Barabaro, Coppolino, Leone, and Sinagra, 1978).

4.2.4 Improved Charcoal

Dry cell batteries are a practical but expensive form of mobile fuel that is used by rural people when moving around at night and for powering radios and other small appliances. The high cost of dry cell batteries is financially constraining for rural households, but their popularity gives a good indication of how valuable a versatile fuel like electricity is in rural areas (Table 6). However, dry cell batteries can constitute an environmental hazard unless they are recycled in a proper fashion. Tables (6-7) further show that direct burning of fuel-wood and crop residues constitute the main usage of biomass, as is the case with many developing countries. In fact, biomass resources play a significant role in energy supply in all developing countries. However, the direct burning of biomass in an inefficient manner causes economic loss and adversely affects human health. In order to address the problem of inefficiency, research centres around the world, e.g., (Hall, and Scrase, 1998) have investigated the viability of converting the resource to a more useful form of improved charcoal, namely solid briquettes and fuel gas. Accordingly, biomass resources should be divided into residues or dedicated resources, the latter including firewood and charcoal can also be produced from forest residues (Table 7). Whichever form of biomass resource used, its sustainability would primarily depend on improved forest and tree management.

4.2.5 Gasification

Gasification is based on the formation of a fuel gas (mostly CO and H_2) by partially oxidising raw solid fuel at high temperatures in the presence of steam or air. The technology can use wood chips, groundnut shells, sugarcane bagasse, and other similar fuels to generate capacities from 3 kW to 100 kW. Many types of gasifier designs have been developed to make use of the diversity of fuel inputs and to meet the requirements of the product gas output (degree of cleanliness, composition, heating value, etc.) (Pernille, 2004).

4.2.6 Biomass and Sustainability

A sustainable energy system includes energy efficiency, energy reliability, energy flexibility, fuel poverty, and environmental impacts. A sustainable biofuel has two favourable properties, which are availability from renewable raw material, and its lower negative environmental impact than that of fossil fuels. Global warming, caused by CO_2 and other substances, has become an international concern in recent years. To protect forestry resources, which act as major absorbers of CO_2, by controlling the ever-increasing deforestation and the increase in the consumption of wood fuels, such as firewood and charcoal, is therefore an urgent issue. Given this, the development of a substitute fuel for charcoal is necessary. Briquette production technology, a type of clean coal technology, can help prevent flooding and serve as a global warming countermeasure by conserving forestry resources through the provision of a stable supply of briquettes as a substitute for charcoal and firewood.

There are many emerging biomass technologies with large and immediate potential applications, e.g., biomass gasifier/gas turbine (BGST) systems for power generation with pilot plants, improved

Table 6. Energy carrier and energy services in rural areas

Energy Carrier	Energy End-Use
Fuel-wood	Cooking Water heating Building materials Animal fodder preparation
Kerosene	Lighting Ignition fires
Dry cell batteries	Lighting Small appliances
Animal power	Transport Land preparation for farming Food preparation (threshing)
Human power	Transport Land preparation for farming Food preparation (threshing)

Table 7. Biomass residues and current use

Type of Residue	Current Use
Wood industry waste	Residues available
Vegetable crop residues	Animal feed
Food processing residue	Energy needs
Sorghum, millet, and wheat residues	Fodder, and building materials
Groundnut shells	Fodder, brick making, and direct fining oil mills
Cotton stalks	Domestic fuel considerable amounts available for short period
Sugar, bagasse, and molasses	Fodder, energy need, and ethanol production (surplus available)
Manure	Fertiliser, brick making, and plastering

techniques for biomass harvesting, transportation and storage. Gasification of crop residues such as rice husks, groundnut shells, etc., with plants already operating in China, India, and Thailand. Treatment of cellulosic materials by steam explosion which may be followed by biological or chemical hydrolysis to produce ethanol or other fuels, cogeneration technologies, hydrogen from biomass, striling energies capable of using biomass fuels efficiently, etc. Table 8 gives a view of the use of biomass and its projection worldwide.

However, a major gap with biomass energy is that research has usually been aimed at obtaining supply and consumption data, with insufficient attention and resources being allocated to basic research, to production, harvesting and conservation processes. Biomass has not been closely examined in terms of a substitute for fossil fuels compared to carbon sequestration and overall environmental benefits related to these different approaches. To achieve the full potential of biomass as a feedstock for energy, food, or any other use, requires the application of considerable scientific and technological inputs (D'Apote, 1998). However, the aim of any modern biomass energy systems must be:

Table 8. Final energy projections including biomass (Mtoe)

Region	1995			
	Biomass	Conventional Energy	Total	Share of Biomass (%)
Africa	205	136	341	60
China	206	649	855	24
East Asia	106	316	422	25
Latin America	73	342	416	18
South Asia	235	188	423	56
Total developing countries	825	1632	2456	34
Other non-OECD countries	24	1037	1061	1
Total non-OECD countries	849	2669	3518	24
OECD countries	81	3044	3125	3
World	**930**	**5713**	**6643**	**14**
Region	2020			
	Biomass	Conventional Energy	Total	Share of Biomass (%)
Africa	371	266	631	59
China	224	1524	1748	13
East Asia	118	813	931	13
Latin America	81	706	787	10
South Asia	276	523	799	35
Total developing countries	1071	3825	4896	22
Other non-OECD countries	26	1669	1695	1
Total non-OECD countries	1097	5494	6591	17
OECD countries	96	3872	3968	2
World	**1193**	**9365**	**10558**	**11**

1. To maximise yields with minimum inputs.
2. Utilise and select adequate plant materials and processes.
3. Optimise use of land, water, and fertiliser.
4. Create an adequate infrastructure and strong research and development (R&D) base.

An afforestation programme appears an attractive option for any country to pursue in order to reduce the level of atmospheric carbon by enhancing carbon sequestration in the nation's forests, which would consequently mitigate climate change. However, it is acknowledged that certain barriers need to be overcome if the objectives are to be fully achieved. These include the followings.

- Low level of public awareness of the economic/environmental benefits of forestry.
- The generally low levels of individuals' income.
- Pressures from population growth.
- The land tenural system, which makes it difficult (if at all possible) for individuals to own or establish forest plantations.
- Poor pricing of forest products especially in the local market.
- Inadequate financial support on the part of governments.
- Weak institutional capabilities of the various Forestry Departments as regards technical manpower to effectively manage tree plantations.

However, social policy conditions are also critical. This is still very much lacking particularly under developing countries conditions. During the 1970s and 1980s different biomass energy technologies were perceived in sub-Saharan Africa as a panacea for solving acute problems. On the account of these expectations, a wide range of activities and projects were initiated. However, despite considerable financial and human efforts, most of these initiatives have unfortunately been a failure.

Therefore, future research efforts should concentrate on the following areas.

- Directed R and D in the most promising areas of biomass to increase energy supply and to improve the technological base.
- Formulate a policy framework to encourage entrepreneurial and integrated process.
- Pay more attention to sustainable production and use of biomass energy feedstocks, methodology of conservation and efficient energy flows.
- More research aimed at pollution abatement.
- Greater attentions to interrelated socio-economic aspects.
- Support R and D on energy efficiency in production and use.
- Improve energy management skills and take maximum advantage of existing local knowledge.
- Closely examine past successes and failures to assist policy makers with well-informed recommendations.

4.3 Combined Heat and Power (CHP)

District Heating (DH), also known as community heating can be a key factor to achieve energy savings, reduce CO_2 emissions and at the same time provide consumers with a high quality heat supply at a competitive price. Generally, DH should only be considered for areas where the heat density is sufficiently high to make DH economical. In countries like Denmark for example, DH may today be economical even to new developments with lower density areas, due to the high level of taxation on oil and gas fuels combined with the efficient production of DH.

Most of the heat used for DH can be produced by large CHP plants (gas-fired combined cycle plants using natural gas, biomass, waste or biogas) as shown in Table 2. DH is energy efficient because of the way the heat is produced and the required temperature level is an important factor. Buildings can be heated to a temperature of 21°C and domestic hot water (DHW) can be supplied at a temperature of 55°C using energy sources other than DH that are most efficient when producing low temperature levels (<95°C) for the DH water (David, 2000). Most of these heat sources are CO_2 neutral or emit low levels. However, only a few of these sources are available to small individual systems at a reasonable cost, whereas DH schemes because of the plant's size and location can have access to most of the heat sources and at a low cost. Low temperature DH, with return temperatures of around 30-40°C can utilise the following heat sources:

- Efficient use of CHP by extracting heat at low calorific value (CV).
- Efficient use of biomass or gas boilers by condensing heat in economisers.
- Efficient utilisation of geothermal energy.
- Direct utilisation of excess low temperature heat from industrial processes.
- Efficient use of large-scale solar heating plants.

Heat tariffs may include a number of components such as a connection charge, a fixed charge and a variable energy charge. Also, consumers may be incentivised to lower the return temperature. Hence, it is difficult to generalise but the heat practice for any DH company, no matter what the ownership structure is, can be highlighted as follows:

- To develop and maintain a development plan for the connection of new consumers.
- To evaluate the options for least cost production of heat.
- To implement the most competitive solutions by signing agreements with other companies or by implementing own investment projects.

- To monitor all internal costs and with the help of benchmarking, improve the efficiency of the company.
- To maintain a good relationship with the consumer and deliver heat supply services at a sufficient quality.

Also, installing DH should be pursued to meet the objectives for improving the environment through the improvement of energy efficiency in the heating sector. At the same time DH can serve the consumer with a reasonable quality of heat at the lowest possible cost. The variety of possible solutions combined with the collaboration between individual companies, the district heating association, the suppliers and consultants can, as it has been in Denmark, be the way forward for developing DH in the United Kingdom.

4.4 Fuel Cells

Platinum is a catalyst for fuel cells and hydrogen-fuelled cars presently use about two ounces of the metal. There is currently no practicable alternative. Reserves are in South Africa (70%), and Russia (22%). Although there are sufficient accessible reserves in South Africa to increase supply by up to 5% per year for the next 50 years, there are significant environmental impacts associated with its mining and refining, such as groundwater pollution and atmospheric emissions of sulphur dioxide ammonia, chlorine and hydrogen chloride. The carbon cost of platinum use equates to 360 kg for a current fuel cell car, or 36 kg for a future car, with the target platinum loading of 0.2 oz, which is negligible compared to the CO_2 currently emitted by vehicles (IHA, 2003). Furthermore, Platinum is almost completely recyclable. At current prices and loading, platinum would cost 3% of the total cost of a fuel cell engine. Also, the likely resource costs of hydrogen as a transport fuel are apparently cheapest if it is reformed from natural gas with pipeline distribution, with or without carbon sequestration. However, this is not as sustainable as using renewable energy sources. Substituting hydrogen for fossils fuels will have a positive environmental impact in reducing both photochemical smog and climate change. There could also be an adverse impact on the ozone layer but this is likely to be small, though potentially more significant if hydrogen was to be used as aviation fuel.

4.5 Hydrogen Production

Hydrogen is now beginning to be accepted as a useful form for storing energy for reuse on, or for export off, the grid. Clean electrical power harvested from wind and wave power projects can be used to produce hydrogen by electrolysis of water. Electrolysers split water molecules into its constituent parts: hydrogen and oxygen. These are collected as gases; hydrogen at the cathode and oxygen at the anode. The process is quite simple. Direct current is applied to the electrodes to initiate the electrolysis process. Production of hydrogen is an elegant environmental solution. Hydrogen is the most abundant element on the planet, it cannot be destroyed (unlike hydrocarbons) it simply changes state (water to hydrogen and back to water) during consumption. There is no CO or CO_2 generation in its production and consumption and, depending upon methods of consumption, even the production of oxides of nitrogen can be avoided too. However, the transition will be very messy, and will take many technological paths to convert fossil fuels and methanol to hydrogen, building hybrid engines and so on. Nevertheless, the future of hydrogen fuel cells is promising. Hydrogen can be used in internal combustion engines, fuel cells, turbines, cookers gas boilers, road-side emergency lighting, traffic lights or signalling where noise and pollution can be a considerable nuisance, but where traffic and pedestrian safety cannot be compromised.

Hydrogen is already produced in huge volumes and used in a variety of industries. Current worldwide production is around 500 billion Nm^3 per year (EWEA, 2003). Most of the hydrogen produced today is consumed on-site, such as at oil refineries, at a cost of around \$0.70/kg and is not sold on the market (Steele, 1997). When hydrogen is sold on the market, the cost of liquefying the hydrogen and transporting it to the user adds considerably to the production cost. The energy required to produce hydrogen via electrolysis (assuming 1.23 V) is about 33 (kWh/kg). For 1 mole (2 g) of hydrogen the energy is about 0.066 (kWh/mole) (Sitarz, 1992). The achieved efficiencies are over 80% and on this basis electrolytic hydrogen can be regarded as a storable form of electricity. Hydrogen can be stored in a variety of forms:

- Cryogenic; this has the highest gravimetric energy density.
- High-pressure cylinders; pressures of 10,000 psi are quite normal.
- Metal hydride absorbs hydrogen, providing a very low pressure and extremely safe mechanism, but is heavy and more expensive than cylinders, and
- Chemical carriers offer an alternative, with anhydrous ammonia offering similar gravimetric and volumetric energy densities to ethanol and methanol.

4.6 Hydropower

Hydropower has a valuable role as a clean and renewable source of energy in meeting a variety of vital human needs. Water is a basic requirement for survival: for drinking, for food, energy production and for good health. As water is a commodity, which is finite and cannot be created, and in view of the increasing requirements as the world population grows, there is no alternative but to store water for use when it is needed. However, the major challenges are to feed the increasing world population, to improve the standards of living in rural areas and to develop and manage land and water in a sustainable way. Hydropower plants are classified by their rated capacity into one of four regimes: micro (<50kW), mini (50-500 kW), small (500 kW-5 MW), and large (>5 MW) (John, and James, 1989).

The total world installed hydro capacity today is around 1000 Giga Watts (GW) and a lot more are currently planned, principally in developing countries in Asia, Africa and South America as shown in Table 9, which is reproduced from (Okkan, 1993). However, the present production of hydroelectricity is only about 18 per cent of the technically feasible potential (and 32 per cent of the economically feasible potential); there is no doubt that a large amount of hydropower development lies ahead (Okkan, 1993).

4.7 Wind Energy

Water is the most natural commodity for the existence of life in the remote desert areas. However, as a condition for settling and growing, the supply of energy is the close second priority. The high cost and the difficulties of mains power line extensions, especially to a low populated region can focus attention on the utilisation of different and more reliable and independent sources of energy like renewable wind energy. Accordingly, the utilisation of wind energy, as a form of energy, is becoming increasingly attractive and is being widely used for the substitution of oil-produced energy, and eventually to minimise atmospheric degradation, particularly in remote areas. Indeed, utilisation of renewables, such as wind energy, has gained considerable momentum since the oil crises of the 1970s. Wind energy, though site-dependent, is non-depleting, non-polluting, and a potential option of the alternative energy source. Wind power could supply 12% of global electricity demand by 2020, according to a report by the European Wind Energy Association and Greenpeace (Njeru, 2013).

Wind energy can and will constitute a significant energy resource when converted into a usable form. As Figure 1 illustrates, information sharing is a four-stage process and effective collaboration must also provide ways in which the other three stages of the 'renewable' cycle: gather, convert and utilise, can be integrated. Efficiency in the renewable energy sector translates into lower gathering, conversion and utilisation (electricity) costs. A great level of installed capacity has already been achieved. Figure 2 clearly shows that the offshore wind sector is developing fast, and this indicates that wind is becoming a major factor in electricity supply with a range of significant technical, commercial and financial hurdles to be overcome. The offshore wind industry has the potential for a very bright future and to emerge as a new industrial sector, as Figure 3 implies.

Table 9. World hydro potential and development

Continent	Africa	Asia	Australia & Oceania	Europe	North & Central America	South America
Gross theoretical hydropower potential (GWhy^{-1})	4×10^6	19.4×10^6	59.4×10^6	3.2×10^6	6×10^6	6.2×10^6
Technically feasible hydropower potential (GWhy^{-1})	1.75×10^6	6.8×10^6	2×10^6	10^6	1.66×10^6	2.7×10^6
Economically feasible hydropower potential (GWhy^{-1})	1.1×10^5	3.6×10^6	90×10^4	79×10^4	10^6	1.6×10^6
Installed hydro capacity (MW)	21×10^3	24.5×10^4	13.3×10^4	17.7×10^4	15.8×10^4	11.4×10^4
Production by hydro plants in 2002 or average (GWhy^{-1})	83.4×10^3	80×10^4	43×10^3	568×10^3	694×10^3	55×10^4
Hydro capacity under construction (MW)	> 3024	$>72.7 \times 10^3$	>177	$>23 \times 10^2$	58×10^2	$>17 \times 10^3$
Planned hydro capacity (MW)	77.5×10^3	$>17.5 \times 10^4$	>647	$>10^3$	$>15 \times 10^3$	$>59 \times 10^3$

Figure 1. The renewable cycle

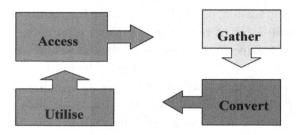

The speed of turbine development is such that more powerful models would supersede the original specification turbines in the time from concept to turbine order. Levels of activities are growing at a phenomenal rate (Figure 4), new prospects developing, new players entering, existing players growing in experience; technology evolving and, quite significantly, politics appear to support the sector.

5. ENERGY AND SUSTAINABLE DEVELOPMENT

Sustainability is defined as the extent to which progress and development should meet the need of the present without compromising the ability of the future generations to meet their own needs (Odeku, Maveneka, Konanani, 2013). This encompasses a variety of levels and scales ranging from economic development and agriculture, to the management of human settlements and building practices. Tables (10-12) indicate the relationship between energy conservation, sustainable development and environment.

The following issues were addressed during the Rio Earth Summit in 1992 (Abdeen, 2009):

- The use of local materials and indigenous building sources.
- Incentive to promote the continuation of traditional techniques, with regional resources and self-help strategies.
- Regulation of energy-efficient design principles.
- International information exchange on all aspects of construction related to the environment, among architects and contractors, particularly non-conventional resources.
- Exploration of methods to encourage and facilitate the recycling and reuse of building materials, especially those requiring intensive energy use during manufacturing, and the use of clean technologies.

And, the following action areas for producers were recommended:

- **Management and measurement tools:** Adopting environmental management systems appropriate for the business.

Figure 2. Global prospects of wind energy utilisation by 2003-2010

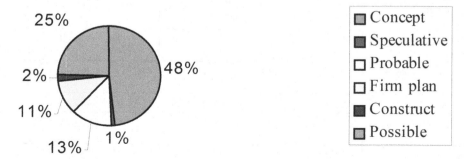

Figure 3. Prospect turbines share for 2003-2010

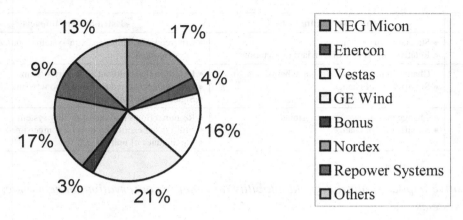

Figure 4. Average windfarm capacity 2003-2010

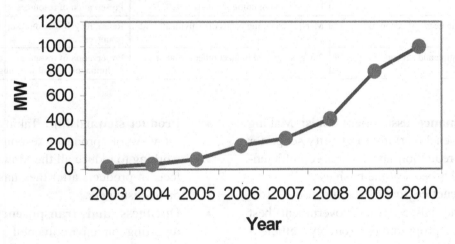

Table 10. Energy and sustainable environment

Technological Criteria	Energy and Environment Criteria	Social and Economic Criteria
Primary energy saving in regional scale	Sustainability according to greenhouse gas pollutant emissions	Labour impact
Technical maturity, and reliability	Sustainable according to other pollutant emissions	Market maturity
Consistence of installation and maintenance requirements with local technical known-how	Land requirement	Compatibility with political, legislative and administrative situation
Continuity and predictability of performance	Sustainability according to other environmental impacts	Cost of saved primary energy

Table 11. Classification of key variables defining facility sustainability

Criteria	Intra-System Impacts	Extra-System Impacts
Stakeholder satisfaction	• Standard expectations met. • Relative importance of standard expectations.	• Covered by attending to extra-system resource base and ecosystem impacts.
Resource base impacts	• Change in intra-system resource bases. • Significance of change.	• Resource flow into/out of facility system. • Unit impact exerted by flow on source/sink system. • Significance of unit impact.
Ecosystem impacts	• Change in intra-system ecosystems. • Significance of change.	• Resource flows into/out of facility system. • Unit impact exerted by how on source/sink system. • Significance of unit impact.

Table 12. Positive impact of durability, adaptability and energy conservation on economic, social and environment systems

Economic System	Social System	Environmental System
Durability	Preservation of cultural values	Preservation of resources
Meeting changing needs of economic development	Meeting changing needs of individuals and society	Reuse, recycling and preservation of resources
Energy conservation and saving	Savings directed to meet other social needs	Preservation of resources, reduction of pollution and global warming

- **Performance assessment tools:** Making use of benchmarking to identify scope for impact reduction and greater eco-efficiency in all aspects of the business.

- **Best practice tools:** Making use of free help and advice from government best practice programmes (energy efficiency, environmental technology, resource savings).

- **Innovation and ecodesign:** Rethinking the delivery of 'value added' by the business, so that impact reduction and resource efficiency are firmly built in at the design stage.

- **Cleaner, leaner production processes:** Pursuing improvements and savings in waste minimisation, energy and water consumption, transport and distribution, as well as reduced emissions.

- **Supply chain management:** Specifying more demanding standards of sustainability from 'upstream' suppliers, while supporting smaller firms to meet those higher standards.

- **Product stewardship:** Taking the broadest view of 'producer responsibility' and working to reduce all the 'downstream' effects of products after they have been sold on to customers.

- **Openness and transparency:** Publicly reporting on environmental performance against meaningful targets; actively using clear labels and declarations so that customers are fully informed; building stakeholder confidence by communicating sustainability aims to the workforce, the shareholders and the local community (Figure 5).

This is the step in a long journey to encourage progressive economy, which continues to provide people with high living standards, but, at the same time helps reduce pollution, waste mountains, other environmental degradation, and environmental rationale for future policy-making and intervention to improve market mechanisms. This vision will be accomplished by:

Figure 5. Link between resources and productivity

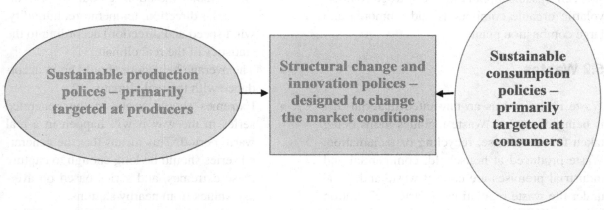

- 'Decoupling' economic growth and environmental degradation. The basket of indicators illustrated in Table 13 shows the progress being made. Decoupling air and water pollution from growth, making good headway with CO_2 emissions from energy, and transport. The environmental impact of our own individual behaviour is more closely linked to consumption expenditure than the economy as a whole.

- Focusing policy on the most important environmental impacts associated with the use of particular resources, rather than on the total level of all resource use.

- Increasing the productivity of material and energy use that are economically efficient by encouraging patterns of supply and demand, which are more efficient in the use of natural resources. The aim is to promote innovation and competitiveness. Investment in areas like energy efficiency, water efficiency and waste minimisation.

- Encouraging and enabling active and informed individual and corporate consumers.

5.1 Chemicals

Humans and wildlife are being contaminated by a host of commonly used chemicals in food packaging and furniture, according to the World Wildlife Federation (WWF) and European Union (Abdeen, 2008). Currently, the chemical industry has been under no obligation to make the information public. However, the new proposed rules would change this. Future dangers will only be averted if the effects of chemicals are exposed and then the dangerous ones are never used. Indeed, chemicals used for jacket waterproofing, food packaging and non-stick coatings have been found in dolphins, whales, cormorants, seals, sea eagles and polar bears from the Mediterranean to the Baltic. The European Commission has adopted an ambitious action plan to improve the development and wider use of environmental technologies such as recycling systems for wastewater in industrial processes, energy-saving car engines and soil remediation techniques, using hydrogen and fuel cells (Abdeen, 2012). The legislation, which has not been implemented in time, concerns the incineration of waste, air quality limit, values for benzene and carbon monoxide, national emission ceilings for sulphur dioxide, nitrogen oxides, volatile organic compounds and ammonia and large combustion plants.

5.2 Wastes

Waste is defined as an unwanted material that is being discarded. Waste includes items being taken for further use, recycling or reclamation. Waste produced at household, commercial and industrial premises are control waste and come under the waste regulations. Waste Incineration Directive (WID) emissions limit values will favour efficient, inherently cleaner technologies that do not rely heavily on abatement. For existing plant, the requirements are likely to lead to improved control of:

- NO_x emissions, by the adoption of infurnace combustion control and abatement techniques.
- Acid gases, by the adoption of abatement techniques and optimisation of their control.
- Particulate control techniques, and their optimisation, e.g., of bag filters and electrostatic precipitators.

The waste and resources action programme has been working hard to reduce demand for virgin aggregates and market uptake of recycled and secondary alternatives. The programme targets are:

- To deliver training and information on the role of recycling and secondary aggregates in sustainable construction for influences in the supply chain; and
- To develop a promotional programme to highlight the new information on websites.

5.3 Global Warming

This results in the following requirements:

- Relevant climate variables should be generated (solar radiation: global, diffuse, direct solar direction, temperature, humidity, wind speed and direction) according to the statistics of the real climate.
- The average behaviour should be in accordance with the real climate.
- Extremes should occur in the generated series in the way it will happen in a real warm period. This means that the generated series should be long enough to capture these extremes, and series based on average values from nearby stations.

On some climate change issues (such as global warming), there is no disagreement among the scientists. The greenhouse effect is unquestionably real; it is essential for life on earth. Water vapour is the most important GHG; followed by carbon dioxide (CO_2). Without a natural greenhouse effect, scientists estimate that the earth's average temperature would be −18°C instead of its present 14°C (Raphael, 2012). There is also no scientific debate over the fact that human activity has increased the concentration of the GHGs in the atmosphere (especially CO_2 from combustion of coal, oil and gas). The greenhouse effect is also being amplified by increased concentrations of other gases, such as methane, nitrous oxide, and CFCs as a result of human emissions. Most scientists predict that rising global temperatures will raise the sea level and increase the frequency of intense rain or snowstorms. Climate change scenarios sources of uncertainty and factors influencing the future climate are:

- The future emission rates of the GHGs (Table 14).
- The effect of this increase in concentration on the energy balance of the atmosphere.
- The effect of these emissions on GHGs concentrations in the atmosphere.
- The effect of this change in energy balance on global and regional climate.

Table 13. The basket of indicators for sustainable consumption and production

Economy-Wide Decoupling Indicators	
1	Greenhouse gas emissions
2	Air pollution
3	Water pollution (river water quality)
4	Commercial and industrial waste arisings and household waste not cycled
Resource Use Indicators	
5	Material use
6	Water abstraction.
7	Homes built on land not previously developed, and number of households
Decoupling Indicators for Specific Sectors	
8	Emissions from electricity generation
9	Motor vehicle kilometres and related emissions
10	Agricultural output, fertiliser use, methane emissions and farmland bird populations
11	Manufacturing output, energy consumption and related emissions
12	Household consumption, expenditure energy, water consumption and waste generated.

It has been known for a long time that urban centres have mean temperatures higher than their less developed surroundings. The urban heat increases the average and peak air temperatures, which in turn affect the demand for heating and cooling. Higher temperatures can be beneficial in the heating season, lowering fuel use, but they exacerbate the energy demand for cooling in the summer times.

Neither heating nor cooling may dominate the fuel use in a building in temperate climates, and the balance of the effect of the heat is less. As the provision of cooling is expensive with higher environmental cost, ways of using innovative alternative systems, like the mop fan will be appreciated. The solar gains would affect energy consumption. Therefore, lower or higher percentages of glazing, or shading devices might affect the balance between annual heating and cooling loads. In addition to conditioning energy, the fan energy needed to provide mechanical ventilation can make a significant further contribution to energy demand. Much depends on the efficiency of design, both in relation to the performance of fans themselves and to the resistance to flow arising from the associated ductwork. Figure 6 illustrates the typical fan and thermal conditioning needs for a variety of ventilation rates and climate conditions.

Table 14. West European states GHG emissions

Country	1990	1999	Change 1990-99	Reduction Target
Austria	76.9	79.2	2.6%	-13%
Belgium	136.7	140.4	2.8%	-7.5%
Denmark	70.0	73.0	4.0%	-21.0%
Finland	77.1	76.2	-1.1%	0.0%
France	545.7	544.5	-0.2%	0.0%
Germany	1206.5	982.4	-18.7%	-21.0%
Greece	105.3	123.2	16.9%	25.0%
Ireland	53.5	65.3	22.1%	13.0%
Italy	518.3	541.1	4.4%	-6.5%
Luxembourg	10.8	6.1	-43.3%	-28.0%
Netherlands	215.8	230.1	6.1%	-6.0%
Portugal	64.6	79.3	22.4%	27.0%
Spain	305.8	380.2	23.2%	15.0%
Sweden	69.5	70.7	1.5%	4.0%
United Kingdom	741.9	637.9	-14.4%	-12.5%
Total EU-15	4199	4030	-4.0%	-8.0%

Figure 6. Energy impact of ventilation

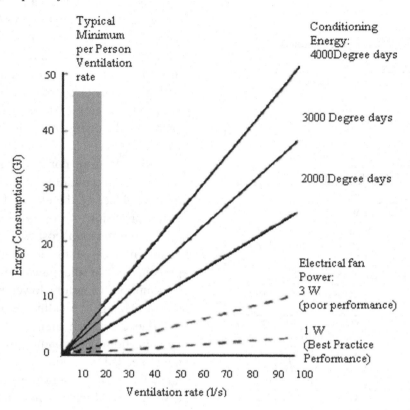

5.4 Ground Source Heat Pumps

The term "ground source heat pump" has become an all-inclusive term to describe a heat pump system that uses the earth, ground water, or surface water as a heat source and/or sink. Some of the most common types of ground source ground-loop heat exchangers configurations are classified in Figure 7. The GSHP systems consist of three loops or cycles as shown in Figure 8. The first loop is on the load side and is either an air/water loop or a water/water loop, depending on the application. The second loop is the refrigerant loop inside a water source heat pump. Thermodynamically, there is no difference between the well-known vapour-compression refrigeration cycle and the heat pump cycle; both systems absorb heat at a low temperature level and reject it to a higher temperature level. However, the difference between the two systems is that a refrigeration application is only concerned with the low temperature effect produced at the evaporator, while a heat pump may be concerned with both the cooling effect produced at the evaporator and the heating effect produced at the condenser. In these dual-mode GSHP systems, a reversing valve is used to switch between heating and cooling modes by reversing the refrigerant flow direction. The third loop in the system is the ground loop in which water or an antifreeze solution exchanges heat with the refrigerant and the earth.

The GSHPs utilise the thermal energy stored in the earth through either vertical or horizontal closed loop heat exchange systems buried in the ground. Many geological factors impact directly on site characterisation and subsequently the design and cost of the system. The solid geology of the United Kingdom varies significantly.

Figure 7. Common types of ground-loop heat exchangers

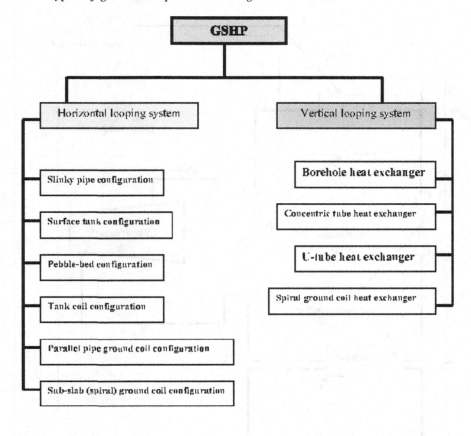

Furthermore there is an extensive and variable rock head cover. The geological prognosis for a site and its anticipated rock properties influence the drilling methods and therefore system costs. Other factors important to system design include predicted subsurface temperatures and the thermal and hydrological properties of strata. The GSHP technology is well established in Sweden, Germany and North America, but has had minimal impact in the United Kingdom space heating and cooling market. Perceived barriers to uptake include geological uncertainty, concerns regarding performance and reliability, high capital costs and lack of infrastructure. System performance concerns relate mostly to uncertainty in design input parameters, especially the temperature and thermal properties of the source. These in turn can impact on the capital cost, much of which is associated with the installation of the external loop in horizontal trenches or vertical boreholes. The climate in the United Kingdom makes the potential for heating in winter and cooling in summer from a ground source less certain owing to the temperature ranges being narrower than those encountered in continental climates. This project will develop an impartial GSHP function on the site to make available information and data on site-specific temperatures and key geotechnical characteristics.

The GSHPs are receiving increasing interest because of their potential to reduce primary energy consumption and thus reduce emissions of greenhouse gases. The technology is well established in North Americas and parts of Europe, but is at the demonstration stage in the United Kingdom. The information will be delivered from digital geoscience's themes that have been developed from observed data held in corporate records. This

Figure 8. Schematic of the GSHP system (heating mode operation)

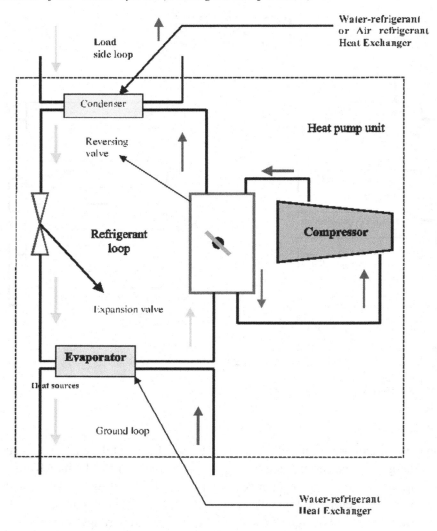

data will be available to the GSHP installers and designers to assist the design process, therefore reducing uncertainties. The research will also be used to help inform the public as to the potential benefits of this technology.

The GSHPs play a key role in geothermal development in Central and Northern Europe. With borehole heat exchangers as heat source, they offer de-central geothermal heating with great flexibility to meet given demands at virtually any location. No space cooling is included in the vast majority of systems, leaving ground-source

heat pumps with some economic constraints. Nevertheless, a promising market development first occurred in Switzerland and Sweden, and now also in Austria and Germany. Approximately 20 years of R and D focusing on borehole heat exchangers resulted in a well-established concept of sustainability for this technology, as well as in sound design and installation criteria. The market success brought Switzerland to the third rank worldwide in geothermal direct use. The future prospects are good, with an increasing range of applications including large systems with thermal energy storage for heating and cooling, ground-source heat pumps in densely populated development areas, borehole heat exchangers for cooling of telecommunication equipment, etc.

Loops can be installed in three ways: horizontally, vertically or in a pond or lake (Figure 9). The type chosen depends on the available land area, soil and rock type at the installation site. These factors help to determine the most economical choice for installation of the ground loop. The GSHP delivers (3-4) times as much energy as it consumes when heating, and cools and dehumidifies for a lower cost than conventional air conditioning. It can cut homes or business heating and cooling costs by 50% and provide hot water free or with substantial savings. The GSHPs can reduce the energy required for space heating, cooling and service water heating in commercial/institutional buildings by as much as 50%.

Efficiencies of the GSHP systems are much greater than conventional air-source heat pump systems. A higher COP (coefficient of performance) can be achieved by a GSHP because the source/sink earth temperature is relatively constant compared to air temperatures. Additionally, heat is absorbed and rejected through water, which is a more desirable heat transfer medium because of its relatively high heat capacity. The GSHP systems rely on the fact that, under normal geothermal gradients of about 0.5°F/100 ft (30°C/km), the earth temperature is roughly constant in a zone extending from about 20 ft (6.1 m) deep to about 150 ft (45.7 m) deep. This constant temperature interval within the earth is the result of a complex interaction of heat fluxes from above (the sun and the atmosphere) and from below (the earth interior). As a result, the temperature of this interval within the earth is approximately equal to the average annual air temperature (Roriz, 2001). Above this zone (less than about 20 feet (6.1 m) deep), the earth temperature is a damped version of the air temperature at the earth's surface. Below this zone (greater than about 150 ft (45.7 m) deep), the earth temperature begins to rise according to the natural geothermal gradient. The storage concept is based on a modular design that will facilitate active control and optimisation of thermal input/output, and it can be adapted for simultaneous heating and cooling often needed in large service and institutional buildings (Strauss, 2013). Loading of the core is done by diverting warm and cold air from the heat pump through the core during periods with excess capacity compared to the current need of the building (Tukahirwa, 2013; Valkila, and Saari, 2012). The cool section of the core can also be loaded directly with air during the night, especially in spring and fall when nights are cold and days may be warm.

Figure 9. The GSHPs extract solar heat stored in the upper layers of the earth

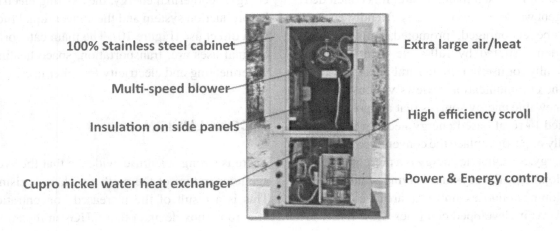

100% Stainless steel cabinet

Multi-speed blower

Insulation on side panels

Cupro nickel water heat exchanger

Extra large air/heat

High efficiency scroll

Power & Energy control

6. DISCUSSIONS

Peoples rely upon oil for primary energy and this for a few more decades. Other conventional sources may be more enduring, but are not without serious disadvantages (Vargas-Parra, 2013). The renewable energy resources are particularly suited for the provision of rural power supplies and a major advantage is that equipment such as flat plate solar driers, wind machines, etc., can be constructed using local resources and without the advantage results from the feasibility of local maintenance and the general encouragement such local manufacture gives to the build up of small-scale rural based industry. This communication comprises a comprehensive review of energy sources, the environment and sustainable development. It includes the renewable energy technologies, energy efficiency systems, energy conservation scenarios, energy savings in greenhouses environment and other mitigation measures necessary to reduce climate change. This study gives some examples of small-scale energy converters, nevertheless it should be noted that small conventional, i.e., engines are currently the major source of power in rural areas and will continue to be so for a long time to come. There is a need for some further development to suit local conditions, to minimise spares holdings, to maximise interchangeability both of engine parts and of the engine application. Emphasis should be placed on full local manufacture. It is concluded that renewable environmentally friendly energy must be encouraged, promoted, implemented and demonstrated by full-scale plant (device) especially for use in remote rural areas.

The communication reviews various options of renewable energy sources that are possibly be applied to rural based energy needs which may wholly or partly replace the conventional sources of energy. Sustainable energy is a prerequisite for development. Energy-based living standards in developing countries, however, are clearly below standards in developed countries. Low levels of access to affordable and environmentally sound energy in both rural and urban low-income areas are therefore a predominant issue in developing countries. In recent years many programmes for development aid or technical assistance have been focusing on improving access to sustainable energy, many of them with impressive results. Apart from success stories, however, experience also shows that positive appraisals of many projects evaporate after completion and vanishing of the implementation expert team. Altogether, the diffusion of sustainable technologies such as energy efficiency and renewable energy for cooking, heating, lighting, electrical appliances and building insulation in developing countries has been slow. Energy efficiency and renewable energy programmes could be more sustainable and pilot studies more effective and pulse releasing if the entire policy and implementation process was considered and redesigned from the outset. New financing and implementation processes, which allow reallocating financial resources and thus enabling countries themselves to achieve a sustainable energy infrastructure, are also needed. The links between the energy policy framework, financing and implementation of renewable energy and energy efficiency projects have to be strengthened and as well as efforts made to increase people's knowledge through training. Different sources of energy, which can be used for different final uses. Those sources are wind power, solar energy, geothermal energy, the existing electricity production system and the conventional fuels with direct use (Figure 10). The main categories of final uses are: transportation, space heating, water heating and electricity for other uses.

7. CONCLUSION

There is strong scientific evidence that the average temperature of the earth's surface is rising. This is a result of the increased concentration of carbon dioxide and other GHGs in the atmo-

Figure 10. Energy sources their final uses

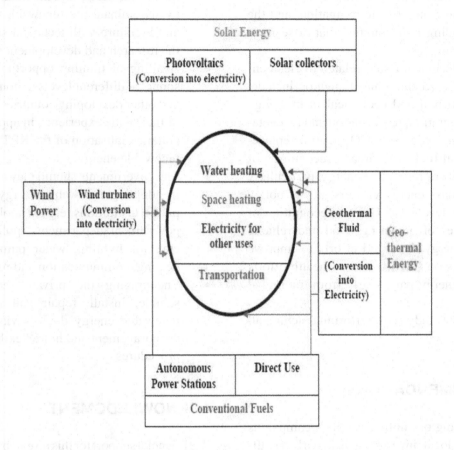

sphere as released by burning fossil fuels. This global warming will eventually lead to substantial changes in the world's climate, which will, in turn, have a major impact on human life and the built environment. Therefore, effort has to be made to reduce fossil energy use and to promote green energy, particularly in the building sector. Energy use reductions can be achieved by minimising the energy demand, rational energy use, recovering heat and the use of more green energy. This study was a step towards achieving this goal.

The adoption of green or sustainable approaches to the way in which society is run is seen as an important strategy in finding a solution to the energy problem. The key factors to reducing and controlling CO_2, which is the major contributor to global warming, are the use of alternative ap-

proaches to energy generation and the exploration of how these alternatives are used today and may be used in the future as green energy sources. Even with modest assumptions about the availability of land, comprehensive fuel-wood farming programmes offer significant energy, economic and environmental benefits. These benefits would be dispersed in rural areas where they are greatly needed and can serve as linkages for further rural economic development.

However, by adopting coherent strategy for alternative clean sustainable energy sources, the world as a whole would benefit from savings in foreign exchange, improved energy security, and socio-economic improvements. With a nine-fold increase in forest–plantation cover, every nation's resource base would be greatly improved while the international community would benefit from pollution reduction, climate mitigation, and the increased trading opportunities that arise from new income sources.

The non-technical issues related to clean energy, which have recently gained attention, include: (1) Environmental and ecological factors, e.g., carbon sequestration, reforestation and revegetation. (2) Renewables as a CO_2 neutral replacement for fossil fuels. (3) Greater recognition of the importance of renewable energy, particularly modern biomass energy carriers, at the policy and planning levels. (4) Greater recognition of the difficulties of gathering good and reliable renewable energy data, and efforts to improve it. (5) Studies on the detrimental health efforts of biomass energy particularly from traditional energy users.

The present study is one effort in touching all these aspects.

8. RECOMMENDATIONS

- Launching of public awareness campaigns among local investors particularly small-scale entrepreneurs and end users of the RET to highlight the importance and benefits of renewable, particularly solar, wind, and biomass energies.
- Amendment of the encouragement of investment act, to include furthers concessions, facilities, tax holidays, and preferential treatment to attract national and foreign capital investment.
- Allocation of a specific percentage of soft loans and grants obtained by governments to augment budgets of the (R&D) related to manufacturing and commercialisation of the RET.
- Governments should give incentives to encourage the household sector to use renewable energy instead of conventional energy. Execute joint investments between

the private sector and the financing entities to disseminate the renewable information and literature with technical support from the research and development entities.

- Availing of training opportunities to personnel at different levels in donor countries and other developing countries to make use of their wide experience in application and commercialisation of the RET particularly renewable energy.
- The governments should play a leading role in adopting renewable energy devices in public institutions, e.g., schools, hospitals, government departments, police stations, etc., for lighting, water pumping, water heating, communication and refrigeration.
- Encouraging the private sector to assemble, install, repair and manufacture renewable energy devices via investment encouragement and more flexible licensing procedures.

ACKNOWLEDGMENT

The financial support for this research work is from the Energy Research Institute (ERI). Thanks to my wife Kawthar Abdelhai Ali for her warmth and love. Her unwavering faith in me, her intelligence, humour, spontaneity, curiosity and wisdom added to this article and to my life.

REFERENCES

Abdeen, M. O. (2008). Green energies and environment. *Renewable & Sustainable Energy Reviews*, *12*, 1789–1821. doi:10.1016/j.rser.2006.05.009

Abdeen, M. O. (2009). Principle of low energy building design: Heating, ventilation and air conditioning, Cooling India. *India's Premier Magazine on the Cooling Industry, Mumbai, India.*, 5(4), 26–46.

Abdeen, M. O. (2012). Clean and green energy technologies: Sustainable development and environment. *Sky J. Agric. Res., 1*(2), 28–50.

ASHRAE. (2003). Energy efficient design of new building except new low-rise residential buildings (BSRIASHRAE proposed standards 90-2P-1993, alternative GA). American Society of Heating, Refrigerating, and Air Conditioning Engineers Inc.

ASHRAE. (2005). *Commercial/Institutional Ground Source Heat Pump Engineering Manual. American Society of heating.* Atlanta, GA, USA: Refrigeration and Air-conditioning Engineers, Inc.

Barabaro, S., Coppolino, S., Leone, C., & Sinagra, E. (1978). Global solar radiation in Italy. *Solar Energy, 20,* 431–435. doi:10.1016/0038-092X(78)90163-9

Baruah, D. (1995). Utilisation pattern of human and fuel energy in the plantation. *Journal of Agriculture and Soil Science, 8*(2), 189–192.

Bendewald, M., & Zhai, Z. J. (2013). Using carrying capacity as a base line for building sustainability assessment. *Habitat International, 37,* 22–32. doi:10.1016/j.habitatint.2011.12.021

Bos, E., My, T., Vu, E., & Bulatao, R. (1994). *World population projection: 1994-95.* Baltimore, London: World Bank by the John Hopkins University Press.

CAEEDAC. (2000). *A descriptive analysis of energy consumption in agriculture and food sector in Canada* (Final Report, February 2000). The Canadian Agricultural Energy End-Use Data and Analysis.

Cantrell, J., & Wepfer, W. (1984). Shallow Ponds for Dissipation of Building Heat: A case Study. *ASHRAE Transactions, 90*(1), 239–246.

D'Apote, S. L. (1998). IEA biomass energy analysis and projections. In *Proceedings of Biomass Energy Conference: Data, analysis and Trends.* Paris: OECD.

David, J. M. (2000). Developing hydrogen and fuel cell products. *Energy World,* (303), 16–17.

Duchin, F. (1995). *Global scenarios about lifestyle and technology, the sustainable future of the global system.* Tokyo: United Nations University.

Duffie, J. A., & Beckman, W. A. (1980). *Solar Engineering of Thermal Processes.* New York: J. Wiley and Sons.

Dutt, B. (1982). Comparative efficiency of energy use in rice production. *Energy, 6,* 25.

EWEA. (2003). Wind force 12. Brussels: European Wind Energy Associaton.

Gerald, S. (2012). Why we disagree about climate change: A different viewpoint. *Energy & Environment, 23*(8), 76–95.

Givoni, B. (1998). *Climate consideration in building and urban design.* New York: Van Nostrand Reinhold.

Glaas, E., & Juhola, S. (2013). New levels of climate adaptation policy: Analysing the institutional interplay in the Baltic Sea Region. *Sustainability, 1,* 56–122.

Hall, O., & Scrase, J. (1998). Will biomass be the environmentally friendly fuel of the future? *Biomass and Bioenergy, 15,* 357–367. doi:10.1016/S0961-9534(98)00030-0

IHA. (2003). *World Atlas & Industry Guide.* United Kingdom: The International Journal Hydropower & Dams.

John, A., & James, S. (1989). *The power of place: bringing together geographical and sociological imaginations, 1989.* Academic Press.

Kammerud, R., Ceballos, E., Curtis, B., Place, W., & Anderson, B. (1984). Ventilation cooling of residential buildings. ASHRAE Trans, 90(1B).

Kavanaugh, S., & Rafferty, K. (1997). *Ground source heat pumps. Design of Geothermal Systems for Commercial and Institutional Buildings. American Society of heating.* Atlanta, GA, USA: Refrigeration and Air-conditioning Engineers, Inc.

Lin, K., & Chang, T. C. (2013). Everyday crises: Marginal society livelihood vulnerability and adaptability to hazards. *Progress in Development Studies, 13*(1), 1–18. doi:10.1177/146499341201300101

Morrow, K. (2012). Rio+20, the green economy and re-orienting sustainable development. *Environmental Law Review, 14*(4), 15–23.

Njeru, J. (2013). 'Donor-driven' neoliberal reform processes and urban environmental change in Kenya: The case of Karura Forest in Nairobi. *Progress in Development Studies, 13*(1), 63–78. doi:10.1177/146499341201300105

Odeku, K. O., Maveneka, A., & Konanani, R. H. (2013). Consequences of Country's Withdrawal from Climate Change Agreements: Implications for Carbon Emissions Reduction. *Journal of Human Ecology (Delhi, India), 41*(1), 17–24.

OECD/IEA. (2004). Renewables for power generation: status and prospect. Paris: Organisation for Economic Co-operation and Development.

Okkan, P. (1993). Reducing CO_2 emissions-How do heat pumps compete with other options? *IEA Heat Pump Centre Newsletter, 11*(3), 24–26.

Pernille, M (2004, March/April). Feature: Danish lessons on district heating. *Energy Resource Sustainable Management and Environmental*, 16-17.

Raphael, A. T. (2012). Energy and Climate Change: Critical reflection on the African Continent; Is There an Ideal REDD+ Program?. *An Analysis of Journal Sustainable Development in Africa, 14*(6), 25–36.

Rees, W. E. (1999). The built environment and the ecosphere: a global perspective. *Building Research and Information, 27*(4), 206–220. doi:10.1080/096132199369336

Roriz, L (2001). *Determining the potential energy and environmental effects reduction of air conditioning systems.* Commission of the European Communities DG TREN.

Shaviv, E. (1989). The influence of the thermal mass on the thermal performance of buildings in summer and winter. In T. C. Steemers, & W. Palz (Eds.), *Science and Technology at the service of architecture* (pp. 470–472). Dordrecht: Kluwer Academic Publishers.

Singh, J. (2000). *On farm energy use pattern in different cropping systems in Haryana, India.* Germany: International Institute of Management-University of Flensburg, Sustainable Energy Systems and Management, Master of Science.

Sitarz, D. (1992). *Agenda 21: The Earth Summit Strategy to save our planet.* Boulder, CO: Earth Press.

Sivkov, S. I. (1964). To the methods of computing possible radiation in Italy. *Trans. Main Geophys. Obs., 1964*, 160.

Sivkov, S. I. (1964). On the computation of the possible and relative duration of sunshine. *Trans. Main Geophys Obs, 160*, 1964.

Steele, J. (1997). *Sustainable architecture: principles, paradigms, and case studies.* New York: McGraw-Hill Inc.

Strauss, J. (2013). Does housing drive state-level job growth? Building permits and consumer expectations forecast a state's economic activity. *Journal of Urban Economics, 73*, 77–65. doi:10.1016/j.jue.2012.07.005

Thakur, C., & Mistra, B. (1993). Energy requirements and energy gaps for production of major crops in India. *Agricultural Situation of India*, *48*, 665–689.

The United Nations Framework Convention on Climate Change (UNFCCC). (2009). The draft of the Copenhagen Climate Change Treaty (pp. 3–181). The United Nations Framework Convention on Climate Change.

Tukahirwa, J. T. (2013). Comparing urban sanitation and solid waste management in East African metropolises: The role of civil society organisations. *Cities (London, England)*, *30*, 204–211. doi:10.1016/j.cities.2012.03.007

United Nations (UN). (2003). World urbanisation project: the 2002 revision. New York: The United Nations Population Division.

Valkila, N., & Saari, A. (2012). Perceptions Held by Finnish Energy Sector Experts Regarding Public Attitudes to Energy Issues. *J. Sustainable Dev.*, *5*(11), 23–45.

Vargas-Parra, M. V. (2013). Applying exergy analysis to rainwater harvesting systems to assess resource efficiency. *Resources, Conservation and Recycling*, *72*, 50–59. doi:10.1016/j.resconrec.2012.12.008

Wu, J., & Boggess, W. (1999). The optimal allocation of conservation funds. *Journal of Environmental Economics and Management*, *38*.

Yaldiz, O., Ozturk, H., & Zeren, Y. (1993). Energy usage in production of field crops in Turkey. In *Proceedings of 5th International Congress on Mechanisation and Energy Use in Agriculture*. Kusadasi.

KEY TERMS AND DEFINITIONS

Biomass Energy: The energy embodied in organic matter ("biomass") that is released when chemical bonds are broken by microbial digestion, combustion, or decomposition. Biofuels are a wide range of fuels, which are in some way derived from biomass. The term covers solid biomass, liquid fuels and various biogases. Biofuels are gaining increased public and scientific attention, driven by factors such as oil price spikes and the need for increased energy security.

Environment: The natural environment, commonly referred to simply as the environment, encompasses all living and non-living things occurring naturally on Earth or some region thereof. The biophysical environment is the symbiosis between the physical environment and the biological life forms within the environment, and includes all variables that comprise the Earth's biosphere.

Geothermal Energy: Geothermal power (from the Greek roots geo, meaning earth, and thermos, meaning heat) is power extracted from heat stored in the earth. This geothermal energy originates from the original formation of the planet, from radioactive decay of minerals, and from solar energy absorbed at the surface. Heat transferred from the earth's molten core to underground deposits of dry steam (steam with no water droplets), wet steam (a mixture of steam and water droplets), hot water, or rocks lying fairly close to the earth's surface.

Greenhouse Gases: Greenhouse gases are gases in an atmosphere that absorb and emit radiation within the thermal infrared range. This process is the fundamental cause of the greenhouse effect. The main greenhouse gases in the Earth's atmosphere are water vapour, carbon dioxide, methane, nitrous oxide, and ozone. Changes in the concentration of certain greenhouse gases, due to human activity such as fossil fuel burning, increase the risk of global climate change.

Hydropower: Hydropower, hydraulic power or waterpower is power that is derived from the force or energy of moving water, which may be harnessed for useful purposes. Hydropower is using water to power machinery or make electricity. Water constantly moves through a vast global cycle, evaporating from lakes and oceans, forming clouds, precipitating as rain or snow, and then flowing back down to the ocean.

Renewable Energy: Renewable energy is energy generated from natural resources such as sunlight, wind, rain, tides, and geothermal heat, which are renewable (naturally replenished). Energy obtained from sources that are essentially inexhaustible (unlike, for example the fossil fuels, of which there is a finite supply). Energy sources that are, within a short time frame relative to the Earth's natural cycles, sustainable, and include non-carbon technologies such as solar energy, hydropower, and wind, as well as carbon-neutral technologies.

Resource Management: Efficient incident management requires a system for identifying available resources at all jurisdictional levels to enable timely and unimpeded access to resources needed to prepare for, respond to, or recover from an incident. Resource management is the efficient and effective deployment for an organisation's resources when they are needed. Such resources may include financial resources, inventory, human skills, production resources, or information technology (IT).

Solar Energy: Energy from the sun that is converted into thermal or electrical energy; "the amount of energy falling on the earth is given by the solar constant, but very little use has been made of solar energy". Energy derived ultimately from the sun. It can be divided into direct and indirect categories. Most energy sources on Earth are forms of indirect solar energy, although we usually do not think of them in that way. Solar energy uses semiconductor material to convert sunlight into electric currents. Although solar energy only provides 0.15% of the world's power and less than 1% of USA energy, experts believe that sunlight has the potential to supply 5,000 times, as much energy as the world currently consumes.

Sustainable Development: Development, which seeks to produce sustainable economic growth, while ensuring future generations' ability to do the same by not exceeding the regenerative capacity of the nature. In other words, it is trying to protect the environment. A process of change in which the resources consumed (both social and ecological) are not depleted to the extent that they cannot be replicated. Environmentally friendly forms of economic growth activities (agriculture, logging, manufacturing, etc.) that allow the continued production of a commodity without damage to the ecosystem (soil, water supplies, biodiversity or other surrounding resources).

Wind Energy: Kinetic energy present in wind motion that can be converted to mechanical energy for driving pumps, mills, and electric power generators. Wind power is the conversion of wind energy into a useful form of energy, such as using wind turbines to make electricity, wind mills for mechanical power, wind pumps for pumping water or drainage, or sails to propel ships.

Chapter 16
New Efficient Evolutionary Algorithm Applied to Optimal Reactive Power Dispatch

Provas Kumar Roy
Dr. B. C. Roy Engineering College, India

ABSTRACT

Evolutionary Algorithms (EAs) are well-known optimization techniques to deal with nonlinear and complex optimization problems. However, most of these population-based algorithms are computationally expensive due to the slow nature of the evolutionary process. To overcome this drawback and to improve the convergence rate, this chapter employs Quasi-Opposition-Based Learning (QOBL) in conventional Biogeography-Based Optimization (BBO) technique. The proposed Quasi-Oppositional BBO (QOBBO) is comprehensively developed and successfully applied for solving the Optimal Reactive Power Dispatch (ORPD) problem by minimizing the transmission loss when both equality and inequality constraints are satisfied. The proposed QOBBO algorithm's performance is studied with comparisons of Canonical Genetic Algorithm (CGA), five versions of Particle Swarm Optimization (PSO), Local Search-Based Self-Adaptive Differential Evolution (L-SADE), Seeker Optimization Algorithm (SOA), and BBO on the IEEE 30-bus, IEEE 57-bus, and IEEE 118-bus power systems. The simulation results show that the proposed QOBBO approach performed better than the other listed algorithms and can be efficiently used to solve small-, medium-, and large-scale ORPD problems.

1. INTRODUCTION

Optimal reactive power dispatch (ORPD) has a growing impact on secure and economical operation of power systems. It is an effective method to minimize the transmission losses and maintain the power system running under normal conditions. All controllable variables, such as voltage of generators, tap ratio of transformers, Var injection of shunt compensators, are determined which minimizes real power losses, satisfying a given set of operational constraints. It is an effective method to improve voltage level, decrease power losses and maintain the power system running under normal conditions.

DOI: 10.4018/978-1-4666-6252-0.ch016

Different classical techniques have been reported in the literature pertaining to ORPD problem, including conventional approaches such as linear programming (LP) (Aoki, Fan & Nishikor, 1988), interior point methods (Granville, 1994; Yan, Yu, Yu, & Bhattarai,2006) and dynamic programming (DP) (Lu, & Hsu, 1995). These methods are local optimizers in nature, i.e., they might converge to local solutions instead of global ones if the initial guess happens to be in the neighborhood of a local solution. DP method may cause the dimensions of the problem to become extremely large, thus requiring enormous computational efforts.

Methods such as evolutionary programming (EP) (Ma & Lai, 1996; Wu & Ma, 1995), genetic algorithm (GA) (Iba, 1994; Lee & Park, 1995; Swarup,Yoshimi & Izui, 1994), particle swarm optimization (PSO) (Kawata, Fukuyama,Takayama & Nakanish, 2000; Li, Cao, Liu, Liu & Jiang, 2009; Zhao, Guo and Cao, 2005), Tabu search (TS) (Yiqin, 2010), differential evolution (DE) (Liang, Chung, Wong & Dual,2007; Varadarajan & Swarup, 2008; Zhang, Chen, Dai & Cai 2010), SOA (Dai, Chen, Zhu & Zhang 2009a; Dai, Chen, Zhu & Zhang 2009b), BBO (Bhattacharya & Chattopadhyay, 2010) do not depend on convexity assumptions and are capable of handling non-linear optimization problems. Saraswat et al. proposed ORPD based hybrid fuzzy multi-objective evolutionary algorithm (HFMOEA) (Saraswat & Saini, 2013) to minimize power loss and voltage stability index simultaneously of IEEE 24 bus Reliability Test System (IEEE 24 bus RTS) and its performance was compared with non-dominated sorting genetic algorithms such (NSGA-II) and modified NSGA-II (MNSGA-II). Roy et al. proposed multi-objective gravitational search algorithm (MOGSA) (Roy, Mandal, & Bhattacharya, 2012) to solve optimal reactive power dispatch problem of IEEE 30-bus and IEEE-57 bus test systems. Abou El-Ela et al. presented ant colony optimization (ACO) (Abou El-Ela, Kinawy, El-Sehiemy & Mouwafi, 2011) to minimize the power loss of IEEE 14-bus, IEEE

30-bus and a real power system at West Delta Network as a part of the Unified Egyptian Network and the simulation results of the proposed method were compared with those of linear programming (LP), genetic algorithm (GA) and particle swarm optimization (PSO) techniques. A pareto based multi-objective differential evolution (MODE) approach (Ramesh, Kannan, & Baskar, 2012) to solve optimal reactive power dispatch (ORPD) which minimized the real power loss and improve bus voltage profile simultaneously was introduced by Ramesh et al. and the effectiveness of the proposed method was tested on IEEE-118 bus and IEEE 300-bus. Granada et al. implemented Lagrangian decomposition method (LDM) (Granada, Rider, Mantovani, & Shahidehpour, 2012) on IEEE RTS-96 system and a 354-bus system for solving ORPD problem. A pareto based ACO algorithm (Jaganathan, Palaniswami, Vignesh, & Mithunraj, 2011) for simultaneous minimization of the real power loss and the voltage stability index of ORPD problem was developed by Jaganathan et al. and the proposed method was implemented on IEEE 30-bus system to test its effectiveness. A multi-objective oppositional-based self-adaptive modified GSA (OMGSA) (Niknam, Narimani, Azizipanah-Abarghooee, & Bahmani-Firouzi, 2013) for solving ORPD problem which simultaneously minimized active power loss, voltage deviation, and voltage stability index was proposed by Niknam et al. Soler et al. in their recent endeavor introduced penalty-based nonlinear optimization technique (Soler, Asada & Costa, 2013). to solve ORPD problem. A fully distributed multiagent-based reinforcement learning method (Xu, Zhang, Liu & Ferrese, 2012) for solving ORPD problem was presented by Xu et al.. Duman et al. developed a ORPD based GSA approach (Duman, Sonmez, Guvenç & Yorukeren, 2012) for optimizing power losses, voltage profile and voltage stability of IEEE 30-bus, IEEE 57-bus and IEEE 118-bus test systems. Khazali and Kalantar introduced harmony search algorithm (HSA) (Khazali, & Kalantar, 2011) to solve ORPD problem. In this article, three different single objectives namely minimization of power loss, improvement of voltage profile and enhancement of voltage stability were used. To proof the superiority, the proposed method was implemented on IEEE 30-bus and IEEE 57-bus test systems and compared its performance with GA and PSO. Mallipeddi et al. implemented an efficient constraint handling method to solve the ORPD problem of IEEE 30-bus and IEEE 57-bus test systems.

Each of the above methods has its own characteristics, strengths and weaknesses; but long computational time is a common drawback for most of them, especially when the solution space is hard to explore. Many efforts have been made to accelerate convergence of these methods. In this article, quasi opposition-based learning (OBL) (Tizhoosh, 2005) is applied on BBO to make it faster and achieve better optimal solution. The concept of OBL is earlier applied to accelerate PSO (Zhang, Ni, Wu & Gu, 2009), DE (Rahnamayan, Tizhoosh & Salama, 2007), ant colony optimization (ACO) (Haiping, Xieyon & Baogen, 2010) and teaching learning based optimization (TLBO) (Mandal & Roy, 2013). The main idea behind the OBL is considering the estimate and opposite estimate (guess and opposite guess) at the same time in order to achieve a better approximation for current candidate solution. Purely random selection of solutions from a given population has the chance of visiting or even revisiting unproductive regions of the search space. The chance of this occurring is lower for opposite numbers than it is for purely random ones. A mathematical proof has been proposed (Haiping, Xieyong & Baogen, 2010) to show that, in general, opposite numbers are more likely to be closer to the optimal solution than purely random ones.

The effectiveness of the proposed QOBBO based ORPD algorithm is tested on IEEE 30-bus, IEEE 57-bus and IEEE 118-bus test systems. The results of QOBBO are compared to those of PSO, comprehensive learning PSO (CLPSO)

(Dai, Chen, Zhun & Zhang, 2009), CGA (Dai, Chen, Zhun & Zhang, 2009), real standard version of PSO (SPSO-07) (Dai, Chen, Zhun & Zhang, 2009), PSO with constriction factor (PSO-cf) (Dai, Chen, Zhun & Zhang, 2009), PSO with adaptive inertia weight (PSO-w) (Dai, Chen, Zhun & Zhang, 2009),, local search based self-adaptive differential evolution (L-SADE) (Dai, Chen, Zhun & Zhang, 2009), seeker optimization algorithm (SOA) (Dai, Chen, Zhun & Zhang, 2009), BBO (Bhattacharya & Chattopadhyay, 2010), BBO (Roy, Ghoshal & Thakur, 2012), interior point based OPF (IP-OPF) (Vlachogiannis & Lee, 2006), Conventional PSO (Vlachogiannis & Lee, 2006), coordinated aggregation (CA) (Vlachogiannis & Lee, 2006), general passive congregation PSO (GPAC) (Vlachogiannis & Lee, 2006) and local passive congregation PSO (LPAC) (Vlachogiannis & Lee, 2006) to make it clear that the proposed method is powerful and reliable.

This article is organized as follows. Section 2 formulates ORPD problems, Section 3 describes the basic theory and algorithm steps of the BBO technique. Opposition-based learning and quasi-oppositional based BBO applied to the ORPD are addressed in Section 4 and Section 5, respectively. Parameter selection and test results are presented in Section 6 and Section 7, respectively. Section 8 provides the conclusion of this article.

2. MATHEMATICAL PROBLEM FORMULATION

The general ORPD problem under normal operating condition may be formulated as follows:

$$Minimize \quad f(u,v) \tag{1}$$

$$\begin{cases} g(u,v) = 0 \\ h(u,v) \leq 0 \end{cases} \tag{2}$$

where $f(u, v)$ is the objective function; $g(u, v) = 0$ are the equality constraints; $h(u, v) = 0$ are the inequality constraints; u is the vector of dependent variables and may be expressed as:

$$u = [V_{L_1}, ..., V_{L_i}, ...V_{L_{NL}}, Q_{G_1}, ..., Q_{G_i}, ...,$$

$$Q_{G_{NG}}, S_{L_1}, ..., S_{L_i}, ..., S_{L_{NTL}}] \text{ where } V_{L_i}$$

is the voltage of the i-th load bus; Q_{G_i} is the reactive power generation of the i-th generator bus; S_{L_i} is the apparent power flow of the i-th branch; NL is the number of load buses; NG is the number of generator buses and NTL is the number of transmission lines.

v is the set of the independent variables, which may be expressed as shown below:

$$v = [V_{G_1}, ..., V_{G_i}, ..., V_{G_{NG}},$$

$$T_1, ..., T_i, ..., T_{NT}, Q_{C_1}, ..., Q_{C_i}, ..., Q_{C_{NC}}] \qquad (4)$$

where V_{G_i} is the voltage of the i-th generator bus; T_i is the tap setting of the i-th regulating transformer; Q_{C_i} is the reactive power generation of the i-th Var source; NT is the number of regulating transformers and NC is the number of shunt compensators.

2.1 Objective

The objective of ORPD problem is to minimize the transmission loss while satisfying all equality and inequality constraints. The transmission loss may be expressed as

$$P_{loss} = \sum_{k=1}^{NTL} G_k \left[V_i^2 + V_j^2 - 2|V_i||V_j| \cos \delta_{ij} \right] \qquad (5)$$

where, P_{loss} is the total power losses; G_k is the conductance of k-th line connected between i-th and j-th buses; V_i, V_j are the voltage of i-th and j-th buses respectively; ∂_{ij} is the phase angle between i-th and j-th bus voltages.

2.2 System Equality and Inequality Constraints

The equality constraints represent the load flow equations, which are given below for i-th bus.

$$\begin{cases} P_{G_i} - P_{L_i} = \sum_{j=1}^{NB} |V_i||V_j| \left(G_{ij} \cos \delta_{ij} + B_{ij} \sin \delta_{ij} \right) \\ Q_{G_i} - Q_{L_i} = \sum_{j=1}^{NB} |V_i||V_j| \left(G_{ij} \sin \delta_{ij} - B_{ij} \cos \delta_{ij} \right) \end{cases}$$

where, P_{G_i}, Q_{G_i} are the active and reactive power of the i-th generator; P_{L_i}, Q_{L_i} are the active and reactive power of the i-th load bus; G_{ij}, B_{ij} are the conductance and susceptance of transmission line connected between the i-th and the j-th bus; NB is the number of buses.

In addition to the equality constraints, the ORPD problem is subject to the following inequality constraints:

1. **Generator Voltage and Reactive Power Constraints:** Voltage and reactive power of the i-th generator bus lies between its operating limits as given below:

$$\begin{cases} V_{G_i}^{\min} \leq V_{G_i} \leq V_{G_i}^{\max} i = 1, 2, \cdots, NG \\ Q_{G_i}^{\min} \leq Q_{G_i} \leq Q_{G_i}^{\max} i = 1, 2, \cdots, NG \end{cases} \qquad (7)$$

where, $V_{G_i}^{\min}, V_{G_i}^{\max}$ are the minimum and maximum voltage of the i-th generating unit; $Q_{G_i}^{\min}, Q_{G_i}^{\max}$ are the minimum and maximum reactive power of the i-th generating unit.

2. **Load Bus Voltage Constraints:** Voltage of load buses must be within their lower and upper operating limits as follows:

$$V_{L_i}^{\min} \leq V_{L_i} \leq V_{L_i}^{\max} \quad i = 1, 2, \cdots, NL \qquad (8)$$

where, $V_{L_i}^{\min}, V_{L_i}^{\max}$ are the minimum and maximum load voltage of the i-th unit.

3. **Transmission Line Loading Constraints:** Line loading of transmission lines must be restricted within their upper limits as follows:

$$S_{Li} \leq S_{L_i}^{\max} \quad i = 1, 2, \cdots, NTL \qquad (9)$$

where, S_{L_i} is the apparent power flow of the i-th branch; $S_{L_i}^{\max}$ is the maximum apparent power flow limit of the i-th branch.

4. **Transformer Tap Settings Constraints:** Transformer tap settings are bounded between upper and lower limits as given below:

$$T_i^{\min} \leq T_i \leq T_i^{\max} \quad i = 1, 2, \cdots, NT \qquad (10)$$

where, $T_i^{\min}, T_i^{\max}$ are the minimum and maximum tap setting limits of the i-th transformer.

5. **Reactive Power Injections Constraints:** Shunt compensation are restricted by their limits as follows:

$$Q_{C_i}^{\min} \leq Q_{C_i} \leq Q_{C_i}^{\max} \quad i = 1, 2, \cdots, NC \qquad (11)$$

where, $Q_{C_i}^{\min}, Q_{C_i}^{\max}$ are the minimum and maximum Var injection limits of the i-th shunt capacitor.

3. BIOGEOGRAPHY-BASED OPTIMIZATION

Biogeography-based optimization (BBO) developed by Simon (Simon, 2008) is a new biogeography inspired algorithm and is an example of how a natural process can be modeled to solve optimization problems. BBO has already been applied successfully to solve economic load dispatch (ELD) (Roy, Ghoshal & Thakur, 2010a) and optimal power flow (OPF) (Roy, Ghoshal & Thakur, 2010b) problems. In BBO, each possible solution is an island and their features that characterize habitability are called suitability index variables (*SIV*). The goodness of each solution is called its habitat suitability index (*HSI*). Over evolutionary periods of time, some islands may tend to accumulate more species than others because they posses certain environmental features that are more suitable to sustaining those species than islands with fewer species. Habitats with high *HSI* have large population, high emigration rate, simply by virtue of large number of species that migrate to other habitats. The immigration rate is low for these habitats as these are already saturated with species. On the other hand, habitats with low *HSI* have high immigration and low emigration rate, because of sparse population.

In BBO, each solution is associated with the fitness which is analogous to *HSI* of a habitat. A good solution is analogous to a habitat having high *HSI* and a poor solution represents a habitat having a low *HSI*. Good solutions share their features with poor solutions by means of migration (immigration and emigration). Good solutions have more resistance to change than poor solutions. On the other hand, poor solutions are more dynamic and accept a lot of new features from good solutions.

The immigration rate and emigration rate of the j-th island may be formulated as follows (Simon, 2008):

$$\lambda_j = I \cdot \left(1 - \frac{j}{n}\right) \qquad (12)$$

$$\mu_j = \frac{E \cdot j}{n} \qquad (13)$$

where λ_j, μ_j are the immigration rate and emigration rate of the j-th individual; I is the maximum possible immigration rate; E is the maximum possible emigration rate; j is the number of species of the j-th individual; and n is the maximum number of species.

In BBO, the mutation is used to increase the diversity of the population to get the good solutions. Mutation operator modifies a habitat's *SIV* randomly based on mutation rate. The mutation rate m_j is expressed as (14) (Simon, 2008).

$$m_j = m_{\max}\left(\frac{1 - P_j}{P_{\max}}\right) \qquad (14)$$

where m_j is the mutation rate for the j-th habitat having j number of species; $m_{\max}$ is the maximum mutation rate; $P_{\max}$ is the maximum species count probability; P_j is the species count probability for the j-th habitat and is given by Simon (2008) as shown below.

$$P_j = \begin{cases} -(\lambda_j + \mu_j)P_j + \mu_{j+1}P_{j+1} & j = 0 \\ -(\lambda_j + \mu_j)P_j + \lambda_{j-1}P_{j-1} + \mu_{j+1}P_{j+1} & 1 \le j \le n-1 \\ -(\lambda_j + \mu_j)P_j + \lambda_{j-1}P_{j-1} & j = n \end{cases}$$
$$(15)$$

where λ_{j+1}, μ_{j+1} are the immigration and emigration rate for the j-th habitat contains $j+1$ species; λ_{j-1}, μ_{j-1} are the immigration and emigration rate for the j-th habitat contains $j-1$ species.

The generic steps of the BBO algorithm are as follows:

Step 1: Generation of initial random set of habitats according to the constraints of the problem.
Step 2: Evaluation of the fitness (*HSI*) of each habitat.
Step 3: Sorting of habitats from best to worst.
Step 4: Identification of elite habitats based on the *HSI* values.
Step 5: Mapping of *HSI* to the number of species.
Step 6: Modification of each habitat with probabilistic migration operation using immigration rate and emigration rate of each habitat.
Step 7: Modification of habitats with probabilistic mutation operation.
Step 8: Verification of feasibility of the newly generated solution.
Step 9: Replacement of infeasible solutions by best feasible solutions.
Step 10: Go to step 2 for the next iteration until a stopping criterion be achieved.

4. QUASI OPPOSITION-BASED LEARNING

Opposition-based learning (OBL), introduced by Tizhoosh (Tizhoosh, 2005), has proven to be an effective method to accelerate PSO (Zhang, Ni, Wu & Gu, 2009), DE (Rahnamayan, Tizhoosh & Salama, 2007), ACO (Haiping, Xieyon & Baogen, 2010), and teaching learning based optimization (TLBO) (Mandal & Roy, 2013). Like other evolutionary algorithms, BBO starts with an initial population string, which is randomly generated when no preliminary knowledge about the solution space is known. The process of evolution terminates when predefined criteria are satisfied. The computation time is directly related to distance of the guess from optimal solution. The chances of getting optimal solutions can be improved by starting with a closer (fitter) solution by checking the opposite solution simultaneously. So the closer solution between the guess solution and the opposite guess solution can be chosen as initial solution. According to probability theory, in 50% of cases the guess is farther to solution than opposite guess; for these cases staring with opposite guess can accelerate convergence. The same approach can be applied not only to initial solutions but also to each solution in the current population.

Before concentrating on OBL, brief introduction of opposite and quasi opposite numbers (Rahnamayan, Tizhoosh & Salama, 2007) have been presented in this section. Purely random selection of solutions from a given population set has the chance of visiting or revisiting local optimal regions instead of global optimal regions of the search space. It has been proved that, in general, opposite numbers are more likely to be closer to the optimal solution than purely random ones (Rahnamayan, Tizhoosh, & Salama, 2008). It has also been proved that the probability of getting better solution using quasi-opposite points is more compare to opposite points (Rahnamayan, Tizhoosh, & Salama, 2007). The opposite number, quasi-opposite number, opposite point and quasi-opposite point may be formulated as follows (Rahnamayan, Tizhoosh & Salama, 2007):

- **Opposite number:** Let $x \in [a,b]$ be a real number. Its opposite number x^o is defined by:

$$x^o = a + b - x \qquad (16)$$

Similarly, the definition may be generalized to higher dimensions as follows:

- **Opposite point:** Let $P(x_1, x_2, ..., x_n)$ be a point in n-dimensional space, where $x_i \in [a,b]$; $i = \{1, 2, ..., n\}$. The opposite point

$$OP(x_1^o, x_2^o, ..., x_n^o)$$

is defined by:

$$x_i^o = a_i + b_i - x_i \qquad (17)$$

- **Quasi-oppositite number and quasi-opposite point:** In (Rahnamayan, Tizhoosh & Salama, 2007), Rahnamayan introduces quasi-opposition-based learning and proves that a quasi-opposite point is more likely to be closer to the solution than the opposite point.

- **Quasi-opposite number:** Let $x \in [a,b]$ be a real number. Its quasi-opposite number x^{qo} is defined by:

$$x^{qo} = rand(c, x^o) \qquad (18)$$

where $rand(c, x^o)$ is a random number uniformly distributed between c and x^o; c is the center of the interval [a, b] and is given by:

$$c = \frac{a+b}{2} \qquad (19)$$

- **Quasi-oppositional point:** Let $P(x_1, x_2, ..., x_n)$ be a point in n-dimensional space, where $x_i \in [a,b]$; $i = \{1, 2, ..., n\}$. The quasi-oppositional point

$$QOP(x_1^{qo}, x_2^{qo}, ..., x_n^{qo})$$

is defined by:

$$x_i^{qo} = rand(c_i, x_i^o) \; i = \{1, 2, ..., n\} \qquad (20)$$

5. QOBBO ALGORITHM APPLIED TO ORPD PROBLEM

The details of different steps of QOBBO algorithm for solving ORPD problems are described below:

Step 1: Initialize the population randomly, i.e. the initial positions of *SIVs* (independent variables such as generators' voltages, tap settings of regulating transformers and reactive power injections of shunt capacitors) of each habitat should be randomly selected while satisfying the equality and inequality constraints. Several numbers of habitats depending upon the population size are being generated. Each habitat represents a potential solution.

Step 2: Calculate quasi-oppositional populations that is represented by

$$QOP_{i,j} = rand(c_j, OP_{i,j}) \; c_j = \frac{a_j + b_j}{2}$$

$$OP_{i,j} = a_j + b_j - P_{i,j} \qquad (21)$$

where $i = 1, 2, ..., N_P; j = 1, 2, ..., N_D$; $rand(c_j, OP_{i,j})$ is a random point uniformly distributed between c_j and $OP_{i,j}$; $P_{i,j}$ is the j-th independent variables of the i-th vector of the population; $OP_{i,j}$ is the j-th independent variables of the i-th vector of the opposite population; N_P is the population size and N_D is the number of independent variables.

Step 3: Determine all dependent variables such as load voltages, active power of slack bus, generators' reactive powers, etc using load flow analysis.

Step 4: Calculate the fitness value (i.e. *HSI*) of each habitat of the population and quasi-oppositional population sets.

Step 5: Select N_P number of fittest vectors from P and QOP as initial *SIVs*.

Step 6: Sorting the fittest vectors from best to worst.

Step 7: Identify few elite habitats based on the *HSI* values.

Step 8: For each j-th habitat, map the *HSI* to the number of species, immigration rate λ_j and emigration rate μ_j.

Step 9: The independent variables (*SIVs*) of each non-elite habitat are modified by performing probabilistically immigration and emigration operation (Simon, 2008).

Step 10: Species count probability of each habitat is updated using (15). Modify the independent variables (*SIVs*) of non-elite habitats by probabilistic mutation operation.

Step 11: Determine all dependent variables such as load voltages, generators' reactive powers, etc using load flow analysis and calculate the fitness value (i.e. *HSI*) of each i-th habitat of the population set.

Step 12: Based on a jumping rate J_r (i.e. jumping probability), after generating new populations by migration and mutation, the quasi-opposite population is calculated and fitness value of objective function (i.e. *HSI*) for each habitat of quasi-opposite population is calculated.

Step 13: Select N_P fittest individuals from the union of the current population and the quasi-oppositional population.

Step 14: Go to Step 6 for the next iteration.

6. PARAMETER SELECTION

The performance of the proposed algorithm depends on input parameters and they should be chosen carefully. After several runs, optimal input control parameters shown in Table 1 are found to be best for optimal performance of the proposed algorithm.

7. NUMERICAL SOLUTIONS

In this section, the performance of the QOBBO approach using three case studies of ORPD is evaluated. The optimization method is imple-

Table 1. Parameters for QOBBO in computation

Habitat modification probability	1	Elitism parameter	4
Mutation probability	0.005	Step size for numerical integration	1
Maximum immigration rate	1	Jumping rate	0.3
Maximum emigration rate	1		

mented in Matlab (MathWorks) using Microsoft Windows XP. All the programs are run on a 2.5 GHz core 2 duo processor with 1GB of random access memory. Due to the inherent randomness involved, the performance of heuristic search based optimization algorithms cannot be judged by the results of a single trial. Therefore, many trials with different initial populations are required to test the robustness of the proposed method. In each case study, 50 independent runs are made to generate 50 different initial trial solutions. In these case studies, the stopping criterion is 100 generations for the proposed QOBBO algorithm.

7.1 IEEE 30-Bus System

The IEEE 30-bus system consists of 41 branches, 6 generator buses and 24 load buses. Four branches 6–9, 6–10, 4–12 and 27–28, are under tap setting transformer branches. In addition, buses 10, 12, 15, 17, 20, 21, 23, 24 and 29 have been selected as shunt Var compensation buses. Bus 1 is selected as slack bus and 2, 5, 8, 11 and 13 are the generator buses. The others are load buses. The total active and reactive load demand on this system are 2.834 *p.u.* and 1.260 *p.u.* respectively. The line data, bus data, generator data of (Lee, Park & Ortiz, 1985) are used for solving this problem. The voltage magnitudes limits of all buses are ($0.95 p.u, 1.1 p.u.$). Tap settings limits of regulating transformers are ($0.9 p.u., 1.1 p.u.$). The Var injection of the shunt capacitors are within the interval of *(0 MVar, 5 MVar)*. The upper and lower limits of reactive power generation are adopted from (Lee, Park & Ortiz, 1985). The optimal control variables and the transmission

loss obtained for the IEEE 30-bus system using various techniques are given in Table 2 while satisfying all the equality and inequality constraints. Simulation results show that the transmission loss obtained by proposed algorithm is the best as compared to PSO (Mahadevann & Kannan, 2010), CLPSO (Mahadevann & Kannan, 2010) and BBO (Bhattacharya & Chattopadhyay, 2010). The convergence of optimal solution using QOBBO is shown in Figure 1.

Owing to the randomness, the proposed algorithm is executed 50 times when applied to the test system. The best, worst and average power losses found by the different methods are tabulated in Table 3. QOBBO shows good consistency by keeping the difference between the best and worst solutions within 0.035%. In addition, the average execution times summarized in Table 3 show that QOBBO is faster than PSO, CLPSO and BBO. The consistency of proposed QOBBO approach in attaining the near optimal value can also be noticed from Table 3. Out of 50 trails, the success rate of QOBBO is higher (98 %) compare to PSO (43%), CLPSO (80%) and BBO (96%).

7.2 IEEE 57-Bus System

In order to evaluate the applicability of the proposed method to larger scale systems, the proposed QOBBO algorithm is also applied to the reactive power dispatch problem of the IEEE 57-bus system. This system consists of 57 buses, 80 transmission lines, 7 generators connected at bus numbers 1, 2, 3, 6, 8, 9 and 12; 15 regulating transformers connected between the line numbers 4-18, 4-18, 21-20, 24-26, 7-29, 34-32, 11-41,

Table 2. Simulation results of ORPD using different techniques for the IEEE 30-bus system

Techniques	Base Case	PSO	CLPSO	BBO	QOBBO
V_1 (p.u.)	1.0500	1.1000	1.1000	1.1000	1.0999
V_2 (p.u.)	1.0400	1.1000	1.1000	1.0944	1.0942
V_5 (p.u.)	1.0100	1.0867	1.0795	1.0749	1.0747
V_8 (p.u.)	1.0100	1.1000	1.1000	1.0768	1.0766
V_{11} (p.u.)	1.0500	1.1000	1.1000	1.0999	1.1000
V_{13} (p.u.)	1.0500	1.1000	1.1000	1.0999	1.0999
TC_{6-9}	1.0780	0.9587	0.9197	1.0435	1.03873
TC_{6-10}	1.0690	1.0543	0.9000	0.90117	0.90000
TC_{4-12}	1.0320	1.0024	0.9000	0.98244	0.97244
TC_{27-28}	1.0680	0.9755	0.9397	0.96918	0.96275
Q_{C10} (Mvar)	0.0000	0.042803	0.049265	0.049998	0.500000
Q_{C12} (Mvar)	0.0000	0.500000	0.500000	0.04987	0.500000
Q_{C15} (Mvar)	0.0000	0.030288	0.500000	0.049906	0.500000
Q_{C17} (Mvar)	0.0000	0.040365	0.500000	0.04997	0.500000
Q_{C20} (Mvar)	0.0000	0.026697	0.500000	0.049901	0.041578
Q_{C21} (Mvar)	0.0000	0.038894	0.500000	0.049946	0.500000
Q_{C23} (Mvar)	0.0000	0.000000	0.500000	0.038753	0.025843
Q_{C24} (Mvar)	0.0000	0.035879	0.500000	0.049867	0.049926
Q_{C29} (Mvar)	0.0000	0.028415	0.500000	0.029098	0.022213
Transmission loss (p.u.)	0.05812	0.046282	0.045615	0.045511	0.045312
P_{Loss}^{Save} %	-	20.36820	21.51583	21.69477	22.03716

Figure 1. Transmission loss convergence characteristic using QOBBO (IEEE 30-bus system)

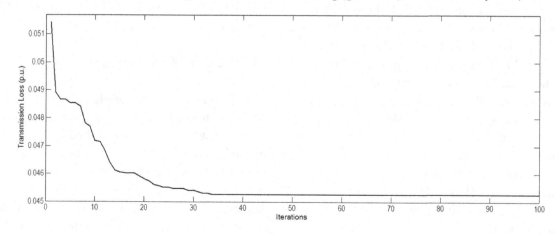

Table 3. Comparison of the result obtained by different methods for the IEEE 30-bus system

Algorithms	Transmission Loss (*p.u.*)			Average Computational Time (Sec.)	Success Rate (%)
	Maximum	Minimum	Average		
PSO	0.047986	0.046282	0.047363	130	43
CLPSO	0.046833	0.045615	0.046397	138	80
BBO	0.045522	0.045511	0.045515	110	96
QOBBO	0.045328	0.045312	0.045319	108	98

15-45, 14-46, 10-51, 13-49, 11-43, 40-56, 39-57 and 9-55; 3 shunt compensators connected at bus numbers 18, 25 and 53. The total load demand on this system is 12.508 *p.u.* The line data, bus data, generator data of (IEEE 57-bus test system) are used for solving this problem. The voltage magnitudes of all buses are considered within the range of ($0.94 p.u., 1.06 p.u.$). Tap settings of regulating transformers are within the range of ($0.9 p.u., 1.1 p.u.$). The Var injection of the shunt capacitors connected at bus numbers 18, 25 and 53 are taken within the interval of *(0 Mvar-10 MVar), (0 Mvar-5.9 MVar)* and *(0 Mvar-6.3 MVar)* respectively. The upper and lower limits of the reactive power generations are adopted from (Dai, Chen, Zhun & Zhang, 2009).

1. **Without Considering Constraints of Reactive Power Generation:** The best, worst and average transmission losses in 50 trial runs using CGA (Dai, Chen, Zhun & Zhang, 2009), CLPSO (Dai, Chen, Zhun & Zhang, 2009), SPSO-07(Dai, Chen, Zhun & Zhang, 2009), L-SADE (Dai, Chen, Zhun & Zhang, 2009), PSO-cf (Dai, Chen, Zhun & Zhang, 2009), PSO-w (Dai, Chen, Zhun & Zhang, 2009), SOA (Dai, Chen, Zhun & Zhang, 2009), BBO (Bhattacharya & Chattopadhyay, 2010) methods are shown in Table 4. Table 5 shows the base case results, optimum results using different techniques for the IEEE 57-bus system ignoring reactive power generation constraints. The simulation results show that the QOBBO method can

obtain lower generation cost than the other mentioned methods. Table 4 also shows that the average cost produced by QOBBO is least compared with other methods emphasizing its better solution quality. For comparing the computational speed, the CPU time requirement for the other recently published methods along with QOBBO are represented in Table 4. It is noted that the QOBBO method is computationally most efficient as time requirement is minimum amongst all the methods. To illustrate the convergence of the proposed algorithm, values of transmission loss over 100 trials are plotted in Figure 2.

2. **Considering Constraints of Reactive Power Generation:** The optimal settings of control variables along with transmission loss obtained using the proposed QOBBO method and BBO method reported in the literature is presented in Table 6. The numerical results indicate that the transmission loss determined by QOBO is more advanced than that found by BBO with all control variables remained within their permissible limits. The best, worst and average active transmission loss obtained using BBO (Bhattacharya & Chattopadhyay, 2010) and QOBBO in 50 independent runs are summarized in Table 7, which show that the proposed QOBBO algorithm obviously performs better than the BBO algorithm. Also, the average CPU time for this case using QOBBO for a population size of 50 and iteration cycles of 100

Table 4. Comparative statistical result of different methods (IEEE 57-bus system case I)

Algorithms	Transmission Loss (p.u.)			Average Computational Time (Sec.)	Success Rate (%)
	Maximum	**Minimum**	**Average**		
CGA	0.2750772	0.2524411	0.2629356	411.38	NA
CLPSO	0.2478083	0.2451520	0.2467307	426.85	NA
SPSO-07	0.2545745	0.2443043	0.2475227	137.35	NA
PSO-cf	0.2603275	0.2428022	0.2469805	408.19	NA
PSO-w	0.2615279	0.2427052	0.2472596	408.48	NA
L-SADE	0.2439142	0.2426739	0.2431129	410.14	NA
SOA	0.2428046	0.2426548	0.2427078	391.32	NA
BBO	0.242621	0.242616	0.242619	232.15	90.00
QOBBO	0.2426142	0.2426096	0.2426106	230.08	97.00

Table 5. Optimal control variable settings of different methods (IEEE 57-bus system case I)

Techniques →	Base Case	CGA	CLPSO	SPSO-07	PSO-cf	PSO-w	L-SADE	SOA	BBO	QOBBO
V_1 (p.u.)	1.0400	0.9686	1.0541	1.0596	1.0600	1.0600	1.0600	1.0600	1.0600	1.0600
V_2 (p.u.)	1.0100	1.0493	1.0529	1.0580	1.0586	1.0578	1.0574	1.0580	1.0580	1.0585
V_3 (p.u.)	0.9850	1.0567	1.0337	1.0488	1.0464	1.04378	1.0438	1.0437	1.0442	1.0460
V_6 (p.u.)	0.9800	0.9877	1.0313	1.0362	1.0415	1.0356	1.0364	1.0352	1.0364	1.0373
V_8 (p.u.)	1.005	1.0223	1.0496	1.0600	1.0600	1.0546	1.0537	1.0548	1.0567	1.0567
V_9 (p.u.)	0.9800	0.9918	1.0302	1.0433	1.0423	1.0369	1.0366	1.0369	1.0377	1.0379
V_{12} (p.u.)	1.015	1.0044	1.0342	1.0356	1.0371	1.0334	1.0323	1.0336	1.0351	1.0351
TC_{4-18}	0.9700	0.92	0.99	0.95	0.98	0.90	0.94	1.00	0.99165	0.98001
TC_{4-18}	0.9780	0.92	0.98	0.99	0.98	1.02	1.00	0.96	0.96447	0.97429
TC_{21-20}	1.0430	0.97	0.99	0.99	1.01	1.01	1.01	1.01	1.0122	1.01460
TC_{24-26}	1.0430	0.90	1.01	1.02	1.01	1.01	1.01	1.01	1.0110	1.00890
TC_{7-29}	0.9670	0.91	0.99	0.97	0.98	0.97	0.97	0.97	0.97127	0.97204
TC_{34-32}	0.9750	1.10	0.93	0.96	0.97	0.97	0.97	0.97	0.97227	0.97450
TC_{11-41}	0.9550	0.94	0.91	0.92	0.90	0.90	0.90	0.90	0.90095	0.90000
TC_{15-45}	0.9550	0.95	0.97	0.96	0.97	0.97	0.97	0.97	0.97063	0.97174
TC_{14-46}	0.9000	1.03	0.95	0.95	0.96	0.95	0.96	0.95	0.95153	0.95010
TC_{10-51}	0.9300	1.09	0.98	0.97	0.97	0.96	0.96	0.96	0.96252	0.96267
TC_{13-49}	0.8950	0.90	0.95	0.92	0.93	0.92	0.92	0.92	0.92227	0.92193
TC_{11-43}	0.9580	0.90	0.95	1.00	0.97	0.96	0.96	0.96	0.95988	0.95986
TC_{40-56}	0.9850	1.00	1.00	1.00	0.99	1.00	1.00	1.00	1.0018	1.00930
TC_{39-57}	0.9800	0.96	0.96	0.95	0.96	0.96	0.96	0.96	0.96567	0.96601
TC_{9-55}	0.9400	1.00	0.97	0.98	0.98	0.97	0.97	0.97	0.97199	0.97096
Q_{C18} (Mvar)	0.0000	0.084	0.09888	0.03936	0.09984	0.05136	0.08112	0.09984	0.09640	0.09425
Q_{C25} (Mvar)	0.0000	0.00816	0.05424	0.05664	0.05904	0.05904	0.05808	0.05904	0.05897	0.05900
Q_{C53} (Mvar)	0.0000	0.05376	0.06288	0.03552	0.06288	0.06288	0.06192	0.06288	0.062948	0.06300
Transmission loss (p.u.)	0.28462	0.2524411	0.245152	0.2443043	0.2428022	0.2427052	0.2426739	0.2426548	0.242616	0.2426096
P_{Loss}^{Sav} %	-	11.3059	13.8669	14.1647	14.6925	14.7266	14.7376	14.7443	14.7579	14.7602

is 230.21 Sec. whereas the CPU time for the BBO algorithm for the same population size and number of iteration cycles is 232.32 Sec. This clearly shows that the new proposed algorithm is capable of giving a better optimum solution with less computational time. Figure 3 shows the active power loss convergence obtained by QOBBO.

Figure 2. Transmission loss convergence characteristic using QOBBO (IEEE 57-bus system-case I)

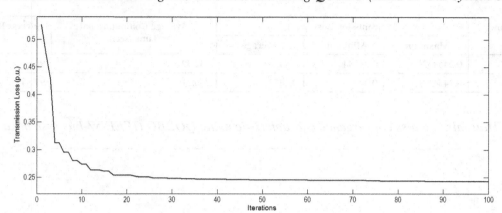

Table 6. Comparative statistical result of different methods (IEEE 57-bus system case II)

Control Variables	BBO	QOBBO	Control Variables	BBO	QOBBO
V_1 (*p.u.*)	1.0600	1.06	TC_{15-45}	0.96602	0.96612
V_2 (*p.u.*)	1.0504	1.0504	TC_{14-46}	0.95079	0.95079
V_3 (*p.u.*)	1.0440	1.0436	TC_{10-51}	0.96414	0.96414
V_6 (*p.u.*)	1.0376	1.0381	TC_{13-49}	0.92462	0.92462
V_8 (*p.u.*)	1.0550	1.0574	TC_{11-43}	0.95022	0.95042
V_9 (*p.u.*)	1.0229	1.0242	TC_{40-56}	0.99666	0.99666
V_{12} (*p.u.*)	1.0323	1.0322	TC_{39-57}	0.96289	0.96289
TC_{4-18}	0.96693	0.96725	TC_{9-55}	0.96001	0.95931
TC_{4-18}	0.99022	0.98393	Q_{C18} (Mvar)	0.09782	0.0996
TC_{21-20}	1.0120	1.0124	Q_{C25} (Mvar)	0.058991	0.059
TC_{24-26}	1.0087	1.0068	Q_{C53} (Mvar)	0.06289	0.063
TC_{7-29}	0.97074	0.97228	Transmission loss (*p.u.*)	0.24544	0.24529
TC_{34-32}	0.96869	0.96869	$P_{Loss}^{Save}\%$	13.7657	13.8184
TC_{11-41}	0.90082	0.90082			

7.3 IEEE 118-Bus System

To proof the efficiency of the proposed QOBBO method for large scale ORPD problem, it is finally applied to IEEE 118-bus test system. This system has 54 generators, 12 synchronous condensers connected at bus numbers 34, 44, 45, 46, 48, 74, 79, 82, 83, 105, 107, 110 and 9 tap changing transformers connected between the transmission lines [5-8], [25–26], [17–30], [37–38], [59–63], [61–64], [65–66], [68–69] and [80–81]. The active and reactive loads of the system are 4242

Table 7. Optimal control variable settings of different methods (IEEE 57-bus system case II)

Algorithms	Transmission Loss (*p.u.*)			Average Computational Time (sec.)	Success Rate (%)
	Maximum	Minimum	Average		
BBO	0.245452	0.24544	0.245445	232.32	96.67
QOBBO	0.24541	0.24529	0.24534	230.21	97.84

Figure 3. Transmission loss convergence characteristic using QOBBO (IEEE 57-bus system case II)

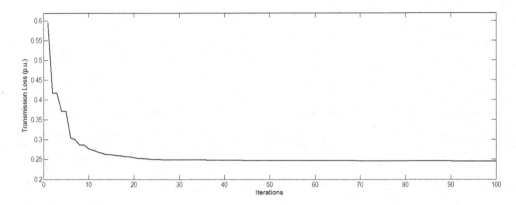

MW and 1438 MVAR, respectively, and the base value of the system is 100 MVA. The complete system data along with minimum and maximum limits of active power of slack bus, reactive power generation limits of the generator buses, reactive power injected by shunt compensators are adopted from (The IEEE 118-bus test system). The voltage magnitude limits of all the generator buses are set to 0.95 p.u for lower bound and to 1.1 p.u for upper bound. The voltage limits of all the load buses are considered within 0.94 p.u. and 1.06 p.u. The maximum and minimum values tap changing transformer control variables are 1.1 and 0.9 in per unit, respectively.

The optimal values of the control variable settings and transmission loss obtained by BBO and QOBBO for this test system are given in Table 8. From the comparison, it is found that the proposed QOBBO algorithm gives the best results for transmission loss without violating any system constraint which demonstrates the superiority of the proposed QOBBO algorithm over BBO algorithm. Figure 4 shows the transmission loss convergence through the QOBBO algorithm,

which brings out smoothness of the convergence characteristic of the algorithm.

The active line loss obtained by using different methods namely QOBBO, BBO (Roy, Ghoshal & Thakur, 2012), interior point based OPF (IP-OPF) (Vlachogiannis & Lee, 2006), Conventional PSO (Vlachogiannis & Lee, 2006), coordinated aggregation (CA) (Vlachogiannis & Lee, 2006), general passive congregation PSO (GPAC) (Vlachogiannis & Lee, 2006) and local passive congregation PSO (LPAC) (Vlachogiannis & Lee, 2006) are listed in Table 9 for this test system. The results depicted in Table 9 clearly show that the proposed QOBBO approach outperforms all the other methods reported in the literature.

8. CONCLUSION AND FUTURE SCOPE OF WORK

This article has demonstrated the feasibility of employing QOBBO approach for efficient solving of ORPD problems. To enrich the searching behavior and to avoid being trapped into local optimum,

Table 8. Simulation results obtained by BBO and QOBBO for the IEEE 118-bus system

Control Variables	BBO	QOBBO	Control Variables	BBO	QOBBO
V_1 (p.u.)	1.0623	1.0063	V_{87} (p.u.)	0.9517	1.0469
V_4 (p.u.)	1.0865	1.0279	V_{89} (p.u.)	1.1000	1.0526
V_6 (p.u.)	1.0760	1.0120	V_{90} (p.u.)	1.0599	1.0136
V_8 (p.u.)	1.1000	1.0239	V_{91} (p.u.)	1.0558	1.0085
V_{10} (p.u.)	1.1000	1.0509	V_{92} (p.u.)	1.0710	1.0461
V_{12} (p.u.)	1.0687	1.0090	V_{99} (p.u.)	1.0454	1.0453
V_{15} (p.u.)	1.0526	0.9948	V_{100} (p.u.)	1.0548	1.0517
V_{18} (p.u.)	1.0503	0.9883	V_{103} (p.u.)	1.0433	1.0498
V_{19} (p.u.)	1.0489	0.9924	V_{104} (p.u.)	1.0272	1.0437
V_{24} (p.u.)	0.9500	1.0438	V_{105} (p.u.)	1.0222	1.0334
V_{25} (p.u.)	1.0289	1.0789	V_{107} (p.u.)	1.0168	1.0165
V_{26} (p.u.)	1.1000	1.0858	V_{110} (p.u.)	1.0399	1.0478
V_{27} (p.u.)	1.0037	1.0420	V_{111} (p.u.)	1.0475	1.0515
V_{31} (p.u.)	1.0074	1.0226	V_{112} (p.u.)	1.0353	1.0272
V_{32} (p.u.)	0.9976	1.0397	V_{113} (p.u.)	1.0490	1.0239
V_{34} (p.u.)	1.0576	1.0118	V_{116} (p.u.)	1.0648	1.0490
V_{36} (p.u.)	1.0535	1.0131	TC_{5-8}	0.9996	0.9879
V_{40} (p.u.)	1.0373	0.9866	TC_{25-26}	1.0782	1.0868
V_{42} (p.u.)	1.0422	0.9770	TC_{17-30}	0.9858	1.0012
V_{46} (p.u.)	1.0482	1.0184	TC_{37-38}	0.9821	1.0095
V_{49} (p.u.)	1.0713	1.0347	TC_{59-63}	0.9778	0.9811
V_{54} (p.u.)	1.0522	1.0013	TC_{61-64}	1.0270	1.0165
V_{55} (p.u.)	1.0520	1.0007	TC_{65-66}	1.1000	0.9572
V_{56} (p.u.)	1.0518	1.0041	TC_{68-69}	0.9773	0.9186
V_{59} (p.u.)	1.0708	1.0370	TC_{80-81}	1.1000	0.9932
V_{61} (p.u.)	1.0672	1.0427	Q_{C34} (Mvar)	1.4400	5.098
V_{62} (p.u.)	1.0673	1.0433	Q_{C44} (Mvar)	20.270	6.341
V_{65} (p.u.)	1.0729	1.0435	Q_{C45} (Mvar)	5.8300	7.887
V_{66} (p.u.)	1.0907	1.0604	Q_{C46} (Mvar)	10.840	8.093
V_{69} (p.u.)	1.0463	1.0651	Q_{C48} (Mvar)	15.040	8.048
V_{70} (p.u.)	1.0114	1.0251	Q_{C74} (Mvar)	22.120	2.663
V_{72} (p.u.)	0.9790	1.0306	Q_{C79} (Mvar)	2.4500	16.719
V_{73} (p.u.)	1.0131	1.0228	Q_{C82} (Mvar)	13.120	16.956
V_{74} (p.u.)	0.9917	1.0105	Q_{C83} (Mvar)	5.8800	5.864
V_{76} (p.u.)	0.9500	1.0123	Q_{C105} (Mvar)	30.000	11.183
V_{77} (p.u.)	1.0262	1.0310	Q_{C107} (Mvar)	6.8100	10.000
V_{80} (p.u.)	1.0396	1.0413	Q_{C110} (Mvar)	19.470	4.405
V_{85} (p.u.)	1.1000	1.0550	Power Loss (MW)	128.9700	119.2623

Figure 4.Transmission loss convergence characteristic obtained by QOBBO (IEEE 118-bus system)

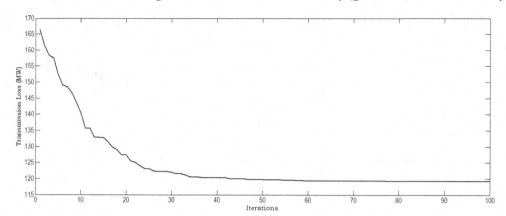

Table 9. Comparison of the result obtained by different methods for the IEEE 118-bus system

Algorithms	QOBBO	BBO	IP-OPF	Conventional PSO	CA	GPAC	LPAC
Power Loss	119.2623	128.97	132.1097	131.9146	131.8638	131.9083	131.9010
Computational Time (Sec.)	25.89	27.418	11.873	26.040	22.453	28.090	13.572

quasi-opposition-based population initialization and quasi-opposition-based generation jumping are incorporated in conventional BBO approach.

The proposed approach has been successfully and effectively implemented on IEEE 30-bus, IEEE 57-bus and IEEE 118-bus test systems to find the optimal settings of the control variables and optimal transmission loss of the small, medium and large scale power system. To demonstrate the effectiveness of the proposed algorithm to solve ORPD problem, the results of the QOBBO algorithm have been compared to those reported in the literature. The comparison confirms the superiority in terms of solution quality of the proposed approach over other heuristic techniques available in the literature. It is also observed from the repeated trail runs that QOBBO converges

to near optimal solution with high success rate, which demonstrates the robustness of the proposed method. Moreover, it is found that the proposed method not only produces minimum transmission loss, but requires lesser computational time compared to other reported results in the literature.

The performance of the proposed QOBBO method may further be tested by applying other areas of power system such as unit commitment (UC), hydrothermal scheduling (HTS), combined heat and power dispatch (CHPD), optimal placement of FACTS devices in transmission network, optimal placement of capacitor and distributed generator (DG) in radial distribution network, optimal tuning of power system stabilizer (PSS) etc. and it is left for the readers.

REFERENCES

Abou El-Ela, A.A., Kinawy, A.M., El-Sehiemy, R.A., & Mouwafi, M.T. (2011). Optimal reactive power dispatch using ant colony optimization algorithm. *Electrical Engineering, 93* (2), 103-116.

Aoki, K., Fan, M., & Nishikori, A. (1988). Optimal VAR planning by approximation method for recursive mixed-integer linear programming. *IEEE Transactions on Power Systems, 3*(4), 1741–1747. doi:10.1109/59.192990

Bhattacharya, A., & Chattopadhyay, P. K. (2010). Solution of optimal reactive power flow using biogeography-based optimization. *International Journal of Electrical and Electronics Engineering, 4*(8), 580–588.

Dai, C., Chen, W., Zhu, Y., & Zhang, X. (2009). Reactive power dispatch considering voltage stability with seeker optimization algorithm. *Electric Power Systems Research, 79,* 1462–1471. doi:10.1016/j.epsr.2009.04.020

Dai, C., Chen, W., Zhu, Y., & Zhang, X. (2009). Seeker optimization algorithm for optimal reactive power dispatch. *IEEE Transactions on Power Systems, 24*(3), 1218–1231. doi:10.1109/TPWRS.2009.2021226

Duman, S., Sonmez, Y., Guvenç, U., & Yorukeren, N. (2012). Optimal reactive power dispatch using a gravitational search algorithm. *IET Generation, Transmission and Distribution, 6* (6), 563-576.

Granada, M., Rider, M. J., Mantovani, J. R. S., & Shahidehpour, M. (2012). A decentralized approach for optimal reactive power dispatch using a Lagrangian decomposition method. *Electric Power Systems Research, 89,* 148–156. doi:10.1016/j.epsr.2012.02.015

Granville, S. (1994). Optimal reactive dispatch through interior point methods. *IEEE Transactions on Power Systems, 9*(1), 136–146. doi:10.1109/59.317548

Haiping, M., Xieyong, R., & Baogen, J. (2010). Oppositional ant colony .optimization algorithm and its application to fault monitoring. In *Proceedings of 2010 29th Chinese Control Conference (CCC),* (pp. 3895 – 3898). CCC.

Iba, K. (1994). Reactive power optimization by genetic algorithm. *IEEE Transactions on Power Systems, 9*(2), 685–692. doi:10.1109/59.317674

IEEE 118-Bus Test System. (n.d.). Available from http://www.ee.washington.edu/research/pstca/pf118/ pg_tca118bus.htm

IEEE 57-Bus Test System. (n.d.). Available from http://www.ee.washington.edu/research/ pstca/pf57/pg_tca57bus.htm

Jaganathan, S., Palaniswami, S., Vignesh, G.M., & Mithunraj, R. (2011). Applications of multi objective optimization to reactive power planning problem using ant colony algorithm. *European Journal of Scientific Research, 51* (2), 241-253.

Kawata, H. K., Fukuyama, Y., Takayama, S., & Nakanishi, Y. (2000). A particle swarm optimization for reactive power and voltage control considering voltage security assessment. *IEEE Transactions on Power Systems, 15*(4), 1232–1239. doi:10.1109/59.898095

Khazali, A. H., & Kalantar, M. (2011). Optimal reactive power dispatch based on harmony search algorithm. *International Journal of Electrical Power & Energy Systems, 33,* 684–692. doi:10.1016/j.ijepes.2010.11.018

Lee, K., Park, Y., & Ortiz, J. (1985). A united approach to optimal real and reactive power dispatch. *IEEE Transactions on Power Apparatus and Systems, 104*(5), 1147–1153. doi:10.1109/TPAS.1985.323466

Lee, K. Y., & Park, Y. M. (1995). Optimization method for reactive power planning by using a modified simple genetic algorithm. *IEEE Transactions on Power Systems, 10*(4), 1843–1850. doi:10.1109/59.476049

Li, Y., Cao, Y., Liu, Z., Liu, Y., & Jiang, Q. (2009). Dynamic optimal reactive power dispatch based on parallel particle swarm optimization algorithm. *Computers & Mathematics with Applications (Oxford, England), 57*, 1835–1842. doi:10.1016/j.camwa.2008.10.049

Liang, C. H., Chung, C. Y., Wong, K. P., & Dual, X. Z. (2007). Parallel optimal reactive power flow based on cooperative co-evolutionary differential evolution and power system decomposition. *IEEE Transactions on Power Systems, 22*(1), 249–257. doi:10.1109/TPWRS.2006.887889

Lu, F. C., & Hsu, Y. Y. (1995). Reactive power/voltage control in a distribution substation using dynamic programming. *IEE Proceedings. Generation, Transmission and Distribution, 142*(6), 639–645. doi:10.1049/ip-gtd:19952210

Ma, J. T., & Lai, L. L. (1996). Evolutionary programming approach to reactive power planning. *IEE Proceedings. Generation, Transmission and Distribution, 143*(4), 365–370. doi:10.1049/ip-gtd:19960296

Mahadevan, K., & Kannan, P. S. (2010). Comprehensive learning particle swarm optimization for reactive power dispatch. *International Journal of Applied Soft Computing, 10*(2), 641–652. doi:10.1016/j.asoc.2009.08.038

Mallipeddi, R., Jeyadevi, S., Suganthan, P.N., & Baskar, S. (2012). Efficient constraint handling for optimal reactive power dispatch problems. *Swarm and Evolutionary Computation, 5*, 28-36.

Mandal, B., & Roy, P. K. (2013). Optimal reactive power dispatch using quasi-oppositional teaching learning based optimization. *International Journal of Electrical Power & Energy Systems, 53*, 123–134. doi:10.1016/j.ijepes.2013.04.011

Niknam, T., Narimani, M.R., Azizipanah-Abarghooee, R., & Bahmani-Firouzi, B. (2013). Multiobjective Optimal Reactive Power Dispatch and Voltage Control: A New Opposition-Based Self-Adaptive Modified Gravitational Search Algorithm. *IEEE Systems Journal.*

Soler, E.M., Asada, E.N., & Costa, G.R.M.(2013). *Penalty-Based Nonlinear Solver for Optimal Reactive Power Dispatch With Discrete Controls.* IEEE Transactions on Power Systems

Rahnamayan, S., Tizhoosh, H. R., & Salama, M. M. A. (2007). Quasi oppositional differential evolution. In *Proceeding of IEEE Congress on Evolutionary Computation CEC 2007*, (pp. 2229–2236). IEEE.

Rahnamayan, S., Tizhoosh, H. R., & Salama, M. M. A. (2008). Opposition versus randomness in soft computing techniques. *Applied Soft Computing, 8*(2), 906–918. doi:10.1016/j.asoc.2007.07.010

Ramesh, S., Kannan, S., & Baskar, S. (2012). An improved generalized differential evolution algorithm for multi-objective reactive power dispatch. *Engineering Optimization, 44* (4), 391-405.

Roy, P. K., Ghoshal, S. P., & Thakur, S. S. (2010). Biogeography-based Optimization for economic load dispatch problems. *Electric Power Components and Systems, 38*(2), 166–181. doi:10.1080/15325000903273379

Roy, P. K., Ghoshal, S. P., & Thakur, S. S. (2010). Biogeography based optimization for multi-constraints optimal power flow with emission and non-smooth cost function. *Expert Systems with Applications, 37*(12), 8221–8228. doi:10.1016/j.eswa.2010.05.064

Roy, P. K., Ghoshal, S. P., & Thakur, S. S. (2012). Optimal VAR control for improvements in voltage profiles and for real power loss minimization using Biogeography Based Optimization. *International Journal of Electrical Power & Energy Systems*, *43*, 830–838. doi:10.1016/j.ijepes.2012.05.032

Saraswat, A., & Saini, A. (2013). Multi-objective optimal reactive power dispatch considering voltage stability in power systems using HF-MOEA. *Engineering Applications of Artificial Intelligence*, *26*, 390–404. doi:10.1016/j.engappai.2012.06.008

Simon, D. (2008). Biogeography-based optimization. *IEEE Transactions on Evolutionary Computation*, *12*(6), 702–713. doi:10.1109/TEVC.2008.919004

Swarup, K. S., Yoshimi, M., & Izui, Y. (1994). Genetic algorithm approach to reactive power planning in power systems. In *Proceedings of the 5th Annual Conference of Power and Energy Society*. IEE.

Tizhoosh, H. (2005). Opposition-based learning: A new scheme for machine intelligence. In *Proceedings of the International Conference on Computational Intelligence for Modelling Control and Automation* (CIMCA-2005). Vienna, Austria: CIMCA.

Varadarajan, M., & Swarup, K. S. (2008). Differential evolution approach for optimal reactive power dispatch. *Applied Soft Computing*, *8*, 1549–1561. doi:10.1016/j.asoc.2007.12.002

Vlachogiannis, J. G., & Lee, K. Y. (2006). A comparative study on particle swarm optimization for optimal steady-state performance of power systems. *IEEE Transactions on Power Systems*, *21*(4), 1718–1728. doi:10.1109/TPWRS.2006.883687

Wu, Q. H., & Ma, J. T. (1995). Power system optimal reactive power dispatch using evolutionary programming. *IEEE Transactions on Power Systems*, *10*(3), 1243–1249. doi:10.1109/59.466531

Xu, Y., Zhang, W., Liu, W., & Ferrese, F. (2012). Multiagent-based reinforcement learning for optimal reactive power dispatch. *IEEE Transactions on Systems, Man and Cybernetics Part C: Applications and Reviews*, *42* (6), 1742-1751.

Yan, W., Yu, J., Yu, D. C., & Bhattarai, K. (2006). A new optimal reactive power flow model in rectangular form and its solution by predictor corrector primal dual interior point method. *IEEE Transactions on Power Systems*, *21*(1), 61–67. doi:10.1109/TPWRS.2005.861978

Yiqin, Z. (2010). Optimal reactive power planning based on improved Tabu search algorithm. In *Proceedings of 2010 International Conference on Electrical and Control Engineering*. Academic Press.

Zhang, C., Ni, Z., Wu, Z., & Gu, L. (2009). A novel swarm model with quasi-oppositional particle. In *Proceedings of 2009 International Forum on Information Technology and Applications*, (pp. 325-330). Academic Press.

Zhang, X., Chen, W., Dai, C., & Cai, W. (2010). Dynamic multi-group self-adaptive differential evolution algorithm for reactive power optimization. *International Journal of Electrical Power & Energy Systems*, *32*, 351–357. doi:10.1016/j.ijepes.2009.11.009

Zhao, B., Guo, C. X., & Cao, Y. J. (2005). A multiagent-based particle swarm optimization approach for optimal reactive power dispatch. *IEEE Transactions on Power Systems*, *20*(2), 1070–1078. doi:10.1109/TPWRS.2005.846064

Chapter 17

Multiobjective Optimization of Bioethanol Production via Hydrolysis Using Hopfield–Enhanced Differential Evolution

T. Ganesan
Universiti Teknologi Petronas, Malaysia

I. Elamvazuthi
Universiti Teknologi Petronas, Malaysia

K. Z. K. Shaari
Universiti Teknologi Petronas, Malaysia

P. Vasant
Universiti Teknologi Petronas, Malaysia

ABSTRACT

Many industrial problems in process optimization are Multi-Objective (MO), where each of the objectives represents different facets of the issue. Thus, having in hand multiple solutions prior to selecting the best solution is a seminal advantage. In this chapter, the weighted sum scalarization approach is used in conjunction with three meta-heuristic algorithms: Differential Evolution (DE), Hopfield-Enhanced Differential Evolution (HEDE), and Gravitational Search Algorithm (GSA). These methods are then employed to trace the approximate Pareto frontier to the bioethanol production problem. The Hypervolume Indicator (HVI) is applied to gauge the capabilities of each algorithm in approximating the Pareto frontier. Some comparative studies are then carried out with the algorithms developed in this chapter. Analysis on the performance as well as the quality of the solutions obtained by these algorithms is shown here.

DOI: 10.4018/978-1-4666-6252-0.ch017

INTRODUCTION

In recent times, emerging technologies in engineering optimization frequently present themselves in multi-objective (MO) settings (Eschenauer *et al.*, 1990; Statnikov and Matusov 1995). Strategies in MO optimization can be simply classified into two groups. First being methods that use the concept of Pareto-optimality to trace out the non-dominated solutions at the Pareto curve, for instance in; Strength Pareto Evolutionary Algorithm (SPEA) (Zitzler and Thiele, 1998) and Non-dominated Sorting Genetic Algorithm II (NSGA-II) by Deb *et al.*, (2002). The second group of methods is known as the scalarization/weighted approaches. During the application of these methods, the objective functions are aggregated into a single weighted function which is then resolved for a finite series of scalar (weight) values. Some established scalarization techniques include the Weighted Sum method (Fishburn, 1967; Triantaphyllou, 2000), Goal Programming (Luyben and Floudas, 1994) and Normal-Boundary Intersection method (NBI) (Das and Dennis, 1998). Using these techniques, the scalars are used to consign relative trade-offs to the objectives during the aggregation procedure. Hence, alternative near-optimal solutions are generated for various values of the scalars. See Eschenauer *et al.*, (1990), Sandgren, (1994) and Statnikov and Matusov (1995) for detail investigations and explanations on MO techniques in engineering optimization.

In MO optimization problems, determining a highly efficient set of solutions can be a very daunting process. Some headway regarding this issue (revolving around concepts such as diversity and convergence) has been proposed in the last years. These ideas were then used as indicators to evaluate the solution set produced by the optimization algorithm (Grosan, 2003). Such assessments were then used to benchmark the algorithm's performance. These concepts unfortunately could not absolutely state and rank the superiority of solution sets produced by an algorithm against other such

sets by other algorithms. The only known concept that can be used generally for the overall ranking of solution sets is the idea of 'Pareto-dominance'. The Hypervolume Indicator (HVI) (Zitzler *et al.*, 2008) is a set measure reflecting the volume enclosed by a Pareto front approximation and a reference set (Knowles and Corne, 2003; Igel *et al.*, 2007; Emmerich *et al.*, 2005). The HVI thus guarantees strict monotonicity regarding Pareto dominance (Fleischer, 2003; Zitzler *et al.*, 2003). This makes the ranking of solution sets and hence algorithms possible for any given MO problem.

In bioethanol production, thermal processes are commonly used to hydrolyze starch to produce fermentable sugars for bioethanol production (see Cardona and Sanchezo, 2007). These processes consume high amounts of energy and may produce undesirable by-products such as; oils and glycerol (Marques *et al.*, 2006). In many fuel-grade ethanol production plants, very high gravity or VHG fermentation is carried out. This technique increases the final ethanol concentration in the mash and productivity (Bao *et al.*, 2011). Hence, for simultaneous sacharification and fermentation in very high gravity mash, a fitting starch hydrolysis strategy is required. Besides, the balancing of the formation and consumption rate of the oligosaccharides is critical for the optimization of the fermentation process. Fermentation time may be longer and ethanol yield may decrease if the initial oligosaccharides concentrations are low. However, if the initial concentration of oligosaccharides is high then the yeast would be vulnerable to osmotic stress and substrate inhibition (Thatipamala, 1992; Hounsa *et al.*, 1998). Thus, the MO optimization of the fermentation process parameters is crucial for the successful economical production of ethanol from starch (Oberoi *et al.*, 2010). In Bao *et al.*, (2011), response surface methodology was employed to model and optimize the cold enzyme starch hydrolysis conditions. Metaheuristic techniques such as Differential Evolution (DE) (Storn and Price, 1995) and Gravitational Search Algorithm

(GSA) (Rashedi *et al.*, 2009) were employed in this work to solve this problem with the aid of measurement metrics (Zitzler and Thiele, 1999).

Gravitational Search Algorithm (GSA) introduced recently by Rashedi *et al.*, (2009) is currently among the most applied meta-heuristic techniques in combinatorial optimization. GSA belong to the group of swarm-based stochastic search methods (such as; Particle Swarm Optimization (PSO) (Kennedy and Eberhart, 1995) and Cuckoo Search Algorithm (CSA) (Yang and Deb, 2009). GSA operates on a population of solutions basedf on Newtonian law of gravity and mass interactions. This algorithm regards agents as objects consisting of different masses. In recent times, GSA has been broadly applied in many industrial settings (Chatterjee and Mahanti, 2010).

Differential Evolution (DE) is a population-based evolutionary algorithm that has been derived from Genetic Algorithms (GA) (Holland, 1992). DE was developed in the nineties by Storn and Price (1995). DE has been used extensively to solve problems which are non-differentiable, non-continuous, non-linear, noisy, flat, multidimensional, have many local minima, constraints or high degree of stochasticity. Lately, DE has been applied to a variety of areas including optimization problems in chemical and process engineering (Babu and Munawar, 2000; Babu and Singh, 2000; Angira and Babu, 2005).

This work aims to produce a set of solutions that dominantly approximates the Pareto frontier in the objective space of the MO optimization of bioethanol production from cold enzyme starch hydrolysis. The problem was tackled using Differential Evolution (DE) (Storn and Price, 1995) and Gravitational Search Algorithm (GSA) (Rashedi *et al.*, 2009) and the proposed Hopfield-enhanced Differential Evolution (HEDE) technique in conjunction with the weighted sum approach to generate a series of solutions that dominantly approximate the Pareto frontier. The dominance

ranking among the frontier approximations produced by the algorithms were carried out using the Hypervolume Indicator (HVI) metric (Zitzler *et al.*, 2008). In addition a convergence metric (Deb and Jain, 2002) was also employed to extract information related to the distribution characteristics for solution options produced by each algorithm. Comparison studies were then conducted on the individual best solutions as well as the obtained frontier approximations.

This paper is organized as follows. The next section elucidates prior art, the computational techniques which are the DE, GSA and the proposed HEDE approaches. The 'Measurement Metrics' section provides details on the convergence and the HVI metrics employed in this work. The bioethanol production problem which consists of three objectives along with four decision variables and constraints are illustrated thereafter. Next, a rigorous analysis and discussion of the computational outcome with the metaheuristic approaches utilized in this work have been reported. This paper ends with some concluding remarks and suggestion for future works.

DIFFERENTIAL EVOLUTION

DE is a class of evolutionary meta-heuristic algorithms first introduced by Storn and Price, (1995). This central idea of this technique is the incorporation of perturbative methods into evolutionary algorithms. DE starts by the initialization of a population of at least four individuals denoted as P. These individuals are real-coded vectors with some size N. The initial population of individual vectors (the first generation denoted $gen = 1$) are randomly generated in appropriate search ranges. One principal parent denoted x^p_i and three auxiliary parents denoted x^a_i is randomly selected from the population, P. In DE, every individual, I in the population, P would become a principle parent,

x^p_i at one generation or the other and thus have a chance in mating with the auxiliary parents, x^a_i. The three auxiliary parents then engage in 'differential mutation' to generate a mutated vector, V_i.

$$V_i = x^a_1 + F(x^a_2 - x^a_3) \tag{1}$$

where F is the real-valued mutation amplification factor which is usually between 0 and 1. Next V_i is then recombined (or exponentially crossed-over) with x^p_i to generate child trial vector, x^{child}_i. The probability of the cross-over, CR is an input parameter set by the user. In DE, the survival selection mechanism into the next generation is called 'knock-out competition'. This is defined as the direct competition between the principle parent, x^p_i and the child trial vector, x^{child}_i to select the survivor of the next generation as follows:

$$x_i(gen+1) = \begin{cases} x^{child}_i(gen) \leftrightarrow \\ x^p_i(gen) \leftrightarrow \end{cases}$$
$$f(x^{child}_i) \, better \, than \, f(x^p_i) \tag{2}$$
$$otherwise$$

Therefore, the knock-out competition mechanism also serves as the fitness evaluation scheme for the DE algorithm. The parameter setting for the DE algorithm is given in Table 1: The algorithm of the DE method is shown in Algorithm 1.

Table 1. DE parameter setting

Parameters	Values
Individual Size, N	6
Population Size, P	7
Mutation amplification factor, F	0.3
Cross-over Probability, CR	0.667

GRAVITATIONAL SEARCH ALGORITHM (GSA)

The GSA algorithm is a meta-heuristic algorithm first developed Rashedi *et al.*, (2009). This technique was inspired by the law of gravity and the idea of interaction of masses. This algorithm uses the Newtonian gravitational laws where the search agents are the associated masses. Thus, the gravitational forces influence the motion of these masses, where lighter masses gravitate towards the heavier masses (which signify good solutions) during these interactions. The gravitational force hence acts as the communication mechanism for the masses (analogous to 'social component' for the particle agents in PSO (Kennedy and Eberhart, 1995)). The position of the masses correlates to the solution space in the search domain while the masses characterize the fitness space. As the iterations increase, and gravitational interactions occur, it is expected that the masses would

Algorithm 1. Differential evolution (DE)

```
Step 1: Initialize  individual size N, P, CR and F
Step 2: Randomly initialize the population vectors, x^G_i.
Step 3: Randomly select one principal parents, x^p_i
Step 4: Randomly select three auxiliary parents, x^a_i
Step 5: Perform differential mutation & generate mutated vector, V_i
Step 6: Recombine V_i with x^p_i to generate child trial vector, x^child_i
Step 7: Perform 'knock-out' competition for next generation survival selection
Step 8: If the fitness criterion is satisfied and t= T_max, halt and print solu-
tions
else proceed to step 3
```

conglomerate at its fittest position and provide an optimal solution to the problem.

Initially the GSA algorithm randomly generates a distribution of masses, $m_i(t)$(search agents) and also sets an initial position for these masses, x_i^d. For a minimization problem, the least fit mass, $m_i^{worst}(t)$ and the fittest mass, $m_i^{best}(t)$ at time t are calculated as follows:

$$m^{best}(t) = \min_{j\in[1,N]} m_j(t) \tag{3}$$

$$m^{worst}(t) = \max_{j\in[1,N]} m_j(t) \tag{4}$$

For a maximization problem, its simply vice versa. The inertial mass, $m_i'(t)$ and gravitational masses, $M_i(t)$ are then computed based on the fitness map developed previously.

$$m_i'(t) = \frac{m_i(t) - m^{worst}(t)}{m^{best}(t) - m^{worst}(t)} \tag{5}$$

$$M_i(t) = \frac{m_i(t)}{\sum_{j=1}^{N} m_j(t)} \tag{6}$$

such that

$$M_{ai} = M_{pi} = M_{ii} = M_i : i \in [1, N] \tag{7}$$

Then the gravitational constant, $G(t+1)$ and the Euclidean distance $R_{ij}(t)$ is computed as the following:

$$G(t+1) = G(t)\exp\left(\frac{-\alpha t}{T_{max}}\right) \tag{8}$$

$$R_{ij}(t) = \sqrt{\left(x_i(t)\right)^2 - \left(x_j(t)\right)^2} \tag{9}$$

where α is some arbitrary constant and T_{max} is the maximum number of iterations, $x_i(t)$ and $x_j(t)$ are the positions of particle i and j at time t. The interaction forces at time t, $F_{ij}^d(t)$ for each of the masses are then computed:

$$F_{ij}^d(t) = G(t)\left(\frac{M_{pi}(t)\times M_{aj}(t)}{R_{ij}(t)+\varepsilon}\right)\times\left(x_j^d(t) - x_i^d(t)\right) \tag{10}$$

where ε is some small parameter. The total force acting on each mass i is given in a stochastic form as the following:

$$F_i^d(t) = \sum_{\substack{j=1\\i\neq j}}^{N} rand(w_j)F_{ij}^d(t) : rand(w_j) \in [0,1] \tag{11}$$

where $rand(w_j)$ is a randomly assigned weight. Consequently, the acceleration of each of the masses, $a_i^d(t)$ is then as follows:

$$a_i^d(t) = \left(\frac{F_i^d(t)}{M_{ii}(t)}\right) \tag{12}$$

After the computation of the particle aceleration, the particle position and velocity is then calculated:

$$v_i^d(t+1) = rand(w_j) + v_i^d(t) + a_i^d(t) \tag{13}$$

$$x_i^d(t+1) = x_i^d(t(t)) + v_i^d(t(t+1)) \tag{14}$$

where $rand(w_j)$ is a randomly assigned weight. The iterations are then continued until the all mass agents are at their fittest positions in the fitness landscape and some stopping criterion which is set by the user is met. The GSA algorithm is presented in Algorithm 2 and the parameter settings are given in Table 2.

Table 2. GSA parameter setting

Parameters	Values
Initial parameter (G_o)	100
Number of mass agents, n	6
Constant parameter, α	20
Constant parameter, ε	0.01

HOPFIELD-ENHANCED DIFFERENTIAL EVOLUTION (HEDE)

The Hopfield enhancement technique employed in this work is based on the idea of Ising spin models Amit *et al.*, (1985) and Hopfield Neural Networks (HNN) (Hopfield, 1982; Hopfield, 1984). The Ising spin model in statistical physics was originally developed in Dyson, (1969) which consequently inspired the creation of the Hopfield Recurrent Artificial Neural Network (HNN) (Hopfield, 1982; Hopfield, 1984). These neural nets were observed to have applications in many optimization-type problems (Lee *et al.*, 1998; Vasant *et al.*, 2012).

One key feature of the HNN is that a decrease in the network energy by a finite amount occurs whenever there is a change in the network's state. This essential property confirms or accentuates the convergence of the output whenever the network state is changed.

HNNs are usually constructed by a finite number of interlinked artificial neurons. These neurons update their weights or their activation values (outputs from threshold neurons) independently relative to other neurons in the network. Since HNNs are back-propagating auto-associator networks, the input of the neurons are updated by the activation values of the output. Therefore, the input of a neuron i at a cycle $t+1$ is as follows:

$$s_i(t + 1) = \sum_{j=1}\sum_{i=1} y_j(t)w_{ji} + \theta \text{ for } j \neq i$$

(15)

where $y_j(t)$ is the activation values from the output, w_{ji} is the neural weights and θ is some arbitrary constant set by the user.

Algorithm 2. Gravitational Search Algorithm (GSA)

```
Step 1: Initialize no of particles, mᵢ and initial positions, xᵢ(0)
Step 2: Initialize algorithm parameters G (0), α.
Step 3: Compute gravitational & inertial masses based on the fitness map
Step 4: Compute the gravitational constant, G(t)
Step 5: Compute distance between agents, Rᵢⱼ(t)
Step 6: Compute total force, Fᵢᵈ(t) and the acceleration aᵢᵈ(t) of each agent.
Step 7: Compute new velocity vᵢ(t) and position xᵢ(t) for each agent
Step 8: If the fitness criterion is satisfied and t= Tₘₐₓ, halt and print solutions
        else proceed to step 3
```

In this work, the central ideas that built the fundamentals of the HNN are applied to the DE algorithm in this work. This was done to improve the convergence capabilities of the DE algorithm. First, the population of vectors, x^G_i was initialized. Then, a set of random weights w_{ij} was introduced and the symmetric property was imposed. The consequence steps are similar to the regular DE algorithm where one principal parent, x^p_i and three auxiliary parents x^a_i are randomly selected. Differential mutation is then performed and the mutated vector, V_i is generated. The V_i is then recombined with x^p_i to generate child trial vector, x^{child}_i. Next the function A, which arguments are the weights w_{ij} and the child trial vector, x^{child}_i is introduced as follows:

$$A_i(t) = \sum_{ij} w_{ij}(t) k^{x^{child}_i} \tag{16}$$

where k is a constant which is a input parameter specified by the user. This way $A_i(t)$ replaces and changes the functionality of the x^{child}_i in the regular DE algorithm. Then the piece-wise threshold function, $s_i(t)$ is computed as the following:

$$s_i(t+1) = \begin{cases} +1 \, iff A_i(t) > U \\ -1 \, iff A_i(t) < U \\ s_i(t) \, iff otherwise \end{cases} \tag{17}$$

where U is a constant which is an input parameter specified by the user. The energy function is then computed as the following:

$$E = -\frac{1}{2} \sum_{j=1} \sum_{i=1} A_j(t+1) A_j(t) w_{ij} - \sum_{i=1} \theta s(t) \tag{18}$$

where θ is a relaxation constant defined by the user. Hence, new variant for the DE algorithm, the Hopfield-Enhanced DE (HEDE) algorithm

was developed. The specified parameter settings and the HEDE algorithm are as in Table 3 and Algorithm 3 respectively. The flowchart for HEDE method is given in Figure 1.

MEASUREMENT METRICS: HYPERVOLUME INDICATOR (HVI) AND CONVERGENCE METRIC

The Hypervolume Indicator (HVI) is the only strictly Pareto-compliant indicator that can be used to measure the quality of solution sets in MO optimization problems (Zitzler *et al.*, 2008). Strictly Pareto-compliant can be defined such that if there exists two solution sets to a particular MO problem, then the solution set that dominates the other would a higher indicator value. The HVI measures the volume of the dominated section of the objective space and can be applied for multi-dimensional scenarios. When using the HVI, a reference point needs to be defined. Relative to this point, the volume of the space of all dominated solutions can be measured. The HVI of a solution set $x_{d\epsilon}X$ can be defined as follows:

Table 3. Parameter settings for the HEDE algorithm

Parameters	Values
Individual Size, N	6
Population Size, P	7
Mutation amplification factor, F	0.15
Max No. of Function Evaluations, T_{max}	3000
Constant, U	100
Constant, k	2.3
Constant, θ	0.02
Cross-over Probabbility, CR	0.667

Algorithm 3. Hopfield DE (HEDE)

Step 1: Initialize individual size N, P, CR and F
Step 2: Randomly initialize the population vectors, x^G_i.
Step 3: Randomly initialize weights, w_{ij} (t)
Step 4: Enforce symmetry condition on weights
Step 5: Randomly select one principal parents, x^P_i
Step 6: Randomly select three auxilary parents, x^a_i
Step 5: Perform differential mutation & generate mutated vector, V_i
Step 7: Recombine V_i with x^P_i to generate child trial vector, x^{child}_i
Step 8: Compute the function $A_i(t)$
Step 8: Compute the energy function, E.
Step 9: Perform 'knock-out' competition for next generation survival selection
Step 10: If $dE<0$, proceed to next step
   else go to Step 4.
Step 11: If the fitness criterion is satisfied and $t= T_{max}$, halt and print solutions, else proceed to

Figure 1. Hopfield DE (HEDE) Flowchart

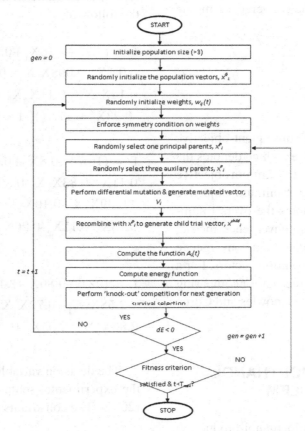

$$HVI(X) = vol\left(\bigcup_{(x_1,...x_d)\in X}[r_1,x_1]\times...\times[r_d,x_d]\right)$$

$$(19)$$

where $r_{1,...,}r_d$ is the reference point and $vol(.)$ being the Lebesgue measure. In this work the HVI is used to measure the quality of the approximation of the Pareto front by the GSA and the DE algorithms when used in conjunction with the weighted sum approach.

The convergence metric used in this work was developed in Deb and Jain, (2002). This metric gauges the convergence property of a solution set with respect to a reference set. In this work, since the Pareto optimal frontier was not known, a target vector $P*$ which was the most dominant vector was employed as the reference set. For a set of solutions for a single run of the program the formulation to compute the convergence metric is as the following:

$$d_i = \min_{j=1}^{|P*|}\sqrt{\sum_{k=1}^{M}\left(\frac{f_k^i - f_k^i}{f_k^{max} - f_k^{min}}\right)} \qquad (20)$$

where i and j denotes the subsequent objective function values, k is the index which denotes the objective function, f_k^{max} is the maximum objective function value, f_k^{min} is the minimum objective function value and M denotes the overall number of objectives. For this convergence metric, low the metric values indicate high convergence characteristics among the solution vectors. For a detail discussions on these metrics for comparing nondominated solutions see Knowles and Corne (2002).

DESCRIPTION OF BIOETHANOL PRODUCTION PROBLEM

The MO optimization of bioethanol production from cold enzyme starch hydrolysis was considered in this work. The MO optimization of

fermentation process parameters is crucial for the successful economical production of bioethanol from starch (Oberoi *et al.*, 2010). In Bao *et al.*, (2011), the response surface methodology was employed to model and optimize the cold enzyme starch hydrolysis conditions. The model presented in Bao *et al.*, (2011) for the MO optimization of bioethanol production with respect to the constraints is as the following:

```
Maximize→Predicted Biomass, f₁
Maximize→Ethanol Concentration, f₂
Maximize→Starch utilization ratio, f₃
subject to process constraints. (21)
```

The normalized objective functions which are the predicted biomass in x 10^8 cells/ml, ethanol concentration in weight % and starch utilization ratio in % as modeled in Bao *et al.*, (2011)are as the following:

$$f_1 = (4.22+0.16X_1+0.17X_2+0.077X_3 \\ +0.1X_4-0.098X_1X_4+0.11X_2X_3+ \\ 0.14X_2X_4+0.11X_3X_4-0.16X_1^2 \\ -0.23X_2^2-0.17X_3^2)(-1\times10^{-4})) \qquad (22)$$

$$f_2 = (16.76+0.8X_1+0.45X_2+0.27X_3+ \\ 0.11X_4-0.83X_1X_2-0.29X_1X_3+0.26X_2X_3 \\ +0.39X_2X_4-0.19X_3X_4+ \\ 0.13X_1^2-0.11X_2^2-0.26X_4^2)(-1\times10^{-4}) \qquad (23)$$

$$f_3 = (92.6+0.86X_1-1.44X_2-2.55X_1X_3 \\ +2.58X_1X_4+0.72X_2X_4+ \\ 2.83X_3X_4- 2.05X_1^2-0.86X_2^2)(-1\times10^{-4}) \qquad (24)$$

The decision variables are constrained as per the experimental setup described in Bao *et al.*, (2011). The constraints are as follows:

$$X_1 \in [214, 264]$$

$X_2 \in [392, 694]$

$X_3 \in [60, 79]$

$X_4 \in [103, 108]$ (25)

where X_1 is the amount of α - amylase (*IU* per *g* starch), X_2 is the amount of glucoamylase (*IU* per *g* starch), X_3 is the liquefaction temperature (*°C*) and X_4 is the liquefaction time (minutes) . The algorithms used in this work were programmed using the C++ programming language on a personal computer (PC) with an Intel dual core processor running at 2 GHz.

COMPUTATIONAL RESULTS AND ANALYSIS

In this work, the solution sets which are the approximations of the Pareto frontier were obtained using the GSA, DE and HEDE methods. The quality of these solutions was measured using the HVI and further solution analysis was carried out using the convergence metric. The nadir point (or the reference point) used in the HVI is a specific point where all the solutions sets produced by the algorithms dominate this point. The nadir point selected in this work is $(r_1, r_2, r_3) = (0, 0, 0)$.

The individual solutions (for specific weights) of the GSA algorithm were gauged with the HVI. The best, median and worst individual solutions were determined. The individual solutions for the GSA algorithm and their respective dominance values are shown in Table 4.

The associated weights (w_1, w_2, w_3) for the best, median and worst solution are (0.5, 0.2, 0.3), (0.4, 0.4, 0.2) and (0.3, 0.3, 0.4). The computational time for the best, median and worst solution is 0.504, 0.159 and 0.024 seconds respectively. As for the approximation of the Pareto frontier, 28 solutions for a range of weights were obtained for both the algorithms. The approximate Pareto frontiers obtained using the GSA algorithm is shown in Figure 2:

The individual solution ranking for the DE algorithm and their individual HVI values are given in Table 5.

The associated weights (w_1, w_2, w_3) for the best, median and worst solutions produced by the DE algorithm are (0.7, 0.2, 0.1), (0.2, 0.5 0.3) and (0.1, 0.8, 0.1). The computational time for the best, median and worst solution is 1.672, 1.051 and 0.0612 seconds respectively. The approximate Pareto frontiers obtained using the DE algorithm is shown in Figure 3:

Table 4. Individual solutions generated by the GSA algorithm

Description		Best	Median	Worst
Objective Function	f_1	3.65868	3.64527	3.64071
	f_2	6.63677	6.60933	6.59878
	f_3	15.6708	15.5948	15.5659
Decision Variable	x_1	214.804	214.265	214.016
	x_2	392.76	392.185	392.021
	x_3	60	60	60
	x_4	103	103	103
Iterations		149	47	17
Dominance		380.516	375.722	373.959

Figure 2. Pareto frontiers of the objectives obtained by the GSA method

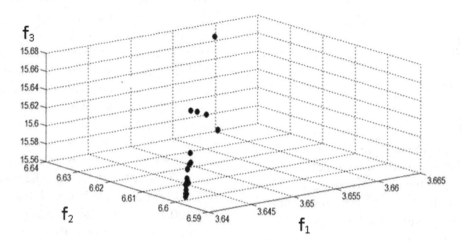

Table 5. Individual solutions generated by the DE algorithm

Description		Best	Median	Worst
Objective Function	f_1	10.8773	10.7006	5.66004
	f_2	16.1959	15.1282	10.2589
	f_3	45.1815	43.3621	25.7811
Decision Variable	x_1	259.172	238.744	262.823
	x_2	692.897	693.02	481.374
	x_3	61.4032	61.1993	60.7709
	x_4	104.403	104.199	103.771
Iterations		217	223	13
HVI		7959.519	7019.492	1496.91

Figure 3. Pareto frontiers of the objectives obtained by the DE method

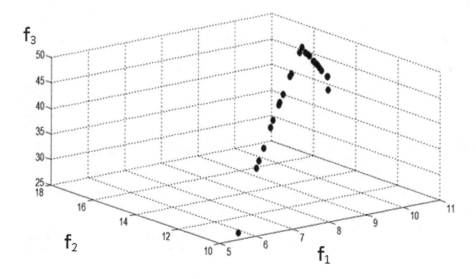

The individual solutions for the HEDE algorithm and their individual HVI values are given in Table 6.

The associated weights (w_1, w_2, w_3) for the best, median and worst solution are (0.5, 0.4, 0.1), (0.1, 0.2, 0.7) and (0.1, 0.6, 0.3). The computational time for the best, median and worst solution is 1.962, 0.148 and 0.250 seconds respectively. The approximate Pareto frontiers obtained using the HEDE algorithm is given in Figure 4.

It can be observed using the HVI that the best solution obtained by HEDE algorithm dominates the best solution produced by the DE and GSA algorithms by 6.79% and 29.42%. The comparison of the best candidate solutions obtained by the methods employed in this work is shown in Table 7.

In Table 7, it can be seen that the best solutions produces by CDE, DE and GSA algorithms are more dominant the PSO approach. The HVI computed for the entire frontier of each solution set produced by an algorithm gives the true measure of dominance when compared with another algorithm. In this work, the HVI for the entire frontier was computed for each of the algorithm. The execution time for each algorithm to generate the entire frontier was also obtained. The HVI for

Table 6. Individual solutions generated by the HEDE algorithm

Description		Best	Median	Worst
Objective Function	f_1	10.9375	10.7297	10.4712
	f_2	16.4561	15.7132	13.8888
	f_3	45.6871	44.1768	41.3627
Decision Variable	x_1	263.811	251.463	216.155
	x_2	693.485	690.265	691.48
	x_3	61.4515	61.3178	60.9686
	x_4	104.451	104.318	103.969
Iterations		431	32	55
HVI		8223.157	7448.117	6015.477

Figure 4. Pareto frontiers of the objectives obtained by the HEDE method

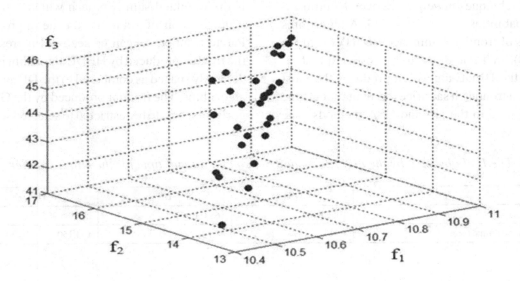

Table 7. The comparison of the best solutions obtained by the algorithms

Description		GSA	DE	HEDE
Objective Function	f_1	3.65868	10.8773	10.9375
	f_2	6.63677	16.1959	16.4561
	f_3	15.6708	45.1815	45.6871
Decision Variable	x_1	214.804	259.172	263.811
	x_2	392.76	692.897	693.485
	x_3	60	61.4032	61.4515
	x_4	103	104.403	104.451
Iterations		149	217	431
HVI		380.516	7959.519	8223.157

the entire frontier for the solution sets produced by the DE, GSA as well as HEDE and the associated execution time is shown in Table 8.

In Table 8, the frontier produced by the HEDE algorithm is more dominant than the one produced by the GSA and DE algorithms by 1863.103% and 22.664% respectively. The dominance ranking of the approximate Pareto frontiers produced by the algorithms is $HEDE \prec DE \prec GSA$ (where the symbol, '$\prec$' denotes as 'more dominant than'). A new optima is achieved by the HEDE method (see Table 7) since it outperforms the DE and GSA methods. The individual best solution of the HEDE method maximizes all the objectives f_1, f_2 and f_3 very effectively as compared to the DE algorithm. Thus, it can be said that the proposed HEDE technique outweighs the overall optimization capabilities of the DE and GSA algorithms in terms of frontier dominance (see HVI value in Table 8). In Table 8, it can be observed that although the HEDE algorithm produces the most dominant frontier, it sacrifices computational time as compared to the DE and GSA methods. The

value of the convergence metric for the approximate frontier produced by the GSA, DE and HEDE techniques are shown in Table 9.

In Table 9, as mentioned in Section 3.2, the smaller the metric value, the more convergent the solution spread at the frontier. The DE technique is observed to be more convergent than the GSA technique by 90.537%. It can be also observed that the HEDE technique outweighs the DE and GSA approaches in terms of frontier convergence by 34.611% and 93.812% respectively. Therefore, the convergence ranking of the approximate Pareto frontiers produced by the algorithms is $HEDE > DE > GSA$ (where the symbol, '$>$' is denoted as 'more convergent than').

In this work the scalarization scheme used is the weighted sum approach which constructs a progression of solutions on the approximate Pareto frontier. As can be seen in Figures 2 - 4, the frontier produced by HEDE algorithm is more diversely spaced as compared to the DE and GSA algorithms. The frontier produced by the GSA algorithm seems to be restricted to selected sections

Table 8. The HVI obtained by the algorithms and the computational time for the entire frontier

	GSA	DE	HEDE
HVI	10523.408	168411.491	206585.995
Computational time (secs)	7.917	45.231	194.150

Table 9. The HVI obtained by the algorithms and the computational time for the entire frontier

	GSA	DE	HEDE
Convergence Value	0.820	0.077597	0.05074

of the objective space (Figure 2). This spacing characteristic heavily influences the ability of the algorithm to efficiently approximate the Pareto frontier. Localized solutions of the frontier such as the ones produced by the GSA algorithm miss out on critical solutions in the objective space. Therefore, this causes the GSA algorithm to have a lower dominance as compared to the DE and HEDE algorithms.

One of the setbacks of employing metaheuristic algorithms in conjunction with the weighted sum framework is that it *does not guarantee Pareto optimality* of the approximate frontier (only in the weak sense (Pradyumn, 2007)). In addition, these sorts of scalarization techniques cannot approximate sections of the Pareto frontier that is *concave*. Although the HVI metric is most effective in benchmarking the dominance of solution sets produced by algorithms, this metric is *very dependent on the choice of the nadir point*. Hence, the nadir point selection is very crucial when using the HVI metric.

In this work, the HEDE, DE and GSA algorithms performed *stable computations* during the computational executions. All Pareto-efficient solutions produced by the algorithms developed in this work violated none of the constraints given in the problem. One of the advantages of using the HEDE algorithm as compared to the other algorithms used in this work is that it produces *highly effective results* in terms of approximating the Pareto frontier.

A new optima is achieved by the HEDE method (see Table 7) since it outperforms the other algorithms used in this work. Thus, it can be said that the HEDE method in this work outweighs the overall optimization capabilities of GSA and DE

approaches (see HVI value in Table 8). In terms of computational time taken for the algorithm to produce the entire approximate Pareto frontier, the HEDE method takes the longest time followed by the GSA and the DE method respectively. In this work, the DE and GSA algorithms performed stable computations during the program executions. This can mostly be attributed to complexity of the HEDE algorithm due to the integration of the Hopfield component as compared to other algorithms implemented in this work.

Referring to Table 9, the Hopfield enhancement of the DE technique is observed to increase the DE algorithm's capabilities to produce solution spreads that are more convergent. It can be inferred that for the bioethanol production problem, *the algorithm that produced the most convergent results also produces the solution spread that is the most dominant (HEDE)*. Therefore, for problems such as this, convergence-inclined algorithms such as HEDE are very suitable for generating dominant solution options that approximate the Pareto frontier.

CONCLUSION

A new local optimum and a highly dominant approximation of the Pareto frontier were attained using the HEDE approach in conjunction with the weighted sum framework. In addition, using the HEDE algorithm, the solution spread of the frontier had a very convergent distribution. When gauged with the HVI metric, the DE and HEDE techniques generated the most dominant Pareto frontier as compared to the GSA method. For future works, other meta-heuristic algorithms such as Genetic

Programming (GP) (Koza, 1992), Analytical Programing (AP) (Zelinka, 2002), Hybrid Neuro-GP (Ganesan, 2011) MO evolutionary algorithm (Qu and Suganthan, 2010), (Ke Li *et al.*, 2011) and Hybrid Neuro-Swarm (Elamvazuthi *et al.*, 2011) should be applied to the bioethanol production problem. The HVI metric should be applied using a variety of nadir points. This would provide more information relating the consequences of these points to the degree of dominance of solution sets. During these numerical experiments, the spacing metric should be measured and compared for the observation of the uniformity of the spreads with respect to the algorithms. More large-scale MO problems should be studied using the HEDE and DE algorithms for a better understanding of the mentioned algorithm's performance and efficiency.

REFERENCES

Amit, D. J., Gutfreund, H., & Sompolinsky, H. (1985). Spin-glass models of neural networks. *Physical Review A.*, *32*(2), 1007–1018. doi:10.1103/PhysRevA.32.1007 PMID:9896156

Angira, R., & Babu, B. V. (2005). Optimization of Non-Linear Chemical Processes Using Modified Differential Evolution (MDE). In *Proceedings of the 2ⁿᵈ Indian International Conference on Artificial Intelligence*. Pune, India: MDE.

Babu, B. V., & Munawar, S. A. (2000). Differential Evolution for the Optimal Design of Heat Exchangers. In *Proceedings of All-India seminar on Chemical Engineering Progress on Resource Development: A Vision 2010 and Beyond*. Bhuvaneshwar.

Babu, B. V., & Singh, R. P. (2000). Synthesis & Optimization of Heat Integrated Distillation Systems Using Differential Evolution. In *Proceedings of All- India seminar on Chemical Engineering Progress on Resource Development: A Vision 2010 and Beyond*. Bhuvaneshwar.

Bao, Y. L., Yan, Z. C., Wang, H. L., & Chen, L. (2011). Optimization of bioethanol production during simultaneous saccharification and fermentation in very high-gravity cassava mash. *Antonie van Leeuwenhoek*, *99*, 329–339. doi:10.1007/s10482-010-9494-5 PMID:20803106

Cardona, C. A., & Sánchezo, J. (2007). Fuel ethanol production: process design trends and integration opportunities. *Bioresource Technology*, *98*(12), 2415–2457. doi:10.1016/j.biortech.2007.01.002 PMID:17336061

Chatterjee, A., & Mahanti, G. K. (2010). Comparative Performance Of Gravitational Search Algorithm And Modified Particle Swarm Optimization Algorithm For Synthesis Of Thinned Scanned Concentric Ring Array Antenna. *Progress In Electromagnetics Research B*, *25*, 331–348. doi:10.2528/PIERB10080405

Das, I., & Dennis, J. E. (1998). Normal-boundary intersection: A new method for generating the Pareto surface in nonlinear multicriteria optimization problems. *SIAM Journal on Optimization*, *8*(3), 631–657. doi:10.1137/S1052623496307510

Deb, K., & Jain, S. (2002). *Running performance metrics for Evolutionary Multiobjective Optimization* (KanGAL Report No. 2002004). Kanpur, India: Kanpur Genetic Algorithms Laboratory, Indian Institute of Technology.

Deb, K., Pratap, A., Agarwal, S., & Meyarivan, T. (2002). A Fast and Elitist Multi-Objective Genetic Algorithm: NSGA-II. *IEEE Transactions on Evolutionary Computation*, *6*(2), 182–197. doi:10.1109/4235.996017

Dyson, F. J. (1969). Existence of a phase-transition in a one-dimensional Ising ferromagnet. *Communications in Mathematical Physics*, *12*, 91–107. doi:10.1007/BF01645907

Elamvazuthi, I., Ganesan, T., & Vasant, P. (2011). A comparative study of HNN and Hybrid HNN-PSO techniques in the optimization of distributed generation (DG) power systems. In *Proceedings of International Conference on Advanced Computer Science & Information System* (ICACSIS), (pp 195 – 200). ICACSIS.

Emmerich, M., Beume, N., & Naujoks, B. (2005). An EMO Algorithm Using the Hypervolume Measure as Selection Criterion. In *Proceedings of Conference on Evolutionary Multi-Criterion Optimization* (EMO 2005). Springer.

Eschenauer, H., Koski, J., & Osyczka, A. (1990). *Multicriteria Design Optimization*. Berlin: Springer-Verlag. doi:10.1007/978-3-642-48697-5

Fishburn, P.C. (1967). *Additive Utilities with Incomplete Product Set: Applications to Priorities and Assignments*. Baltimore, MD: Operations Research Society of America (ORSA).

Fleischer, M. (2003). The measure of Pareto optima: Applications to multi-objective metaheuristics. In *Proceedings of Conference on Evolutionary Multi-Criterion Optimization* (EMO 2003), (pp 519–533). EMO.

Ganesan, T., Vasant, P., & Elamvazuthi, I. (2011). *Optimization of nonlinear geological structure mapping using hybrid neuro-genetic techniques*. Mathematical and Computer Modelling, *54* (11-12), 2913 – 2922.

Grosan, C. (2003). Performance metrics for multiobjective optimization evolutionary algorithms. In *Proceedings of Conference on Applied and Industrial Mathematics* (CAIM). CAIM.

Holland, J. H. (1992). *Adaptation in Natural and Artificial Systems: An Introductory Analysis with Applications to Biology, Control and Artificial Intelligence*. USA: MIT Press.

Hopfield, J. J. (1982). Neural Networks and Physical Systems with Emergent Collective Computational Abilities. *Proceedings of the National Academy of Sciences of the United States of America*, *79*, 2554–2558. doi:10.1073/pnas.79.8.2554 PMID:6953413

Hopfield, J. J. (1984). Neurons with Graded Response have Collective Computational Properties like those of Two-State Neurons. *Proceedings of the National Academy of Sciences of the United States of America*, *81*, 3088–3092. doi:10.1073/pnas.81.10.3088 PMID:6587342

Hounsa, C. G., Brandt, E. V., Johan, T., Stefan, H., & Bernard, A. P. (1998). Role of trehalose in survival of Saccharomyces cerevisiae under osmotic stress. *Microbiology*, *144*, 671–680. doi:10.1099/00221287-144-3-671 PMID:9534237

Igel, C., Hansen, N., & Roth, S. (2007). Covariance Matrix Adaptation for Multi-objective Optimization. *Evolutionary Computation*, *15*(1), 1–28. doi:10.1162/evco.2007.15.1.1 PMID:17388777

Kennedy, J., & Eberhart, R. (1995). Particle Swarm Optimization. In *Proceedings of the International Conference on Neural Networks*. Perth, Australia: IEEE.

Knowles, J., & Corne, D. (2002). On metrics for comparing nondominated sets. In *Proceedings, World Congress on Computational Intelligence* (CEC'02), (pp. 711 – 716). IEEE.

Knowles, J., & Corne, D. (2003). Properties of an Adaptive Archiving Algorithm for Storing Nondominated Vectors. *IEEE Transactions on Evolutionary Computation*, *7*(2), 100–116. doi:10.1109/TEVC.2003.810755

Koza, J. R. (1992). *Genetic Programming: On the Programming of Computers by means of Natural Selection*. USA: MIT Press.

Lee, K. Y., Sode-Yome, A., & Park, J. H. (1998). Adaptive Hopfield Neural Networks for Economic Load Dispatch. *IEEE Transactions on Power Systems, USA, 13*(2), 519–526. doi:10.1109/59.667377

Li, , K., Kwong, S., Cao, J., Li, M., Zheng, J., & Shen, R. (2011). Achieving Balance Between Proximity And Diversity In Multi-Objective Evolutionary Algorithm. *Information Sciences, 182*, 220–242. doi:10.1016/j.ins.2011.08.027

Luyben, M. L., & Floudas, C. A. (1994). Analyzing the interaction of design and control. 1. A multiobjective framework and application to binary distillation synthesis. *Computers & Chemical Engineering, 18*(10), 933–969. doi:10.1016/0098-1354(94)E0013-D

Marques, P. T., Perego, C., Le Meins, J. F., Borsali, R., & Soldi, V. (2006). Study of gelatinization process and viscoelastic properties of cassava starch: effect of sodium hydroxide and ethylene glycol diacrylate as cross-linking agent. *Carbohydrate Polymers, 66*(3), 396–407. doi:10.1016/j.carbpol.2006.03.028

Oberoi, H. S., Vadlani, P. V., Madl, R. L., Saida, L., & Abeykoon, J. P. (2010). Ethanol production from orange peels: two-stage hydrolysis and fermentation studies using optimized parameters through experimental design. *Journal of Agricultural and Food Chemistry, 58*(6), 3422–3429. doi:10.1021/jf903163t PMID:20158208

Pradyumn, S. K. (2007). On the Normal Boundary Intersection Method for Generation of Efficient Front. In Y. Shi et al. (Eds.), *ICCS 2007, Part I, LNCS 4487* (pp. 310–317). Springer-Verlag Berlin Heidelberg.

Qu, B. Y., & Suganthan, P. N. (2010). Multi-objective evolutionary algorithms based on the summationof normalized objectives and diversified selection. *Information Sciences, 180*, 3170–3181. doi:10.1016/j.ins.2010.05.013

Rashedi, E., Nezamabadi-pour, H., & Saryazdi, S. (2009). GSA: A Gravitational Search Algorithm. *Information Sciences, 179*, 2232–2248. doi:10.1016/j.ins.2009.03.004

Sandgren, E. (1994). Multicriteria design optimization by goal programming. In H. Adeli (Ed.), *Advances in Design Optimization* (pp. 225–265). London: Chapman & Hall.

Sandgren, E. (1994). Multicriteria design optimization by goal programming. In H. Adeli (Ed.), *Advances in Design Optimization* (pp. 225–265). London: Chapman & Hall.

Statnikov, R. B., & Matusov, J.B. (1995). Multicriteria Optimization and Engineering. New York: Chapman and Hall.

Storn, R., & Price, K. V. (1995). *Differential evolution – A simple and efficient adaptive scheme for global optimization over continuous spaces* (Technical Report TR-95-012). ICSI.

Tamiz, M. (1996). *Multi-objective programming and goal programming: Theories and multicriteria design optimization*. Berlin: Springer-Verlag. doi:10.1007/978-3-642-87561-8

Thatipamala, R., Rohani, S., & Hill, G. A. (1992). Effects of high product and substrate inhibitions on the kinetics and biomass and product yields during ethanol batch fermentation. *Biotechnology and Bioengineering, 40*(2), 289–297. doi:10.1002/bit.260400213 PMID:18601115

Triantaphyllou, E. (2000). *Multi-Criteria Decision Making: A Comparative Study*. Dordrecht, The Netherlands: Kluwer Academic Publishers.

Vasant, P., Ganesan, T., & Elamvazuthi, I. (2012). Hybrid tabu search Hopfield recurrent ANN fuzzy technique to the production planning problems: a case study of crude oil in refinery industry. *International Journal of Manufacturing, Materials, and Mechanical Engineering, 2*(1), 47 - 65.

Yang, X. S., & Deb, S. (2009). Cuckoo search via L'evy flights. In *Proc. of World Congress on Nature & Biologically Inspired Computing (NaBIC 2009)*. IEEE Publications.

Zelinka, I. (2002). Analytic programming by Means of SOMA Algorithm. In *Proc. 8th, International Conference on Soft Computing Mendel'02*. Brno, Czech Republic: Mendel.

Zitzler, E., Knowles, J., & Thiele, L. (2008). Quality Assessment of Pareto Set Approximations. In J. Branke et al. (Eds.), Multiobjective Optimization (LNCS) (vol. 5252, pp. 373-494). Springer-Verlag.

Zitzler, E., & Thiele, L. (1998). Multiobjective optimization using evolutionary algorithms—A comparative case study. In A. E. Eiben, T. B̈ack, M. Schoenauer, & H. P. Schwefel (Eds.), *Parallel Problem Solving from Nature,* (vol. 5, pp. 292–301). Springer. doi:10.1007/BFb0056872

Zitzler, E., & Thiele, L. (1999). Multiobjective evolutionary algorithms: a comparative case study and the strength Pareto approach. *IEEE Transactions on Evolutionary Computation, 3*(4), 257–271. doi:10.1109/4235.797969

Zitzler, E., Thiele, L., Laumanns, M., Fonseca, C. M., & Grunert da Fonseca, V. (2003). Performance Assessment of Multiobjective Optimizers: An Analysis and Review. *IEEE Transactions on Evolutionary Computation, 7*(2), 117–132. doi:10.1109/TEVC.2003.810758

KEY TERMS AND DEFINITIONS

Bioethanol Production Process: Bioethanol in this context refers to ethanol extracted from a biological/natural source (for instance in this work starch). Bioethanol Production Process commonly involves fermentation, distillation, dehydration, hydrolysis and denaturing processes.

Decision Making: Searching an optimal solution (or decision) with respect to other factors (constraints), in this context, with the aid of computer algorithms.

Differential Evolution (DE): DE is a population-based evolutionary algorithm which is a type of metaheuristic approach. DE employs perturbation methods for population mutation for consistent improvement of the solution set.

Gravitational Search Algorithm (GSA): A swarm-based metaheuristic algorithm that utilizes concepts of mass interactions and dynamics of motion from Newtonian gravitational laws.

Hopfield Artificial Neural Networks (HNN): The Hopfield Artificial Neural Networks (HNN) were developed in Hopfield (1982) and Hopfield (1984) are neural nets that have an energy function that is correlated to the network state and the property of convergence.

Hopfield-Enhanced Differential Evolution (HEDE): HEDE is the proposed algorithm developed in this work to enhance/improve the original DE algorithm by integrating it with ideas from the HNN with aim to improve the capabilities of the DE algorithm to obtain convergent and dominant solutions.

Hypervolume Indicator: The Hypervolume Indicator (HVI) is an n-dimensional metric that returns a unary value which measures the closeness between the solution spread on the Pareto frontier and the optimal/dominant Pareto frontier.

Multi-Objective (MO) Optimization: MO Optimization is class of mathematical optimization problems that involve the simultaneous optimization of multiple objectives which may or may not be with respect to constraint(s).

Weighted Sum Approach: A MO solution procedure which involves the assignment of scalar/weight values to indicate objective trade-offs among the solutions of the problem.

APPENDIX: NOTATION

- DE Algorithm:
  - **N:** Individual Size vector.
  - **P:** Population Size.
  - **F:** Mutation amplification factor.
  - **CR:** Cross-over probability.
  - $\mathbf{x}^G_i$: Population vectors.
  - $\mathbf{x}^p_i$: Principal parents.
  - $\mathbf{x}^a_i$: Auxiliary parents.
  - $\mathbf{V}_i$: Mutated vector.
  - $\mathbf{x}^{child}_i$: Child trial vector.
  - $\mathbf{T}_{max}$: Maximum number of iterations.
- GSA Algorithm:
  - $\mathbf{G(t)}$: Gravitational constant.
  - **N:** Number of mass agents.
  - α, ε : Constant parameters.
  - $\mathbf{R}_{ij}\mathbf{(t)}$: Distance between agents.
  - $\mathbf{F}_{id}\mathbf{(t)}$: Total force of each agent.
  - $\mathbf{a}_{id}\mathbf{(t)}$: Acceleration of each agent.
  - $\mathbf{v}_i\mathbf{(t)}$: Velocity of each mass agent.
  - $\mathbf{x}_i\mathbf{(t)}$: Position of each mass agent.
  - **T:** Function Evaluations.
- HEDE Algorithm:
  - $\mathbf{y}_j\mathbf{(t)}$: The activation values.
  - $\mathbf{w}_{ji}$: The neural weights.
  - θ : Arbitrary constant.
  - **k, U:** Constant parameter.
  - $\mathbf{A}_i\mathbf{(t)}$: Defined aggregate function.
  - $\mathbf{s}_i\mathbf{(t)}$: Piece-wise threshold function.
  - **E:** Energy function.
- Measurement Metrics:
  - **k':** Index denoting the objectives.
  - $\mathbf{f}_k$: Objective function value.
  - **P*:** Target vector.
  - $\mathbf{d}_i$: Convergence metric value.
  - $\mathbf{x}_d$: Solutions in set *X*.
  - $\mathbf{r}_{1,...,}\mathbf{r}_d$: Reference point.
  - **vol(.):** Lebesgue measure.

- Bioethatnol Production:
  - f_1: Predicted biomass in x 10^8 cells/ml.
  - f_2: Ethanol concentration in weight %.
  - f_3: Starch utilization ratio in %.
  - X_1: Amount of α - amylase (*IU* per *g* starch).
  - X_2: Amount of glucoamylase (*IU* per *g* starch).
  - X_3: The liquefaction temperature (^oC).
  - X_4: The liquefaction time (minutes).

Compilation of References

(1965). Yuan, X. (1997). New cut sets and their applications. *Fuzzy Systems and Mathematics*, *11*, 37-43.

(2008). Selection of optimal conditions for CNC multitool drilling system using non-traditional techniques. *International Journal of Machining and Machinability of Materials*, *3*(1), 190–207.Satishkumar, S.Asokan, P.

Abadi, D. (2009). Data Management in the Cloud: Limitations and Opportunities. Data Engineering.

Abate, A., Nappi, M., Riccio, D., & Sabatino, G. (2007). 2D and 3D face recognition: A survey. *Pattern Recognition Letters*, *28*(14), 1885–1906. doi:10.1016/j.patrec.2006.12.018

Abdeen, M. O. (2008). Green energies and environment. *Renewable & Sustainable Energy Reviews*, *12*, 1789–1821. doi:10.1016/j.rser.2006.05.009

Abdeen, M. O. (2009). Principle of low energy building design: Heating, ventilation and air conditioning, Cooling India. *India's Premier Magazine on the Cooling Industry, Mumbai, India.*, *5*(4), 26–46.

Abdeen, M. O. (2012). Clean and green energy technologies: Sustainable development and environment. *Sky J. Agric. Res.*, *1*(2), 28–50.

Abecker, A., Bernardi, A., Hinkelmann, K., Kühn, O., & Sintek, M. (1998). Toward a Technology for Organisational Memories. *IEEE Intelligent Systems*, *13*(3), 40–48. doi:10.1109/5254.683209

Abecker, A., Mentzas, G., Ntioudis, S., & Papavassiliou, G. (2003). Business Process Modelling and Enactment for Task-Specific Information Support. *Wirtschaftsinformatik*, *2003*(1), 977–996.

Abou El-Ela, A.A., Kinawy, A.M., El-Sehiemy, R.A., & Mouwafi, M.T. (2011). Optimal reactive power dispatch using ant colony optimization algorithm. *Electrical Engineering*, *93* (2), 103-116.

Aboulnaga, A., Salem, K., Soror, A. A., Minhas, U. F., Kokosielis, P., & Kamath, S. (2009). *Deploying Database Appliances in the Cloud. IEEE Data Eng. Bull.*

Abrahamson, E. (2000). Change Without Pain. *Harvard Business Review*, (July-August): 75–79.

Abrikosov, A. A. (1957). On the magnetic properties of superconductors of the second group.[English Translation]. *Soviet Physics, JETP*, *5*, 1174–1182.

Adini, A. R., Redlich, M., & Tenne, R. (2011). Medical applications of inorganic fullerene-like nanoparticles. *Journal of Materials Chemistry*, *21*, 15121–15131. doi:10.1039/c1jm11799h

Adobbati, R., Marshall, A., Scholer, A., Tejada, S., Kaminka, G., Schaffer, S., & Sollitto, C. (2001). Gamebots: A 3D Virtual World Test-Bed For Multi-Agent Research. In *Proc. of 2nd Workshop on Infrastructure for Agents*, (pp. 47-52). Academic Press.

Agbinya, J. I., & Silva, S. D. (2005). Face recognition programming on mobile handsets. In *Proc. 12th Int. Conf. on Telecommunications*. Cape Town, South Africa: Academic Press.

Aggelidis, V. P., & Chatzoglou, P. D. (2012). Hospital information systems: Measuring end user computing satisfaction (EUCS). *Journal of Biomedical Informatics*, *45*, 566–579. doi:10.1016/j.jbi.2012.02.009 PMID:22426283

Agress, C. M., Wegner, S., Bleifer, D. J., Lindsey, A., Van Houten, J., Schroyer, K., & Estrin, H. M. (1964). The common origin of precordial vibrations. *The American Journal of Cardiology, 13*(2), 226–231. doi:10.1016/0002-9149(64)90177-8 PMID:14122011

Aguilera-Sigalat, J., Casas-Solvas, J. M., Morant-Miñana, M. C., Vargas-Berenguel, A., Galian, R. E., & Pérez-Prieto, J. (2012a). Quantum dot/*cyclo*dextrin supramolecular systems based on efficient molecular recognition and their use for sensing. *Chemical Communications, 48*, 2573–2575. doi:10.1039/c1cc15312a PMID:22080219

Aguilera-Sigalat, J., Rocton, S., Galian, R. E., & Pérez-Prieto, J. (2011). Fluorescence enhancement of amine-capped CdSe/ZnS quantum dots by thiol addition. *Canadian Journal of Chemistry, 89*, 359–363. doi:10.1139/V10-160

Aguilera-Sigalat, J., Rocton, S., Sánchez-Royo, J. F., Galian, R. E., & Pérez-Prieto, J. (2012b). Highly fluorescent and photostable organic- and water-soluble CdSe/ZnS core–shell quantum dots capped with thiols. *RSC Advances, 2*, 1632–1638. doi:10.1039/c1ra01005k

Aguilera-Sigalat, J., Sanchez-SanMartín, J., Agudelo-Morales, C. E., Zaballos, E., Galian, R. E., & Pérez-Prieto, J. (2012c). Further insight into the photostability of the pyrene fluorophore in halogenated solvents. *ChemPhysChem, 13*, 835–844. doi:10.1002/cphc.201100843 PMID:22271708

Ahlquist, J., & Novak, J. (2007). *Game Development Essentials: Game Artificial Intelligence*. Delmar Cengage Learning.

AIM@SHAPE. (2008). Retrieved from http://www.aimatshape.net

Akhbardeh, A., Tavakolian, K., Gurev, V., Lee, T., New, W., Kaminska, B., & Trayanova, N. (2009). Comparative analysis of three different modalities for characterization of the seismocardiogram. In *Proceedings of the Annual International Conference of the IEEE Engineering in Medicine and Biology Society*. IEEE.

Aladwani, A. M., & Palvia, P. C. (2002). Developing and validating an instrument for measuring user-perceived web quality. *Information & Management, 39*(6), 467–476. doi:10.1016/S0378-7206(01)00113-6

Albertson, M. O., Grossman, S., & Haas, R. (2000). Partial list colorings. *Discrete Mathematics, 214*(1-3), 235–240. doi:10.1016/S0012-365X(99)00315-5

Álvares, A. J., Ferreira, J. C. E., & Lorenzo, R. M. (2008). An integrated web-based CAD/CAPP/CAM system for the remote design and manufacture of feature-based cylindrical parts. *Journal of Intelligent Manufacturing, 19*(6), 643–659. doi:10.1007/s10845-008-0117-1

Amazon web services. (n.d.). Retrieved from http://aws.amazon.com/

Amit, D. J., Gutfreund, H., & Sompolinsky, H. (1985). Spin-glass models of neural networks. *Physical Review A., 32*(2), 1007–1018. doi:10.1103/PhysRevA.32.1007 PMID:9896156

Angira, R., & Babu, B. V. (2005). Optimization of Non-Linear Chemical Processes Using Modified Differential Evolution (MDE). In *Proceedings of the 2nd Indian International Conference on Artificial Intelligence*. Pune, India: MDE.

Anson, D., Eck, C. L., King, J., Mooney, R., Sansom, C., Wilkerson, B., & Wychulis, D. (2001). *Efficacy of alternate keyboard configurations: Dvorak vs. Reverse-QWERTY*. Retrieved March 27, 2013, from http://atri.misericordia.edu/Papers/Dvorak.php

Aoki, K., Fan, M., & Nishikori, A. (1988). Optimal VAR planning by approximation method for recursive mixed-integer linear programming. *IEEE Transactions on Power Systems, 3*(4), 1741–1747. doi:10.1109/59.192990

Armstrong, A. G., & Hagel, J. (1996). The real value of online communities. *Harvard Business Review, 73*(3), 134–141.

Arrabales, R., & Muñoz, J. (2010). *The Awakening of Conscious Bots: Inside the Mind of the 2K BotPrize 2010 Winner*. Retrieved from http://aigamedev.com/open/articles/conscious-bot/

Arrabales, R., Ledezma, A., & Sanchis, A. (2009). CERA-CRANIUM: A Test Bed for Machine Consciousness Research. In *Proceedings of International Workshop on Machine Consciousness*. Academic Press.

Ashley, S. (1995). Rapid prototyping is coming of age. *Mechanical Engineering (New York, N.Y.)*, 63.

ASHRAE. (2003). Energy efficient design of new building except new low-rise residential buildings (BSRI-ASHRAE proposed standards 90-2P-1993, alternative GA). American Society of Heating, Refrigerating, and Air Conditioning Engineers Inc.

ASHRAE. (2005). *Commercial/Institutional Ground Source Heat Pump Engineering Manual. American Society of heating.* Atlanta, GA, USA: Refrigeration and Air-conditioning Engineers, Inc.

Atanassov, K. (1986). Intuitionistic fuzzy sets. *Fuzzy Sets and Systems, 20,* 87–96. doi:10.1016/S0165-0114(86)80034-3

Atanassov, K. (1989). More on intuitionistic fuzzy sets. *Fuzzy Sets and Systems, 33,* 37–46. doi:10.1016/0165-0114(89)90215-7

Atanassov, K. (1994). Operators over interval-valued intuitionistic fuzzy sets. *Fuzzy Sets and Systems, 64,* 159–174. doi:10.1016/0165-0114(94)90331-X

Atanassov, K., & Gargov, G. (1989). Interval-valued intuitionistic fuzzy sets. *Fuzzy Sets and Systems, 31,* 343–349. doi:10.1016/0165-0114(89)90205-4

Auer, S., & Herre, H. (2007). RapidOWL - An Agile Knowledge Engineering Methodology. In *Perspectives of Systems Informatics* (pp. 424–430). Springer Berlin Heidelberg. doi:10.1007/978-3-540-70881-0_36

Autodesk. (2013a). *CAD software defined.* Retrieved January 10, 2013 from http://usa.autodesk.com/adsk/servlet/item?siteID=123112&id=17690382

Autodesk. (2013b). *Digital prototyping.* Retrieved January 10, 2013 from http://usa.autodesk.com/digital-prototyping/

Babu, B. V., & Munawar, S. A. (2000). Differential Evolution for the Optimal Design of Heat Exchangers. In *Proceedings of All-India seminar on Chemical Engineering Progress on Resource Development: A Vision 2010 and Beyond.* Bhuvaneshwar.

Babu, B. V., & Singh, R. P. (2000). Synthesis & Optimization of Heat Integrated Distillation Systems Using Differential Evolution. In *Proceedings of All- India seminar on Chemical Engineering Progress on Resource Development: A Vision 2010 and Beyond.* Bhuvaneshwar.

Baevsky, R., Bogomolov, V., Funtova, I., Slepchenkova, I., & Chernikova, A. (2011). Prospects of medical monitoring of long-duration space flights by means of non-contact recording of physiological functions during sleep time. *Human Physiology, 37*(7), 816–820. doi:10.1134/S036211971107005X

Baevsky, R., Egorov, A., & Kazarian, L. (1964). Metodika seismokardiografii. *Kardiologiia, 18,* 87–89.

Baker, J., & Kudrolli, A. (2010). Maximum and minimum stable random packings of Platonic solids. *Physical Review E: Statistical, Nonlinear, and Soft Matter Physics, 82,* 061304–1–5. doi:10.1103/PhysRevE.82.061304

Bakkes, S., Spronck, P., & van den Herik, J. (2011). A CBR-Inspired Approach to Rapid and Reliable Adaption of Video Game AI. In *Proc. of the 19th International Conference on Case-Based Reasoning,* (pp. 17-26). Academic Press.

Bakkes, S., Spronck, P., & van den Herik, J. (2009). Rapid and Reliable Adaptation of Video Game AI. *IEEE Transactions on Computational Intelligence and AI in Games, 1*(2), 93–104. doi:10.1109/TCIAIG.2009.2029084

Balaban, A. T., & Klein, D. J. (2009). Claromatic carbon nanostructures. *The Journal of Physical Chemistry C, 113,* 19123–19133. doi:10.1021/jp9082618

Balaban, A. T., Klein, D. J., & Liu, X. (1994). Graphitic cones. *Carbon, 32,* 357–359. doi:10.1016/0008-6223(94)90203-8

Balic, J., Kovacic, M., & Vaupotic, B. (2006). Intelligent Programming of CNC Turning Operations using Genetic Algorithm. *Journal of Intelligent Manufacturing, 17*(3), 331–340. doi:10.1007/s10845-005-0001-1

Balla, R.-K., & Fern, A. (2009). UCT for Tactical Assault Planning in Real-Time Strategy Games. In *Proceedings of 21st International Joint Conference on Artificial Intelligence*, (pp. 40-45). Academic Press.

Bao, Y. L., Yan, Z. C., Wang, H. L., & Chen, L. (2011). Optimization of bioethanol production during simultaneous saccharification and fermentation in very high-gravity cassava mash. *Antonie van Leeuwenhoek*, *99*, 329–339. doi:10.1007/s10482-010-9494-5 PMID:20803106

Barabaro, S., Coppolino, S., Leone, C., & Sinagra, E. (1978). Global solar radiation in Italy. *Solar Energy*, *20*, 431–435. doi:10.1016/0038-092X(78)90163-9

Bardhan, R. (2008). Global Financial Integration and real estate security returns. *Real Estate Economics*, *36*, 285–381. doi:10.1111/j.1540-6229.2008.00214.x

Bar, M. (2004). Visual objects in context. *Nature Reviews. Neuroscience*, *5*, 619–629. doi:10.1038/nrn1476 PMID:15263892

Bar-Nahum, G., Epshtein, V., Ruckenstein, A. E., Rafikov, R., Mustaev, A., & Nudler, E. (2005). A ratchet mechanism of transcription elongation and its control. *Cell*, *120*, 183–193. doi:10.1016/j.cell.2004.11.045 PMID:15680325

Barney, J. B. (1991). Firm resources and sustained competitive advantage. *Journal of Management*, *17*(1), 99–120. doi:10.1177/014920639101700108

Barquin, R. (2010).: Knowledge Management in the Federal Government: A 2010 Update; http://www.b-eye-network.com/view/14527

Barsegyan, A. A., Kupriyanov, M. S., Stepanenko, V. V., & Holod, I. I. (2008). *Technologies for data analysis: data mining, visual mining, text mining, OLAP*. Sankt-Peterburg, Russia: BHV-Peterburg.

Baruah, D. (1995). Utilisation pattern of human and fuel energy in the plantation. *Journal of Agriculture and Soil Science*, *8*(2), 189–192.

Bates, J. (1994). The Role of Emotion in Believable Characters. *Communications of the ACM*, *37*, 122–125. doi:10.1145/176789.176803

Bell, M. (2008). Toward a Definition of "Virtual Worlds". *Journal of Virtual Worlds Research*, *1*(1).

Bendewald, M., & Zhai, Z. J. (2013). Using carrying capacity as a base line for building sustainability assessment. *Habitat International*, *37*, 22–32. doi:10.1016/j.habitatint.2011.12.021

Bérard, B., Bidoit, M., Finkel, A., Laroussinie, F., Petit, A., Petrucci, L., & Schnoebelen, Ph. (2001). *Systems and Software Verification: Model-Checking Techniques and Tools*. Springer. doi:10.1007/978-3-662-04558-9

Berne, R. M., & Levy, M. N. (1977). Cardiovascular physiology (3rd ed.). Saint Louis: Mosby.

Bernstein, P. A., & Melnik, S. (2007). Model management 2.0: manipulating richer mappings. In *Proceedings of the 2007 ACM SIGMOD international conference on Management of data*, (pp. 1-12). ACM.

Berretti, S., Del Bimbo, A., & Pala, P. (2010). 3D face recognition using iso-geodesic stripes. *IEEE Trans. PAMI*, *32*(12), 2162–2177. doi:10.1109/TPAMI.2010.43

Berry, L. L., & Parasuraman, A. (1991). *Marketing services: Competing through quality*. New York, NY: The Free Press.

Berry, M. W. (2003). *Survey of text mining: clustering, classification, and retrieval*. Springer.

Bertolazzi, S., Brivio, J., Radenovic, A., Kis, A., Wilson, H., Prisbrey, L., … Proksch, R. (2013). Exploring flatland: AFM of mechanical and electrical properties of graphene, MoS_2 and other low-dimensional materials. *Microscopy and Analysis*, (5), 21-24.

Bertolazzi, S., Brivio, J., & Kis, A. (2011). Stretching and breaking of ultrathin MoS_2. *ACS Nano*, *5*, 9703–9709. doi:10.1021/nn203879f PMID:22087740

Betke, U., & Henk, M. (2000). Densest lattice packings of 3-polytopes. *Computational Geometry*, *16*, 157–186. doi:10.1016/S0925-7721(00)00007-9

Bezmel'nitsyn, V. N., Eletskii, A. V., & Okun', M. V. (1998). Fullerenes in solutions. *Physics–Uspekhi*, *41*, 1091–1114.

Bhattacharya, A., & Chattopadhyay, P. K. (2010). Solution of optimal reactive power flow using biogeography-based optimization. *International Journal of Electrical and Electronics Engineering*, *4*(8), 580–588.

Bhowmik, M., & Pal, M. (2009). Partition of generalized interval-valued intuitionistic fuzzy sets and some properties. *International Journal of Applied Mathematical Analysis and Applications*, *4*(1), 1–10.

Bhowmik, M., & Pal, M. (2010). Generalized interval-valued intuitionistic fuzzy sets. *The Journal of Fuzzy Mathematics*, *18*(2), 357–371.

Bi, H. X., Li, S. J. & Zhang, Y. R. (2011). The geometric modeling of pieces in virtual milling simulation. *Advanced Materials Research*, *291*, 2262-2265.

Biederman, I., & Kalocsai, P. (1997). Neurocomputational bases of object and face recognition. *Philosoph. Trans. R. Soc.: Biol. Sci.*, *352*, 1203–1219. doi:10.1098/rstb.1997.0103 PMID:9304687

Bieniek, D., Dyess, R., Hotek, M., Loria, J., Machanic, A., Soto, A., & Wiernik, A. (2006). *Microsoft SQL Server 2005 implementation and maintenance – training kit.* Microsoft Press.

Biever, C. (2012, September). *Mimicry Beats Consciousness in Gaming's Turing Test.* Retrieved from http://www.newscientist.com/article/dn22305-mimicry-beats-consciousness-in-gamings-turing-test.html

Binning, G., Quate, C. F., & Gerber, C. (1986). Atomic force microscope. *Physical Review Letters*, *56*, 930–933. doi:10.1103/PhysRevLett.56.930 PMID:10033323

Bixby, R., & Kennedy, K. & Kremer, U. (1993). *Automatic data layout using 0-1 integer programming* (Tech. Rep. CRPC-TR93349-S). Houston, TX: Rice University, Center for Research on Parallel Computation.

Blank, I., & Yove, G. (2011). The structure of face–space is tolerant to lighting and viewpoint transformations. *Journal of Vision (Charlottesville, Va.)*, *11*(8), 1–13. doi:10.1167/11.8.15 PMID:21795412

Blizzard. (2010). *World of Warcraft Terms of Use.* Retrieved from http://us.blizzard.com/en-us/company/legal/wow_tou.html

Bloodgood, J. M., & Salisbury, W. D. (2001). Understanding the influence of organizational change strategies on information technology and knowledge management strategies. *Decision Support System Journal*, *31*, 55–69. doi:10.1016/S0167-9236(00)00119-6

Boatwright, P., & Cagan, J. (2010). *Product emotion: The way to captive customers.* Academic Press.

Bonacina, S., Lanzi, P., & Loiacono, D. (2008). Evolving Dodging Behavior for OpenArena using Neuroevolution of Augmenting Topologies. In *Proceedings of PPSN'08 Workshop (Computational Intelligence and Games).* PPSN.

Bonse, R., Kockelkorn, W., Smelik, R., Veelders, P., & Moerman, W. (2004). *Learning Agents in Quake III (Technical Report).* University of Utrecht, Department of Computer Science.

Booth, M. (2004). The Official Counter-Strike Bot. In *Proceedings of Game Developers Conference'04.* Academic Press.

Borodin, O. V., Kostochka, A. V., & Woodall, D. R. (1998). Total colourings of planar graphs with large girth. *European Journal of Combinatorics*, *19*(1), 19–24. doi:10.1006/eujc.1997.0152

Bos, E., My, T., Vu, E., & Bulatao, R. (1994). *World population projection: 1994-95.* Baltimore, London: World Bank by the John Hopkins University Press.

Bouneb, Z., & Saïdouni, D. (2009). Parallel state space construction for a model checking based on maximality semantics. In *Proceedings of the 2nd Mediterranean Conference on Intelligent Systems and Automation* (Vol. 1107, pp. 7-12). Zarzis, Tunisia: Academic Press. doi:10.1063/1.3106517.

Bourgeois, L., Bando, Y., Han, W. Q., & Sato, T. (2000). Structure of boron nitride nanoscale cones: Ordered stacking of 240° and 300° disclinations. *Physical Review B: Condensed Matter and Materials Physics*, *61*, 7686–7691. doi:10.1103/PhysRevB.61.7686

Bourgeois, L., Bando, Y., Shinozaki, S., Kurashima, K., & Sato, T. (1999). Boron nitride cones: Structure determination by transmission electron microscopy. *Acta Crystallographica. Section A, Foundations of Crystallography*, *55*, 168–177. doi:10.1107/S0108767398008642 PMID:10927246

Bouzenada, M., Bensouyad, M., Guidoum, N., Reghioua, A., & Saïdouni, D. (2012). A Generalized Graph Strict Strong Coloring Algorithm. *International Journal of Applied Metaheuristic Computing, 3*(1), 24–33. doi:10.4018/jamc.2012010103

Bowyer, K., Chang, K., & Flynn, P. (2006). A survey of approaches and challenges in 3D and multi-modal 3D + 2D face recognition. *Computer Vision and Image Understanding, 101*(1), 1–15. doi:10.1016/j.cviu.2005.05.005

Boyd, D. M., & Ellison, N. B. (2008). Social network sites: Definition, history and scholarship. *Journal of Computer-Mediated Communication, 13*(1), 210–230. doi:10.1111/j.1083-6101.2007.00393.x

Bozhenko, B. S. (1961). Seismocardiography--a new method in the study of functional conditions of the heart. *Terapevticheskii Arkhiv, 33*, 55–64. PMID:13872234

Brain, Z., & Addicoat, M. (2010). Using meta-genetic algorithms to tune parameters of genetic algorithms to find lowest energy molecular conformers. In *Proceedings of the Alife XII Conference* (pp. 378-385). Odense, Denmark: The MIT Press.

Brantner, M., Florescu, D., Graf, D., Kossmann, D., & Kraska, T. (2008). Building a Database on S3. In Proceedings of ACM SIGMOD 2008. ACM.

Bray, D. A. (2008). *Information pollution, knowledge overload, limited attention spans, and our responsibilities as IS professionals.* Paper presented in Global Information Technology Management Association (GITMA) World Conference. Atlanta, GA.

Bruker. (2013). Atomic force microscopy reveals DNA double helix. *Microscopy and Analysis, (3).*

Buckley, J. J., & Jovers, L. J. (2006). *Simulating Continuous Fuzzy Systems, Studies in Fuzziness and Soft Computing* (Vol. 188). Springer-Verlag Berlin Heidelberg.

Buckley, J. J., Reilly, K., & Zhang, X. (2004). Fuzzy probabilities for web planning. *Soft Computing, 8*, 464–476. doi:10.1007/s00500-003-0305-z

Bueno Alejo, C. J., Fasciani, C., Grenier, M., Netto-Ferreira, J. C., & Scaiano, J. C. (2011). Reduction of resazurin to resorufin catalyzed by gold nanoparticles: Dramatic reaction acceleration by laser or LED plasmon excitation. *Catalysis Science & Technology, 1*, 1506–1511. doi:10.1039/c1cy00236h

Bueno-Alejo, C. J., D'Alfonso, C., Pacioni, N. L., González-Béjar, M., Grenier, M., & Lanzalunga, O. et al. (2012). Ultraclean derivatized monodisperse gold nanoparticles through laser drop ablation customization of polymorph gold nanostructures. *Langmuir, 28*, 8183–8189. doi:10.1021/la3010689 PMID:22591001

BulTreeBank Group. (2010). *Available linguistic resources for Bulgarian.* Retrieved March 27, 2013, from http://www.bultreebank.org/Resources.html

Burrell, M. (2009). *Serbian Dvorak.* Retrieved March 27, 2013, from http://www.csd.uwo.ca/~mburrel/software/serbian-dvorak

Bustince, H., & Burillo, P. (1995). Correlation of interval-valued intuitionistic fuzzy sets. *Fuzzy Sets and Systems, 74*, 237–244. doi:10.1016/0165-0114(94)00343-6

Bustince, H., & Burillo, P. (1996). Vague sets are intuitionistic fuzzy sets. *Fuzzy Sets and Systems, 79*, 403–405. doi:10.1016/0165-0114(95)00154-9

Buyya1, R., & Murshed, M. (2002) GridSim: A toolkit for the modeling and simulation of distributed resource management and scheduling for Grid computing. *Concurrency and Computation: Practice and Experience, 14*(13-15), 1175–1220.

Buyya1, R., Branson, K., Giddy, J., & Abramson, D. (2003). The virtual laboratory: A toolset to enable distributed molecular modelling for drug design on the World-Wide Grid. *Concurrency and Computation: Practice and Experience, 15*(1)1–25.

Buyya, R., Yeo, C. S., Venugopal, S., Broberg, J., & Brandic, I. (2009). Cloud computing and emerging IT platforms: Vision, hype, and reality for delivering computing as the 5th utility. *Future Generation Computer Systems, 25*(6). doi:10.1016/j.future.2008.12.001 PMID:21308003

Buzdin, A. I. (1993). Multiple-quanta vortices at columnar defects. *Physical Review B: Condensed Matter and Materials Physics*, *47*, 11416–11419. doi:10.1103/PhysRevB.47.11416 PMID:10005280

CAEEDAC. (2000). *A descriptive analysis of energy consumption in agriculture and food sector in Canada* (Final Report, February 2000). Author.

Camarinha-Matos, L. M., & Afsarmanesh, H. (1999). The virtual enterprise concept. In *Proceedings of the IFIP TC5WG5.3/PRODNET Working Conference on Infrastructures for Virtual Enterprises: Networking Industrial Enterprises* (Vol. 153, pp. 3-4). Academic Press.

Cantrell, J., & Wepfer, W. (1984). Shallow Ponds for Dissipation of Building Heat: A case Study. *ASHRAE Transactions*, *90*(1), 239–246.

Caragiannisa, I., Kaklamanisa, C., & Persianob, P. (2002). Edge coloring of bipartite graphs with constraints. *Theoretical Computer Science*, *270*(1-2), 361–399. doi:10.1016/S0304-3975(00)00400-X

Cardona, C. A., & Sánchezo, J. (2007). Fuel ethanol production: process design trends and integration opportunities. *Bioresource Technology*, *98*(12), 2415–2457. doi:10.1016/j.biortech.2007.01.002 PMID:17336061

Carl Zeiss Microscopy. (2013). *Cover story. Microscopy and Analysis Directory.*

Carlson, R. (1997). *Experienced cognition.* Mahwah, NJ: Lawrence Erlbaum.

Carroll, D. L., Redlich, P., Ajayan, P. M., Charlier, J.-C., Blase, X., de Vita, A., & Car, R. (1997). Electronic structure and localized states at carbon nanotube tips. *Physical Review Letters*, *78*, 2811–2814. doi:10.1103/PhysRevLett.78.2811

Castiglioni, P., Faini, A., Parati, G., & Di Rienzo, M. (2007). Wearable seismocardiography. In *Proceedings of Engineering in Medicine and Biology Society, 2007.* IEEE.

Castiglioni, P., Meriggi, P., Rizzo, F., Vaini, E., Faini, A., Parati, G., & Di Rienzo, M. (2012). Seismocardiography while sleeping at high altitude. In *Proceedings of Engineering in Medicine and Biology Society* (EMBC). IEEE.

Castiglioni, P., Meriggi, P., Rizzo, F., Vaini, E., Faini, A., Parati, G., et al. (2011). Cardiac sounds from a wearable device for sternal seismocardiography. In *Proceedings of Engineering in Medicine and Biology Society.* IEEE.

Celenk, M., & Aljarrah, I. (2006). Internal shape-deformation invariant 3D surface matching using 2D principal component analysis. In *Proc. of SPIE-IS&T Electronic Imaging*, (vol. 6056, pp. 118-129). SPIE.

Champandard, A. (2011). *This Year in Game AI: Analysis, Trends from 2010 and Predictions for 2011.* Retrieved 02.10.2011, from http://aigamedev.com/open/editorial/2010-retrospective/

Champandard, A. (2007). Most Influental AI Games. *AIGameDev.com.* Retrieved from http://aigamedev.com/open/highlights/top-ai-games/

Chang, I. C., Li, Y. C., Wu, T. Y., & Yen, D. C. (2012). Electronic medical record quality and its impact on user satisfaction - Healthcare providers' point of view. *Government Information Quarterly*, *29*, 235–242. doi:10.1016/j.giq.2011.07.006

Chapman, J. (2009). Design for emotionally durability. *Design Issues*, *25*(4), 29–35. doi:10.1162/desi.2009.25.4.29

Chatterjee, A., & Mahanti, G. K. (2010). Comparative Performance Of Gravitational Search Algorithm And Modified Particle Swarm Optimization Algorithm For Synthesis Of Thinned Scanned Concentric Ring Array Antenna. *Progress In Electromagnetics Research B*, *25*, 331–348. doi:10.2528/PIERB10080405

Chaudhuri, S., & Dayal, U. (1997). An overview of data warehousing and OLAP technology. *SIGMOD Record*, *26*(1), 65–74. doi:10.1145/248603.248616

Chau, P. K., Au, G., & Tam, K. Y. (2000). Impact of information presentation modes on online shopping: An empirical evaluation of a broadband interactive shopping service. *Journal of Organizational Computing and Electronic Commerce*, *10*(1), 1–22.

Chellali, M., & Volkmann, L. (2004). Relations between the lower domination parameters and the chromatic number of a graph. *Discrete Mathematics*, *274*(1-3), 1–8. doi:10.1016/S0012-365X(03)00093-1

Chen, G., Gyarfas, A., & Schelp, R. (1998). Vertex colorings with a distance restriction. *Discrete Mathematics*, *191*(1-3), 65–82. doi:10.1016/S0012-365X(98)00094-6

Chen, J. H., Yeh, S. S., & Sun, J. T. (2011). An S-curve acceleration/deceleration design for CNC machine tools using quintic feedrate function. *Computer-Aided Design and Applications*, *8*(4), 583-592.

Chen, J., & Lee, B. (2011). Parameter optimization of a five-axis tool grinder using Grey Relational analysis. Key Engineering Materials, 458, 246-251.

Chen, Y., Lochegnies, D., Defontaine, R., Anton, J., Aben, H. & Langlais, R. (2013). Measuring the 2D residual surface stress mapping in tempered glass under the cooling jets: The influence of process parameters on the stress homogeneity and isotropy. *Strain*, *49*(1), 60-67.

Chen, E. R., Engel, M., & Glotzer, S. C. (2010). Dense crystalline dimer packings of regular tetrahedra. *Discrete & Computational Geometry*, *44*, 253–280. doi:10.1007/s00454-010-9273-0

Chen, R. F., & Hsiao, J. L. (2012). An investigation on physicians' acceptance of hospital information systems: A case study. *International Journal of Medical Informatics*, *81*, 810–820. doi:10.1016/j.ijmedinf.2012.05.003 PMID:22652011

Chen, S. M., & Tan, J. M. (1994). Handling multi-criteria fuzzy decision making problems based on vague sets. *Fuzzy Sets and Systems*, *67*, 163–172. doi:10.1016/0165-0114(94)90084-1

Chernova, S., & Veloso, M. (2007). Multiagent Collaborative Task Learning through Imitation. In *Proc. of the 4th International Symposium on Imitation in Animals and Artifacts*, (pp. 74-79). Academic Press.

Chiang, D. A., & Lin, N. P. (1999). Correlation of fuzzy sets. *Fuzzy Sets and Systems*, *102*, 221–226. doi:10.1016/S0165-0114(97)00127-9

Chiou, J. S. (2005). The antecedents of consumers' loyalty toward Internet service providers. *Information & Management*, *41*(6), 685–695. doi:10.1016/j.im.2003.08.006

Choi, D., Konik, T., Nejati, N., Park, C., & Langley, P. (2007). A Believable Agent for First-Person Perspective Games. In *Proc. of the 3rd Artificial Intelligence and Interactive Digital Entertainment International Conference*. Academic Press.

Choi, D., Kim, H., & Kim, J. (1999). Toward the Construction of Fun Computer Games: Differences in the Views of Developers and Players. *Personal and Ubiquitous Computing*, *3*(3), 92–104.

Chopra, N. G., Luyken, R. J., Cherrey, K., Crespi, V. H., Cohen, M. L., Louie, S. G., & Zettl, A. (1995). Boron nitride nanotubes. *Science*, *269*, 966–967. doi:10.1126/science.269.5226.966 PMID:17807732

Choy, H. S., & Chan, K. W. (2003). A corner-looping based tool path for pocket milling. *Computer Aided Design*, *35*(2), 155–166. doi:10.1016/S0010-4485(02)00049-0

Cioffi, C., Campidelli, S., Brunetti, F. G., Meneghetti, M., & Prato, M. (2006). Functionalisation of carbon nanohorns. *Chemical Communications*, *2006*, 2129–2131. doi:10.1039/b601176d PMID:16703130

Cioffi, C., Campidelli, S., Sooambar, C., Marcaccio, M., Marcolongo, G., & Meneghetti, M. et al. (2007). Synthesis, characterization, and photoinduced electron transfer in functionalized single wall carbon nanohorns. *Journal of the American Chemical Society*, *129*, 3938–3945. doi:10.1021/ja068007p PMID:17343379

Clarke, E., Grumberg, O., & Peled, D. (1999). *Model Checking*. Cambridge, MA: The MIT Press.

Cohen, W. W., Kumar, P. R., & Fienberg, S. E. (2003). A comparison of string distance metrics for name matching tasks. In *Proceedings of IJCAI Workshop on Information Integration on the Web*, (pp. 73-78).

Cole, N., Louis, S., & Miles, C. (2004). Using a Genetic Algorithm to Tune First-Person Shooter Bots. In *Proc. of the International Congress on Evolutionary Computation*, (pp. 139-145). Academic Press.

Computer news. (1999). *Computer linguistics*. Retrieved March 27, 2013, from http://kv.minsk.by/index1999262201.htm

Conway, J. H., & Torquato, S. (2006). Packing, tiling, and covering with tetrahedra. *Proceedings of the National Academy of Sciences of the United States of America*, *103*, 10612–10617. doi:10.1073/pnas.0601389103 PMID:16818891

Coronado, E., Galán-Mascarós, J. R., Monrabal-Capilla, M., García-Martínez, J., & Pardo-Ibáñez, P. (2007). Bistable spin-crossover nanoparticles showing magnetic thermal hysteresis near room temperature. *Advanced Materials*, *19*, 1359–1361. doi:10.1002/adma.200700559

Counts, S., & Fisher, K. E. (2010). Mobile social networking as information ground: A case study. *Library & Information Science Research*, *32*(2), 98–115. doi:10.1016/j.lisr.2009.10.003

Crossly, L. (2003). Building emotions in design, PDD group. *The Design Journal*, *6*(3), 35–45. doi:10.2752/146069203789355264

Crow, R. S., Hannan, P., Jacobs, D., Hedquist, L., & Salerno, D. M. (1994). Relationship between seismocardiogram and echocardiogram for events in the cardiac cycle. *American Journal of Noninvasive Cardiology*, *8*(1), 39–46.

Csikszentmihalyi, M. (1991). *Flow: The Psychology of Optimal Experience*. New York: Harper Perennial.

CTIOA. (2011). *Ceramic tile and stone standards*. Retrieved November 28, 2011, from http://www.ctioa.org

Cui, G., Lu, Y., Li, J., Gao, D. & Yao, Y. (2012). Geometric error compensation software system for CNC machine tools based on NC program reconstructing. *International Journal of Advanced Manufacturing Technology*, *63*(1-4), 169-180.

Curta, F. (2006). Southeastern Europe in the Middle Ages, 500-1250. Cambridge University Press.

Cyr, D., Head, M., & Ivanoc, A. (2006). Design aesthetics leading to m-loyalty in mobile commerce. *Information & Management*, *43*(8), 950–963. doi:10.1016/j.im.2006.08.009

D'Apote, S. L. (1998). IEA biomass energy analysis and projections. In *Proceedings of Biomass Energy Conference: Data, analysis and Trends*. Paris: OECD.

Dai, C., Chen, W., Zhu, Y., & Zhang, X. (2009). Reactive power dispatch considering voltage stability with seeker optimization algorithm. *Electric Power Systems Research*, *79*, 1462–1471. doi:10.1016/j.epsr.2009.04.020

Dai, C., Chen, W., Zhu, Y., & Zhang, X. (2009). Seeker optimization algorithm for optimal reactive power dispatch. *IEEE Transactions on Power Systems*, *24*(3), 1218–1231. doi:10.1109/TPWRS.2009.2021226

Dalkir, K. (2013). *Knowledge management in theory and practice*. Routledge.

Das Sarma, A., Dong, X., & Halevy, A. Y. (2008). Bootstrapping pay-as-you-go data integration systems. In Proceedings of SIGMOD 2008. ACM.

Das, I., & Dennis, J. E. (1998). Normal-boundary intersection: A new method for generating the Pareto surface in nonlinear multicriteria optimization problems. *SIAM Journal on Optimization*, *8*(3), 631–657. doi:10.1137/S1052623496307510

Davenport, T. H., Long, D. W., & Beers, M. C. (1998). Successful Knowledge Management Projects. *Sloan Management Review*, *39*, 43–57.

David, J. M. (2000). Developing hydrogen and fuel cell products. *Energy World*, (303), 16–17.

Davis, F. D. (1989). Perceived usefulness, perceived ease of use, and user acceptance of information technology. *Management Information Systems Quarterly*, *13*(3), 319–340. doi:10.2307/249008

Davis, F. D., Bagozzi, R. P., & Warshaw, P. R. (1992). Extrinsic and intrinsic motivation to use computers in the workplace. *Journal of Applied Social Psychology*, *22*(14), 1111–1132. doi:10.1111/j.1559-1816.1992.tb00945.x

Day, J. D., & Wendler, J. C. (1998). Best Practice and Beyond: Knowledge Strategies. *The McKinsey Quarterly*, *1*, 19–25.

De Ridder, S., Migeotte, P. F., Neyt, X., Pattyn, N., & Prisk, G. (2011). Three-dimensional ballistocardiography in microgravity: A review of past research. In *Proceedings of Engineering in Medicine and Biology Society*. IEEE.

Deb, K., & Jain, S. (2002). *Running performance metrics for Evolutionary Multiobjective Optimization* (KanGAL Report No. 2002004). Kanpur, India: Kanpur Genetic Algorithms Laboratory, Indian Institute of Technology.

Deb, K., Pratap, A., Agarwal, S., & Meyarivan, T. (2002). A Fast and Elitist Multi-Objective Genetic Algorithm: NSGA-II. *IEEE Transactions on Evolutionary Computation, 6*(2), 182–197. doi:10.1109/4235.996017

Deco, G., & Rolls, E. T. (2004). A neurodynamical cortical model of visual attention and invariant object recognition. *Vision Research, 44*(6), 621–642. doi:10.1016/j.visres.2003.09.037 PMID:14693189

Dehkordi, P. K., Marzencki, M., Tavakolian, K., Kaminska, M., & Kaminska, B. (2011). Validation of respiratory signal derived from suprasternal notch acceleration for sleep apnea detection. In *Proceedings of Engineering in Medicine and Biology Society*. IEEE.

Dehkordi, P., Marzencki, M., Tavakolian, K., Kaminska, M., & Kaminska, B. (2012). Monitoring torso acceleration for estimating the respiratory flow and efforts for sleep apnea detection. In *Proceedings of Engineering in Medicine and Biology Society* (EMBC). IEEE.

Deighton, J., & Grayson, K. (1995). Marketing and seduction: Building exchange relationships by managing social consensus. *The Journal of Consumer Research, 21*(4), 660–676. doi:10.1086/209426

DeLone, W. H., & McLean, E. R. (1992). Information systems success: The quest for the dependent variable. *Information Systems Research, 3*(1), 154–171. doi:10.1287/isre.3.1.60

Densham, P. J., & Armstrong, M. P. (1987). *A spatial Decision Support System for locational planning: Design implementation and operation.* Paper presented at the Eighth International Symposium on Computer-Assisted Cartography. Baltimore, MD.

Design, C.-A. (2008) In *The Columbia Encyclopedia* (6th ed.). Retrieved February 26, 2009, from http://www.encyclopedia.com/1E1-ComputerAD.html

Desmet, P. (2002). *Designing emotions.* Delft, The Netherlands: Delft University Press.

Desmet, P. M. A. (2003a). A multilayered model of product emotions. *The Design Journal, 6*(2), 4–13. doi:10.2752/146069203789355480

Desmet, P. M. A. (2003b). Measuring emotion: development and application of an instrument to measure emotional responses to products. In M. Blythe, K. Overbeeke, A. F. Monk, & P. Wright (Eds.), *Funology: From Usability to Enjoyment* (pp. 111–123). Dordrecht: Kluwer Academic Publishers.

Dharwadker, A. (2006). The independent set algorithm. Retrieved from http://www.dharwadker.org/independent_set.

Di Rienzo, M., Meriggi, P., Rizzo, F., Vaini, E., Faini, A., Merati, G., et al. (2011). A wearable system for the seismocardiogram assessment in daily life conditions. In *Proceedings of Engineering in Medicine and Biology Society*. IEEE.

Di Rienzo, M., Meriggi, P., Vaini, E., Castiglioni, P., & Rizzo, F. (2012). 24h seismocardiogram monitoring in ambulant subjects. In *Proceedings of Engineering in Medicine and Biology Society (EMBC), 2012 Annual International Conference of the IEEE*. San Diego, CA: IEEE.

Dijkstra, E. W. (1965). Solution of a problem in concurrent programming control. *CACM, 8*(9), 569. doi:10.1145/365559.365617

Dimond, E. G. (1964). Precordial vibrations clinical clues from palpation. *Circulation, 30*(2), 284–300. doi:10.1161/01.CIR.30.2.284 PMID:14205557

Dinh, A. (2011). Design of a seismocardiography using tri-axial accelerometer embedded with electrocardiogram. In *Proceedings of the World Congress on Engineering and Computer Science 2011*. Academic Press.

Dinh, A., Choi, Y., & Ko, S. B. (2011). A heart rate sensor based on seismocardiography for vital sign monitoring systems. In *Proceedings of Electrical and Computer Engineering* (CCECE). IEEE.

Dittrich, J. P., & Salles, M. A. V. (2006). iDM: A unified and versatile data model for personal dataspace management. In Proceedings of VLDB 2006, (pp. 367–378). VLDB.

Doan, A. H., Domingos, P., & Halevy, A. Y. (2001). Reconciling schemas of disparate data sources: A machine learning approach. *SIGMOD Record*, *30*, 509–520. doi:10.1145/376284.375731

Doan, A., & Halevy, A. Y. (2005). Semantic integration research in the database community. *AI Magazine*, *26*, 83–94.

Doney, P. M., & Cannon, J. P. (1997). An examination of the nature of trust in buyer-seller relationships. *Journal of Marketing*, *61*(2), 35–51. doi:10.2307/1251829

Dong, X., & Halevy, A. Y. (2007). Indexing dataspaces. In *Proceedings of SIGMOD Conference*, (pp. 43–54). ACM.

du Buf, J. M. H., Terzic, K., & Rodrigues, J. M. H. (2013). Phase-differencing in stereo vision: solving the localisation problem. In *Proc. 6th Int. Conf. on Bio-inspired Systems and Signal Processing*, (pp. 254-263). Academic Press.

Du, J. & Yan, X. (2012). Multi-agent system for process planning in STEP-NC based manufacturing. *Research Journal of Applied Sciences, Engineering and Technology*, *4*(20), 3865-3871.

Duchin, F. (1995). *Global scenarios about lifestyle and technology, the sustainable future of the global system*. Tokyo: United Nations University.

Duffie, J. A., & Beckman, W. A. (1980). *Solar Engineering of Thermal Processes*. New York: J. Wiley and Sons.

Duman, S., Sonmez, Y., Guvenç, U., & Yorukeren, N. (2012). Optimal reactive power dispatch using a gravitational search algorithm. *IET Generation, Transmission and Distribution*, *6*(6), 563-576.

Dutt, B. (1982). Comparative efficiency of energy use in rice production. *Energy*, *6*, 25.

Dyson, F. J. (1969). Existence of a phase-transition in a one-dimensional Ising ferromagnet. *Communications in Mathematical Physics*, *12*, 91–107. doi:10.1007/BF01645907

Eco_Friendly Super Computing, Dell Case Study. (n.d.). Retrieved April, 4, 2014 from http://www.cit.sunderland.ac.uk/downloads/files/Sunderland_University.pdf

EIS. (2010). *Expressive Intelligence Studio: 2010 StarCraft AI Competition Results*. Retrieved 30.09.2011, from http://eis.ucsc.edu/StarCraftAICompetition#Results

El Ouafi, A., Guillot, M., & Bedrouni, A. (2000). Accuracy enhancement of multi-axis CNC machines through on-line neurocompensation. *Journal of Intelligent Manufacturing*, *11*(6), 535-545.

El Rhalibi, A., & Merabti, M. (2008). A Hybrid Fuzzy ANN System for Agent Adaptation in a First Person Shooter. *International Journal of Computer Games Technology*, 1–18. doi:10.1155/2008/432365

Elamvazuthi, I., Ganesan, T., & Vasant, P. (2011). A comparative study of HNN and Hybrid HNN-PSO techniques in the optimization of distributed generation (DG) power systems. In *Proceedings of International Conference on Advanced Computer Science & Information System (ICACSIS)*, (pp 195 – 200). ICACSIS.

Elliott, R. (1998). A model of emotion-driven choice. *Journal of Marketing Management*, *14*, 95-108.

Elliott, R. V., Packard, R. G., & Kyrazis, D. T. (1954). Acceleration ballistocardiography: Design, construction, and application of a new instrument. *Circulation*, *9*(2), 281–291. doi:10.1161/01.CIR.9.2.281 PMID:13127190

Emmerich, M., Beume, N., & Naujoks, B. (2005). An EMO Algorithm Using the Hypervolume Measure as Selection Criterion. In *Proceedings of Conference on Evolutionary Multi-Criterion Optimization* (EMO 2005). Springer.

Encyclopædia Britannica. (2012). *Traditional ceramics*. Retrieved May 1, 2012, from http://www.britannica.com/EBchecked/topic/601792/traditional -ceramics

Encyclopedia Britannica. (2009). *Cyrillic alphabet. Encyclopedia Britannica 2009 Student and Home Edition*. Chicago: Encyclopedia Britannica.

Eschenauer, H., Koski, J., & Osyczka, A. (1990). *Multicriteria Design Optimization*. Berlin: Springer-Verlag. doi:10.1007/978-3-642-48697-5

EWEA. (2003). Wind force 12. Brussels: Author.

Eyewitness: Complete AI Interviews. (2002, September 18). *PC Gamer*. Retrieved 30.09.2011 from http://tinyurl.com/eyewitness-2002-09-18

Fadaifard, H., Wolberg, G., & Haralick, R. (2013). Multiscale 3D feature extraction and matching with an application to 3D face recognition. *Graphical Models*, *75*(4), 157–176. doi:10.1016/j.gmod.2013.01.002

Faraday, M. (1857). The Bakerian Lecture: Experimental relations of gold (and other metals) to light. *Philosophical Transactions of the Royal Society of London*, *147*, 145–181. doi:10.1098/rstl.1857.0011

Farivar, R. (2009). Dorsal-ventral integration in object recognition. *Brain Research. Brain Research Reviews*, *61*(2), 144–153. doi:10.1016/j.brainresrev.2009.05.006 PMID:19481571

Farrajota, M., Rodrigues, J. M. F., & du Buf, J. M. H. (2011). Optical flow by multi-scale annotated keypoints: A biological approach. In *Proc. Int. Conf. on Bio-inspired Systems and Signal Processing*, (pp. 307-315). Academic Press.

Farrajota, M., Saleiro, S., Terzic, K., & Rodrigues, J. M. H & du Buf, J.M.H (2012). Multi-scale cortical keypoints for realtime hand tracking and gesture recognition. In *Proc 1st Int. Workshop on Cognitive Assistive Systems: Closing the Action-Perception Loop, in conjunction with IEEE/RSJ Int. Conf. on Intelligent Robots and Systems*, (pp. 9-15). Academic Press.

Fasciani, C., Bueno Alejo, C. J., Grenier, M., Netto-Ferreira, J. C., & Scaiano, J. C. (2011). High-temperature organic reactions at room temperature using plasmon excitation: Decomposition of dicumyl peroxide. *Organic Letters*, *13*, 204–207. doi:10.1021/ol1026427 PMID:21142017

Fenzi, M., Dragon, R., Leal-Taixé, L., Rosenhahn, B., & Ostermann, J. (2012). 3D Object recognition and pose estimation for multiple objects using multi-prioritized RANSAC and model updating. *Pattern Recognition*, *LNCS, 7476*, 123–133. doi:10.1007/978-3-642-32717-9_13

Fishburn, P.C. (1967). *Additive Utilities with Incomplete Product Set: Applications to Priorities and Assignments*. Baltimore, MD: Operations Research Society of America (ORSA).

Fleischer, M. (2003). The measure of Pareto optima: Applications to multi-objective metaheuristics. In *Proceedings of Conference on Evolutionary Multi-Criterion Optimization* (EMO 2003), (pp 519–533). EMO.

Forte, C., & De Rossi, B. (1974). *Principi di economia ed estimo*. Milano: Etas libri.

Franklin, M. J., Halevy, A. Y., & Maier, D. (2005). From databases to dataspaces: a new abstraction for information management. *SIGMOD Record*, *34*(4), 27–33. doi:10.1145/1107499.1107502

Friedman, D., Steed, A., & Slater, M. (2007). Spatial Social Behavior in Second Life. *Lecture Notes in Computer Science*, *4722*, 252–263. doi:10.1007/978-3-540-74997-4_23

Frijda, N. H. (1994). Varieties of affect: emotions and episodes, moods, and sentiments. In P. Ekman & R.J. Davidson (Eds.), The nature of emotion, fundamental questions (pp. 59-67). Oxford, UK: Oxford University Press.

Fujishima, A., Rao, T. N., & Tryk, D. A. (2000). Titanium dioxide photocatalysis. *Journal of Photochemistry and Photobiology A Chemistry*, *1*, 1–21. doi:10.1016/S1389-5567(00)00002-2

Functional Multilingual Extensions to European Keyboard Layouts. (2008). *The Bulgarian alphabet and keyboard in the context of EU communications*. Retrieved March 27, 2013, from http://www.csc.fi/english/pages/meek/The-Bulgarian-Alphabet-and-Keyboard

Fung, R. K. K., & Lee, M. K. O. (1999). EC-Trust (trust in electronic commerce): Exploring the antecedent factors. In *Proceedings of the 5th American Conference on Information Systems*, (pp. 517-519). Academic Press.

Galleguillos, C., & Belongie, S. (2010). Context based object categorization: A critical survey. *Computer Vision and Image Understanding*, *114*(6), 712–722. doi:10.1016/j.cviu.2010.02.004

Ganapathi, A., Kuno, H., Dayal, U., Wiener, J. L., Fox, A., Jordan, M., & Patterson, D. (2009). Predicting Multiple Metrics for Queries: Better Decisions Enabled by Machine Learning. In *Proceedings of the 2009 IEEE International Conference on Data Engineering*. IEEE.

Ganesan, T., Vasant, P., & Elamvazuthi, I. (2011). *Optimization of nonlinear geological structure mapping using hybrid neuro-genetic techniques.* Mathematical and Computer Modelling,*54* (11-12), 2913 – 2922.

Garcia-Molina, H., Ullman, J. D., & Widom, J. (2002). *Database systems: The complete book.* Moscow, Russia: Williams.

Garrett, J. J. (2003). *The elements of user experience: User-centered design for the web.* Indianapolis, IN: New Riders.

Gasser, U., Weeks, E. R., Schofield, A., Pusey, P. N., & Weitz, D. A. (2001). Real-space imaging of nucleation and growth in colloidal crystallization. *Science, 292,* 258–262. doi:10.1126/science.1058457 PMID:11303095

Gaussian 09 Reference Manual (n.d.). Retrieved April 2014 from http://www.gaussian.com/g_tech/g09w_ref.htm

GaussView 5 Reference Table Contents. (n.d.). Retrieved April 4, 2014 from http://www.gaussian.com/g_tech/gv5ref/gv5ref_toc.htm

Gau, W. L., & Buehrer, D. J. (1994). Vague sets, IEEE Transactions on Systems, *Man and Cybernetics. Part A, 23,* 610–614.

Gefen, D., Pavlou, P. A., Benbasat, I., McKnight, D. H., Stewart, K., & Straub, D. W. (2006). Should institutional trust matter in information systems research? *Communications of the AIS, 19*(7), 205–222.

Gerald, S. (2012). Why we disagree about climate change: A different viewpoint. *Energy & Environment, 23*(8), 76–95.

Gerstenkorn, T., & Manko, J. (1991). Correlation of intuitionistic fuzzy sets. *Fuzzy Sets and Systems, 44,* 39–43. doi:10.1016/0165-0114(91)90031-K

Ginty, K., Tindle, J., & Tindle, S. J. (2009). Cluster systems – An open-access design solution. In *Proceedings of International Conference on Systems Engineering (ICSE).* Coventry University.

Giorgis, L., Hernandez, A. I., Amblard, A., Senhadji, L., Cazeau, S., Jauvert, G., & Donal, E. (2008). Analysis of cardiac micro-acceleration signals for the estimation of systolic and diastolic time intervals in cardiac resynchronization therapy. *Computers in Cardiology, 2008,* 393–396.

Giovangrandi, L., Inan, O. T., Wiard, R. M., Etemadi, M., & Kovacs, G. (2011). Ballistocardiography—A method worth revisiting. In *Proceedings of the 30th Annual International Conference of the IEEE Engineering in Medicine and Biology Society,* (pp. 4279-4282). IEEE.

Givoni, B. (1998). *Climate consideration in building and urban design.* New York: Van Nostrand Reinhold.

Glaas, E., & Juhola, S. (2013). New levels of climate adaptation policy: Analysing the institutional interplay in the Baltic Sea Region. *Sustainability, 1,* 56–122.

Glende, A. (2004). Agent Design to Pass Computer Games. In *Proc. of the 42nd Annual ACM Southeast Regional Conference,* (pp. 414-415). ACM.

Goffaux, V. & van Zon, J, & Schiltz, C. (2011). The horizontal tuning of face perception relies on the processing of intermediate and high spatial frequencies. *Journal of Vision, 11*(10), 1-9.

Gollisch, T., & Meister, M. (2010). Eye smarter than scientists believed: neural computations in circuits of the retina. *Neuron, 65*(2), 150–164. doi:10.1016/j.neuron.2009.12.009 PMID:20152123

Gordon, J. (1877). Certain molar movements of the human body produced by the circulation of the blood. *Journal of Anatomy and Physiology, 11*(3), 533–536. PMID:17231163

Gorman, B., Thurau, C., Bauckhage, C., & Humphrys, M. (2006). Believability Testing and Bayesian Imitation in Interactive Computer Games. *Lecture Notes in Computer Science, 4095,* 655–666. doi:10.1007/11840541_54

Graesser, A., Lang, K., & Roberts, R. (1991). Question Answering in the Context of Stories. *Journal of Experimental Psychology. General, 120*(3), 254–277. doi:10.1037/0096-3445.120.3.254

Granada, M., Rider, M. J., Mantovani, J. R. S., & Shahidehpour, M. (2012). A decentralized approach for optimal reactive power dispatch using a Lagrangian decomposition method. *Electric Power Systems Research*, *89*, 148–156. doi:10.1016/j.epsr.2012.02.015

Granville, S. (1994). Optimal reactive dispatch through interior point methods. *IEEE Transactions on Power Systems*, *9*(1), 136–146. doi:10.1109/59.317548

Gratzel, M. (2001). Photoelectrochemical cells. *Nature*, *414*, 338–344. doi:10.1038/35104607 PMID:11713540

Grosan, C. (2003). Performance metrics for multiobjective optimization evolutionary algorithms. In *Proceedings of Conference on Applied and Industrial Mathematics* (CAIM). CAIM.

Grossberg, S., Srinivasan, K., & Yazdanbakhsh, A. (2011). On the road to invariant object recognition: How cortical area V2 transforms absolute to relative disparity during 3D vision. *Neural Netw*, *24*(7), 686-92.

Grubbs, F. E. (1950). Sample criteria for testing outlying observations. *Annals of Mathematical Statistics*, *21*, 27–58. doi:10.1214/aoms/1177729885

Grubbs, F. E. (1969). Procedures for detecting outlying observations in samples. *Technometrics*, *11*(1), 1–21. doi:10.1080/00401706.1969.10490657

Gruber, M. (2001). *Mastering SQL*. Sofia, Bulgaria: SoftPress.

Gruber, T. R. (1993). A translation approach to portable ontology specifications. *Knowledge Acquisition*, *5*(2), 199–220. doi:10.1006/knac.1993.1008

Grudev, I. (1999). *The first Slavonic-Bulgarian alphabet – The Cyrillic*. Retrieved June 03, 2010, from http://www.fortunecity.com/victorian/coldwater/293/pyr_k.htm

Guidoum, N., Bensouyad, M., & Saïdouni, D. (2013). The strict strong coloring based graph distribution algorithm. [IJAMC]. *International Journal of Applied Metaheuristic Computing*, *4*(1). doi:10.4018/jamc.2013010104

Gurev, V., Tavakolian, K., Constantino, J., Kaminska, B., Blaber, A. P., & Trayanova, N. A. (2012). Mechanisms underlying the isovolumic and ejection peaks in seismocardiogram morphology. *Journal of Medical and Biological Engineering*, *32*(2), 103–110. doi:10.5405/jmbe.847 PMID:23105942

Haddad, M., Dekar, L., & Kheddouci, H. (2008). A distributed strict strong coloring algorithm for broadcast applications in ad hoc networks. In *Proceedings of the 8th International Conference on New Technologies in Distributed Systems*. Lyon, France: Academic Press.

Haddad, M., & Kheddouci, H. (2009). A strict strong coloring of trees. *Information Processing Letters*, *109*(18), 1047–1054. doi:10.1016/j.ipl.2009.06.012

Hagelbäck, J., & Johansson, S. (2009). A Multiagent Potential Field-Based Bot for Real-Time Strategy Games. *International Journal of Computer Games Technology*, 1–10. doi:10.1155/2009/910819

Haggie, K. & Kingston, J. (2003, June). Choosing Your Knowledge Management Strategy. *Journal of Knowledge Management Practice*, 1–24.

Haiping, M., Xieyong, R., & Baogen, J. (2010). Oppositional ant colony .optimization algorithm and its application to fault monitoring. In *Proceedings of 2010 29th Chinese Control Conference* (CCC), (pp. 3895 – 3898). CCC.

Hair, J. F., Black, B., Babin, B., Anderson, R. E., & Tatham, R. L. (2010). *Multivariate data analysis: A global perspective*. New Jersey: Pearson Education Inc.

Halevy, A. Y., Franklin, M. J., & Maier, D. (2006). Principles of dataspace systems. In *Stijn Vansummeren* (pp. 1–9). ACM.

Hall, O., & Scrase, J. (1998). Will biomass be the environmentally friendly fuel of the future? *Biomass and Bioenergy*, *15*, 357–367. doi:10.1016/S0961-9534(98)00030-0

Haluska, C. K., Riske, K. A., Marchi-Artzner, V., Lehn, J.-M., Lipowsky, R., & Dimova, R. (2006). Time scales of membrane fusion revealed by direct imaging of vesicle fusion with high temporal resolution. *Proceedings of the National Academy of Sciences of the United States of America*, *103*, 15841–15846. doi:10.1073/pnas.0602766103 PMID:17043227

Hamilton, E. J. M., Dolan, S. E., Mann, C. M., Colijn, H. O., McDonald, C. A., & Shore, S. G. (1993). Preparation of amorphous boron nitride and its conversion to a turbostratic, tubular form. *Science*, *260*, 659–661. doi:10.1126/science.260.5108.659 PMID:17812224

Hamilton, E. J. M., Dolan, S. E., Mann, C. M., Colijn, H. O., & Shore, S. G. (1995). Preparation of amorphous boron nitride from the reaction of haloborazines with alkali metals and formation of a novel tubular morphology by thermal annealing. *Chemistry of Materials*, 7, 111–117. doi:10.1021/cm00049a017

Hamker, F. (2005). The reentry hypothesis: the putative interaction of the frontal eye field, ventrolateral prefrontal cortex, and areas V4, IT for attention and eye movement. *Cerebral Cortex*, 15, 431–447. doi:10.1093/cercor/bhh146 PMID:15749987

Han, J., & Jaffe, R. (1998). Energetics and geometries of carbon nanocone tips. *The Journal of Chemical Physics*, 108, 2817–2823. doi:10.1063/1.475672

Hans, D. D. (2004). Agile Knowledge Management in Practice. In G. Melnik, & H. Holz (Eds.), *Advances in Learning Software Organizations* (Vol. 137–143). Lecture Notes in Computer ScienceHeidelberg: Springer-Verlag.

Hansen, M. T., Nohria, N., & Tierney, T. (1999). What's Your Strategy for Managing Knowledge? *Harvard Business Review*, (March-April): 106–116. PMID:10387767

Harada, K., Kamimura, O., Kasai, H., Matsuda, T., Tonomura, A., & Moshchalkov, V. V. (1996). Direct observation of vortex dynamics in superconducting films with regular arrays of defects. *Science*, 274, 1167–1170. doi:10.1126/science.274.5290.1167 PMID:8895460

Haridy, S., Wu, Z., & Shafik, A. (2012). An educational scheme for a CNC drilling machine. *International Journal of Manufacturing, Materials, and Mechanical Engineering*, 2(2), 1–11. doi:10.4018/ijmmme.2012040101

Hartmann, U. (1985). *Theory of noncontact force microscopy: Scanning tunneling microscopy III. Theory of STM and related scanning techniques* (R. Wiensendanger, & J. H. Guntherodt, Eds.). Berlin: Springer.

Hassanein, K., & Head, M. (2007). Manipulating social presence through the web interface and its impact on consumer attitude towards online shopping. *International Journal of Human-Computer Studies*, 65(8), 689–708. doi:10.1016/j.ijhcs.2006.11.018

Haxby, J., Hoffman, E., & Gobbini, M. (2002). Human neural systems for face recognition and social communication. *Biological Psychiatry*, 51(1), 59–67. doi:10.1016/S0006-3223(01)01330-0 PMID:11801231

Hayes, J. (2002). *The theory and practice of change management*. Palgrave, Basingstone.

Heaney, R., & Sriananthakumar, S. (2012, September). Time-varying correlation between stock market returns and real estate returns. *Journal of Empirical Finance*, 19(4), 583–594. doi:10.1016/j.jempfin.2012.03.006

Hecker, C. (2011). *My Liner Notes for Spore*. Retrieved 20.09.2011, from http://chrishecker.com/My_liner_notes_for_spore

Hedeler, C., Belhajjame, K., Paton, N. W., Fernandes, A. A. A., Embury, S. M., Mao, L., & Guo, C. (2011). Pay-As-You-Go Mapping Selection in Dataspaces. In Proceedings of SIGMOD 2011, (pp. 1279-1282). ACM.

Heeks, R. (2006). *Implementing and Managing eGovernment*. London: Sage Publications.

Heitger, F. et al. (1992). Simulation of neural contour mechanisms: from simple to end-stopped cells. *Vision Research*, 32(5), 963–981. doi:10.1016/0042-6989(92)90039-L PMID:1604865

Himma, K. (2007). The concept of information overload: A preliminary step in understanding the nature of a harmful information-related condition. *Ethics and Information Technology*, 9(4), 259–272. doi:10.1007/s10676-007-9140-8

Hingston, P. (2009). A Turing Test for Computer Game Bots. *IEEE Transactions on Computational Intelligence and AI in Games*, 1(3), 169–186. doi:10.1109/TCIAIG.2009.2032534

Hirono, D., & Thawonmas, R. (2009). Implementation of a Human-Like Bot in a First Person Shooter: Second Place Bot at BotPrize 2008. In *Proc. of Asia Simulation Conference*. Academic Press.

Hofstadter, D. (1995). Preface 4: The Ineradicable Eliza Effect and Its Dangers. In *Fluid Concepts and Creative Analogies: Computer Models of the Fundamental Mechanisms of Thought*. New York: Basic Books.

Holland, J. H. (1992). *Adaptation in Natural and Artificial Systems: An Introductory Analysis with Applications to Biology, Control and Artificial Intelligence*. USA: MIT Press.

Holsapple, C. W. (2003). Knowledge and its attributes. In C. W. Holsapple (Ed.), *Handbook on Knowledge Management 1: Knowledge Matters*. Heidelberg: Springer-Verlag. doi:10.1007/978-3-540-24748-7

Hong, D. H., & Choi, D. H. (2000). Multicriteria fuzzy decision making problems based on vague set theory. *Fuzzy Sets and Systems*, *114*, 103–113. doi:10.1016/S0165-0114(98)00271-1

Hong, D. H., & Hwang, S. W. (1995). Correlation of intuitionistic fuzzy sets in probability spaces. *Fuzzy Sets and Systems*, *75*, 77–81. doi:10.1016/0165-0114(94)00330-A

Hopfield, J. J. (1982). Neural Networks and Physical Systems with Emergent Collective Computational Abilities. *Proceedings of the National Academy of Sciences of the United States of America*, *79*, 2554–2558. doi:10.1073/pnas.79.8.2554 PMID:6953413

Hopfield, J. J. (1984). Neurons with Graded Response have Collective Computational Properties like those of Two-State Neurons. *Proceedings of the National Academy of Sciences of the United States of America*, *81*, 3088–3092. doi:10.1073/pnas.81.10.3088 PMID:6587342

Houlette, F. (2001). *SQL: A beginner's guide*. Sofia, Bulgaria: SoftPress.

Hounsa, C. G., Brandt, E. V., Johan, T., Stefan, H., & Bernard, A. P. (1998). Role of trehalose in survival of Saccharomyces cerevisiae under osmotic stress. *Microbiology*, *144*, 671–680. doi:10.1099/00221287-144-3-671 PMID:9534237

Hsu, C. L., & Lu, H. P. (2004). Why do people play games? An extended TAM with social influences and flow experience. *Information & Management*, *41*(7), 853–868. doi:10.1016/j.im.2003.08.014

Huang, C. N., & Motavalli, S. (1994). Reverse engineering of planar parts using machine vision. *Computers & Industrial Engineering*, *26*(2), 369–379. doi:10.1016/0360-8352(94)90070-1

Huang, H. (2013). Some properties on the cut sets of intuitionistic fuzzy sets. *Annals of Fuzzy Mathematics and Informatics*, *5*(3), 475–481.

Huang, M. H. (2006). Flow, enduring, and situational involvement in the web environment: A tripartite second-order examination. *Psychology and Marketing*, *23*(5), 383–411. doi:10.1002/mar.20118

Hubel, D. H. (1995). *Eye, brain and vision*. Scientific American Library.

Hung, W. L., & Wu, J. W. (2002). Correlation of intuitionistic fuzzy sets by centroid method. *Information Sciences*, *144*, 219–225. doi:10.1016/S0020-0255(02)00181-0

Hu, X., & Zhou, Q. (2013). Health and ecosystem risks of graphene. *Chemical Reviews*, *113*, 3815–3835. doi:10.1021/cr300045n PMID:23327673

Hwang, C. L., & Yoon, K. (1981). *Multiple Attributes Decision Making Methods and Applications*. Berlin, Heidelberg: Springer. doi:10.1007/978-3-642-48318-9

Iba, K. (1994). Reactive power optimization by genetic algorithm. *IEEE Transactions on Power Systems*, *9*(2), 685–692. doi:10.1109/59.317674

ICARUS. (2007). *ICARUS Project*. Retrieved from http://cll.stanford.edu/research/ongoing/icarus/

IEEE 118-Bus Test System. (n.d.). Available from http://www.ee.washington.edu/research/pstca/ pf118/ pg_tca-118bus.htm

IEEE 57-Bus Test System. (n.d.). Available from http://www.ee.washington.edu/research/ pstca/ pf57/pg_tca-57bus.htm

Igbaria, M., Livari, J., & Maragahh, H. (1995). Why do individual use computer technology: A finish case study. *Information & Management*, *29*(5), 227–238. doi:10.1016/0378-7206(95)00031-0

Igel, C., Hansen, N., & Roth, S. (2007). Covariance Matrix Adaptation for Multi-objective Optimization. *Evolutionary Computation*, *15*(1), 1–28. doi:10.1162/evco.2007.15.1.1 PMID:17388777

IHA. (2003). *World Atlas & Industry Guide*. United Kingdom: The International Journal Hydropower & Dams.

Ijaz, K., Bogdanovych, A., & Simoff, S. (2011). Enhancing the believability of embodied conversational agents through environment-, self-and interaction-awareness. In *Proc. of Australasian Compuer Science Conference*. Academic Press.

Ilsever, J., Cyr, D., & Parent, M. (2007). Extending models of flow and e-loyalty. *Journal of Information Science and Technology*, *4*(2), 10–13.

Inmon, W. (1996). The data warehouse and data mining. *Communications of the ACM*, *39*(11), 49–50. doi:10.1145/240455.240470

Intriligator, J., & Cavanagh, P. (2001). The spatial resolution of visual attention. *Cognitive Psychology*, *43*(3), 171–216. doi:10.1006/cogp.2001.0755 PMID:11689021

Isla, D. (2005). Handling Complexity in the Halo 2 AI. In *Proceedings ofGame Developers Conference'05*. Academic Press.

Jackie, C. (2013). *What is CAD?*. Retrieved January 10, 2013, from http://architecture. about.com/od/software/g/CAD.htm

Jaganathan, S., Palaniswami, S., Vignesh, G.M., & Mithunraj, R. (2011). Applications of multi objective optimization to reactive power planning problem using ant colony algorithm. *European Journal of Scientific Research*, *51* (2), 241-253.

Janic, M. (2003). Multicriteria evaluation of high-speed rail, trans rapid maglev and air passenger transport in Europe. *Trans Plan Technol.*, *26*(6), 491–512. doi:10.1080/0308106032000167373

Jarke, M., Lenzerini, M., Vassiliou, Y., & Vassiliadis, P. (2003). *Fundamentals of data warehouses*. Springer Verlag. doi:10.1007/978-3-662-05153-5

Jashapara, A. (2011). Knowledge Management: An Integrated Approach (second edition). Prentice Hall, Pearson Education Limited, United Kingdom.

Jeffery, S. R., Franklin, M. J., & Halevy, A. Y. (2008). Pay-as-you-go user feedback for dataspace systems. In *Proceedings of the ACM SIGMOD International Conference on Management of Data*, (pp. 847-860). ACM.

Jerosch-Herold, M., Zanetti, J., Merkle, H., Poliac, L., Huang, H., & Mansoor, A. et al. (1999). The seismocardiogram as magnetic-field-compatible alternative to the electrocardiogram for cardiac stress monitoring. *International Journal of Cardiac Imaging*, *15*(6), 523–531. doi:10.1023/A:1006364518204 PMID:10768746

Jiao, Y., & Torquato, S. (2011). Communication: A packing of truncated tetrahedra that nearly fills all of space and its melting properties. *The Journal of Chemical Physics*, *135*, 151101–1–4. doi:10.1063/1.3653938 PMID:22029288

Jimoda, L. A., Oke, E. O., & Salam, K. K. (2013). Modelling of mass transfer rate during biocoagulation-flocculation of coal-rich wastewater. *Journal of Scientific Research Reports*, *2*, 376–390. doi:10.9734/JSRR/2013/3492

John, A., & James, S. (1989). *The power of place: bringing together geographical and sociological imaginations, 1989*. Academic Press.

Jones, R. M., Laird, J. E., Nielsen, P. E., Coulter, K. J., Kenny, P., & Koss, F. (1999). Automated intelligent pilots for combat flight simulation. *AI Magazine*, *20*(1), 27–41.

Jordan, P. (2002). *Designing pleasurable products: An introduction to the new human factors*. London: Taylor & Francis.

Kaelbling, L., Littman, M., & Moore, A. (1996). Reinforcement Learning: A Survey. *Journal of Artificial Intelligence Research*, *4*, 237–285.

Kaiser, U., Schwarz, A., & Wiesendanger, R. (2007). Magnetic exchange force microscopy with atomic resolution. *Nature*, *446*, 522–525. doi:10.1038/nature05617 PMID:17392782

Kakumanu, P., Makrogiannis, S., & Bourbakis, N. (2007). A survey of skin-color modeling and detection methods. *Pattern Recognition*, *40*(3), 1106–1122. doi:10.1016/j.patcog.2006.06.010

Kallus, Y., Elser, V., & Gravel, S. (2010). Gravel, Dense periodic packings of tetrahedra with small repeating units. *Discrete & Computational Geometry*, *44*, 245–252. doi:10.1007/s00454-010-9254-3

Kammerud, R., Ceballos, E., Curtis, B., Place, W., & Anderson, B. (1984). Ventilation cooling of residential buildings. ASHRAE Trans, 90(1B).

Kao, C., & Liu, S. T. (2002). Fuzzy measures for correlation coefficient of fuzzy numbers. *Fuzzy Sets and Systems*, *128*, 267–275. doi:10.1016/S0165-0114(01)00199-3

Karp, R. M. (1972). Reducibility among combinatorial problems. In *Proceedings of the Symposium on the Complexity of Computer Computations* (pp. 85-103). Academic Press.

Kavanaugh, S., & Rafferty, K. (1997). *Ground source heat pumps. Design of Geothermal Systems for Commercial and Institutional Buildings. American Society of heating*. Atlanta, GA, USA: Refrigeration and Air-conditioning Engineers, Inc.

Kawata, H. K., Fukuyama, Y., Takayama, S., & Nakanishi, Y. (2000). A particle swarm optimization for reactive power and voltage control considering voltage security assessment. *IEEE Transactions on Power Systems*, *15*(4), 1232–1239. doi:10.1109/59.898095

Keen, P., Ballance, C., Chan, S., & Schrump, S. (2000). *Electronic commerce relationships: Trust by design*. Upper Saddle River, NJ: Prentice Hall.

Kemmerling, M., Ackermann, N., Beume, N., Preuss, M., Uellenbeck, S., & Walz, W. (2009). Is Human-Like and Well Playing Contradictory for Diplomacy Bots?. In *Proceedings ofIEEE Symposium on Computational Intelligence and Games*, (pp. 209-216). IEEE.

Kennedy, J., & Eberhart, R. (1995). Particle Swarm Optimization. In *Proceedings of the International Conference on Neural Networks*. Perth, Australia: IEEE.

Khazali, A. H., & Kalantar, M. (2011). Optimal reactive power dispatch based on harmony search algorithm. *International Journal of Electrical Power & Energy Systems*, *33*, 684–692. doi:10.1016/j.ijepes.2010.11.018

Kim, G., Shin, B., & Lee, H. G. (2009). Understanding dynamics between initial trust and usage intentions of mobile banking. *Information Systems Journal*, *19*(3), 283–311. doi:10.1111/j.1365-2575.2007.00269.x

Kim, P., Odom, T. W., Huang, J.-L., & Lieber, C. M. (1999). Electronic density of states of atomically resolved single-walled carbon nanotubes: Van Hove singularities and end states. *Physical Review Letters*, *82*, 1225–1228. doi:10.1103/PhysRevLett.82.1225

Kim, S., & Park, H. (2013). Effects of various characteristics of social commerce (s-commerce) on consumers' trust and trust performance. *International Journal of Information Management*, *33*, 318–332. doi:10.1016/j.ijinfomgt.2012.11.006

Kingery, W. D., Bowen, H. K., & Uhlmann, D. R. (2006). *Introduction of ceramics* (2nd ed.). New York, NY: Wiley-Interscience.

Kismihók, G., Mol, S., Sancin, C., Van der Voort, N., Costello, V., Sorrentino, G., & Zoino, F. (2010). Ontology based competency matching between the vocational education and the workplace: The OntoHR project. *Proceedings of AICA, l'Aquila, Italy*.

Kitano, H., Asada, M., Kuniyoshi, Y., Noda, I., Osawai, E., & Matsubara, H. (1998). RoboCup: A Challenge Problem for AI and Robotics. *Lecture Notes in Computer Science*, *1395*, 1–19. doi:10.1007/3-540-64473-3_46

Klabunde, R. (2005). *Cardiovascular physiology concepts*. LWW.

Klein, D. J., & Balaban, A. T. (2011). Clarology for conjugated carbon nano-structures: Molecules, polymers, graphene, defected graphene, fractal benzenoids, fullerenes, nano-tubes, nano-cones, nano-tori, etc. *Open Organic Chemistry Journal*, *5*(Suppl. 1-M3), 27-61.

Klein, D. J. (1992). Aromaticity via Kekule structures and conjugated circuits. *Journal of Chemical Education*, *69*, 691–694. doi:10.1021/ed069p691

Klein, D. J. (2002). Topo-combinatoric categorization of quasi-local graphitic defects. *Physical Chemistry Chemical Physics*, *4*, 2099–2110. doi:10.1039/b110618j

Klein, D. J., & Balaban, A. T. (2006). The eight classes of positive-curvature graphitic nanocones. *Journal of Chemical Information and Modeling*, *46*, 307–320. doi:10.1021/ci0503356 PMID:16426066

Klimkó, G. (2001). *Mapping Organisational Knowledge*. (Unpublished doctoral dissertation). Corvinus University of Budapest, Budapest, Hungary

Klotz, W. (2002). *Graph coloring algorithms* (Tech. Rep. No. 5). Clausthal, Germany: Clausthal University of Technology.

Knafla, B. (2011). *Introduction to Behavior Trees*. Retrieved 15.09.2011, from http://bjoernknafla.com/introduction-to-behavior-trees

Knowles, J., & Corne, D. (2002). On metrics for comparing nondominated sets. In *Proceedings, World Congress on Computational Intelligence* (CEC'02), (pp. 711 – 716). IEEE.

Knowles, J., & Corne, D. (2003). Properties of an Adaptive Archiving Algorithm for Storing Nondominated Vectors. *IEEE Transactions on Evolutionary Computation*, *7*(2), 100–116. doi:10.1109/TEVC.2003.810755

Kő, A., & Klimkó, G. (2009). Towards a Framework of Information Technology Tools for Supporting Knowledge Management. In E. Noszkay (Ed.), *The Capital of Intelligence - the Intelligence of Capital* (pp. 65–85). Budapest: Foundation for Information Society.

Kohler-Redlich, P., Terrones, M., Manteca-Diego, C., Hsu, W. K., Terrones, H., & Rühle, M. et al. (1999). Stable BC_2N nanostructures: Low-temperature production of segregated C/BN layered materials. *Chemical Physics Letters*, *310*, 459–465. doi:10.1016/S0009-2614(99)00845-3

Kolluri, S. P., & Tseng, A. A. (1989). Simulation of CNC Controller Features in Graphics-Based Programming. *Computers in Industry*, *11*(2), 135–146. doi:10.1016/0166-3615(89)90101-2

Kotter, J. (2011). Change management vs. change leadership: What's the difference? *Forbes*. Retrieved April 15, 2013

Kotter, J. P. (1995). Leading change: Why transformation efforts fail. *Harvard Business Review*, (March-April): 59–67.

Kotter, J. P. (1997). On leading change: A conversation with John P. Kotter. *Strategy and Leadership*, *25*(1), 18–23. doi:10.1108/eb054576

Koufaris, M. (2002). Applying the technology acceptance model and flow theory to online consumer behavior. *Information Systems Research*, *13*(2), 205–223. doi:10.1287/isre.13.2.205.83

Kourtzi, Z., & Connor, C. (2011). Neural representations for object perception: structure, category, and adaptive coding. *Annual Review of Neuroscience*, *34*, 45–67. doi:10.1146/annurev-neuro-060909-153218 PMID:21438683

Koza, J. R. (1992). *Genetic Programming: On the Programming of Computers by means of Natural Selection*. USA: MIT Press.

Krishnan, A., Dujardin, E., Treacy, M. M. J., Hugdahl, J., Lynum, S., & Ebbesen, T. W. (1997). Photoisomerization in dendrimers by harvesting of low-energy photons. *Nature*, *388*, 451–454. doi:10.1038/41284

Kroenke, D. M. (2003). *Database processing*. Moscow, Russia: Piter.

Kroto, H. W. (1987). The stability of the fullerenes C_n, with $n = 24, 28, 32, 36, 50, 60$ and 70. *Nature*, *329*, 529–531. doi:10.1038/329529a0

Kumar, D. N. T., & Wei, Q. (2013). Analysis of quantum dots for nano–bio applications as the technological platform of the future. *Research Journal of Biotechnology*, *8*(5), 78–82.

Kurada, S., & Bradley, C. (1997). A machine vision system for tool wear assessment. *Tribology International*, *30*(4), 295–304. doi:10.1016/S0301-679X(96)00058-8

Kurosu, M. & Kashimura, K. (1995). *Apparent usability vs. inherent usablity: experimental analysis on the determinants of the apparent usability*. Academic Press.

Kurtz, K. J. (1990). Bruits and hums of the head and neck. In H. K. Walker, W. D. Hall, & J. W. Hurst (Eds.), *Clinical methods: The history, physical, and laboratory examinations* (3rd ed.). Boston: Butterworth Publishers, a division of Reed Publishing.

Laird, J. (2002). Research in Human-level AI using Computer Games. *Communications of the ACM*, *45*, 32–35. doi:10.1145/502269.502290

Lam, R., & du Buf, J. M. H. (2011). Retrieval of 3D polygonal objects based on multiresolution signatures. In *Proc. Int. Symp. Visual Computing*, (LNCS) (vol. 6939, pp. 136–147). Berlin: Springer.

Langley, P., Choi, D., & Rogers, S. (2005). *Interleaving Learning, Problem-Solving, and Execution in the ICARUS Architecture (Technical Report)*. Computational Learning Laboratory, Stanford University.

Larson, j., & Cheng, H. H. (2000). Object-oriented cam design through the internet. *Journal of Intelligent Manufacturing*, *11*(6), 515-534.

Lawes, C. M. M., Hoorn, S. V., & Rodgers, A. (2008). Global burden of blood-pressure-related disease, 2001. *Lancet*, *371*(9623), 1513–1518. doi:10.1016/S0140-6736(08)60655-8 PMID:18456100

Le Hy, R., Arrigoni, A., Bessière, P., & Lebeltel, O. (2004). Teaching Bayesian Behaviours to Video Game Characters. *Robotics and Autonomous Systems*, *47*, 177–185. doi:10.1016/j.robot.2004.03.012

Lee, F., & Gamard, S. (2003). Hide and Seek: Using Computational Cognitive Models to Develop and Test Autonomous Cognitive Agents for Complex Dynamic Tasks. In *Proc. of the 25th Annual Conference of the Cognitive Science Society*. Academic Press.

Lee, E. S. (1999). *Essays about computer security*. University of Cambridge Computer Laboratory.

Lee, K. Y., & Park, Y. M. (1995). Optimization method for reactive power planning by using a modified simple genetic algorithm. *IEEE Transactions on Power Systems*, *10*(4), 1843–1850. doi:10.1109/59.476049

Lee, K. Y., Sode-Yome, A., & Park, J. H. (1998). Adaptive Hopfield Neural Networks for Economic Load Dispatch. *IEEE Transactions on Power Systems, USA*, *13*(2), 519–526. doi:10.1109/59.667377

Lee, K., Park, Y., & Ortiz, J. (1985). A united approach to optimal real and reactive power dispatch. *IEEE Transactions on Power Apparatus and Systems*, *104*(5), 1147–1153. doi:10.1109/TPAS.1985.323466

Leighton, F. (1979). A graph coloring algorithm for large scheduling problems. *Journal of Research of the National Bureau of Standards*, *84*, 489–505. doi:10.6028/jres.084.024

Leszczynski, J., & Shukla, M. K. (Eds.). (2009). *Practical aspects of computational chemistry*. Berlin: Springer.

LetterFrequency. (2010). *Letter & Word Frequency in English / Other Language Frequencies*. Retrieved March 27, 2013, from http://www.letterfrequency.org

Lewand, R. E. (2000). *Cryptological mathematics*. The Mathematical Association of America.

Li, J., & Li, H. (2008). The cut sets, decomposition theorems and representation theorems on R-fuzzy sets. *International Journal of Information and systems sciences*, *6*(1), 61-71.

Li, , K., Kwong, S., Cao, J., Li, M., Zheng, J., & Shen, R. (2011). Achieving Balance Between Proximity And Diversity In Multi-Objective Evolutionary Algorithm. *Information Sciences*, *182*, 220–242. doi:10.1016/j.ins.2011.08.027

Li, X., Jia, T., & Zhang, H. (2009) Expression-insensitive 3D face recognition using sparse representation. In *Proc. IEEE Conf. on Computer Vision and Pattern Recognition* (pp. 2575-2582). IEEE.

Liang, C. H., Chung, C. Y., Wong, K. P., & Dual, X. Z. (2007). Parallel optimal reactive power flow based on co-operative co-evolutionary differential evolution and power system decomposition. *IEEE Transactions on Power Systems*, *22*(1), 249–257. doi:10.1109/TPWRS.2006.887889

Liaw, C., Wang, W.-H., Tsai, C.-T., Ko, C.-H., & Hao, G. (2013). Evolving A Team In A First-Person Shooter Game By Using A Genetic Algorithm. *Applied Artificial Intelligence*, *27*(3), 199–212. doi:10.1080/08839514.2013.768883

Lichocki, P., Krawiec, K., & Jaśkowski, W. (2009). Evolving Teams of Cooperating Agents for Real-Time Strategy Game. *Lecture Notes in Computer Science*, *5484*, 333–342. doi:10.1007/978-3-642-01129-0_37

Li, F., & Rao, Y. (2001). Weighted multi-criteria decision making based on vague sets. *Computer Science*, *28*(7), 60–65.

Lind, D. A., Marchal, W. G., & Wathen, S. A. (2010), Basic statistics for business and economics. 7thed. United States: McGraw-Hills.

Lin, K., & Chang, T. C. (2013). Everyday crises: Marginal society livelihood vulnerability and adaptability to hazards. *Progress in Development Studies*, *13*(1), 1–18. doi:10.1177/146499341201300101

Linke, H. (Ed.). (2002). Special issue on Ratchets and Brownian Motors: Basics, Experiments and Applications. *Applied Physics. A, Materials Science & Processing, 75,* 167–354. doi:10.1007/s003390201401

Linke, H., Alemán, B. J., Melling, L. D., Taormina, M. J., Francis, M. J., & Dow-Hygelund, C. C. et al. (2006). Self-propelled Leidenfrost droplets. *Physical Review Letters, 96,* 154502-1–4. doi:10.1103/PhysRevLett.96.154502 PMID:16712160

Lippitt, R., Watson, J., & Westley, B. (1958). *The Dynamics of Planned Change*. New York: Harcourt, Brace.

Li, S. Z., & Jain, A. K. (2011). *Handbook of Face Recognition*. London: Springer. doi:10.1007/978-0-85729-932-1

Liu, P. D. (2009). Multi-Attribute decision-making method research based on interval vague set and TOPSIS method, *Technological and Economic Development of Economy. Baltic Journal of Sustainability., 15*(3), 453–463.

Liu, P. D., & Guan, Z. L. (2008). Research on group decision making based on the vague set and hybrid aggregation operators. *Journal of Wuhan University of Technology, 30*(10), 152–155.

Liu, P. D., & Guan, Z. L. (2009). An approach for multiple attribute decision-making based on Vague sets. *Journal of Harbin Engineering University, 30*(1), 106–110.

Livingstone, D. (2006). Turing's Test and Believable AI in Games. *Computers in Entertainment, 4*(1), 6–18. doi:10.1145/1111293.1111303

Li, Y., Cao, Y., Liu, Z., Liu, Y., & Jiang, Q. (2009). Dynamic optimal reactive power dispatch based on parallel particle swarm optimization algorithm. *Computers & Mathematics with Applications (Oxford, England), 57,* 1835–1842. doi:10.1016/j.camwa.2008.10.049

Loiseau, A., Willaime, F., Demoncy, N., Hug, G., & Pascard, H. (1996). Boron nitride nanotubes with reduced numbers of layers synthesized by arc discharge. *Physical Review Letters, 76,* 4737–4740. doi:10.1103/PhysRevLett.76.4737 PMID:10061368

Louridas, P. (2008). Orchestrating web services with BPEL. *IEEE Software,* 85–87. doi:10.1109/MS.2008.42

Lowe, D. G. (2004). Distinctive image features from scale-invariant keypoints. *International Journal of Computer Vision, 60*(2), 91–110. doi:10.1023/B:VISI.0000029664.99615.94

Lu, A., & Ng, W. (2005). Lecture Notes in Computer Science: Vol. 3716. *Vague sets or intuitionistic fuzzy sets for handling vague data: Which one is better* (pp. 401–416). Springer.

Lu, A., & Ng, W. (2009). Maintaining consistency of vague databases using data dependencies. *Data & Knowledge Engineering, 68*(7), 622–641. doi:10.1016/j.datak.2009.02.007

Lucinda, C., & Martin, N. (1999). *Oxford English Dictionary* (4th ed.). Oxford, UK: Oxford University Press.

Lu, F. C., & Hsu, Y. Y. (1995). Reactive power/voltage control in a distribution substation using dynamic programming. *IEE Proceedings. Generation, Transmission and Distribution, 142*(6), 639–645. doi:10.1049/ip-gtd:19952210

Luke, W. (2009). *The structure, influence and application of emotion in product design*. Leicester, UK: De Montfort University.

Lundahl, D. (2006). A holistic approach to product development. *Food Technology,* 28–33.

Luyben, M. L., & Floudas, C. A. (1994). Analyzing the interaction of design and control. 1. A multiobjective framework and application to binary distillation synthesis. *Computers & Chemical Engineering, 18*(10), 933–969. doi:10.1016/0098-1354(94)E0013-D

Lynden, S., Mukherjee, A., Hume, A. C., Fernandes, A. A. A., Paton, N. W., Sakellariou, R., & Watson, P. (2009). The design and implementation of OGSA-DQP: A service-based distributed query processor. *Future Generation Computer Systems, 25*(3), 224–236. doi:10.1016/j.future.2008.08.003

Macan, T. H., Shahani, C., Dipboye, R. L., & Phillips, A. P. (1990). College students' time management: Correlations with academic performance and stress. *Journal of Educational Psychology, 82*(4), 760–768. doi:10.1037/0022-0663.82.4.760

Machado, M., Mota, R., & Piquini, P. (2003a). Electronic properties of BN nanocones under electric fields. *Microelectronics Journal*, *34*, 545–547. doi:10.1016/S0026-2692(03)00044-2

Machado, M., Piquini, P., & Mota, R. (2003b). Energetics and electronic properties of BN nanocones with pentagonal rings at their apexes. *The European Physical Journal D*, *23*, 91–93. doi:10.1140/epjd/e2003-00040-x

Machado, M., Piquini, P., & Mota, R. (2003c). Electronic properties of selected BN nanocones. *Materials Characterization*, *50*, 179–182. doi:10.1016/S1044-5803(03)00085-8

Machado, M., Piquini, P., & Mota, R. (2004). Charge distributions in BN nanocones: Electric field and tip termination effects. *Chemical Physics Letters*, *392*, 428–432. doi:10.1016/j.cplett.2004.05.088

Machado, M., Piquini, P., & Mota, R. (2005). The influence of the tip structure and the electric field on BN nanocones. *Nanotechnology*, *16*, 302–306. doi:10.1088/0957-4484/16/2/022 PMID:21727440

Madden, J. D. W. (2009). Stiffer than steel. *Science*, *323*, 1571–1572. doi:10.1126/science.1171169 PMID:19299609

Mahadevan, K., & Kannan, P. S. (2010). Comprehensive learning particle swarm optimization for reactive power dispatch. *International Journal of Applied Soft Computing*, *10*(2), 641–652. doi:10.1016/j.asoc.2009.08.038

Ma, J. T., & Lai, L. L. (1996). Evolutionary programming approach to reactive power planning. *IEE Proceedings. Generation, Transmission and Distribution*, *143*(4), 365–370. doi:10.1049/ip-gtd:19960296

Mallipeddi, R., Jeyadevi, S., Suganthan, P.N., & Baskar, S. (2012). Efficient constraint handling for optimal reactive power dispatch problems. *Swarm and Evolutionary Computation*, *5*, 28-36.

Malone, T. (1981). What Makes Computer Games Fun? *Byte*, *6*(12), 258–278.

Manasco, B. (1996). Leading Firms Develop Knowledge Strategies. *Knowledge Inc.*, *1*(6), 26–35.

Mandal, B., & Roy, P. K. (2013). Optimal reactive power dispatch using quasi-oppositional teaching learning based optimization. *International Journal of Electrical Power & Energy Systems*, *53*, 123–134. doi:10.1016/j.ijepes.2013.04.011

Mandelbaum, H., & Mandelbaum, R. A. (1953). Studies utilizing the portable electromagnetic ballistocardiograph: IV. the clinical significance of serial ballistocardiograms following acute myocardial infarction. *Circulation*, *7*(6), 663–673. doi:10.1161/01.CIR.7.6.910 PMID:13051833

Manojlovich, J., Prasithsangaree, P., Hughes, S., Chen, J., & Lewis, M. (2003). UTSAF: A Multi-agent-based Framework for Supporting Military-based Distributed Interactive Simulations in 3D Virtual Environments. In *Proc. of 2003 Simulation Conference*. Academic Press.

Mansour, S. (2002). Automatic generation of part programs for milling sculptured surfaces. *Journal of Materials Processing Technology*, *127*(1), 31-39.

Marchi, G., & Argiolas, M. (2008). A GIS based technology for representing and analyzing real estate values. In *Proceedings of UDMS 2007*, (pp. 345-354). UDMS.

Margulis, L., Salitra, G., Tenne, R., & Talianker, M. (1993). Nested fullerene-like structures. *Nature*, *365*, 113–114. doi:10.1038/365113b0 PMID:8371754

Marques, P. T., Perego, C., Le Meins, J. F., Borsali, R., & Soldi, V. (2006). Study of gelatinization process and viscoelastic properties of cassava starch: effect of sodium hydroxide and ethylene glycol diacrylate as cross-linking agent. *Carbohydrate Polymers*, *66*(3), 396–407. doi:10.1016/j.carbpol.2006.03.028

Martins, J. A., Rodrigues, J. M. F., & du Buf, J. M. H. (2009) Focus of attention and region segregation by low-level geometry. In *Proc. Int. Conf. on Computer Vision - Theory and Applications*, (vol. 2, pp. 267-272). Academic Press.

Martin, Y., & Wickramasinghe, H. K. (1987). Magnetic imaging by *force microscopy* with 1000Å resolution. *Applied Physics Letters*, *50*, 1455–1457. doi:10.1063/1.97800

Marvizadeh, S. Z. & Choobineh, F. F. (2013). Reducing the number of setups for CNC punch presses. *Omega*, *41*(2), 226-235.

McDonagh-Philip, D., & Lebbon, C. (2000). The emotional domain in product design. *The Design Journal*, *3*(1), 31–43. doi:10.2752/146069200789393562

McKay, W. P. S., Gregson, P. H., McKay, B. W. S., & Militzer, J. (1999). Sternal acceleration ballistocardiography and arterial pressure wave analysis to determine stroke volume. *Clinical and Investigative Medicine. Medecine Clinique et Experimentale*, *22*(1), 4–14. PMID:10079990

McKnight, D. H., Choudhury, V., & Kacmar, C. (2002). The impact of initial consumer trust on intentions to transact with a web site: A trust building model. *The Journal of Strategic Information Systems*, *11*(3-4), 297–323. doi:10.1016/S0963-8687(02)00020-3

Mehta, M., Ontañón, S., & Ram, A. (2010). Meta-Level Behavior Adaptation in Real- Time Strategy Games. In *Proceedings of ICCBR 2010 Workshop on Case Based Reasoning for Computer Games*. ICCBR.

Mell, P., & Grance, T. (2011). *The NIST Definition of Cloud Computing*. NIST Special Publication 800-145.

Menkiti, M. C., & Onukwuli, O. D. (2010). Coag-flocculation studies of *Moringa oleifera* coagulant (MOC) in brewery effluent: Nephelometric approach. *Journal of American Science*, *6*(12), 788–806.

Mentzas, G., Draganidis, F., & Chamopoulou, P. (2006). An Ontology Based Tool for Competency Management and Learning Path. Presented on I-KNOW 06 conference, Graz, Austria

Microsoft Compute Cluster Pack. (n.d.). Retrieved April 4, 2014 from http://msdn.microsoft.com/en-us/library/cc136762%28v=vs.85%29.aspx

Microsoft Corporation. (2001). *MCSE training: Microsoft SQL Server 2000 – design and implementing databases*. Sofia, Bulgaria: SoftPress.

Microsoft Corporation. (2008). *Transact SQL*. Retrieved March 27, 2013, from http://www.microsoft.com/sql

Milward, D. (2009). *List of Neverwinter Nights 2 NPCs*. Retrieved 03.10.2011, from http://www.sorcerers.net/Games/NWN2/Walkthrough/NPCList.php

Mintzberg, H. (1991). The effective organization: forces and forms. *Sloan Management Review*, *32*(2), 57–67.

Mirchev, K. (1963). Konstantin-Cyril, the creator of the Old-Bulgarian literary language. *Journal "Bulgarian Language"*, *13*(3).

Mirza, H. T., Chen, L., & Chen, G. (2010). Practicability of Dataspace Systems. *International Journal of Digital Content Technology and its Applications*, *4*(3), 233-243.

Misra, A., Klein, D. J., & Morikawa, T. (2009a). Clar theory for molecular benzenoids. *The Journal of Physical Chemistry A*, *113*, 1151–1158. doi:10.1021/jp8038797 PMID:19132846

Misra, A., Schmalz, T. G., & Klein, D. J. (2009b). Clar theory for radical benzenoids. *Journal of Chemical Information and Modeling*, *49*, 2670–2676. doi:10.1021/ci900321e PMID:19916509

Mitchell, D. (1995). *From MUDs to Virtual Worlds*. Microsoft Virtual Worlds Group.

Mittal, B. (1988). The role of affective choice mode in the consumer purchase of expressive products. *Journal of Economic Psychology*, *9*, 499–524. doi:10.1016/0167-4870(88)90016-5

Miyamoto, Y., Rubio, A., Cohen, M. L., & Louie, S. G. (1994). Chiral tubules of hexagonal BC_2N. *Physical Review B: Condensed Matter and Materials Physics*, *50*, 4976–4979. doi:10.1103/PhysRevB.50.4976 PMID:9976827

Mkrtchyan, G. S., & Shmidt, V. V. (1972). Interaction between a cavity and a vortex in a superconductor of the second kind.[English Translation]. *Soviet Physics, JETP*, *34*, 195–197.

Mondal, T. K., & Samanta, S. K. (2002). Generalized intuitionistic fuzzy sets. *The Journal of Fuzzy Mathematics*, *10*(4), 839–862.

Moreno, A. B., & Sanchez, A. (2004) GavabDB: A 3D face database. In *Proc. 2nd COST275 Workshop on Biometrics on the Internet*, (pp. 77-85). Academic Press.

Morie, J., Chance, E., Haynes, K., & Purohit, D. (2012). Storytelling with Storyteller Agents in Second Life. In *Proc. of International Conference on Cyberworlds*, (pp. 165-170). Academic Press.

Morrow, K. (2012). Rio+20, the green economy and re-orienting sustainable development. *Environmental Law Review*, *14*(4), 15–23.

Mota, R., Machado, M., & Piquini, P. (2003). Structural and electronic properties of 240° nanocones. *Physica Status Solidi*, *0*(c), 799–802. doi:10.1002/pssc.200306216

Mounsey, P. (1957). Praecordial ballistocardiography. *British Heart Journal*, *19*(2), 259. doi:10.1136/hrt.19.2.259 PMID:13413014

Mozgovoy, M., & Umarov, I. (2010a). Building a Believable Agent for a 3D Boxing Simulation Game. In *Proc. of the 2nd International Conference on Computer Research and Development*, (pp. 46-50). Academic Press.

Mozgovoy, M., & Umarov, I. (2010b). Building a Believable and Effective Agent for a 3D Boxing Simulation Game. In *Proc. of the 3rd IEEE International Conference on Computer Science and Information Technology*, (pp. 14-18). IEEE.

Murphy, C. J., & Coffer, J. L. (2002). Quantum dots: A primer. *Applied Spectroscopy*, *56*, 16A–27A. doi:10.1366/0003702021954214

Murphy, C. J., Thompson, L. B., Alkilany, A. M., Sisco, P. N., Boulos, S. P., & Sivapalan, S. T. et al. (2010). The many faces of gold nanorods. *Journal of Physical Chemistry Letters*, *1*, 2867–2875. doi:10.1021/jz100992x

Naemura, K., & Iseki, H. (2003). Vibration isolation for seismocardiogram measurement in the OpenMRI-guided operating theater. *JSME International Journal Series C*, *46*(4), 1426–1433. doi:10.1299/jsmec.46.1426

Naithani, B., & Chauhan, S. (2012). Mathematical modelling approach for determining optimal machining parameters in turning with computer numerical control (CNC) machines. *International Journal of Computer Aided Engineering and Technology*, *4*(5), 403–419. doi:10.1504/IJCAET.2012.048838

Namasivayam, V., & Günther, R. (2007). A Fast Flexible Molecular Docking Program Based on Swarm Intelligence. *Journalism*, *70*(6), 475–484. Chemical Biology and Drug Design PMID:17986206

Nanfara, F., Uccello, T., & Murphy, D. (1995). *The CNC Workbook: An Introduction to Computer Numerical Control*. Addison-Wesley Publishing Company.

Naveed, M., Kitchin, D., & Crampton, A. (2010). Monte-Carlo Planning for Pathfinding in Real-Time Strategy Games. In *Proceedings of PlanSIG Workshop*, (pp. 125-132). PlanSIG.

Nayagam, L. G., Muralikrishnan, S., & Sivaraman, G. (2011). Multi-Criteria Decision Making based on Interval-Valued Intuitionistic Fuzzy Sets. *Expert Systems with Applications*, *38*, 1464–1467. doi:10.1016/j.eswa.2010.07.055

Neary, J., MacQuarrie, D., Jamnik, V., Gledhill, S., & Busse, E. (2011). Assessment of mechanical cardiac function in elite athletes. *Open Sports Medicine Journal*, *5*, 26–37. doi:10.2174/1874387001105010026

Nel, A., Zhao, Y., & Mädler, L. (2013). Environmental health and safety considerations for nanotechnology. *Accounts of Chemical Research*, *46*, 605–606. doi:10.1021/ar400005v PMID:23964654

Nelson, R. R., & Todd, P. A. (2005). Antecedents of information and system quality: An empirical examination within the context of data warehousing. *Journal of Management Information Systems*, *21*(4), 199–235.

Neu, J. C., Cañizo, J. A., & Bonilla, L. L. (2002). Three eras of micellization. *Physical Review E*, *66*, 61406–1-9.

Niknam, T., Narimani, M.R., Azizipanah-Abarghooee, R., & Bahmani-Firouzi, B. (2013). Multiobjective Optimal Reactive Power Dispatch and Voltage Control: A New Opposition-Based Self-Adaptive Modified Gravitational Search Algorithm. *IEEE Systems Journal*.

Njeru, J. (2013). 'Donor-driven' neoliberal reform processes and urban environmental change in Kenya: The case of Karura Forest in Nairobi. *Progress in Development Studies*, *13*(1), 63–78. doi:10.1177/146499341201300105

Nonaka, I., & Takeuchi, H. (1995). *The Knowledge-Creating Company: How Japanese Companies Create the Dynamics of Innovation*. Oxford University Press.

Norman, D. (2006, August 19). *A discussion with Don Norman on what makes great design prt1: Icon-o-Cast by Lunar Design* [Podcast]. Retrieved from http://phobos.apple.com/WebObjects/MZStore.woa/wa/viewPodcast?id=78230141&s=143444

Norman, D. (2004). *Emotion design: Why we love (or hate) everyday things.* New York, NY: Basic Books.

Notman, R., Noro, M., O'Malley, B., & Anwar, J. (2006). Molecular basis for dimethylsulfoxide (DMSO) action on lipid membranes. *Journal of the American Chemical Society, 128,* 13982–13983. doi:10.1021/ja063363t PMID:17061853

Oberdörster, G., Maynard, A., Donaldson, K., Castranova, V., Fitzpatrick, J., Ausman, K., ... Yang, H. (2005). A report from the ILSI Research Foundation/Risk Science Institute Nanomaterial Toxicity Screening Working Group. *Particle and Fibre Toxicology, 2,* 8-1-35.

Oberoi, H. S., Vadlani, P. V., Madl, R. L., Saida, L., & Abeykoon, J. P. (2010). Ethanol production from orange peels: two-stage hydrolysis and fermentation studies using optimized parameters through experimental design. *Journal of Agricultural and Food Chemistry, 58*(6), 3422–3429. doi:10.1021/jf903163t PMID:20158208

Odeku, K. O., Maveneka, A., & Konanani, R. H. (2013). Consequences of Country's Withdrawal from Climate Change Agreements: Implications for Carbon Emissions Reduction. *Journal of Human Ecology (Delhi, India), 41*(1), 17–24.

OECD/IEA. (2004). Renewables for power generation: status and prospect. Paris: Author.

Okkan, P. (1993). Reducing CO_2 emissions-How do heat pumps compete with other options? *IEA Heat Pump Centre Newsletter, 11*(3), 24–26.

Oliva, A., & Torralba, A. (2006). Building the gist of a scene: the role of global image features in recognition. Progress in Brain Res. *Visual Perception, 155,* 23–26.

Ontañón, S., Mishra, K., Sugandh, N., & Ram, A. (2007). Case-based Planning and Execution for Real-time Strategy Games. *Lecture Notes in Computer Science, 4626,* 164–178. doi:10.1007/978-3-540-74141-1_12

Orkin, J. (2006). Three States and a Plan: the AI of FEAR. In *Proceedings of Game Developers Conference'06.* Academic Press.

Ortega-Villar, N., Thompson, A. L., Muñoz, M. C., Ugalde-Saldívar, V. M., Goeta, A. E., Moreno-Esparza, R., & Real, J. A. (2005). Solid- and solution-state studies of the novel μ-dicyanamide-bridged dinuclear spin-crossover system $\{[(Fe(bztpen)]_2[\mu\text{-}N(CN)_2]\}(PF_6)_3 \cdot nH_2O$. *Chemistry (Weinheim an der Bergstrasse, Germany), 11,* 5721–5734. doi:10.1002/chem.200500171 PMID:16028299

Ortony, A., Clore, G. L., & Collins, A. (1988). *The cognitive structure of emotions.* Cambridge: Cambridge University Press. doi:10.1017/CBO9780511571299

Orzan, S., van de Pol, J., & Valero Espada, M. (2005). A state space distribution policy based on abstract interpretation. *Electronic Notes in Theoretical Computer Science, 128*(3), 35–45. doi:10.1016/j.entcs.2004.10.017

Overbeeke, C. J., & Hekkert, P. (Eds.). (1999). *Proceedings of the first international conference on Design and Emotion.* Delft: Department of Industrial Design.

Pagona, G., Fan, J., Maigne, A., Yudasaka, M., Iijima, S., & Tagmatarchis, N. (2007a). Aqueous carbon nanohorn–pyrene–porphyrin nanoensembles: Controlling charge-transfer interactions. *Diamond and Related Materials, 16,* 1150–1153. doi:10.1016/j.diamond.2006.11.071

Pagona, G., Fan, J., Tagmatarchis, N., Yudasaka, M., & Iijima, S. (2006a). Cone-end functionalization of carbon nanohorns. *Chemistry of Materials, 18,* 3918–3920. doi:10.1021/cm0604864

Pagona, G., Sandanayaka, A. S. D., Araki, Y., Fan, J., Tagmatarchis, N., & Charalambidis, G. et al. (2007b). Covalent functionalization of carbon nanohorns with porphyrins: Nanohybrid formation and photoinduced electron and energy transfer. *Advances in Functionalized Materials, 17,* 1705–1711. doi:10.1002/adfm.200700039

Pagona, G., Sandanayaka, A. S. D., Araki, Y., Fan, J., Tagmatarchis, N., & Yudasaka, M. et al. (2006b). Electronic interplay on illuminated aqueous carbon nanohorn–porphyrin ensembles. *The Journal of Physical Chemistry B, 110,* 20729–20732. doi:10.1021/jp064685m PMID:17048875

Panait, L., & Luke, S. (2005). Cooperative Multi-Agent Learning: The State of the Art. *Autonomous Agents and Multi-Agent Systems*, 11(3), 387–434. doi:10.1007/s10458-005-2631-2

Pandia, K., Inan, O. T., Kovacs, G. T. A., & Giovangrandi, L. (2012). Extracting respiratory information from seismocardiogram signals acquired on the chest using a miniature accelerometer. *Physiological Measurement*, 33(10), 1643–1660. doi:10.1088/0967-3334/33/10/1643 PMID:22986375

Panigrahi, M., & Nanda, S. (2006). A comparison between intuitionistic fuzzy sets and generalized intuitionistic fuzzy sets. *The Journal of Fuzzy Mathematics*, 14(2), 407–421.

Pao, H.-K., Chen, K.-T., & Chang, H.-C. (2010). Game Bot Detection via Avatar Trajectory Analysis. *IEEE Transactions on Computational Intelligence and AI in Games*, 2(3), 162–175. doi:10.1109/TCIAIG.2010.2072506

Papadakis, A. (2006). *D5 - As Is Analysis*. SAKE Project Documentation.

Park, D. G., Kwun, Y. C., Park, J. H., & Park, I. Y. (2009). Correlation coefficient of interval-valued intuitionistic fuzzy sets and its application to multiple attribute group decision making problems. *Mathematical and Computer Modelling*, 50, 1279–1293. doi:10.1016/j.mcm.2009.06.010

Parkhurst, D., Law, K., & Niebur, E. (2002). Modelling the role of salience in the allocation of overt visual attention. *Vision Research*, 42(1), 107–123. doi:10.1016/S0042-6989(01)00250-4 PMID:11804636

Passalis, G., Kakadiaris, I., & Theoharis, T. (2007). Intraclass retrieval of nonrigid 3D objects: application to face recognition. *IEEE Trans. PAMI*, 29(2), 218–229. doi:10.1109/TPAMI.2007.37 PMID:17170476

Paukkunen, M., Linnavuo, M., Haukilehto, H., & Sepponen, R. (2012). A system for detection of three-dimensional precordial vibrations.[IJMTIE]. *International Journal of Measurement Technologies and Instrumentation Engineering*, 2(1), 52–66. doi:10.4018/ijmtie.2012010104

Paukkunen, M., Linnavuo, M., & Sepponen, R. (2013). A portable measurement system for the superior-inferior axis of the seismocardiogram. *Journal of Bioengineering & Biomedical Science*, 3(1). doi: doi:10.4172/2155-9538.1000123

Paul, J., II. (1985). *Encyclical epistle slavorum apostoli of the supreme pontiff John Paul II to the bishops, priests and religious families and to all the Christian faithful in commemoration of the eleventh centenary of the evangelizing work of SAINTS CYRIL AND METHODIUS*. Retrieved March 27, 2013, from http://www.vatican.va/holy_father/john_paul_ii/encyclicals/documents/hf_jp-ii_enc_19850602_slavorum-apostoli_en.html

Pavlou, P. A., Liang, H., & Xue, Y. (2007). Understanding and mitigating uncertainty in online exchange relationships: A principal-agent perspective. *Management Information Systems Quarterly*, 31(1), 105–136.

Pearson, W. (2004). *MS Access for the business environment: stored procedures from the MS Access client*. Retrieved March 27, 2013, from http://www.databasejournal.com/features/msaccess/article.php/3363511

Penkov, B., Obretenov, A., Sendov, B., Kirpikova, T., & Joukanov, T. (1962). Frequencies of letters in written Bulgarian. *Acad. bulgare Sci.*, 15, 243–244.

Pernille, M (2004, March/April). Feature: Danish lessons on district heating. *Energy Resource Sustainable Management and Environmental*, 16-17.

Piepgrass, D. (2006). *The Asset Keyboard*. Retrieved March 27, 2013, from http://millikeys.sourceforge.net/asset

Pierpont, W. G. (1998). *The Art & Skill of Radio-Telegraphy* (2nd rev. ed.). Retrieved March 27, 2013, from http://www.zerobeat.net/tasrt/c28.htm

Pilke, E. M. (2004). Flow experience in information technology use. *International Journal of Human-Computer Studies*, 61(3), 347–357. doi:10.1016/j.ijhcs.2004.01.004

Pillosu, R. (2009). *Coordinating Agents with Behavior Trees: Synchronizing Multiple Agents in CryEngine 2*. Retrieved from AIGameDev.com

Pinto, N., Barhomi, Y., Cox, D., & DiCarlo, J. (2010). Comparing state-of-the-art visual features on invariant object recognition tasks. In *Proc. IEEE Workshop on Applications of Computer Vision*, (pp. 463-470). IEEE.

Plantevit, M., Charnois, T., Klema, J., Rigotti, C., & Cremilleux, B. (2009). Combining sequence and itemset mining to discover named entities in biomedical texts: a new type of pattern. *International Journal of Data Mining. Modelling and Management*, *1*(2), 119–148.

Pong, B. K., Trout, B. L., & Lee, J. Y. (2008). Modified ligand-exchange for efficient solubilization of CdSe/ZnS quantum dots in water: A procedure guided by computational studies. *Langmuir*, *24*, 5270–5276. doi:10.1021/la703431j PMID:18412382

Pradyumn, S. K. (2007). On the Normal Boundary Intersection Method for Generation of Efficient Front. In Y. Shi et al. (Eds.), *ICCS 2007, Part I, LNCS 4487* (pp. 310–317). Springer-Verlag Berlin Heidelberg.

Precision contouring control of machine tools. (2013). *The* International Journal of Advanced Manufacturing Technology, *64*(1-4), 319–333.

Prins, F., Monrabal-Capilla, M., Osorio, E. A., Coronado, E., & van der Zant, H. S. J. (2011). Room-temperature electrical addressing of a bistable spin-crossover molecular system. *Advanced Materials*, *23*, 1545–1549. doi:10.1002/adma.201003821 PMID:21449059

Prochaska, J. O., & DiClemente, C. C. (1986). Toward a comprehensive model of change. In W. R. Miller, & N. Heather (Eds.), *Treating addictive behaviors: processes of change* (pp. 3–27). New York: Plenum Press. doi:10.1007/978-1-4613-2191-0_1

Puzyn, T., Leszczynska, D., & Leszczynski, J. (2009). Toward the development of *nano-QSARs*: Advances and challenges. *Small*, *5*, 2494–2509. doi:10.1002/smll.200900179 PMID:19787675

Pylyshyn, Z. W., & Storm, R. W. (1988). Tracking multiple independent targets: Evidence for a parallel tracking mechanism. *Spatial Vision*, *3*(3), 179–197. doi:10.1163/156856888X00122 PMID:3153671

Quaresma, P. (2008). *Frequency analysis of the Portuguese language*. Centre for Informatics and Systems of University of Coimbra, TR 2008/003, ISSN 0874-338X.

Qu, B. Y., & Suganthan, P. N. (2010). Multi-objective evolutionary algorithms based on the summation of normalized objectives and diversified selection. *Information Sciences*, *180*, 3170–3181. doi:10.1016/j.ins.2010.05.013

Rahm, E., & Bernstein, P. A. (2001). A survey of approaches to automatic schema matching. *The VLDB Journal*, *10*, 334–350. doi:10.1007/s007780100057

Rahnamayan, S., Tizhoosh, H. R., & Salama, M. M. A. (2007). Quasi oppositional differential evolution. In *Proceeding of IEEE Congress on Evolutionary Computation CEC 2007*, (pp. 2229–2236). IEEE.

Rahnamayan, S., Tizhoosh, H. R., & Salama, M. M. A. (2008). Opposition versus randomness in soft computing techniques. *Applied Soft Computing*, *8*(2), 906–918. doi:10.1016/j.asoc.2007.07.010

Ramesh, S., Kannan, S., & Baskar, S. (2012). An improved generalized differential evolution algorithm for multi-objective reactive power dispatch. *Engineering Optimization*, *44* (4), 391-405.

Ramirez-Valdez, L., & Hasimoto-Beltran, R. (2009). 3D-facial expression synthesis and its application to face recognition systems. *J. of Applied Research and Technology*, *7*, 323–339.

Ramos-Castro, J., Moreno, J., Miranda-Vidal, H., Garcia-Gonzalez, M., Fernández-Chimeno, M., Rodas, G., & Capdevila, L. (2012). Heart rate variability analysis using a seismocardiogram signal. In *Proceedings of Engineering in Medicine and Biology Society (EMBC), 2012 Annual International Conference of the IEEE*, (pp. 5642-5645). IEEE.

Ranathunga, S., Cranefield, S., & Purvis, M. (2011). Interfacing a Cognitive Agent Platform with a Virtual World: a Case Study using Second Life. In *Proc. of the 10th International Conference on Autonomous Agents and Multiagent Systems*, (vol. 3, pp. 1181-1182). Academic Press.

Raphael, A. T. (2012). Energy and Climate Change: Critical reflection on the African Continent; Is There an Ideal REDD+ Program?. *An Analysis of Journal Sustainable Development in Africa*, *14*(6), 25–36.

Rashad, A., Hamdy, A., Saleh, M., & Eladawy, M. (2009). 3D face recognition using 2DPCA. Int. *J. of Computer Science and Network Security*, *9*(12), 149–155.

Rashedi, E., Nezamabadi-pour, H., & Saryazdi, S. (2009). GSA: A Gravitational Search Algorithm. *Information Sciences*, *179*, 2232–2248. doi:10.1016/j.ins.2009.03.004

Rees, W. E. (1999). The built environment and the ecosphere: a global perspective. *Building Research and Information*, *27*(4), 206–220. doi:10.1080/096132199369336

Reines, D., Conaway, R. C., & Conaway, J. W. (1999). Mechanism and regulation of transcriptional elongation by RNA polymerase II. *Current Opinion in Cell Biology*, *11*, 342–346. doi:10.1016/S0955-0674(99)80047-7 PMID:10395562

Reinhart, G., & Weissenberger, M. (1999). Multibody simulation of machine tools as mechatronic systems for optimization of motion dynamics in the design process. In *Proceedings of Advanced Intelligent Mechatronics*, (pp. 605-610). IEEE.

Riedl, M., & Young, R. (2005). *An Objective Character Believability Evaluation Procedure for Multi-Agent Story Generation Systems* (pp. 278–291). Intelligent Virtual Agents. doi:10.1007/11550617_24

Riege, A., & Lindsay, N. (2006). Knowledge management in the public sector: stakeholder partnerships in the public policy development. *Journal of Knowledge Management*, *10*(3), 24–39. doi:10.1108/13673270610670830

Rinner, C. (2003). Web-based Spatial Decision Support: Status and Research Directions. *Journal of Geographic Information and Decision Analysis*, *7*(1), 14–31.

Rinner, C., Keßler, C., & Andrulis, S. (2008). The Use of Web 2.0 Concepts to Support Deliberation in Spatial Decision-Making. *Computers, Environment and Urban Systems*, *32*(5), 386–395. doi:10.1016/j.compenvurbsys.2008.08.004

Robertson, J., & Good, J. (2005). Adventure Author: an Authoring Tool for 3D Virtual Reality Story Construction. In *Proceedings of AIED-05 Workshop on Narrative Learning Environments*, (pp. 63-69). Academic Press.

Robinson, J. P., & Amirtharaj, E. C. H. (2012b). A Search for the Correlation coefficient of Triangular and Trapezoidal intuitionistic Fuzzy sets for Multiple Attribute Group Decision Making. Communications in Computer and Information Science, 283, 333-342.

Robinson, J. P., & Amirtharaj, E. C. H. (2011a). A short primer on the Correlation coefficient of Vague sets. *International Journal of Fuzzy System Applications*, *1*(2), 55–69. doi:10.4018/ijfsa.2011040105

Robinson, J. P., & Amirtharaj, E. C. H. (2011b). Extended TOPSIS with correlation coefficient of Triangular Intuitionistic fuzzy sets for Multiple Attribute Group Decision Making. *International Journal of Decision Support System Technology*, *3*(3), 15–40. doi:10.4018/jdsst.2011070102

Robinson, J. P., & Amirtharaj, E. C. H. (2012a). Vague Correlation coefficient of Interval Vague sets. *International Journal of Fuzzy System Applications*, *2*(1), 18–34. doi:10.4018/ijfsa.2012010102

Robinson, J. P., & Amirtharaj, E. C. H. (in press). Efficient Multiple Attribute Group Decision Making models with Correlation coefficient of Vague sets. *International Journal of Operations Research and Information Systems*.

Rodrigues, J. M. F., & du Buf, J. M. H. (2011). A cortical framework for scene categorization. In *Proc. Int. Conf. on Computer Vision, Imaging and Computer Graphics - Theory and Applications*, (pp. 364-371). Academic Press.

Rodrigues, J. M. F., Martins, J., Lam, R., & du Buf, J. M. H. (2012b). Cortical multiscale line-edge disparity model. In *Proc. Int. Conf. on Image Analysis and Recognition* (LNCS) (vol. 7324, pp. 296-303). Berlin: Springer.

Rodrigues, J., & du Buf, J. M. H. (2004). Visual cortex frontend: integrating lines, edges, keypoints and disparity. In *Proc. Int. Conf. Image Anal. Recogn.* (LNCS) (Vol. 3211, pp. 664-671). Berlin: Springer.

Rodrigues, J. M. F., Lam, R., & du Buf, J. M. H. (2012a). Cortical 3D face and object recognition using 2D projections. *International Journal of Creative Interfaces and Computer Graphics*, *3*(1), 45–62. doi:10.4018/jcicg.2012010104

Rodrigues, J., & du Buf, J. M. H. (2006). Multi-scale keypoints in V1 and beyond: object segregation, scale selection, saliency maps and face detection. *Bio Systems*, *2*, 75–90. doi:10.1016/j.biosystems.2006.02.019 PMID:16870327

Rodrigues, J., & du Buf, J. M. H. (2009a). Multi-scale lines and edges in V1 and beyond: brightness, object categorization and recognition, and consciousness. *Bio Systems*, *95*, 206–226. doi:10.1016/j.biosystems.2008.10.006 PMID:19026712

Rodrigues, J., & du Buf, J. M. H. (2009b). A cortical framework for invariant object categorization and recognition. *Cognitive Processing*, *10*(3), 243–261. doi:10.1007/s10339-009-0262-2 PMID:19471984

Roriz, L (2001). *Determining the potential energy and environmental effects reduction of air conditioning systems.* Commission of the European Communities DG TREN.

Ros, R., Veloso, M., de Mántaras, R., Sierra, C., & Arcos, J. (2007). Beyond Individualism: Modeling Team Playing Behavior. *Proc. of the National Conference on Artificial Intelligence*, *22*(2), 1671-1674.

Roscoe, J. T. (1975). *Fundamental research statistics for the behavioural sciences* (2nd ed.). New York: Holt, Rinehart and Winston.

Roseman, I. J., & Smith, G. A. (2001). Appraisal theory: Overview, assumptions, varieties, controversies. In K. R. Scherer, A. Schorr, & T. Johnstone (Eds.), *Appraisal processes in emotion: Theory, methods, research (Series in affective science)* (pp. 3–19). New York, NY: Oxford University Press.

Roy, P. K., Ghoshal, S. P., & Thakur, S. S. (2010). Biogeography based optimization for multi-constraints optimal power flow with emission and non-smooth cost function. *Expert Systems with Applications*, *37*(12), 8221–8228. doi:10.1016/j.eswa.2010.05.064

Roy, P. K., Ghoshal, S. P., & Thakur, S. S. (2010). Biogeography-based Optimization for economic load dispatch problems. *Electric Power Components and Systems*, *38*(2), 166–181. doi:10.1080/15325000903273379

Roy, P. K., Ghoshal, S. P., & Thakur, S. S. (2012). Optimal VAR control for improvements in voltage profiles and for real power loss minimization using Biogeography Based Optimization. *International Journal of Electrical Power & Energy Systems*, *43*, 830–838. doi:10.1016/j.ijepes.2012.05.032

Rubio, A., Corkill, J. L., & Cohen, M. L. (1994). Theory of graphitic boron nitride nanotubes. *Physical Review B: Condensed Matter and Materials Physics*, *49*, 5081–5084. doi:10.1103/PhysRevB.49.5081 PMID:10011453

Rugar, D., Mamin, H. J., Guethner, P., Lambert, S. E., Stern, J. E., McFadyen, I., & Yogi, T. (1990). Magnetic force microscopy: General principles and application to longitudinal recording media. *Journal of Applied Physics*, *68*, 1169–1183. doi:10.1063/1.346713

Salerno, D. M., & Zanetti, J. (1991). Seismocardiography for monitoring changes in left ventricular function during ischemia. *Chest*, *100*(4), 991–993. doi:10.1378/chest.100.4.991 PMID:1914618

Salerno, D. M., Zanetti, J. M., Green, L. A., Mooney, M. R., Madison, J. D., & Van Tassel, R. A. (1991). Seismocardiographic changes associated with obstruction of coronary blood flow during balloon angioplasty. *The American Journal of Cardiology*, *68*(2), 201–207. doi:10.1016/0002-9149(91)90744-6 PMID:2063782

Salerno, D., & Zanetti, J. (1990). Seismocardiography: A new technique for recording cardiac vibrations. concept, method, and initial observations. *Journal of Cardiovascular Technology*, *9*(2), 111–118.

Samiotis, K. (Ed.). (2009) *D28 Evaluation Report.* SAKE Project Documentation.

Sánchez-Crespo Dalmau, D. (2005, March). Postcard from GDC 2005: Tutorial — Machine Learning. *Gamasutra, 8.*

Sandbach, G., Zafeiriou, S., Pantic, M., & Yin, L. (2012). Static and dynamic 3D facial expression recognition: A comprehensive survey. *Image and Vision Computing*, *30*(10), 683–697. doi:10.1016/j.imavis.2012.06.005

Sandgren, E. (1994). Multicriteria design optimization by goal programming. In H. Adeli (Ed.), *Advances in Design Optimization* (pp. 225–265). London: Chapman & Hall.

Saraswat, A., & Saini, A. (2013). Multi-objective optimal reactive power dispatch considering voltage stability in power systems using HFMOEA. *Engineering Applications of Artificial Intelligence, 26*, 390–404. doi:10.1016/j.engappai.2012.06.008

Sarawagi, S., & Bhamidipaty, A. (2002). Interactive deduplication using active learning. In *Proceedings of the eighth international conference on Knowledge discovery and data mining*, (pp. 269-278). Academic Press.

Sastry1, K., Johnson, D. D., Thompson, A. L., Goldberg, D. E., Martinez, T. J., Leiding, J., & Owens, J. (2007). Optimization of Semiempirical Quantum Chemistry Methods via Multiobjective Genetic Algorithms: Accurate Photodynamics for Larger Molecules and Longer Time Scales. *Materials and Manufacturing Processes, 22*(5), 553–561.

Sato, R. (2012). Mathematical Model of a CNC Rotary Table Driven by a Worm Gear.[IJIMR]. *International Journal of Intelligent Mechatronics and Robotics, 2*(4), 27–40. doi:10.4018/ijimr.2012100103

Scaiano, J. C., Stamplecoskie, K. G., & Hallett-Tapley, G. L. (2012). Photochemical Norrish type I reaction as a tool for metal nanoparticle synthesis: Importance of proton coupled electron transfer. *Chemical Communications, 48*, 4798–4808. doi:10.1039/c2cc30615h PMID:22498952

Schellman, J. A. (1975). Macromolecular binding. *Biopolymers, 14*, 999–1018. doi:10.1002/bip.1975.360140509

Schreiber, G. (2000). *Knowledge Engineering and Management, The CommonKADS Methodology*. The MIT Press.

Schrum, J., Karpov, I., & Miikkulainen, R. (2011). UT²: Human-like Behavior via Neuroevolution of Combat Behavior and Replay of Human Traces. In *Proc. of IEEE Conference on Computational Intelligence and Games*, (pp. 329-336). IEEE.

Schwarzenbach, G. (1952). Der chelateffekt. *Helvetica Chimica Acta, 35*, 2344–2359. doi:10.1002/hlca.19520350721

Shanthi, S., & Priya, K. S. (2012). Photo degradation of dyes from their aqueous solutions of their binary mixture, using TiO_2 as the oxidant with different sources of energy. *Journal of Chemistry & Chemical Engineering, 6*, 951–955.

Sharma, P. K. (2011). (α,β) cut for intuitionistic fuzzy groups. *International Mathematical Forum, 6*(53), 2605–2614.

Shaviv, E. (1989). The influence of the thermal mass on the thermal performance of buildings in summer and winter. In T. C. Steemers, & W. Palz (Eds.), *Science and Technology at the service of architecture* (pp. 470–472). Dordrecht: Kluwer Academic Publishers.

Shevchenko, V. Y., Madison, A. E., & Shudegov, V. E. (2003). The structural diversity of the nanoworld. *Glass Physics and Chemistry, 29*, 577–582. doi:10.1023/B:GPAC.0000007934.93203.f3

Shilatifard, A., Conaway, J. W., & Conaway, R. C. (1997). Mechanism and regulation of transcriptional elongation and termination by RNA polymerase II. *Current Opinion in Genetics & Development, 7*, 199–204. doi:10.1016/S0959-437X(97)80129-3 PMID:9115429

Shiller, R. J. (2008). *The Subprime Solution*. Princetown University Press.

Shukla, D., Ahearn, W. G., & Farid, S. (2005). Chain amplification in photoreactions of *N*-alkoxypyridinium salts with alcohols: Mechanism and kinetics. *The Journal of Organic Chemistry, 70*, 6809–6819. doi:10.1021/jo050726j PMID:16095300

Shukla, D., Ahearn, W. G., & Farid, S. (2006). Enhancement of chain amplification in photoreactions of *N*-methoxypyridinium salts with alcohols. *Photochemistry and Photobiology, 82*, 146–151. doi:10.1562/2005-06-28-RA-594 PMID:16178662

Siekpe, J. S. (2005). An examination of the multidimensionality of the flow construct in a computer-mediated environment. *Journal of Electronic Commerce Research, 6*(1), 31–43.

Sigurd, B. (1968). Rank-frequency distributions for phonemes. *Phonetica*, *18*, 1–15. doi:10.1159/000258595

Sigurd, B., Eeg-Olofsson, M., & Weijer, J. (2004). Word length, sentence length and frequency-Zipf revisited. *Studia Linguistica*, *58*(1), 37–52. doi:10.1111/j.0039-3193.2004.00109.x

Silaghi-Dumitrescu, I., Haiduc, I., & Sowerby, D. B. (1993). Fully inorganic (carbon-free) fullerenes? The boron-nitrogen case. *Inorganic Chemistry*, *32*, 3755–3758. doi:10.1021/ic00069a034

Simon, S. (2008). *Definitions of correlation. Children's Mercy*. Retrieved February 9, 2014, from http://www.childrens-mercy.org/stats/definitions/correlation.htm.

Simon, D. (2008). Biogeography-based optimization. *IEEE Transactions on Evolutionary Computation*, *12*(6), 702–713. doi:10.1109/TEVC.2008.919004

Simov, K., Peev, Z., Kouylekov, M., Simov, A., Dimitrov, M., & Kiryakov, A. (2001). CLaRK – An XML-based system for corpora development. In *Proceedings of the Conference on Corpus Linguistics* (pp. 558-560). Academic Press.

Singh, J. (2000). *On farm energy use pattern in different cropping systems in Haryana, India*. Germany: International Institute of Management-University of Flensburg, Sustainable Energy Systems and Management, Master of Science.

Sitarz, D. (1992). *Agenda 21: The Earth Summit Strategy to save our planet*. Boulder, CO: Earth Press.

Sivkov, S. I. (1964). On the computation of the possible and relative duration of sunshine. *Trans. Main Geophys Obs*, *160*, 1964.

Sivkov, S. I. (1964). To the methods of computing possible radiation in Italy. *Trans. Main Geophys. Obs.*, *1964*, 160.

Skordev, D. (2007). *Some consideration in relation with the Bulgarian keyboard layouts*. Retrieved March 27, 2013, from http://www.fmi.uni-sofia.bg/fmi/logic/skordev/bg_layouts0.htm

Sledgianowski, D., & Kulviwat, S. (2009). Using social network sites: The effects of playfulness, critical mass and trust in a hedonic context. *Journal of Computer Information Systems*, *49*(4), 74–83.

Smeets, D., Claes, P., Vandermeulen, D., & Clement, J. (2010). Objective 3D face recognition: Evolution, approaches and challenges. *Forensic Science International*, *1-3*, 125–132. doi:10.1016/j.forsciint.2010.03.023 PMID:20395086

Smith, M., Lee-Urban, S., & Munoz-Avila, H. (2007). RETALIATE: Learning Winning Policies in First-person Shooter Games. In *Proc. of the National Conference on Artificial Intelligence*, (pp. 1801-1806). Academic Press.

Smith, R. (2012). Distinct word length frequencies: distributions and symbol entropies. *Glottometrics*, *23*, 7–22.

Socialbakers. (2013). *Malaysia Facebook statistics*. Retrieved January 2, 2014 from http://www.socialbakers.com/facebook-statistics/malaysia.

Soler, E.M., Asada, E.N., & Costa, G.R.M .(2013). *Penalty-Based Nonlinear Solver for Optimal Reactive Power Dispatch With Discrete Controls*.IEEE Transactions on Power Systems

Soni, B., & Hingston, P. (2008). Bots Trained to Play Like a Human are More Fun. In *Proceedings ofIEEE International Joint Conference on Neural Networks*, (pp. 363-369). IEEE.

Soror, A. A., Minhas, U. F., Aboulnaga, A., & Salem, K. Kokosielis, & P., Kamath, S. (2008). Automatic Virtual Machine Configuration for Database Workloads. In Proceedings of ACM SIGMOD 2008. ACM.

Sousa, R., Rodrigues, J. M. F., & du Buf, J. M. H. (2010) Recognition of facial expressions by cortical multi-scale line and edge coding. In *Proc. Int. Conf. on Image Analysis and Recognition*, (vol. 1, pp. 415-424). Academic Press.

Spronck, P., Ponsen, M., Sprinkhuizen-Kuyper, I., & Postma, E. (2006). Adaptive Game AI with Dynamic Scripting. *Machine Learning*, *63*, 217–248. doi:10.1007/s10994-006-6205-6

Stamplecoskie, K. G., Fasciani, C., & Scaiano, J. C. (2012). Dual-stage lithography from a light-driven, plasmon-assisted process: A hierarchical approach to subwavelength features. *Langmuir*, *28*, 10957–10961. doi:10.1021/la301728r PMID:22803690

Stamplecoskie, K. G., Pacioni, N. L., Larson, D., & Scaiano, J. C. (2011). Plasmon-mediated photopolymerization maps plasmon fields for silver nanoparticles. *Journal of the American Chemical Society*, *133*, 9160–9163. doi:10.1021/ja201139z PMID:21615121

Stamplecoskie, K. G., & Scaiano, J. C. (2010). Light emitting diode irradiation can control the morphology and optical properties of silver nanoparticles. *Journal of the American Chemical Society*, *132*, 1825–1827. doi:10.1021/ja910010b PMID:20102152

Starr, I., Rawson, A., Schroeder, H., & Joseph, N. (1939). Studies on the estimation of cardiac ouptut in man, and of abnormalities in cardiac function, from the heart's recoil and the blood's impacts, the ballistocardiogram. *American Journal of Physiology: Legacy Content*, *127*(1), 1-28.

Starr, I., & Wood, F. C. (1961). Twenty-year studies with the ballistocardiograph: The relation between the amplitude of the first record of "healthy" adults and eventual mortality and morbidity from heart disease. *Circulation*, *23*(5), 714–732. doi:10.1161/01.CIR.23.5.714

Statnikov, R. B., & Matusov, J.B. (1995). Multicriteria Optimization and Engineering. New York: Chapman and Hall.

Steele, J. (1997). *Sustainable architecture: principles, paradigms, and case studies*. New York: McGraw-Hill Inc.

Stefanov, B., & Birdanova, V. (1997). Hygienic-ergonomic evaluation of the computer keyboard layouts. *Computer*, *2*, 56–62.

Stinson, D. (2006). *Cryptography: theory and practice*. CRC Press.

Stojanovic, N., Apostolou, D., Dioudis, S., Gábor, A., Kovács, B., Kő A., … Kasprzycki, J. (2008). *D24 – Integration plan*. SAKE Project Documentation.

Stojanovic, N., Kovács, B, Kő, A., Papadakis, A., Apostolou, D., Dioudis, D., Gabor, A., … Kasprzycki, J. (2007). *D16B – 1st Iteration Prototype of Semantic-based Content Management System*. SAKE Project Documentation.

Stone, P., Kaminka, G., Kraus, S., & Rosenschein, J. (2010). Ad Hoc Autonomous Agent Teams: Collaboration without Pre-Coordination. In *Proc. of the 24th AAAI Conference on Artificial Intelligence*, (pp. 1504-1509). AAAI.

Stork, M., & Trefny, Z. (2010). *Quantitative seismocardiography system with separate QRS detection*. Academic Press.

Storn, R., & Price, K. V. (1995). *Differential evolution – A simple and efficient adaptive scheme for global optimization over continuous spaces* (Technical Report TR-95-012). ICSI.

Strauss, J. (2013). Does housing drive state-level job growth? Building permits andconsumer expectations forecast a state's economic activity. *Journal of Urban Economics*, *73*, 77–65. doi:10.1016/j.jue.2012.07.005

Strebel, P. (1996). Why Do Employees Resist Change? *Harvard Business Review*, (May-June), 86–92.

Su, T., Lin, C., Lin, P., & Hu, J. (2006). Shape memorization and recognition of 3D objects using a similarity-based aspect-graph approach. In *Proc. IEEE Int. Conf. on Systems, Man, and Cybernetics*, (pp. 4920-4925). IEEE.

Sudholta, W., Baldridgea, K. K., Abramson, D., Enticott, C., Garic, S., Kondric, C., & Nguyen, D. (2005). Application of grid computing to parameter sweeps and optimizations in molecular modelling. *Future Generation Computer Systems*, *21*(1), 27–35. doi:10.1016/j.future.2004.09.010

Sugumaran, R., & DeGroote, J. (2011). Spatial Decision Support Systems: Principles and Practices. Boca Raton, FL: CRC Press, Taylor & Francis.

Sugumaran, V., & Sugumaran, R. (2007). Web-based Spatial Decision Support Systems (WebSDSS): Evolution, Architecture, Examples and Challenges. *Communications of the Association for Information Systems*, *19*, 40.

Sutjipto, A. G. E., Muhida, R., & Konneh, M. (2011). Virtual simulation and remote desktop interface for CNC milling operation. *Advanced Materials Research*, *264*, 1643-1647.

Swarup, K. S., Yoshimi, M., & Izui, Y. (1994). Genetic algorithm approach to reactive power planning in power systems. In *Proceedings of the 5th Annual Conference of Power and Energy Society*. IEE.

Sweetser, P., & Wyeth, P. (2005). *GameFlow: a Model for Evaluating Player Enjoyment in Games*(Vol. 3, p. 3). Computers in Entertainment.

Taatgen, N., van Oploo, M., Braaksma, J., & Niemantsverdriet, J. (2003). How to Construct a Believable Opponent using Cognitive Modeling in the Game of Set. In *Proc. of the 5th International Conference on Cognitive Modeling*, (pp. 201-206). Academic Press.

Tagmatarchis, N., Maigne, A., Yudasaka, M., & Iijima, S. (2006). Functionalization of carbon nanohorns with azomethine ylides: Towards solubility enhancement and electron-transfer processes. *Small*, *2*, 490–494. doi:10.1002/smll.200500393 PMID:17193072

Tailor, D., Finkel, L., & Buchsbaum, G. (2000). Color-opponent receptive fields derived from independent component analysis of natural images. *Vision Research*, *40*(19), 2671–2676. doi:10.1016/S0042-6989(00)00105-X PMID:10958917

Takezawa, N., & Fukushima, K. (1994). Optimal size of a cylindrical insulating inclusion acting as a pinning center for magnetic flux in superconductors. *Physica. C, Superconductivity*, *228*, 149–159. doi:10.1016/0921-4534(94)90186-4

Takezawa, N., & Fukushima, K. (1997). Optimal size of an insulating inclusion acting as a pinning center for magnetic flux in superconductors: Calculation of pinning force. *Physica. C, Superconductivity*, *290*, 31–37. doi:10.1016/S0921-4534(97)01574-8

Tambovtsev, Y., & Martindale, C. (2007). Phoneme Frequencies Follow a Yule Distribution. *SKASE Journal of Theoretical Linguistics*, *4*(2), 1–11.

Tamiz, M. (1996). *Multi-objective programming and goal programming: Theories and multicriteria design optimization*. Berlin: Springer-Verlag. doi:10.1007/978-3-642-87561-8

Tamura, R., & Tsukada, M. (1995). Electronic states of the cap structure in the carbon nanotube. *Physical Review B: Condensed Matter and Materials Physics*, *52*, 6015–6026. doi:10.1103/PhysRevB.52.6015 PMID:9981793

Tan, C. F., Singh, R. S., & Kher, V. K. (2012). An expert carbide cutting tools selection system for CNC Lathe machine. *International Review of Mechanical Engineering*, *6*(7), 1402-1405.

Tangelder, J., & Veltkamp, R. (2008). A survey of content based 3D shape retrieval methods. *Multimedia Tools and Applications*, *39*, 441–471. doi:10.1007/s11042-007-0181-0

Tavakolian, K., Blaber, A. P., Ngai, B., & Kaminska, B. (2010). Estimation of hemodynamic parameters from seismocardiogram. In *Proceedings of the Computing in Cardiology*, (pp. 1055-1058). Academic Press.

Tavakolian, K., Khosrow-Khavar, F., Kajbafzadeh, B., Marzencki, M., Rohani, S., Kaminska, B., & Menon, C. (2012b). Seismocardiographic adjustment of diastolic timed vibrations. In *Proceedings of Engineering in Medicine and Biology Society (EMBC), 2012 Annual International Conference of the IEEE*, (pp. 3797-3800). IEEE.

Tavakolian, K., Ngai, B., Blaber, A. P., & Kaminska, B. (2011). Infrasonic cardiac signals: Complementary windows to cardiovascular dynamics. In *Proceedings of Engineering in Medicine and Biology Society*. IEEE.

Tavakolian, K., Portacio, G., Tamddondoust, N. R., Jahns, G., Ngai, B., Dumont, G. A., & Blaber, A. P. (2012a). Myocardial contractility: A seismocardiography approach. In *Proceedings of Engineering in Medicine and Biology Society (EMBC), 2012 Annual International Conference of the IEEE*, (pp. 3801-3804). IEEE.

Tavakolian, K., Khosrow-Khavar, F., Kajbafzadeh, B., Marzencki, M., Blaber, A., Kaminska, B., & Menon, C. (2013). Precordial acceleration signals improve the performance of diastolic timed vibrations. *Medical Engineering & Physics*, *35*(8), 1133–1140. doi:10.1016/j.medengphy.2012.12.001 PMID:23291107

Tavakolian, K., Vaseghi, A., & Kaminska, B. (2008). Improvement of ballistocardiogram processing by inclusion of respiration information. *Physiological Measurement*, *29*, 771–781. doi:10.1088/0967-3334/29/7/006 PMID:18560054

Tencé, F., & Buche, C. (2008). Automatable Evaluation Method Oriented toward Behaviour Believability for Video Games. In *Proceedings of International Conference on Intelligent Games and Simulation*, (pp. 39-43). Academic Press.

Tenne, R., Margulis, L., Genut, M., & Hodes, G. (1992). Polyhedral and cylindrical structures of tungsten disulphide. *Nature, 360*, 444–446. doi:10.1038/360444a0

Tenne, R., & Redlich, M. (2010). Recent progress in the research of inorganic fullerene-like nanoparticles and inorganic nanotubes. *Chemical Society Reviews, 39*, 1423–1434. doi:10.1039/b901466g PMID:20419198

Terauchi, M., Tanaka, M., Suzuki, K., Ogino, A., & Kimura, K. (2000). Production of zigzag-type BN nanotubes and BN cones by thermal annealing. *Chemical Physics Letters, 324*, 359–364. doi:10.1016/S0009-2614(00)00637-0

Teresawa, M., Takezawa, N., Fukushima, K., Mitamura, T., Fan, X., & Tsubakino, H. et al. (1998). Flux pinning and flux creep in $La_{2-x}Sr_xCuO_4$ with splayed columnar defects. *Physica. C, Superconductivity, 296*, 57–64. doi:10.1016/S0921-4534(97)01822-4

Terrones, M., Benito, A. M., Manteca-Diego, C., Hsu, W. K., Osman, O. I., & Hare, J. P. et al. (1996). Pyrolytically grown $B_xC_yN_z$ nanomaterials: Nanofibres and nanotubes. *Chemical Physics Letters, 257*, 576–582. doi:10.1016/0009-2614(96)00594-5

Terzić, K., Rodrigues, J. M. F., & du Buf, J. M. H. (2013a). Real-Time object recognition based on cortical multi-scale keypoints. In J. Sanches, L. Micó, & J. Cardoso (Eds.), Pattern Recognition and Image Analysis SE - 37 (Vol. 7887, pp. 314–321). Berlin: Springer. doi:doi:10.1007/978-3-642-38628-2_37 doi:10.1007/978-3-642-38628-2_37

Terzić, K., Rodrigues, J. M. F., & du Buf, J. M. H. (2013b). Fast cortical keypoints for real-time object recognition. In *Proc. IEEE Int. Conf. on Image Processing*, (pp. 3372-3376). IEEE.

Thakur, C., & Mistra, B. (1993). Energy requirements and energy gaps for production of major crops in India. *Agricultural Situation of India, 48*, 665–689.

Thatipamala, R., Rohani, S., & Hill, G. A. (1992). Effects of high product and substrate inhibitions on the kinetics and biomass and product yields during ethanol batch fermentation. *Biotechnology and Bioengineering, 40*(2), 289–297. doi:10.1002/bit.260400213 PMID:18601115

The United Nations Framework Convention on Climate Change (UNFCCC). (2009). The draft of the Copenhagen Climate Change Treaty (pp. 3–181). Author.

Thesing, L. A., Piquini, P., & Kar, T. (2006). Theoretical investigation on the stability and properties of III-nitride nanotubes: BN-AlN junction. *Nanotechnology, 17*, 1637–1641. doi:10.1088/0957-4484/17/6/016

Thomsen, R. (2008). *Elements in the validation process*. Retrieved 05.03.2008, from http://www.nordvux.net/page/481/cases.htm

Thurau, C., Bauckhage, C., & Sagerer, G. (2004). Learning Human-like Movement Behavior for Computer Games. In *Proc. of the 8th International Conference on the Simulation of Adaptive Behavior (SAB'04)*. SAB.

Tilborg, H. C. A. (2000). *Fundamentals of cryptology*. Kluwer Academy Publisher.

Tindle, J., Ginty, K., & Tindle, S. J. (2009) Rendering 3D Computer Graphics on a Parallel Computer. In *Proceedings of International Conference on Systems Engineering (ICSE)*. Coventry University.

Tindle, J., Gray, M., Warrender, R. L., Ginty, K., & Dawson, P. K. D. (2012). Application Framework for Computational Chemistry (AFCC) Applied to New Drug Discovery. *International Journal of Grid and High Performance Computing, 4*(2), 46–62. doi:10.4018/jghpc.2012040104

Tizhoosh, H. (2005). Opposition-based learning: A new scheme for machine intelligence. In *Proceedings of the International Conference on Computational Intelligence for Modelling Control and Automation (CIMCA-2005)*. Vienna, Austria: CIMCA.

Torrens, F., & Castellano, G. (2013b). Bundlet model of single-wall carbon, BC_2N and BN nanotubes, cones and horns in organic solvents. *Journal of Nanomaterials & Molecular Nanotechnology, 2*, 1000107-1-9.

Torrens, F., & Castellano, G. (2005). Cluster origin of the solubility of single-wall carbon nanotubes. *Computing Letters*, *1*, 331–336. doi:10.1163/157404005776611303

Torrens, F., & Castellano, G. (2007a). Cluster nature of the solvation features of single-wall carbon nanotubes. *Current Research in Nanotechnology*, *1*, 1–29.

Torrens, F., & Castellano, G. (2007b). Effect of packing on the cluster nature of C nanotubes: An information entropy analysis. *Microelectronics Journal*, *38*, 1109–1122. doi:10.1016/j.mejo.2006.04.004

Torrens, F., & Castellano, G. (2007c). Cluster origin of the transfer phenomena of single-wall carbon nanotubes. *Journal of Computational and Theoretical Nanoscience*, *4*, 588–603.

Torrens, F., & Castellano, G. (2007d). Asymptotic analysis of coagulation–fragmentation equations of carbon nanotube clusters. *Nanoscale Research Letters*, *2*, 337–349. doi:10.1007/s11671-007-9070-8

Torrens, F., & Castellano, G. (2010). Cluster nature of the solvent features of single-wall carbon nanohorns. *International Journal of Quantum Chemistry*, *110*, 563–570. doi:10.1002/qua.22054

Torrens, F., & Castellano, G. (2011). (Co-)solvent selection for single-wall carbon nanotubes: *Best* solvents, acids, superacids and guest–host inclusion complexes. *Nanoscale*, *3*, 2494–2510. doi:10.1039/c0nr00922a PMID:21331393

Torrens, F., & Castellano, G. (2012). *Bundlet* model for single-wall carbon nanotubes, nanocones and nanohorns. *International Journal of Chemoinformatics and Chemical Engineering*, *2*(1), 48–98. doi:10.4018/IJCCE.2012010105

Torrens, F., & Castellano, G. (2013a). Solvent features of cluster single-wall C, BC_2N and BN nanotubes, cones and horns. *Microelectronic Engineering*, *108*, 127–133. doi:10.1016/j.mee.2013.02.046

Trefný, Z., Svačinka, J., Kittnar, O., Slavíček, J., Trefný, M., Filatova, E., . . . Loučka, M. (2011). Quantitative ballistocardiography (Q-BCG) for measurement of cardiovascular dynamics. *Academia Scientiarum Bohemoslovaca, 60*(4), 617.

Triantaphyllou, E. (2000). *Multi-Criteria Decision Making: A Comparative Study*. Dordrecht, The Netherlands: Kluwer Academic Publishers.

Trifonov, T., & Georgieva-Trifonova, T. (2012). Research on letter and word frequency in the modern Bulgarian language. *International Journal of Knowledge-Based Organizations*, *2*(3), 74–90. doi:10.4018/ijkbo.2012070105

Tseng, A. A., Kolluri, S. P., & Radhakrishnan, P. (1989). A CNC machining system for education. *Journal of Manufacturing Systems*, *8*(3), 207–214. doi:10.1016/0278-6125(89)90042-3

Tsohou, A., Lee, H., Al-Yafi, K., Weerakkody, V., El-Haddadeh, R., & Irani, Z. et al. (2012). Supporting Public Policy Making Processes with Workflow Technology: Lessons Learned From Cases in Four European Countries. *International Journal of Electronic Government Research*, *8*(3), 63–77. doi:10.4018/jegr.2012070104

Tukahirwa, J. T. (2013). Comparing urban sanitation and solid waste management in East African metropolises: The role of civil society organisations. *Cities (London, England)*, *30*, 204–211. doi:10.1016/j.cities.2012.03.007

Turing, A. (1950). Computing Machinery and Intelligence. *Mind*, *59*, 433. doi:10.1093/mind/LIX.236.433

Tuttle, R., Little, G., Corney, J., & Clark, D. E. R. (1998). Feature recognition for NC part programming. *Computers in Industry*, *35*(3), 275–289. doi:10.1016/S0166-3615(97)00089-4

United Nations (UN). (2003). World urbanisation project: the 2002 revision. New York: The United Nations Population Division.

Uptain, S. M., Kane, C. M., & Chamberlin, M. J. (1997). Basic mechanisms of transcript elongation and its regulation. *Annual Review of Biochemistry*, *66*, 117–172. doi:10.1146/annurev.biochem.66.1.117 PMID:9242904

Valentin, D., Abdi, H., & Edelman, B. (1997). What represents a face? A computational approach for the integration of physiological and psychological data. *Perception*, *26*(10), 1271–1288. doi:10.1068/p261271 PMID:9604063

Valkila, N., & Saari, A. (2012). Perceptions Held by Finnish Energy Sector Experts Regarding Public Attitudes to Energy Issues. *J. Sustainable Dev.*, *5*(11), 23–45.

Valmari, A. (1998). The State Explosion Problem. Lectures on Petri Nets I: Basic Models, 1491, 429–528.

Valvo, E. L., Licari, R., & Adornetto, A. (2012). CNC milling machine simulation in engineering education. *International Journal of Online Engineering, 8*(2), 33-38.

van der Heijden, M., Bakkes, S., & Spronck, P. (2008). Dynamic Formations in Real-Time Strategy Games. In *Proceedings of IEEE Symposium on Computational Intelligence and Games*, (pp. 47-54). IEEE.

Vance, A., Christophe, E. D. C., & Straub, D. W. (2008). Examining trust in information technology artefacts: The effects of system quality and culture. *Journal of Management Information Systems, 24*(4), 73–100. doi:10.2753/MIS0742-1222240403

Varadarajan, M., & Swarup, K. S. (2008). Differential evolution approach for optimal reactive power dispatch. *Applied Soft Computing, 8*, 1549–1561. doi:10.1016/j.asoc.2007.12.002

Vargas-Parra, M. V. (2013). Applying exergy analysis to rainwater harvesting systems to assess resource efficiency. *Resources, Conservation and Recycling, 72*, 50–59. doi:10.1016/j.resconrec.2012.12.008

Vasant, P., Ganesan, T., & Elamvazuthi, I. (2012). Hybrid tabu search Hopfield recurrent ANN fuzzy technique to the production planning problems: a case study of crude oil in refinery industry. *International Journal of Manufacturing, Materials, and Mechanical Engineering, 2*(1), 47 - 65.

Vazov, I. (1999). Under the yoke. *Slovoto*. Retrieved March 27, 2013, from http://www.slovo.bg/showwork.php3?AuID=14&WorkID=5778&Level=1

Veltkamp, R. C., Giezeman, G. J., Bast, H., Baumbach, T., Furuya, T., Giesen, J., et al. (2010) Shrec 2010 track: Large scale retrieval. In *Proc. Eurographics/ACM SIGGRAPH Symp. on 3D Object Retrieval* (pp. 63–69). ACM.

Venuvinod, P. K., & Ma, W. (2004). *Rapid prototyping: Laser-based & other technologies*. Boston, MA: Kluwer Academic. doi:10.1007/978-1-4757-6361-4

Vescoukis, V., Doulamis, N., & Karagiorgou, S. (2012). A service-oriented architecture for decision support systems in environmental crisis management. *Future Generation Computer Systems, 28*, 593–604. doi:10.1016/j.future.2011.03.010

Vigne, R., Mangler, J., Schikuta, E., & Rinderle-Ma, S. (2012). A structured marketplace for arbitrary services. *Future Generation Computer Systems, 28*, 48–57. doi:10.1016/j.future.2011.05.024

Vinter, J. G., Davis, A., & Saunders, M. R. (1987). Strategic approaches to drug design. An integrated software framework for molecular modelling. *Journal of Computer-Aided Molecular Design, 1*(1), 31–51. doi:10.1007/BF01680556 PMID:3505586

Vlachogiannis, J. G., & Lee, K. Y. (2006). A comparative study on particle swarm optimization for optimal steady-state performance of power systems. *IEEE Transactions on Power Systems, 21*(4), 1718–1728. doi:10.1109/TPWRS.2006.883687

Vogt, E., MacQuarrie, D., & Neary, J. P. (2012). Using ballistocardiography to measure cardiac performance: A brief review of its history and future significance. *Clinical Physiology and Functional Imaging*. doi:10.1111/j.1475-097X.2012.01150.x PMID:23031061

Wadhavane, P. D., Galian, R. E., Izquierdo, M. A., Aguilera-Sigalat, J., Galindo, F., & Schmidt, L. et al. (2012). Photoluminiscence enhancement of CdSe quantum dots: A case of organogel–nanoparticle symbiosis. *Journal of the American Chemical Society, 134*, 20554–20563. doi:10.1021/ja310508r PMID:23214451

Wang, B. F. (2011). Research and development of embedded CNC system for drilling based on ARM. *Advanced Materials Research, 291*, 2733-2736.

Wang, C. S., Wiegers, T. & Vergeest, J. S. (2011). An implementation of intelligent CNC machine tools. *Applied Mechanics and Materials, 44*, 557-561.

Wang, H., Shen, C., & Ritterfeld, U. (2009). Enjoyment of Digital Games. In U. Ritterfeld, M. Cody, & P. Vorderer (Eds.), Serious Games: Mechanisms and Effects (pp. 25–47). Academic Press.

Wang, L., & Cheng, Q. (2006). Web-Based Collaborative Decision Support Services: Concept, Challenges and Application. In *Proceedings of the ISPRS Symposium*. ISPRS.

Wang, G., & Li, X. (1999). Correlation of information energy of interval valued fuzzy numbers. *Fuzzy Sets and Systems*, *103*, 169–175. doi:10.1016/S0165-0114(97)00303-5

Wang, J. Q. (2006). Multi-criteria interval intuitionistic fuzzy decision making approach with incomplete certain information. *Control and Decision*, *11*, 1253–1256.

Wang, J., Zhang, J., & Liu, S.-Y. (2006). A new score function for Fuzzy MCDM based on Vague set theory. *International Journal of Computational Cognition*, *4*(1), 44–48.

Wang, L. C., Baker, J., Wagner, J. A., & Wakefield, K. (2007). Can a retail web site be social? *Journal of Marketing*, *71*(3), 143–157. doi:10.1509/jmkg.71.3.143

Wang, Q. H., Kalantar-Zadeh, K., Kis, A., Coleman, J. N., & Strano, M. S. (2012). Electronics and optoelectronics of two-dimensional transition metal dichalcogenides. *Nature Nanotechnology*, *7*, 699–712. doi:10.1038/nnano.2012.193 PMID:23132225

Wang, Y. S., Wang, Y. M., Lin, H. H., & Tang, T. I. (2003). Determinants of user acceptance of Internet banking: An empirical study. *International Journal of Service Industry Management*, *14*(5), 501–519. doi:10.1108/09564230310500192

Warrender, R. L., Tindle, J., & Nelson, D. (2013). Job Scheduling in a High Performance Computing Environment. In *Proceedings of International Conference on High Performance Computing & Simulation (HPCS2013)*. Helsinki, Finland: HPCS.

Warrender, R. L., Tindle, J., & Nelson, D. (2013). Evaluating The Use of Virtual Machines in High Performance Clusters. *International Journal of Advanced Computer Technology*, *2*(5), 25–30.

Weber, G. (1975). Energetics of ligand binding to proteins. *Advances in Protein Chemistry*, *29*, 1–83. doi:10.1016/S0065-3233(08)60410-6 PMID:1136898

Weinland, D., Ronfard, R., & Boyer, E. (2011). A survey of vision-based methods for action representation, segmentation and recognition. *Computer Vision and Image Understanding*, *115*(2), 224–241. doi:10.1016/j.cviu.2010.10.002

Weng-Sieh, Z., Cherrey, K., Chopra, N. G., Blase, X., Miyamoto, Y., & Rubio, A. et al. (1995). Synthesis of $B_xC_yN_z$ nanotubules. *Physical Review B: Condensed Matter and Materials Physics*, *51*, 11229–11232. doi:10.1103/PhysRevB.51.11229 PMID:9977849

Wernerfelt, B. (1984). A resource-based view of the firm. *Strategic Management Journal*, *5*, 171–180. doi:10.1002/smj.4250050207

Westra, J., & Dignum, F. (2009). Evolutionary Neural Networks for Non-Player Characters in Quake III. In *Proceedings of IEEE Symposium on Computational Intelligence and Games*, (pp. 302-309). Academic Press.

What is Microsoft's High Performance Computing HPC Server?. (n.d.). Retrieved April 4, 2014 from http://www.microsoft.com/hpc/en/us/product/cluster-computing.aspx

Wiig, K. M. (1997). Knowledge Management: Where Did It Come From and Where Will It Go? *Expert Systems with Applications*, *13*(1), 1–14. doi:10.1016/S0957-4174(97)00018-3

William, P. (1998). *Rapid Prototyping Primer*. Retrieved January 10, 2013, from http://www.me.psu.edu/lamancusa/rapidpro/primer/chapter2.htm

Wilson, R. A., Bamrah, V. S., Lindsay, J., Schwaiger, M., & Morganroth, J. (1993). Diagnostic accuracy of seismocardiography compared with electrocardiography for the anatomic and physiologic diagnosis of coronary artery disease during exercise testing. *The American Journal of Cardiology*, *71*(7), 536–545. doi:10.1016/0002-9149(93)90508-A PMID:8438739

Wintermute, S., Xu, J., & Irizarry, J. (2007). *SORTS Tech Report. Artificial Intelligence Lab*. University of Michigan.

Wong, Y. K., & Hsu, C. J. (2008). A confidence-based framework for business to consumer (B2C) mobile commerce adoption. *Personal and Ubiquitous Computing*, *12*(1), 77–84. doi:10.1007/s00779-006-0120-5

Woodward, C. (1996). *Computer aided industrial design for ceramics and glass industries.* Finland: Dest Artes Oy.

Wrigley, C., Popovic, V. Chamorro-Koc, & Marianella. (2009). A methodological approach to visceral hedonic rhetoric. In Proceedings of the International Association of Societies of Design Research Conference 2009. COEX.

Wu, W., Yu, C., Doan, A. H., & Meng, W. (2004). An interactive clustering based approach to integrating source query interfaces on the deep web. In *Proceedings of the ACM SIGMOD 2004*, (pp. 95-106). ACM.

Wu, H. C. (2009). Statistical confidence intervals for fuzzy data. *Expert Systems with Applications, 36*, 2670–2676. doi:10.1016/j.eswa.2008.01.022

Wuister, S. F., de Mello Donegá, C., & Meijerink, A. (2004). Influence of thiol capping on the exciton liminiscence and decay kinetics of CdTe and CdSe quantum dots. *The Journal of Physical Chemistry B, 108*, 17393–17397. doi:10.1021/jp047078c

Wu, J. J., & Chang, Y. S. (2005). Towards understanding members' interactivity, trust, and flow in online travel community. *Industrial Management & Data Systems, 105*(7), 937–954. doi:10.1108/02635570510616120

Wu, J., & Boggess, W. (1999). The optimal allocation of conservation funds. *Journal of Environmental Economics and Management, 38*.

Wu, Q. H., & Ma, J. T. (1995). Power system optimal reactive power dispatch using evolutionary programming. *IEEE Transactions on Power Systems, 10*(3), 1243–1249. doi:10.1109/59.466531

Xia, X., Jelski, D. A., Bowser, J. R., & George, T. F. (1992). MNDO study of boron-nitrogen analogues of buckminsterfullerene. *Journal of the American Chemical Society, 114*, 6493–6496. doi:10.1021/ja00042a032

Xie, X., Xu, A. F., Lu, X. C., & Wang, B. (2012). Research of the numerical control machining simulation. *Advanced Materials Research, 546*, 767-771.

Xu, Y., Zhang, W., Liu, W., & Ferrese, F. (2012). Multiagent-based reinforcement learning for optimal reactive power dispatch. *IEEE Transactions on Systems, Man and Cybernetics Part C: Applications and Reviews, 42* (6), 1742-1751.

Xue, X.-B., & Zhou, Z.-H. (2009). Distributional features for text categorization. *IEEE Transactions on Knowledge and Data Engineering, 21*(3), 428–442. doi:10.1109/TKDE.2008.166

Xu, Z. S. (2007). Methods for aggregating interval-valued intuitionistic fuzzy information and their application to decision making. *Control and Decision, 22*(2), 215–219.

Yaldiz, O., Ozturk, H., & Zeren, Y. (1993). Energy usage in production of field crops in Turkey. In *Proceedings of 5th International Congress on Mechanisation and Energy Use in Agriculture.* Kusadasi.

Yang, X. S., & Deb, S. (2009). Cuckoo search via L'evy flights. In *Proc. of World Congress on Nature & Biologically Inspired Computing* (NaBIC 2009). IEEE Publications.

Yannakakis, G., & Hallam, J. (2004). *Evolving Opponents for Interesting Interactive Computer Games* (Vol. 8, pp. 499–508). From Animals to Animats.

Yannakakis, G., & Hallam, J. (2005). A Generic Approach for Obtaining Higher Entertainment in Predator/Prey Computer Games. *Journal of Game Development, 1*(3), 23–50.

Yannakakis, G., & Hallam, J. (2007). Towards Optimizing Entertainment in Computer Games. *Applied Artificial Intelligence, 21*, 933–971. doi:10.1080/08839510701527580

Yan, W., Yu, J., Yu, D. C., & Bhattarai, K. (2006). A new optimal reactive power flow model in rectangular form and its solution by predictor corrector primal dual interior point method. *IEEE Transactions on Power Systems, 21*(1), 61–67. doi:10.1109/TPWRS.2005.861978

Yiqin, Z. (2010). Optimal reactive power planning based on improved Tabu search algorithm. In *Proceedings of 2010 International Conference on Electrical and Control Engineering.* Academic Press.

Young, J. B. (2004). The global epidemiology of heart failure. *The Medical Clinics of North America, 88*(5), 1135–1143. doi:10.1016/j.mcna.2004.06.001 PMID:15331310

Yuan, X., Li, H., Xing, & Sun, K. (2011). The cut sets, decomposition theorems and representation theorems on intuitionistic fuzzy sets and interval valued fuzzy sets. *Science China Information Sciences*, *54*(1), 91-110.

Yu, C. (1993). Correlation of fuzzy numbers. *Fuzzy Sets and Systems*, *55*, 303–307. doi:10.1016/0165-0114(93)90256-H

Yvette, S., & Karine, F. (2001). Information quality: Meeting the needs of the consumer. *International Journal of Information System*, *21*(1), 21–37.

Zadeh, L.A. (1965) Fuzzy sets. *Information and Control*, *8*, 338–353. doi:10.1016/S0019-9958(65)90241-X

Zadeh, L. A. (1978). Fuzzy sets as a basis for a theory of possibility. *Fuzzy Sets and Systems*, *1*, 3–28. doi:10.1016/0165-0114(78)90029-5

Zajonc, R. (1980). Feeling and thinking: Preferences need no inferences. *The American Psychologist*, *35*, 151–175. doi:10.1037/0003-066X.35.2.151

Zanetti, J., Poliac, M., & Crow, R. (1991). Seismocardiography: Waveform identification and noise analysis. *Proceedings of the Computers in Cardiology*, *1991*, 49–52. doi:10.1109/CIC.1991.169042

Zelinka, I. (2002). Analytic programming by Means of SOMA Algorithm. In *Proc. 8ᵗʰ, International Conference on Soft Computing Mendel'02*. Brno, Czech Republic: Mendel.

Zeng, W., & Li, H. (2007). Correlation Coefficient of Intuitionistic Fuzzy sets. *Journal of Industrial Engineering International*, *3*, 33–40.

Zhang, C., Li, D., Lai, Y., & Tu, Y.(2013). Dependence-Aware task scheduling for resource-constrained CNC systems. *Advances in Information Sciences and Service Sciences*, *5*, 607–615.

Zhang, C., Ni, Z., Wu, Z., & Gu, L. (2009). A novel swarm model with quasi-oppositional particle. In *Proceedings of 2009 International Forum on Information Technology and Applications*, (pp. 325-330). Academic Press.

Zhang, L. B., You, Y. P., & Yang, X. F. (2013). A control strategy with motion smoothness and machining precision for multi-axis coordinated motion CNC machine tools. *International Journal of Advanced Manufacturing Technology*, *64*(1-4), 335-348.

Zhang, X. T., & Song, Z. (2012). An iterative feedrate optimization method for real-time NURBS interpolator. *International Journal of Advanced Manufacturing Technology*, *62*, 1273-1280.

Zhang, Y., Rauch, M., Xie, H., Zhao, Y., Xu, X., & Liu, Y. (2011). Machining simulation - A technical review and a proposed concept model. *International Journal of Internet Manufacturing and Services*, *3*, 59-75.

Zhang, X., Chen, W., Dai, C., & Cai, W. (2010). Dynamic multi-group self-adaptive differential evolution algorithm for reactive power optimization. *International Journal of Electrical Power & Energy Systems*, *32*, 351–357. doi:10.1016/j.ijepes.2009.11.009

Zhao, B., Guo, C. X., & Cao, Y. J. (2005). A multiagent-based particle swarm optimization approach for optimal reactive power dispatch. *IEEE Transactions on Power Systems*, *20*(2), 1070–1078. doi:10.1109/TPWRS.2005.846064

Zhi-feng, Ma., Cheng, Z.H., Xiaomei, Z. (2001). Interval valued vague decision systems and an approach for its rule generation. *Acta Electronica Sinica*, *29*(5), 585–589.

Zhong, B., Hardin, M., & Sun, T. (2011). Less effortful thinking leads to more social networking? The associations between the use of social network sites and personality traits. *Computers in Human Behavior*, *27*(3), 1265–1271. doi:10.1016/j.chb.2011.01.008

Zhou, T. (2013). An empirical examination of continuance intention of mobile payment services. *Decision Support Systems*, *54*, 1085–1091. doi:10.1016/j.dss.2012.10.034

Zhou, T., Li, H., & Liu, Y. (2010). The effect of flow experience on mobile SNS users' loyalty. *Industrial Management & Data Systems*, *110*(6), 930–946. doi:10.1108/02635571011055126

Zhou, Z., & Wu, Q. Z. (2006). Multi-criteria decision making based on interval valued vague sets. *Transactions of Beijing Institute of Technology*, *8*, 693–696.

Zhu, J., Kase, D., Shiba, K., Kasuya, D., Yudasaka, M., & Iijima, S. (2003). Binary nanomaterials based on nanocarbons: A case for probing carbon nanohorns' biorecognition properties. *Nano Letters*, *3*, 1033–1036. doi:10.1021/nl034266q

Zipf, G. K. (1932). *Selective Studies and the Principle of Relative Frequency in Language*. Cambridge: Harvard University Press. MA doi:10.4159/harvard.9780674434929

Zipf, G. K. (1949). *Human Behavior and the Principle of Least Effort*. Cambridge, MA: Addison-Wesley Press.

Zitzler, E., Knowles, J., & Thiele, L. (2008). Quality Assessment of Pareto Set Approximations. In J. Branke et al. (Eds.), Multiobjective Optimization (LNCS) (vol. 5252, pp. 373-494). Springer-Verlag.

Zitzler, E., & Thiele, L. (1998). Multiobjective optimization using evolutionary algorithms—A comparative case study. In A. E. Eiben, T. B̈ack, M. Schoenauer, & H. P. Schwefel (Eds.), *Parallel Problem Solving from Nature*, (vol. 5, pp. 292–301). Springer. doi:10.1007/BFb0056872

Zitzler, E., & Thiele, L. (1999). Multiobjective evolutionary algorithms: a comparative case study and the strength Pareto approach. *IEEE Transactions on Evolutionary Computation*, *3*(4), 257–271. doi:10.1109/4235.797969

Zitzler, E., Thiele, L., Laumanns, M., Fonseca, C. M., & Grunert da Fonseca, V. (2003). Performance Assessment of Multiobjective Optimizers: An Analysis and Review. *IEEE Transactions on Evolutionary Computation*, *7*(2), 117–132. doi:10.1109/TEVC.2003.810758

Zverovich, I. E. (2006). A new kind of graph coloring. *Journal of Algorithms*, *58*(2), 118–133. doi:10.1016/j.jalgor.2005.0

Zyda, M., Hiles, J., Mayberry, A., Wardynski, C., Capps, M., & Osborn, B. et al. (2003). The MOVES Institute's Army Game Project: Entertainment R&D for Defense. *IEEE Computer Graphics and Applications*, *23*, 28–36. doi:10.1109/MCG.2003.1159611

About the Contributors

Mehdi Khosrow-Pour, DBA, received his Doctorate in Business Administration from the Nova Southeastern University (Florida, USA). Dr. Khosrow-Pour taught undergraduate and graduate information system courses at the Pennsylvania State University – Harrisburg for 20 years. He is currently Executive Editor at IGI Global (www.igi-global.com). He also serves as Executive Director of the Information Resources Management Association (IRMA) (www.irma-international.org), and Executive Director and President of the World Forgotten Children's Foundation (www.world-forgotten-children.org). He is the author/editor of over 20 books in information technology management. He is also the editor-in-chief of the *Information Resources Management Journal*, the *Journal of Cases on Information Technology*, the *Journal of Electronic Commerce in Organizations*, and the *Journal of Information Technology Research*, and has authored more than 50 articles published in various conference proceedings and scholarly journals.

* * *

Amal Kumar Adak received his MSc degree in Mathematics and PhD from Vidyasagar University, West Bengal, India in 2006 and 2013, respectively. He is an Assistant Teachers in Department of Mathematics of Jafuly Deshpran School, West Bengal, India since 2007. His research interest includes fuzzy and intuitionistic fuzzy sets, intuitionistic fuzzy matrices, and operations research.

Henry Amirtharaj is working as Associate Professor of Mathematics, PG and Research Department of Mathematics, Bishop Heber College, Tiruchirappalli, India. He has a teaching experience of nearly 25 years. He is a Research Guide for MPhil and PhD in Mathematics. His areas of research are Numerical Analysis, Mathematical Statistics, Operations Research, and Fuzzy Set Theory. He completed PhD in the year 2002 from Regional Engineering College, Bharathidasan University, Tiruchirappalli, India. His papers are published in several international journals, and he has presented papers in several international conferences.

Michele Argiolas was born on March 1976, in Cagliari, Italy. In 2000, he completed a five-year Engineering Master Degree in Building Engineering at the Faculty of Engineering of the University of Cagliari with summa cum laude. In 2006, he completed his Phd in "Ingegneria del Territorio" (Real Estate Appraisal, Urban Planning, Hydraulic, Transportation Department) at the University of Cagliari (Italy). From 2011 is Assistant Professor (Ricercatore TD) of Real Estate Appraisal at the Department of Civil, Environmental Engineering and Architecture. His research interests are centered on housing market analysis, with particular reference to housing market affordability, taxation policies, and market supply analysis.

Maurizio Atzori was born in 1978 in Italy. He graduated in Computer Science (Informatica) summa cum laude in 2002, from the University of Pisa. He holds a PhD in Computer Science from the School for Graduate Studies "Galileo Galilei," University of Pisa, obtained in 2006. He has been member of the ISTI-CNR, holding a research fellowship from CNR of Pisa, and a member of Knowledge Discovery and Delivery Laboratory. He has been visiting scholar at Purdue Univesity (Indiana, USA), working with Prof. Christopher W. Clifton and his research team. He has been visiting resercher working with Prof. Yucel Saygin at Sabanci University (Istanbul, Turkey) and at UCLA, collaborating with Prof. Carlo Zaniolo. Since December 2010, he is Assistant Professor (Ricercatore Universitario, Professore Aggregato) at the Department of Mathematics and Computer Science of the University of Cagliari (Italy). His major research interests regard databases, Web of data, data integration, data mining and privacy-preserving algorithms for data management.

Meriem Bensouyad was born in Constantine, Algeria in 1988. In July 2011, she obtained a Master's degree in Computing Sciences from Mentouri University of Constantine, Algeria. Since 2011, she has been a PhD student at CFSC research group of MISC laboratory in Constantine 2 University, Constantine, Algeria. Her research interests include the graphs partitioning, distribution and especially coloring problems.

Monoranjan Bhowmik received his MSc in Mathematics from Indian Institute of Technology, Kharagpur, West Bengal, India and PhD from Vidyasagar University, India in 1995 and 2008, respectively. Currently, he is an Assistant Professor of VTT College, Paschim Midnapore, West Bengal, India. He is Associate-Editor of *International Journal of Fuzzy Mathematical Archive*. He is a reviewer of several international journals. His main scientific interest concentrates on fuzzy and intuitionistic fuzzy sets, fuzzy and intuitionistic fuzzy matrices and fuzzy algebras.

Mourad Bouzenada was born and brought up in Constantine where he graduated in 1990 at Mentouri University. He began his career as a computer science engineer with mechanical public company. During his seven years with this company, he spent most time in the development of applications before returning to university to take a PhD degree in 2008. Currently, he is an associate professor at Constantine 2 University and he is a member of MISC laboratory. His research interests include computer vision and real-time tracking for augmented reality. He is also interested in the distributed computing aspects of real-time systems. More recently, he studies graph coloring for distribution.

Gloria Castellano received her PhD in Chemistry. She is a full-time Associated Professor in organic chemistry of the Universidad Católica de Valencia *San Vicente Mártir* in the Faculty of Veterinary and Experimental Sciences. Her research is in Natural Products and computational Chemistry in the Universidad Católica de Valencia *San Vicente Mártir*. She is the Editor-in-Chief of Nereis: Latin American Journal of Methods, Modelling and Simulation in Interdisciplinary Technology. She has 37 research articles published in indexed journals.

P. K. D. Dawson is employed as a Researcher in the Department of Health and Well Being in the Faculty of Science at the University of Sunderland. His research interests are primarily focused upon drug discovery using molecular modelling methods and the program Gaussian09.

Nicoletta Dessi is associated professor of Computer Science at University of Cagliari, where she currently teaches Two Database courses (Fundamental and Advanced). She received the PhD degree in Mathematics from University of Cagliari, in 1970. From 2004-2010, she has been deputy head of the Department of Mathematics and Computer Science at University of Cagliari. Previously, she has been the director of the Scientific Computing Centre at University of Cagliari (94-04). Her main research interests are in the area of data mining and information systems, with current focus on bioinformatics. She is also involved in data integration research based on Cloud, data integration, Web services, and trusted cooperation. She has published her research results in international journals and the refereed proceedings of the major conferences of the field. Currently, she is the principal investigator and the responsible of the research project "DENIS: Dataspaces Enhancing the New Internet in Sardinia," funded by RAS, Regione Autonoma della Sardegna (Italy) in 2012.

Hans du Buf obtained a MSc degree from the Techical University of Eindhoven (The Netherlands) in 1983 and a PhD degree from the same university in 1987, working at the Institute for Perception Research (IPO). He worked for seven years at the Swiss Federal Institute of Technology in Lausanne – EPFL (Switzerland) before moving to the University of the Algarve in Faro (Portugal) in 1994. His teaching includes digital systems, computer architecture, computer graphics as well as image processing. He is the head of the Vision Laboratory at UAlg, where his current work focuses on models of visual perception and cognitive robotics.

Irraivan Elamvazuthi obtained his PhD from Department of Automatic Control and Systems Engineering, University of Sheffield, UK in 2002. He is currently an Associate Professor at the Department of Electrical and Electronic Engineering, Universiti Teknologi PETRONAS (UTP), Malaysia. His research interests include Control, Robotics, Mechatronics, Power Systems, and Bio-medical Applications.

Olalere Folasayo Enoch is a Researcher at Universiti Malaysia Kelantan. He holds BTech in Industrial Design at Federal University of Technology Akure, Nigeria and Master of Arts in Product Design at Universiti Malaysia Kelantan, Malaysia. Presently, he is a PhD Candidate at Universiti Malaysia Kelantan, where he is exploring on the new area of intersection between heritage values and contemporary design. His main research interests are ceramics art and design, computer-aided design, user-centre design, design theory, art appreciation, and heritage studies.

András Gábor, PhD, CISA, is a managing director of Corvinno Ltd, Associate Professor and Head of the IT Institute of Corvinus University of Budapest. He is an economist, graduated from the then Karl Marx University of Economics. He has a second degree in Computer Science (1979) and earned his PhD in 1983, CISA (Certified Information Systems Auditor) since 1999. His research field includes systems design, information management, intelligent systems, and knowledge management. He is participating in several national and international research project and author of several Hungarian and international publication. He was visiting scholar at DePaul University, Chicago, Imperial College, London, and University of Amsterdam. He worked as a consultant on behalf of the Ministry of Education concerning MIS development in Higher Education between 2003 and 2006.

T. Ganesan is currently a faculty member with the Department of Chemical Engineering Universiti Teknologi Petronas (UTP), Tronoh, Malaysia. He holds a bachelor's degree in Chemical Engineering (Hons.) and a Master of Science in Computational Fluid Dynamics from UTP. He completed a PhD in Process Optimization. His research interests include multi-objective optimization and computational intelligence.

Tsvetanka Georgieva-Trifonova received her MSc degree in Mathematics and Informatics in 1997 and her PhD degree in Computer Science in 2009 from University of Veliko Tarnovo, Bulgaria. Currently she is Associate Professor at the University of Veliko Tarnovo, Bulgaria and teaches Databases, Information Systems Modeling, Multimedia Information Systems, and Data Warehousing and Mining. She has published over 30 papers in refereed journals and international conferences, mainly in the fields of databases, collaborative filtering, and data warehousing. She joined several national research projects on the above areas. Her current research interests include multidimensional modeling, data mining, collaborative filtering, and information systems.

K. Ginty is employed as a Researcher Manager in the Department of Computing, Engineering, and Technology DCET in the Faculty of Applied Sciences at the University of Sunderland. His research interests are primarily focused upon the development of applications that run in a networking environment and information systems standards.

M. Gray is employed as a Senior Lecturer in the Department of Health and Well Being in the Faculty of Science at the University of Sunderland. His research interests are primarily focused upon drug discovery using computational chemistry and molecular modelling methods.

Nousseiba Guidoum was born in Constantine, Algeria, on March 28th 1989. She received her research Master's degree in Computer Science in July 2011 from Mentouri University of Constantine, Algeria. Since 2011, she has been a PhD student at CFSC research group of MISC laboratory, Constantine 2 University of Constantine, Algeria.

Salah Haridy is currently a postdoctoral research associate in the Department of Mechanical and Industrial Engineering at Northeastern University, USA. He received his PhD in 2014 in Systems and Engineering Management from Nanyang Technological University, Singapore. He received his BSc and MSc in 2004 and 2008, respectively, in Mechanical Engineering and Technology from Benha University, Egypt. His research work focuses on statistical process control, applied statistics, process capability, healthcare systems engineering and design of experiments. He has authored more than 15 articles published in various scholarly journals and conference proceedings. He serves as a reviewer for reputable journals in his expertise. He is the recipient of the 2013 Mary G. and Joseph Natrella Scholarship.

Andrea Kő, PhD, CISA is an Associate Professor at the Department of Information Systems of Corvinus University of Budapest from 2005. She has MSc in Mathematics and Physics from Eötvös Lóránd University of Budapest, Hungary (1988), a University Doctoral degree in Computer Science (1992) from Corvinus University of Budapest, Hungary, and a PhD degree in Management and Business Administration (2005) from Corvinus University of Budapest, Hungary. She participated in several international and national research projects in the areas of: knowledge management; semantic technologies and e-government (recently she was a researcher in Ubipol [Ubiquitous Participation Platform for Policy Making]; FP7- ICT-2009.7.3, ICT for Governance and Policy Modelling; 2009-2012) project. She has published more than 50 papers in international scientific journals and conferences.

Barna Kovács is a research associate at the Department of Information Systems of Corvinus University of Budapest. He is an economist and graduated from the Corvinus University of Budapest in 2003.He received his PhD in the topic of managing information overload in organizational workflow systems in 2011. His research interests include systems design, information management. He was a visiting scholar at University of Kuopio (Finland) in 2005. He participated various national and European Union research projects.

Roberto Lam graduated in Informatics at the University of the Algarve (UAlg, Portugal) in 1994 and obtained his MSc degree in Computer Systems Engineering in 2001. He was appointed Adjoint Professor at Instituto Superior de Engenharia. Since 1996, he has been teaching Computer Science, Algorithms, and Web technologies. In 1999, he joined the Vision Laboratory at UAlg and in 2001 he was integrated in the Institute for Systems and Robotics (ISR/IST-Lisbon). He has participated in national research projects and his major research interests are modelling and recognition of 3D objects.

Matti Linnavuo is a senior researcher at Aalto University School of Electrical Engineering (Department of Electrical Engineering and Automation). He received his MSc in 1978 and his LSc in 1982 at Helsinki University of Technology. Before beginning his academic career at Helsinki University of Technology, he worked in R&D of medical and industrial measurement devices. Currently, his research interests include technological advancements in physiological measurements, ubiquitous healthcare, and rehabilitation.

Maxim Mozgovoy is an associate professor at the University of Aizu (Japan), where he studies practical game-oriented observation-based AI systems. The main purpose of his research is to demonstrate the advantages of machine learning and case-based reasoning over traditional approaches to game AI development that often require enormous handwork. His other research interests are focused around natural language processing technologies. In particular, he is currently working on a "virtual language lab" that will combine natural language processing algorithms with a computer-assisted language-learning environment. Maxim Mozgovoy is also an author of several books on programming and computer science.

Abdeen Mustafa Omer (BSc, MSc, PhD) is an Associate Researcher at Energy Research Institute (ERI). He obtained both his PhD degree in the Built Environment and Master of Philosophy degree in Renewable Energy Technologies from the University of Nottingham. He is qualified Mechanical Engineer with a proven track record within the water industry and renewable energy technologies. He graduated from University of El Menoufia, Egypt, BSc in Mechanical Engineering. His previous experience involved being a member of the research team at the National Council for Research/Energy Research Institute in Sudan and working director of research and development for National Water Equipment Manufacturing Co. Ltd., Sudan. He has been listed in the book WHO'S WHO in the World 2005, 2006, 2007, and 2010. He has published over 300 papers in peer-reviewed journals, 100 review articles, 5 books, and 100 chapters in books.

Madhumangal Pal is a Professor of Applied Mathematics, Vidyasagar University, India. He has received Gold and Silver medals from Vidyasagar University for rank first and second in MSc and BSc examinations respectively. In addition, he received, jointly with Prof. G.P. Bhattacherjee, "Computer Division Medal" from Institute of Engineers (India) in 1996 for best research work. He received Bharat Jyoti Award from International Friend Ship Society, New Delhi in 2012. Prof. Pal has successfully guided 16 research scholars for PhD degrees and has published more than 140 articles in international and national journals, 31 articles in edited book and in conference proceedings. His specializations include Computational Graph Theory, Genetic Algorithms and Parallel Algorithms, Fuzzy Correlation & Regression, Fuzzy Game Theory, Fuzzy Matrices, Fuzzy Algebra. He is the Editor-in-Chief of *Journal of Physical Sciences* and *Annals of Pure and Applied Mathematics*, and member of the editorial boards of several journals. Prof. Pal is the author of the eight books published from India and Oxford, UK. He organized several national seminars/ conferences/ workshop. In addition, he visited China, Malaysia, Thailand, and Bangladesh to participate and deliver invited talks and chaired national and international seminars/conferences/refresher course, etc.

Mikko Paukkunen is a doctoral student at Aalto University School of Electrical Engineering (Department of Electrical Engineering and Automation). He received his BSc in 2011 (Aalto University School of Electrical Engineering) and his MSc also in 2011 (Aalto University School of Electrical Engineering). His research interests include biomedical systems and circuits, biomedical signal processing, and physiological measurements.

Barbara Pes was born in Cagliari, Italy, in 1976. She obtained her Laurea degree in Physics from the University of Cagliari in 2001. From 2002 to 2005, she collaborated with the Database and Data Mining Group at the Department of Mathematics and Computer Science, University of Cagliari. Since 2006, she has been working as Assistant Professor (Ricercatore Universitario) at the Science Faculty, University of Cagliari, where she teaches Foundations of CS and Data Mining courses. She is author or co-author of more than 30 international papers. Her research interests include Service Oriented Architectures and Web Services, Data Mining and Knowledge Discovery in Databases, Bio-Informatics, Feature Selection, and Classification of Micro-Array Data.

John Robinson is working as Assistant Professor of Mathematics, PG and Research Department of Mathematics, Bishop Heber College, Tiruchirappalli, India. He has more than eight years of teaching experience. His areas of research are Fuzzy set Theory, Fuzzy Decision Analysis, Fuzzy Data Mining, and Fuzzy Optimization. He has completed PhD degree programme in 2013 at Bharathidasan University, Tiruchirappalli, India. He has published several research papers in International journals in the area of Fuzzy Decision Analysis and Fuzzy Data Mining and presented several papers in international conferences.

João Rodrigues graduated in Electrical Engineering in 1993 at the University of Trás-os-Montes and Alto Douro (Portugal). He got an MSc degree in Computer Systems Engineering in 1998 and a PhD degree in Electronics and Computer Engineering in 2008 from the University of the Algarve, Faro (Portugal). He is an Adjoint Professor at Instituto Superior de Engenharia at UAlg, where he has been teaching Computer Science and Computer Vision disciplines since 1994. He joined the Vision Laboratory at UAlg in 1996, in 1998 also the Institute for Systems and Robotics (ISR/IST-Lisbon). He has participated in 11 scientific projects. His major research interests lie in computer and human vision, accessibility, and system integration.

Provas Kumar Roy was born in 1973 at Mejia, Bankura, West Bengal, India. He received the BE degree in Electrical Engineering from R. E. College, Durgapur, Burdwan, India in 1997; ME degree In Electrical Machine from Jadavpur University, Kolkata, India in 2001; and PhD from NIT Durgapur in 2011. Presently, he is working as Professor in the department of Electrical Engineering, Dr. B. C. Roy Engineering College, Durgapur, India. He has published more than 30 research papers in international journals. His field of research interest includes Economic Load Dispatch, Combined Heat and Power Dispatch, Optimal Power Flow, FACTS, Unit Commitment, Automatic Generation Control, State Estimation, Radial Distribution System, Power System Stabilizer, and Evolutionary Computing Techniques, etc.

Djamel Eddine Saidouni was born in Algeria in 1968. In 1996, he received his PhD degree in Theoretical Computer Science from the university Paul Sabatier of Toulouse, France. Currently, he is a professor at the Department of Computer Science and its applications of Constantine 2 University of Constantine, Algeria. In addition, he is the head of the CFSC research group of MISC laboratory. His main research domain interests formal models for specifying and verifying dynamic and real time systems, true concurrency models, and state space explosion problem.

Amro Shafik received his BSc and MSc degrees in Mechanical Engineering from Benha Faculty of Engineering, Benha University, Egypt, in 2004 and 2010, respectively. He is an assistant lecturer at the same university in the Department of Mechanical Engineering. His general research interests are automation, mechatronics, and robotics. He is currently pursuing his PhD in the field of Advanced Mechatronics at University of Toronto, Canada.

Ab. Aziz Shuaib is an Associate Professor and a lecturer in Faculty of Creative Technology and Heritage, Universiti Malaysia Kelantan, Malaysia. His research interests are architecture, design theory, ergonomic, aesthetic appreciation, traditional art and design, and heritage.

Norazah Mohd Suki is an associate professor at the Labuan School of International Business and Finance, Universiti Malaysia Sabah, Labuan International Campus. She has successfully supervised several postgraduate students at MBA and PhD level. Her research interests include Electronic Marketing, E-Commerce, M-Commerce, Consumer Behaviour, Mobile Learning, and areas related to Marketing. She actively publishes articles in international journals. She is the editor-in-chief to *Labuan e-Journal of Muamalat & Society*, a member in advisory board for several outstanding journals. She has sound experiences as speaker to public and private universities, government bodies on courses related to Structural Equation Modelling (SEM), Statistical Package for Social Sciences (SPSS), Research Methodology.

Norbayah Mohd Suki is a senior lecturer at the Labuan School of Informatics Science, Universiti Malaysia Sabah. Her research interests include Film, Animation, Creative Multimedia, Mobile Learning, ICT, Human Computer Interaction, and Educational Technology. She actively publishes articles in international journals. She has sound experiences as multimedia specialist.

Kasim Terzic obtained a BEng degree in Electronic Engineering from the University of East Anglia, Norwich (UK) in 1999 and an MSc degree in Information and Communication Systems from the Hamburg University of Technology (Germany) in 2003. In 2011, he received a Dr.rer.nat. degree in Computer Science from the University of Hamburg. Since 2011, he has been working as a post-doctoral fellow at the Vision Laboratory at the University of the Algarve (UAlg) in Faro (Portugal). He has worked on four international and one national research project. His interests lie in object recognition, scene understanding, and models of human and computer vision.

J. Tindle is emeritus Professor of Telecommunications Engineering at the University of Sunderland. He has been closely involved in the design and development of the University of Sunderland Cluster Computer. The cluster computer has been used in a number of areas, for example, drug discovery using molecular modelling and computational chemistry methods, dynamic finite element analysis for vehicle crash analysis, and 3D computer graphics rendering for media applications. In addition, a number of industrial sponsored projects have been completed including the development of software tools that are used to plan the layout of large telecommunications networks. These tools are based upon intelligent and evolutionary computing methods.

Francisco Torrens is lecturer in physical chemistry at the Universitat de València. After obtaining a PhD in molecular associations in Azines and Macrocycles from the Universitat de València, Dr. Torrens undertook postdoctoral research with Professor Rivail at the Université de Nancy I. More recently, Dr. Torrens has collaborated on projects with Professor Tomás-Vert. Major research projects include characterization of the electronic structure of electrically conductive organic materials, theoretical study of new electrically conductive organic materials, protein modelling, electronic correlation, development and applications of high-precision mono and multi-referential electronic correlation methods, development and application of high-precision quantum methods, methodological developments and applications of quantum methods, molecular modelling and chemistry-computer applications for the description and prediction of molecular properties, development and integration of a computational system for the discovery of active drugs against AIDS, cancer pandemics and other microbial diseases of high social impact, starting an electronic journal of scientific-technological and gender spreading, computational design, chemical obtaining and biological evaluation of new antiprotozoal and anticancer drugs, prediction of the environmental impact of chemical substances using chemobioinformatics tools, discovery of new inhibitors of tyrosinase: computational design, synthesis, characterization and experimental corroboration, search for new antimicrobial agents that inhibit the synthesis of the bacterial cell wall and minimal active domains of proteins of the Bcl-2 family. His scientific accomplishments include the first implementation in a computer at the Universitat de València of a program for the elucidation of crystallographic structures, and the construction of the first computational-chemistry program adapted to a vector-facility supercomputer in a Spanish university.

Tihomir Trifonov received the MSc degree in Electrical and Communication Engineering from the National Technical University of Ukraine, in 1983, and the PhD degree in Mathematical Modeling and Applied Mathematics from the Institute of Hydromechanics, National Academy of Sciences, Ukraine, in 1991. He is currently working as an Associate Professor at the Veliko Tarnovo University and at the National Military University, Veliko Tarnovo, Bulgaria. His research interests include underwater acoustics information systems, mathematical modeling in various areas of technique and economics, information security, and applied cryptography. He has authored and coauthored more than 100 papers in journals and conference proceedings, some books, and student manuals in mathematics and statistics. He is a member of the IEEE Computer Society and IEEE Communication Society, International Statistical Institute, and the Union of Bulgarian Mathematicians. He is a member of the 2010 Top 100 Educators of the International Biographical Centre, Cambridge, and he is included in the 2010 Edition of Marquis Who's Who in the World.

Iskander Umarov is the inventor of behavior-capture AI technology Artificial Contender, co-owner of TruSoft Int'l Inc and currently the Creative Director at Konami Digital Entertainment. Iskander's research focuses on implementations and applications of case-based reasoning and learning by observation AI systems for the purposes of simplification of the knowledge, behavior and skills transfer from human experts to computer agents. His other research and work interests include general machine learning, spatial reasoning and AI behaviors. During the last 15 years, Iskander worked at and with such companies as SONY, Electronic Arts, Konami, Irrational Games and Lockheed Martin, and gained hands-on experience on AI for a range of video games, including, recently, Bioshock Infinite and Pro Evolution Soccer 2015.

P. Vasant is a senior lecturer in the Department of Fundamental and Applied Sciences, Universiti Teknologi Petronas (UTP), Tronoh, Malaysia. His research interests are Soft Computing and Computational Intelligence.

R. L. Warrender is a Senior Lecturer at the University of Sunderland within the Department of Computing Engineering Technology DCET in the Faculty of Applied Sciences. Currently studying for a professional doctorate related to his work on cluster computing, he is working on collaborative research projects with different groups around the University who have high computational requirements. As well as being involved in the development and upgrade of the cluster, he has helped introduce cluster computing to the undergraduate teaching curriculum at the university.

Ku Zilati is an Associate Professor at the Chemical Engineering Department, Faculty of Engineering, Universiti Teknologi Petronas (UTP). She holds a degree in Chemical Engineering (Hons.) (University of Detroit Mercy, MI, USA) and Master in Chemical Engineering (West Virginia University, WV, USA). She completed her PhD in 2007 at West Virginia University, WV, USA. Her areas of expertise are powder technology, particle coating, and computational fluid dynamics.

Index